A HISTORY OF MILITARISM

CONTENTS

PART II THE DEVELOPMENT AND MILITARIZATION OF MASS ARMIES

PART III THE MILITARY AND POLITICS

PREFACE

This book was originally written and published on the eve of the Second World War, in the early expectation of a large conflict to come, into which the war-unwilling democracies would be drawn at a time when they might not be prepared for the worst, when there was danger that they might prove unprepared thanks to a militarism on the part of their soldiers which would limit their best efficiency and impede the highest usefulness of their arms. Happily, not very much of such dreaded militarism came into effect. What appeared instead was the militarism of civilian leaders, showing itself in many lands. Civilian militarism was nothing new in the 1920's and 1930's—the new development was rather that it came into power and governance in the totalitarian states, such as Russia, Italy, Germany, Spain, gaining sooner or later control over the military establishments. In Germany of the Third Reich this happened in 1938, the year after the publication of this book. It seemed best at this time to leave the twelve chapters of the original work *essentially* untouched (although there are numerous minor changes), omitting even the opportunity to make use of later insights or of highly competent kindred writings since published, useful to and on the whole confirming our thesis, such as Gerhard Ritter's magistral *Staatskunst und Kriegshandwerk* I (1954), Gordon Craig's *Politics of the Prussian Army: 1640-1945* (1955), Harold J. Gordon's *The Reichswehr and the German Republic* (1957), Samuel P. Huntington's *Soldier and the State* (1957), and the author's own *Defense and Diplomacy* (1956). To cover the newer phenomena, variations, and ideas of militarism, two chapters, based on recent literature, have been added to the original text.

January 1959   *A. V.*

A HISTORY OF MILITARISM

Every war is fought, every army is maintained in a military way and in a militaristic way. The distinction is fundamental and fateful. The military way is marked by a primary concentration of men and materials on winning specific objectives of power with the utmost efficiency, that is, with the least expenditure of blood and treasure. It is limited in scope, confined to one function, and scientific in its essential qualities. Militarism, on the other hand, presents a vast array of customs, interests, prestige, actions, and thought associated with armies and wars and yet transcending true military purposes. Indeed, militarism is so constituted that it may hamper and defeat the purposes of the military way. Its influence is unlimited in scope. It may permeate all society and become dominant over all industry and arts. Rejecting the scientific character of the military way, militarism displays the qualities of caste and cult, authority and belief.

The Distinction Between Militarism and the Military Way

It is not militarism in this sense, therefore, when armies call for and make efficient, rational, up-to-date, and to a certain extent, humane use of the materials and forces available to them; when they prepare themselves for war decided upon, not by themselves, but by the civilian powers of the state; when they refrain from perpetuating themselves for the purpose of drawing money, enjoying power and honor, governing soldiers in peacetime, and drilling them in accordance with the rules of previous wars; when they get ready for the true future war which is not "in the air," but which takes the form of an image deduced from the general economy of contemporary society and from the materials it produces as war potentials.

The full realization that the military way and the militaristic way are two separate and distinct aspects of the use of men and materials by armies came late, however, and first in France. There, under the Second Empire, the word and the concept of "militarism" arose in political struggles. It was employed, like the coeval concept, "imperialism," by the Empire's republican and socialist enemies. From that time forward in France, in English usage after 1864, and in Germany since 1870, militarism has connoted a domination of the military man over the civilian, an undue preponderance of military demands, an emphasis on military considerations, spirit, ideals, and scales of value, in the life of states.[1] It has meant also the imposition of heavy burdens on a people for military purposes, to the neglect of welfare and culture, and the waste of the nation's best man power in unproductive army service.

Complaints against militarism are, of course, old. In the ninth century A.D., before the knights took over the arms-bearing monopoly in Europe, the freeholder groaned about the burdens laid upon him by the numerous Carolingian war enterprises, much as liberals, in the nineteenth century, deplored the strain put upon national economy by armaments. But militarism has become a political issue only recently—an issue raised in the struggles of domestic politics as a reproach to parties and institutions which unduly further military desires.

In the international sphere militarism has provided fuel for those recriminations which were supposed to find a solution and end in the war-guilt paragraph of the Versailles Treaty—recriminations in which each nation charges another with building up disproportionate armaments that threaten peace and force pacific nations to follow suit. This reproach was long aimed in the main at Germany by England and the United States, whose insular situation and historic development had kept their armies small and permitted reliance on their navies instead. With her own gigantic army, France was not in a comparable position for criticizing Germany. As France went on increasing her forces after 1918, when Germany was disarmed—agreeing with Clemenceau's position in March 1918, that "by bleating peace you cannot disarm German militarism"[2]—she found herself open to similar reproaches. These came in part from German writers who were active, between 1919 and 1933, in the campaign of "innocence," designed to prove Germany guiltless,[3] a campaign which the Versailles paragraph had launched. Yet reproaches also came from those elements in the Anglo-Saxon countries which sought the pacification of the world through the reduction of armies.

With imperialism, as a coeval term, militarism shares the tendency to extend dominion. The former generally seeks size, the latter, strength. Where the one looks primarily for more territory, the other covets more men and more money. The two hardly ever exist by themselves. Both are tendencies largely "justified" by history —that is, they cover their new demands with a cloak of tradition, the one invoking the images of emperors long dead, the other recalling past glories of action. And, in fact, history has examples of both to show.

Militarism in non-European regions, by 1939 seemingly extinguished except among the Japanese, once had many features in common with that of the modern West. For example, the Sikhs were taught "to devote their energies to steel alone among material things, ever carrying arms and ever waging war." [4] The ancient Assyrians afford the clearest demonstration of past imperialism and militarism. They were a rude folk from one of those frontiers of civilization which have ever proved the revitalizers of war, providing fresh ambition, new weapons, and still more barbaric methods for breaking up the war patterns of settled societies. Their army was the earliest fighting organization of great efficiency, complete from the emperor's life guards and baggage train to army chaplains. In her rise, frontier energy, "smartness," and disregard of humanity, Assyria seemed so like Prussia to the great German orientalist Hugo Winckler, that he kept exclaiming: "Prussia is Assur!" as he uncovered fresh similarities between the ancient conquerors and those who overran his native Saxony in 1756 and 1866.

Modern militarism has, nevertheless, specific traits. Since modern armies are not so constantly engaged in combat as were the ancient armies, they are more liable to forget their true purpose, war, and the maintenance of the state to which they belong. Becoming narcissistic, they dream that they exist for themselves alone. An army so built that it serves military men, not war, is militaristic; so is everything in an army which is not preparation for fighting, but merely exists for diversion or to satisfy peacetime whims like the long-anachronistic cavalry. This was well expressed by the Russian grand duke who admitted that he hated war "because it spoils the armies."

Generally speaking, militarism flourishes more in peacetime than in war. In wartime, however, the pursuit of ends not identical with the winning of victory is militaristic; enterprises for sheer glory or the reputation of leaders, which reduce the fighting strength of armies and wreck them from within, come under that head. Such features have appeared in every war and have been sharply condemned by competent military commanders. Napoleon, for instance, considered it "the greatest crime that man can commit on earth to kill on purpose men whose lives are entrusted to his direction and honor." [5] Again, Colonel T. E. Lawrence, after a certain battle, found it impossible to share the satisfaction of the British officers who had directed it: "To me an unnecessary action, or shot, or casualty, was not only waste but sin. I was unable to take the professional view that all successful actions were gains. . . . Even from the purely military point of view the assault seemed to me a blunder. The 200 Turks in Wejh had no transport and no food, and if left alone a few days must have surrendered." [6]

The acid test of an army is war—not the good opinion it entertains of itself or wins by "indoctrination" or other "promotional activities" before the war, or even sometimes after a defeat. War is the criterion, and war only. The rest is advertisement, including Moltke's claim that "the army is the most outstanding institution in every country, for it alone makes possible the existence of all civic institutions." This is no more true than the pacifist contention that armies as such constantly endanger the existence of civic institutions, and it ignores the paramount purpose of armies. Armies may protect society, if they prepare intelligently for defense; they may threaten it if they lose a sense of proportion between their own interests and those of the rest of society. It has happened that armies become so involved in contemplating domestic critics and foes, liberals in an earlier age, socialists later, and Communists more recently, that they have forgotten to concentrate on the enemy abroad—or that they have even sympathized with foreign armies and made common front with them against internal antagonists. In so doing, militarists have sharpened conflicts at home and permitted political views to cloud considerations of military efficiency.

One instance of this was the tendency of the old German army to overestimate the Russian soldiers, to whom Frederick the Great had paid the compliment: "It is not sufficient to kill the Russians. One has to knock them over too." The ancient Russo-Prussian comradeship in arms blinded Germans to fatal deficiencies in the Czarist machine; on the other hand, the army's antagonism to socialist labor led it to underestimate the war potential of native German industrial workers.

After 1918, various generals like Hoffmann in Germany and Fuller in England were so anti-Communist that they regarded Russia as *the* enemy even when their own governments were considering her as a potential ally against an aggressor. Another example of unmilitary thinking was presented by Major General John F. O'Ryan, a former police commissioner of New York, who, even after the American presidential campaign of 1936 had revealed less than 100,000 votes for the Communists, insisted that military training must be increased to check the alarming spread of Communism: "If we should come to war with a Communistic government, we shall have to fight a foe within as well as a foe without." [7] If Communists were really so strong in the United States, a more strictly military logic, it seems, would have required choosing an enemy, such as Japan, against whom all groups, including Communists, could fight together; or, if the future enemy was to be a fascist power, which seemed as likely, should not the army have favored and educated anti-fascists for military ends?

Militarism is thus not the opposite of pacifism; its true counterpart is civilianism. Love of war, bellicosity, is the counterpart of the love of peace, pacifism; but militarism is more, and sometimes less, than the love of war. It covers every system of thinking and valuing and every complex of feelings which rank military institutions and ways above the ways of civilian life, carrying military mentality and modes of acting and decision into the civilian sphere.[8] Under that definition, the "militarism of moods and opinions" has been more clearly in evidence in Germany than elsewhere, except in Japan, because there the soldier has been admired in peacetime, and not, as in other lands, mostly in war. Even in peace, the German seemed, until 1945, inclined to acknowledge the primacy of the military and accept its absolute good regardless of its use in war, its victories or defeats. This militarism was, however, not confined to Germany; it is far-reaching and deeply rooted, although in the Occident it is relatively modern.

Beginnings of Mass Militarism

The beginnings of such militarism of sentiment and conviction as a mass phenomenon may be placed in the romantic age, opening in the latter part of the eighteenth century. At that time, the old rationalism of the Enlightenment, which had regarded the soldier as a drilled murderer, was being submerged in resurgent emotionalism, and the glory of "romance" was being spread over the drab realities of war and the commonplaces of the industrial revolution. The carriers of this tendency were not the middle classes, represented by English utilitarians, Continental liberals and American rationalists of the constitutional period; these were distrustful of militarism, fearing to lose the fruits of their emancipation by such backward yearning for times and institutions hostile to their own developing interests. The makers of romanticism were rather the upper and the lower classes, the captivating and the captivated classes—the former, the Tory, or conservative forces, strove to re-erect what Edmund Burke called the state of the "knights and saints," and sought mass support through its romantic appeals.

Materially, this movement was all in favor of the churches, the nobility, and the armies. As Novalis, himself a nobleman and romantic poet, defined romanticism, it "is nothing but a qualitative transvaluation. . . . In giving a high sense to the common thing, a mysterious look to the commonplace, to the well-known the dignity of the unknown, to the final thing an infinite appearance, I romanticize it." [9] Through such transfiguration, old powers were re-established in public esteem. In the Middle Ages, up to then despised, was found a storehouse of such magic, by which Prussian soldiers in the Wars of the Liberation appeared as "crusaders," while their French enemies became the "Saracens." Or again, Prussia was discovered to be Sparta reincarnated; her war was dignified by comparison with that of the old Dorians, which was called

rather less of an effective activity directed toward the ruin of others than an impersonating activity which was to show the most beautiful aspect of the people in unanimous and flexible movement, like a vigorous and well-exercised body in the joyous consciousness of its strength.[10]

In that time of envelopment in historic and poetic association, the military profession won a high social position and moral value, and was ranked second only to the clergy by Metternich, who said that the one "labors through the word from the pulpit for the moral truth, the other on the battlefield by their deeds for right and justice. Church and army are serving order through the power of discipline and through hierarchical arrangement." [11] This elevation of the soldier, attained in the romantic age proper, was only increased by other movements in the later nineteenth and early twentieth centuries. In 1908, Walther Rathenau saw approaching yet another kind of romanticism with similar effect:

Romanticism of race. It is going to glorify the pure Nordic blood and create new concepts of virtue and vice. The tendency toward materialism will check this romanticism for a time. Then it will vanish, because the world needs, besides the blond temperament, the dark intellectuality, and because the demoniacal insists upon its rights. But the traces of this last romanticism will never disappear.[12]

All these social romantic movements sprang from reactionary grievances and desires, including in every case the grievances and desires of resentful military elements. In France, for instance, the military elements felt badly treated under the Bourbon Restoration, when the old officers of Napoleon were ousted in favor of noblemen who had never served in the army. They also cherished resentments under the ensuing bourgeois kingdom, when middle-class scorn for army service was at its height. As Alfred de Vigny, himself an officer for some fifteen years after 1814, complained, the citizens, absorbed by business, had only contempt for the idleness of the soldier: "The man for hire, the soldier, is a poor braggart, victim, and executioner, a scapegoat daily sacrificed to his people and for his people, who make sport of him; he is a martyr ferocious and humble at the same time." [13] But not only officers resented this attitude. A complex basis of feeling was formed among the common men who had served under Napoleon—a basis akin to that on which the veterans' organizations of the nineteenth and twentieth centuries were to flourish. At bottom this was the romanticization of an experience which, while it lasted, had been considered anything but romantic by the majority. Yet as the cult of Napoleon was built up, as memories and *gloire* were celebrated, the post-Napoleonic time became in many ways more militaristic than the Empire of Napoleon had been, when the nation had at last become truly war-weary.

The military of the Napoleonic school were glad to find a broad basis for support among the masses in their anti-Bourbon policies by re-picturing Napoleon. The same General Lamarque who had scorned the peaceful policy of France after 1815 as a "halt in the mud" and emphasized the need of re-employing the war-experienced officers of the old Empire to rebuild a strong army, was happy to discover with the masses "one point of contact; this is, the memory of past glory in which the meanest hamlet, the smallest straggling village, has taken an active part; for in every hamlet, under the roofs of all cottages, live the warriors of the Old Army." [14] Thus memory was militarized and made to serve as the ally of professional military interest, temporarily out of power. In this endeavor, artists and poets assisted, among them Heine and Béranger. The latter made more good poetry out of the dead Napoleon than had the panegyrists of his lifetime:

On parlera de la gloire
Sous la chaume bien longtemps.
L'humble toit dans cinquante ans
Ne connaîtra plus d'autre histoire.

(*They will speak of glory
In the cottages long afterward.
The humble roof in fifty years
Will know no other history.*) [15]

If the cottagers were soon to "know no other history," that was also the work of the historian-politicians, notably Thiers. Like the lark in his song, Thiers made his way upward by his panegyrical treatment of the military performances of the generals—Hoche, Kléber, Desaix, and then Bonaparte. Thiers became one of the first middle-class politicians to play on military mass instincts and make antirevolutionary, as well as imperialistic, use of military force; changing from an enemy of the Algerian enterprise under Charles X, he made himself its most exuberant apologist. In Thiers, the generals who took "a grand view" of the Algerian scheme found a protector with still grander views. He, the pint-sized bourgeois who had never seen military service, granted the army as much glory and romance in the present as in the past. In his history of the Empire, Thiers makes Napoleon the civilian-militarist superman—censured when found necessary with a servility which craves forgiveness for its humble presumption—a superman who plays like an artist upon that instrument of grandeur, the soldier of France. In this soldier Thiers sees no mere cannon fodder, but a person endowed with a mission, a missionary unconscious of the need for his own enfranchisement. "Cult of the Revolution, cult of the glory of arms, cult of the great Emperor, that is for Thiers the trinity of belief. It is also that of the French commoner." [16] Indeed, Thiers is among the first in that line of bourgeois civilian writers given to the praise of militarism, whose hybrid figures haunted Carlyle, Treitschke, Theodore Roosevelt, Nietzsche, Barrès, Charles Maurras, and Kipling. They all praised army institutions and army men, some for obedience and others for leadership, exulting as in the case of Carlyle over "the commander of men; he, to whose will other wills are to be subordinated, and loyally surrender themselves, and find their welfare in so doing, may be reckoned the most important of Great Men."

This sentiment echoed among those who had learned to feel the horrors and uncertainties of industrialization. While even those who fared comfortably sometimes turned backward in nostalgic appreciation of the Middle Ages, millions of workers and farmers, finding no great profit or enjoyment in their new freedom, sought solace for their isolation in the growing life of societies, clubs, and party organizations. What is more, even though they hated it personally and individually, they sought solace in war.

The contradictory attitude of the nineteenth-century masses toward wars is brought out by Lorenz von Stein: "It is true that victory brings to the sum total of the state, to the people, the highest profits, whereas at the same time it remains forever unable to restore to the individual what it has taken from him. . . . It is therefore natural that the individual hates war when at the same time he willingly surrenders his all to it. Forever an educated people will consider war as a misfortune, forever war will be combated in the name of humanity, and still after a victory a nation will seldom doubt that it is worth as much as it cost." [17]

This "forever" was laid down under the influence of the short wars of the nineteenth century and would not have held true immediately after 1918 under the mass disillusionment. But there is no doubt that the attitude of even modern masses toward militarism is a composite of contradictions. Péguy, one of the justest men of our time, has pointed to this inconsistency in the demands popularly made upon armies:

To demand of war, of the military, first cortèges such as only they can provide, secondly objects of malediction such as only they can furnish, thirdly and above all subjects for inspiration which cannot be demanded of peace: in this lies an undeniable, an insufferable duplicity, a peculiar triplicity. This is really making them serve three altogether contradictory purposes. . . . The people demand of the military parades, reviews of the 14th of July, . . . of war and the military, an occasion for the exercise of their curses and their moral, sentimental, public, oratorical, official, philanthropic, scientific, eloquent, learned, socialist, materialist, historical, syndicalist-revolutionary reprobation; thirdly, they demand of war and the military a motive of inspiration, an action of the imagination, when, reading back into the past, interpreting the present, anticipating the future, they want to make themselves believe that they have not lost the taste for adventures, when, finally, they are tired of being bored by the images of peace.[18]

Carried beyond their immediate uses and romantic associations, military arrangements and discipline have become a great pattern for individual employers or managers under industrialism, and finally for the order conceived of by Fascism and Communism. To a certain extent also, even the Salvation Army represents an attempt to get hold of military instincts in the service of religious philanthropy. Various church organizations have likewise made use of military forms and inclinations: the Jesuits from an early time imitated military institutions and condoned un-Christian features in militarism, like dueling.[19] Even of late the Jesuits have had a great hold on such officers as Boisdeffre, Foch, and Weygand. The Order of the Assumptionists was founded around 1850, and reconstituted in the 1880's for the purpose of extending the reign of Christ, to preserve and widen "the conquests of the Church," with the help of lay chevaliers.[20] The Knights of Columbus, founded in 1882, like the Knights of Labor, founded in 1869, is rooted in similar regions of feudal-military feelings.

In a world which becomes increasingly secularized, the ceremonial function of soldiers and the military arrangement of mass ceremonies grow in equal measure. Ever since the rise of standing armies, the soldier has been employed to a varying degree as a ceremonial appurtenance. This function has increased everywhere. Soldiers have formed the largest element and recently almost the whole of the inauguration parade of the American president. Soldiers appear as main performers on national holidays in France, and as participants in the English coronation ceremonies, for which new uniforms, more splendid than the drab khaki, were introduced. This development reached its extreme form in the completely militarized mass assemblies of the fascist states. The ceremonial function of the armies largely contributed to the continued existence of guards in the monarchies, or their revival in some of the fascist countries where bodies like Hitler's protective guard reunited the two original functions of guards: protection of the sovereign, who thinks he needs it again, and ceremonial duties. Exclusively ceremonial soldiers have formed the Swiss Guard of the Vatican since the termination of the Papal State. The ceremonial function of troops further contributed to the preservation of cavalry and the continued use of horses. When the British field artillery was mechanized in the 1930's, one battery of Horse was excepted "for ceremonial purposes." [21]

The prolonged existence of army militarism has been in part guaranteed by civilian militarism, which sees in armies the embodiment of certain, usually conservative, desires of its own: the desire for survival, at least impersonally, and security; the desire for discipline and command, for employs not immediately concerned with material profit, and the corresponding forms of organization —a hierarchy, coupled with the desire for comradeship. Moreover, where the hope for individual happiness becomes dubious to great numbers, where they become tired of peace and comfort, or of living safely in poverty, where their place in society seems wrong and private endeavor to lead nowhere, where the party strife seems senseless and literary production anarchic, then life with and within military bodies appears to offer a desirable pattern, at least for a time. Declaring "we are against the comfortable life," Mussolini turned just such desires to the uses of Fascism.

This love of "the strenuous life," for "the hard virtues," this hope for the *sabre libérateur*,[22] may in many cases be extremely short-lived and its lovers may all too soon repent their thirst for "living dangerously"; some such breaking-point occurs in the life of every militarist, even if he denies it upon recovery. But where the scramble for jobs seems hopeless, especially if made so by what appears to be corruption or bad luck or absence of plan, the desire arises to be put in one's right place from above, as members of military bodies seem to be placed, under a venerable head, and according to carefully devised schemes.

At the very bottom of the civilian order the isolated individual wants to find himself in a more congenial, less quarrelsome company than that provided by his business employment or his relatives. He may find this relief in the mass movements and processions in which the equal step, the music of bands, and mass chanting drown out, temporarily, the dissensions of ordinary life. As far as this charm is "remembered" by the ex-soldier, it is false memory, for there is very little in it that corresponds to actual experience in marching, which is hateful to every soldier, overburdened as he is, sweating, dusty, nauseated by the stench of the column, wishing nothing more fervently than to be away by himself in the fields. There is no true "repetition" in the formal march of men buoyed up by music, drink, and holiday freedom from a humdrum existence, saluted by crowds and the dignitaries of the reviewing stand. It is the same with the search for the round table of good comradeship, a much rarer article in actual military service than afterward. But by way of such illusions militarization has overtaken a large sector of the elements that are known in the United States as "joiners," comprising not only ex-soldiers, but marchers called by "knightly" names and bearing "knightly" insignia, and the class warriors.

Military History as a Phase of Militarism

In the process of militarizing minds, no small role has been played by writers of military history. By and large, these have been written with polemical purpose for the justification of individuals or armies and with small regard for socially relevant facts. The disputing of such works is made extremely difficult because war and battle are in many respects the outcome of neither art nor science; the products of the latter are clearly on record, to be examined at will, but the record of a battle is more or less confused at best. It would be hard to discover or prove what actually occurred in the brief heat of combat, even were nations not so eager to ascribe victory at once, on the evening of the same day, to one side or another, to one individual or another.

In order to meet the requirements of their contemporaries and of posterity it has been a habit of generals and their staffs not only to edit the reports of battles but also to word their orders in such an oracular fashion that victory, if it comes, can be traced to them, while failure, if it befalls, can be excused as a misreading by those lower in command.[23] For instance, when Leonard Wood's brigade at San Juan Hill was lying under heavy fire, to which it could hardly reply, and its commander saw no way out but to attack, the command gave a "Delphic response" to his report: "The Commanding General would deplore any loss of life, but he does expect general officers to use all their men to best advantage." Tired of inaction and losses, Wood attacked with his brigade, but he and Roosevelt were quick enough to claim for themselves, as against such "orders," the credit for the success.[24]

Again, a rival for high command may go on record in order to prove that his proposals were right, rather than those of the actual commander who failed. General Hoffmann, on occasion, remarked that "one really ought to found an insurance business against lost glory of war," and was only a little less ready than others to claim successes as the exclusive outcome of his own ideas. He considered the long-drawn-out rivalry between Falkenhayn and Hindenburg-Ludendorff as rather purposeless: "But H. and L. want to have it for the historical documents. To those I am more or less indifferent. I have now for the first time during the whole war observed a 'history' from nearby and know that it takes place in an entirely different manner from what posterity learns. Since it is so, some trifles or false descriptions more or less do not matter." [25]

Hoffmann's superiors had been very assiduous in cultivating their reputations ever since they had been favored at Tannenberg. Popular belief persisted in maintaining that Hindenburg had planned that battle some twenty-five years before, whereas in fact the plans had all been worked out by his unlucky predecessor in office. It was his good fortune that the Germans intercepted the Russian wireless, betraying their plans at every stage, for this did more to win the battle than Hindenburg. Taking account of the popular desire to ascribe victory to one man—or at the most to two men, co-operating closely—and the workings of chance, one can hardly avoid sharing Hoffmann's conclusion that "no one has won the battle," [26] a conclusion that might well be extended to most battles, at least in modern times.

The self-presentation of the military man in the form of memoirs thus tends to be controversial. It may contain admission of errors, though that is rare, but there is nothing in military documentation which would resemble an unreserved confession in the style of Rousseau. True, Frederick the Great in his *History of My Times* (1742 and 1746) conceded that no general had ever committed as many faults as he did in the First Silesian War, when he was learning the art of arms with the Austrian enemy as preceptor.[27] At Dresden in 1813 Napoleon admitted "with magnanimity that he was author of the greatest faults in the Russian campaign." [28] Blücher, on the evening after the battle at the Katzbach, confessed his good luck, saying to Gneisenau: "The battle we have won, nobody can deny us that; but now I wonder how we shall go about making the people understand how cleverly we have devised that." [29] Grant regretted that the "last assault at Cold Harbor was ever made." [30]

But little beyond this has ever been confessed, if this is indeed confession and not the pleasantry of victorious but gallant generals.

The Prince de Ligne thought it required greatness to acknowledge a military error,[31] which is one way of saying that the soldier is far more eager to be right than to concede right. If confession is one test of truthfulness, then there is little of reality in military memoirs. And since—apparently, constitutionally so—there can be but little of such realism, the Prussian general Constantin von Alvensleben, an upright and conservative man, laid down the rule that "a Prussian general dies but does not leave any memoirs." Prussian tradition long forbade the public appearance of the individual officer in his lifetime or posthumously.[32] Memoir writing might not be to the good of the memorialist's service, or, if to the supposed good, it might not be truthful.

A very large part of military history is written, if not for express purposes of supporting an army's authority and prestige, at least with the intention of not hurting it, not revealing its secrets, avoiding the betrayal of weakness, vacillation, or distemper; it is usually designed with a future war in mind, in its inspiring treatment of some particular war in the past. To doubt and attack such prestige by historical criticism even Moltke resented as "unpatriotic." [33] Military history wishes to save authority, especially when the writer is closely identified with the past to be treated. This tendency is the vice of most of the historical productions in which general staffs collaborate, through their historical departments—those "Historical Sections of the General Staff of the Army," which nearly all armies have successively acquired. They are the instruments which keep history a fiction agreed upon, *"une fable convenue,"* as Napoleon regarded it, and no other field of history is more open to the charge than that of the military.

The work of the Prussian General Staff on the Franco-Prussian War, for instance, is written in the style of a heroic epos, leading up to victory by ingeniously harmonized methods. Recalling Homer's ever recurring epithets for his heroes, this history constantly remarks, when speaking of the order of a general to a subordinate, that the latter was on the point of doing just that from his own insight and resolution.[34] Thus a harmony is established between the puerile thinking of the King, who allowed himself on occasions to interfere with Moltke's arrangements—to the latter's great disadvantage—and the genius of Moltke, by placing both men on the same level. This is obedience-history for the purposes of a hereditary monarchy under which the grandson of the first William tried to make out of his ancestor a William the Great, a change which could not be put across even in Germany.[35]

Officers who had participated in the Austrian campaigns of 1849 admitted that the General Staff history had caused accidental engagements to appear well planned in advance and that many a great battle disposition had been written after the battle.[36] A lieutenant colonel who criticized the Austrian General Staff's history —treated the official sources unofficially, as he said—was stricken from the lists of the imperial and royal officer corps.[37] Battle orders, which the naïve or patriotic historian is inclined to accept as the most genuine documentation of a commander's intentions, are often enough shaped with the intention "to cover up and not to spout out truth," and therefore often assume a sibylline character.

The rigor of authority, or its wish to "leave well enough alone," has generally suppressed critical treatment. The Prussian military authorities of pre-1914 times punished, refuted, persecuted, ostracized critical officer writers over whom they still exercised disciplinary powers and whose irregular opinions were taken for proof of "disloyalty." The nearest approach to a German Dreyfus case arose for reasons of military history. An ex-captain, one Hoenig, crippled in the Franco-Prussian War, for a long time well appreciated as a military writer, later made himself objectionable by severe judgments passed on the historical writings of the General Staff. General von Bernhardi, the well-known author of *Germany and the Next War,* challenged Hoenig to a duel, but the half-blind, invalided writer declined to fight a duel on such grounds. A court of honor, before which old colleagues of Hoenig tried to compromise him but merely compromised themselves, deprived him of the right to wear the uniform.[38]

Much of military history is, therefore, misleading as a result of the authors' deliberate intentions, and much of the rest is merely convention-ridden in the interest of militarism. It is dominated by stereotypes, such as the eternal story of the bayonet fight, for which hardly any historical sources worth the name are available, but which cannot be left out of any description lest the knightly hand-to-hand encounter of manly valor be missing.[39] And unconsciously, perhaps, the average writer is filled with the images which Napoleon consciously used or invented for his own advancement. The Emperor was, of course, the most gifted self-manipulator of his fame, and did not need such public relations counselors as those who wrote an autobiography for Hindenburg and managed his candidature and elections. Bonaparte wrote or edited his own war bulletins; "lying like a bulletin" became a saying of his time. When anyone pointed out the untruthful character of the bulletins, he would say: "My dear fellow, you are a dunderhead; you don't understand it." [40] He wrote and talked as much of his own history as possible; at St. Helena, twenty years after the event, he dictated the famous address to the Army of Italy in 1796: "Soldiers, you are unclad, badly nourished; the government owes you much, it can give you nothing. . . . I will lead you into the most fertile plains of the world. Rich provinces, great towns will be in your power; you will find there honor, glory, and riches." [41] Of other proclamations from his own pen, he later remarked: "That is a little of the charlatan." [42]

Always asking of himself, "What will they say in France?" Napoleon sought to fit himself into those ready-made situations and garments which popular imagination holds out for the hero to wear. Mishaps for which he was directly responsible he attributed to dead men or others not in a position to defend themselves. He invented the story about his conversation with Mohammedan leaders on religious questions inside a pyramid;[43] and took good care that paintings of Arcole showed him with the tricolor in his hand on the bridge, instead of in the dirt and water at the foot of the dike where he really was, for the first and only time, in personal danger—and in circumstances none too glorious.[44]

The historical record of warfare is thus dependent to a large extent on the writers' desire to preserve reputations, their tendency to clichés, and confusion of history as experience and history as authority. All this makes the teaching of war through the historical method a dubious enterprise. Yet no other art or science has so definitely clung to the thought and teachings of the past as guidance for the future, or so far ignored the alterations of circumstances brought by time. To call a battle of today a "Cannae" is about as much justified as naming a brand of synthetic perfume "Psyche," but the military officer, unlike the capitalist, looks backward in order to prepare for the future.

The capitalist, if he reads today the Fugger newsletters of the sixteenth century, thinks of them as utterly unrelated to his own letters. Only with respect to credit is he ready to pay respect to age; like regiments, business firms are inclined to point to their respectable age if they have acquired one. Otherwise, the businessman is emancipated to an extreme degree from the past; and if he troubles himself about military affairs, as did Johann von Bloch, he asks the military: "What is the use of talking about the past when you are dealing with an altogether new set of considerations?"

Within military institutions, however, exists a peculiar contradiction: their members are dominated by a conservative view of things while at the same time they prepare for a task which is truly in the future and which, when discharged, will be potentially revolutionary in procedure and effect on society. Unamuno once spoke of the "historical present" which does not allow a people like the Spanish to find its way into the real present. Most armies have been or are living in such a historical present. Militarism is in this sense mere "historicism" and armies are of all groups in society the ones most subdued to historical memoirs in their methods and honor concepts: "duty as our fathers understood it." [45]

So Foch, for example, employed history in directing the Ecole de Guerre. With no schooling for historical criticism, but a great conviction of the need for authority, which the Jesuits seem to have given him, Foch proceeded, he said, "from the facts which history delivers to us"—delivers, apparently, as a factory produces goods. "Our models and the facts on which we shall base a theory," he announced, "we shall draw from the Revolution and from the Empire." In choosing such periods arbitrarily, he generally avoided the latest wars; his own studies referred largely to the Prusso-Austrian War of 1866. But the remoteness of an experience did not matter to him, for he discounted recent changes in the composition and machinery of armies. He did not heed the warning of Napoleon who, although invoking the great warriors of the past as his ancestors for purposes of government, declared that warfare depended upon equipment, that the example of the ancients did not teach us anything because their arms were so different, and that tactics should be changed every ten years. The result of such French teaching was that the experience of 1870-1, which fully demonstrated the inviolability of the fronts was, shocking as it had been, forgotten. As General Colin writes, "The heroism of the military writers had to manifest itself on paper by the firm resolution to make the impossible real": that is, to insist on the open mass attack, the *offensive à l'outrance*,[46] which left the French less ready than they should have been to meet 1914.

This tendency to connect the present battle with the long line of past conflicts is naturally stronger in older Europe than America. Less burdened with military relics, General Ulysses S. Grant felt that historical luggage impeded forward movement. He was convinced that some of the Union generals—he might have had Halleck in mind especially—"failed because they worked out everything by rule."

They knew what Frederick did at one place, and Napoleon at another. They were always thinking about what Napoleon would do. Unfortunately for their plans, the rebels would be thinking about something else. I don't underrate the value of military knowledge, but if men make war in slavish obedience to rules, they will fail. No rules will apply to conditions of war as different as those which exist in Europe and America. Consequently, while our generals were working out problems of an ideal character . . . practical facts were neglected. To that extent I consider remembrances of old campaigns a disadvantage. . . . *War is progressive*.[47]

In this search for lessons in the past, the military man is hampered by conventional images, the pressure of official polemic and personal rivalry, and a too narrow conception of history which concentrates upon particular details of battles, campaigns, and wars. This may be highly misleading, even if accurate, and is apt to give a distorted picture of reality. As a French colonel and teacher of discipline exclaimed: "No one will understand that, in order to know tomorrow, it is necessary to be acquainted with yesterday, and yesterday is nowhere sincerely written down. It is only in the memory of those who know how to remember because they know how to see, and these have not spoken." [48]

At the opposite extreme lies another concept of history, which hunts for the ideal, constant, and not time-conditioned laws of war, to be traced through the centuries from Cannae to the Marne. In the denial of the time-conditioned character of war, the military writer approaches the theologian, likewise unwilling to admit temporary influences upon his eternal beliefs. This inclination to make absolute order through military history makes even judicious men like Liddell Hart say that thought is the most influential factor in history, although maintaining in the same breath that "the nature of armies is determined by the nature of the civilization in which they exist," and admitting that the thought of the Renaissance "did not really begin to affect the military world until the seventeenth century." [49]

The dangers of this absolute school of history were pointed out by General von Clausewitz in his *On War*. Former wars, he thought, form a collection of reminders, an association of ideas for the general to choose from, not repeatable experiences. Though unwilling to agree with the thinkers of the age of Rousseau who considered warfare "a natural function of man," requiring no aid from knowledge, he emphasized the limits of the latter:

No activity of the human spirit is possible without a certain richness of ideas and images, and those are not inborn but acquired; they constitute man's knowledge. . . . Theory must educate the future leader or rather guide him in his education, but not accompany him to the battlefield. . . . As things are, there exist no laws at all for warfare. [50]

Between the narrow specialist concept of military history, and that which seeks to formulate abstract philosophy, there is another, the socio-economic, which would integrate the development of armies and warfare with that of the state, business and finance, society as a whole and its ideas. But so broad a view is repugnant to the ordinary military mind, if not to certain individuals. The average military mind is conservative in its relation to the revolutionary processes of history from the Protestant Reformation to our own times. This is inherent in the nature of armies and their management. As it takes many years to organize and equip an army, a long-time stability is necessary in the structure and functions of the society in which the preparation of the army is made. Hence the army by the very nature of things depends for its existence, honors, emoluments, and privileges upon the order in which it takes form; and in self-defense, if nothing more, it is conservative in relation to the order in which it thrives, whether that order be agrarian, capitalistic, or communistic.

So it has come about that, generally speaking, the great modern revolutions have been, in their origins, foreign to and remote from armies—the Reformation, the rise of capitalism, the industrial revolution, the American Revolution, and the other world-shaking upheavals from the eighteenth century to the twentieth century. So it has also come about that armies have always been closely associated with suppressions, reactions, and counterrevolutions. In the religious counterrevolution of the sixteenth century, for example, the former army officer Loyola furnished the scheme of organization and force for the Jesuits, whose first general he was; army men supported the armed feudalism which survived in the armies of the capitalistic states—armies maintained at the expense of the capitalists and the lower classes prevented the industrial revolution from working out to logical forms; army men aided the monarchists and imperialists who overcame the revolutions in England, France, and Germany; and army men have supported the fascisms which combated the Russian and other revolutions.

The resistance of the armies and their leaders to such revolutions is based to some extent on their professional conservatism, which loves order, sees order merely in the established arrangements, and cannot discern a new one amid popular turmoil. The technological, psychological, and other changes wrought by a revolution have to be enforced from the outside upon army men; often this is only possible when the old army has been beaten. The soldier and revolutions, leaving aside mere revolts, thus stand in antithesis. A soldier is not a revolutionary, though a revolutionary may turn into a soldier, as Cromwell did. Masses of men, ideas, machinery, appear to be breaking loose in such an eruption, and thus can only be distressing to the soldier's order-approving mind; so Bonaparte, watching the Paris riots, longed to fire canister shot among the milling people to bring them back to order. Clinging to tradition, which in itself is a means for him to maintain authority, the soldier is averse to acknowledging and embracing changes forced upon him, particularly if they do not appear to favor his immediate interests.

Accustomed to commanding masses, the officer hates to see masses in seeming command. He prefers his own dependence upon individual persons of disciplined minds, and this strong sense for the individual is accentuated by the constant prospect of personal danger, of being wiped out in battle. But though so determinedly individual, the soldier can never be very individualistic. Tradition predetermines his behavior and mode of thought; all his patterns are cut for him, and he seeks more or less eagerly to conform to them. His sphere of action even in war is severely limited under modern conditions, far more so than the popular imagination, filled with inherited images, will allow. The soldier becomes an individual only in moments of danger, or when he attains high rank; the rest of the time he is a subordinate, and stereotyped. He is, in truth, much like those old-fashioned pictures which German conscripts used to buy, showing a soldier in three poses—on guard duty, on horseback, and in full dress—with empty spots left for the face of the individual, which were carefully filled by pasting photographic cut-outs in the vacancies.

The conservatism of the soldier is strengthened by the fact that the public now places an inordinate expectation upon the individual military leader, the theoretically insulated personality, although the conditions of modern warfare actually tend to minimize the authority and power of decision of the solitary leader. The public still insists upon giving the credit for military victory to the single hero, ignoring the fact that this credit is nowadays more than ever indivisible. And the method of rewarding officers and men continues the tradition. Technical progress would permit the proper measuring and distributing of success; it should be possible to determine which officer obtained his objective with the least expenditure of life and material, and to award honors in due proportion. But the officer, though he becomes more like an engineer, is not rewarded in fact according to any such standards. Distinctions still go customarily to those officers who have personally survived tremendous disasters, to which their own errors may have largely contributed. Marks of distinction are accorded to those wounded in battle, but not perhaps for especially courageous actions or painful and damaging illnesses incurred in war. Thus, survival in battle is honored in modern war when it is often merely the result of chance, just as survival used to be when it was necessarily a result of valor and strength.

Actually, the relations of individual danger and group success are less close today than at any previous time. In medieval warfare, when the individual was the unit of combat, the prowess of the single man was the basis of the whole party's victory. Now, on the other hand, the soldier has become a cipher; yet he continues to feel, and to be regarded by others, like a knight instead of a workman or technician of destruction. We may hold with Jung that this inclination is rooted in the "medieval stratum of our unconscious mind," at the same time rooting other more barbaric phenomena of warfare in a berserk stratum of that unconsciousness. For purposes of social history, however, this tracing back of emotions is hardly as important as tracing the forces and conditions which preserve them.

The popular feeling that flatters the soldier as such is doubtless part of the general elevation of the common man. The old caricature of the *miles gloriosus,* so long representing civilian resentment at the professional braggart and swashbuckler, seems to have vanished from stage and fiction; the new stereotypes are more flattering. "I want a hero!" exclaimed Byron. And the public cries: "We want *one* hero; we cannot admire a whole headquarters, an aggregation of committees." Hence of all successes and performances that of the military man is still most personal. As a Prussian high official wrote, when the question of his biography was discussed: "Among soldiers the personality is the symbol. . . . Of Alexander and Epaminondas all the world knows how to talk; of Pericles only a few, and the few only a little." [51] The general, and other officers, are eager to live up to, and perhaps to die for, a largely fictitious convention established around them, for them, and finally by them. The soldier is, therefore, to be regarded as an *imaginary individual* in a social scene.

Both the conservatism and the individualism of the soldier make him feel resentful at civilian interference in his affairs. He becomes restive under demands that he submit to civilian control, wishing to preserve that independence which seems his by right and tradition; he ignores or tries to escape the fact that powerful social and technological changes have already been exerting pressure upon him and that he cannot remain immune from them. He is unable to see that strict interdependence exists between the military institutions to which he belongs and the general political economy of the nation in which they have arisen. To his mind, armies still grow in a vacuum, according to ideal plans, formed by well-considered, expert wish and will. This conviction is strengthened by the extreme conventionality of military history, which is far behind other branches of history in recognizing social, cultural, and material backgrounds for the play of events.

The Uses and Lessons of Military History

The present confusion in the civilian mind and the true military mind respecting the purposes of armies and limits of warfare is attributable to many circumstances. Among them, no doubt, is the character of military history as it has commonly been written. Ordinary citizens are lacking in the raw experiences of combat, or deficient in technical knowledge, and inclined to leave the compilation of military records to "experts" in such affairs. Writers on general history have tended to neglect the broader aspects of military issues; confining themselves to accounts of campaigns and battles, handled often in a cursory fashion, they have usually written on the wars of their respective countries in order to glorify their prowess, with little or no reference to the question whether these wars were conducted in the military way of high efficiency or in the militaristic way, which wastes blood and treasure.

Even more often, in recent times, general historians have neglected military affairs and restricted their reflections to what they are pleased to call "the causes and consequences of wars"; or they have even omitted them altogether. This neglect may be ascribed to many sources. The first is, perhaps, a recognition of the brutal fact that the old descriptions of campaigns are actually of so little use to civilians and military alike. Another has been the growing emphasis on economic and social fields deemed "normal" and the distaste of economic and social historians for war, which appears so disturbing to the normal course of events. Although Adam Smith included a chapter on military defense in his *Wealth of Nations* as a regular part of the subject, modern economists concentrate on capital, wages, interest, rent, and other features of peaceful economic pursuits, largely forgetting war as a phase of all economy, ancient or modern. When they mention the subject of armies and military defense, these are commonly referred to as institutions and actions which interrupt the regular balance of economic life. And a third source of indifference is the effort of pacifists and peace advocates to exclude wars and military affairs from general histories, with a view to uprooting any military or militaristic tendencies from the public mind, on the curious assumption that by ignoring realities the realities themselves will disappear.

This lack of a general fund of widely disseminated military information is perilous to the maintenance of civilian power in government. The civilian mind, presumably concerned with the maintenance of peace and the shaping of policies by the limits of efficient military defense, can derive no instruction from acrimonious disputes between militarists, limitless in their demands, and pacifists, lost in utopian visions. Where the civilians fail to comprehend and guide military policies, the true military men, as distinguished from the militarists, are also imperiled. For these, the executors of civilian will, dedicated to the preparation of defense and war with the utmost regard for efficiency, are dependent upon the former.

Again and again, military men have seen themselves hurled into war by the ambitions, passions, and blunders of civilian governments, almost wholly uninformed as to the limits of their military potentials and almost recklessly indifferent to the military requirements of the wars they let loose. Aware that they may again be thrown by civilians into an unforeseen conflict, perhaps with a foe they have not envisaged, these realistic military men find themselves unable to do anything save demand all the men, guns, and supplies they can possibly wring from the civilians, in the hope that they may be prepared or half prepared for whatever may befall them. In so doing they inevitably find themselves associated with militaristic military men who demand all they can get merely for the sake of having it, without reference to ends. It is this prospect which has led military men, engaged in relating armies to the context of society and its potentials of warfare, to demand the formulation of civilian policy.

To promote this understanding and co-operation between civilians and their military executors, armies and war cannot be considered aside from their relations to society; the potentials of war must be recognized in the practical arts, forms of government, and public policies, for the potentials of power indicate the limitations of power. At the same time civilians should acquaint themselves with the roots, growth, nature, proclivities, and psychology of armies and their management by officers—the character of the military estate and the interests attached to it. This only the broadest interpretation of history and its dissemination can provide.

Military men themselves have been on the whole quicker to see the interrelations of armies and societies than civilians. As long ago as 1770, Comte de Guibert, in his *Essai général de tactique,* recognized the intimate connection of war and social institutions, emphasizing the fact that every improvement in the army must be preceded by an improvement in the state to which it belongs. With an insight uncommon for the times, he also saw that standing armies, besides being a burden on the people, did not provide the highest potentials and declared that the hegemony over Europe would fall to the nation that created a "national army." In the same century, on the other side of the Rhine, a nonmilitary but bureaucratic historian, Justus Möser, perceived that his absolutist contemporaries were inclined to absolutize war, and that other ages had also reflected their characteristics in war no less than in art:

> The style of all arts, and even of the dispatches and love letters of a Duke of Richelieu stand to one another in some relation. Each war has a tone of its own, and the actions of state have their coloring, their costumes, and their manner, in connection with religion and the sciences. . . . The hasty French genius shows itself in state actions as well as in the novel. One can discover it under the ground by the line along which it follows and gathers in a rich vein of ore. . . . Each time has a style of its own.[52]

On their part some general historians, such as Leopold von

Ranke, have recognized the correspondence of military institutions and modes of warfare to the state of society. This conception was greatly elaborated by the founders of historical materialism. To them, indeed, "nothing was more dependent on economic conditions than an army and navy." [53] Army history, more than any other, exhibited to them the interrelation between the forces of production and social conditions. War, Marx wrote, "is earlier developed to perfection than peace." He pointed to the way in which certain economic relationships, like that of labor and employer, had been evolved earlier for war in the armies than for peace in a capitalist society.[54] Division of labor, Marx and Engels thought, had been first achieved within one branch of human activity, in war; machinery had first been used on a large scale and the value of metals enhanced.[55] The labor of later non-Marxist researchers has gone to substantiate, in large part, the contention that progress in war often has preceded progress in peace; that war immensely stimulated certain phases of capitalist development, and yet was in turn dependent upon economic conditions.

This was indeed the opinion of the foremost teacher of military history in Moltke's era, Major Max Jähns, who sought to prove that everywhere the forms of war constitutions corresponded to those of political economy. Thus medieval economy, based on land ownership, produced its specific forms of war in armies of barons and knights; so did early capitalism with its mercenary armies; mercantilism brought impressment and recruiting; general conscription was related to modern capitalism. Fascism and its institutions he did not live to see. But writing in days when Darwinism had just been embraced, and railways and the telegraph had for the first time been applied in war, Jähns even maintained that all the intellectual progress of tribal societies had been made through war: "These progressive steps have been the more manifold and quick, the more various and the more difficult has been the struggle of peoples for survival." [56]

Leaving open the question whether military development was always so close to and contributory to other steps in the growth of society, we may say that each stage of social progress or regress has produced military institutions in conformity with its needs and ideas, its culture as well as its economics. As Goethe observed, "The quality of its courts of law and its armies gives the most minute insight into the essence of an empire." That is to say, army conditions reflect the state of society generally. Hence the task of the historian remains to show in any given case or period how the army of a state fits into the system of national or international division of labor; how armies are interrelated, by what means and interests they are kept up, and how the manning and paying of armies affect society, finances, and national economy; how the thought of military men stands in relation to the thought of their own time.

From such history it is impossible to lay down inexorably the patterns of a coming conflict. More often than not, war emancipates itself from the past conditions as it goes on, creating new forms and laws, under the guidance of great military thinkers and leaders. Military history can at best deduce the possibilities of future innovations. It can, however, show the dependence of military institutions on the conceptions and values of the dominant interests in a society and the derivation of war patterns from the social values and practices of the warmaking party. In the beginning, at least, war is always fought with the means and thoughts of an earlier time; its character is fixed at the outbreak by the repressions and brake-frictions imposed by the socio-economic frame of the previous peace.

If there is no sure and absolute guidance for the future in the past, history can at least be made to yield certain limited and specific lessons. One of these is the necessity for facing the difficulties and peculiarities of coalition warfare, as Pershing and others were unready to do in the First World War. Another is the cold fact that national policy is military policy, no matter in what fine phrases it is couched. If civilian policies are constructed without regard to their military implications, with reckless disregard of war potentials, and money is voted for military establishments blindly, without knowing whether it is too meager or excessive, or whether it is to be spent in a military or a militaristic manner, the maintenance of peace and of society itself is threatened.

If, through a broader kind of military history, civilians could learn to relate ends and means, much of the friction between them and the military would be eliminated; both would be controlled by an informed and realistic conception of society's interests, and the militaristic men could be subordinated to the military; the nearest approach would be made to a rational adjustment of international controversies which the present state of world affairs would permit. Or at least, under a comprehensive review of its military institutions, any given nation might come closer to attaining security—now the avowed aim of armies, though often imperiled by the pursuit of the militaristic way on the part of the military and their blind followers in the civilian sphere.

Postscript 1958: Post-1945 military history has not quite lived up to this prescription, if prescription it was. The history of the Second World War has indeed been undertaken by the two great Western belligerents with great promptness, though not with the undue haste shown by the Berlin General Staff when it went over to the "historiographical offensive," as the French General Staff complained, and began to publish its own version of the Franco-Prussian War as early as 1872, thus capturing world opinion. Only after the most careful preparations, including the sequestering of German records and the use of German captive leaders to provide their version of the recent battles, was writing and publishing begun. In both Britain and the United States the general staffs largely renounced their role as history writers—their censoring function is somewhat unclear—and instead agreed to let civilian professional historians compose the voluminous histories of the Second World War. It cannot be said that this change resulted in a civilianization of war history, but rather in a militarization of civilian writers more anxious not to err on the side of military detail than to bring the latest of the wars into the larger frame of a general history of wars. The result, too often, was case histories, each assignment left flowering or withering by itself, like potted plants, and not all themes of war assigned or handled, with organization and operations most fully treated and problems like military-civilian relations or morale least, if at all.

The downgrading to which Stalin from 1945 on, if not earlier, submitted the victorious Soviet army, included its war history as well and stood in the way of its being written as the army itself would have liked and as it thought it had deserved. Following Stalin's own downgrading, army hopes revived that now at last a true or desirable history would be written, a hope that vanished when the army's fugleman, Marshal Zhukov, was in turn downgraded by Khrushchev. Soviet marshals were either not permitted to write their memoirs or found this inadvisable, whereas Western generals proceeded to do so even before going into retirement and with a promptness that suggested the market demands for the "crusades" of western generals or the "passion plays" which German generals had participated in under Hitler no less than the need or desire for justification. The more cautious generals like Montgomery or Alanbrooke held their retaliatory fire longest, but none of them equaled the literary style, breadth of view, and depth of insight of Winston Churchill's history-memoirs. In that respect, at least, the civilian side of civilian-military relations remained superior.

FROM THE FEUDAL WARRIOR TO THE MASS ARMY

If militarism comprises all the activities, institutions, and qualities not actually needed for war, then the standing army in peacetime is the greatest of all militaristic institutions. At least it would have appeared so to the men of the Middle Ages, who were accustomed to consider the usefulness of an army over with the conclusion of war. When the last battle was won, armed forces were expected to dissolve and return to their homes; the notion of maintaining large numbers of fighting men in idleness, constantly ready for combat, was utterly foreign to early writers on military topics.

1
From the Mounted Warrior to the Standing Army

The Breakdown of the Feudal Array

Under the feudal system, the warrior was permanent, but not the army. Always awaiting trial of his strength, to which he was bound by duty, inclination, and education, the knight with his followers assembled at the summons to arms—or at least he was expected to do so. But once the campaign was over, he rode back to his castle. Not only did the feudal army disperse when peace was made, but even during war it operated on principles peculiar to the times. It was an aggregation of individuals who considered themselves equals and their followers as tools and did not know leaders in a modern sense. They fought in a single line, *la haie*, the hedge, each man insisting on a front position. The bourgeois notion of a reserve in store was antipathetic to the chivalric mind.

As far as their power went, the feudal noblemen tried to monopolize the arms-bearing privilege, both for fighting and hunting. Under the medieval formula of the division of labor in society, the knights were appointed to do battle, as the clergy to pray and the people to work. Drastic punishment was meted out to those inferiors who could be caught infringing on their rights: in 1078, peasants of southern Germany who had taken up arms for their Emperor, Henry IV, were, after their defeat, castrated by the feudal armies for their presumption in bearing tools reserved to the knighthood.[1] The glory of death on the battlefield was reserved for the armored man on horseback; and though common men were permitted to come to his assistance in some extreme cases, this was regarded as abnormal and monstrous. If they perished by his side, it was viewed with lusty mockery as a joke. Describing the battle of Senlis in 1418, a French chronicler said: "There was a captain who had a crowd of foot-men who all died, and there was great laughter because they were all men of poor estate."[2]

Of course, this reduced the military strength of all peoples under feudalism. Had the German peasants been allowed to own long-bows and crossbows, the resistance of Germany to foreign marauders in the Thirty Years' War might have been more effective. This fact was even perceived by some at the time, and an English voice was raised to protest against the hunting monopoly: "Is not the safety of the country worth more than the saving of a few wild fowl?" But the feudal nobleman remained impervious to such considerations; even though he saw the ability of foot soldiers demonstrated, as in the Crusades, when so many steeds died and could not be replaced, he was not interested in enlarging warfare. Nor could he have done so under the conditions of land-economy, when cash was too scarce to permit such progress in war. He moved within a simple, much-restricted frame, and resisted with jealous pride the forces which soon began to break down his ideal system of privileges.

Even in the Middle Ages, the Swiss peasant communities had managed to preserve a prefeudal, communal system in their mountains, which they defended with success against the formidable array of armored knights. Swiss foot soldiers defeated feudal armies at Morgarten in 1315, at Sempach in 1386, at Granson and Murten in 1476; growing aggressive, they won outside their own land at Nancy in 1477. Still primitive, they did not have a true leader, only an *Ordner,* a regulator who ordered the crowds without commanding them; the throng was kept together by the drum beat and swinging of banners. In this society which had escaped the sway of feudal knights, there was a reservoir of popular military strength which could be drawn upon and hired later by more modern armies.

The latent fighting power of the common man was also demonstrated by the uprisings of the Hussites, peasants and townsmen inspired by religious zeal to create a heaven on earth, embodying more than Luther's, the Reformation Militant. Judged by such standards as military leadership, the Hussites were more advanced than the Swiss, for they followed a commander; everywhere that their strength was pitted against feudal armies, they were victorious; they collapsed only when undermined on the home front, with the defeat of the radical Taborites in 1434.

During the Middle Ages, townspeople had remained to a large extent outside the system of feudalism, and did their own fighting, though along feudal lines, as in the wars of Italian city-states after Legnano (1176), of Flemish towns (Courtrai, 1302), and of the German Hanse towns (first German victory at sea, 1254). These towns won and kept their liberties by shedding the blood of their own citizens in incessant struggle against chivalric forces. They also resorted to war for purposes unknown to the nobility: for the protection and development of trade, for territorial conquest around their cities, and in the interests of mobile property. As their wealth increased from enlarged traffic, the cities, with their money-economy, larger fluid resources, and higher technology, began more and more to challenge the feudal system based upon immobile wealth in land and simple barter.

Soon, indeed, the burghers preferred not to fight their own battles any longer. They found that the growth of population in towns, the increasing number of workers cut loose from the soil and standing outside the guilds, provided more men willing to earn their bread by risking their bodies for brawls and wars. These mercenaries, or soldiers (the word comes from the Latin *solidus,* a heavy, solid coin), could be organized under the leadership of war entrepreneurs, the *condottieri,* to fight for the towns. By this division of labor, the burghers could pursue trade and finance, devote themselves to politics and the refinements of leisure. No longer did they reckon man power as the chief "nerve of war" (*nervo della guerra*) as feudalism did; they esteemed more highly other elements, iron, money, and bread. They tended to forget, though Machiavelli reminded them, that men and iron could always find them bread and money, but money and bread could not always secure good men.

The chief sources of footloose men were Swiss and German at first. Political governors of the former, in return for money for themselves and their cantons, permitted foreign powers to recruit there. But the true organizer of war was rather to be found in the beginning among the Germans, where a prince or war lord in need of an army called upon and authorized some well-known colonel to found regiments. On his part, the colonel relied on captains as subcontractors to bring in the men, who were not bound but free soldiers, *Landsknechte,* appearing in large numbers by the end of the fifteenth century. Usually the colonel was of noble origin or was knighted before receiving his commission—an early indication of the leadership monopoly which the nobility was to retain in various European countries. Thus an essentially capitalistic enterprise was hidden behind a patent of nobility; and this patent proved its value in terms of international as well as national profit when the business of supplying men for mercenary armies became fully cosmopolitan in the seventeenth century.

Enlargement of troops was necessary to make effective use of the bow. As Comines remarked, on the occasion of the battle of Montlhéry (1476): "The supreme thing for battles are the archers, but let them be by the thousands, for in small numbers they are worth nothing, and let them be badly mounted so that they feel no regret at losing their horses."[3] The rivalry in numbers so evoked then aroused the deepest resentment among feudal knights, who had been accustomed to aproximately equal opposing forces, and to equality of weapons as well. It was not chivalrous to be superior in numbers or differently armed, or to fight at a distance. The knight did not consider the bow and arrow "fair weapons." The sword knew where it struck the adversary, the arrow did not. And it was far worse when the gun was introduced with which, as Hegel said, the soldier shoots into the void. The new modes of warfare, at the end of the fifteenth century, seemed treacherous and dishonorable to those looking back wistfully to a nobler age, now closed:

In olden times he received great praise and honor who let his enemy have equal arms. Challenges went out in good order to those who were good knightly people. Now no one is a good captain who cannot beat his handicapped enemy. Now he is praised and extolled in war, who is able and knows how to cheat his enemy.[4]

With the introduction of artillery, the antagonism of bourgeois and noble increased. These devices were the products of urban arts and crafts; they resulted from the economic, social, and intellectual changes that disintegrated feudalism and were manufactured by the foes of feudalism—the city bourgeois and the artisans. In a strict sense, gunpowder, muskets, and cannon did not "smash feudalism"; plebeian foot soldiers without firearms had already beaten chivalric bodies before their introduction; moreover, the last feudal armies had themselves employed guns, as Charles the Bold did against the Swiss. The notion that artillery alone had the revolutionary effect as a smasher of feudalism was rather a part of the self-praise of later gunners. One of those who started the legend was an artillery captain, Michael Mieth, in the Emperor's service in 1683, who exulted:

Where are now those numerous robber castles, built on high mountains, in which not a few shamefully robbing and burning murderers, preserving themselves safely, not only made whole territories unsafe, but even defied the highest and crowned heads? Have they not been intimidated by the guns, like chickens, and are their residences not turned into stone-heaps and dens of owls, snakes, and bad spirits?

Mieth also developed the argument that the use of artillery or even newer weapons is at bottom more humane. Had the Greeks and Trojans known gunpowder, he surmised, the former would not have lost 80,800,000 men [!] before Troy. Moreover, gunpowder increased the abilities of Christendom to spread faith:

Before the discovery of gunpowder, both the Indies were in the jaws of hellish Satan and in the very darkest obscurity, more like cattle or wild beasts in customs and beliefs than like reasonable creatures of the great God. Gunnery has been the only means by which the command of Christ could be performed (Luke 14:23: "Urge them to come in that My house may become full.").[5]

Despite the self-satisfaction of Mieth, it was more than the change of weapons which overcame feudalism: the weapons themselves were the fruit of a long period of development in which urban independence was growing and money-economy spreading, challenging the old social system based on the soil. Artillery was made and introduced, however, by antifeudal classes, it is true, and it remained in bourgeois hands henceforth. The noblemen who later commanded national armies never became fully accustomed to such arms, or quite reconciled to their use. The artillery was stationed on the left of the battle front throughout the eighteenth century, to indicate that it must yield precedence and honor to the rest of the army.

The resentment of the nobleman against the artillery was part of that large heritage carried over from feudal times into modern warfare, which included the most variegated complex of antiquated sentiments, convictions, valuations, and a general disinclination for technological progress. This survival of many feudal traits helped determine the future course of war development.

The Standing Army as an Institution of Militarism

Although the burgher enlarged and improved his troops, he still expected to be able to disband them at the end of a war as the forces of medieval chivalry had been scattered when peace was made. But this proved less and less easy, as armies grew in size and strength. The *condottieri* and other bands demonstrated to their employers their unwillingness to stop their corporate activities, to give up what Machiavelli called their "living by war." The Italian city-states resorted to all kinds of tricks, from poison to bribes, to get rid of their hirelings. But the situation was most difficult in France at the end of the Hundred Years' War, after a century of strife between France and England, when the former was left with a multitude of warriors who did not remember peace and often had no homes to which they might return. The only way to overawe such hosts and persuade them to disarm and disperse seemed to be that suggested to Charles VII by the rich merchant Jacques Cœur: to select a small, picked minority to chase away the rest after they had been paid off with the money Cœur provided. Thus the nucleus of the first real standing army was formed.[6]

The first standing army was thus, paradoxically, the outcome of the idea that armies should not be permanent. It arose as an institution to liquidate bothersome military groups seeking to perpetuate their existence by marauding. The idea behind the scheme came from the finance-capitalism of the times, which Cœur represented, eager for order in an age when the seat of power had not yet been fixed. The same middle-class elements supported the rise of national armies under the direction of sovereigns, and the suppression of the small, private armies of lords, in other countries, as in England under Henry VII (1485-1509), France under Louis XI (1461-83), or the Spain of Ferdinand (1479-1516) and Isabella. They proffered loans to assist in the formation of the new territorial states, the nations of Europe. "Remember that you would not have obtained your crown without my help," wrote Jakob Fugger, the rich merchant of Germany whose power later paralleled or surpassed that of Cœur in France, to Charles V, in a rare moment of bourgeois exaltation mingled with anxiety for the sums which Charles owed him.[7]

But very rapidly the new standing armies which were formed, though they offered relief from the feudal anarchy that was upsetting to business, proved themselves a threatening incubus upon money-economy. This was because, in most lands, the bourgeois refrained from trying to become his own soldier or governor. As had been demonstrated in the various attempts at militia-making among citizenry in the towns, the bourgeois was not willing to do his own war work. He wanted to buy it like any other labor. But he was not willing even to direct the soldiers he hired; and when the national armies were made, he left the beginning and end of wars in the hands of princes. By disdaining military matters, the new money-economy created in the long run its own worst enemy and rival—armies and the warrior. It indulged in wars, or suffered them without attempt at honest contradiction, paying no heed to occasional good advice, like that of the Spanish writer who warned that wars must not be undertaken unless the hope of profit bulked larger than the fear of losses: "It will otherwise be best to remain quiet. It will not be a wise proceeding to make war on the poor." [8]

Although the bourgeois left the direction of war to the princes, the princes did not themselves control their armies entirely in the beginning: rather they contracted with private entrepreneurs for the collection, organization, disciplining, and feeding of forces. Thus the bourgeois financed wars they did not start—kings started wars they did not fully manage. These war entrepreneurs, who continued their activities under new names, had already been noblemen in the majority of cases, usually of the lesser and impecunious brackets. The higher aristocracy did not bestir itself so energetically as a Montluc, a Wallenstein, a Marlborough. These men indicated what forces were still left in a class that had, for a time, seemed likely to go down helplessly before the rising, money-making bourgeoisie. They became the true beneficiaries of the standing army, whereas the bourgeois profit through armies was largely restricted to the purveyor's business. The nobility even officered the standing army more than the old impermanent forces of the *condottieri*. It was essentially created in their favor, for the employment and sustenance of a feudal class which could not make a living otherwise, after the feudal system broke down.

Only in England were the middle-class citizens able to maintain some parliamentary control over the military system, and hold the purse strings through Parliament; they were aroused to this assumption of power by the terrifying experience with Cromwellian militarism in the mid-seventeenth century, when the army for a time emancipated itself from the parties and ran the country. This clear view of an army in the ascendant shocked Englishmen into a sense of responsibility ever afterward. Elsewhere (leaving Holland aside), however, the bourgeois were not so fortunate in attempts to restrict the mandates handed to the sovereign for standing armies. They indeed sought through their estates and parliaments to cut down the grants of money for military purposes to small sums and short periods; but in France and Germany the balance of power between the estates was so even that the monarch and his bureaucracy obtained the upper hand. Inclining toward the nobility, the monarchs gave them preference and honors, while granting the bourgeois, instead of honor, a chance to build up manufactures and commerce. Thus a silent deal was consummated at the expense of the peasantry and the common laborer, the beasts of burden of absolutism as a military and industrial system. This was illustrated in Brandenburg-Prussia, where the Estates in 1653

granted their Elector six years' taxes and a standing army, and in
return the Elector gave the nobility permission to proceed almost
at their pleasure against the peasant, binding him to the soil.[9] The
Elector got his *miles perpetuus*, the perpetual or standing soldier,
while the nobleman got his perpetual serf.

The entrenchment of the nobility in the standing army, the existence of which the bourgeoisie began to regret, fixed that institution upon nations. There were indeed protests against it, especially
in England of the seventeenth and eighteenth centuries, and on
the Continent during the Enlightenment. But the defenders of the
standing army could by then, with a great show of military logic,
claim that for one country to dispense with it would be a one-sided
and dangerous disarmament. "In ancient time," as a speaker justified the institution in Parliament in 1733, "no Prince in Europe
had a standing force, now they have all, which makes it necessary
for us to have it, for the Militia is nothing against trained soldiers.
The eighteen thousand men proposed bears no proportion to the
numbers kept up by our neighbours." [10]

If Britain's insular situation allowed her to keep her army out of
relation to others, the rest saw themselves inextricably caught in a
power-competition for which the statisticians of the time provided
the measures. The limit of military rivalry, as far as numbers went,
was then believed to have been reached when the labor of the non-
soldiers of a country was no longer able to support the army, the
rest of the government, and themselves—this proportion had been
20 to 25 per cent in the old Greek city-states, but was only around
one per cent in the latter half of the eighteenth century.[11] This
limitation, generally accepted, then kept the armies small, but to
the civilian minds they seemed already overgrown: "Europe is
crowded with soldiers," someone cried in 1788. "Almost all the
governments are military. . . . It is necessary finally to put a stop
to these immense and permanent armies which devour Europe."
In vain did a few military experts add their wishes for a reduction
in the number of soldiers to the civilian taxpayers' pleas. It seemed
far better to Marshal Saxe "to have a small number of troops, who
are well kept up and well disciplined than to have a great number
who are not. Not large armies win battles but good ones do." [12]

The Christian world was not alone in creating institutions of militarism. Faraway Japan did likewise and at about the same time as
Europe—after 1600—building up a similar martial noblesse, not
for war, since there was none for two and a half centuries, but for
the sake of the nobility. Here the theoretical position of the monarch was very high and exalted, but his actual weakness much
more apparent than in Europe. The reign of the Tokugawas, the
usurping Shoguns, reduced his role to insignificance; it also held the

small feudal clans of samurai, up to then as anarchic as in early Europe, in a lacquered order which preserved a largely feudal system of values and economy. The first of the Tokugawas, after the battle of Sekigahara in which he conquered all competitors, uttered the famous saying: "After the victory, tie the helmet faster!" The helmets *were* tied faster, but not for war—for the preservation of the feudal order of Japanese society.

The Japanese division of labor gave to the knight the function of defending the country and to the peasant that of feeding it. As a book on the duties of the knight (*Yamaga Soko*) lays it down: "The knight need not work in the field and worry about daily bread. Neither does he have to be concerned about his clothing. Instead he has the separate and difficult task of upholding morale." A feudal poet, contemplating the lot of the peasantry, seemed to feel that the exchange was not even: "Every morning and evening, when I consume rice, I remember the peasants whose gifts I enjoy without returning it by special favors." These functions determined the standing of classes in society: first came the knight, then the peasant, third were the handicraftsmen, and fourth the despised class of traders and merchants, on whom, as the *corpus vile,* the knight might try his sword. The relative elevation of the peasant was the feature most unlike Europe. Otherwise, as in Europe, the nobleman held the arms-bearing right and the honor monopoly; and his honor was enhanced by emphasis on ancestral glories.[13]

The Standing Army as a Foundation for the Postfeudal Nobleman, His Living and His Honor, His Outdoor Relief

There was no military necessity, except such as these standing armies themselves created, for having armies in perpetual existence; and there were, originally, no special military gifts distinguishing the nobility which should have made that class the more or less exclusive furnisher of officers. Members of other classes had shown military talents quite as well, Cromwell above all. Brandenburg drove a Swedish force out of the country in 1675 with the help of a peasant militia, and the best generals of the Great Elector were Derfflinger, once a tailor's apprentice, and Hennings, a burgher's son. But only in a few places was the citizens' militia allowed to survive, as in England, where (after the Bill of Rights, 1689) it formed a counterforce against the standing army, the latter entrusted to the King as far as "government, command, and disposition" were concerned, but the former put under the lieutenants of the counties, who were responsible to Parliament for raising and controlling their militia. Where such a militia was absent, the abilities of nonnobles received no military training or testing ground.

In the long run, the standing army provided livings principally for noblemen, which were, at least by comparison, sinecures. Even though they were by no means all as comfortable as clerical berths, the economy of the standing army ensured regular, steady incomes to its beneficiaries, with no break between one war and the next. This solved what had been a grave problem for the nobles of Europe generally, the question of what they should do when the feudal economy was shattered. It saved them from ruin.

By the sixteenth century, a whole estate, that of the aristocracy in several lands, had been faced with the necessity of finding some new employment, after the rise of strong kings and rich towns. As early as 1524 a German book on *Nobility and War* complained that the wealth and luxuries of townsmen, particularly of merchants, were casting noblemen into the shade. To restore the aristocracy, the author advocated the replacement of the clerical hierarchy by a military hierarchy supported by the income of secularized bishoprics and manned by nobles. The members should wear a "livery" distinguishing them from the rest of the people and golden medals to indicate their noble rank and military functions.[14] But the religious reformation did not, as this writer expected, work out to the direct and immediate profit of the aristocracy in Germany; rather it diminished the authoritarian position of the nobleman in society and in the armies. In France as well, the issue was acute; in the 1570's, Montluc, a man of the lower noblesse, felt that a new crusade would not answer the purpose. "One must not renew the wars for the Holy Land, for we are not as devout as the good people of times past." But he thought some outlet could be found for young bloods in the New World, following the Spanish example.[15]

Only a small, rich section of the high nobility could avoid this pressing question and, as great landowners, contribute to the original accumulation which made early capitalism possible by producing grain and wool in grand style. Trade was closed to the noblesse of France and Germany generally; only in England could a few, like Sir Walter Raleigh, consecrate themselves *"tam Marti quam Mercurio,"* not only to Mars but to the merchant god, Mercury.[16] For the lower nobility and squirearchy of Europe in the main there seemed no future but a steady sinking down into boorish sloth on their meager estates.

Where could they go? The clergy had become more bourgeois and church offices less remunerative; but they did strive to break into that field: the effort of nobles to recover prestige and posts in the Church formed part of the Jesuit movement, which was a counterrevolution of nobles as well as a Counter Reformation in religion. This did not solve the problem; nor did the law offer an answer.

That expanding profession, preparing and providing for a slowly growing bureaucracy, was monopolized by the keen-witted sons of townsmen. By their pens the nobles could not support themselves; they contributed little to the thought, learning, or poetry of the time. On the contrary, the nobility developed a resentment against the pen and against the power of finance, though not against property and income, which it was to hand on to succeeding generations of officers.

Originally a "noble" resentment against the too intelligent or wealthy rivals in towns, this feeling was spread among soldiers generally, from the officers down. Under noble influence, armies came to hate the lawyer with the parliamentarians. Colonel Thomas Pride, of Pride's Purge, expressed the hope "that the lawyers' gowns might all be hung up beside the Scots' colours yet." It was the same animosity *"pour les avocats"* of the Directorate that animated Bonaparte when he wanted to conquer lands in his own name instead of theirs. This resentment was to go on growing, breaking out in various forms against diplomats, lawyers, financiers—all those among whom the nobleman had not originally been able to find a place and make a name.

There remained the army. But at first it seemed that even this sphere would be invaded by expensive and ambitious townsmen. Writers like the Elizabethan dramatists Beaumont and Fletcher, however, encouraged courtiers and noblemen by their ridicule of the so-called trained bands of the bourgeois London militia. *The Knight of the Burning Pestle* makes the ludicrous captain of such a company harangue his men in mock-heroic vein:

Gentlemen, countrymen, friends, and my fellow-soldiers. I have brought you this day from the shops of security and the counters of content, to measure out honour by the ell and prowess by the pound. Remember then, whose cause you have in hand. And like a set of true-born scavengers, scour me this famous realm of enemies.[17]

The blunt Blaise de Montluc, who rose in fifty years of army service to the high post of Maréchal de France, was an enemy of the Huguenots, not merely from religious conviction, but also because "the majority of all those who mix themselves up with finances are of that religion; for such is the temper of man always to love novelties; and the worst, from which all misfortune has started, is that the men of the law . . . have forsaken the ancient religion of the King, in order to embrace the new." Such adversaries, by their devilish legal finesse, he thought, caused the Catholic party to lose what it won by its arms. Royal and law courts in France, he wrote, absorbed two-thirds of those who were by nature fit to become good captains and who, in such employ, became poltroons and incidentally ruined the nobility; its whole decay, he felt, was occasioned by litigation and the bad counsels of advocates.[18]

As these resentments all too clearly indicate, the sixteenth century witnessed an eclipse of the nobility. Driven by hunger from their cold castles, they were for hire and could not always make their own conditions. They had to compete in armies with townsmen. For a time, under Francis I and Henry II, the younger noblemen of France actually served an apprenticeship on entering military service, either as archers in the ordnance companies or even as lance corporals in the infantry. In the second half of the sixteenth century, however, the aristocrat began to resist such apprenticeship and expected through noble birth to attain the rank formerly won only by long service. Consequently, the quality of French armies deteriorated as the conviction of the nobleman about his inherent military value and right to command became intensified.[19] Even a military sage like Montluc assumed that experiences in battle had taught him that "fifty *gentilshommes* have more effect than two hundred soldiers: we retain some of that honor which our fathers have obtained for us, in gaining it through this beautiful title of noble." But they would be still better military men if they became "doctors of war." [20]

The way out of the dilemma was found in giving them a monopoly of officers' posts, recognizing their sense of position and importance, and also in requiring them to submit their unruly spirits to a certain discipline and a modicum of education.

The Noble Officer and Education

The notion of the Académie des Nobles did not take root at once, since the nobles, having received the privilege of officer service, saw no necessity for applying themselves to the war sciences, and still believed that it was quite enough if a soldier could sign his name. Again and again they had to be forced to accept book learning. As a class, the nobility continued to shun education, which was not easily obtainable under rural conditions of life where, as the complaints under Louis XV disclosed, the noblesse taught their children nothing but hunting and killing the enemies of their clan.[21] They shunned education even more in the military field than in law, insisting on preferment in service, not for superior knowledge, but solely on grounds of birth. Military schools did not flourish in France, for the noblemen sought to suppress all institutions of the kind that forced them to show themselves worthy of employment.[22]

Profoundly averse to a theoretical training, the nobles thought that war taught what was needful for an officer to know. Such a conviction inspired them to send their children to service as soon as possible. The young noble officer could be found on the battle-field at as tender an age as twelve. A French cornet of twelve was reported as having received a saber cut across his face and being made prisoner. More usually, this child labor on the part of the nobility began with the fourteenth or fifteenth year, either as a volunteer or ensign or provided with a patent for a sublieutenancy.

Serving as a volunteer was thought to bring the future officer too easily into an intimacy with the common soldiery he was soon to command, and whose respect he might forfeit by betraying weak-nesses inherent in extreme youth. To avoid that risk and yet ex-ercise the novice the cadets were taken out of the regiments by Louvois in 1682 and drilled together in nine companies. Inciden-tally they received some other, more school-like education, but so little discipline that Louis XIV, who could not brook insubordina-tion, dissolved the cadet companies after Louvois's death in 1692, whereas such institutions were imported to Prussia among the in-novations brought there by Huguenot refugees.[23]

France again tried the cadet companies, nurseries of infantry officers, in the years from 1726 to 1733, but once more they proved unsatisfactory. This institution had been forced on the recalcitrant beneficiaries from the outside, and the same was true of the next set-up by the French government: the Ecole Militaire. Like the first Austrian school for the education of future officers, founded im-mediately after the close of the Thirty Years' War by a private capitalist with the ominous name of Baron de Chaos (who left the whole of his considerable fortune for an institution to teach the art of engineering and war),[24] the French school was due to the proposals of a financier—one of the brothers Paris, the greatest French capitalists of the eighteenth century, whose fortunes had arisen from trading in war supplies.[25] Paris persuaded La Pompa-dour to win over the King, Louis XV, to the idea. It was sustained by the perseverance of D'Argenson and in part financed by a lot-tery, so that the beneficiaries had nothing to contribute except their younger sons, the cadets. To persuade them to take advantage of it, the King told the *hobereaux,* the French Junkers, that an educa-tion was advisable for an army career. "It is necessary," said the founding decree, "that the ancient prejudice which has instilled the belief that bravery alone makes the man of war should give place imperceptibly to a taste for the military studies which we have in-troduced" (1751).[26]

The Ecole Militaire was to receive five hundred young impecu-nious noblemen, "born without fortune," by preference sons and orphans of noble officers and families of "old race," who had fallen into misery and were too poor to educate their children elsewhere or put them into the army as officers. The intendants were ordered to send such children, aged from nine to eleven, to Paris from the provinces where the *hobereaux* were living on a level with and close to the peasantry. Their poverty destined these pupils from the beginning for service in the infantry and made it easier for their professors to break their self-will than it had been for officers to subdue the cadets. This made the Ecole Militaire the most Spartan institution for military education in France; but still a number of graduates left without being able to speak and write correctly. After 1776 it became a higher institution of military education for the best graduates—those who received royal fellowships—of the military colleges in the provinces, founded in that year; and it also took sons of families rich enough to pay an annual sum of two thousand crowns. Among the first of its products was the young Napoleon Bonaparte, who had graduated from the Collège Militaire of Brienne in 1783.[27]

The smallest amount of actual education, military or otherwise, was presumably offered to the *pages* with whom the reigning princes and the greatest *grands seigneurs* surrounded themselves. But since pages in such entourages were expected to obtain favors, among them lieutenancies and even companies, such employment and patronage were eagerly sought by noble families. Dissipation, distraction, loose morals, sumptuous habits of living, were more often and readily acquired in the *pageries* than military discipline and knowledge; but the contact with courtiers might prove helpful long afterward, as well as the connections made there with others coming into influence.[28]

In Prussia as in France the problem of the relation of the nobles to the standing army also made trouble for the monarch. To bring the hard-riding and hard-drinking Junker to the desk of the military student was not easy. But Frederick the Great and his father adopted strong measures designed to force education upon the men who expected to serve the Prussian Crown in the armies. So schools were opened and, on top of the Berlin *corps de cadets à selecta,* an Académie des Nobles, "to furnish, for that part of the young nobility to whom Nature has given only talents instead of other fortune, a most careful education." In addition, officers with theoretical gifts received special instruction during the winter months, and the twelve best were taken into Frederick's suite to learn directly from him the arts of war. Thus an officer elite, able to do the work of a general staff, was formed. The King's preferred occasions for experimenting, teaching, and examining were the annual autumn maneuvers. The old-time "musters" had been turned by him, after 1743, into actual exercises for war and finally into a high school of formal tactics after the Seven Years' War, into an *imago belli,* modern peacetime maneuvers.[29]

But not enough of the officers came forward or were accepted, and their influence for reform was not sufficient to outweigh the old Prussian inertia. Reform proposals of the post-Frederician times could not avail against the powers which had protection in the shadow of the great King and continued to hinder the "unreserved opening of officers' positions to educated outsiders; this alone would force the noble officers to educate themselves too, in order not to remain behind, and would obtain good officers for us," as a staff officer's reform proposal declared.[30]

The superiority of the eighteenth-century bourgeoisie in intelligence and wealth made the old powers apprehensive, even in Prussia, where "questions of civilization played a relatively subordinate role," [31] down to the beginning of the nineteenth century. But the nobility managed, nonetheless, to cling to its high prerogatives. The French noblesse claimed all officers' jobs for itself; and meanwhile a Prussian reformer proposed to raise the salaries of officers in order to preserve the country gentry: "If in the face of the ruling opinion one intends to preserve for some time all the privileges of birth, for the inherited nobility—certainly no easy enterprise—in the Prussian state, the officer estate which forms the largest part of the nobility must be raised." [32]

At length, toward the middle of the eighteenth century, in the dusk of the feudal regime, some nobles began to study seriously;[33] they began to realize that education was one of the means of defending the officer monopoly of the nobility, and that it involved holding a monopoly on the military institutes. The *noblesse de race* in France thus won in 1781 a decree that only its members should be admitted to the military schools of France which they had for so long shunned. Hard-driven nobles in Prussia as well as in France even entered the artillery and engineer corps and soon tried to make these special bodies also their own. When an Academy of Engineers was founded in 1768 in Potsdam, its charter declared that among the pupils "noble origin should very much be insisted upon because experience teaches that the corps into which many bourgeois have crept does not enjoy the full esteem in the army that most of the other corps do . . . and further because the country nobility is numerous, and there exist within it fewer gradations than among the bourgeois from whom the master mechanic, too, might finally make claims to have his sons accepted as pupils. Only an excellent genius could replace the want of descent, and the test [for outsiders] would be a complete examination in all the sciences which are taught in the topmost class." [34]

Examination and competition, the value of which Hume praised so highly, were largely reserved for the bourgeois; they were accustomed to that in their own schools. The military would not have such tests for themselves, except in those schools founded for the

neglected children of the common soldiers, or in the less honorary
bodies like the Saxon artillery where, after 1766, in case of a vacancy, the six officers next in line were examined and the best man
given the vacant post, provided his family "connections" were not
too much against him and the examiners were in a position to
appreciate the talents of the examined.[35]

Outside France, where military education underwent so many
shifts, institutions for this purpose became one of the manias of
eighteenth-century absolutism. To even the smallest German prince
they were either a means of government or a hobby. Men like the
poet Schiller and Scharnhorst were brought up in such places, the
former to be an army surgeon, the latter an officer. Only in England were such institutions completely ignored. Vainly did Defoe
outline a program for one, in his *Essay upon Projects,* written in
1692 and published in 1697. This typical urban schemer, one in the
long line of advice-givers of his time, proposed a Royal Academy
for Military Exercises, with four colleges complete with study plan
and a yearly budget of £90,000. He realized that "war is the best
academy in the world, where men study by necessity and practice
by force, and both to some purpose, with duty in the action, and
a reward in the end." The English nation had had no recent war
experience and William III, then Defoe's protector, was in need of
experienced officers whom he could only find among foreigners, not
among the best families of England; he had entrusted sixteen regiments to gentlemen of these families who had never seen any service
and knew very little about commanding. Defoe recommended that
the Englishmen as future officers learn something if they wanted
to dispense with the foreigners, against whose competition they
grumbled. But his project was never realized.

As heretofore in England, the great public schools like Win-
chester, Eton, and Harrow were considered, during most of the
century, sufficient to supply education for officers, that is, if any
at all was required for a military man. Most of the gentry up to
the middle of the eighteenth century were not so very different in
this respect from Junkers in Prussia, or from their own servants,
or from the captain in Swift's *Hamilton Bawn:*

A scholard, when just from his college broke loose,
Can hardly tell how to cry bo *to a goose;*
Your Noveds, and Blutarchs, and Omers, and stuff,
'Fore George, they don't signify this pinch of snuff.

To give a young gentleman right education,
The army's the only good school in the nation;
My schoolmaster called me a dunce and a fool,
But at cuffs I was always the cock of the school.

Despite divergences in the forms of education for army officers, the requirement of technical training tended to strengthen the hold of the nobles on army positions. They were by no means able to exclude all bourgeois from military colleges and to prevent absolutely the rise of common men from the lower ranges to higher places; yet for a long time their grip on officers' posts was so firm as to amount almost to a monopoly. Such technical training as they did receive fortified them in their notions of "nobility," "honor," and prestige which, in their estimation, lifted them far above the bourgeois, the peasants, the yokels, laborers, and "scum of the cities" swept into the standing armies by impressment.

The Nobleman's Price for Service: Monopoly of Military Posts and Prestige

The hauteur of the noble officer, which so often covered up his lack of education, was enhanced by the scarcity value he acquired in certain periods. At the end of long campaigns the circles of nobility were left decimated, as in Prussia at the close of the Seven Years' War, during which even Frederick the Great had to take some bourgeois officers. In such moments the nobleman was able to exact a yet higher price, in the form of special privileges, from the state and society for his military services.

As a rule he was rewarded by exemptions from taxes. In France he was relieved from the *taille,* from customs duties and the excise, from billeting, carting, and other compulsory service with horses, all of which fell on the peasants and to some extent on townspeople. What was taken from his shoulders fell on the peasants, who were permitted few exemptions anywhere and none in Prussia and Russia. Down to about 1735 in Prussia, the cavalry was quartered on them; each peasant received two thalers monthly for every such unwelcome guest, who cost him actually four to five thalers.[36] The argument for freeing the nobleman was that he paid an *"impôt de sang,"* a blood tax on the battlefield, and therefore should be excused from the *taille,* originally a tax levied for war purposes. This might have been true at the early period, when the nobleman served at his own expense, but the argument was no longer so cogent when he served for money and perquisites.

A further reward for the nobility was the privilege of proceeding almost at their pleasure against the peasant; in part of Prussia, for instance, where he had not been a serf in the Middle Ages, he became so as part of the favor accorded to the Junker officer. In all countries, the nobleman's salaries and other compensations were raised; additional satisfaction was given him in the form of prestige; to appease his hunger for advancement he was given so great a preference in army advancement that he virtually recovered the monopolistic status that he had enjoyed in the Middle Ages, when he had been the supreme warrior, haloed with glory and dowered with hunting and arms-bearing rights. War became again, often enough, what it had been in the past, an exercise for the chivalric ardor; it was urged by the Marshal de Berwick in 1727 that more campaigns be conducted to benefit noblemen: "This monarchy had sustained itself so brilliantly only by the valor of the nobility; therefore one should think that in order to exercise it, some war would be necessary from time to time." [37]

With this situation the city bourgeois was relatively well satisfied. He was indeed subject to harassing contributions and suffered much from coinage debasement for war purposes and other interferences with economic life, but he was relieved from the risk and pains of military service himself. The methods of eighteenth-century warfare were comparatively humane and rational: wars were on a small scale, conducted with more regard to strategic effect than ruthless destruction, since the noblemen, who had recovered charge of military affairs, reintroduced some feudal ideals and were ready to treat one another, even as enemies, with certain courtesies. This meant the sparing of captured towns and a greater regard for property rights than in earlier or later times.

That the city bourgeois was being shut out from the real seat of power he hardly perceived, so busy was he in developing his expanding commerce; he desired little more than to be left alone. But constantly the doors to army posts were closing against him, or, if he entered them, he found they led nowhere. In the artillery or the engineering divisions, he indeed found room, but these were despised branches; he could not penetrate the "better" regiments, especially the cavalry, which the upper aristocracy arrogated to itself. In the work of army administration, naturally, the man of the middle classes, who found such tasks congenial or was more intelligent than the aristocrat, was welcomed, but he did not find it easy to exert his powers over the noble officer; the attempts of such administrators to interfere with the noblemen caused much rekindling of ancient antagonisms.

The metamorphosis of a bourgeois into an officer might take place only by the expenditure of large sums of money. Whereas in France this process generally included the buying of certain offices in the government, carrying titles which ennobled the purchaser, it was more indirect in England and Prussia; there the aspirant had usually to pass through the landholding aristocracy. This was hardest in Prussia, where at times bourgeois were prohibited from acquiring so-called noble estates. It was easier in England, where the army was the appendage of the landed lords, and their circle was more open to newcomers from trade; in England money counted for more than in other armies because here the purchase system for officers' commissions was more thoroughgoing. But even in England, money must not be too new. Scornfully as Napoleon spoke of the English—*"sono mercanti"*—the English officer was inclined to regard the shopkeepers of his own nation in similar terms. General Wolfe, who was stationed for a time in Glasgow, found the citizens there "civil, designing and treacherous, with their immediate interests always in view; they pursue trade with warmth and the necessary mercantile spirit, arising from the baseness of their other qualifications." [38]

Being excluded from real power in military affairs, the city middle classes were subjected to more and more contempt and down-right ill treatment at the hands of the haughty military noble; their liberties were lost to the grasping bureaucracy which grew up side by side with the army, and their self-respect was trampled upon by the military and bureaucrats in eager competition. When protests against such behavior came before Frederick William I of Prussia, he declined to punish the culprits by dismissing them from service: "If I should let them go, finally it would come my own turn. Therefore I must sustain my officers and servants, if I want to sustain myself." [39] Under his son, the military took unquestioned precedence over everyone; the youngest lieutenant outranked the highest civilian official, if the latter were not noble. The governor of Breslau called the topmost officials in that town "asses," and was not rebuked for it. In cases of quarrels between officers and officials, the King always agreed with the former. If the commandant of Berlin knocked out some citizens' teeth with his stick, the injured parties had simply no redress. To have social intercourse with the bourgeoisie was prohibited for the officer.[40]

The French bourgeoisie fared only a little better at the hands of officers whenever the two separate estates came into contact, as when the military were quartered on civilians, or both met in theaters where officers claimed the best seats and took care to obtain them by placing sentries where they intended to sit. In spite of the high, and sometimes even superior, position of the civilian bureaucracy in France, its members had to suffer much maltreatment by officers. Generally an officer who had abused an official got off with a reminder "to be more circumspect with public personages.' But the restraining power over the military remained somewhat greater in France than in Prussia; an officer, "insulted" by a bourgeois of Bordeaux, broke the insulter's arm with the butt of his pistol and was thereupon condemned to pay an indemnity of seventy-five thousand livres.[41]

Though everywhere he suffered from the standing armies, which he had himself created but had permitted to fall into the hands of feudal castes, the citizen's situation varied in different countries. His own wealth was one factor. The character of the nobleman who assumed military direction was another.

Nobility and the French Army

In France the reward of the nobility for army services tended especially to take the shape of many extra jobs, which were created for the benefit of younger sons. In 1702, for instance, 7,000 officers' commissions were created there for the place-hunting young nobility,[42] to the exclusion of long-serving noncoms and the *roturiers* generally. A little later there were as many pensioned officers in the pay of the King as there were officers in actual service, thus giving him a double set. How superfluous many of these posts were was shown in 1787, when there existed 36,000 officers of all grades, apparently all drawing pay, but only 13,000 of them on active duty. By the time of the election for the States General, on the eve of the Revolution, there were 9,578 officers in the actual establishment of the French army, of whom 6,633 were noble, 1,845 bourgeois, and 1,100 officers of fortune, usually of middle-class origin; besides these, some 2,500 more were on the payrolls of the army. The pay of these 12,000 officers absorbed more than one-half of the yearly expenditure.

In the overstaffed French army the number of generals had waxed out of all proportion to the need. There were no less than 1,171 of them in the French army as against only 80 in the Prussian, which was slightly larger than the French forces, and about 350 in the Austrian army, which was nearly the same size. By the first of January, 1791, the sweep of the Revolution had reduced the number of French generals to a mere 34 among a total of 9,406 officers.[43]

Up to the Revolution attempts to reform the army, whether to raise its efficiency or reduce expenses, were shattered on the rock of the noblemen's defense of vested rights. The cry, "It is necessary, however, to place the gentlemen," stopped all mouths. Moreover, the military qualifications of the aristocracy, in particular of the *grands seigneurs,* did not tend to increase; indeed, Minister d'Argenson thought the race had deteriorated and ought probably to be drowned "like a race of hounds" which had become worthless.[44] Mere birth as qualification for army service began to be doubted.

Of course, bourgeois of means elbowed their way into the French nobility. Ever since the financial crash of the Law Bubble in 1720, which cured them of a liking for governmental shares, they turned to investments in lands, which they often made pay by rationalization of agriculture. The power of money, sanctified by land, rendered them eligible for titles; their descendants, slightly mellowed, might seek officer positions. By the middle of the century there were about four thousand officers of such plebeian origin in the French army; but they did not make their way into the uppermost posts, and their advance was steadily resisted by the angry *noblesse de race* which bewailed the rise of "sons of *roturiers,* used to effeminate ways, who have never heard their fathers speak of anything but interest and other things relative to their profession." It strove to stop the tide by decree.

Much against the will of those who thought primarily of military efficiency, the *noblesse de race* obtained in 1781 an order that candidates for the grade of sublieutenant had to show a pedigree of at least four noble ancestors.[45] A bourgeois grandfather excluded one from candidacy, much as a Jewish grandmother in Hitler's Germany, with the difference, however, that the *race* requirements of the eighteenth century did not apply to bourgeois seeking lower posts up to the grade of lieutenant, ensign, or cornet, or those from military schools. This exclusion decree added a powerful impetus to prerevolutionary sentiment against the nobility.

To the group jealousies in the *ancien régime* was added a subdivision in military monopoly between the *haute* or court *noblesse,* who held most of the higher posts, and the impoverished *petite noblesse* of the provinces, the *hobereaux,* who filled the lower ranks, especially in the infantry. About this pernicious division, a reforming war minister expressed the opinion: "Some have all without meriting anything; the others do not get anywhere, whatever they deserve." He was not alone in his judgment that the military virtues of the provincials, ignorant and surly as they often were, their sobriety, endurance of hardships, courage, and feeling of honor were far superior to those of the spoiled children of the exalted nobility. But belonging to the higher group automatically gave commanding positions.[46]

Family importance and court favor combined to give the court noble his colonelcy, sometimes even before his twentieth year. He rarely commanded his regiment himself but lived at the court, his troops being taken care of in the meanwhile by the eldest captain as lieutenant colonel. Both kinds of nobles started their careers from low rank, but the courtier jumped ahead while the *hobereau* waited for his turn in the vacancies, hoping that, as he became eldest lieutenant, he could buy the captaincy offered for sale by some superannuated incumbent. This was only possible if the lieutenant had by then managed to scratch together several thousand livres for the purchase.

Poverty made the small nobles job-hungry; they could start in the army with a lieutenancy free of charge, but the higher offices had to be bought. Yet other fields were closed: even if they had an inclination for bureaucratic positions, these had also a price, which the bourgeois was more often able to pay. The animosity, therefore, between the two groups of nobles split the solidarity of that class and entered a wedge between it and the Crown. The provincial nobles became so wroth with the King that some even proposed that the army should swear allegiance to the nation, that is, to the Estates, instead. To that extent, therefore, members of the nobility and army shared revolutionary sentiments; and the Revolution, in that aspect, was a product of the perpetual French *Fronde* of provincial petty noblemen against the monarchy. Too late, then, the nobility discovered that the Revolution was directed at its own monopoly of privileges entirely—too late, the nobility rallied around the Crown.

Military Nobility in Prussia

The specifically French problem of the split in the ranks of noblemen was not duplicated in Prussia, which had no high aristocracy, or in England, where the high aristocracy went into politics instead of war, on the whole, leaving the military field free for the lesser gentlemen. A greater solidarity, accordingly, was to be found in either of the latter.

In Prussia the striving of the nobility for exclusive rights in the army was crowned with a more complete success than in France, although, as the country was poorer, this did not mean so rich a reward financially. But the monopoly of military posts was not won at once. When the standing army was formed there, the Prussian Junker had to share jobs with such foreign nobles and non-nobles, even peasant sons, as had had military experience in the Thirty Years' War. Then the young nobleman had to serve "from the pike up." Irked by this, the feudal estate petitioned the Elector to spare them this humiliating equality with burghers and peasants.[47]

The hour struck for the nobleman in Prussia when he became a war entrepreneur as chief of his company. This scheme was developed after 1721; the captain, if he was a Junker, could then take his own serfs, or those of his relatives, into the service, exercise them a few months every year, and then give them furlough to work on the land again. This did not waste the King's money abroad for recruits and was favored by the so-called absolutist monarchs, Frederick William I and his son, Frederick the Great. They approved of it from the standpoint of economy, but were not blind to its dangers. The former cursed the noblemen for their pride and interference and swore: "They shall dance according to my piping, or the Devil take me. I shall hang and broil them as the Czar does and treat them as rebels. . . . I stabilize sovereignty and put the Crown firmly like a *rocher de bronce* and leave to the Junkers the hot air of the Landtag." But though he wanted to "ruin the Junkers for their officiousness," he achieved little in his attempts to lay heavier taxes on them, or protect the peasants from their rule.[48]

It was indeed not always easy even to pretend that the King was governing in Prussia. The first King confessed in his Political Testament that he had to "dissimulate" his worries about the recalcitrance of his field marshal "because the latter had such a large following in the army and commanded my guards, which consisted of four thousand men." [49] The Prussian kings felt that there was a difference between state interest and that of the military nobles and endeavored to form a bureaucracy which contained a certain balancing weight of plebeians. Frederick William I also considered it wise to enlarge the royal domain by buying feudal estates and thus raising grain which could be used to hinder Junker profiteering in grain and other markets, to the peril of army supplies. But his son, Frederick the Great, did not permit the rise of a bourgeois class which might have offset the Junkers; he expressly forbade the acquisition of feudal estates by the bourgeois, insisting that their capital be restricted to trade and manufacturing. In cases of conflict, between royal domains and the Junkers' estates, over boundaries, he rather preferred, as he wrote, "to do wrong to myself, for what is a small loss to me is a great profit to the nobleman whose sons defend the country; in this the race is so good that it deserves to be rewarded and preserved in every way." This was his manner, autocratic in appearance more than in fact, of admitting the dominant fact of Prussian history, that the Junkers have been the "real regents of the Prussian state." [50]

Although he employed numerous bourgeois officers when he could not find others, Frederick the Great ignored their good services and coldly sent them away at the end of campaigning. He insisted instead that his noblemen must serve on, although these might have grown tired of war and its shocking losses—four thousand Prussian officers seem to have died in the Seven Years' War alone.[51] Much as they sought retirement, the King declared it was "more necessary and more becoming to the nobleman to serve as an officer than to live in the country and feed chickens." [52] He had been suspicious of nonnobles, even as a crown prince, feeling that they lacked honor, seeking profit instead. The nobleman would be forced to behave himself because if he failed in the army, he could not take up other employments, like the bourgeois, or find refuge even in his father's house.

When the exclusively noble character of the Prussian officer corps as a whole was fully established by Frederick, he proceeded in his later years to measures aimed at preventing too much caste solidarity. He sought to divide them by emphasizing the distinctions of rank. As officers complained, he injected the principle of *divide et impera* to spoil their unity: the "apple of discord" was thrown among them to "raise jealousy, rancor and distrust," and create spies who betrayed their secrets.[53]

In numbers this privilege of the Junker expresses itself in the following manner: in 1739, near the close of Frederick William's reign, all the thirty-four Prussian general officers were noble, among the fifty-seven colonels there was one nonnoble only, among the forty-six lieutenant colonels there were but two, and two among the one hundred and eight majors. The corps of engineers, with a special list of officers, had one noble and one nonnoble colonel each, one nonnoble lieutenant colonel and three noble and nonnoble majors each. The Prussian army list of 1786 has among the fifty-two general officers of the infantry not one nonnoble, but sixteen noble foreigners; among the fifty-nine colonels is not one nonnoble, but there are twenty-seven noble foreigners; among the twenty-three lieutenant colonels appears one nonnoble, but there are six noble foreigners; among one hundred and eighty-five majors, there are two nonnobles but forty-seven noble foreigners. In the field artillery were found one major general (noble), four colonels of whom three were nobles, three lieutenant colonels, all noble, and thirteen majors, of whom two were nonnoble and two foreigners. The cavalry (aside from the Hussars with three bourgeois majors) had not one single nonnoble among the staff officers.[54]

Up to the year 1791, the Prussian army had counted 895 general officers from 518 different noble families—among them were fourteen by the name of Kleist, eleven Schwerin, ten Goltz, nine Berck and nine Bredow, seven Dohna and seven Marwitz. Among the seven to eight thousand officers in the Prussian army list for 1806, only 695 were nonnobles as against more than a thousand with French names, some of old families of refugees, others newcomers. Of these 695, some 30 were staff officers, as against at least 360 foreigners as staff officers; 289 served in the artillery, 131 in the regular infantry (83 in the depot battalions), 76 in the light infantry, and so on.[55] Thus middle-class Prussians were outnumbered by foreigners in their own army; this lent color to the saying that Prussia was not a country that had an army, but an army that had a country.

The beneficiaries of this system did not want to see any changes, even when the victories of the French showed glaring faults in it. They did not want their incomes, prestige, or even their baggage trains reduced; although they saw France, Austria, and Russia abandon riding horses for subaltern officers, for instance, they refused to follow foreign example. It was irrelevant, said a Prussian:

The numerous nobility who serve as subalterns in our army and, in a way which all Europe recognizes, constitute the greatest strength and the greatest superiority of our army, would be humiliated, mortified and, degraded below a status which birth and education granted them up to now, by measures which would make them the equals of the common soldiers. This would make them vexed and dissatisfied with their estate. The well-to-do would leave the service, and those serving out of need would lose their self-confidence; the subalterns and officers generally would sink in the estimation of the common soldier, and this, the most beautiful ornament and the greatest superiority of our army, would be lost.[56]

Not until the crushing victory of the French under Napoleon, at Jena, was this privilege system defeated, which had been maintained in spite of attempts at reform, and the introduction of a merit system. It had become, as a German liberal condemned it, an "old-Frederician *caput mortuum* or rather, if you prefer, the grotesque flowering of Junkerdom, the ostentatious display of its stupidity and presumption." [57]

Gentry and Army in England

Originally, in Brandenburg-Prussia, militarism had begun with the avowed aim of promoting the general welfare: when the Great Elector first demanded a standing army in 1666, he did so with the argument that permanent institutions, fortresses, and troops would assure the security of the country, the protection of all individuals.[58] If the military predominated there, it was because other interests were weak, like that of commerce, or silent, permitting the army and government bureaucracy to absorb the state. Thus in Prussia, the army transgressed the purely military sphere, becoming far more militaristic than that of England. There, other interests were vocal and active, particularly those of commerce; since they shouldered so much of the work of governing, the army was more nearly restricted to its primal function. Power was sought by England, therefore, not so much for its own sake, as on the Continent, as for *maximal welfare,* the ideal laid down by Bentham in the very days of Frederick. England was not constantly organized for power, like Prussia, except on the seas, and hence her military efforts at that time were generally very ineffectual.

If military tasks were to be performed, members of England's upper class took it upon themselves to lead her regiments and small armies; and it was her good fortune if she chanced to find a Marlborough or a Wellington, who came from the lesser gentry, in command of her forces, instead of Peterboroughs, Howes, and Burgoynes. In England the first people in the state held the military positions, and not, as Frederick demanded in Prussia, the reverse—the military taking the uppermost state positions. This, however, meant a diffusion of English energies over the political field: in 1761, at the very time when more than twenty each of Schwerins, Kleists, Gröbens, Bülows, and other members of Prussian country gentlemen's families held commissions in the army, five Townsends, five Manners, four Cavendishes, four Yorkes, and three Walpoles were holding seats in the English Parliament.

If any members of the English gentry wanted commissions in the British army, they could most easily obtain them through the parliamentary "interest." Many army officers were members of Parliament themselves: fifty-four in the Parliaments of 1732-3 and 1754, all of them "for" the government, and sixty-four in that of 1761, including John Burgoyne, William Howe, and Charles Cornwallis, all of them soldiers actually in service at the time; besides there were many members who had seen service earlier. That was, as Lord Chesterfield said, "the known way to military preferment," even if not to the benefit of the service itself, for their seat in Parliament enabled "young subaltern puppys" to force themselves "into higher posts than they are fit for." Those higher up already were no less eager to advance their careers through the first and more effective rule for promotion, "interest and seniority." [59]

The large number of officers in Parliament—eighty-five out of about five hundred members in 1761, if naval officers be included —did not make for an English militarism. The officers were more partisans of the government than of the military institutions. This situation produced the peculiarly British inefficiency around the middle of the eighteenth century, when only the great endeavors of the German Hanoverian kings of England kept parliamentary patronage from running completely away with all the better army positions. It was a struggle to hold the officers to their duties, "discipline not being so natural to Us as I could wish," as George III remarked with an unmistakable yearning for improvement in the German direction. [60]

Honor and Other Feudal Heritage in the Army

As the noblemen won back their old position of superiority in society, not least through mastery of the standing armies of the several nations, they reasserted their particular scales of values. These were in the main as foreign to the ideas of city bourgeois as had been the chivalric ideals of the medieval knights, their ancestors. The nobleman cared little for the "bourgeois virtues," industriousness, thrift, education and knowledge, living up to contracts; but he exalted instead his peculiar concept of "honor," as the prerogative of a high-born estate, which could not be shared with inferiors.

This in turn affected the development of armies in the period: had their generals been educated bourgeois more emphasis would certainly have been placed on technical advance and efficiency, less upon punctilio, birth, and prestige, points which might hinder true effectiveness in warfare and, being superfluous to it, were hence militaristic rather than military. These honor concepts were similar in the countries of Western Europe at that time, since enough of a common heritage of feudalism had survived in them all; only Russia, lacking the earlier chivalry, remained outside the codes. Among the rest, there was a supranational sentiment of honor which even enforced greater courtesies to a foreign foe of equal rank than to bourgeois of one's own country; this again had been a trait of feudal armies in the Middle Ages.

This heritage of feudalism might easily have been swept away in the tide of change, including religious reformation movements, the spread of high finance and the growth of large-scale manufacture, which transformed Europe in the sixteenth, seventeenth, and eighteenth centuries. But through the standing army, the citadel and last retreat of feudalism, it was preserved with all its fateful consequences to later military history. To be sure, the city bourgeois might have refused to acquiesce in such a scheme of things; but, like Molière's comic apostate to his class, the *Bourgeois Gentilhomme,* M. Jourdain, the bourgeois betrayed his usual suicidal tendency to embrace concepts which he considers above his own because they are martial and hence seem less selfish than he knows his own to be, and the selfishness of the knights, in the corporate interest more than in the personal one, he does not penetrate.

Although merchants themselves might retain some pride in their own occupation, as they did in certain places, their sons were very apt to forsake their father's trade for the lawyer's gown or the sword. They bought offices and lands to which honor was attached, like the son of Anton Fugger who turned from his family's trading and finance to imitate the ways of noblemen. A first step in this process of ennoblement was often to become "horsy." Marcus Fugger wrote a book on studs (*Von der Gestüterey,* 1578) to this end. "The horse became so to speak the mobile pedestal of the nobleman, from which he surveyed the bourgeois as from a great height. The first titles of the nobility and army are derived from this animal, which had also been admitted to be noble; *chevaliers, écuyers* (squires), *connétables,* and marshals draw their names from the horse and the care dedicated to this useful and occasionally superb helpmeet of the warrior." [61]

When the man of the middle classes took a title, however, he did not merely add dignity to his person, but moved entirely out of his former sphere with its principal ideals. The nobleman's honor concept had little to do with the chief bourgeois concept, that of individual virtue. As Montesquieu admitted, virtue was not the regulative force in the aristocratic system: "Ambition in laziness, meanness in pride, the desire to become rich without labor, aversion to truth, flattery, betrayal, perfidy, the breaking of all one's engagements, contempt for the duties of a citizen . . . and more than all that, ridicule heaped upon virtue, form the character of courtiers at all times and in all places." [62] Honor, that is, the search for distinctions and higher rank, stood in the place of virtue as the animating principle in the noblemen's society.

This honor was essentially that of a caste, not of the individual. It was distinct from that idea of inner honor, springing from soul and mind, guided by individual conscience, which some rare persons and small groups have at times endeavored to hold up as a model. Such "personal honor" might well clash with the demands of group honor, based on lineage and tradition, and so prove prejudicial to military hierarchy. The individual's conscience might lead him to emphasize the Christian virtues of humility and universal love, incompatible with the fierce pride that constituted the honor of the nobleman; it might even force him to admit himself in the wrong, a thing the nobleman's honor, and the statesman's as well, forbade. To a certain extent, writers have tried to bring the two disparate ideals together; Schopenhauer defined them by the dictum: "Honor is the outward conscience and conscience the inward honor." The officer and good churchman Mahan, trying to preserve the compatibility of honor and Christianity, thought that "honor does not forbid a nation to acknowledge that it is wrong, or to recede from a step which it has taken through wrong notions or mistaken reasons." [63] But in practice, he would hardly have been able to name a case where a nation's statesmen have, on the basis of honor, admitted that they were in the wrong. National honor has arisen, closely intertwined with feudal honor, although the exact hour of its appearance is still unsettled; there were stirrings of national honor in feudal society itself, during the Crusades, for instance, long before Schiller's famous line: "Unworthy is the nation that does not set its all on honor."

The honor of the military noble was, then, exclusive, the possession of a high estate. He was adamant about refusing to share it with his countrymen, commoners in the army or out. In France it was said in 1601: "If there is contempt in the world; it goes to the merchant." Even a hundred and fifty years later, it was the opinion of Montesquieu that to admit bourgeois to honor would destroy that quality itself: "All is lost if the lucrative profession of the trader should succeed by its riches in ever becoming an honored profession. . . . A disgust then seizes all the other estates, honor loses all its esteem, the slow and natural means of distinguishing oneself do not apply any longer, and the government is stricken in principle." [64] So, too, Frederick the Great in Prussia maintained that bourgeois must be kept in their places in order to heighten the officers' feeling of honor; if the officer enjoys supreme prestige in peacetime, he will be readier to sacrifice himself in war: "I have myself undertaken war and have seen how several times a colonel has decided the fate of the state. On such decisive days, one learns to appreciate the value of good officers; then one learns to love these men, seeing with what high-minded contempt of death, with what unshakable strength of mind they oppose the enemy and force him to evacuate the field."

Since honor was regarded as their exclusive prerogative by the noblemen, they would not brook interference with it, or supervision, by outsiders, not even their king. The king was indeed the bestower of favors, titles, berths, and medals, but when he was called, as in England, "the fountain of honor," this meant, in reality, only the fountain of *honors*. Over honor itself he had little control. The monarch in Calderón's *Medico de su Honra* admits this to a confidant: "Honor is the sacred place where the soul resides altogether. I am not the king over souls."

The honors awarded by the king needed the tacit approval of members of the honor class, which might not be forthcoming. Each member of the privileged group felt that he had a right to vote on the case in question, that "honor is the esteem of our peers," and would not be complete without that general assent. This independence of the sovereign made easier any severance of loyalty pledged to him, when such loyalty to a Crown conflicted with that to the interest of the nobility. Such a shifting took place in the Glorious Revolution in England, when William III expected the leaders of the British army not to permit themselves "to be abused by a false notion of honor" pledging themselves to the Stuarts, but to transfer allegiance to him, remembering what they owed to themselves and their posterity, which they, "as Men of Honour, ought to prefer to all private considerations and engagements forever." [65] This hope was justified: the Stuarts retained only a little more of their former officers' and nobles' allegiance than the last of the Hohenzollerns after 1918—both Marlborough and Hindenburg indeed entertained some treasonable relations with the fallen sovereigns after their ignominious flights, but both were at the time under a cloud of disfavor.

It was this jealous group solidarity of the noblemen which helped make the officer castes of the European armies into self-governing bodies, divorced from civilian control and even impatient of royal meddling—ruling themselves by their members' own traditions or corporate whims. The institution of the duel was the sharp reminder of this group independence and power. Contrary to the usual belief in its old Germanic character, it spread from Spain, and it was possibly in the beginning a form of knightly protest against the societal consequences, like commercialization, of the influx of the precious metals from the Indies. It was one of the means by which the noble estate governed itself; and officers were convinced that the privilege of dueling was the essential basis of their group reputation. Glory must be acquired, as Schopenhauer said, but honor must not be lost. The former could be obtained in war, the latter had to be preserved in peacetime by the *code duello*.

Minor differences in rank, of course, existed in this honor society. But officers of lower rank might cross sabers with superiors; and even cadets, not yet officers, could challenge those to whom they were entrusted for their education. They were on an equal footing in the group, as members of a class admitted to possess honor, compelled to maintain it by demanding or giving "satisfaction" on occasions when it was slighted. Judgment as to what constituted such a slight was left to the challenger, the challenged, and the group of their immediate colleagues. Attempts of various governments to interfere in such affairs of honor, in the interests of military efficiency, were furiously resented.

England was least caught by the general "duellomania," in part because the lines were not so clearly drawn between noble and gentleman. Birth, highly as it was revered there, was endowed with fewer privileges than on the Continent. If one were recognized as a gentleman, which might be attained through fortune or in other ways than by the accident of birth, that established one's standing among peers. To be an acceptable officer called for behavior worthy of a gentleman, a broader term than noble: conduct "unbecoming the character of an officer and a gentleman" disqualified from further service. Even so, the Royalist side in the Civil War found it necessary to forbid, under penalties, "reproachful or provoking speeches or acts" and challenges to fight duels.[66] With the triumph of more bourgeois forces, cases of libel were more often taken to the courts than on the Continent, more and more so because of the attractively heavy indemnities awarded to the damaged party. Public opinion turned more and more against the duel; as early as the 1690's, Defoe urged that it be punished and a challenger be denied the character of gentleman.[67]

The more feudal spirit of the French noblemen led to a greater insistence upon self-determination in that respect. It is said that in the first eighteen years of the reign of Henry IV, around four thousand gentlemen had been killed in duels, and again as many during that of Louis XIII.[68] As the absolute monarchy strove to put down this lordly pride, it attacked the duel system. Louis XIII had two noblemen of high rank beheaded because of a duel, and from the mid-seventeenth century on, increasing edicts prohibited such affairs, often putting them on a level with ordinary brawling. Under Louis XIV, when the edicts were actually applied with punishment as well as threat, dueling became for a time almost extinct, though by the end of Louis XV's reign it so far revived that there was said to be more of it in France than in all the rest of Europe put together. The reasons for mortal combat were often trifling: a remark on one's dress, a struggle over a theater seat, a trial of the courage of a newcomer to a regiment.[69]

Officers usually condoned the offense, and if murder was the outcome, helped the culprit to evade prosecution. The courts were generally not very anxious to punish him; the government shrank from the more drastic means, like degradation of duelists, or preventive measures, such as the suppression of fencing masters. But some order was brought into the regiments through a "tribunal of the point of honor," a court of last appeal on all such conflicts, composed of the marshals of France.

Officers, and in particular regimental ones, were throughout the age inclined to evade laws against dueling. The law had no majesty for them, and indeed jurists and other governmental officials connived at the practice, aspiring themselves to join the honor society; the official and the student frequently wore swords like the officer. This led so far as to condone dueling even among the common soldiers, who contracted a mania for such combat, which in France lasted right down to the Revolution. General Hoche, as a private, took it upon himself to provoke a brutal corporal to a duel in order to punish him. At times, the disputes set regiments at odds: on one occasion, fifty men of one regiment were fighting an equal number of another on the *glacis* of Maubeuge; when they were separated, two men were dead and thirty-seven wounded. The best way found to suppress this spirit was putting whole companies to onerous peacetime duties.[70]

Though the state was strong in Prussia, and most determined efforts were made there to tame the officer bodies, they were likewise doomed to failure. The state declared that duelers showed contempt of divine law by risking the salvation of Christian souls, and also affronted the state, in harming its servants. Once capital punishment was threatened. But the self-will of the noble officers was not broken by an edict, and the actual punishment, if inflicted at all, remained an honorable confinement in comfort. Frederick the Great himself, who disliked the duel and berated his officers for the wrong-headed prejudice that cost him valuable lives, had to condone it and indeed excuse it by admitting that the officer who refused to duel would find no employment anywhere else in Europe. Toward the end of his reign, however, as enlightened humanitarianism made headway even in his service, a Prussian court of honor was set up on the French model, consisting of the peers of the parties involved in an affair. This left it to the officers themselves to decide whether one of their number had been guilty of infamous conduct, but still that seemed irksome interference to them.[71]

The actual result in most countries, therefore, of the struggle between law and the officer was the triumph of the latter. Despite attempts to impose discipline from above, the officers of noble birth preserved their own rules and will, and this was to the benefit of their estate as a whole. If their private acts appear quixotic, their behavior never ran contrary to the true interest of the group. Battling officers set the tone in the regiments and often wrecked the discipline of the rest; they prevented the "expert" from attaining eminence in peacetime, at least, by repulsing or hampering him. It was often necessary for the state, as in Austria, to ennoble such outsiders in order to insure their standing in the honor group. Officer bodies became more exclusive castes than they would otherwise have been, holding back talent from advancement to the detriment of the service.

It proved extremely difficult for the absolutist system to extend "honor" from the officer to the common soldier. Though the officers' "word of honor" was a contractual pledge observed fairly well between peers, in capitulations or armistices between armies, it was binding only among peers. It could be broken to others, as in 1756, when English volunteers were urged to present themselves for service which, they were promised, would not take them out of the United Kingdom; they were promptly put on board transports and shipped to Gibraltar, and, as further recruiting naturally suffered by this breach of faith, Hanoverians and Hessians had to be bought for the defense of England.[72] Honor did not forbid pillaging occupied towns and territories, or incurring debts and not paying them, except at gaming tables, or dishonoring innocent girls below the officers' own estate. Nor was it applicable to the man in the ranks. "Both have their principles," stated the Saxon-Polish Field Service Rules of 1752:

For the officer, honor is reserved, for the common man obedience and loyalty. . . . From honor flows intrepidity and equanimity in danger, zeal to win ability and experience, respect for superiors, modesty toward one's equals, condescension toward inferiors, severity against criminals. . . . Nothing therefore must incite the officer but honor, which carries its own recompense; but the soldier is driven and restrained and educated to discipline by reward and fear. . . . The worst soldier is an officer without honor, a common man without discipline.[73]

With this guiding principle in view, decorations were withheld from the common soldier in most armies, notably the English and Prussian, thus maintaining the feudal character of such distinctions. Only in France were certain attempts made to recognize his bravery and faithfulness. Golden rings had been granted to some men in the early provincial militia to stir up emulation; Henry IV formed a plan to found an order attainable by common men, but died before he could carry it out; his son, Louis XIII, took up this idea and created an order in 1633, open equally to officers and men. This was overshadowed in 1679 by the Ordre Militaire de Saint-Louis, founded by Louis XIV, which might be bestowed upon soldiers as well as officers who had served at least ten years, and carried with it a pension of from two hundred to eight hundred livres. Veterans with twenty-four years of service were presented with a medal.[74] But, in spite of such advances in France, the way was still closed to a modern army, with its broad extension of honor to millions and to the yet more recent national and race honor concepts.

Even before the French Revolution, however, this next development was foreseen, or urged, by various writers. In the first part of the eighteenth century, the Marshal Saxe, a German nobleman in French army service, published a plea for universal military service in that country. To increase the number of soldiers and heighten their excellence he advised the admission of all to honor; if military service were widespread, this would be inevitable: the poor bourgeois would be consoled by watching the rich serve, and the rich would not dare complain as they followed the noble, and all would be elevated in mutual esteem. This was the counsel of a military practitioner and grand seigneur, with insight into the psychological machinery which worked or might be made to work in armies.[75]

Somewhat later, in the 1770's, another German—not in Prussia but in the little oak-surrounded town of Osnabrück—the headstrong Justus Möser, proposed something similar in his *Patriotische Phantasien*. He indeed approached it from another angle: whereas Marshal Saxe wanted a better and bigger army by extending honor to the people, it was the hope of Möser, the bureaucratic official, to make people into soldiers in order to give them honor, pride, and self-respect. Pride could be restored to the Germans, Möser thought, by permitting them to bear arms:

The Nordic peoples, and in particular the Germans, connect honor mainly with weapons, and in the long run despise those who

are not entitled to carry and use them. And therefore there is no
other way but to tie up again the sword with the handicrafts, if we
wish to obtain the necessary honor for this estate. . . . Many will
think it would be dangerous to allow so many people the right to
carry arms and exercise them in the same way as regulars. But that
would be a policy suitable to despots who would allow their free
subjects the right to complain, but not the right to give their words
emphasis. A hundred years from now, the national militia will
everywhere be the main thing and will reaffirm liberty and property which would perish were our present constitution to be continued.

The dream of Möser and Marshal Saxe of great national armies,
of armed nations, was approaching realization as they wrote. The
end of the narrow and exclusive period of caste domination by
military nobility was drawing to a close in the eighteenth century,
just as, in the fifteenth, the arms-bearing monopoly of the old
medieval chivalry was being challenged successfully by the city
bourgeois and the state.

Yet the bourgeois, who once again attacked the nobleman for his
honor privilege and commanding position in society, was not
animated by a positive desire for martial honors for himself. The
thirst to engage and rise in army service was certainly not one of the
factors contributing to revolutionary sentiment. What he did wish to
see was armies molded more strictly according to utilitarian ideas of
usefulness, instead of by feudal concepts of distinction. "Utility
determines what we esteem," wrote Hume, and Holbach also
declared: "Honour, like virtue, can only be based on usefulness." [76]
Even to the less radical Montesquieu "virtue is the basis (*ressort*)
of the Republic, honor—false honor—that of the Monarchy." [77]
The bourgeois thinkers of the Enlightenment wished to identify
honor with service to society, and in that light they did not find
armies as they knew them particularly useful institutions. The aim of
the forerunners of the Revolution was, accordingly, thinking more of
tearing down the previously existing arrangements than of setting
up new models of their own.

Under the formal, finished surfaces of the old society in the eighteenth century, new forces were stirring which took effect in the military as in other spheres. Poets, philosophers, economists, and thinkers of the Enlightenment generally were revolted by the artificialities and injustices of the ossified social scheme—as far as their own class was affected: carrying forward the humanism and secularism of the Renaissance, they sought to lead humanity in the direction of greater freedom under more rational principles. Nature, Democracy, and Reason were the ideas in which they viewed a possible salvation.

2

The Military Thought of the Enlightenment

Antimilitary Thought

As they turned the searchlight of critical examination on every phase of society, government, economy, theology, education, and the arts, the military system was not spared. The caste-ridden standing army, composed of soldier automatons, the bulwark of the absolutist monarchy, was contrary to Nature, Rights of Man, and Reason. Many chief figures of the Enlightenment assailed the army and warfare of absolutism, but usually without a clear idea of what might be substituted in the more natural and rational society they wished to form. What would a more "natural" army be like? Nature they were learning to admire afresh in the so-called "English gardens," but these, though far freer than the old formal parks with hedges clipped in monstrous shapes, were still far from nature in the raw. A natural army, they imagined, would disband after a war was over; it would be composed of all able-bodied citizens, equal in arms. But how should this "democratic" army, a mass army, be controlled? They supposed: by the third guiding principle, Reason. Poor psychologists—and this was the weakness of thinkers in the Enlightenment generally—they foresaw rationality progressing in equal strides with nature and democracy, binding and teaching both; they failed to envisage a world in which the third, and most vital, element would remain by far the feeblest, leaving "Nature" to go back to the jungle and "Democracy" to unfold blindly its terrible strength.

Shrewd as critics, if not as prophets, the French exposed the militarism of their age. Diderot objected to monarchies which, to preserve their power, subordinated everything, science, art, or philosophy, to the military group; in which the king was the first soldier of his army and the science of warfare was held the only useful science. Carrying over into his study of political science this civilian perspective, Montesquieu denounced as a new epidemic the desire of kings to enlarge their forces endlessly; each king, he said, was maintaining too many troops and thus grinding his people down to starvation—a state of things which was called peace, but was in reality leading only to poverty and degradation. Although he did not advocate a complete dissolution of the army, Montesquieu was afraid it might destroy the balance of his three powers of government if too much strength were given to the prince at its head; he left it to the legislature to dissolve the army if it found that appropriate.

Far sharper was Voltaire. He called soldiers hired murderers and the scum of the nation, poor devils in cheap blue cloth at a hundred and ten sous an ell, with the new-style conqueror at their head for whom some genealogist had proved his claims to a province. Since Sulla the standing armies, paid with the money of the citizens, had been used even more to subjugate the citizens at home than the enemies abroad. That the burgher of the eighteenth century was to a large extent spared the ravages of war was not enough for Voltaire. War was damaging to the peoples who were not parties to the case threshed out by arms. It was absurd and barbaric for nations to perish for the interests of two sovereigns: "Let them battle in an enclosed field if they want to; but that a whole people should be sacrified for their interests, that is a horror." Peoples should have a right of self-determination.

Turgot called war and conquest mere aberrations or crime, and he and Quesnay considered the standing army the most unproductive of all estates, which ought to be replaced by a militia. For Herder, the army, and in particular the Prussian army, was a "hired, thoughtless, strengthless, will-less machine."

The fiery exponent of leveling democracy, Rousseau, said armies were the pest which depopulated Europe, appointed to attack and subjugate either neighbors or their own peoples. He wanted a militia in the Swiss manner: "Every citizen shall be a soldier from duty; none by profession. Every citizen shall be ready, but only when need calls for it." Where the other thinkers appear as liberals in their military policies as in other hopes, Rousseau foreshadows the claims for military and other duties toward the state which democracy is always readier to demand than to offer. There is but one step from the general to the specific, from his postulate that "every good citizen owes his talents and lights to society," to the first French law of conscription, proclaiming that "every Frenchman is a soldier and owes himself to the defense of his country."

Across the Atlantic, the American Declaration of Independence took up several of these complaints and demands and condemned the King of England, who "has kept among us, in times of peace, standing armies without the consent of our legislatures," and who "has affected to render the Military independent of and superior to the Civil Power." The American Revolution particularly inflamed the enemies of standing armies in Europe, since the British "hirelings" had apparently failed miserably against the militia composed of men who had rushed forward from their plows in the hour of danger.

The outcome of the Coalition Wars against revolutionary France, so shameful for the old standing armies, confirmed the doubts about their value and added to the number of the doubters, who were joined by Fichte and Kant. The former found throughout history a tendency on the part of all monarchs inclining inwardly to absolutism and outwardly to universal dominion. To enforce their will monarchs created the soldier estate—an order of men "tied to their estate by the very thing which hardens their estate, severe discipline; and by the laws of discipline written in blood, they find their honor in their degradation, and their indemnification for the other burdens of their condition by being left unpunished in case of crimes against burgher and peasant." [1] Kant confidently voiced the hope that standing armies would come to an end as time went on; for "they threaten other states continually with war by their readiness to appear always ready for war; they incite states to excel in the number of armed men, to which no limit is set; and when by the costs it involves, peace becomes even more burdensome than a short war, armies themselves furnish the reason for aggressive war in order to get rid of this burden." [2] Kant, like one of the old Greek sages, was convinced that war is evil in that it makes more bad people than it destroys.

Particularly significant for military affairs were the writings of the economists. It is true that some of them came vigorously to the defense of the standing-army system. Adam Smith in his *Wealth of Nations* (1776) took up the cudgel in its support. He found it the cheapest and most efficacious instrument for what he called "certainly the noblest of arts—warfare." As befitted the endless wars on the borders of the expanding British Empire, Smith saw, in the army and the firearm, agencies "favorable both to the permanency and the extension of civilization." But in exploring the processes of creating wealth and adding to the welfare and economic security of peoples, the economists, the physiocrats writing against the mercantilist army, encountered the costs of maintaining armies and the problems of gigantic debts created by warfare. If none of them made a frontal attack upon military systems as such, all of them had to consider the relations of agriculture, industry, and labor to military instrumentalities and fiscal charges. In so doing they helped a few military writers to see that the nature of armies and warfare, including the prospects of victory, was really grounded in the economic life and operations of society. Military men, as distinguished from militaristic men, began to review the petrifying traditions associated with the standing-army system.

French and British Military Thought

The thought of the new economists was centered on the freedom of the individual from state intervention, liberty of competitive activity, immunity in the management of his private property. Paralleling the rise of this conception in economics is the rise, during the Enlightenment, of the conception of the *genius*—the greatest, freest, and most creative personality. The genius is born for greatness even though his original rank may be low. The genius frees himself from his native tongue, his class, his body, the bonds of rococo formalism and military traditionalism. He escapes the narrow expertness of military engineers who had no right, as the Comte de Guibert, a pathbreaker in French military thought, mockingly said, to derive their beautiful name, *corps de génie,* from genius, when it really belonged to an engine alone.[3]

Influenced by the Enlightenment and all the turmoil of spirit that accompanied it, a large number of military men let their minds play somewhat freely over armies and warfare in relation to supreme ends and society itself. Among this group were Marshal Maurice Comte de Saxe, Guibert, Bourcet, and several others who, rather than Napoleon, may be said to have initiated the ideas of the new military age. The Revolution, to be sure, came between these thinkers and Bonaparte. It made possible the realization of the new ideas. But the thinkers were the precursors.

Saxe, undoubtedly a military genius himself and a man of wide experience in warfare, summed up his philosophy of arms, significantly enough, in a weird book called *Mes Rêveries,* published after his death. Although Carlyle, with his blind admiration of the passing system of Frederick the Great, thought this book was a farrago of nonsense, it was in fact an unconventional and revolutionary exploration of war systems and war psychology better deserving the name of "classic."

Like Machiavelli and like another *grand seigneur,* the Prince de Ligne, Saxe possessed a flair for military psychology. He knew that the drilling of men in his time, which treated the soldier in closed ranks—a product as finished as any manufactured goods packed for sale—could not alone guarantee the quality of the troops, that rather "the *imbécilité du cœur* was among all things in war the most important, that to which the greatest attention should be paid." On this feeling he intended to play with regimental music; not unlike some modern employers, he wanted to apply music to make the men forget the hardships of long marches—that was the *tactique* too. The Greeks and Romans had not invented military music merely to confound their senses but to make troops march in cadence. Music would make them forget the exertion as it inspires people to dance to music all night who cannot continue two hours without it.

Instead of being satisfied with the traditional military organization as a tool to work with, Saxe advocated the combined use of light and regular infantry, the former to be placed some one hundred or two hundred paces in front of the "century," to disquiet the enemy, to inflict losses on him and hide the maneuvers of the "centuries." They were the forerunners, attacking in battle in the same way and with the same effect as those disturbing ideologues who slung missiles at persons and institutions which seemed only little, if at all, disturbed by their shots, till the masses from the rear followed up the preparatory work, charging through and bringing about the decision. Saxe shared the fate of the ideologues at the hands of Napoleon, the grim heir of the Revolution, who spoke very disparagingly about the *Rêveries* and their author and was far from admitting any real obligation to him.

All infantry was to be armed with breech-loading fusils, an arm not yet invented, but proposed by Saxe, which makes us think of the very different relation of later officers to the arms maker. Firing was not to be at the word of command, as that only cramped the natural style of aiming and shooting. In the soldiers' training, jumping, running, marksmanship were to play a considerable role. The infantry was to act in close connection with the other arms, cavalry and artillery; the smallest caliber of the latter were to be infantry cannon for uses similar to those reserved to the machine gun of today. Saxe wanted to see these arms—four regiments, each consisting of four heavy centuries, a half-century each of light infantry and of cavalry—united into a legion, thus foreshadowing the modern military divisions.

In an age when competition between states and armies, and

therefore war, was restricted largely by feudal codes, Saxe demanded that it be freed, regardless of the consequences of the adoption of innovations—they would favor the one party which used them first. If the enemy were to adopt them and thereby neutralize an initial advantage, that would only be a proof of the excellence of the new weapon; enemies were bound to persist in their old errors for some time and adopt the new thing only after several defeats. "So reluctant are all nations," meaning armies, "to give up old customs." This is a conception of military competition only accepted in the second half of the nineteenth century.

The *Rêveries* of Saxe were not altogether free of absurdities. He wanted to equip the infantry with sandals. He very reasonably proposed to have the soldier's hair cut short but, to please the artificial inclinations of the time, they were to wear perukes of lambskins over their round heads. In order to bring forth a more warlike race, he proposed marriages to last only five years, an idea reflecting his own caste and birth and his own activities in the line of propagation—a notion which reappeared in Nazi eugenics designed, like Saxe's, to produce more soldiers and thereafter diminish them. It would mean putting the youth of a nation into a military orphans' home.

Another explorer of military affairs in the age of the Enlightenment was William Lloyd, son of an English divine. Lloyd was a military adventurer, who in turn served the French, the Pretender, the French, the Prussians, the Austrians, the Prussians, the British— as a political agent—and the Russians. In his *Military Memoirs* (1781) he divides the art of war into a mechanical part which with its rules anyone may learn, and one which can neither be explained nor taught. Genius alone can show the right way and is itself the free gift of nature. The art of war resembles poetry or eloquence. Many know the rules of either very well, but few possess the true talent. Even if works are composed according to the rules, they remain cold and tasteless if they are not permeated by that divine fire which constitutes the true character of genius. The natural genius must have the natural soldier to use—not too natural, however, because Lloyd is not a revolutionary. Looking at the senseless uniforms of the time, he demands that the soldier be clad and armed according to the nature of his tasks; that he be taught nothing but what is really useful to him before the enemy; that he be directed toward everything that might become useful to him somehow. Since the pike, which would have been so useful against cavalry, has disappeared, Lloyd wants the flintlock musket lengthened by a four-foot-long lance, and to be loadable from the breech. For the protection of the infantry he advises heavy leather helmets and cuirasses.

The commanding general, in Lloyd's theory, must know the

military genius of the nations and regulate his warfare as well as the structure of his own army in accordance with their peculiarities. The natural talents must be guided and not destroyed; therefore Lloyd condemns the attempt of the French War Minister, Comte de Saint-Germain, to introduce Prussian discipline. The latter alone keeps the heterogeneous Prussian army together, a complicated machine formidable only as long as it is permeated by a spirit like that of Frederick. Should this motive power weaken even for a moment, the whole heterogeneous machine would fall apart. The subjects of a despot learn submissiveness and obedience from early youth; they are therefore preferable to those of a republic, if the latter are not animated, as in a defensive war, by a fanaticism for liberty, which can be replaced in subjects of a despotism by religious fanaticism.

With all that, Lloyd condemns the Frederician maxim that the soldier must fear his officers more than his enemies, not from any humanitarian motive, but because he is convinced that passive obedience, springing from fear of punishment, makes man passive in everything. The warrior ought to be active and enterprising and all moral levers which can bring him to that state of mind ought to be used. Clearly, Lloyd wants to have the suppressed and neglected energies resuscitated and the imponderables newly appreciated.

The activity of the military genius Lloyd wants to see rationalized by mathematics and geography; topography determines the direction of marches, camps, and positions. The general who knows these things can direct war enterprises with geometrical precision and lead a continual war without ever getting into the necessity of giving battle.

This conception makes Lloyd another adherent of the battleless war—certainly a notion even more non-Napoleonic than anti-Frederician. Frederick used to call a battle an unpleasant emetic, necessary from time to time. Whereas both these military leaders could not conceive of armies too large, even if they outran their possibilities of control, Lloyd thought that an army strength of from fifty to sixty thousand men was sufficient for all undertakings, and that more was needless. The idea of the small army, proposed by Puységur and others, seems at bottom due to the bourgeois notion which is not fully antimilitaristic but would prefer to engage in war with only a moderate or restricted amount of expense. The aim in the offensive war is still pre-Napoleonic and the conquest of a restricted territory of the enemy, holding it in pawn, has nothing in it of the modern aggressive warfare involving large masses and large territories.

Lloyd's cosmopolitan employment, which included fighting under the Pretender and preparing plans for a later French invasion of his native England in support of the Pretender's claims to the throne, prevented him from appreciating one important imponderable in the military field—that is, nationalism. After Percy and Herder had announced the doctrine, each nation was supposed to have a genius, a genius not originally competitive in a bellicose way, but hovering about the wells of its poetry and folklore. This national genius was, however, claimed for army purposes by the Comte de Guibert's *Essai général de tactique* (1770). Guibert pointed to the stalemate in which the wars of the century had ended as a rule, in spite of the heavy burdens which the large standing armies put upon the states. Then he insisted that the dominion over Europe would go to the nation which had a vigorous government, possessed the manly virtues, and raised a popular army. Such a nation could carry on war at low expense and make it profitable by its victories. The truly strong army must be national, not composed, like the Prussian, in large part of foreigners, mercenaries, vagabonds, driven by fickleness and need to serve under these colors where they were retained by discipline. The successes of such troops are due to the ignorance of their enemies and the skill of their King, who had created new tactics. If he has a weak successor, this ephemeral power, Prussia, will sink back into the sphere to which her real means point.

To prepare for the national force, according to Guibert's scheme, every nerve must be strained to develop inner strength. This could be done only if the sovereign limited his powers and told his people: "I return to you the overgrown power, which I have not misused, which my successors shall not misuse either. I call upon you to share in the government. I retain nothing but the dignity of the Crown, the right to propose to you wise laws, the power to apply them as soon as you have approved of them, and, in all accidents threatening the state, I shall have the authority of dictatorship." This proposal is nothing less than a call for constitutional government and limited monarchy for the military reason that they make the nation strong. "Modern tactics can be relied upon only as long as the spirit of European constitutions remains the same; as soon as it meets in an enemy a phalanx of moral powers it will go the way of all human inventions."

In common with other reformers, Guibert wanted the emancipation of the body through gymnastics. Gymnastics and *Turnen* were to become elements of national education, applied for military use. Exercises like swimming, running, and climbing were to be more a part of the soldier's training, and manual exercises and evolutions were to be less conspicuous, for the former, rather than the latter, bring to the soldier an idea of the accidents that might befall in war. These exercises were to limber up the soldier and enable him to take a quicker step—one hundred and twenty paces per minute as against the customary seventy—which, finally introduced into service in the French army, enabled it to outmarch the enemy.[4]

Not all of Guibert's proposals pointed to an actual future; he remained on the whole an enemy, though not an obstinate one, of column tactics, the deep array, the *ordre profond,* about which a lively argument was going on in the schools and salons during the 1770's and 1780's. Guibert, at least, destroyed the metaphor which lay at the bottom of the *ordre profond:* the belief that it was possible to heighten the strength of troops by adding to their depth, that the shock itself was the product of mass and celerity on the part of the infantry and "heavy cavalry." He reminded the tacticians that they were not dealing with atoms but with individuals, whose nature was wasted in columns where the mechanical and sheepish instinct of men drove them to disorder.

Relying again on the individual, Guibert demanded individual aiming, independent firing, musketry practice against war targets, concentrating effective fire on a given point. The idea of quick firing, hitherto the fashion, he said, seemed to be based on the notion that the mere noise of it was deadly. No wonder that in a battle where five hundred thousand musket shots were spent, losses amounted only to two thousand.

The dispute about the shallow array, the *ordre mince,* and the *ordre profond* foreshadowed the use to which national troops would be put. The reliable, individual national soldier was to be placed with the skirmishers, the mass or the mob of the nation in heavy, dense columns. The predilection of the one and the other among the tacticians is conditioned by their estimation, high or low, of the masses. Only rarely was use made of both orders, the combination of columns and skirmishers, as advocated by De Lessac in his *De l'esprit militaire* (1783).

The Frederician armies had been one large unit moving under the command and direction of the King-Commander himself, with very little for the general to do in battle except set an example to officers and men and die with them; thirty-one Prussian generals were slain in the Seven Years' War. It was one large organization, like the economy of mercantilism, which wanted to bring everything under the one roof of the state. To delegate authority, not always strong enough to stretch directly over a whole army, to create units for the subdivision of the battle labor, to standardize and accelerate movements of bodies larger than regiments and smaller than armies, Guibert and others before him wanted—especially for the purposes of march movements and of supply—the army grouped in sub-armies, complete with all arms, or, in other words, in *divisions.*

Though rather earlier in point of time, the *division* in the army compares with the *atelier concentré,* the gathering of many processes of manufacture under one roof with division of labor in an industrial plant. The military transformation accompanied the industrial revolution or evolution. From the standpoint of national economy, the *atelier concentré* in eighteenth-century France indicated the decentralization of control, or delegation of powers, except in the most important state affairs, in order to achieve higher efficiency. The same process toward efficiency took place in the armies. The divisions, long discussed in France, were introduced into the French armies by the Convention of 1793 and were later taken up by nearly all European armies.

In order to obtain the proper delegation of authority, Guibert wanted the artillery to be concentrated on specific points, those where the enemy is to be attacked or from which he might attack, and no more dispersion of fire along the front with the vague hope of disabling enemies. Moreover, he wanted the army itself to be concentrated in its efforts toward those specific points—always *"serrée, unie, rassemblée, et disposée au combat."*

To complete the emancipation of the army, Guibert advocated discarding the old system of supply: "What I want to avoid is that my supplies should command me." He reminded his contemporaries that the Romans and others had lived on and at the expense of the country in which they were fighting; that Cato had said: war must support war; and that the Romans felt themselves best served, not by those generals who had conducted glorious campaigns, but by those who supplied their troops the best and brought the most money home to the public treasury. Fertile countries like Flanders and parts of Germany lent themselves particularly well to this kind of warfare. But since war was to be carried on in other parts, too, supply trains, magazines, transport systems would remain necessary to armies. Guibert, however, wanted to see them militarized under the direction of officers, for the "bureaux, not to speak of the contractors, are the born enemies of all that tends to put the details of military administration into military hands." He thus foreshadowed the days when everyone belonging to the army, down to drivers, and veterinarians and women auxiliaries—and many not in the army at all—would be in uniform.

German Military Thought

Guibert was by no means the only military man to demand a nationalization of armies, to insist that the states should no longer fight through substitutes, a small number of mercenaries maintained by the states to fight their, or rather their governors', quarrels. A petty German prince, regent of less than a hundred square miles—

to which he added by building an island in the middle of a large lake in his country—Count William of Schaumburg, the teacher of Scharnhorst in the 1770's, also wanted the whole nation to take part in war. No longer should the "defensive" people, robbed of their defensive strength by ambitious rulers, look helplessly on as witnesses of their own misfortunes, while their fates were decided by substitutes. The Count believed in close co-operation between the substitutes, forming the framework of an army, and the people; he introduced conscription in his own nation of Bückeburg.[5]

During this period there were adherents of military nationalism even in Prussia, where the bourgeoisie was comfortably balancing its specific interests by a vague, peaceful cosmopolitanism, and still enjoyed its exemptions from military service, though it was theoretically put on a basis of general conscription in 1792.

The Duke of Brunswick, the commander at Valmy, was convinced as early as 1791 that small Prussia could preserve herself only by excellent institutions, the courage and patriotism of all estates, and the inner strength of the army; steps should be taken to make patriotism more alive, particularly military patriotism, and lower bureaucratic offices should be reserved for old soldiers in order to raise the inclination for army service. But King Frederick William II and the generals were averse to all ideas of a people in arms and considered it dangerous politics. The acquisition of large Polish territories was viewed not nationally, but as providing more and cheaper recruits, and this in turn made the Prussians cling to their old tactical orders, for they could not expect the newly acquired Poles to skirmish for them.[6]

Only the younger intelligence among the Prussian officers was struck by the superiority of the French revolutionary armies, which were national as long as they were revolutionary. Reformers in Prussia demanded in 1798 a reduction by one-half of the number of foreigners, who still amounted to about 50 per cent of the privates, and the naturalization of the rest of them. In case of disturbances, during the time when the native soldiers were on leave, the dissatisfied foreigners could not be relied upon and would plunder, while in case of war they would all desert; for their interest, the only thing that móved them, was too small to keep them to the Prussian service. The system of using foreigners preserved all the demoralizing features of discipline, and their low morals were infecting those of the inlanders and the whole people.[7]

The long-despised militia reappears in proposals of 1803. The advantages of a militia well organized in peacetime were said to consist in the greater number of soldiers it supplied, in the exercise of the nation in arms, in adding to the political weight of the state without adding greatly to its burdens. It was declared highly important to "gain the public opinion of the nation for this new institution," a thing the French understood so well. The French could inculcate patriotism and the thought that nothing was more honorable than the defense of one's country through instruction in rural and urban schools, especially by giving historical examples showing that king and nobility had always stood in the fore when danger to the fatherland was to be warded off. This example Prussians might well follow:

One must demonstrate and teach—the teacher himself filled with enthusiasm and inner conviction—that Prussia's constitution is the best and happiest of all; one must animate the attention directed toward public affairs by the distribution of pamphlets; one must, in short, interest the people in state and government. Teach them to appreciate the latter; then they will not think of the affairs of state as different from their own; and when they consider both as *one* thing, as it is, they will consider each controversy of the state as their own personal one, and willingly take up arms for it and defend it.

There was said to exist no antagonism in Prussia against the soldier estate as such, but only against the "great constraint and those artificial movements which rob man, born after all as an individual, of independence, and which are not needed in actual war." The standing army should preserve its elegance of movements. In particular, the Prussian army could not do without it, or else it would lose its credit abroad, which was based on that appearance. The militia were to be taught everything concerning reality in war, but nothing of the military arts of peace.

Nevertheless, the general officers turned down such comprehensive proposals, condemned the idea of individualizing the common man, and insisted on further exercising the bodies of troops toward the perfection of great machines in which the individual was to disappear like an atom. The old-fashioned position was stated in the following terms:

Personal bravery of a single individual alone does not decide on the day of battle, but bravery of the corps, and the latter rests on the good opinion and the confidence that each individual places in the corps to which he belongs. This confidence is, however, produced and promoted by that so-called pedantry. The exterior splendor, the regularity of movements, the adroitness and at the same time firmness of the mass—all this gives the individual soldier the safe and calming conviction that nothing can withstand his particular regiment or battalion.[8]

In other words, *esprit de corps* was considered by the officer nobility as militarily superior to nationalism. Against their resistance, reform proposals were shattered. Scharnhorst (April 1806) vainly demanded an increase of the regular army plus a national militia. For Scharnhorst, nationalism is the basis of a more numerous army: a weak militia is more harmful than useful; "only the whole mass can make an impression and lead to great results." A national militia could raise the number of the Prussian army from two hundred and twenty thousand to five hundred and twenty thousand men. For purposes of propaganda, Scharnhorst recommended a special war newspaper with all the news that would arouse aspiration to do great things; for this purpose, initial successes, even if unimportant, should be utilized. He even deprecated the prevailing opinion that the talent of the general was the sole deciding factor. He put strength of will and character higher. Resolute nations can win even under mediocre leaders: "When the necessity of a war is once recognized by a nation, nothing further is needed than the resolution of the leader to conquer or to die; this alone now decides between subjugation and liberty." [9]

Those Prussian officers who resisted the thought that nationalism should be enlisted in warfare, and the passions and activities of the masses exploited "in newly created fanatical army masses," were mortally afraid of many things in changing tactics and strategy. Especially were they afraid that a deployed infantry would fall into disorder. Although men of this school were in the majority, they were challenged by one of their peers and ex-comrades, Dietrich Heinrich von Bülow: "to give an order to disorder; that will always end better than when fright is the originator of the disorder among the subordinate." Bülow (1757-1807) was that rare thing, a military genius and an eccentric, a student of Rousseau, in turn a Prussian officer, director of a band of actors, a traveler and trader in the United States between 1792 and 1795 (where he met Steuben), and a prolific writer on military and political affairs. Bülow was later a worshipper of Napoleon and his universal monarchy, since "God had ordained the French for dominion because they mitigate by honor and decency the general corruption." For writing unfavorably about Russia's part in the War of 1805, he was handed over to the Czar's government by his fellow countrymen, and died in a Russian dungeon. Bülow was the originator of the modern terminology of war literature: for instance, he defined strategy and tactics as far as they bear definition and introduced the basis of operations. He also demanded examinations for officers.[10]

A few sentences out of Bülow's writings[11] indicate his grasp of the new powers and his understanding of the old ones: "The battles of the future will be decided by *tirailleur* fighting." "A *carré* surrounded by skirmishing light infantry belongs to the most pitiable of objects." "Discipline and courage are only contributing forces; the mass, the quantity, of the combatants decides." "The others [non-Napoleonic generals] always lead war as if they had learned it from their governesses. Everything so conventional, so well-bred, so modest, so aesthetic, war for war's sake. It was reserved to the genius of Napoleon to make unmannerly war." Bülow also lauds Napoleon's proclamations: "One must praise the men in order to make them worthy of the praise. The others only know orders of the day, full of bitter and cold phrases like the sour wine with which they refresh themselves. Happy the nation that can still be governed by phrases, that you can make believe a thing; the others are only susceptible to beatings and curses."

Bülow had taken part in the Prussian discussion about the reduction of the baggage train before 1806, which was decided in favor of the old order. The subaltern officers kept their riding and pack horses because, as General von Rüchel declared, "a Prussian nobleman does not walk." [12] "Knights," they answered Bülow (who was one by origin though he demanded that feather beds should stay at home) "knights must ride." When he also advocated the reduction of officers' commissions he was asked: "Where does the author put our dead nobility, the horseless knights?" [13]

The ideas, plans, proposals that appeared singly—rather than in such totality as in the thought of Guibert or Lloyd—in the ensuing revolutionary wars, were based on those potentialities of the rising bourgeoisie that might be turned to military use. This bourgeoisie, however, did not itself develop the military thought destined to mobilize its energies; this was as a rule done by military professionals —Guibert, Lloyd, Behrenhorst, Washington (the nearest to a professional in America), Napoleon and his marshals. True bourgeois thought, from the Abbé de Saint-Pierre to Kant, was directed toward abolishing war; war appeared to it as senseless, profitless to the people in general—though profitable to a few—indecisive, lacking in order.

The latter quality of war struck no one more than an old military man who had been caught by Kantian thought, Georg Heinrich von Behrenhorst (1733-1814), once an aide-de-camp of Frederick, like Steuben and, like the latter, estranged from that monarch. His "Considerations on the Art of War, Its Progresses, Its Contradictions, and Its Trustworthiness," published anonymously in 1797,[14] were written down when the first French war successes had already been achieved. At that time the "science of strangling according to rules," as he called it, had entered upon a new stage. It was by then too late to warn the bourgeoisie of the new militarism which had got hold of it and was shortly to achieve the *coup d'état* of the 18th Brumaire, when no more civilian protests would be heard. As Kant points out the limits of human cognition, Behrenhorst shows from the development of the art of war how unreliable it is and how full of contradictions. Neither his own nor any other time has accepted the view, but has preferred to derive from Kant his objective ethics, applicable to military service, rather than his peace ideology, to which Behrenhorst contributes the proofs of the military expert.

"The art of war," says Behrenhorst, "calls for a vaster amount of knowledge and more inborn talents than any of the other arts, in order to form a system of mechanics which does not, like the actual one, rest upon immutable laws, but upon unknown and therefore indirectable indications of the soul, and works with levers and windlasses which have feeling and will. Through fate it has received in modern times a primary moving force, i.e., gunpowder—to which human courage and human strength are unequal and will remain so."

Warfare is too much subjected to accident to be either art or science, Behrenhorst thought. If ever there were beginnings of a science in warfare, the introduction of the firearm had cut through such developments. The wide distance between the parties of a battle, the powder smoke which covered a battlefield, the suddenness of mass losses marred all calculations. In vain had Maurice of Orange, Gustavus Adolphus, Turenne, and Frederick tried to limit chance; always not the wisest but the most fortunate had gained victory, notably Frederick himself.

That king had become a complete illusionary in his drill-ground tactics while he had lost all sense of practicability in actual battle. Frederick had wrecked the moral springs in the soldier, either through royal negligence or contempt; he left courage and thinking, the internal values, without healthful nursing; by repulsive and foreign customs, he undermined the people's constitution which his country had challenged him to develop. The general disease of Frederician and post-Frederician tacticians was to plague themselves with empty things—things highly appreciated because they were difficult and, when once the execution succeeded, produced the delusion of having performed something really important. In no science is there anything more useless, more dazzling, and more like child's play than the over-refinement of modern tactics.

"*Drauf! Drauf!* (Up! Up and at them!), the old watchword of the Swedes under Charles XII, of the Prussians in their early wars, that is the pith, the quintessence, of the whole practical art of war." To make the soldier natural again, Behrenhorst advocated a reasonable haircut and a uniform as comfortable as that of the sailor. Bülow thought soldiers ought to be garbed as naturally as the Iroquois, i.e., nearly naked.

Watching the fall of French royalty without any resistance on the part of their military supports, Behrenhorst decided that large standing armies for interior purposes were useless because not immune to public opinion. He wanted the standing army reduced, and the rest used for productive labor in peacetime in order to spare the strength of the state for war purposes. "What the Dutch once could do, what the Americans could do without a standing army, what France could do after her standing army had largely emigrated, deserted, and become disorganized, what these states could do when they had their enemies in their own countries, every nation can do which loves its constitution and is not willing to be conquered and subjected. Courage, arms, fortified places, money, and the mere frameworks of regiments; then in case of serious trouble the regent entrusted with the general confidence—that is, a constitutional monarch—full of confidence returned to him, has only to stamp with the foot and the necessary filling of the cadres will flow from a thousand wells out of the population." War would exercise the troops thus raised and war would produce the generals, as in America and in France.

While recommending the small standing army to the bourgeois —he said he was writing for "laymen too if they only knew history" —Behrenhorst warned them at the same time not to trust to progress in warfare: "The new inventions allow passing advantages, then they become general, and then the whole thing reduces itself to a mere bare manslaughter, just as things stood in the beginning. The art of fighting *en masse,* since it necessarily frustrates itself constantly by its own development, cannot possibly belong to those steps of progress which mankind is destined to make." Insofar as Behrenhorst was a military pacifist, he hoped that his writing would contribute "a few drops to the bath" that might soften the "hard tumor of the war-and-destruction disease in the heart of the great." And as a pacifist he remained an expert of war, advising in July 1812 the direction of the war against Napoleon as it was soon afterward to be conducted, "without a premeditated plan: avoid great battles; be liberal with barren ground; then war will annul itself by the monstrousness of its own means." [15]

Against these far-ranging and widely shared doubts about the usefulness of war and the standing armies, which a considerable group of military experts had accepted, a defense was organized on the part of those who were bound to suffer from a reduction, or abolition, of such armies, or from the deprecation of their honor and reputation. For Germany this defense started from Hanover, where the existence of the army was threatened by the modern antimilitary tendency, as well as by the ancient opposition of the Estates. Convinced of the great danger which threatened their estate as well as their commonwealth, in Hanover a number of officers united in order to fight the wrong opinions spread about the standing armies. The medium of their defense was bourgeois—books and a periodical, the *Neue Militärische Journal.* Foremost among them was a professional soldier, not a nobleman born into this soldier estate but a peasant son educated for it in one of the military schools of absolutism, a talented author on military affairs—**Scharnhorst**. By a strange turn of affairs the ideologue of militarism, even though militarism remained a domain of the nobles, was a nonnoble. Scharnhorst himself became convinced from personal experience in the Hanoverian army that in wartime "the dumbest cattle gets ahead almost as well here as the most intelligent man; the latter is slighted because he is not noble." So strong had the feeling of exasperation become in him at one time that the hatred of the French was eclipsed by his own class feeling: "We are slighted by the aristocrats and yet fight for the aristocrats." [16] Still the great military preceptor went on teaching like any old pedagogue in a school of titled time-wasters, and refused for a long time to heed any such Rousseau-tinged ideas as that government and administration, and perhaps even armies, needed a selection from those below.

It is evident from this meager outline of military thought during the Enlightenment that a new intellectual setting was being prepared for all thinking about war and the system of standing armies, including its tactics and strategy. War had been accepted as a "natural" and a "noble art" by the members of the feudal array and by the directors of standing armies. Now the very art was challenged as "senseless," "brutal," and "unworthy of mankind." Kant's clarion call for "perpetual peace" was running through the philosophic circle and was in time to reach masses of people. Economists were asking embarrassing questions: What are the economic advantages of war? How are the costs of armies and wars to be met? How large are the charges which the economy of a given society can bear? [17] A German critic asked the statisticians of his time: "How great can the number of standing soldiers become in comparison with the number of working subjects before neither have anything to eat?" [18]

Nor were the writings of military men less disturbing to the defenders of the standing-army traditions. They, too, were asking sharp questions: Are standing armies after all the most efficient fighting forces available? Can we not evoke genius from below? Will not men who fight for their homes and their nation be more effective on the field than the impressed rabble of town and country and mercenary foreigners, no matter how severely disciplined and flogged? May not the "disorderly" methods of scattering skirmishers and deployed infantry, composed of men fighting for something besides pay and fear, prove superior to the "systematic" methods of the old armies? Such ideas were rejected, to be sure, by the majority of military men who, according to their wont, looked backward as they stumbled forward. But these were the civil and military ideas which were to make history as they accompanied the transformation of the standing army into the mass army.

Even before the weight of debts contracted in wars, the Enlightenment and economic changes brought absolutism and its standing army crashing to the ground in France; the American Revolution split open the military as well as the political thought of Western civilization. On the side of political institutions this Revolution brought into existence a large-scale republic—the very antithesis to the absolute monarchy which formed the core of European militarism. It extended the principle of representative government and civilian control over armies to a continental domain.

On the military side the war of the American Revolution was in part a revolt against the British standing army of "bloody backs" and "hirelings," as Americans were fond of calling British mercenaries. It was a protest against the reinforcement of British government by military regulars and the quartering of regulars on the people of the colonies. In its inception at Lexington and Concord the Revolution was literally an attack by militiamen on British regulars—an uprising of embattled farmers who had homes to fight for against disciplined regulars who had no homes and fought for pay under fear.

At the end of the Revolution, America presented the scene of a society without a monarch, without a privileged aristocracy to monopolize the offices of the army, without a state church to bless the banners of war. That was a menacing challenge to the European military system and the political system which enclosed it. This Revolution was three thousand miles away from the Continent, but repercussions of the conflict reached all parts of Europe. "Veterans in diplo-

3

The American Revolution Challenges the Standing Army

macy and in affairs of state consider us as a kind of militia," wrote John Adams in 1782, "and hold us, perhaps, as is natural, in some degree of contempt, but wise men know that militia sometimes gain victories over regular troops, even by departing from the rules." [1]

The Military Thought and Practice of the Revolutionary War

The American War of Independence furnished the demonstration ground on which were tested old and new military policies and tactics. From it European military theorists found proof or disproof, largely, it must be said, according to their preconceptions, of the contentions which they had long been discussing in a vacuum. That the colonists had won their liberty, arms in their hands, strengthened the belief in militia institutions and in the "natural" soldier springing from the outdoor bourgeois and farmer. Actually many of the older military institutions were introduced in the American army before victory was won. The initial successes of militiamen at Concord and Bunker Hill were later challenged, and it was contended that the Congress of the United States and European friends of "freer" military institutions had been deceived. Indeed, as early as September 1776, convinced that the militia had been, on the whole, more hurtful than serviceable,[2] Washington began his long struggle with Congress for a regular army of men enlisted for the duration of the war. Yet neither during the war nor afterward did the belief in the fighting power of militiamen disappear from American thought and practice.

This war was in point of style a mixed war: almost the last mercantilistic war insofar as, for instance, the French help is concerned. Through it the French intended to diminish the superior weight which England exercised in the balance of power, of which the colonies were assumed to be an integral part. On the other hand, it was almost the first revolutionary war of modern times. In part, it still lies on the Frederician side, or even pre-Frederician with respect to slow-moving tactics of the British; but it also inaugurates the age of revolutionary warfare in Europe. Giving and receiving battle were almost as often avoided on both sides as in the typical European war of the time. Dependence on the magazine supply was the same on both sides of the ocean. On the other hand, everything with the Americans was improvised, the making of paper money included. As revolutionaries, the Americans, or at any rate a sufficient number of them, accepted these tokens as money and fought for the revolutionary cause in the field in defense of their rights in the beginning, and for independence later.

Yet their spontaneous way of entering war, the action of minutemen, was soon found insufficient to raise and keep the required number of soldiers in the field. As early as January 1776, Washington advised "coercive measures" to bring the regiments up to their strength. The colonists were as eager to employ foreigners, deserters, and prisoners of war as any European general of the times. They did not even shrink from holding back Burgoyne's troops, which they had agreed to transport instantly to England, in the hope of persuading them to join the American service.[3] The states used deserters as substitutes for their own inhabitants who were liable to service, as well as Negroes free and freed after entering military service—an American application of the old Germanic rule that "war makes free." Foreign officers were far less welcome to the leaders of the revolutionary armies who thought themselves provided with enough candidates for such service, except artillery officers and engineers. If, after all, this war was a national war, a war that not only brought forth a nation but was undertaken by one, it was not wholly so by the free choice of those who had entered upon it.

Substitutes were not sufficient to fill the quotas of the states, which in fact were never filled. Recourse to the draft and to the endowment of Washington with dictatorial powers for two periods was found necessary to obtain men and materials. But owing to its unwillingness to tax the colonists heavily with military duties and to its inclination to spread the actual burden of service among as many men as possible, the Congress could not make up its mind to let Washington build up an army of permanent soldiers, inured to war and discipline. The Congress would not accept a division of labor among the people as Washington advised, the division of labor which the military system of the mercantilist age involved, observing that "the frequent calls upon the militia have interrupted the cultivation of the land, and of course have lessened the quantity of its produce, occasioned a scarcity, and enhanced the prices." Washington wanted "a good army rather than a large one."[4] But the Congress preferred to let great masses, almost four hundred thousand men from beginning to end, pass for short and different periods through the army service. So far as it was the intention of the Congress to ease the burdens of war by making many men share them, the result was contrary to expectations. The soldiers remained raw, uninformed, unseasoned. More lives were lost than would have been the case with permanent troops, and no doubt the iron discipline introduced by Washington increased the deep antipathy of Americans to all permanent army service.

Another more obvious fear of European militarism was reflected in the dread of a standing army which might usurp power. This dread was from the beginning to the end uppermost in the minds of the delegates in the Congress, who only realized very late that such an idea was utterly foreign to Washington; before that realization his actions were often hampered by the distrust and interference of the Congress.

The so-called "natural" qualities, on which the enemies of the standing army sought to rely for their military organization, were partly preparing the American for war and partly disqualifying him. "The Americans possess as much natural bravery as any people on earth," wrote General Greene in 1776; "but," he added, "habit must form the soldier." [5] Life on the frontier produced expert riflemen, to an even greater number proportionally than on the *lisières* of Europe where the hunting monopoly of the princes and the nobles kept rifle shooting and the military use of the rifleman in narrow bounds.[6] Such considerations moved European governments to turn down proposals to found more "military colonies" along their eastern borders where, as Lloyd and others thought, they might be kept "in constant contact with war" and thus be prevented from ever forgetting it.

Where the American countrymen could be employed with their accustomed rifle and spade, they proved useful, inflicting from behind trees and stone walls heavy losses; on one occasion their own and the British losses were as one to fifty in casualties.[7] Another feature of natural warfare was the scant respect the Americans paid to the European tradition of winter quarters. In the southern theater of war the climate allowed warfare through the winter. In the north the Hessians found their beloved Christmas celebrations rudely interrupted by the continuous activity of Washington.

The Americans also made a specialty of picking off the British officers, so easily recognizable, as at Bunker Hill and Bemis Heights and Cowpens, and thus took the braces out of the British structure of discipline. This individual aiming was foreign to the "shooting machine" of the European infantry. Though "ungentlemanlike," it taught the British a lesson, for on occasions they too used loyalist marksmen, united in partisan formations, to pick off the American officers in their turn.[8] They also formed a light infantry or cavalry clad in green as "without comparison the best color of light troops . . . if put on in the spring, by autumn it nearly fades with the leaves, preserving its characteristics of being scarcely discoverable at a distance." [9]

Yet it was one thing for the British to learn something under the immediate stress of American fighting, and another for them or for any other European country to draw from the American experiences the final lesson, that is, the value of irregular, or *tirailleur*, warfare. Such warfare had probably won the Americans their chief victories in the field. They had applied this order, or seeming disorder, *à l'impromptu*, under the spur of the moment and of the battlefield. Eventually Steuben put this disorder under rules for light infantry for which, contrary to Frederick's opinion, he thought the best men good enough.

The spur was new. The lesson was vitalized by it rather than by the conscious remembrance of such experiences as the wilderness battle—Braddock's defeat of 1755.[10] The obvious success of the light troops on both sides and the lesson of the superiority of the shooting arm convinced most of the officers who had fought in North America that its adaptation by European forces was inevitable. To acknowledge this revolution in tactics, in addition to recognizing the revolutionary Republic, was, however, more than the British military could undertake. In spite of their own losses and the conviction of the officers who had fought in North America that a change in tactics was necessary, the British were more impressed by the wonderfully exact peacetime maneuvers of Frederick the Great near Berlin. Under this impression the first general drillbook for the British army was written and published in 1788. Only a few American experiences were accepted in England: among them the later change from the triple to the double rank. Others were neglected; for example, the advantage of mounted infantry as against cavalry proper and the use of mimicry in warfare.[11]

To maintain the old discipline, the old uniform and in particular its impractical color were retained. When it was proposed on the Continent in the 1790's to dull the luster of firearms, as had been found advisable in the American war, a military author protested: the soldier would then have too little to polish, and "lose his *point d'honneur* of cleanliness." This "expert's" opinion prevailed and not that of Scharnhorst, who wanted the soldier to lose this particular *point d'honneur* because it destroyed him. Rather should he be taught to know his musket well and keep it fit for action; other useful activities should be made his *point d'honneur* instead of the care he had to apply to his altogether unsuitable uniform and pieces of equipment.[12] Such protests were of as little avail as Bülow's paradoxical advice to the Prussians, whose uniform was so impractical that a soldier did not even know where to place a tobacco pipe: "The Miami Indians are clad much more to the purpose. A woolen blanket round the shoulders. It would be advisable to send the officers of the light infantry to school among the Indians in order to learn the thing." [13]

Another American lesson was spurned by military officers in Europe: the American demonstration of "shooting to kill." Owing to intermarriages among the nobility of Europe and the sense of class solidarity, European army officers had been rather tender of one another even when arrayed on opposing sides; by sticking to certain points of "honor," as they conceived it, they had refused to resort to certain "tricks" even to gain advantages in war. To such feudal conceptions of warfare American revolutionists did not adhere. They were out to win independence. Their officers, as bourgeois in the European sense of the term, were absolute enemies of the feudal officers on the other side; they were not friendly associates of a class, temporarily on opposite sides. The depth of this enmity led Americans to resort to methods which the British regarded as contrary to the rules of "civilized" warfare, although the latter were by no means tender in the use of Indians as their allies.

For example, numerous American officers under breach of parole took up arms again after their release. At Huberton, sixty Americans approached the British lines with rifles clubbed, as if they were to surrender; allowed to come unharmed within close distance, they suddenly stopped, fired a volley and ran away to the forest. At Bennington on August 16, 1777, the British were attacked by five hundred militiamen in front, "while five hundred others in rustic attire, many of whom had sworn allegiance on the previous day," came round upon their rear. Some Americans entered the British army as pretended loyalists and turned to the patriot side when occasion arose; Cornwallis had some such "traitors" hanged, but refrained from further measures because the revolutionaries were in a position to make reprisals. Washington himself, generally scrupulous in such things, on one occasion suggested that members of an American regiment who happened to wear red coats put on buttons of an English regiment, pass through the English lines and kidnap General Clinton.[14]

The Officer in the American Revolution

Officers were more easily to be found for the War of Independence than men. American politicians were as firmly convinced as British politicians that they knew who could best officer their bands. None was considered more fit than the man who knew how to raise the greatest number of men; it was thought that his persuasive power would keep them together as well as it had brought them together. Their intriguing and dickering, with little consideration for previous military experience and worth, produced many poor officers with a few very good ones, including Washington. It is not inconceivable that the politicians selected for his office the richest man in their midst, partly in order to have the credit that went with his name; at all events, he had to pledge it and on at least one occasion convince his men that they would actually receive a promised bounty.[15] Thrice did the richest man of the land command armies in the mercantilist age: Wallenstein, Soubise, and Washington—not to mention Medina-Sidonia, the commander of the Spanish Armada, and the Duke of Marlborough.

The Frenchman in that group left his name more properly in the pages of cookbooks than of war works. Of the others, two, both great landowners, displayed terrific energy, directed to organization and political relations with their employer as well as to command in battle; they exercised an intermediary function between camp and political authority. In both cases the political authority was weak, tempting Wallenstein to extreme ambitions, but never tempting Washington, though he was twice a dictator. In this stand midway between the Congress and the officers whose demands he recognized as just, Washington far surpassed in strength Oliver Cromwell who, a hundred years before, had exercised a similar function as mediator between officers and the English Parliament and had become a militarist subject to his own officers, in the end.

Washington and Wallenstein had the common task of making armies and holding them together. The American general had the special task of making and unmaking officers. In carrying it out he eliminated as far as possible the democratic processes of selection and election and in its stead employed his own authority as general, as the first gentleman in the army and the country. He had to instill into the officers a sense of subordination and of honor which General Nathanael Greene, the blacksmith from Rhode Island, contended was not natural among the American people: "The common people are exceedingly avaricious; the genius of the people is commercial from the long intercourse of trade. The sentiment of honor, the true characteristic of a soldier, has not yet got the better of interest." [16]

Their commercial habits also brought a great predilection for the service of supply. Steuben found more quartermasters and commissaries at Valley Forge, he said, than in all the armies of Europe together.[17] Yet the supply system never became efficient. Washington had to stop the ancient corrupt European practice of the *passevolants,* officers drawing pay for men not enrolled or sent away from camp to work on the officers' farms. As the colonies did not provide a class or stratum to whom officer duty seemed natural and reward of no immediate concern—a class with its well-established concepts of military honor and behavior—such standards had to be introduced or emphasized.

To provide a material basis Washington urged the Congress again and again to vote "good pay" for the officer. He realized that an expert, not bound by the obligation of an estate to which he was born, had to be paid well if he was to remain in the service—the service which the best of officers often threatened to quit unless better provided for.[18]

This will induce gentlemen and men of character to engage [argued Washington], and till the bulk of your officers is composed of such persons as are actuated by principles of honor and a spirit of enterprise, you have little to expect from them. They ought to have such allowances as will enable them to live like and support the character of gentlemen, and not be driven by the scanty pittance to the low and dirty arts which many of them practise to filch from the public more than the difference of pay would amount to upon an ample allowance. . . . There is nothing that gives a man consequence and renders him fit for command like a support that renders him independent of everybody but the State he serves. . . . If such pay be allowed the officer as will induce gentlemen of character and liberal sentiments to engage, and proper care and precaution are used in the nomination, more regard being had to the character of persons than to the number of men they can enlist, we should in a little time have an army able to cope with any that can be opposed to it, as there are excellent materials to form one out of.[19]

Higher pay, on which Washington insisted, and with him the southern colonists, was intended in part to overcome the egalitarian notions of the New Englanders and to make for real distinctions between officers and men. These in the beginning hardly existed. For instance, a Lieutenant Whitney was tried and convicted for "infamous conduct in degrading himself by doing the duty of an orderly sergeant." [20] In other respects, officers brought along or quickly acquired the notion of the English gentleman-officer that to drill recruits was sergeant's duty and beneath the station of an officer.

Steuben, who as a Prussian officer since his fourteenth year had passed through all the ranks from private upward, mainly for the purpose of learning, and learning to teach, the manual of exercise, had to take the musket himself and demonstrate at Valley Forge the manual of exercise which he wanted to introduce. He made the officers undergo the gymnastics of the Prussian cadet so that they could instruct their men. With this teaching went the minimum of discipline that served the purposes of the American army, instead of the Frederician maximum, which underwent a considerable humanization on the way across the Atlantic. Steuben remembered too well the abuses which the men in Europe suffered at the hands of their officers. In the first standard set of regulations for the American army, he made it "the first object" of the captain "to gain the love of his men by treating them with every possible kindness and humanity," recommending "means of preserving the lives of many valuable men" by increasing care. He did not forget the economy in the Prussian army which strictly forbade the use of enlisted men as officers' servants, a habit rapidly developed in the American army; he had the servants returned to their original duty.[21]

The considerate treatment of the common soldier finally led to the beginnings of mass honor—a revolutionary idea. To the American soldier was given a share of the general honors and distinctions gained in war by the introduction of so-called "service stripes"—insignia connoting three years' service with "bravery, fidelity and good conduct." [22] Since the Congress did not specially honor the officers, they united, just before the army was dissolved, to honor themselves and the memory of the war, through the medium of the Order of the Cincinnati.

This was the first American honor society with a military character. It was at the same time the first organization of ex-servicemen, combining the ancient honor element—personal, as well as national—with the element of mutual aid. It also united the eighteenth-century predilection for secret societies with the still older inclination to bequeath honors to descendants, for the Order of the Cincinnati was to survive by passing membership on to the eldest male representative of the family of a deceased member. And the brotherhood-in-arms with the French was acknowledged by the admission of French officers who had fought on American soil. That made the Order international in the eyes of American patriots who cried out against this European "importation" and even more against the hereditary principle in the Order, which seemed to contain the germs of a hereditary aristocracy in the United States.

Taking account of the outcry, Washington persuaded the Cincinnati to abandon that feature at their first annual meeting in 1784.[23] Afraid of an aristocracy which would abet a standing army and of a standing army which would abet an aristocracy, to which so "many persons of elevated views and ideal habits in these states" would like to change, as Rufus King noted in 1785,[24] the authors of the Constitution of 1787 expressly provided against a nobility in the United States.

The "self-made" man of America wanted no "ancestor-made man," for the latter is the true antithesis to the former. Like Jefferson, he repudiated the "standing army in time of peace [or] a navy, which by its own expense and the eternal wars in which it [*sic*] will implicate us, will grind us with public burthens, and sink us under them." [25] The time was not yet come in the United States when birth, appearing as *race*, would be claimed as the carrier of privilege by a *plantocracy*.

The curious thing about the chief military lessons to be drawn from the War of Independence is that they were little heeded in the United States and likewise at the moment in the European armies. The conservatism of the latter naturally led them to stick blindly to their traditional tactics. When Frederick the Great in 1785 admitted the young Gneisenau, just returned from America, to some of his worst infantry, the so-called free battalions, he did it with the remark that "the people returning from America think a great deal of themselves and of their knowledge of war, and they still must learn war all over again in Europe." [26] The conservatism of the Americans was equally great, however; it convinced them quickly, as the *Federalist* intimates, that the militia had really won the war, that the services of Steuben had not been necessary,[27] that a standing army would not be needed, that it might be as dangerous to the new liberties as Rome's military triumphs had been to her liberties.

The Establishment of the American Military System

Yet after victory had been won in 1783, out of the experience of the revolutionary war and their thought respecting the place of the military in their society, Americans effected a settlement which presented certain striking features. Between the close of the war and the settlement, however, came a severe struggle aligning a party or faction that included the principal officers of the war against the party or faction composed of leaders among the embattled farmers or militiamen. Indeed this conflict had started before the war had come to an end. Among the officers in the army were a few men who frankly distrusted a republican form of government and desired either a monarchy or some kind of authoritarian system. One of these officers wrote a letter to Washington in which he expressed contempt for a republic and suggested the establishment of a military state, at least in part of the huge territory open to settlement.

Although Washington replied in a stinging rebuke, there is no doubt that some of the army officers toyed with the idea of overthrowing the government under the Articles of Confederation by a military stroke.[28] As Mrs. Mercy Warren, the wife of a revolutionary leader, observed in 1787:

Many of the younger Class, particularly the students at Law and the youth of fortune and pleasure, are crying out for a monarchy and a standing army to support it. . . . These joined by the whole class of Cincinnati who are panting for a nobility, and with the eagle dangling at their breast, assume distinctions that are yet new in this Country—these parties make a formidable body ready to bow to the sceptre of a king, provided they may be the lordlings who in splendid idleness may riot on the hard earnings of the peasant and the mechanic:—These plead the necessity of a standing army to suppress the murmurs of a few who yet cherish that spirit of freedom which only calls forth the exertions and leads to the best improvement of the human mind.[29]

Mrs. Warren's fears were not entirely groundless. Noah Webster observed that in 1785 "certain military characters" agreed "in case of civil convulsion to rally the officers and soldiers of the late army, and with the help of supplies to be furnished by some rich merchants, to give a government to this country by force." Webster added that agents having some such plans had gone from Connecticut to the "military gentlemen" in Massachusetts.[30]

The alarms of military officers were increased by an uprising of farmers in Massachusetts, led by a former officer in the revolutionary army, Daniel Shays (1786-7). In the course of this disturbance, protests arose against heavy taxes and debts, against the rich, against creditors, lawyers, and courts. At the same time radical demands were put forth in the name of the farmers. It was openly said that militiamen had offered their lives to their country, had saved the property of the rich, and were entitled to special consideration in the apportionment of economic benefits springing from victory.

Standing between these two factions was Washington. He was frightened by the Shays rebellion and looked upon this commoners' upheaval with horror. Nevertheless, he was equally firm in rejecting all thought of erecting a military dictatorship. Other conservative men shared his views and preferred, with him, to establish a new constitution by the peaceful process of a convention and ratification than by the violent method of arms. The upshot of the domestic struggles that followed the Revolution was the Constitution of the United States, which furnished the outlines of a settled military policy for the country—the outlines that presented striking contrasts to European absolutism.

The central feature of the Constitution in respect to the army and navy was the establishment of civilian control in government over the military branches. By its provisions, Congress alone can raise and support armies, provide for their government, control the militia, vote money for military purposes (for no longer than two years at a time), and declare war. The President of the United States, a civilian, is made commander-in-chief of the army and navy—the supreme war lord. In the original Constitution, drafted by conservatives, it was provided that the privileges of the civil writ of habeas corpus shall not be suspended unless in cases of rebellion or invasion the public safety may require it. To this Constitution were soon added two amendments in the spirit of Jeffersonian agrarianism: a well-regulated militia being necessary to the security of a free state, the right of the people to keep and bear arms shall not be infringed; and the quartering of soldiers on householders, without their consent, is forbidden in time of peace, and allowed in time of war only under the limitations of law—that is, law made by civilians, an embodiment and revision of the English heritage, establishing supremacy of the civilian over the military. Congress provided better for a standing institution of military learning than for a standing army.

In the military system later developed within the framework of the Constitution, many details also stood out in sharp contrast to the Continental system and even the British system: (1) although Congress was given unlimited power to raise armies, the principal reliance for man power was long placed upon the militia of the states, with its democratic relations between officers and men; (2) the standing army, though added to the militia, was kept small, even minute at times, until the end of the nineteenth century; (3) training for officers was finally provided by the establishment of the military academy at West Point, but this provision was countered in a manner to prevent the rise of a hereditary officer caste— by the distribution of cadetships among all the states and congressional districts through the agency of political senators and representatives; (4) the concentration of army discipline was upon immediate usefulness in civil disturbances and wars rather than upon displays and ceremonials, as often in Europe; the army was restricted by what was considered usefulness, which included the guarding of the frontier and public works; and (5) reliance was placed upon volunteers for the standing army in time of peace and hence upon foot-loose youths usually from the lower strata of society.

In other words, the American system at the outset was a military system, not a militaristic system. It conceived of the army as an agency of civil power, to be organized and disciplined with that purpose in view, and not as an end in itself. Although military heroes were fascinating to Americans and were frequently elevated to the presidency of the United States, militarism with its glamour and hard service scarcely got a hold on American imagination until after the opening of the twentieth century. Certainly at the end of the eighteenth century, the American system challenged the attention of European thinkers, especially of the Enlightenment, who were preparing the way for the downfall of the French monarchy and the substitution of the mass army for the standing army, so long the cherished institution of absolutism.

When George Washington was inaugurated under a constitution establishing civil supremacy over the military, the storm was already at the gates of absolutism in France. There the standing army had been undermined from within by dissensions among the noblemen, who largely formed its officers, and by quarrels between this estate and the Crown. Authority within the army, from the King down, was weak when it met the Revolution. The victory of the French revolutionists was easy, therefore, since they did not collide with a unified army interest in the beginning. Within six years they had overturned the monarchy, beheaded the King, deprived the nobles of economic and other privileges, stripped the Church of property and attempted the establishment of a constitution asserting civilian supremacy.

During the first period of the Revolution, the superiority of civilian government could be maintained, for the old standing army was thoroughly discredited. The Republic had, however, to form a defense force of its own when it became embroiled in war with the absolutisms of the mid-Continent, to which was soon added the weight of British sea and land power. Mass armies were created as protectors of the Republic and spreaders of revolution throughout Europe. Then, in 1795, the bourgeois government of the Directorate found itself threatened by counterrevolutionary elements on one side and by the hyperrevolutionary working class of France, denied the suffrage, on the other. The agent chosen to blow away opposition with cannon shot was a young artillery officer, the son of a Corsican lawyer, Napoleon Bonaparte; at this hour the bourgeoisie saw a savior in that ex-

4

Mass Armies: The French Revolution and Napoleon

ponent of the army, and opened to him the career which led, with
the aid of the new mass armies, to the Consulate and the Empire,
to the triumph and ruin of France.

The Old Military System Breaks Down

The old standing armies were seldom used for purposes of suppression at home—not that they were averse to it, but occasions had
been few since the French *dragonnades,* when Huguenots were
literally eaten out of house and home by soldiers quartered upon
them. The eighteenth century was at bottom orderly. Only in England, where the beginnings of industrialism led to disturbances,
did need arise for using troops in "keeping order." There they
were put to use in riots, as among the Gloucestershire weavers in
1756 or silk weavers in 1765, in a sailors' strike in 1768 and in
other emergencies.[1] As a rule these soldiers served the government
well, not feeling any solidarity with the rioters; an unusual officer,
Wolfe, sent to support the civil power in 1756, sensed the injustice
of their case better than his men, whom he restrained from drastic
actions against the "poor, half-starved weavers of broadcloth." [2]
In the 1790's, a great many small barracks were built in England;
in them soldiers were quartered for police purposes,[3] as constables
of the counterrevolution, in which England was an ally of Continental powers at home no less than in the field.

This function the army had rarely exercised in France, and when
Louis XVI and his entourage relied upon it to guard absolutism
against social upheaval, they were soon disillusioned. That drilled
force quickly began to dissolve. It proved to be not a machine but
an aggregation of men. As early as July 1789, the guards, to whom
the King might look for safety, showed that they had been permeated by bourgeois propaganda and money, through long resi-
dence in Paris and constant intercourse with the people.[4] They
helped to storm the Bastille and fought on the side of the populace
against the foreign regiments in French service. Thus even the elite
guards were no more immune to currents of thought running
through society than were other regiments. Many of the soldiers,
of course, did their "duty," but not enough to save the Crown. The
cynical Duc de Châtelet, owner of the Guardes Françaises, had
said that it was necessary to confine soldiers closely, that is, protect
them against thought, "in order to have in pressing cases the children of the *canaille* to use on the *canaille.*" But his hopes were
disappointed; the two kinds of *canaille* fraternized.[5]

Nor was Louis XVI able to count upon the effective support of
the nobles who monopolized offices in the army—to count upon
them as members of their class or as officers. Almost at the outset

of his troubles, the Chamber of Nobles in the States General was divided into the minority of the *grands seigneurs* who wanted to retain the *status quo,* satisfactory to them, and preserve the absolute monarchy, and, on the other hand, the majority of the country noblemen, who demanded reforms to favor their specific interests, such as the opening of all officer positions to all noblemen equally and to no other class. Of the 285 elected members of the noble estate, no less than 154 were officers and about one-third of them sympathized with popular ideas. In other words, the strength of their class was broken by their own inner dissensions almost as much as by the onslaughts of the bourgeoisie. So they lost their hold on the soldiers as well as on the nonnoble *officiers de fortune,* who resented their restriction to the very lowest ranks, and on the noncommissioned officers who were likewise prevented from rising to the rank of officers. In this way, the army was torn asunder on the eve of the Revolution.

All privileges of the nobility were abolished by the Revolution, and after the system of purchasing commissions was ended, all military ranks and positions were opened to the bourgeoisie. The nobility was "reduced to the level of the nation." [6] Die-hard nobles went abroad and prepared war against revolutionary France, many of them remaining in the pay of the King; others stayed behind to work against the Revolution from within the regiments, much as the German officers in the Reichswehr did after 1919; the Girondin nobles eagerly approved of foreign war, hoping thereby to regain their control over the soldiers and recover their ancient position in the nation.

In that age, when soldiers and officers served regularly abroad, no old concept of nationalism stood in the way of this activity in the interest of a class. "*La patrie,* that was for the majority of *émigrés* not the soil on which they had been born; it was the ensemble of the ancient institutions and traditions, under the protection of which they and their fathers had been brought up." [7] The nationalism which proscribed *émigrés* and their activities was new and inspired by the new governing interests, born of civil, not of foreign, war. Clinging to the customs of foreign war, the regular French troops usually treated the nobles as honorable and loyal enemies, whereas the volunteers massacred them as traitors.

When the old officers who stayed behind rallied around the King and under the old symbol of the white cockade, it was too late. It only added to the fury of the masses to learn that officers had trampled on the new national symbol, the tricolor, to the strains of "*O Richard, ô mon roi, l'univers t'a abandonné.*" The nation now insisted on respect for the new symbol with an earnestness which had heretofore been reserved for religious emblems. The new symbol was worn as a cockade by the soldiers like the old white one, which incidentally was not so ancient after all since it dated only from 1767.[8] The tricolor gratified emotions previously enjoyed only by the nobility. In short, the whole nation became the nobility, considering its foes outside the pale. The introduction of this nationalist symbolism opened a new era of mass manipulation through symbols, and particularly of armies; many armies took it up later, consciously imitating the French,[9] when defeats proved to them that they, too, needed such devices to conjure up popular emotions which no mere word of command could stir. As a means of persuasion the symbol belongs midway between the command and the oration.

The New Military Way Is Opened

In the course of the early constitutional reforms and especially after war began with the absolutist powers, the revolutionists reconstructed the military system of France. In accordance with the physiocratic and other philosophical ideas of free competition, the nobles' monopoly of army offices was abolished and careers were thrown open to talent from whatever source. Hopes were entertained that in the military field, where the social privileges had been the greatest hindrance to talent, genius might arise as in the sciences and the arts, where it was of low extraction, as Diderot had pointed out.[10] Thus energies were tapped which had been latent for the one hundred and fifty years of the aristocratic regime in the armies—ever since the time, described in Grimmelshausen's *Simplicissimus,* the German epic of the Thirty Years' War, in which the nobleman is shown discussing with the *"Feldweibel,"* advocate of the common man, the respective roles of their classes. The latter declares that no fool would serve and expose himself to obvious danger of death if he was not allowed to hope that his good behavior would promote him; his old colonel had often said that he did not want a soldier in his regiment who was not firmly persuaded that by his bravery he would become a general. This very old ambition, smothered for over a century, was appealed to by the French regulations, the law of February 1790 providing that everyone had to start at the bottom and rise necessarily through each grade.[11] Despite the demonstration of its failure in America, the elective principle was introduced in the promotion of French officers and noncoms.

In order to defend the position it had won, the Third Estate organized everywhere National Guards from its own midst. Lafayette, first in command of the Paris National Guard and then in the field, was considered the person who could most safely be entrusted by the "real shareholders in the great national concern" with the power to defend their gains against not only the aristocrats but also the proletariat—the "machines for work," as Sieyès called them, who were not regarded as fit machines for voting or serving in the National Guard.[12] Lafayette may have remembered conflicts between Continentals and militia in America, when he took care not to estrange the middle-class Guard from the regular regiments, but rather to associate them. When, however, he tried to restore order among the regulars by energetic measures, he aroused the distrust of the Jacobins. Hoping to get rid of the undesirables of the Revolution by some other way than pursuing war energetically, though the chances for France were then good and the slow-moving enemy was not yet in the field, Lafayette held treasonable intercourse with the foreign powers with a view to aiding their march upon Paris, scattering the Jacobins, revising the Constitution, and concluding peace. In turn the Jacobins, by their propaganda which Lafayette, like a liberal such as Kerensky, suffered to continue, undermined the confidence of soldiers under him; and rather than present himself to the Assembly, Lafayette forsook his own men for the enemy, who trusted him just as little.

It was relatively simple, of course, to throw open offices in the army and to organize guards. More perplexing was the problem of raising men for the rank and file. In the beginning the bourgeois were uncertain how to solve this problem. They knew something about popular hatred for conscription from the protests which the people had made against the operation of old laws. They did not want a mass army. As long as they could, they tried to rely on volunteers and the remaining portion of the old Line. But as the crisis deepened and the peril of foreign invasion loomed on the horizon, a law was passed in February 1793, ordering a levy of three hundred thousand men to be furnished in contingents by the communities. After exempting politicians or elected officials, married men, and some others, the Convention left the picking of the remainder to local politics, as was also the case under the American draft acts of 1917 and 1940. Where the aristocrats were still sufficiently strong, in some places, they chose Republicans for the honor of serving; where the latter were in the majority, they made the aristocrats or refractory priests go. More often poor men were chosen—in effect impressed—and the rich, for the privilege of staying at home, were obliged to pay a bonus to the *"héros à 500 livres."* This act of February was supplemented in August by the law for the *levée en masse.*[13]

Despite the violent opposition to the levy by requisition and despite the necessity of compromising with rebellious regions, the revolutionists continued to raise men by that process, while welcoming volunteers. The following year the difference between the regulars and volunteers was abolished and the two branches were amalgamated. As the wars proceeded, two cries, coupled with the compulsions of the law, rallied an increasing number of men from the masses to the colors: "The Revolution is in danger!" and "The country is in danger!" In time the two were fused into one mighty passion. They became incarnate in the *"Marseillaise,"* sung by marching men who carried French arms and revolutionary ideas to all parts of Europe and threatened even the supremacy of Great Britain in the balance of power throughout the world.

The strength of the revolutionary army was increased by the support of the artillery, early won over. It proved to be the best arm of the service at Valmy, where the invaders were turned back, and again at Jemappes. The artillery had always been the least feudalized branch, although sufficiently full of the guild spirit to resist the introduction of the revolutionary decimal system.[14] Thanks to the reforms it had undergone since the close of the Seven Years' War, it had become more mobile and more standardized in equipment, the calibers being reduced to twelve-, eight-, and four-pounders. It had accepted the Revolution readily, most of its officers being sympathetic, and the Revolution found it advisable and practical to leave its personnel untouched. Dumouriez, who had called the artillery "the strength of the French army," could not persuade any part of this branch to follow him in his desertion to the Austrians. All this the victorious Revolution appreciated by changing the precedence in the army in 1797, giving the artillery, once ranked behind the 64th regiment of infantry, the lead over all other branches, being followed by the engineers, and then the infantry and cavalry.[15] Honor corresponds to usefulness, according to bourgeois notions.

Being directors of machines—the creations of technology, requiring exact knowledge rather than feudal honor in operation—artillery officers had stood somewhat apart from the other branches of the old standing army. They were by training and instinct more akin to manufacturers, artisans, and business men generally than to ordinary proud nobles who loved parades, decorations, and honorifics. It is not to be forgotten that Bonaparte belonged to this branch and won his first spurs in the service of the Revolution by his display of genius for artillery at Toulon in the early days of upheaval. Had the King taken the lead in self-defense, Bonaparte would have served him; but the King was weak and futile, so Bonaparte served the bourgeois state that was rising on the ruins of absolutism—that is, he served it until he was able to take charge of it himself and bend it to his militaristic ambitions. Though an artillerist, however, he was conservative and his rise actually blocked

war-technological progress; for instance, he suppressed the balloon-
ists in the army and turned down Fulton's invention.

With masses of men drawn into the army and the war of arms
associated with a war of revolutionary ideas against the ideas of
feudalism and absolutism, propaganda was employed on an impressive scale. This was not new, to be sure. To go no further back in
history, propaganda figured in the Puritan Revolution in England,
when religious and democratic ideas were brought into the service
of Cromwell's army. It appeared also in the American Revolution
on both sides. But the wars of the French Revolution and the wars
of Napoleon were made wars of ideas, wars of a world revolution,
and as soldiers like young Murat saw it,[16] the use of ideas in raising
and inspiring armies was recognized as an indispensable part of
domestic struggles and foreign wars. The Girondists tried to induce
great numbers of enemy troops to desert by promising them an
annual pension of one hundred francs with reversion to their wives
and a gratuity of fifty livres; broadsides with this promise were
spread along the boundaries and among the foreign troops.[17]

The Allies disliked this propaganda, this "new French method of
attack, not with sword or cannon, but with far more dangerous
weapons, by which they tried to inspire the common soldier with
Republican sentiments," as a Prussian participant of the War of
1792 complained,[18] apparently oblivious to the fact that Frederick
the Great himself had used propaganda among foreigners. "If you
can animate a people on account of liberty of conscience, and also
convince it that it is oppressed by the priesthood and the devout,"
he had said, "you can surely reckon on this people. This really means
to move heaven and hell in your interest. In an occupied country
like Saxony, one plays the role of a protector of the Lutheran
religion; in the Catholic country, one speaks of nothing but toler-
ance." Thus Frederick, himself an unbeliever, had attempted to
manipulate Christian beliefs. The new belief of the French was,
however, secular. If its devotees did not convince foreign soldiers
in great numbers, they persuaded themselves—a circumstance of
no less importance.

Groups of French soldiers sometimes appeared unarmed at the
outposts of the enemy and announced that they were friends; many
were German-speaking Alsatians who told the Prussians that they
ought to sever the unnatural connection with their old enemies, the
Austrians. They left behind large packages of leaflets in which the
harmony of French and Prussian interests was pointed out, and
liberty and equality hymned in language which the soldier could
understand.

The Allies had to forbid such visits and insinuations. They failed
to comprehend this new mode of warfare, or use it when there were

occasions to turn to account defeatist sentiments in the French armies. Indeed, from the very beginning, they simply could not understand how to conduct this war of opinion. Brunswick had intended to send out a proclamation addressed to the National Guard, telling it that no war was intended against the French nation; that there would be no interference with their liberties and constitution, but that the coalition merely wanted to obtain justice for the German princes whose Alsatian property had been taken away.[19] His actual Manifesto of 1792, however, written by an *émigré*, helped only the Jacobins and damaged the cause of monarchy. When the British occupied Toulon, they did the same thing by declaring in a manifesto prepared by the Cabinet that they held the place in trust for Louis XVII and would continue the occupation until monarchy could be restored, all conquered territories returned, just reparations paid, and due assurances as to future good behavior rendered.[20]

Given mass armies inspired to frenzy by the passions and ideas of the Revolution, warfare took on novel aspects. Within and around the regular troops of the old style were large numbers of men, more individualized and more ruthless in combat than any soldiers of a standing army, drilled and commanded by noble officers accustomed to the conceptions and customs of feudal honor. Recruiting under the February law brought 180,000; the *levée en masse* some 450,000 men. By January 1, 1794, some 770,000 men belonged to the diverse armies and 500,000 of them stood along the exterior front.

Sheer numerical superiority gained them successes at Hondschooten and Wattignies in September and October 1793, where 50,000 and 45,000 Frenchmen, respectively, battled 15,000 and 18,000 Allies. Little-exercised masses faced, or rather encountered, overexercised mercenaries who slowly retired, cursing the "furious fools" that lost three times as many men as they themselves and yet continued to advance.[21] Still the Allies were convinced, as an instruction by the Austrian Mack laid down the principle, that the two- or threefold numerical superiority of the French was completely balanced by the miserable quality of their generals, officers, and soldiers; that the French could yet be beaten by the long front of the Allies; and that the Allied troops must not in terror allow the battle to "deteriorate" into skirmishing.[22]

The masses, which soon faced the very Hessian regiments who had encountered their like in America before, immediately began to grope for some adequate form of combat which would prove effective and still give a survival chance to the soldier, indoctrinated now and for a long time to come with the idea that he as an individual was entitled to live. Like the Americans previously, these far greater masses were untrained and therefore unable to apply the traditional forms of warfare by advancing in stiff lines and firing volleys. Time and other circumstances did not allow instruction in such maneuvers. Instead they were led to attack in deep columns, a formation which called for less drill-instilled order, and were preceded and flanked by swarms of *tirailleurs,* who took over the function of the shooting machine of the infantry and supplanted the firing effect of the linear tactics. Whereas the light infantry before had largely been used for scouting or patrolling, and not in close connection with the infantry of the line, they were now an essential part of the battle infantry. Indeed they usually proved to be the best part when the mob, inclined to get panicky, was thrown together in the columns.

Skirmishing was left unregulated by the drill rules, since it was thought that regulation might harm the spirit of initiative. Therein the revolutionary soldiers "found" the column formation and adapted it to their use in connection with the *tirailleur* tactics, dropping what they had not time to teach to the constantly growing and renewed soldiery. The single tactical elements were old; their combination, however, was new. Yet none of the soldiers' contemporaries regarded it as new or considered it equally revolutionary with the constitutional and social changes occurring at the same time.[23]

By terming Bonaparte a genius, the history of the tactical development of the French revolutionary armies became so firmly telescoped that, for nearly a century, the nature of this change was overlooked, and the fact was ignored that the genius had the media of his successes ready made for him. The contemporary foes of the French Revolution and the Consulate were so tightly bound up in the general antirevolutionary constitution of their own countries that they could not understand, much less take over, the military achievements worked out by the Revolution. Even obvious and proved military achievements of the French, like the discarding of the larger part of the impedimenta of the train, were spurned by the Prussians, though they were fully advised that much of the French success was due to such changes.[24] Only an enthusiasm equal to that of the French could have brought others to such a sacrifice of comfort. There was thus no bridge of understanding between the two camps, no expertness on the Allied side for adapting the French institutions. Social conservativism blinded the experts to a degree never again comparable.

In the French armies, the Allies saw only disorder; irregularities in the size of formations, equipment, and dress; poor horses; and unheard-of liberties during the marches. If the French achieved any successes, presumably it was in spite of the lack of discipline and the *égalité,* which in military terms means an equal chance for everybody to live and rise. In fact the French were exceedingly helped by the errors of the coalition. Strategy, as Hans Delbrück used to say, consists in making at least one error less than the enemy.

The "Instruction for the Whole Royal Prussian Infantry" of 1798, largely a work of the new King Frederick William III himself and therefore reactionary, insisted on a very different kind of *égalité,* equality in death: "*Égalité* is the first beauty of the soldiery, and in a body which is to act and maneuver together, regularity and accord are necessary." The perfection of this uniformity and the reassertion of the claim to absolute surrender by the soldier to the higher will is the Prussian parade step, described in the Instruction, if not introduced there in its final form: "In the training of the soldier he shall neither stamp the ground with the heel nor stir it up with the tip of the shoe, but the foot must be so put down with the knee stiff that on firm ground the foot leaves a mark on the earth." [25] The reason why the Prussian goose step became so profoundly antipathetic or ridiculous to Western democracies lies in its origin and purpose: its expression of counterrevolution.

The ruthless use of French masses in the face of death was, after all, an outcome of the same Jacobin egalitarianism which, as Robespierre expressed it, would rather see ten thousand men perish than a principle. The French were carrying the mercilessness of the civil war into foreign lands. None of that supranational memory of feudal courtesy survived. The Allied armies now found a ghost as their enemy and it could not be vanquished by their platoon fire. Before Dunkirk in 1793 and at Jena in 1806, the British, Hessians, Hanoverians, and Prussians, in their array of three ranks deep, received a deadly fire from Frenchmen hiding behind hedges, bushes, fences, or in ditches—men who could not be reached by the platoon fire of the serried foe. When the Allies charged with the bayonet, these skirmishers ran away before the attack and took refuge behind new cover. This was as exhausting as shadow boxing to the Prussians, whose rules forbade them to take even the little cover they could have found by lying down, and also to the Austrians, who abstained from the use of field fortification lest it damage the agricultural land of Belgium. This old-fashioned form of warfare could not disappear until the system of government for which it stood had been reformed or annihilated.

To make war loss more permanent, the ransoming of prisoners of war was prohibited by French decrees of September 1792, and May 1793; it might restore fighters to the enemy, more in need of them than the French. A Frenchman had warned the Prussian King: "You can only repair your losses by training at great expense new recruits at home; one thousand soldiers will cost you as much as one hundred thousand of the French." [26] The enemy abroad as well as at home was to be destroyed, if the Jacobins were to have their way. In fact, it was they, rather than the generals, who started the large-scale consumption of men in war; the officers merely accepted the masses provided for them—and were accused by the Jacobins of not being as efficient as the guillotine. Among the civilians the strategic foreign-war aim was essentially the same as in civil war. That aim was to destroy the enemy, at least up to the moment where "the death of an enemy soldier becomes useless to liberty." [27] Up to that moment, at least, each enemy soldier was to be considered as a foe having nothing in common with the revolutionist, largely because he was of a different class.

Carnot made it a general rule, in February 1794, "to act in mass formation and take the offensive. Join action with the bayonet on every occasion. Give battle on a large scale and pursue the enemy till he is utterly destroyed." [28] The enemy especially threatened with destruction was the body of *émigrés*—some twenty thousand of them—fighting on the side of the coalition. When caught they were to be killed; upward of three hundred suffered death as prisoners. Shortly before his own overthrow, Robespierre even proceeded to do away with war rules which the armies had up to then observed by decreeing that no quarter be shown to British and Hanoverian soldiers.[29] But the French troops in the field and Carnot himself took good care to disobey this order, for it did not suit armies as self-preserving bodies or, if one preferred, the supranational concept of honorable warfare. It cost poor General Honchard his life when a search among his papers revealed that he had corresponded in polite terms with enemy generals about the exchange of prisoners; his conduct was regarded as treasonable intercourse with the enemy.[30] When the Convention later decreed that no more Spanish were to be made prisoners, it was pointed out on the part of the army "that those who were themselves exposed to reprisals had to reckon with the future." Nevertheless, and even though the Spanish did not apply reprisals in 1795, some eight to nine thousand of them were massacred.[31]

To teach the destruction of others was proclaimed the aim of Jacobin military education. Robespierre wanted the pupils of the new school, the Ecole de Mars, who were to complete the work of the Revolution, to be engineers of destruction. Instead of drawing the students from the upper classes of the French nation, they were henceforth to take them from *sans-culottes* families. The former students in military schools, he said, learned a little mathematics, drew plans and profiles of fortresses, knew the Prussian drill rules, but did not kill a Prussian. The new disciples of Mars were to be trained in the French way, that is, to learn how to use the bayonet and the *pas de charge,* and finish this education in a practical way, in three months and a half, in a camp of tents instead of in the palace where the old Ecole Militaire was housed.

This Martian training camp was to be under the immediate control of the Committee of Public Safety, who were to select the teachers and the inmates, half to be drawn from the country and half from cities and towns. Those selected and assembled in July 1794 on the plains of Sablons were generally sons of the Jacobins, clad in a half-Greek, half-Roman costume designed by David. After the Thermidor, this "young Robespierrian breed" was dissolved without leaving much behind to indicate its value or the reverse. Instead, the Ecole Centrale des Travaux Publiques was founded, which changed its name to Ecole Polytechnique in 1795, for the education of artillery and engineer officers—those who were in a narrower sense the technicians of destruction. In 1802 Napoleon re-established the Ecole Militaire much as he had known that institution under the old régime.[32]

The Ninth Thermidor liquidated inflation and class struggle in France; it marked the beginning of the end of civilian preponderance over the military. And yet the military had been profoundly influenced in their thinking by the Jacobin class-war notion of totally destroying the enemy, an idea up to then foreign to them. Even when class conflict and Jacobinism were put down, the idea of total destruction was to prove ineradicable; out of it came a new strategy aimed at incapacitating the enemy for further resistance through material or psychological means. As Clausewitz phrased it: "The destruction of the enemy forces is among all purposes which might be pursued in war always the most imperative one." One of the heritages of Jacobinism is terror in war, in the use of which Napoleon fancied himself a connoisseur.

Theoretically Napoleon had been caught by the Jacobin idea. In a fit of bad temper on St. Helena, he raved against the "rose-water war" made nowadays, whereas formerly the vanquished were massacred or enslaved and their women violated; he declared that if he had ordered such extreme measures in Vienna in 1809, the powers would not have come to Paris so easily. He was angry when his retinue reminded him that if everything on the enemy side were destroyed, conquests would be more difficult, for the foe would defend himself to the uttermost: "The gun had brought about equality among men; look at Spain. We have behaved there as was formerly done, but the whole population has arisen and driven us out."[33] A certain limitation on destruction was imposed, not by humanitarian scruples, but military considerations and the need of armies to preserve themselves in interludes between battles. Actually, Napoleon used terror sparingly. But he and his marshals often applied rules of war which the Allies did not consider compatible with honor.[34] And, on the whole, the balance in the observance of the rules of honor favors his enemies.

Since the mass armies and their warfare were at first in the service of the new bourgeois state, the "lawful" representatives of that state—whether the Legislative Assembly, the Convention, or the Directory—sought to maintain civilian control over the Leviathan that they had called into being. The whole process was illustrated and symbolized in the career of Lazare Carnot, the organizer of victory.

Significantly enough, Carnot was the son of a mere notary and acquainted with military engineering. He was a member of the Legislative Assembly, the Convention, and the dread Committee of Public Safety. He helped to draft the law for the *levée en masse* in August 1793—the law which sought to bring the entire man power and all national resources into the service of warfare. He operated, if he did not invent, the civil agencies of the representative body, the so-called "deputies on mission," who controlled the armies at the front by the summary promotion and demotion of officers and the execution of generals who failed to achieve victory.

This was terror at the front, while terror behind the lines suppressed counterrevolutionary movements in the French population. When civilian ideologues, such as Robespierre and Saint-Just, sought to interfere with Carnot for using even aristocratic experts in his operations, he shouted at them: "You are ridiculous dictators!" And went his way. (This conflict was repeated in the Russian Revolution, between Trotsky, who used experts, and Stalin, who thought good Bolsheviks could do the work.) While he was at the head of affairs the bourgeois of the Revolution had an efficient spokesman and master in their attempt to control the military forces. It was he who "liquidated" Robespierre, and in time Carnot found his own master. He helped to make Bonaparte commander of the Army of Italy, lived to serve that imperious lord of war, and died an exile when the Bourbons were restored to the throne in France.

Napoleon Turns the Mass System to Militaristic Ends

The civilian dreamers of the Revolution, who sought to create a new social order in France, may have imagined that the mass armies designed to defend the Revolution at home and abroad would docilely serve the lawyers and ideologues at Paris to the end. If so, they were quickly disillusioned. When the Directory employed

Bonaparte to save it from another revolution on the Left and a counterrevolution on the Right, it unwittingly rang its own death knell. After all, the new mass system had not entirely destroyed the old standing-army system; nor could it in the nature of things. It had necessarily relied upon the technical knowledge of the officers and men who rose out of the standing-army system, and in the early phases of war and revolution another elite of officers had sprung up.

As things stood in April 1791, among these rising officers, Kellermann, their senior, was almost fifty-seven years old, Sérurier forty-nine, Berthier and Pérignon thirty-eight, Moncey thirty-seven, Lefèbvre and Masséna thirty-six, Augerau thirty-four, Jourdan thirty, Bernadotte and Brune twenty-nine, Bonaparte twenty-two, Marmont seventeen. On the enemy side, Wurmser was sixty-seven, Suvorov sixty-two, Brunswick fifty-seven, Blücher forty-nine, Wellington twenty-three.[35] If we take the future twenty-five marshals of Napoleon, excluding the Pole Poniatowski, as prototypes of the new elite, most of them were not violent revolutionaries in a political sense—except three—and some, like Lefèbvre, had been throughout the confusion men of order, protecting banking and other institutions from the plundering crowd.[36]

Nor were they revolutionary soldiers in the sense that their military service started under the Revolution. Almost all of them were at least as well educated as Blücher. Six only of the future marshals belonged to the civilian class; the majority had been officers (nine) or soldiers (ten) in the time of the monarchy. All of the nine officers with one exception were nobles, though mostly of the lower ranks. Of the thirty-two general officers of the Armée d'Orient when it sailed for Egypt in 1798, sixteen had served as officers and eleven as nonofficers in the army before 1789, and only five began their career as revolutionary soldiers. As is the case in every struggle for survival, there is no way to tell whether the fittest for military performances had survived death by the guillotine or in the field. But good generals did survive those ordeals, carrying the war far beyond the frontiers of France.

Their victories revived the military sets of values which the Revolution had eclipsed. The normal ambitions and rivalries among generals returned. As late as 1795 they had vied, as in the Armée du Rhin, to see "who should *not* be the chief"; they had run from the honor of command and excused themselves on the ground of youth and inexperience. For a time there existed a strange moratorium on ambition among the generals and consequently a solidarity of interests among them. But in the campaign of 1796, it is said, Moreau, "really influenced by sheer military selfishness alone," ruined Jourdan as he wrecked Macdonald in 1799.[37]

At the same time, the distinction of rank was reasserted from above—the distinction which had been forgotten for a time, owing to the (often more pretended than real) common origin of officers and men and the concept of the superior being as in the main a war technician. In November 1796, General Ney observed "with pain that, contrary to good order and delicacy, the majority of the officers mixed with the soldiers and were drinking with them in the cabarets." He ordered such officers to be imprisoned and in case of relapse to lose their rank.[38] The law about the election of officers was by this time generally ignored. It was forbidden to promote an illiterate even to the rank of corporal. So the officer regained an authoritative position between the soldier and the civilian governors, beginning with 1794 when the attendance of soldier deputations upon the Convention was prohibited.[39] Thus ended the second attempt of the common soldier to take a part in state counsels.

Among these officers, one was able to become master of all the soldiers and of the bourgeois state created by the Revolution: Napoleon Bonaparte. Much as historians have debated the secret of his achievement, no formula has been found to "explain" the "mystery." Nor is the cryptic word "genius" sufficient to account for it —"he seems to be above men," as a Paris paper wrote on his Italian successes.[40] However, the stages of his climb are clear; winning command of the Army of Italy, he attacked the enemies at their feeblest points, which they proceeded to weaken for him yet further.[41] With the glory of this campaigning he helped to destroy the civilian Directory and establish the Consulate and finally an Empire on its ruins. At home he defended the obvious property interests of the bourgeois and many gains of the Revolution, meantime making them pay dearly for the defense. In his enterprises abroad he exploited the manhood of France, enfranchised or not, in one war after another, waged for militaristic purposes: that is, not for the defense of France and the Revolution, but to realize his dreams of military power. Whether these dreams were the emanations of genius or the fantasies of a "conquering beast," he, the liquidator of the Revolution, wasted the assets which he had seized. Among his dissimulative and manipulative methods are many which illustrate the process by which the military way was transformed into a militaristic and Caesarian way.

First of all Bonaparte was no mere *capitaine canon* of the Vendémiaire. He was a watcher of events who studied class interests in conflict during and after the Revolution, familiarizing himself with civil concerns at stake, including finance and economy, observing closely the officers around him, and penetrating the psychology of the soldier and of the nation as a joyful recipient of "glory." He threaded his way carefully through the mazes of civilian conflicts until he came to the "hour" when action could be taken with some assurance of triumph. On his return from Egypt whence he reported, after his landing, new victories which were actually defeats, the personal credit of Bonaparte was unimpaired with the French nation. But he did not then throw it into the scales of one of the warring parties, who were making the public tired of parliamentarism. For the time being he was waiting. "Where I am, I command or am silent," he told someone who wanted his early intercession. Nevertheless, he was secretly conspiring with civilians and with military men; many of the latter, attacked for their presumptions by publicists, whom they in turn flogged, felt themselves more apart as a corps than ever. By 1799 the expression *citoyen général* had fallen into desuetude.[42] Bonaparte's military entourage was set to work to establish connections with officers who could be trusted when the hour for imposing a new order of things would call for their assistance and that of their soldiers.[43]

Lefèbvre, the Commandant of Paris, was won over by Bonaparte's flatteries. When handed the sword which Bonaparte had carried to the Pyramids, he declared himself, with tears and curses, ready "to throw the lawyers into the river." [44] The lawyers at whom such *noyades* were directed were the Thermidorians, the survivors of Jacobinism. By this time Bonaparte had cast in his lot with the party of order which, rather than the military men themselves, engineered the coup. It triumphed on the 18th and 19th Brumaire with military help; while the parliamentarians were influenced by the memory of Cromwell, the soldiers were agitated by the rumor that an attempt had been made on the life of the Great General.

Now Bonaparte joined the government as First Consul. Whatever had threatened her, France "felt saved" after the 18th Brumaire, as after the 18th Brumaire of Louis Napoleon later, as Germany felt after Hindenburg's *coup d'état* of 1933. Emissaries went to the armies to tell them that "the new order of things was all to their advantage." Some were aware, no doubt, that the elevation of Bonaparte was a first step toward an absolute government, the end of liberty, a violation of the principles to which they attributed the great French successes won up to that time.[45] But more were convinced, as one of Ney's military friends wrote, that "order had arrived"; that the new constitution of the year VII "in nominating a general First Consul makes the whole weight fall back on the military estate; and that is the more due to us since the nature of our condition has already given us the physical weight." [46]

The army had now become the only arms bearer in the Republic, a monopoly which armies have always been eager to obtain; for Bonaparte's first act of government on his accession to the Con-

sulate was to suppress the Garde nationale which, as a citizens'
army, had shown some resistance. It was not to be restored until
1806, when he told his state council that this Garde was "the tu-
telary genius of the *boutiques;* when you arm the mob, you make
revolutions; when you arm property, you prevent them." [47] The
army was elated and most of the officers presumably felt like
Coignet: "The army was now so numerous and so beautiful that
it would have liked best to fight all Europe." [48]

Through the First Consul, the 18th Brumaire transferred a rank
to the soldiers that elevated them above the bourgeois, or at least
above those civilians who wanted to interfere with the army. But,
as Bonaparte understood the soldiers, "they were not republicans;
accustomed to obey, they were content to see the bourgeois subdued like themselves. Armies are essentially monarchist." [49] That
some officers were not, the conspiracy in which Pichegru and
Moreau were involved demonstrated all too plainly. And yet those
who surrounded the First Consul almost like a court were monarchists at heart, without being Bourbon legitimists, and the officers
among them regarded that system as for the best of the service
and their own interest. As Montluc had said: "Let us own that we
soldiers would be nothing without kings. If we obey them, that is
obeying the orders of God without trying to obtain reward by reproaches and importunities; and the wrong is not the kings' if
someone is poorly recognized, but is the fault of those who are
around them and do not make known to them who serve well or
badly." [50]

The First Consul himself, after the 18th Brumaire, had drawn
up as a pamphlet a "Parallel between Caesar, Cromwell, Monck,
and Bonaparte," and sent it out as a trial balloon. He had pointed
to himself as the man with the firm and clever hand which would
hold and sustain the gains of the Revolution, itself greater in deeds
than in men. When this parallel did not find acclaim, he resigned
his ambitions—for the time being: the pear was not yet ripe.[51] But
it did ripen when the army, assembled in the camp of Boulogne
in 1804, pronounced its monarchist desires, led apparently by Ney,
in petitions addressed to the First Consul, and called upon him to
proclaim himself Emperor and establish a dynasty. They found him
grateful and responsive. On the 18th of May a *senatus consultum*
conferred the imperial crown on Bonaparte and he in turn on the
19th made the fourteen corps commanders marshals of France.
"The army viewed the establishment of the Empire with pleasure;
the new order of things could only become more and more favorable to it." [52]

Having threaded his way to the top, Bonaparte made use of
military psychology by drawing his marshals into an honor system

to support his scheme of government. He "did not believe in the virtue of men but he believed in their honor." He gave a certain scope to dueling even though as a general he regretted the losses of good officers it might occasion; aside from that, he thought, dueling would uphold politeness in society. Those fought with pistols he deemed ignoble; "the fight with swords is that of brave men." [53] He maintained that he himself as an artillery lieutenant fought such a duel, of which, however, historiography knows nothing.

Napoleon's honor arrangements were never so devised that they excluded anyone beforehand, as did the feudal scheme. "I ennoble all Frenchmen," he said, "every one can be proud." [54] The Legion of Honor, founded by him under the Consulate, included civilians as well as military of all ranks. The legionaries swore "by their honor" to devote themselves to the service of the Republic, "to fight, by all means which justice, reason, and the laws authorize, every enterprise which tends to re-establish the feudal regime, to produce again titles and qualities which were the attributes thereof; finally, to contribute with all my power to maintaining liberty and equality." [55]

This first honor system was then decidedly antifeudal; the later systems which emanated from the Emperor were somewhat less so, but still did not destroy the equality in society which the Revolution had produced, even though, through the system of donations for the marshal dukes, he brought back some of the costliness of feudal honoring. With the creation of the marshals, he resumed old traditions as well, and also in connection with the guards, which he restored in 1804. These did not, however, form a court institution but rather the elite corps of his fighting troops, fifty-six thousand strong in 1812. In imitation of the Roman habits of the Africani and Coriolani, the marshals bore the name of the battle where they had distinguished themselves most; they were sufficiently well equipped with estates and other income to maintain a noble establishment.

With the return of many noble *émigrés* to France, the honor society under the Empire regained many feudal aspects. Marshals and generals had their family records searched to show an ancient noble origin. One of them, Clarke, Duc de Feltre, simple *gentil-homme,* "ruined himself buying titles and getting a genealogy for himself." He induced Las Cases to indicate in his writings that he was a descendant of the Plantagenets. With these prepossessions, it was easy for Clarke to embrace the Bourbons after they returned and become an ardent royalist.[56] Davout, himself of the lowest nobility, as marshal surrounded himself with the *jeune noblesse* as closely as many a sovereign. His chief of staff was a count; several of his aides-de-camp and orderly officers were counts and dukes.[57]

To most marshals, the feudal military side of Napoleon's system of government was far more sympathetic than the uses he made of religion for the same purpose. Some of them who had entered churches mainly for taking away treasures protested, as did Lannes and Augereau, against the reinstallation of *l'infâme.* They wanted to jump out of their equipages when they found that they were being carried to Mass in Notre Dame, and were only restrained by the First Consul's military command. When he afterward asked Augereau what he thought about the ceremony, the marshal answered, much to the irritation of Bonaparte: "Very nice; only a million men are missing who allowed themselves to be killed in order to destroy what we re-establish." Caesarism, Augereau evidently thought, was enough religion for the Napoleonic armies.[58]

To the general need and desire for legitimizing his regime, Napoleon himself paid homage by marrying into the House of Hapsburg and arranging intermarriages between other royal and princely houses and those members of his own family who had not already married sons of innkeepers, like Murat—whom the First Consul had not wanted as a brother-in-law, complaining that "in the rank where fortune and glory have placed me, I cannot mix his blood with mine." For purposes of government, at least, Napoleon behaved as if his own blood, once so red and new, had already turned to blue. He wanted to age his governmental system rapidly by the use of ancient imperialist symbols and associations with the ancient families—"that is, what has always existed," he said on St. Helena.[59] He who smashed so many feudal institutions, for instance, that old German Empire, which before him "consisted of great fiefs," now wanted to reign over complexes of mixed feelings and intents which, originally feudal, had become largely militarist and easily held in check.

Such were his *moyens de gouvernement,* consisting rather of psychological manipulations altering from day to day, than of systems of thought such as ideologues would devise. Thus operating, he raised himself in the estimation of others. As a fatal consequence this obedience, coupled with his military achievements and good luck, raised his own estimate of himself and led to his ruin.

It was not enough to attach to his cause the "honor" of high military officers and signs of legitimacy. After all, millions of privates had to fight and die for the realization of his ambitions. So Bonaparte gave attention to winning the affections of the rank and file. He made a point of remembering or seeming to remember old warriors who had fought at Arcole or Wagram or Austerlitz; such a point, indeed, that thousands of veterans must have felt themselves to be personal friends of their commander. In his numerous proclamations to the armies—terse, inflammatory, and insinuating—

Napoleon carried propaganda to a high point and impregnated the armies with the kind of ideas for which they would fight, at least ostensibly. Had he been less of a literary artist, he might have been less of a military commander. Either deliberately or for genuine military purposes, Napoleon displayed on occasion an interest in the comfort and welfare of soldiers, even descending to such details as making sure that their underwear had buttons. Whether on his initiative, or accidentally, stories of his solicitude circulated among the soldiers who fought, suffered, starved, and died for him.

Nor was Bonaparte oblivious to the sentiments of the French bourgeois when he contemplated the cost of his military undertakings. He sought as far as possible to make war "pay its way" by living on conquered countries.[60] For example, after his early triumphs over the Austrians in Italy he levied tribute on the Italian victims whom he had "liberated." Parma, the first state to buy itself free and feed the war and the French Republic by its contributions, paid two million francs, twelve hundred horses with harness, two thousand oxen, ten thousand bushels of grain, and twenty pictures. The other states followed with similar contributions to Paris.

Bonaparte had supplies to spare over and beyond the needs of his army and sent loot to Paris to please and bribe the government and the nation, now beginning to believe that war was not only glorious but practical. In three months, Bonaparte obtained fifty-three million francs in money and three times that in requisitioned goods, not counting the art treasures either sold on the spot or forwarded to Paris, or the quickly dissipated loot allocated to officers and soldiers. Of a consignment from Genoa to a value of a million francs, Bonaparte remarked that the six months of active warfare had cost the Republic an outlay of only four hundred and fifty thousand francs. This kind of war was as appealing to the businessmen as the profits from a small initial investment in a lucky goldmining venture.

In several other respects Bonaparte's campaign resembled a bonanza. The original material outlay was inconsiderable for France, since men were cheap in that populous country; and the *remplaçants* (substitutes) who were permitted after 1800 were not very costly to men of property allowed to purchase service exemptions. France had only to furnish the soldier with a cheap musket and uniform and just a little "priming" before the war was started and he was carried into the enemy's land to be fed there. For this practice a precedent was available in the Thirty Years' War; then the armies had moved to regions where supplies were to be found, and often battle was avoided or postponed when a decision for political or military purposes was needed, thereby prolonging warfare. But Napoleon reversed the thing: he was eager for the decisive battle, to be rid forthwith of care about his supplies. Once the battle was finished, the enemy's country, or a large part of it, was at his service. Frequently, moreover, the enemy had no available reserves; and, with the loss of the capital, seat of a highly centralized government, he was not in a position to organize new levies and other local resistance.

Military leaders have at all times supported the tendency toward centralization, in part for reasons of military bureaucracy, in part out of the conviction that centralism strengthens the offensive. Yet it undeniably produces a weakness in the defensive, a fact which the military policy of the civilians in the United States has never been able to forget since the burning of Washington in 1813. At all events, the weakness inherent in the overcentralization of absolutism led to Bonaparte's "mania for dashing at capitals," as Saint-Cyr condemned it later, when the Emperor continued to indulge in it, although the possession of a capital like Moscow did not mean the same thing as the possession of Berlin after the decisive battle of Jena. Since Napoleon had not beaten the Russians in the field, he could not dictate peace to them from the capital. From the military standpoint, the advisable thing would have been to stop at Smolensk, to reconstruct Poland, to rest and provision the armies.[61] But until the Russian campaign, when the Emperor overreached himself, the warning which Dumouriez gave the Prussians after Austerlitz held good: "According to this manner of warfare, every sovereign is lost who is driven out of his capital; the examples of Austria and Sardinia have proved it." [62]

Certainly wars so directed brought surpluses: the income from contributions in the first Austrian War of 1805 was 75 million francs; in the second of 1809, 88 millions; from Prussia Napoleon maintained he had drawn a billion francs, whereas the intendant for these contributions insists it was a mere 482 millions, plus 125 millions more from the rest of northern Germany. From 1805 to 1809 the intake of this extraordinary treasury amounted to 743 millions. The exactions from Prussia were made particularly heavy by Napoleon in order to make rearmament more difficult for her; he pointed out to the complaining Prussians that their financial difficulties would soon be ended if they would simply dissolve their army.[63]

In curtailing the costs of war for the French bourgeois, Napoleon partly freed the movement of his armies from the shackles of lumbering supply trains; he was more interested in speeding up the legs of the soldier than his arms. The baggage of the officer was cut down; the subaltern lost his horse, and the soldiers their tents, previously carried along by horses. It has been estimated that by comparison the baggage train of a body of French infantry in 1806 amounted to only one-eighth or one-tenth that of an equal body of

Prussian infantry.[64] Other elements helped in this speed-up: since the Seven Years' War, metaled roads had been built all over central Europe, Napoleon himself adding hundreds of miles. And from about the same time, as Delbrück points out, the cultivation of the potato had spread widely; it had already given one war, that of the Bavarian Succession, the nickname of the "potato war," the potato offering the soldiers a more immediate source of consumption than other foodstuffs when they outmarched their supply system.[65]

Nevertheless all such devices came closer to winning time than to gaining battles. In 1796 Napoleon had said: "In the future I may lose a battle but I shall never lose a minute" [66]—a boast that sets him closer to the time-winning record breaker than to the business man who believes that time is money. And it may help to solve the still open question as to why Napoleon, "the conquest brute," undertook so many wars; perhaps it was to show that he could make them faster, better in that sense than others. Yet haste, if it did not cause him to lose a battle as in Russia in 1812, did make him lose that war:

However much had been done to assemble and bring up the needs of supply, still all these arrangements were useless; for right from the beginning of the war the speed of the movements by which Napoleon was hurried forward in order to obtain a main battle, separated the supply system and the army. They did not see one another again.[67]

His speeding of men was as little economic in conception as his spending of men. Still his wars, which, as Clausewitz had said, he made "the business of the whole people," were "cheap and easy wars" for the French upper bourgeoisie. They enjoyed his national wars only as long as he did not nationalize business, but spared their enterprises and their sons. Nationalism had become the great energy source for war; when it claimed too much, however, and the burden put on the French national economy and life by Napoleon became excessive, the bourgeois grew restive. When the Goddess of Victory abandoned the Emperor, so did they and some of his marshals.

Drawing upon masses of men, Napoleon acted more and more in a militaristic spirit, destroying men with the prodigality of a spendthrift when his egomania was enlarged by victories and then threatened by defeats; he welcomed vaccination because it would give him more lives to spend. To the diplomat Metternich he boasted: "You cannot stop me; I spend thirty thousand men a month." He was always sure of his supply of French conscripts and labor, in addition to soldiers wrung from his satraps. He made battle more extensive—at Jena, Prussia opposed to him the largest army she had yet raised—although not in the beginning more bloody than in the Seven Years' War, or at Bunker Hill, where the British lost nearly half of a small force. At Castiglione and Arcole in 1796 the losses of the French and Austrians amounted to about 20 per cent; at Würzburg in the same year, where Bonaparte did not command, the French lost 7 per cent, the Austrians less than 4. An energizer like Suvorov drove up this percentage temporarily in 1799 at the Trebbia, where the losses amounted on both sides to from 30 to 55 per cent, and at Novi to 23 per cent on the French and 16 per cent on the Allied side. At Marengo in 1800, where 24,500 French faced 32,000 Austrians, the former lost 20 per cent, the latter 19.

After Marengo, where the losses amounted to about 20 per cent, the members of the Military Society of Berlin, which united the intelligence of the Prussian army, discussed the recent battles of the French and ascertained that in no case had the losses been as great as in the glorious Frederician battles of Prague or Torgau, where it was thought three times as many men had been lost as at Marengo. Thus they convinced themselves that the French could not be so fearful after all, judging the value of the troops merely according to the losses. They believed that the Prussians knew better how to die and therefore to conquer. When the Prussian army, in the politically favorable situation of 1805, pressed to enter the war against France, Scharnhorst exclaimed: "We have now the best opportunity to acquire a great reputation for ourselves. But we must crave death—and then make peace quickly!" He overlooked the fact that the French knew better how to survive and conquer in the new way: that for the time being the will to survive was objectively stronger than the readiness to die, and that it only contributed to Prussia's defeat when her soldiers did not dare to lie down as the French *voltigeur* fire was pouring upon them.[68]

The figures covering Napoleon's "glorious losses" by no means indicate the full extent of the losses to which the "rage for numbers" of Bonaparte and of those whom he forced to follow his example was leading. Besides the total losses in battle, where, as Lannes said of Montebello, the bones cracked like hail falling against the windows,[69] there were losses outside the battles—losses far higher. Napoleon was always a waster of men. He was averse to treating his troops economically, allowing them liberties at times but not regular supplies. He was ever ready to call up new regiments. In the ten years from 1804 to 1813 he drafted 2,400,000 men, in addition to the volunteers—50,000 in the same period—enrolled seamen, and *gardes d'honneur*. After 1804, when the period of constant war started, few of these were ever dismissed as long as they were fit for service, even though the service age was presumed to be over at twenty-five; far less than half of them ever returned home at the end of the Empire. Up to 1806, the losses of France, within her boundaries of 1793, amounted to 1,700,000 in dead out of 29,000,-000 inhabitants.[70]

The losses in battle were far less than those due to illness. Of the 450,000 men who had passed the Niemen in the summer of 1812, only a few thousands returned half a year later. Davout's corps came out best of all: they had counted 66,000 men on June 15 and returned with some 3,000 men, of whom 674 officers and 1,600 men were still fit for service. Saint-Cyr's corps left Vilna with 25,000 on the 14th of July; up to August 7 it had lost 13,500 men without having seen the enemy, all losses being due to fatigue and want of food. Of those 13,500 men, 8,000 were dead and the rest had little hope of survival, most of them victims of dysentery which, with many, "was complicated by homesickness." By August 16 the corps —mostly Bavarians—was reduced to 11,000 men; by early October to 9,500. Of the French losses from Moscow to the Beresina, eleven-twelfths were due to bad clothing and feeding, and one-twelfth only to the enemy's fire.[71] It was extremely fortunate for Napoleon that most of the survivors of the *grande armée* were officers, noncommissioned and long-serving men who formed the skeleton of the next army. Aside from losses in battle—"troops are made to get killed" as Napoleon defined their purpose[72]—the mortality among the men was as a rule considerably higher than among officers.

Decimation due to sickness was everywhere great in this time of mass armies. Twice Gneisenau saw, in peaceful cantonments, half his companies dying, after they had survived the hardships of a campaign. One-third of the Prussian army in Poland in 1794-5 died in hospitals. With such experiences behind him, Gneisenau—who was himself to die in a cholera epidemic—hoped in the summer of 1812 that cantonments in Russia and the climate would destroy what part of the French army the Russian sword had spared.[73] The fever spots of Europe and its colonies left few of the soldiers condemned to go there untouched. On the island of Walcheren, five-sixths of the French troops that occupied that "home of fever" in 1795 were struck by typhoid and malaria.[74]

When Napoleon's military head was swollen into a militaristic head, the beginning of his end came in sight. "In war men are nothing, *one* man is everything," he wrote. His regard for men sank steadily as he advanced into the last phase, while his self-esteem, his inclination "to make images" out of touch with reality, grew and he was possessed by the *"rage des nombres."* The size of his armies outgrew his actual control, though he tried persistently to retain it by insisting on constant reports about the strength of the divisions. It is highly dubious whether he ever knew, or did not constantly overestimate, the exact number of men at his disposal on the day of

battle.[75] In such uncertainty he was inclined to convince himself by
the sight of the masses of his troops; it gave him an intoxication
from which the reports available on paper should have protected
him.[76] It was as if a merchant trusted for exact information the sight
of his filled storehouse more than the written list of its contents.

The growing recklessness in the wasting of men and the rising
distrust of the individual soldier, which none of the popular tricks
of the *petit caporal* could hide, led to a tactical use of soldiers that
was different from practice under the Republic, the Consulate, and
the very first years of the Empire. This became particularly obvious
in French attacks against an enemy in fortified positions. Instead of
using, as before, *tirailleurs* in great bands, only companies of the
light infantry in the regiments were deployed. For the main effect,
reliance was placed on the moral shock of the close columns,
advancing with drums beating. This tactical form was constantly employed in the Peninsular War. From beginning to end, none of the
generals, Napoleon included, recognized that this was the main
source of all the French disasters in Spain, whereas Wellington after
Vimeiro (1808) acknowledged that such attack in column against
an infantry not previously shaken by the fire of infantry or artillery
had as little chance as a cavalry attack against an intact infantry.[77]
So by his growing disregard for the lives of his men and by his
resort to wasteful tactics, Napoleon wore out the human resources
upon which he relied for his very predominance over France and
Spain.

In the light of this record showing the transformation of Bonaparte, the soldier, into Napoleon, the militarist, some reasons for
his downfall and the collapse of his system become apparent. As his
egomania grew in size, he lost all sense of the proportions among
things and of the limitations on human power, however great it
may be at a given moment. The absence of this sense is a prime
characteristic of militarism, and distinguishes it from the military
way. In Napoleon's case it meant more than a loosening of his
mental and physical grip on the material and human resources at his
command. It meant a blind and stubborn incapacity to understand
the imponderables in front of him. In the reckless use of mass
armies for the attainment of his ambitions, he evoked from the
bosom of half-slumbering feudal societies opposed to him the very
force of mass armies and nationalism which smashed his system
and sent him reeling into exile, where he tried, for the benefit of
simpletons, to create a fiction of himself as the spirit of the
Revolution incarnate—to cover his true significance as the spirit
of militaristic counterrevolution incarnate.

As Napoleon extended the *imperium* of his will and presumption, and the general became the Emperor, his military enemies—though by no means all of them—recognized that he must be conquered by his own instruments of victory; their own strength, in part at least, must be made similar to that of France. The small, rigidly drilled but spiritless armies with which they had been accustomed to playing fine games of strategy were no match in size, tempo, or tactics for this onward sweep of fire-spreading crusaders, carrying their "rights of man" propaganda. The old powers were forced to envisage an alteration of methods, possibly even a crack in their caste system; Archduke Charles, at one time commanding armies against the French, said to Gneisenau that the world could be saved from Napoleon "only by a man not born into princely station." [1]

5

Mass Armies Employed in the Wars of Liberation Against Napoleon

The governmental problem was how to form mass armies inspired by an ardor equal in effect, even if not in kind, to that of the revolutionary Napoleonic forces without making a revolution themselves. Shrinking with dismay from the spectacle of the Reign of Terror, and dreading above everything a repetition of such class upheaval in their own lands, the ruling groups of Britain, Russia, Austria, and Prussia pondered the question of obtaining a new military efficiency without granting too much liberty or opening the door too wide for the germs of revolution. In various ways, these countries tried to mobilize their various potentials—the money power and conservative sturdiness of Britain, the primitive religious loyalty of the Russians—a people "easily satisfied, obedient and brave, born, as it were, for war," in the words of Scharnhorst[2]—and the aroused nationalism of the Prussian bourgeoisie, whose cosmopolitan hopes of winning freedom through Napoleon were frustrated by his reparation policies and other acts of oppression. It was the last of these, Prussia, that best understood the powers available and understood best how to arouse without unchaining them. There, however much they hated the French Revolution, the military men admired its astonishing release of war energies and were inspired to a most radical remaking of their own system. As Gneisenau said in 1807:

The new time needs more than old names, titles, and parchments; it needs new action and strength. The Revolution has mobilized the whole national strength of the French people, and by equalizing the different estates and by the equal taxing of property has transformed into a usurious capital the living power of man and the dead hand of property and has abolished the equilibrium based on these two. If the rest of the states want to restore this equilibrium, then they ought to open up and make use of the same resources.[3]

Prussian Reformers Seek to Awaken Mass Forces Against Napoleon

"Get us a national army," Blücher implored those entrusted with military reforms in Prussia between 1807 and 1813. The small regiments of half-enslaved and overexercised professionals, wheeling and forming according to the rigid Frederician rules of tactics, must be abandoned and the nation called to arms:

It is not as difficult as one thinks; the foot-rule must be abandoned, no one in the world must be exempt, and it must become a shame not to have served except in case of infirmities. . . . It is a conceit to suppose that an exercised soldier would forget so much in two years that he could not be used again after a week. The French have proved to us that it is otherwise; our useless pedantries the soldier might very well forget altogether. The army must be arranged in divisions; the divisions must be composed of all sorts of troops and must have autumn maneuvers against one another.[4]

The problem the reformers faced was how to create this vast new army for a poor and exhausted Prussia, quickly, efficiently, and without great expenditure. The cheapest army could be formed by conscripting the Prussians and inducing them to believe that such patriotic service was honorable—the idea put to work with such good effect in the French army. But under the old order in Prussia, the dominion of the Junkers had estranged everyone else from state and army so that the call to patriotism might evoke little response; during the War of 1806-7 the foreign mercenaries had often, if not as a whole, shown more attachment to the colors than the born Prussians. But foreigners would be too expensive for Prussia to hire in the future; the native popular strength must be awakened and tapped. Were the right methods found, this reserve power would be as great in that country as anywhere else, the reformers cried:

What infinite resources there are slumbering in the womb of a nation, undeveloped and unused! Within the breast of thousands and thousands of people a great genius lived whose upward-striving wings their low conditions paralyze. . . . Why did the courts not grasp the simple and sure means to open a career to genius whenever it shows itself, to encourage talents and virtue from whichever class or rank they may spring? Why did they not choose this way to raise their strength a thousand times and open to the bourgeoisie the *porta triumphalis* by which now only the nobleman is allowed to enter? [In France the Revolution] had awakened all powers and given to each power its adequate sphere of action. Thus heroes had come to the head of armies, statesmen to the first places of government, and finally to the head of a great nation came the greatest man from among them.[5]

These reformers were anything but protagonists of the rising classes, however. Their primary interest was in military victory, to which social reform was but the means. In themselves they constituted a group of officers hampered in their careers by Old Prussian restrictions, keeping down men of modest or non-Prussian origin, such as they were. Recognizing this, Napoleon remarked to a Prussian diplomat that, whereas in France the *canaille* had made the Revolution, in Prussia the army did it, hinting that the Crown and those closest to it were to be on their guard against these military Jacobins, about whose real qualifications he himself was rather poorly advised. In fact Scharnhorst was reported by his spies to be a "former professor of mathematics; German pedant," and Gneisenau a "hothead." [6]

To such army officers, reform and war seemed the likeliest means to attain promotion, which peace and the old framework made so difficult. As Clausewitz, poor and shy, engaged to a countess whom he could not marry until 1810 when he had risen to a higher rank, confided to his fiancée before Jena:

My country needs the war and—let us admit openly—the war only can bring me to the happy goal. In whichever way I might like to connect my own life with the rest of the world, my way always takes me across a great battlefield; without my entering upon it, no permanent happiness will come to me. Much I hope to obtain for myself . . . great demands I have to address to my fortune.[7]

Hence the nationalism of the Prussians was not an autonomous, spontaneous popular growth from below; it was induced by artificial pressure from without and from above. Almost exclusively the ideologues who urged the rise against Napoleon were bureaucrats. This was also true of the philosopher Fichte and the poet Schenkendorf, to whom Napoleon was the most recent monstrosity of Babel, and who found in him the goal for that crusading spirit which is the feudal heritage of us all. "The nation must be inspired with independence; it must be given occasion to become acquainted with itself, so that it takes an interest in itself. . . . Only then will it respect itself and know how to enforce the respect of others," insisted Scharnhorst in 1807. Stein also was convinced that "only by bringing the mind of the nations into excitement and fermentation, can they be brought to an unfolding of all their moral and physical powers." [8]

What the advice of these reformers involved was not a revolution, but a counterrevolution by reform. Some concessions must be made in order to stimulate popular enthusiasm, without for a moment endangering the established order as a whole. Since classlessness is essential to any nationalism—nationalism viewed as a hypnotic suggestion of equality in the presence of death while denying equality in life—Stein proposed in 1808 to abolish the poorer nobility, since it had not even wealth to show or to preserve its worth:

> The preponderance of one class over its co-nationals is injurious, a disturbance of the social order, and it ought to be abolished. The nobility in the Prussian countries is burdensome to the nation, because it is numerous, largely poor and full of claims to salaries, offices, and privileges of all kinds. A consequence of its poverty is its want of education. . . . This great number of half-educated people now exercise their presumptions in their double quality of noblemen and officials as a burden to their co-citizens.[9]

The reformers were willing to go thus far in sacrifice, by abandoning the discredited Junkers, in order to win over the bourgeois for the army and to re-establish with his help the credit of the military. They would allow him to share in the honor which went with army service and positions. The dividing line between the military and bureaucrats on the one side, who began their symbiosis in this reform period, and on the other the bourgeois, had become less marked ever since the death of Frederick the Great, and the reformers proposed to efface it further. Some of the reformers and other officers and officials conspired with the bourgeoisie against the

French in the *Tugendbund*, or Association of Virtue. Blücher held high degrees in the Masonic Orders and was a speaker of unusual gifts, playing at the same time on the warlike and on the humanitarian instincts that co-exist in man, celebrating in Masonry the harmony of society which would exist after the Wars of Liberation were over.

It was necessary to make such gestures because the Prussian bourgeois had been disappointed that the army of 1806 had failed to provide the security which it once boastfully promised, and they did not hesitate to express this resentment in pamphlets and other writings. The citizenry felt their own military prowess had been insufficiently recognized, as at the siege of Kolberg in 1807, directed by Gneisenau, when they rendered efficient support. The claims of the Kolberg burghers found their way into the public papers and aroused the military to violent and injudicious contradiction. During the disputes over apportionment of glory which followed, Gneisenau, as the former commandant, had to admonish the officers at Kolberg to watch with particular care over their behavior, since the recent defeat of the army, once so highly thought of, "has stirred up *Schadenfreude* in many minds which take hold avidly of everything that may serve to defame our estate." [10] He was eager not to estrange such a citizenry.

In their conciliatory policy, the reformers admitted a widening of the jurisdiction of the civil law over the members of the army, but they did not place the majesty of the law so high as to bring under its jurisdiction all conflicts arising within the army. The prohibition of dueling, as it stood on the law books, the officers refused to recognize as binding on themselves. A court martial of 1809 claimed that in such questions not the law of the land but rather that of honor was applicable. The King, however, did not quite allow this claim, but rather reserved for himself the right to mediate in the conflict between the law and the ancient prejudice by an act of his own mercy.

The reformers had induced him before this to regulate to a certain extent questions of honor in connection with the problem of disciplining officers. Under a decree of August 3, 1808, a majority of three-quarters of the officers of a regiment, constituted as a "court of honor," were to decide whether an officer had shown himself unworthy of further service among them; meanness of character was to be the criterion of removal; in order to exclude the possibility of systematic proscription on the part of his comrades, an officer was entitled to demand an investigation of his case by another regiment. Officers were also admonished to reduce the sources of honor conflicts by mutual supervision and by having the older officers warn the younger in time. The submission of cases of insult to such courts was foreshadowed, though it did not actually and regularly take place till twenty years later.[11]

To serve army purposes better, Gneisenau demanded that Prussians were first to become, or to be made, free or freer. Hitherto they had been used as taxpayers or other passive objects of the state machinery, but almost nothing had been done to make the Prussian free, noble, and independent, to induce in him a feeling of being a part of the whole with a dignity of his own. The new argument ran in this vein: to those who only serve a purpose unknown to them it does not matter whom they serve, but the citizen in a state, who knows his country and knows how to appreciate the happiness of a just government under mild laws, offers his sacrifice gladly in order to secure these highest of all goods, if not for himself for those after him. To the much-lamented enervation and degeneration of the peoples nothing has contributed more than the standing armies; they have destroyed the war-readiness and public spirit of the peoples. They are as a power more imaginary than real, the prop of ambition and the tool of its designs, which surpass all the strength of the state. The strongest power of the rulers is its people, but their mutual interests are separated by the standing armies. The way to unite them is to give the peoples constitutions envied by others and in that manner prepare ways and means to be armed for the decisive hour and to survive other states. It leads them through property, enlightenment, morality, civil liberty. If the members of a whole nation are to be made soldiers, they must be filled with a military spirit in time of peace. The diverse and wide-flung provinces of Prussia can be united into a nation only by the common tie of a constitution. In short, Gneisenau and his friends were convinced that the burden of general conscription must be balanced by a right of the people, however limited, to co-operate in the deliberations about war and peace and the financing of war. Once these conditions were fulfilled, armies thrice as large as the present ones would become possible.[12] And they would be much cheaper armies, too.

Although novel to many Prussians in 1807, this proposal for universal service was even older than the French Revolution. A relative of Goethe, a Prussian civilian bureaucrat, had advised, as early as 1744, a perpetual and national militia in the place of mercenary and foreign soldiers as being far cheaper and more reliable than the prevailing system, particularly when military service was made to appear an honorable duty, for honor is the source of all martial efficiency.[13] Another bureaucrat in the Prussian service, though born abroad, Thomas Abbt, professor in the University of Frankfurt on the Oder, in his book *On Death for the Fatherland* (1761), had taught the Prussians how noble it was to die fighting for their country; how dying an individual death was merely following "the laws of perfection which preserve the whole, if necessary, by the loss of a part."

In pressing forward with their projects, Prussia's military Jacobins —Scharnhorst, Gneisenau, Blücher, Boyen, Grolman, Clausewitz— encountered vigorous opposition from the Old Prussian nobility. In fact, none of the reformers was an Old Prussian and a member of those families that had long given Prussia most of her officers.

For Old Prussians there was too much intelligence and too many foreigners, including the Westphalian Von Stein, and the Hanoverian Von Hardenberg, in the reforming circle. They tried to block everything advocated by these men; thus the Old Prussian nobility opposed Stein's agrarian reforms and gladly saw French troops of occupation repress peasant revolts. To them the defeat at Jena was a mere mishap and was not regarded as disproving the value of Frederician tactics. *Tirailleur* tactics were to them, before Jena and long after, "suspicious in political respects and superfluous in military ones." A reactionary of Old Prussia, Field Marshal von Kalckreuth, whom Hardenberg called *"ce vieux méchant fou,"* bemoaned in 1808 the passing of the linear tactics and the platoon fire and their replacement by dispersed fighting—this organized disorder. "The platoon fire was the true palladium of the Prussians," and the new kind "might be good for the French, a vivacious race, but it dishonors the Germans, and particularly the Prussians, peoples with a countenance. Yes, it means dishonoring their national character by taking away the famous firing from them." [14]

Such enemies of reform, who were always closer to the King than the reformers, naturally did not want to see the bourgeoisie enter the officer class, except perhaps in wartime, or with exceptions for the sons of rich bourgeois. At all times, the majority of officer positions were to be reserved for the poor and numerous nobility. To this contention the reformers frankly replied that the usurpation by the nobility of all honorable employments in the army had lost for the army the talents and knowledge of the nation as a whole; that, since the nobility, freed of competition, had felt no need to acquire military talents in order to reach the highest positions, the education and knowledge of the officers had sunk to a low level. To lead the army back to its true destiny, Scharnhorst insisted that a claim to an officer's commission in peacetime should only be based on knowledge and education; in wartime on special bravery, activity, and good judgment. Out of the whole nation all individuals who possessed these qualities must, therefore, be enabled to climb to the highest positions of honor.[15]

It was a strange liberation, a Prussian liberation, coming from above, a passing liberalism for military purposes, and it raised the obvious question: was it intended sincerely on the part of its proponents? It seemed to be. This contention is amply supported by the hatred of their enemies and rivals, which they encountered in the work of reorganization, and by the later history of the reformers. Their radicalism was of a varying degree. Gneisenau said of Grolman, who in Germany after 1918 would have been called a National Bolshevik, that "he was prepossessed by the crassest forms of Jacobinism and would sacrifice everything to them in a bloody way." [16] But he himself believed, as he told the King, that an insurrection was not so easily knocked down as an army in battle; and he grew impatient with the King's irresolution, with the fight put up by the cliques within the army, and with the insinuations that the aspirations of his own group were revolutionary. Early in 1812 he exclaimed: "Would a popular war lead to revolution? Yes, if the peoples, betrayed and forsaken by their governments, should turn to self-help. Then the regents might easily be forgotten for lucky leaders." [17] That was to say, if a Hohenzollern did not place himself at the head of such a movement he might go by the board.

To the deep disappointment of the reformers there was then too little readiness for insurrection and revolution in the Prussian people. And how could it be otherwise among the masses who had been serfs up to the present and then suddenly had their ancient burden changed into the terms of a money economy? Or among an urban population that had just been relieved of the Junker domination by the defeat of this hateful class and had vented its spite by cruel jokes at the expense of Junkers and guard officers? Could it be expected that the insurrections in the Vendée, in Spain, in Tyrol—all of them Catholic regions, by the way—would inspire a spontaneous rising in Prussia, a Landsturm consisting of all men— men who were ready and able, even without previous practice, to handle a weapon of whatever kind and thus more completely resembled a nation in arms than a militia?

The Prussian nation was, in truth, not ready to join an early military insurrection. It needed more French oppression and exactions, more indoctrination on the part of the secret societies like the Tugendbund, or the bureaucrats, who insisted with Stein that the exasperation existing in Germany be nourished by "patriotic emissaries." Only in these ways could the Prussians and other Germans be prepared for a rising against Napoleon. This took time and the Emperor did much to block it. He prolonged occupation and took other military measures to obtain security and keep Prussia down. He obtained the dismissal of Stein and the punishment of some other despised "ideologues." In more indirect ways he secured the removal of almost all the reformers from the Prussian service, some of whom had been previously denounced to the French by their bitter enemies within Prussia herself.[18]

Reforms Are Instituted Without Revolution

Only in the face of stout opposition, and by various steps, did the Reformers manage to reconstitute the social order in Prussia and at last to make possible the *levée en masse* against Napoleon. The history of this process is complicated. Only the barest outlines can be given here.

On the civilian side, though with reference to military ends, many of the social changes wrought by revolution in France were effected in Prussia by law and decree, without violence from below. Serfdom was abolished. Great breaches were made in the feudal class system. Members of the lower social strata were permitted freely to purchase and hold landed property and engage in business enterprises. The spirit of this transformation was expressed in the royal decree of 1807 declaring the purpose of the King "to remove every obstacle that has hitherto prevented the individual from attaining such a degree of prosperity as he is capable of reaching." Thus the individualism so cherished by the British and French bourgeois was introduced into the thought and law of Prussia, although in a restrained and modified form.

But the people of Prussia were not to dominate the making and administration of law in Prussia through a legislative body, or even share in the process of government through any type of representative agency. If, then, Prussian civil reforms presented revolutionary aspects, they were not British or French; they were peculiar and hybrid in character. Yet, such as they were, they contributed to the attainment of military reforms and military objectives in war.

In the domain of military affairs, strictly speaking, the Prussian reformers likewise made impressive, though partial, gains. They early encountered the problem of purging the army. They sought to oust men guilty of ignominies in the War of 1806. But the Old Prussians forced a compromise. Expulsion was confined to a few cases of treason and cowardice, such as that of Hindenburg's little-mentioned ancestor, who had not defended the fortress of Spandau entrusted to him. The superiority of French leadership had demonstrated how necessary it was to open new avenues for military talent and young blood. So a thorough rejuvenation of the generals and staff officers was made. Of the 143 Prussian generals on active duty in 1803, only eight remained in 1812; and of these only two, one of them Blücher, held a command in 1813-15. The reformers would have preferred to eliminate seniority altogether and see officers promoted through the election of their peers: officers of a rank in which a vacancy had occurred should present three candidates and the officers of the next highest rank should select from among them, but on this project the reformers were defeated.

Other more sweeping proposals, borrowed from the French Revolution, like the selection of subaltern officers by the noncommissioned officers and of the latter by the privates, the reformers turned down from the beginning. Yet they provided that in wartime everyone who had distinguished himself by exceptional bravery could become an officer; in peacetime those who had served three months as a common soldier and had passed an examination. In 1809 war schools and in 1810 a war academy for ensigns and lieutenants were founded.[19]

In the leveling operation riding and pack horses were taken away from subaltern officers of the infantry. Not only did the reformers want to reduce the baggage train, they wanted the officer to come down closer to the level of the private and give the latter a constant example of enduring hardships. The number of horses in a regiment of infantry was reduced to one-sixth. The bread wagon practically disappeared, indicating the readiness to live by requisition in another war, like the French. Tents were abolished and greatcoats introduced instead. Comfort in war was to end. An ascetic element was to be enforced, against very considerable opposition, it being the principle "that the moral potency of officer and man was to be strained higher than heretofore, that he was to be made more independent of matter and concentrated upon himself. The mere technical, ever present need of warfare to reduce expenditure and heighten mobility by cutting down the baggage train received its strongest impetus by the general change in thought." [20]

Their greatest demand the reformers did not see fulfilled in peacetime—general conscription, with its affiliates, the Landwehr, a country defense or enrolled militia, and the Landsturm, a kind of *levée en masse*. Nevertheless, for economy's sake, recruiting abroad was ended and the old foreigners in the army were used only as long as they lasted. The new recruits were furnished exclusively through the cantonal system of recruiting. When Napoleon forced the reduction of the Prussian army to forty-two thousand men, less than a third of its former strength, the service time was shortened in order to build up an invisible army instead. But the demand of the reformers on this or other occasions to have every able-bodied Prussian serve for such a period, which might be reduced for the educated, could not overcome the interests which enjoyed the exemptions, nor the opposition of the King and the majority of the civilian ministers. The only use the narrow-minded King saw in conscription was that it might stop desertion, by no means ended after 1807.

Spokesmen of the small but influential group of the university-trained bureaucracy called conscription the tomb of civilization, of the sciences, of the handicrafts, of civil liberty, and all human happiness; only fanatics could adopt this idea, so inimical to all culture and hatched by coarse captains. The bureaus in Königsberg, where the Prussian government resided for the time being, were teeming, it was said, with a democratic, truly revolutionary spirit.[21]

The more powerful nobility, who were already protesting against the loss of their exemption from taxation and of their serfs and who feared a sweeping loss of all privileges of their estates as in France, petitioned the King against general conscription. They called it an outcome of the French swindle of Liberty and Equality, impossible to achieve outside the Greek polis; they said it would lead to the destruction of hereditary nobility, the reliable support of the throne of Frederick and his successors. Some of the reform bureaucracy were willing to have conscription in time of war, when the higher classes would volunteer, but rejected it for peacetime, because it would cause mass emigration from Prussia and the undermining of all civilization.

The military reformers, however, insisted on conscription in peacetime; the acts of war demanded preparation before the outbreak of hostilities, and they declined to trust to the readiness of the higher classes to serve in case of need. The officers answered the civilian argument that the poorer classes were far better fit for army service, because of their muscular strength, by pointing out that these classes could not be expected to show a permanent loyalty to the nation which provided such poor fare for them and did not grant them tax exemption even when they served in the army.[22]

Not until September 3, 1814, was it possible to put into effect the military law designed by Boyen to draw every able-bodied male into the army, in the service of the fatherland. The institution of the Landwehr, first formed in East Prussia only, as well as of the Landsturm, was accepted by the Prussian government in March 1813; it called upon the provinces to organize these popular levies. All exemptions were abolished. Not without a great deal of persuasion from the civilian side was the King moved to admit the potentialities of the Landwehr in a popular war; and even Scharnhorst was slow to do so, for at bottom he could only imagine an army of regulars and had a low, and not entirely unjustified, opinion of the value of the American militia, as shown in the War of 1812.[23]

The Landwehr was officered by well-to-do and respected citizen volunteers or by ex-officers whom the Line could not absorb. The masses of the Prussian armies were supplied by the "freed" peasantry, whose ancient servitude was changed to a precarious liberty, with little protection against their former overlords, who repaid themselves for the loss of serf services by an enclosure of lands. Freed peasants supplied in general an obedient mass, though after some especially severe hardships, including bloody battles, they would revolt against their officers and mistreat them.

Thus the political question, who was to lead them, very early became acute in the military field, that is, within the Landwehr, an omen of the contest among the rural landlords, urban capitalists, and intelligentsia over leadership of the proletariat and peasantry in Prussia. This contest was outlined in the Landwehr edict of March 17, 1813, which declared in effect that owners of feudal estates and royal officials, unless elected officers of the Landwehr, in order to retain respect must not serve in it as privates or non-commissioned officers, but stay at home with the Landsturm instead.[24]

Some old officers thought it beneath their dignity to fight in the Landwehr as staff officers, side by side with men who were really civilians elected by their fellows. Others, with a more realistic Junker instinct, were determined to help prevent the Landwehr from turning into "a small burghers' club." [25] Generally the Junker officers of the regular army did their best to discredit the Landwehr formations, to attribute all successes to the regulars, to claim more distinctions and honors, and better quarters for themselves. So insistent were they that a cabinet order in 1815 had to censure their presumption and tell the regulars that Line and Landwehr were "equally brave and of equal birth." [26]

Actually the Landwehr, though very poorly equipped by the provincial Estates, managed, after the first inclinations to panic had been overcome, to satisfy the Prussian army reformers by its military services and value. Glad to have the army tripled by the Landwehr, and almost surprised to see that so many served "without any property and therefore without attachment to their fatherland," Blücher in his primitive way said of them: "The Landwehr battalions were only so-so at first; but once they had tasted plenty of powder, they did as well as the battalions of the Line." [27] On his part, Napoleon remained so much the *troupier* that he despised the Landwehr like any other kind of armed popular insurrection; this *"armée de mauvaises troupes"* would blow apart like dust; they seemed to him, or at least he denounced them as, dangerous to property—Jacobins, "apostles of all aims, who stir up the mob against the proprietors and are eager to exert the spirit of lawlessness." [28]

Before the war had gone very far, the Landsturm, regarded as the more elementary expression of the popular wrath against the French, had to be curtailed, particularly in its self-governing features, as well as in the tendency to equalize the burden of Landsturm duty irrespective of wealth and other distinctions. The higher bourgeoisie became frightened by the arms in the hands of the populace under elected leaders. The bureaucracy, whose egotism has rarely been surpassed outside Prussia, complained that it would have to face the lower classes as well as the enemy. And "what consequences would it have, if two hundred presidents, counselors, and assessors should be lost at once!" a high bureaucrat exclaimed, fretting about the Landsturm burdens put on his colleagues. The ministers instructed the police "to observe minutely the fermentation which the party spirit produces, and in particular those persons of whom it might be expected that they could endanger the state." [29]

The military value of the Landsturm cannot be said to have been very considerable; still, the fears that it aroused among many of the governors were "unspeakably great." [30] The treatment the most popular armed force received, even before Napoleon had been overcome, was prophetic of what would be the peacetime reward for the war services of the citizenry at large. The French Emperor, the revolutionary peril abroad, were hardly more dreaded by the governors of the time than a revolution at home, in Prussia no less than in England. While invasion threatened from the Camp of Boulogne, the Duke of Richmond wished to avoid as much as possible the distribution of pikes by the Ordnance Department, "thinking the introduction of them into the hands of the lower orders of the people, after the use that had been made of them in Ireland, a very dangerous measure." [31]

In the quest for man power and military efficiency, the Prussian reformers gave the artillery and the engineers the place to which they belonged, despite the antibourgeois ideas of the King and the Junkers. They had suffered in respect and in usefulness ever since Frederick had branded them with the charge that in the Seven Years' War they had merely tried to surpass one another in mistakes. Bent on winning wars, however, rather than maintaining class prestige, the reformers were quick to recognize the potentials of artillery and the engineers.

In keeping with the "popularization" of the army the Order of the Iron Cross was founded at the opening of the war against Napoleon. The Cross was to be given to everyone who distinguished himself during the war, either in the foreign field or at home. Everyone in this Order had, so to speak, to serve from the bottom up; only after having received the lower-class degree was a knight to rise to the higher ones. So much democratic illusion was found necessary even in Prussia. As the founding decree of the Iron Cross declared:

In the present great catastrophe in which everything is at stake for the Nation, the vigorous spirit which elevates the Nation so high deserves to be honored and perpetuated by quite peculiar monuments. That the perseverance by which the Nation endured the irresistible evils of an iron age did not shrink to timidity is proved by the high courage which now animates every breast and which could survive only because it was based on religion and true loyalty to King and Country.

In short, the Prussian bureaucracy, military and civilian, was at last convinced that the war could not be won without the active and loyal help of the people; that it was absolutely necessary, as Scharnhorst wrote to Stein, "to draw the people into your interest because a safe success could by no means be obtained through a standing army alone." Should the Landsturm prove worthless, it would at least "accustom languid people to the idea of defense, to an existence of he-men." [32]

Amid the work of reconstructing the social system and the army came the problem of supreme leadership in arms. The crowning irregularity of all war measures was, to the pedants in Prussia from the King down, the entrusting of the Prussian high command to Blücher, almost seventy years old, a reckless talker, a wild gambler, and a psychopath, visited by severe fits of senile melancholy and fancies. Time and again Blücher believed that, on account of his sins, he was pregnant with an elephant produced by a French soldier, as he told Wellington. At other times he thought the French had bribed his servants to heat his room so hot from under the floor that he would burn his feet unless he jumped or walked on the tips of his toes. Nevertheless, Scharnhorst thought that the old man was the only one to command Prussia's army, and told the King that, even with a thousand imagined elephants, Blücher must have the command. To a far slighter extent than Hindenburg was influenced by Ludendorff, the aged Blücher allowed himself to be guided by Gneisenau, his Quartermaster-General, but for his bolder proposals the inveterate gambler had always an open ear. [33]

The reformers recognized that the Prussian nation, nation though it scarcely was, needed at its head, if it was to follow their war cry, such a figure as Blücher, who was and looked the ancient hero, venerable and dashing at the same time. They pushed aside conventionalities, as Lincoln did when Grant was denounced to him as a drunkard, or like George II who, when told Wolfe was mad, hoped he would bite some of his other generals. Blücher was the true antagonist of Napoleon in a war that was, if not to end war, to end the demi-wargod who had destroyed—as it seemed, forever —prosperity, homes, and families. Now old Blücher went out against Napoleon with the Landwehr to make possible again those supreme elements of civil life whose values conservative statesmen and theorists were constantly emphasizing, whatever their own private behavior. In selecting Blücher and in other ways the reformers were opening the potentialities of irrationality in war, which the old kind of warmakers had tried to eliminate. They were ready to meet contingency by contingency, by more unconventionality. "War is always and everywhere a state of contingency," Gneisenau wrote the Prussian Prime Minister at the beginning of the campaign, "and good luck will have its share in it." [34]

In undertaking the War of Liberation the Prussian reformers took one last leaf out of Napoleon's book by deciding to make war without money. Clausewitz, invoking Guibert, whose prophecies Napoleon and France had fulfilled, had urged as early as 1812 that it could be done: "Formerly money was the nerve of war. It is no longer so." France, twice bankrupt, without a national treasury, had conquered without money. "Why should we not be able to do the same? What do we need money for? To pay the army wages? The army must be fed, and therefore does not need large pay; the little that is necessary the state will yet be able to afford and would have to procure in peacetime too. . . . No, since Guibert's prophecy is fulfilled, the time does not return when vain money is the nerve of war and of nations. The history of our own days proves that the most vigorous war can be conducted with little money but by plenty of courage and good will." Prussia need not wait for England's money to arrive.[35]

When the war came around, however, Prussia, in fact, still needed such subsidies. Her war treasury contained in March 1813 only three thousand thalers; pay remained in arrears for weeks. It was then rediscovered that what making war without money involves is really making war with bad money. Some reformers like Stein were eager to see Prussia enter upon a heavy inflation on this occasion in order to free landholders of their debts in the same way as the highly indebted Austrian nobility had recently re-established itself. This, however, was partly avoided by the sound money bureaucracy close to the banking capital in Prussia. Even so, in January 1813 paper money was issued which everybody was forced to accept at a fixed rate. The volunteers were expected to supply their own equipment with the exception of arms. The expense of fitting out the Landwehr was unloaded on the provincial Estates, which had regained some of their old importance in the adversity that had befallen the Prussian Crown.[36]

British Military Renovations

While the reconstruction of the Prussian army was, at least from the French point of view, revolutionary to some extent, British army institutions and forms of warfare remained frankly prerevolutionary, indeed counterrevolutionary. To combat the French forces more effectively, Whig notions of parliamentary control over army affairs were given a setback at the outset of 1793, when a permanent Commander-in-Chief, with the so-called Horse Guards as his office, was created by the side of the hitherto all-powerful Secretary-at-War, at the War Office. Through the Commander-in-Chief it was hoped to eliminate the jobbery of the political parties which centered around the Secretary-at-War, to establish a discipline even for officers, and incidentally to depoliticize them. After that the eighteenth-century type of officer, who held a commission in the army and was at the same time a member of Parliament, began to vanish. Ex-officers entered Parliament and officer politics took on new forms—extraparliamentary and so largely withdrawn from the public eye.

Faced with the dilemma of either allowing the members of the army to express their political opinions like their fellow-citizens and thus ruin discipline, or taking their political rights away, British parliamentarism preferred, as the lesser evil, to have the soldier— that is, largely the officer—nonpolitical. As Sir Robert Peel said later: "It would be utterly impossible to maintain discipline if soldiers were allowed to be political partisans, correspondents to newspapers, or members of political clubs. Then, indeed, a standing army would be in truth a curse; then might they bid farewell to civil liberty." [37]

One of the consequences of depoliticizing the British officer was his turning to militarism instead, at least potentially so; he became more inclined to place special military interests above general or civilian interests. This tendency was strengthened by other institutions, like those for military education and the Horse Guards. In 1794 a new secretary of state, the Secretary of State for War and Colonies, responsible to Parliament as far as military operations and related affairs were concerned, was set above the Secretary-at-War and the Commander-in-Chief. This official might have served to balance their powers had he not been too much absorbed by his colonial duties; but for a long time their powers remained to a large extent undefined. So this "dual control" of the British army led to constant interdepartmental strife, lasting well into the second half of the nineteenth century, in which the Horse Guards represented the military and the War Office the more civilian claims.[38] Bureaucratic rearrangements in part signified shifts in the power positions of the ruling classes in England after they went to war against the Revolution in 1793. In different ways they were meant to meet two revolutions: the industrial one at home and the military one abroad.

The military issue abroad England tried to meet by means largely taken from the arsenal of the eighteenth century. From the beginning to the end of the wars against the French, she paid in subsidies to her allies fully fifty-two million pounds. (Not until the Second World War and the "cold war" following it were subsidies —now going under names like "lend lease"—paid again on such a lavish scale.) In the eyes of many Englishmen this was far too much, but actually hardly more than an insurance premium when it is considered that the subsidies helped to keep Napoleon out of England and from wrecking it, as he did Germany. Germany suffered the more disastrous effects of the wars, while England was able to forge ahead with her industrial revolution.

Since it was evident that the industrial development, trade, merchant marine, and navy needed many hands, and hands were therefore scarcer for the army, English statesmen thought that they could neither afford nor dare to send as many men into the field as the Continental armies numbered. The British soldier remained an expensive article whose price advanced despite the growth of population which, in England alone, rose from 6,000,000 in 1750 to 7.2 in 1770, to 8.9 in 1801, and to 10.1 millions in 1811.

Realization of the cost kept the English statesmen and generals from laying heavier claims upon the mounting population. While it was possible to raise men by general conscription, the change might have induced the dreaded revolution. Instead, therefore, they turned to the heavy war expenditure of eight hundred and thirty million pounds, of which 6½ per cent went as subsidies to Continental allies.[39] This meant paying for British soldiers and the foreign soldiers, and buying off a domestic revolution which could not have been restricted to the field of military policy, if conscription had been attempted.

For such reasons the soldier supply remained largely the same as in the eighteenth century. The citizenry did not go to war, neither did the industrial wage earner. Yet child labor appeared in the army as well as in the industries, as if in emulation of the gentry, whose younger sons went into the army. In 1815, three battalions of the guards contained four hundred men too young and weak for service in the field; one regiment had to wait for active work till the boys in its ranks, both officers and men, had aged, indicating the scarcity value of the British soldier.[40]

In the field, the nature of the British soldiery kept the generals from applying the column tactics of Napoleon, which the Continentals often took over from him although it appeared a clumsy and expensive formation to Wellington. The latter's tactics were Frederician, tempered not by a humanitarian consideration of men, but by an essentially economic and technological appreciation of their scarcity value—a thing which Pitt, for instance, had never grasped when he squandered men on tropical expeditions. Wellington finally carried out the long-recommended change from the three-deep line to one only two-deep, giving a maximum firing efficiency to closed formations. In the old line the fire of the third man had been almost lost and, in the column of divisions, seven-ninths of the men had been unable to use their muskets.[41]

To protect this infantry from the generally superior French artillery, Wellington took great care to have it hidden as long as possible—screened before the moment of actual clash on the slopes or in woods; he also had his infantry well covered on its flanks with the help of natural surroundings or by cavalry and in front by a line of skirmishers who would block the French *tirailleurs*. This light infantry, a modern element which the English had been forced to introduce in the American theater of war and had thereafter dissolved or forgotten, was reintroduced reluctantly in 1798. In that year the first green-coated British rifle battalion was founded; others followed, mainly German in composition. The British men still deepest in the feudal nexus, such as Highlanders, showed little inclination to give up their custom of standing shoulder to shoulder, even where it was most out of place as in street fighting.

Soldiers from the British Isles—only twenty-five thousand strong at Waterloo—were unshakable in battle, where they were controlled by the officers every minute; but they were little fit for skirmishing or outpost duty, or pursuit on a large scale to rout an enemy, partly on account of their habit of engaging in immediate plundering. After Waterloo the British soldier rested on his arms, whereas the Prussians, under Gneisenau's own command, making use of the new energies, completed the defeat of Napoleon by a merciless pursuit far into the night, and captured innumerable trophies. Whereas the English mercenaries plundered ruthlessly even in cities of friendly powers, the needy Prussians, embracing the Napoleonic policy of reparations, in addition insisted on contributions and other payments from France after victory, regardless of the odium which such extortions might throw on the Bourbons, whom the Allies wanted to see re-established in Paris.

Wellington's organization and use of his army mark in many ways the ultimate perfection of eighteenth-century warfare. The high point was Waterloo. He made the infantry into a precise firing body, and, as might be expected from the general of a country then making the greatest industrial progress, most effectively turned men into machines, according to the eighteenth-century idea of the *homme machine*. However, he had not taken the further step to the new, progressive, liberal notion of putting machines in place of men in order to heighten the effect of their numbers. The Duke's use of men was still basically that of the employer of rural labor, growing scarcer at that time, but the main source of his supply; he did not have the mentality of the industrial employer.

To Wellington, the infantry was the measure of all things. Despite his countrymen's bent for mechanics, he had little understanding of artillery and its specific functions and possibilities; he did not respect engineers and appreciate discoveries, such as Congreve's rocket, a battery of which, doing great work, represented English war technology in the battle of the Nations at Leipzig.[42] In other words, the English army, at a time when urban energies were turning to industries, was left to the care and handling of officers from the rural governing classes, who managed to use an antiquated army device effectively against the by now war-worn troops of Napoleon.

Wellington and most of his officers were Tories, though the apparition of a Whig and almost liberal general, like Thomas Graham, emerged on occasion. The army had been forced to admit many "undesirable elements" among the officers, but the most undesirable were weeded out by court martial. In the main, the governing type was still the officer supplied by the rural gentry. Officers from this class, as an officer of the Rifle Brigade observed, "were able to secure more willing obedience with less effort than others," born as they were into the habit of command and authority.

The honor arrangements in the army commanded by Wellington were generally in favor of those already privileged by birth or in other ways, such as the Guards. As a colonel serving under him complained, "The Duke was occasionally not above writing in his dispatches to please the aristocracy. . . . It used to be a common thing with general officers." This was merely one method used by the classes ruling Britain to deprecate the services of those without whom, under the stress of the times, they could not manage war. Soon after 1815 officers' commissions as a common thing reverted to the class which had held them before the Napoleonic disturbances, the younger sons of the landed gentry.[43]

Even after 1815, under a regulation dating from the days of Charles II, soldiers remained excluded from public parks and gardens in London.[44] England was most reluctant in granting mass honor. The soldiers had small thanks for having fought for the preservation of the gentlemen which, according to Sir John Fortescue, was Wellington's basic aim in the war against Napoleon. "He believed in the England that produced such gentlemen and was resolved to save her and them. He took over his army as an instrument to that end, just as an engineer might take over a gang of labourers to dig a canal, having no love for the gang itself, but determined to make the best of it as a matter of duty. . . . When his purpose was fulfilled, he threw the instrument aside without compunction, having no further use for it and little or no sentiment about it." [45] This is to say that Wellington was a Tory and not primarily a military man, and least so in peacetime.[46]

Coalition Policies and the Austrian Way

The wars against Napoleon were, of necessity, coalition wars, and all the problems of co-operation among allies in the conduct of warfare arose to vex the directors of operations. Then became evident the importance of the civil objective, hitherto hidden amid the smoke of battle. At bottom the Allies against Napoleon were divided in policy and over the conception of the kind of European order to be desired at the end of the conflict. Not even a will to annihilate Napoleon provided a common denominator for all endeavors from the beginning to the end.

For the longest time Austria was willing to see him conquered, but not annihilated, conquered in the eighteenth-century style of moderate policy and warfare, which received its stamp from the tendency to restore the balance of power in Europe. Austria's military endeavors were directly conditioned by Metternich's policy of the restoration of Europe to a balanced unity, receptive even to a chastened Napoleon. As late as March 1814 Metternich secretly advised Napoleon that, without Austria's protracting endeavors, the Allies would have proceeded to extreme measures. As against the kind of warfare and war aims the Prussian Jacobins were pursuing, Metternich and Gentz, who wanted to preserve Austria from being wrecked by the nationalism of her component parts, were anxious lest "the war of Liberation should become not unlike a war of liberty, that the downfall of a despotism, instead of bringing about a real Restoration, might lead to another Revolution." [47]

In complete subservience to Metternich's policy of preventing victory from becoming too overwhelming, the Austrian way of warfare reverted to eighteenth-century ideas of strategy; it overestimated the importance of strategic points and positions, like the plateau of Langres, which the reactionaries of Austria and Prussia thought should be the final objective. There the armies were to remain because, as an Old Prussian member of this school declared, "beyond Chalons and Troyes it would become impossible to determine any one obtainable object as aim and limit of the operations." Therefore the Allies should remain at this place and leave the initiative to the enemy, who, it was expected, would not dare to attack such a domineering position, but would rather accept a tolerable peace. Yet, much to the chagrin of the theoreticians, Napoleon left the region of Langres severely alone.

So close, so subservient to the spirit and aims of diplomacy had warfare become that it was impossible for the Austrian generals, as the English representative in the Allied headquarters observed, to do without complicated marches and laborious maneuvers in order to turn the flank of positions that were not occupied and get across hills and rivers that were not defended. The Russian Chief of Staff did not know of a single case "where a disposition which originated among Austrian generals would have led our troops on the shortest way against the enemy. And still it is well enough to know that quickness in movement prepares success." [48]

In contrast to the Austrians, Prussians such as Gneisenau and Blücher were more filled with the Napoleonic spirit and drove toward Paris "with such a truly childish fury," as Schwarzenberg, the Austrian and Allied Supreme Commander, complained. "They trample with their feet on all rules of war. Without concerning themselves with their back and flanks, they only make plans for *parties fines* in the Palais Royal; that is really miserable in such an important movement as this." The Austrians even allowed themselves to be frightened by Napoleon's threats that the English policy against him and the hatred of Czar Alexander for him might lead to a return of the Jacobins in France.[49]

The Austrians had to be told the obvious thing by the Russians, speaking through another Corsican, Pozzo di Borgo: "While the war is unfinished it is impossible to decide whether its aim has been reached; rather, as long as it lasts, its results remain dependent upon the success of the aims. Only if this principle is adhered to can the Allied Powers hope to see their views accomplished. They must endeavor to destroy the war power of the enemy," and in a hurry at that, lest Napoleon recuperate his strength too quickly, and behold his only chances in the disunion of the Allies.[50]

Their mixture of civil and military policy came close to reintroducing toward the end the cordon system of the First War of the Coalition against the Revolution—a front of over two hundred miles in length from Holland to southern France—after they had crossed the Rhine. Again in Belgium in 1815 the double command of the Allies, nearly twice as strong as the French, gave Napoleon almost his only chance of victory. He threw himself between the two, and first upon the Prussians. After Ligny, he sent part of his troops under Grouchy in vain pursuit of the beaten Prussians eastward, where he insisted they had marched off. Actually, instead of clinging to their line of retreat toward their own boundaries, they went to join Wellington. "These animals have learned something," admitted Napoleon, if contemptuously. Waterloo marked clearly the decline of Napoleon's strategy; there nearly one-third of his strength was absent and could not be thrown into the scales of the final decision. Moreover, this third was kept away by an enemy force of only half its strength.[51]

The difficulties involved in coalition warfare were many in the wars from 1813 to 1815. They were largely caused by the divergences of opinion about the degree to which Napoleon ought to

be beaten. Nevertheless, Katzbach and Waterloo, and to a somewhat lesser degree Leipzig, demonstrated successes which could be
achieved by and in spite of coalition warfare. To its inherent difficulties a new one was added during these wars, the difficulty created
by mobilized nationalism, excited rather by the armies than by the
diplomacies whose war aims against Napoleon were so different.
Nationalism made an army like the Prussian self-willed and insistent upon separation from the command of nonnationals, if only
in part.

Such separation of all Prussian troops was urged upon the King
by Gneisenau at the time the Inter-Allied War Plan of Trachenberg
was devised. "They would inexorably have to share the blame of a
possible defeat with other troops; on the other hand the Prussian
name would never be mentioned in case of a victory, even though
by now 250,000 of Your Majesty's subjects carry arms. The national honor would thus be mortified, or the feeling for it weakened." [52] This was in substance the problem which the Americans
long afterward faced when they entered the world wars; Pershing
advocated solving it in the same way and for the same reasons
employed by Gneisenau a little over a hundred years before, and
the Second World War, though the best fought of all wars of coalition, brought it up once more.

The "despotism of diplomats," as Blücher called their constant
interference in warfare,[53] had to wait till after victory, which they
had retarded, was completed. Only then could it exert full sway.
Not before that day could the diplomats follow their desire to re-
introduce order and stability into the immense disorder of Europe
—a disorder that had been so much heightened by the levies of
the masses. All through the war their desire had been directly reflected in the military thought of the conservatives on their side.
When Moreau, who fought his old rival Napoleon in the camp of
the Allies, saw at Dresden the great bodies of troops assembling
and being ordered, he said that the direction of such masses seemed
to surpass the abilities of the human spirit.[54] Neither he, once a
revolutionary general, nor the generals closest to the Allied sovereigns, could admit the working of any moral self-directing forces
in those masses, capable of helping to overcome the technical difficulties of military control.

Out of the masses came the urge, voiced by Gneisenau, "to hang
the Emperor," [55] and inflict on France annexations, reparations,
humiliations, in order to obtain "security against the restless spirit
of a wicked though able and brave nation." [56] From 1813 to 1815
France had to pay for the maintenance of the Allied armies, for
contributions, claims, and other purposes 1,659 million francs—a
sum still somewhat less than 10 per cent of the total of Napoleon's

extortions.[57] The reduction of France in territory and consequently in population seemed to the Allies the right way to restore the equilibrium in numbers which France had disturbed by her conquests since the reign of Louis XIV. The Prussian army, chief sufferer among the Allies, called on the King and Hardenberg, the Prime Minister, to hold out for better conditions for Prussia. Blücher's great popularity was used to strengthen this pressure. He resigned his command in a demonstrative way, assured, as a Prussian officer confided to an Englishman, that the Prussian army and the Prussian people approved so unanimously of Blücher's opinions that the King would hardly dare to accept his resignation.[58]

To the very end, the language of the peacemakers was disagreeable to the military men. As they understood it, the diplomat was saying to the soldier: "Friend, you are a coarse fellow who does not know how to treat people. The diplomats are much better educated than you, and want to be spoken to in well-rounded phrases. You only know how to speak with cannon. Shut up then. We shall take care of you, so that you need not run around in rags any longer, and perhaps you will get a viaticum." [59] By the public willfulness of the Prussian Jacobins, as obstinate as the French Jacobins, little inclined "to go home and commence a civil life," Castlereagh and Metternich thought,[60] their own King felt humiliated and justified in his steadily closer adherence to the Holy Alliance and his own Old Prussians. He confided to the Russians his fears of their reformist policies and his determination to get rid of them when the proper time arrived. Yet he rewarded them rather royally and better than most of the Allies treated their generals.

In the struggle for political influence over the King, the reformers were defeated by the reaction within Prussia and without, and henceforth were restricted to the purely military field. They had to be satisfied, for the time being, with the territorial gains obtained for Prussia at the Congress of Vienna, together with the acquisition, specially demanded by the army, of the town of Suhl, the seat of the largest German arms factories. They had to let pass the moment when the sword could be drawn against Prussia's so-called friends, when at certain moments of the Vienna Congress Gneisenau seemed ready to shake hands with the devil Napoleon and to revolutionize the nationalities of Austria-Hungary and undertake other Prussian steps in the direction of a German nation.[61] But the expansion of Prussia in Germany, of which Metternich forced a postponement, particularly upon the Prussian military, was clearly forecast by their demands for Prussia's military defense system. This, as conceived by Grolman, to be the first chief of the future general staff, ran on its western side from the Fichtelgebirge north to the Weser: "All the states enclosed within this line Prussia must forever consider as belonging to her, and their acquisition must never be lost sight of." [62]

So at the end it was evident that the French Revolution and Napoleon had called forth a nationalist mass army to oppose their mass army; a kind of revolution from the top had been made in Prussia, and men of military discipline and aims had been raised to high places, thrown into competition with the feudal reactionaries, and set on the way to their test of militarism. But in Prussia as well as in the other countries of the coalition the one great danger that conservative statesmen had stood in awe of—that the Revolution might get hold of war[63]—was averted in the end, at least for 125 years.

THE DEVELOPMENT AND MILITARIZATION OF MASS ARMIES

For a hundred years after the overthrow of Napoleon, Europe was spared another general conflagration. Wars, to be sure, were fought, within and between nations and on the borders of expanding empires overseas. There were domestic wars of nationalism to establish or perfect national unities—in Germany, Italy, and the United States. Britain, France, Sardinia, and Turkey waged war on Russia in the Crimea. France and then Prussia waged war on Austria. Prussia and France girded themselves for the conflict of 1870-1. But, although the Civil War in the United States became a war of conscripted men, none of the struggles in Europe evoked such mass energies as had the wars of the French Revolution and the Napoleonic period. On the whole the time following the Restoration in 1815 and closing only with the Great War of 1914 was one of relative quiet. Between Waterloo and Marne stretched a dull period of tranquillity, designated scornfully by a French general as a "halt in the mud."

This peace permitted what appeared to be enormous strides for liberalism. The unparalleled expansion of world industry and commerce brought about by the mechanical inventions of the modern era, created a widespread wealth in the business class which enabled its possessors to win greater influence in governments. The political rise of the bourgeois was shared by masses below him to some extent in most Western lands. The suffrage was extended in the states of the American Union, in Great Britain, and in France. Serfs were liberated in Russia and slaves emancipated in America. Constitutions were set up in Italy and the Austro-Hungarian Em-

6
The Consolidation of Military Forces

pire. Under the constitutions of the North German Federation and of the Reich, equal manhood suffrage, paralleling "equal" military duty, was granted by Bismarck.

Although such brilliant progress in democracy and representative government seemed recorded with every decade, the period also witnessed a less evident but none the less real advance and consolidation of military power. This, ironically enough, was also made possible by the prolonged peace. Since there was no shake-up in the officer bodies through war, promotion was slowed down to a snail's pace, and many an officer in every army bewailed his inglorious drudgery as "a Danaïd business, eternal preparation and no deed." [1] A decided hardening of the arteries was the result in the general staffs, evidenced in their reluctance to consider technological innovations; how utterly averse they were to changes in material was discovered to their great chagrin by industrialists like Colt, Krupp, and Whitworth, and the military inventor and officer Werner Siemens grew so disgusted with the Prussian service that he gave it up to go into industry. Especially in the first part of the nineteenth century, before Moltke and Grant, the officer remained a sheer romantic in the industrial age.

Aloof from the technical and economic transformations about him, he was also socially remote from the rising bourgeois. Generally the officer who set the tone was the son of the classes of reaction, the large landowners, in the German states, in England, in Russia, France, and the southern states of America. Such men were filled with notions of false feudalism; though most had become officials with regular salaries, they pretended not to be bureaucrats but knights; in the partly restored state of Burke's "knights and saints," they claimed to be the "saints and martyrs of the religion of honor." [2] Not only was the officer largely of the agrarian class, but the soldier material was rural to a surprising degree, in Russia and Austria naturally, somewhat less in France and Prussia, but decidedly so in England, where the army wanted "respectable, docile country lads, brought up by careful, thrifty parents in a decent cottage home." [3] At bottom the army wanted no others, though they pretended it was because the health of urban workers was often too poor for service.[4]

To a very large extent the history of this postwar militarism is again identical with the history of postfeudal nobility everywhere, even in America in the first part of the century, where the visiting Tocqueville found "some loose notions of the old aristocratic honour," [5] and where they were especially strong among the southern plantocracy. The armies were the mainstay of large-scale agriculture which, without the chance to provide grain and mounts to them and to place the younger sons in army and other governmental employs, would in many places have crumbled under the impact of industrialism. The classes from which officers sprang, in Europe, were favored by Corn Laws and other measures, showing that the agrarian still exacted a price from society for his martial aid. With so little interpenetration of the bourgeois and military classes, it was possible for the latter to maintain the attitude of superiority which it had worn since medieval days. But this pride was not based on exactly the same points as before; it could not be so exclusive, the prerogative only of high birth, since so many bourgeois had joined the officer corps, even though social leadership might be in the hands of noblemen. A new type, an assimilating pride, was discovered in the doctrine of *race*. A member of the old French nobility *de race*, Comte de Gobineau, in his essay on the *Inequality of Races* (1853-5) in a way feudalized Darwinism, conceding good race to certain masses who were thereby set above other, inferior masses. These former were declared to constitute an aristocracy of breed, if not of birth; inevitably the best born, the oldest nobility, became or remained the leaders under this new scheme of things.

The race theory counteracted the class theory, which was then menacing the older order and making labor and the middle classes self-conscious, impatient with the pretensions of landed gentry. Gobineau and his followers effaced class lines to some extent by extending their pride to the masses, admitting them into the pseudo-nobility of race; they became the more eager supporters of the leaders of the race in warfare against other races. In effect, this was promising to let the crowds in "on the ground floor" while conducting them to an empty top attic.

The militant menace inherent in the race theory was first exemplified on a large scale in the United States, where the southern planters, not born of high lineage but self-made "aristocrats," extended their pride, the pride of membership in the "white race," to the poor whites, thus solidifying elements otherwise furiously antagonistic to them in the Civil War. This lasted until the stark realities of class tore asunder the poor whites and rich whites—an experience which does not speak for the permanent effectiveness of race theories in war.

During the period under review, accordingly, militarism and liberalism grew up side by side, as bourgeois enriched himself and officer entrenched himself. Neither element made trial of the other's strength; but though the nobility recognized and feared the growth of liberalism and sought constantly to hinder it, the liberals tended to ignore the military problem and left the conduct of military affairs carelessly in other hands.

Democracy Evolves No Philosophy or Agencies of Control Over the Military

Although wars often enriched the bourgeois and gave employment to artisans, neither class looked upon war as a regular occupation or a main source of prosperity; their pursuits and interests were in the main those of peace, for only a small percentage of industry's products at that time were sold to military establishments. Their pamphleteers and publicists generally agreed that war was a threat, and control of the military by civil policy an essential of security and progress. With great elaboration, Herbert Spencer, in his *Principles of Sociology*, placed the industrial type of society high above the militant, in the scale of morals as well as economy. When the sanction of hard-headed economists was thus added to that of Christian pacifism, expressed in plans for perpetual peace, the movement for the outlawing of war was accelerated.

Though agreed on general theory, the bourgeois developed neither the political philosophy nor the practical agencies required to put their views into effect. Their spokesmen rarely approached military questions as experts; scarcely one of them ever took the trouble, which should not have been prohibitive, to acquaint himself with such matters, except from the side of budgeting. The one specialist among the English radicals was Joseph Hume, who had served as an army doctor; the only experts on military questions to be found in the Frankfurt Parliament of 1848, which wanted to see Germany defended but not constituted as a military state, were Rightists —former officers. The usual proposals of liberalism for the best constitution in armies was the national militia with elected officers as the ideal arrangement; and as the more immediate practical plan, a reduction of existing armies to a smaller scale than conservatives and armies themselves wished to concede.[6]

The typical underlying conviction was one inherited from British party politics of the eighteenth century, generally Whiggish, that "a numerous class of warriors and the institution of a standing army cannot *per se* be very compatible with a constitutional monarchy." [7] Liberalism sought to extend law over the whole military body, partly by making ministers of war responsible to Parliament, partly by dividing departments under Secretaries of War and at War, Masters General of Ordnance, and the Exchequer, to check and balance the army force; another device was setting Landwehr against regular army. Even at that, the suspicion or belief of liberals continued that "a standing army can never be turned into a moral institution" (Gladstone).

The first man in Great Britain to set himself up as a watchdog for budgetary control over military expenditure—which the corruption of the old party system had left as a source to feed its dependents—was the Scotsman Hume. In Parliament after 1818 he applied principles of household economy to a branch which gentlemen, up to that time, looked upon as their proper spoil to be divided without reckoning. This was resented by the majority, including that most "romantic" and most indebted Scotsman of the time, Sir Walter Scott, who called Hume the night watchman trying to make a living on diminutive abuses.[8] His own army service had given Hume a unique insight into the behavior of officers, particularly the wealthy, many of whom he had observed in India shirking their unpleasant duties. Besides, Hume had a sincere interest in the well-being of the British soldier.[9]

The most "practical" demand of liberals usually was for retrenchment—reducing the establishment and the budget; they were well aware that this meant curtailing that part of the people's money which went to conservative political enemies who still had the army in their hands. Generally, the liberals accompanied the downward turn of the business cycle with a cry for retrenchment, whereas the military and their friends in Parliament promptly greeted the upturns with demands for higher budgets. If the international situation was not too ominous, each party usually had its wish fulfilled, at least in England where the army was most exposed to the vicissitudes of business life. As Joseph Hume complained in 1826, after an economic crisis had arrived: "In 1823, the army was 59,100. Unfortunately, about this period the price of corn advanced, affairs wore a more cheerful aspect, the poor were better employed, and ministers did not lose the opportunity of augmenting the military establishments. Since then, the numbers have been swelled and the expense increased; in 1824, the number of men was 73,000 and in 1825, 86,438." [10]

The traditional liberal argument was based on the view that English liberties flourished best with the smallest standing army. This contention the Tories tried to counter by calling the army, as it existed or was desired, "a protection rather than any detriment to Liberty. We permitted a licentiousness which under any other constitution might be fatal to the public peace. Meetings were held and language was used which no other empire would permit and which nothing but the confidence of the Crown in the Standing Army would justify even our Government in permitting." [11]

But this argument could not long survive the introduction of the police in England. In granting military bills liberals were ordinarily more reluctant to allot funds for soldiers, who would be taken off the labor market, than to vote money for tangible goods. Instead of seeking to put the army on a popular footing, however, liberals were inclined to furnish money for guns that could be stored, fortifications that could be built and seen, even if they were never finished, and other material things.

When Palmerston raised the scare of a French invasion and recommended strengthening the army, Peel, who was closer to the industries, answered that the country could not support a large standing army, but he devoted one million pounds to fortifying arsenals and dockyards. Work was started in fourteen different places without achieving anything useful. The outcome was such that two forts, for instance, were equipped with 339 and 175 guns, respectively, and had only half a man to each gun; one foreign station in 1847 had 335 guns and a garrison which when complete contained only half as many men.[12]

The fateful character of the constant rise in army expenditures, due to the as yet minor technical improvements in arms and other equipment and increasing sales pressure, led the Cobden-Bright group to present their peace proposals: arbitration and disarmament. Without these, Cobden pointed out, there could be "no necessary or logical end to the increase of our establishments; for the progress of scientific knowledge will lead to a constant increase of expenditure. There is no limit but the limit of taxation." [13] But this was in fact widened far beyond what Cobden would have deemed the limit.

The civil liberties to which liberalism aspired, however, did suffer certain restrictions among the armed forces and with the acquiescence of liberals as a rule. Some or all of these liberties were curtailed for military men in one or other of the following ways: (1) emigration without permission, on the part of persons liable to military duty, was considered desertion in most countries with general conscription, though the degree to which the allegiance of the emigrant for his home country was claimed varied from country to country and from time to time; (2) most armies demanded a permit from the authorities before officers or men could marry; (3) most armies forbade the membership of military persons in political societies; the right of assembly and of union was very much curtailed for soldiers if not strictly forbidden. English Army Regulations of 1868, for instance, forbade members of the army "to institute or take part in any meetings, demonstrations, or processions for party or political purposes in barracks, quarters, camps, or elsewhere." (4) Most armies forbade their active members to engage in any private business.[14]

Against the onrush of liberalism the parties and groups on the defensive could not, especially between wars, present much evidence to prove their superior competence in military affairs, except their past record. Their usual demands for improvements laid before the respective parliaments amounted either to the essential preservation of institutions, like corporal punishment in the British army, or were merely quantitative, not fundamental, improvements. The only important change which Wellington, in his later years, seems to have sponsored was a project for an increase in the army. In such proposals, even if they were declared to be for the "betterment of the King's Service," liberals could detect nothing but an attempt at helping the landed gentry, who had suffered considerably owing to the repeal of the Corn Laws. As a Berlin liberal said under similar conditions: "The military aristocracy wants *itself*, nothing else." [15] The true meaning of *"noblesse oblige,"* Napoleon III cynically remarked, was still *"noblesse exempte."*

There was nothing in England's army which could have convinced liberals, if they had been interested in such things, that it was progressive and primarily concerned in the military way as distinguished from the militaristic way. It was an institution preserved by Wellington and his authority on the *status quo* of Waterloo, in point of equipment, drill, discipline, trains, and origin and education of officers and men. When finally the criticism of Hume and Cobden induced the Horse Guards, the authority of command, to order that ensigns and lieutenants in the future undergo an examination before receiving promotion, the order came so late that it was received with derision on account of its tardy and rather perfunctory character.[16]

In Prussia such liberalism as appeared was concerned with the composition of the army rather than control over it. Men like Boyen and Schön were wholly free from the "demagogue baiting" of their time—the panicky fear and persecution of liberals in Prussia and Germany. They trusted the Landwehr as a military value and did not share the dread of its revolutionary potentialities which filled the reactionaries. Even Clausewitz, more conservative in politics than they, after weighing the pros and cons of the Landwehr, and examining the question whether an invasion or a revolution was a more serious danger to Prussia, approved it. True, he wrote in 1819 that in times of internal commotions and resistance on the part of the lower classes, and after all means of persuasion have been used in vain, governments must be prepared to consider the sword as the *ultima ratio* of the right; the sword is a weak support if the government is not the only sword bearer. But he also thought that if it be in some respects dangerous to have a people in arms, it is much more risky to govern over an unarmed one. The Landwehr as the armed nation makes possible a resistance against invasions from the outside, which no standing army can effect. Whatever the army institutions, force never can be maintained as cheaply as through the Landwehr system. The Landwehr adds to the danger of a revolution: disarmament of the people to the danger of inva-

sion. The latter risk Germany had often known, the former not.[17]
Thus the difference of opinion about the revolutionary character
of the Landwehr at bottom divided military reformers and reactionaries in Prussia.

Under no circumstances were these reformers willing to let the
masses, least of all the bourgeoisie, revert to their eighteenth-century
relation to the army and war. They observed that, though the willingness of the rank and file to serve had not grown, the discipline
of those once in the army was improving as the industries developed. Through the disciplining processes of the army passed a
larger part of the soldiers in Prussia than in those more industrial-
ized countries where the true factory worker did not go into the
army at all, but rather left that service to the poor misfits of town
and rural regions. With good reason did Clausewitz insist that war
must be made "with the whole weight of the national power." The
reformers were the most nationalistic group in the army, mainly
because "national feeling," together with the talents of the commander and the military virtue of the army, formed, according to
Clausewitz, the chief quality for war.

In appreciating the military utility of the civilian part of the
Prussian reforms since 1807, Boyen and his friends probably relied
far too much on the availability and usefulness, and on the energies
and power tendencies, of the rising bourgeois. Eager as the latter
were for more freedom in their economic pursuits, they were lacking in their understanding of the role of power, particularly in a
state like Prussia, and they failed to maintain and widen avenues
to liberties. To the bourgeois, military duties in the army and the
Landwehr were a physical nuisance and a direct loss of money; the
artisan, merchant, industrialist, busy throughout the year, were in
fact more hurt by their Landwehr duties than the landowners and
other rural inhabitants, whose seasonal occupation made it easy to
arrange convenient dates for the Landwehr exercises. Furthermore
the Prussian army, in the strength which Boyen and his friends
thought necessary, formed a terrific financial burden for all classes.
For the year 1816 the War Minister demanded no less than 28,000,-
000 thalers whereas the Minister of Finance estimated the total state
income at 45,000,000 at the utmost, and only granted 19,000,000
for the army; for 1817 the army expenditure amounted to 26,000,-
000, more than half of Prussia's total budget.[18]

All this assisted the Prussian aristocrats in their reactionary movement against the Landwehr, which they feared as "the most important lever for the emancipation of the middle classes." They
were willing to lighten the military burdens and thus renounce
Prussia's military potency and with it her influence in foreign politics, which the reformers had wanted to assure by putting a high

strain on her resources; in so doing, they could restore the ancient influence of the nobility in the state and the army. Class privilege they valued higher than military efficiency and potentialities. Above all they wanted to see the Landwehr atrophy, because such a militia might mean arming the nation for resistance and revolution. They insisted that conscription in the long run was incompatible with the monarchical principle, based as the latter was on honor, rank, nobility, privilege, and that it was also inimical to military discipline, said to be endangered by the intermixture and equalization of the classes. They even pointed to the conservative peace doctrines of the Holy Alliance, based on Christian teachings of love, as forbidding such a force as Prussia maintained by spending about one-half of her total income on the army, as against one-sixth in Austria, one-fourth in Bavaria, one-third in Württemberg, and one-ninth in Baden, the most liberal of all the German states.[19]

In France, as in England and Germany, confusion rather than clarification was the characteristic in military policies. In their opinions, military men as well as politicians were divided. Survivors of the Emperor's wars cherished memories of bygone glories and hated the Bourbon defenders. Politicians were split up into factions— Bourbons, Bonapartists, Liberals, and Republicans. In deference to bourgeois wishes, which coincided with those of the nobility, the dangerous conscription was abolished by the Charter of 1814. But all Frenchmen were declared equal before the law and "equally admissible to civil and military employments." Similar provisions were made in the later constitutions, that after the upheaval of 1848 saying: "Citizens ought to love the fatherland, to serve the Republic, and to defend it at the price of their lives"; that "every Frenchman, with the exceptions fixed by law, owes service to the army and National Guard"—to be organized by law.

The French bourgeoisie understood this as giving it freedom from army duty. Although French generals after 1815 were constantly pleading for actual conscription, urging upon industrialists that "French youth would learn the habit of order and subordination" in the army,[20] the system of *remplaçants,* so agreeable to bourgeois tastes, was kept up. Those who could pay for substitutes might go to agents who made a business of providing such men, and the insurance companies covered the risk of being called to the colors.[21] So long as this liberty was purchasable the comfortable civilians were not interested in real army reorganization or even in civilian control over it. It was with the aid of the army that Louis Napoleon, as Napoleon the Third—or as Hitler the First— transformed himself into an Emperor, richly recompensing the generals who had helped him up. He made them marshals "in consideration of the ability and courage deployed in the defense of order." This nomination of field marshals for services not in the field of war but in assisting a putsch regime set a precedent not followed again until Hitler elevated Von Blomberg.

In the main, the army of the Empire that was to be dedicated to peace—*"l'Empire c'est la paix"*—was dedicated to its own advancement. It remained in the hands of conservative, especially landed families, and those sons of rich bourgeois who joined it were eager to conform to traditions. With all their lust for power, the bourgeois of France, as everywhere else, refused to grapple with militarism.

That the bourgeois, despite their plans for peace, were really not at bottom averse to war, but might at times express war emotions more violently than the true soldier, was demonstrated in England, apparently the least militaristic of countries. There Palmerston employed "spirited foreign policies" partly to allay domestic discontent and stall reforms. His crowning performance was the Crimean War, a by-product of the industrial revolution, which had produced social toxins to plague the foremost of industrial nations. This opened an era of "national" wars about which Moltke wrote:

It is no longer the ambition of princes; it is the moods of the people, the discomfort in the face of interior conditions, the doings of parties, particularly of their leaders, which endanger peace. The great battles of recent history have started against the wish and the will of the governors. The Exchange has obtained in our days an influence which is able to call the armed forces into the field for their interest.[22]

In Britain the sting of the epithet "nation of shopkeepers," was only *now* being felt, after nearly forty years of peace, which at last began to seem ignominious. As a *Times* editor declared: "This nation is a good deal enervated by a long peace, by easy habits of intercourse, by peace societies, and false economy." [23] As they began to yearn for a more romantic action, to revive the knightly qualities which had been submerged in commercialization, the public was delighted when its statesmen challenged foreign nations, or their diplomacies. Both wish and fear were interwoven with the dream of a French invasion of England, evoked by the figure of Napoleon III. Judged by the new sentiments which filled it, the Englishman's home became indeed a castle—hardly well enough fortified by nature, Palmerston thought—within which the Nevil Beauchamps penned personal taunts to French statesmen by way of throwing down gauntlets. In this mental state of Englishmen, the Crimean War was a relief: they were going to undertake a crusade and, to make more complete the irony to which they were impervious, it was to be a crusade for the protection of the Saracen himself. War with such an ally, writers urged, would bring forth "the most heroic and Christian virtues in every citizen." [24]

As a matter of fact, the choice of an enemy against whom this emotionalism might find vent was rather fortuitous. It took a long time for the tide of British war lust to turn against the Russians rather than the French and Napoleon III, who was suspected of seeking "revenge for Waterloo." Finally the Czar won the ambivalent British hatred. Judging from the measure of the pent-up feelings in England, the Crimean War was not, as Disraeli said, "a just but unnecessary war"—rather was it a necessary but unjust war. It was also a war of the middle classes caught between the two peace schools: the Manchester school of free-trade pacifism and the Conservative school of peace-by-diplomacy. Least of all was it a war desired by the British army.

The army had not been constructed for any war with such a foe as Russia. It was scarcely designed for any war at all except within the Empire. It was still left as it had been in the era of Restoration policy which Canning had discarded for England, that is, it was not planned as a competing force. As Charles Butler said in 1839, the military arrangements were utterly at variance with England's foreign relations; no government had "ever consented to admit in practice that foreign affairs have anything to do with military policy. Military men have said for years: 'Tell us for what purposes you keep an army, and we will tell you of what strength it should be and in what manner it should be trained'; but they have never yet received an answer, and it is not likely they ever will." [25]

One thing was certain. This war did not rise out of a long-existing competition of armies and armaments. In the comparatively slow armament race at the time, the competitor of England was not Russia but France, her ally in the war; the competing arm of Britain, moreover, was her navy. "Our army," as Cobden quite rightly expressed the consensus of opinion including that of the army itself, "is maintained without reference to the armies of the Continent, and the armies of the Continent are never formed or maintained with reference to the army of England. . . . The armies of the Continent are not kept up by the governments of those countries for the sake of meeting foreign enemies, but for the purpose of repressing their own subjects." France, however, besides building her navy frankly in competition with England, had been measuring her army and its size by the Russian—and other armies on the Continent—in a fixed relationship, say five men to eight Russians.[26]

In short, the nonmilitary were warlike and the military were not; the latter had to make the war and the former were not themselves going to war in the army, with that "devoted band of paladins." [27] They were, however, willing to pay for it, in the conviction common to the Western bourgeoisie of the mid-century that the division of labor included paying cash instead of blood—the *impôt du sang*. Accordingly, the expense per soldier in this war amounted to the unheard-of sum of five thousand francs,[28] paid in the widely spread belief that a "large indemnity" from the Czar would bring that money back. Besides money, the completely civilian middle classes were, like Kingsley, giving "Brave Words to Brave Soldiers," but not their own sons, hoping that the working people would offer theirs, as far as not absolutely needed for the industries which had absorbed most of the hands and mitigated the old fears of overpopulation. In France, similarly, the army was hardly less foreign to the rich than in England; it had become a service for the upperclass poor, the middle-class poor, and the lowest-class poor, none of whom viewed the bourgeois enrichment with friendly eyes.

If, after that bloody conflict, British economists could discover no distinct advantage in the balance sheet—for the Czar did not pay the expected reparations—the middle classes were at least warmed by the praise of Victorian men of letters celebrating the Crimean War as a glorious demonstration of British justice. All that uncritical romanticism, which offered refuge from the increasingly humdrum actuality of industrialism, was unfolded in Tennyson's *Charge of the Light Brigade*, celebrating a death which the middle classes admired but had managed not to suffer:

Some one had blunder'd:
Theirs not to make reply,
Theirs not to reason why,
Theirs but to do and die.
Into the valley of Death
  Rode the Six Hundred.

Conservatives in Control of Military Affairs

With the liberals uninformed as to military affairs and unable, or unwilling, to take charge, even where they had nominal power, the military in all countries remained substantially undisturbed. The classes managing the armies remained, or became again, the same as before the downfall of the first Napoleon.

In the Prussian army the spirit of 1806 and earlier rose anew. Generals began again to compete for "long fellows." [29] The reformers reduced their moderate liberalism and constitutional hopes in order to save the organization of the army, as they conceived it, from the growing reaction. To the reactionaries, Gneisenau, Boyen, Grolman, and the rest were still the Jacobins. But rather faithlessly the reformers discarded their ideological auxiliaries like Arndt, Jahn, and Görres, who had drawn from the late wars conclusions of their own about military organization and were inclined to trust the citizen soldier and militia. As one of Gneisenau's assistants wrote before the army had even fully returned from France:

> It was quite proper to use them as *piqueurs* who, with the moral hunting-whip, drove the lazy dogs as long as the hunt lasted. But when they sat down to dine with the hunting society and then made table-music with their hunting-whips, it became time to show them the door, since they can do nothing but indecently crack the whip.

Gneisenau, who had once appeared moved by revolutionary wrath, now admitted that all had been mere heat lightning, "that all improvements of our condition have to come from above and must not happen from below." [30] Richly rewarded by the King, promoted and ennobled, by the time of the July Revolution Gneisenau had become almost a reactionary himself.

The Prussian army, in peacetime, was no more eager for a constitution, not to speak of a liberal one under which it would be subordinated, than most other armies. The reforms granted to the Prussian bourgeoisie and peasantry before 1813 seemed to the military leaders more than a sufficient price for general conscription service in the army. The performances of this bourgeoisie in the late wars were flatly denied. Metternich's amanuensis, Gentz, in newspaper articles, gainsaid any claims that the people had helped free Germany and Europe from French supremacy; he insisted that it had been done in the main by "the sublime resolutions of the princes, the wisdom and concord of their cabinets, the genius of their generals and the bravery of their regular armies." [31]

Needless to say, this was the conviction of the nobility in the army and without, whose influence grew again in Prussia and other parts of Germany, after the War of Liberation was over. Varnhagen, a Berlin liberal, attributed the deepest insight into state affairs to a drunkard who, when he heard the salvos fired on the occasion of the news of the fall of Paris, muttered: "There you have it; the war is over; the nobles have won." [32] This was to say they had won the war for themselves, rather than by themselves.

The maddest of the Junkers, Marwitz, even demanded that a special feudal nobility corps be formed as a nursery for all the officers of the army; if a nobleman could not pass the officer examination, he should serve as a noble private.[33] The King's own brother-in-law, a Duke of Mecklenburg, wanted a praetorian army not primarily intended for use against outside foes, for Metternich preserved peace, but to strike and stab the revolution threatening from within.[34] Even if the ultras among the conservative romantics could not obtain full victory for that conception, they wore down the weakening resistance of those officers who proudly remembered their bourgeois origins or recalled the services rendered by the civilian population in the wars. The reactionaries carried through their plan of weeding out the undesirables and liberals and above all made their own concept of an officer estate, as against an officer profession, the ruling one.

Whole regiments, not to speak of the guards, became domains of the nobility, where nobles locked themselves in as in their castles. To that extent the Prussian officer became refeudalized. And until the fall of the monarchy, the ancient, convenient fiction was re-established that each officer stood in the very particular personal relation of a vassal to the King—a notion of loyalty which the reformers had not possessed. Indeed they had attempted to abolish it, considering themselves and all other officers not as members of a privileged estate but of the whole nation, and as such connected with the Prussian Crown.[35]

The bureaucratic organ for making possible this relationship between the officer and the Crown was the so-called Military Cabinet of the Prussian kings and—later—of the German emperors;[36] the other two military monarchies, Russia and Austria-Hungary, had exact counterparts in their military chancelleries. The term itself dates from 1814 when the fight against Napoleon and the era of cabinet wars was thought to be over. If the bureaucratic arrangements under that term are somewhat older, the very name indicates the new assertion of military prerogatives on the part of the no-longer so absolute sovereign, who was persuaded to claim them by the military reactionaries. The Military Cabinet was the institution of the irresponsible military half of the self-running bureaucracy. It represented the group in that bureaucracy momentarily at the top—a group that employed the Cabinet to induce the King to endorse its decisions and plans rather than those of a responsible ministry. Naturally the kings liked it, for it affirmed their tastes for absolutism in an age when they were being limited in other directions. It promoted, as Haller phrased it, their "precious, soul-elevating happiness of being completely independent."

By this Cabinet, a never strictly-defined office, a very important section of the military affairs was removed from the jurisdiction of the War Ministry, under which the reformers had originally hoped to place all military management. This end they had obtained only from 1808 to 1814. After 1814, slowly and with setbacks, a rift developed which split off the Military Cabinet and, somewhat later, the General Staff, and enabled them to acquire an immediate position under the King, thus insuring their bureaucratic independence. The business of the Cabinet was especially concerned with the personal affairs of officers, such as appointments, promotion, rewards, discharge, law cases, and petitions for aid.

In Great Britain, as well as in Prussia, military officers, still closely affiliated with the landed gentry, managed to keep control over commands, rewards, promotions, and services. As Palmerston declared early in the nineteenth century: "If ever the day came when the power of rewarding military services should be transferred from the Crown to the House of Commons, those who saw it might say that they had witnessed the death blow to the Constitution." Macaulay, Secretary of War from 1839 to 1841, said: "Above all other prerogatives, in all well-organized States, the control of the army, and the awarding of rewards and punishments to military men, were considered most exclusively to belong to the Supreme Executive authority. . . . Such matters ought not to be submitted to large popular assemblies of men, who are apt to be influenced by party and factious impulse. . . ." Parliament agreed with him. So did Palmerston and later upholders of the prerogatives of the Crown—prerogatives which in point of fact amount to arrangements by when honor or punishment are retired from public discussion, lest rewards and penalties, which should be above doubt if they are to be effective, be called into question.

This did not exclude, however, all the influence which parliamentarians might exercise in such questions; but they had to operate largely outside Parliament through their party affiliations and the slowly growing military bureaucracy. The constitutional arrangements amounted to this: the Secretary of War presented claims for rewards to the sovereign, as Minister of the Crown, and not as the parliamentary officer he was at the same time.

The screen of constitutional arrangements served to maintain the gentry in the enjoyment of its practical monopoly of providing officers for the army and navy. Numerous promotions, as the radical opposition insisted with good reason, were "a mode of pensioning individuals," a way in which the aristocracy of the country got relatives and friends "pensioned on the public." In other cases, as ex-officers freely admitted in Parliament, the services of fathers were remembered in favor of their sons. A former naval officer gave away the whole pretense of cloaking parliamentary influence on promotions in the name of the sovereign, when he described the typical character of such intercession: he himself "had taken two deserving youths by the hand, who had done themselves honor in the service; they were the sons of an officer of distinguished merit, but they were for a time overlooked. He no sooner made their case known to the Admiralty than their promotion was secured to them."

The opposition could wish for no better illustration of the habits to which they objected.[37]

The reformed Parliament after 1832 was scarcely less lenient in tolerating the habits by which the gentry supported itself in a branch for which the bourgeoisie as such cared little—a branch which it did not even care to see opened to free competition. Parliament was not deeply moved when Joseph Hume, the indefatigable but completely unsuccessful specialist in army reform—of all reforms in Britain, the latest—reminded it in 1836 that of the 390 then existing British generals none had been raised from the ranks.[38] Rather was it willing to have this state of things continue and keep the country gentlemen, as before, in the army. So great was the influx from their side that the British army possessed a larger proportion of officers' posts than any other force in Europe.[39] This situation was in part due to the free trade which gave predominance to manufacture, reduced agriculture, and forced the "younger sons" of country families to look, even more than before, to the army for employment.

This class situation also led to a condition in which progress became excluded from the army. The middle classes left it to the gentry. The gentry, with the fear of Cobden in their hearts, clung the more tenaciously to the ideas about army organization cherished by Wellington—who, as long as he lived, exerted his influence for conservativism, for linear tactics, the sale of officers' commissions for cash, corporal punishment, and neglect of provisions for sanitation and transportation in war-time. Only in 1852 was a rifled musket introduced and that against the opposition of Raglan, the heir of Wellington's ideas, which he applied to the prosecution of the Crimean War. Practically no innovations were admitted by such leaders.

Conceding that "command, preferment, and honour" came to the constitutional army from the Crown, Parliament trusted for the control of "that most unmanageable instrument of power, a standing army," merely to the Mutiny Bill, which, as Sir James Mackintosh said in 1816, "renders the means of maintaining discipline annually dependent on the pleasure of Parliament. This check is held by the whole legislature. Another, and the only control exclusively vested in the House of Commons, is the annual grant of money for the support of the army." The reminder of its financial control addressed to Parliament was provoked by the attempt of a Tory ministry to withdraw from such control the army of occupation in France, where it was paid by French contributions.[40] As such, it stood at the opening of a whole century of combat for and against parliamentary control over armies in Europe. In England this control was to a large extent maintained, superficially at least, though even here the army continued to be an increasingly permanent bureaucracy under the ancient name of the "Military Forces of the Crown." Hiding behind the screening function of the sovereign, it found ways to recede from parliamentary influence. On the Continent, armies as bureaucratic organizations grew up earlier and in many places proved to be stronger than the parliamentary institutions.

The powers which the army as an estate drew from the class position of its officers and their protection against parliamentary institutions were strengthened by the exclusive character of military education. In Prussia, the work of the reformers in breaking down old controls over the selection and promotion of officers was largely canceled by allowing the nobility or its stupidest members to escape the educational test. They wanted to abolish the cadet corps as military schools, for the schools were really nurseries of class prejudice while pretending to give the sons of the Junkers at least a modicum of education. But the King would not listen to the reformers. He insisted in 1811 on keeping these institutions open and on maintaining regulations which admitted only sons of officers who had died in the field or to whom he wished to give proof of his kindness, and he declined all proposals to remove ruthlessly the less gifted pupils. That allowed the King or his Military Cabinet to restrict the choice of pupils to sons of the officer nobility. Still another way of avoiding free competition was found in the demands for the character qualifications of the officer as laid down in 1808: good and useful character and superior knowledge as requirements were placed side by side. But in truth these requirements continually warred with each other for the chief position in evaluating the cadet and officer in the Prussian as in all modern armies.

Character, the less objectively measurable quality, was henceforward found first of all in the aspirants from the nobility. It turned out to be a simple class criterion. The military schools in Prussia were little more than "golden bridges" for the sons of the nobility, viewed from their side; they formed "bridges for asses" as viewed by the bourgeoisie, proud of its own progress in knowledge and science, while the privileged nobility seemed to contribute nothing in those fields commensurate with its position. When, in the Revolution of 1848, the German bourgeoisie felt itself once more on the ascent, it resolved through its central representative organ, the Frankfurt National Assembly, that "all exclusively military institutions of education are to be abolished"; that "for the higher military studies, chairs for the sciences of war are to be founded in several universities." The resolution remained an empty vow.[41]

In spite of the lowering of the educational standards for officers, the officers themselves thought not a little of their own education and the army's educational mission for the Prussian nation. They did so in the hope of duly impressing the education-hungry bourgeoisie. However derisive was the echo to their claim of being the nation's educators, the officers, if on later occasions conceding that the battle of Königgrätz was won by the Prussian schoolmaster, never weakened in asserting their right to this function.

Proud of its own progress in thinking and education, on the other hand, the bourgeoisie throughout the nineteenth century assailed the citadel of ignorance that it observed in the armies, and there more than in the navies. To the bourgeoisie knowledge was useful; to the working class, knowledge came to be power. But these contradictions were denied vigorously by the military, somehow convinced that their power was itself the sign of knowledge on their part, a conviction that only defeats could shake from time to time. In England, General Sir John Fox Burgoyne took a decided stand in 1852 against the great popular demand for educational tests for the army as "uncalled for, delusive and mischievous. . . . At the public school will be found one set of boys who apply to their studies, and make the greater progress in them; another set take to cricket, boating, swimming, etc. Now of the two, I should prefer the latter, as much more likely to make good officers, but they are to be absolutely rejected and forever, unless they can come up to the mark in other matters, which are of no absolute use to them in their profession. . . ." The educational ideals of the agrarians, the hunters of the fox and stag, with all their anti-intellectualism, were also to remain the ideals of the armies; as late as 1930 a British major general, fifty-three years old, was "adversely reported on for not playing field games." [42]

The Guards

> "Where the Guards appear, there is no democracy."
> Emperor William II

In the institution of the guards, as well as in military education, military conservatives entrenched themselves. Everywhere in Europe the guards were indices of the military standstill or reaction, except in Austria, which did without guards and yet exhibited many other marks of the reaction. The respect and pampering they received from the Crown and command were largely unjustified by their performances in the late wars, and where their performances might have warranted consideration, as in the case of Napoleon's guards, it was withheld from them after 1814. When these battalions of Napoleon, composed of the best soldiers the regiments could muster, offered their services to the Bourbons and mounted guard at their accustomed places in Paris, they were then and there replaced by a mounted National Guard, made up of rich young gentlemen who had not fought in the war, and later by the *compagnies rouges,* this "Gothic entourage" of the King, formed completely by officers. After 1815, the twice-returned Bourbons founded the very expensive Royal Guard, a whole army corps of guards.[43]

The Napoleonic guards had been the best war soldiers; the guards of their enemies were conceived of as the best peacetime soldiers. When the Allies retired from Dresden into Bohemia in 1813, Russian generals opposed certain plans because the guards would be thereby endangered; they did not dare to face the Czar with a defeat or heavy losses on the part of those regiments. They insisted that other regiments do the dirty work, even if the whole of the operation was thereby endangered; then they reported to the Czar that the bravery of his guards had warded off all danger. During the campaign in 1814 Alexander was afraid that the beautiful Light Horse Guards might suffer if constantly used like other light cavalry. During the last attacks on Paris in a certain decisive place a superiority of the Allies might easily have been established if the Russian guards could have been used like the Prussian guards.[44]

But they were to be spared for the triumphal march into Paris. This crowning act of the popular War for Liberation was performed by the guards, as far as Russia and Prussia were concerned. With good reason could a Berlin wit in 1816 say of the guards that preferably

they march into the fire which burns in the bosom of the beautiful. . . . Proud, nobly smiling, the guards refrain from battle; leave to the Landwehr the bloody field. Only around the punch-bowl is everyone a hero. But when the dangers are happily over, the guards' feathered cohorts hurry to Paris for the splendid occasion, decorate themselves with laurel and orders, whereas noble horror banishes far away the dispensable hordes of the Landwehr.[45]

After their return from the war, the guards received many favors at the hands of their sovereigns, who kept them under their direct orders and promoted them directly.[46] Many other preferences were given to the noble and generally rich guard officers, all of which harmonized little in the Prussian army with the proposal of Boyen and others that every citizen and every soldier be equally near to the state and its head.[47] Their special uniforms, their stationing in the divers capitals, the large role given to the cavalry, the higher pay, made the guards the most expensive and at the same time the most envied though hardly the most useful part of an army.

To the utilitarians in England this uselessness was particularly obvious since the guards did not serve abroad. Joseph Hume and his friends repeatedly demanded that the guards—privileged without merit and "solely from station," and yet better paid—be dissolved. Since the seven guard formations were stationed in London, Windsor, and Dublin, their defenders argued that they needed better pay. Seventy-five regiments of the Line were out in the colonies, and only twenty-five of them in temperate climate; consequently the mortality of the officers of those regiments of the Line was three times as high as in the guards. The higher rank of the guard officer enabled him to rise faster and obtain an undue proportion of the posts of general officers, one-half of whom were from the guards, and of staff officers. In 1836 the English guards furnished seventy, the rest of the infantry but one hundred and twenty-six, lieutenant colonels.

English radicals considered equalization within the army as only a necessary concomitant to parliamentary reform. In the one sphere as in the other the powers of the aristocracy were to be reduced. The guards, they said, were not even the needful decorations and appendages of royalty—France had given them up since the July Revolution—but merely "the pageants of the aristocracy; a specious device, by means of which the wealthy and the powerful are enabled to promote their offspring over the heads of hard-worked and worn-out veterans, and the means by which the aristocracy had contrived to accumulate upon themselves the rank, the honours, and the emoluments of the military profession, without depriving themselves of any of the enjoyments of civil life," and almost without doing actual military service. But the utilitarianism of the British nation proved on such occasions infinitely weaker than its antiquarianism in military affairs; an amendment proposed by Hume to reduce the army by five thousand men and dissolve the Foot Guards was defeated by a vote of 217 to 46 in 1836 and by similar votes on similar occasions.[48]

That purely military reasons justified the further existence of the guards not even Wellington was willing to maintain. Yet to him they were a nursery of the indispensable English gentleman. He believed that they were "superior to the Line—not as being picked men like the French [under Napoleon] but from the goodness of the non-commissioned officers. They do in fact all that the commissioned officers in the Line are expected to do—and don't do. This must be as long as the present system lasts—and I am all for it—of having gentlemen for officers; you cannot require them to do many things that should be done." [49] A more competent testimony as to the laziness of the aristocracy in military matters is hardly required.

At any rate, in spite of the introduction of metropolitan police in England, the guards sought to justify their prolonged existence by appealing to the desire of the bourgeoisie for security; that seemed a plausible reason for their being left in a bourgeois world. As a commander of the Coldstream Guards represented the situation to a parliamentary commission in 1835: guards "have the honor to guard their Sovereign." Incidentally, on their "loyalty and good conduct, as they are stationed in the metropolis, the repose of the capital and the security of the property and persons of its inhabitants in a great measure depend. These troops are surrounded with temptations of every description, and it will be at all times the policy of revolutionists and destructives to endeavour to fill their minds with discontent and dissatisfaction . . . and to estrange the officers from the affection of the private soldiers and the good opinion of the public." As measures to preserve the loyalties of the privates, the colonel therefore recommended: removal of the incurable offenders, who would always be most easily open to seditious proposals, retention of punishment by flogging, and a military jail where the soldier culprit would not come into contact with criminal elements from the civilian world.[50]

Yet as a matter of cold fact, the sovereigns, whose life and body the guards were everywhere expected to protect, and the aristocracies, who officered the guards down to the First World War, discovered in almost all the revolutions of the nineteenth and twentieth centuries the unreliability of the guards as antirevolutionary forces. The guard officers' revolt of the Dekabrists, or Decembrists, in Russia, stands midway between the officers' conspiracies of the eighteenth century and the social revolutions of the twentieth century, both equally dangerous to the Czars. The Petersburg garrison, mostly composed of the guards, failed the monarchy as well as the Kerensky government in 1917, when they declined to leave for field service because, as they said, they had "to defend the Revolution." In the July Revolution in France in 1830 the guards did nothing to protect the Bourbons. Afterward they were dissolved and the Swiss Guards were sent home, and thus the "nationalization" of the French army was completed—aside from the Foreign Legion, which was founded soon after the July Revolution.

Honor in the Armies

As a supplement to the solidifying force of class feeling and military education, the principle of self-regulation under their own code of *honor* helped to unify the military estate and protect it against civilian intervention. This form of military insulation was weakest in England, where officers did not consider themselves so much apart from the rest of society. Yet even there the code of honor was long upheld against parliamentary interference.

Duels became rather more numerous in the post-Napoleonic time, both within the army and outside, as a phase of the false feudalism of the period. Wellington fought one in 1829 with a political adversary. "Very juvenile!" Greville afterward remarked to the Duke. But the Duke did not see how he could have done otherwise.[51] Against this practice, the morality of the Victorian Age protested, in North America as in Europe, insisting that duels were avoidable and in fact were sinful, unreasonable, contrary to human and divine law. In 1843, a society for the suppression of dueling was founded in England, based on "morality," its members pledged to combat the practice by influence and example; among its 416 members were 35 generals and admirals and some 200 other officers. Commissions for conciliation and arbitration were appointed to aid in the settlement of honor questions. In the War Articles of 1844, the Queen was made to say that she approved of the behavior of officers who avoided duels either by giving or accepting an honorable atonement, that those who insisted upon fighting or aiding others to do so should be punished, and that the friends of those officers who suffered or inflicted injuries should be in a position to bring about a conciliation. Duels were then expressly forbidden as well by the War Articles of 1874 and 1881. In the English army the Articles of War were interpreted as giving every officer, regardless of rank, power to part disputants and quell quarrels, frays, and disorders—if need be, to place the contentious parties under arrest.[52]

The preservation of the honor of the officers was to a large extent entrusted to the Secretary of War. He was responsible for seeing that none remained even on the half-pay list after he had been found guilty of conduct inconsistent with the character of an officer and a gentleman. So far beyond the circle of those actually in service did this honor jurisdiction—though not the power of the court martial—go even in England that, for instance, in 1843 a colonel who was on half-pay was removed because his conduct in some financial affairs had attracted unpleasant notice, if not that of the criminal prosecutor.[53]

The Continental armies were far less susceptible than the Anglo-Saxon ones to the morality concepts of the contemporary bourgeoisie. They preserved and developed their own notions in questions of honor, if they did not, as in Prussia, begin to superimpose these concepts on parts of civilian society. The French bourgeoisie of the July Monarchy left the duelists of the army pretty much alone. The law courts could not agree whether death by duel was manslaughter or not. Affairs of honor were rather numerous in the French and German armies of the time, as if to emphasize that here at least was a sphere where the categorical imperative of the *"Enrichissez-vous!"* was not valid. In peacetime, the army naturally began "to eat into itself for lack of somebody to hew and hack." "Those insane quarrels, those deplorable combats, in which so much bravery was wasted, kept up the cult of honor and the disdain for danger," said a later Marshal of France approving and yet censuring conditions in the army under Louis Philippe. With a certain nostalgia he added: "In those times honor was honored, conscience always in action, bravery glorified, the hierarchy respected, and camaraderie imposed by traditional practices." [54]

The most elaborate systems for upholding and cultivating honor were worked out in the German armies because there, more than anywhere else, the officers wanted to seem apart from other classes and indicate that superiority by some striking trait. Honor was this something apart; unable in their poverty to equal the "conspicuous waste" of wealth of the new rich, they showed a "conspicuous waste" of blood, incidentally making the duel an *imago belli*. As a Prussian general wrote in 1821, the officer needed

aside from the cement which is essentially active in war, the holy respect for King and Country, a medium of cohesion and regulation for peacetime use, in order to enable him at times of great leisure, larger wants, lesser income, and a much more divided interest, to live in harmony with his fellows, co-estates, and himself. This he finds for certain only in his own honor and that of his estate, provided it is tenderly treated and immaculately preserved; more efficiently than by the best disciplinary laws is the officer estate—not well-to-do, rather needy—thereby kept unified and pure, retaining the respect of the educated and uneducated of all other classes of the people.[55]

Almost every month after 1815 a duel between officers occurred in Prussia. But this duellomania, as yet largely restricted to officers, was carried to such excesses that it was found necessary to curb it by regulations issued under the name of the King. In 1821 and 1828 it was decreed that courts of honor should pass, not merely on cases where the officer had degraded himself, but on those damaging to the general honor of the estate. They could, but need not, interfere in order to obtain a peaceful solution of honor conflicts among their fellow officers; they could decide whether a party to such conflicts should be dismissed and removed from the list of the officers. The King reserved to himself the right to confirm such sentences and gave divisional commanders the function of determining whether a conflict was amenable to the honor courts or not.

Thus the way seemed opened to abolishing the duel and substituting an individual concept of honor, had not the conviction been so firmly rooted in the officer body about the value of personal combat as the ultimate expression of group ethics. A military commission of 1837, dealing with the question of punishing challenges and duels between officers, declared that it did not matter to those whose honor had been injured whether the offender was punished in accordance with the civil law; of more consequence to him than even his life was the fact that through the fight the offender and the honor society gained a better opinion of his worth, while the libelous one was refuted. In this belief the "wonderful strength and vital power" of dueling was said to be rooted.

Such convictions, feudal in their insistence on the equality of all members and of members only in point of honor and, insofar, anti-authoritarian, led in 1843 to legalizing, more or less, the duel, in accordance with the wishes prevalent in the officer corps. Boyen in his military liberalism took the stand that, since laws were to leave every citizen the greatest possible liberty compatible with the purposes of the state, duels might be left outside the range of state interference. This weird *laisser faire* helped only to strengthen the bulwark of military feudalism in Prussia, intensively and extensively. The jurisdiction of the courts of honor was now made to include officers of the *gendarmerie,* the rural police, as well as inactive officers on half-pay, discharged with the right to wear the uniform. Special courts of honor were provided for staff officers. And since the officers of the Landwehr were already under such courts, a large body of Prussians was thus made to live under feudal concepts, even in civilian life; they were kept outside the general laws and practically unpunishable for breaches of certain laws.

The Prussian officers practically had it all their own way. Jurists were excluded from their honor procedures. Officers of a regiment could punish fellow officers, though certain punishments, like setbacks in promotion, were outside their jurisdiction. The offenses contrary to honor which officers could commit were of necessity loosely defined, like "want of resolution," or a behavior "contrary to the right feeling of honor or the conditions of the officer estate." With a two-thirds majority, they could get rid of all the disagreeable or irregular characters in their midst, and strengthen their homogeneity, if not always their corporate intelligence—not to speak of the corporate morality which the Rules of 1808 had tried to establish by making meanness of character, "a low way of thinking," the determinant for exclusion. Contrary to their vaunted declarations of service to the state, they decided who was to serve and whether a life that might be precious to the state was to be risked in a duel. Here again class prejudice was, to say the least, theoretically in the way of a potential highest military efficiency; state service was made subordinate to caste interest.[56]

Even conscription, which some liberals hoped to employ in the direction of popular politics, was turned by the military into an instrument of their own estate. The Prussian army law of September

3, 1814, pronounced general conscription for all able-bodied Prussians from the seventeenth to the fiftieth year of age. By no means all served who could do so—Prussia provided more recruits than the army could take, for the country was still too poor to support more soldiers. The desire for economy and for conciliating the bourgeoisie led to the institution of the one-year volunteer: the well-to-do, who could afford to send their sons to secondary schools, were privileged to let them serve merely one year in the army instead of two or three like commoners, provided they paid for their upkeep. The bourgeois took this sop from the state, instead of arrogating for themselves power over the state; and in part the middle-class German became educated in order to avoid the burdens put upon him by militarism.

Liability to universal service had no correlative political effect. The men who were to die for their country were given no voice in its government. Military officers surrounding the Prussian kings made sure that their dominion over the war machine was not shaken by allowing merit, irrespective of class, to rise in the army. The soldier-citizen's influence was not measurably larger than it had been in the eighteenth century.

Military Attachés

Not content with control over the army, with independence in matters of military education and insulation under codes of honor, with an internal consolidation of their forces, the military branched out into international diplomacy through the institution of military attachés stationed in foreign countries. Scarcely any other development of the period was more significant for the future of international relations.

In the general settlement of 1814-15, diplomats, under the leadership of Metternich, had energetically taken affairs out of the hands of soldiers and assumed direction in the interest of the civil powers. So the military decided to become diplomats themselves in order to take care of war. Paradoxically, at the very time when peace diplomacy was more sincerely than ever trying to preserve international order, it allowed military attachés to be added to the staffs of embassies and legations. The demand for these agents was older by at least fifteen years than its realization. The unfortunate Massenbach, chief of staff of the Duke of Brunswick at Jena, had insisted as early as 1800 that "we ought to attach to our legations in Petersburg, Vienna, Paris, London, etc., officers who are destined to the higher command in the army and who during their stay at these courts may make it their business to study the character of those who might be put in the future at the head of hostile or allied

armies. Only in this way shall we prepare in an appropriate fashion
for war." [57] Before this and for some time after, spying on the
foreign armies was taken care of by the regular diplomats who
might know something about such matters, particularly if they were
themselves officers like Napoleon's "general-diplomats." Such specialists might also be supplemented by traveling officers who received
detailed instruction about the military features which they were to
observe abroad. Frederick the Great insisted that his ministers send
him very specific information about foreign armies, their estimates,
maneuvers, or new evolutions.[58]

After 1816 the diplomats attached military observers to the staffs
of their representatives abroad—in the case of Prussia at the demand
of the military.[59] These observers were to be subordinates, not
always very submissive, of the chiefs of embassies or legations, and
report through these agencies to the minister of foreign affairs, the
minister of war, and later to general staffs about their military
observations, to which function they were restricted.

A special representation of military interests and reactionary
sympathies developed between Prussia and Russia after the War
of Liberation. The two monarchs appointed "military plenipo-
tentiaries," who were to be the medium of a direct intercourse between them; these agents were placed in the immediate entourage
of Czar and King and were not subordinated to the heads of the
embassies or the foreign ministers, but reported directly to the
sovereign. Such attachés formed the peculiar connecting link between Russian and Prussian reaction, from the beginning, when
Frederick William III regarded the Czar as his savior from the
French Revolution, down to the end, that is to 1914. Throughout,
all attempts to bring this irresponsible *"Flügeladjutant"* under constitutional or at least diplomatic control were defied.[60]

The Philosophy of War in the Nineteenth and Twentieth Centuries

The power of the military was augmented by writers who created
the ideology of war under the new conditions in Europe. Although
this development may have seemed remote from the interests of the
private or ordinary routineer in the officer class, it was of the utmost
value in confirming the high military in their predilections and
furnishing them a *raison d'être* for their existence and claims. As
Mahan afterward formulated the philosophy of sea power for
Americans and all others with ambitions on the seas, so before the
middle of the nineteenth century military commentators cloaked land
war in a garment of necessity, fact, logic, and justification.

The most powerful writers of this group were Henri Jomini and

Clausewitz. Jomini was a Swiss bank clerk who turned to war and held commissions in both the French and Russian armies, thus offering like Friedrich Engels, the enthusiast for military tactics and self-appointed "general" of the class war, the rare spectacle of the military expert arising from business. After the publication of his *Traité des grandes opérations militaires* in 1804-5, he continued to issue studies and essays until near his death in 1869. Perhaps out of his banking experience he evolved his fundamental rules: economy of time and forces, the winning of superiority at the decisive point, and victory by mobility and surprise. Jomini believed that an army, like a capital investment, was governed by the chance of profit: "Offensive operations should be proportioned to the end in mind."

Jomini preserved some of that supranational Europeanism of Metternich-Castlereagh-Talleyrand, which restricted competition within the European society of nations. As against Napoleon he wanted to keep within bounds the extent to which the resources of Europe, seen as a whole, were to be applied to war by nationalism and its generals. To him the first aim of warfare is indeed Napoleonic —the annihilation of the enemy army; the enemy's country would thereafter fall automatically to the victor. But, in his opinion, the investment of forces and the way of disposing them must be conditioned by the nature of the war theater, which Napoleon had left out of consideration in Spain and Russia: "The excessive abuse which this system suffered at the hands of Napoleon does not exclude the actual advantage it offers, so long as one knows how to limit one's own successes and to keep one's enterprises in right relation to the respective condition of the neighboring armies and nations."

To a considerable extent, Jomini's teachings of war are close to the conception of limited war—war controlled by a sense for a stabilized Europe and social order. Indeed he brings order into war itself, along rational lines, symbolized by diagrams and designs. He attempts to introduce system into it, but he neglects the one great element which stays outside the realm of order and law—the enemy and his behavior. The deficiency of Jomini's teachings lies mainly in his neglect to conceive strategy as *"Klugheitslehre im Verhältnis der Heere zu einander"*—the teachings of wisdom about the relation of armies to one another.[61] Yet he tries to eliminate the unforeseen in the behavior of the enemy. His code of competition is pre-Darwinian and has its seat in the charted fields of standardized conduct instead of the pathless jungles of nationalistic cutthroat struggle.

Karl von Clausewitz' *On War* (*Vom Kriege*) is essentially a contemplation of war experience, rather than a textbook like the works of Jomini.[62] For Clausewitz it was in the nature of war that it could be thought better than taught. This has not saved his writing from being interpreted as an exhortation instead of a philosophy. In a later, so-called realistic time, when philosophical thought was no longer part of the mental equipment of the soldier, and he was no longer able to produce the apology for his own contemporary war or preparation for the next war, it was to Clausewitz that men turned for such aid. Then he was read and expounded by those whom no historical sense warned that writing on the philosophy of war is, even more than theology, time-conditioned. At the moment when Clausewitz pondered the image of war, he was viewing it not from the standpoint of a practical lesson, but in the abstract:

He who uses force unsparingly, without reference to the bloodshed involved, must obtain a superiority if his adversary uses less vigor in its application. The former then dictates the law to the latter, and both proceed to extremities, to which the only limitations are those imposed by the amount of counteracting force on each side. . . . To introduce into a philosophy of war a principle of moderation would be an absurdity. War is an act of violence pushed to its utmost bounds.

In 1841 Varnhagen, a liberal in Berlin, discovered that in the ten years since the posthumous publication of Clausewitz's work his authority had become inordinate, that the Prussian officers swore by him and made it a question of honor to insist that he was the best author on war and that no Prussian officer should pretend to a view different from his.[63] Friedrich Engels read *On War* as philosophy and found it excellent, acclaiming in particular the fact that Clausewitz, confronted with the question whether war was art or science, had said that war most closely resembled trade, that battle in war is the same as cash settlement in trade—rarely as it may occur in reality, everything is still directed toward it, it has to take place eventually, and it decides everything.[64] But rarely was the work understood in such a way, at least by the military profession, to whom it was a superstructural ideology of military bureaucratism.

In defining war as "nothing but a continuation of state policy by other means," Clausewitz went less far in his claims to military influence on state policy than his contemporaries, the military Jacobins of Prussia; and he did not go to the extent indicated by a reversal of this definition which would be Darwinian—"peace is only a continuation of war by other means." In his "continuation," war was not defined as a thing existing in itself but as belonging primarily to politics, both united by the concept of power—politics the application of peaceful power and war that of unpeaceful means.

From his own experiences Clausewitz knew that it was in the nature of war that its processes as such must release forces and produce effects which raise claims of their own and are able then to interfere in the sphere of politics, that military methods might usurp the function of determining political aims. Thus the political purpose would no longer be the lawgiver to war; it would itself have to conform to the means of war and would be changed thereby. Then we would have militarism.

After this warning, which the military might well understand as encouragement, Clausewitz proceeded to an elaboration of his concept of the "absolute war." It was to him the logical, if not necessarily the real, outcome of the tremendous development in the ways of warfare before and after the French Revolution, marked by the growth of armies and the increasing absoluteness in the antagonism between the enemies: "The more magnificent and the stronger are the motives of war, the more they inclose the whole existence of the nations, the more violent is the tension which precedes war; all the more will war approach its absolute form and the question become how to cast down the enemy; the more will the aim of war and the political purpose coincide, and the more warlike and the less political will war *appear* to be."

Clausewitz adds, however, that war had never appeared in its absolute form and had always been limited by customs, laws, the nature of the constitutions of the parties to a war and of their interests. Absolute war suffered constantly "a modification in the reality," and so did its objective—the unconditioned disarming or overthrow of the enemy, which in reality is never the only and necessary condition for war and, therefore, "must by no means be laid down in theory as a law."

Such opinions make Clausewitz's book more nearly a disquisition on the nature of war. But the theory of absoluteness developed by him was understood as advice to approximate just that kind of war. His followers imagined the "absolute war" to be disassociated from everything, even the thing for which it was presumably fought: the national interest. The national interest could thus become subordinate to the best possible war for the military and to the interests which called for war.

That Clausewitz wrote as he did and was read as he was read was largely the outcome of the completed process of bureaucratization in the armies. His teachings, as they were apprehended, were embraced where and when this process was completed. The dates of the translation of his work into French, 1849, and English, 1873, are indicative of this fact. One feature of that bureaucratization was the separation of armies from the generality of interests in their states. Home politics to Clausewitz, when measured by considerations of foreign policy and outside defense, constituted merely *faux frais*.[65] He ranks the military profession supreme over all; among the intellectually determined activities of man, the "warlike genius" takes the highest rank. Having Napoleon in mind, he rates that commander of men no whit higher than Goethe had done, but in so doing Clausewitz incidentally rates his own profession as the highest.

In effect, for the subsequent benefit of his profession, Clausewitz develops the "absolute war" concept and the idea of battle as the single means to attain the end of war. This excludes "philanthropic" thought, an error which must be extirpated, presupposing that "there is a skillful method of disarming and overcoming an enemy without great bloodshed and that this is the proper tendency of the art of war. . . . We do not like to hear of generals who are victorious without the shedding of blood. If bloody battling is a dreadful spectacle, that should merely be the reason to appreciate war more and not to allow our swords to grow blunt by and by, through humanitarianism, until someone steps in with a sharp sword and cuts our arms off our body."

However much this contains a reason for the existence of armies, Clausewitz qualifies his absolute demands: "The political object, as the original motive of the war, should be the standard for determining both the aim of the military force and also the amount of effect to be made." Too much effect is not only wasteful but deadly— therefore: "The waste of our own military forces must, *ceteris paribus,* always be greater the more our aim is directed upon the destruction of the enemy's power. The danger lies within—that the greater efficiency which we seek recoils on ourselves, and therefore has worse consequences in case we fail of success."

In his appraisal of forces and moments, Clausewitz rates those pertaining to the moral sphere more highly than does Jomini, his contemporary, and the eighteenth-century military writers, with their lack of appreciation for imponderables, including the surprise attack, which the young Frederick had scorned at Mollwitz. This makes it the more remarkable that Clausewitz values numerical superiority so highly. It is not all that counts in strategy to him; but in the face of what he regarded as the essential similarity of all armies in his own time, he was convinced "that superiority in numbers becomes every day more decisive, that the principle of assembling the greatest possible numbers may therefore be regarded as more important than ever." This is merely another way of saying that man equals man in armies, as if the revolutionary demand for *égalité* had been realized at least inside and between armies. It makes man-number the yardstick of comparison in military competition: "Battle is a measuring of spiritual and corporeal forces by means of the latter." This led in peace to the demand of the armies for more men; in war to the use of battle masses.

Such dicta, to be explained in Clausewitz by the technical standstill in armies for forty years, were in fact pronounced on the eve of the technical revolution in the military field. They were based on the experience of the Wars of Liberation, coupled with Clausewitz's overrating of the peasant masses in the Russian armies with whom he had fought—a mistake shared by many generations of conservative Prussians after him. If this reveals the time-conditioned character of some of his thought, should he be blamed for the "rage of numbers" in the armies that came after his day, even if this rage was justified by reference to his writings? The answer lies in his warning: "We must then reconcile ourselves to construe war as it is to be, not out of a mere idea, but leave space for everything foreign which interferes with it and clings to it, for all the natural specific weight and friction of the parts—the whole inconsistency, obscurity, and faint-heartedness of the human spirit. We must embrace the view that war, and the shape it is given, rises from ideas, feelings, and conditions prevailing *at the given moment. . . .*"

Theory has to admit all this according to Clausewitz. But, he proceeds: "It is its duty to rank supreme the absolute force in war and to use it as a general directing point, in order that he who wants to learn something from theory, may accustom himself never to lose sight of it, to consider it as the original measure of all his hopes and fears, in order to approximate it wherever he is able or forced to do so." Here indeed *Krieg an sich,* war in itself, becomes very nearly identified with the application of absolute, utmost force which finds its one and only means in battle and though perhaps never attained may constantly be approximated.

Here Clausewitz becomes the apparent promoter of that militarism which thinks solely of war and does not, as the Prince de Ligne recommended to soldiers, think of peace on the first days of war and of war on the first days of peace, but dreams only of war and disregards its economy. In that case, with "violence pushed to its utmost bounds" and after the maximum of exertion, war may not leave much that is worthwhile even to the victorious nation. At all events it was for the unconditioned and absolute war that the military in Germany and France finally prepared in the light of Clausewitz's teaching.

With mass armies under their management, since the Napoleonic wars, the problem of obtaining and keeping national backing became more and more pressing for the military. The rural parts of the nations generally presented little difficulty, for the peasantry served placidly as recruits and the gentry furnished sons as officers and sold grain, meat, and mounts to the troops. In cities, however, the military were regarded with more suspicion as possible disturbers of economic life. This attitude changed when a series of domestic revolutions swept Europe like a tidal wave in 1848-9. Then armies were clearly seen to have a function in preserving inner order and tranquillity and assuring economic stability. As such, they were increasingly agreeable to larger elements among the urban civilians.

The revolutions of 1848-9, frightening the third estate by the "too far-going demands" of the fourth estate of industrial labor, threatened the old order of Europe, as Metternich exclaimed, with another 1792. The Continental armies bowed down temporarily before the storms of February and March, except in Russia, where the Czar declared he had "too much of the Russian blood in him to suffer that the workers should govern Europe." [1] In England, the Chartist march on London dissolved before the troops called out under Wellington's command, thus avoiding a second Peterloo Massacre. Prussian officers admittedly suffered "an inner Jena," not so much an outward military defeat as a nervous breakdown of their belief in their office and usefulness.[2] But everywhere the officers recouped, first in France, where Cavaignac restored order in Paris in "the bloody June days," and

7

Preparations for the Embattlement of Nations in the First World War

then in Austria and Germany. In the latter the armies had formerly kept order by merely standing still, but they now became actively antirevolutionary, putting an end to "the golden age of German *Gemütlichkeit*," as Count von Roon said, replacing it by one of brutality, convincing the soldiers that atrocities had been committed by the revolutionaries and that such barbarism must be fought with barbarism.[3]

The inner wars of 1848-9 were followed by outer wars. The Prussian success story of 1864-71 inspired other nations to follow her, competing militarily as well as industrially. France followed her conqueror most closely. Before long the United States Army was shaken out of somnolence by Elihu Root as Secretary of War; a general staff was established and the scattered and almost independent state militias were assimilated to the regular army. It was not the fault of Leonard Wood if this reorganization took over no more Prussian forms.[4] In England, the attempt of Lord Roberts and others to bring about conscription or universal military service failed, but the Liberal Minister, Haldane, overhauled the forces of the country and prepared them for quick transportation to the Continent, when and if the appropriate day arrived. While apparent efforts were made to counter the perils presented by this increasing militarization of the world—by "peace conferences" at The Hague—those parleys really originated in Russian military motives and were doomed to futility, as far as large objectives were concerned, by military and naval "experts," who held the pacific sentiments of the civilians, such as they were, within "practical" limits. By 1914 the stage had been set for transforming the war of mass armies into a war of nations almost totally mobilized.

The Military in Prussia and the New German Empire

Such political renovations as were made in Germany after the great fright of 1848 were made "from above" by military men and their spokesmen and, like the "revolution from above" in the earlier days of Stein, Hardenberg, Scharnhorst, and Boyen, left those above in their old position with full power to manipulate the results of the "progress." The Prussian constitution of 1850, a charter granted by the King, though it watered down the promises of 1848, nominally gave to the Diet a control over military budgets and the war ministry, but this provision was easily circumvented by the military. The discussions of the constitution of the North German Confederation were not allowed to "get out of hand" by Bismarck, leader of the Junker and the military estate; in its final form, the constitution compelled the other states to reconstruct their armies on standards of Prussian efficiency and to put them under the command of the King of Prussia as President of the Confederation. When, in 1871, this constitution was transformed into one for the new German Empire, with the King of Prussia as Kaiser, the leadership and independence of the Prussian military were confirmed and continued, despite the civilian control over budgets legally vested in the Reichstag.

At each successive stage and crisis in German history, the military gained their principal ends, winning victory by operations in public and behind scenes. To describe these would require volumes: instead of resorting to swift generalizations necessarily vague, it seems best to give a somewhat detailed view of a single episode in the advance of the military estate—the triumph of the military over the Prussian Diet after 1850.

As finally drawn by royal advisers, the Prussian constitution of 1850 left the Landtag a certain sphere of parliamentary control over army affairs—through the annual budget and ministerial responsibility including the Minister of War. But other features of parliamentary control, such as having the army swear to support the constitution, had carefully been removed from the document by military men near the King.[5] Moreover, the officers and other conservatives insisted, as did Roon, in 1861, that this constitution was "the result of the free will of the King" and that, in effect, the King could change the constitution if he chose.[6]

Although at first the Prussian court camarilla left that document alone and submitted fairly moderate financial demands to the Landtag, they soon started their antirevolutionary measures from within the army and through the medium of an institution which, though absolutely unconstitutional and incompatible with ministerial responsibility toward parliament, had survived the storms of 1848: the Military Cabinet.[7] Against ministerial responsibility and thus against the Minister of War, the military entourage of the King made him assert poorly defined rights which, he was made to say, belonged to his position as Commander-in-Chief of the army—a power which the Prussian constitution, like that of England, Belgium, and the United States, had vested in the head of the government. As supreme war lord he claimed a peculiarly close quasi-personal connection with the officers such as had existed for over a hundred years between them and the Prussian Crown, and he employed the position of Commander-in-Chief to eliminate the parliamentary influence exerted through the Minister of War. Outside the latter's control remained the direct correspondence between the King—i.e., the Military Cabinet—and the generals commanding army corps. More and more, the Chief of the General Staff came under the immediate direction of the King, as the Minister of War lost all save a nominal control over the General Staff.[8]

From his war ministers the King claimed a double responsibility: one toward the Landtag in administrative questions, and another, the higher one, toward the sovereign, in "purely military affairs." The less effectively the war ministers could combine these difficult responsibilities, the more the irresponsible, frankly antirevolutionary entourage of the King gained influence—in foreign affairs no less than in questions of army personnel, which became again the particular business of the Military Cabinet.

At its head after 1857 stood an Old Prussian general, Edwin von Manteuffel, a man whose hero was the English Strafford, who, condemned to death for ultra-Royalism, beseeched the King to confirm the death sentence because his own execution seemed the only way to save the Crown at that particular moment.[9] Manteuffel was just the man to begin the long-hoped-for army reform, first by cutting the Military Cabinet free from the semiliberal War Ministry and then by getting rid of officers who might be infected by liberalism, or who harbored doubts about the supremacy of the army.

By the army reorganization of 1861 all power over the army was concentrated in the Crown. As Lassalle had clearly foretold: "As soon as it has been settled that the King can fill all positions in the army, and the army gets into a special relation with him, the King will have, all by himself, not only as much, but ten times as much power as the whole country taken together. Even then, in truth the actual power of the country might be ten, twenty, and fifty times as great as the power of the army." The great, but unorganized, strength of the nation could be overcome by the lesser but organized strength of the army.[10]

In this clean-up, demands for military efficiency coincided with antirevolutionary, or at any rate antiliberal, desires. To get rid of the undesirables, bourgeois officers who did not conform and even noble officers whose intelligence was too far below the minimum requirements of their caste were forced out. "It was my greatest political achievement," boasted Manteuffel later. "Without this cleaning up, the victories of 1864, 1866, and 1870 would not have been possible." [11] At the end of his housecleaning in 1860, fewer than 1,000 nonnoble officers among the 2,900 of the line infantry remained, and of these 2,900 at least 1,800 had passed through the institution for cadets, that is, were mainly sons of the poor nobility. Aside from the line, in nearly all the higher ranks nobles held the officer commissions in the guards, the cavalry—100 per cent in the guard cavalry, 95 per cent in the other cavalry—and the "better" infantry regiments.[12]

Only the artillery and the engineers were still left to be officered by nonnobles, who held up to 80 per cent of the commissions in this branch, still standing lowest in the respect of the rest of the army.

They were "sons of mail carriers and tax officials, students who had failed, postal clerks . . . the welcome dumping-ground for those who could not find admission in the other arms," as the inspector general of the artillery complained in the middle of the 1850's, when he proceeded to exclude such candidates for the future.[13] Some artillery officers like Werner von Siemens, disgusted with political reaction and technological standstill even in their branch, went over to the industries and to liberalism. These exclusions established the watertight compartmental system which the Prussian army was to form, as far as the officers were concerned, against parliamentarism and other civilian influence.

How small numerically and relatively was the entrenched interest of the Prussian nobility appears from the following considerations: among the 18,000,000 inhabitants in Prussia in 1861, there were 68,000 nobles. On the basis of an absolute parity the nobility should have had 46 officers' commissions out of a total of 12,000. According to contemporary calculations, there was a stratum of about 2,500,000 in Prussia who were fitted through education, property, and culture to supply officers. On the basis of parity that would have given the nobility 333 officers' commissions. But actually, of 997 generals and staff officers, 799 were noblemen, when on a parity basis 970 should have been nonnoble.[14]

When following some semiliberals Roon entered the Ministry of War at the end of 1859 it was "on the fixed principle of maintaining the war lord position of the King with respect to the Supreme Command as against the spreading constitutional confusion of ideas," as Manteuffel defined his task for him. The small inroads which parliamentary government had made on Prussian army autocracy were to be blocked. The War Minister, with his countersignature to the orders of the King, was supposed to submit to the general laws, for the observance of which he was responsible to parliament. But Roon, who had early declared his poor opinion of constitutional doctrines, merely pretended to submit to the *fait accompli*. In fact, he used his position as minister to surrender all the influence that his office might have over the supreme command, leaving that as far as possible to the completely irresponsible Military Cabinet. When his liberal colleagues in the Cabinet demanded from the King a widening of ministerial responsibility, and the King was unwilling to grant it, Roon declared that as a general of the Prussian army he was bound to obey the orders of the King as his Commander-in-Chief.[15]

The liberals protested against the withdrawal of the most important army matters into the hands of irresponsible bureaucrats. One of their leaders, Von Twesten, published a sharp pamphlet, *"Was uns noch retten kann"* ("Our Only Salvation") in April 1861, against the doings of the Military Cabinet:

The position of a Civil and Military Cabinet as separate agencies by the side of responsible ministers is more than ever incompatible with the present constitution of the state. The Military Cabinet maintains as a fundamental principle that army affairs have to be kept separate from the rest of the state organism, the pretext being that the army must be reserved for the King's unconditioned and exclusive disposition; that neither ministers nor chambers have a say in the matter. That is the principle of the Roman Imperators. Tacitus relates how a Senator, Junius Gallio, in order to flatter Tiberius, proposed to the Senate new honors for the imperial guards. Thereupon the Emperor scolded him furiously, insisting that none but he had a say about the soldiers. The unhappy man had to be glad to get off alive and atone in hard exile for the crime of having had thoughts about the army. According to constitution and law the army is in no way different from any other branch of state government; the King holds the Commandership-in-Chief as the executive power generally; he appoints the officers as he, directly or indirectly, appoints all the other officials of the state.

Touched in his honor, Manteuffel challenged Twesten and shot his adversary's right hand to pieces in a pistol duel.

Still cherishing resentments against the revolution, the generals demanded a hierarchical order, a discipline extending over the whole of society, on which to build up the army. Not on patriotism and enthusiasm did Roon want to see the army reared, but on a stern war discipline which, in his opinion, suited the character of the people and the spirit of the army. Implicit, "cadaverous" obedience, they thought—and none more than the Prince of Prussia, the later William I—could be instilled only by a return to three-year service for all soldiers. The third year was necessary to produce the "true soldier spirit." While admitting that, even with a great number of illiterates, the technical things could be taught within two years, the generals pointed to the experiences of 1848-9, when the Landwehr of the guards and the cavalry had proved loyal, but the infantry of the line, not to speak of the Landwehr generally, had wavered, if not openly resisted. They attributed this to the sole fact that the loyal troops had served their three years, not to the circumstance that these troops were largely recruited from rural and other classes without revolutionary tendencies—in particular from the rural laborers who recognized in the officer the Junker of the landed estate on which they worked in semiservitude. With this purpose in mind, a service term of two and a half years was introduced in 1852 in the whole infantry, and one of three years in 1856.[16]

The same period was proposed in the army bill of 1860, which gave rise to the constitutional conflict in Prussia. The military authors of this bill wanted an army largely for the officers and for the narrow purposes of their class. The legitimism of the Metternich era strongly survived in many of them, and the army reform was not conceived with any specific war in their minds. They were resolved not to take any dictation from Austria, but Austria was not yet "the enemy." Uppermost now was the desire "to get out of the mud," where the wheels of the apparatus of advancement and promotion turned furiously and yet did not carry them forward as rapidly as the victorious bourgeois were shooting ahead in other fields. The demand was for an army almost twice as large as the old army and for a twofold increase of the number of officers; for a rejuvenation of the army which was to take the field, by eliminating the Landwehr altogether from the field army, and by forming the latter out of a larger peace army and the four classes which had just left the army —the reserve. Thus the future field army was to consist exclusively of regiments of the line, which were filled up by the reserve.

By eliminating the Landwehr regiments, the war army was to become quite homogeneous. The quality of the army became more standardized than ever; every division and subdivision was to be used interchangeably—a process, however, which still stopped short of the guards. The Landwehr was to be employed only for secondary purposes, like occupation of enemy territory and fortresses; and the Landwehr II, containing men from the thirty-sixth year on, was to be dismissed altogether. The maximum age of the field soldier was reduced from thirty-three to twenty-eight. It was thought that the rejuvenation would assure prompter obedience and that a younger army would not be inclined to think politically for itself, as might the Landwehr, whose independence could hamper the actions of the army in case of revolutionary trouble, as well as in an unpopular foreign war. Such an army would win back to the Crown and all the military men who flocked around it a large part of that power which in weak moments had been conceded to the bourgeoisie and its Landtag.

This part of the army reform did away with the Landwehr soldier —the popular element considered dangerous; another was intended to do away with the Landwehr officer. He, too, was far too often liberal and in opposition to the policies of the Crown and military bureaucracy. To stop the *embourgeoisement* of the Landwehr, if not of the army itself, the institution of officer of the reserve was called into existence. Though the design was not realized to the full until many years later, the reserve officer was to resemble as closely as possible the professional officer who took for his model, in turn, the Junker officer, from the small Prussian nobility. To insure this end, the reserve officer was to be elected by the officer body of an active regiment, whereas the Landwehr officer was elected by the Landwehr officers of his home district.

The Liberals dominating the Landtag saw the purposes of the

army bill well enough, and for their own reasons opposed the elimination of the Landwehr, and even more the lengthening of the "active" service period. They were not averse to enlarging the army, particularly the yearly quota, and to granting the additional sums this would require; their own proposals about the numerical strength of the wartime army went beyond the plans of the army itself. But they insisted tenaciously upon a return to the two-year term of service in order to ease the great burden which other features of the bill put upon the people. To them this burden largely consisted in the loss of productive labor to the national economy.

In the face of a troubled scene in foreign affairs at the time, the liberals postponed the outbreak of the interior conflict for a few years, partly to see what the Prussian officers would do with the larger army put at their disposal, especially what they would do to serve the bourgeois' own aspirations for a unification of Germany under Prussian leadership, or for a dissolving of Prussia in the greater Germany. They were willing to pay for the army if it would help bring about such an achievement; but in their plans the army must serve a purpose beyond that of merely providing the Junkers with a living. While the Junkers regarded the army mainly as an institution to furnish berths and to secure power at home, the liberals considered it an instrument to be applied abroad, not for a *coup d'état* at home.

The reform brought with it a much larger army, almost a doubling of the number of officers. Advancement, which the long peace years had reduced almost to a snail's pace, was speeded up. One part of the newly required officers was drawn from the upper classes of the cadet academies, from the nobility generally favored by the 1860 reform.[17] The extra berths were given to politically reliable Landwehr officers, even though they came from those classes "which only in exceptional cases supply useful material for the officer class," as a general wrote to Manteuffel in 1862, full of worry over the threat to the old "chivalric" qualities of the Prussian officer.

These worries led to the assembling of statistics about the social standing of the 2,516 candidates for officers' examinations in 1862-3, 1863-4, and 1866-7; of these candidates 49 per cent were still noble; grouped according to their fathers' professions, 33 per cent were sons of officers, 26 per cent sons of higher officials, 20 per cent sons of large landowners, 7 per cent sons of teachers, and 6 per cent sons of smaller officials; 5 per cent were sons of merchants and industrialists, while only 3 per cent came from the rentier class.

All "better classes" were welcome, but least the sons of capitalists. The motives of the latter were distrusted by the generals. It was actually supposed that only "the quicker advancement of recent times has attracted them and they hope to make better business in the army than elsewhere." [18] Riches and the offspring of rich men were not then so prized in the Prussian army as they later came to be, partly because rich men still belonged to the classes and parties which stood in opposition to the government. Possessing the old self-governing privilege, the officers of a regiment could decide by election whom they wanted to admit to their midst and could turn down the undesirable rich, even if they came up to the educational requirements. This exclusiveness on the part of the army governors foreshadowed the later policy which perilously limited Germany's war strength, when, just before the First World War, the size of the army was made dependent on the number of "reliable" officers available and not upon the size of the population fit to bear arms.

The better education which the sons of the bourgeois might have received and which the army needed more than ever, with the steady advance in machinery applicable to warfare, did not make them any more welcome. Bourgeois sons and education were considered necessary evils, by the army corps commanders and the Military Cabinet rather than by heads of the departments where intelligence was better appreciated, that is, by the War Ministry and the General Staff. Indeed, the latter obtained at last two concessions for education. In 1859 studies in the war schools were made obligatory for future officers, except for those who had studied in universities, and candidates for the officer's entrance examination, the first of two such tests, who were found deficient in knowledge of German grammar and spelling, were in the future to be rejected.

Against such concessions to education those feudal elements whose grammar was often not up to the passing mark protested violently. They objected to ending the feudal privilege and the "historical right" of mistreating the mother language by establishing the "homogeneity" of the Prussian officer corps. Manteuffel was asked peremptorily: "Would that rule insure the further supply of the army with sons of the old aristocracy? Or would it not rather change the composition of the corps, and let sons of enriched bankers in to replace the Dönhoffs and Dohnas in the *Garde du corps,* noblest of the Prussian regiments?" ("Dumb as a Dönhoff" was a standing Prussian expression.) Would such an altered officer body show the same loyalty as that of 1848 in putting down revolution? "Would it not be dangerous to irritate the nobility too much?"

Manteuffel shared this distrust of bourgeois pride in education and the fear that educational standards would keep men of the "old disposition" from the army. Such requirements had already turned away from service the otherwise desirable gentry of Mecklenburg, the "darkest Africa" of Germany. He reminded the War Minister of the old *pons asinorum* for those less cultivated but useful elements —presence of mind, punctuality and order, and decent behavior.

These, he insisted, the officer had to possess as well as an education, and the King's grace and benevolence had in many cases considered such qualities sufficient to admit candidates who had failed three or four times in the entrance examinations. Overeducation of the officer was to Manteuffel and like-minded generals a real danger. One of the latter was convinced that by no means the worst candidates had failed in the high schools, "where often enough haughty teachers, as a rule full of hostility toward the better classes, proud of their fancied scholarship, in brutal ways kill the true feeling of honor and, saturated with the destructive tendencies of the time, almost exclusively rationalist, educate for everything else but character." By these representations the King was deeply moved and allowed an easing and postponement of the strict entrance requirements in order to hold the door open for the "Old Prussians."

In the prolonged struggle between the War Ministry, as that part of the bureaucracy which wanted educated officers competent to deal with the increasingly complicated service, and the Military Cabinet, primarily interested in "reliable" men for political ends, the latter triumphed. For political reasons it was decided in 1870—and the decision prevailed more or less down to 1914—that educational weaknesses in the candidate should be overlooked if his "character" and other gifts were promising. Consequently, the educational level of the successful candidates was constantly lowered and army service became a career for ungifted sons of the well-to-do, noble or not. In view of the fact that actually the character of the candidate was seldom fully disclosed to the examining commissions, the objective criteria were as a rule those of his origin, his father's profession and wealth; in other words, class was the criterion.

Speaking of the worst 120 pupils in the war schools, an inspection report for 1883-4 says "an unpleasantly large proportion of them carry names which for generations have traditionally belonged to our officer corps." [19] This lowering of the standards of the Prussian officer, so little in accordance with the usual reputation of education in Prussia, was to the German liberals, the party of progressive capitalism and education, merely one more indication that the army was being turned into a nursery of the nobility instead of into a field of contest, open to the competition of the whole nation's best minds. It would have shocked them no end had they known that the greatest German historian of the century, Ranke, newly ennobled in 1867, had written Manteuffel that "the *von* was proving very useful" to his soldier son.[20]

With justified scorn, the liberals spurned the claim of the standing army to be a school of war for the whole nation.[21] They could only see in the army an institution for lowering and violating standards of thought and initiative and for reducing their own sons to the level of the East Elbian rural workers. It also angered them to observe the government's complete inaction on an issue which deeply stirred them as much as their liberal contemporaries in other countries, the question of nationalism, the desire for a wider consolidation of local units within a larger territorial frame, furnishing a greater market. This at length provoked the conflict in Prussia.

Thus it was liberalism, not conservatism, that pursued the dreams of the German Empire yet to come. It was a Prussian liberal to whom it had occurred in 1836 that Holland ought to become Prussian because it was rather a necessity for Prussia and would be a benefit for Holland. It was the same liberal who found the word of the Prussian King, in 1848, that Prussia was to be dissolved in Germany, a word of tremendous potentiality: "It might come about that we would demand Alsace and Lorraine from France, the Baltic countries from Russia. Such things Black-Gold-Red can do. Up to now this has just been a beginning." [22]

The Prussian liberal intelligentsia, even when in bureaucratic employ, now insisted that "the German question is a power question, and without proof of the national application and success of power, it will never be solved." That writer, in 1861 a maker of Prussian public opinion by order of a war ministry, was himself pressing for a forward policy against France, or Denmark, or any other country that offered an occasion for action on the part of ossified Prussia. "Only in the field of facts and deeds can the German question be solved, and only our absolute inactivity, our own endless gabbling has of necessity nursed the talkers" of the Prussian opposition.[23]

To overcome this inactivity and put the new army to use, liberals formed in Prussia in 1861 the *Deutsche Fortschrittspartei*, the German Progress Party, which declared itself to be the executive of German nationalism; Prussia was to be realizer of German unity. For this purpose the party, the largest in the Landtag though by no means a party of masses, demanded parliamentary government, including control not only over the military budget but over all details of army organization as well, thus curtailing the rights of the Crown and the army—a Cavour-like policy.

Such demands, however, were unbearable for the King and his military counselors. Roon wrote to the monarch: "My Prussian soldier-heart cannot stand the thought that my King and Master has to place another will above his own." As the mandatory of the officer body, he played the greatest role by barring the adoption of the parliamentary system in Prussia. When he seemed to weaken temporarily and wanted to resign, high officers wrote him that "the King must know that such a change would deeply shake the officer body of the army" and that he must remember that "only soldiers can protect and help him against democrats." [24]

These democrats, by achieving a huge success in the elections at the end of 1861, threw the military party into the greatest alarm. It prepared detailed operations for a march on Berlin with thirty-five thousand infantry and engineer troops, and one hundred cannon; and the troops in Berlin were handed war munitions. Military men entreated the King to dismiss the somewhat liberal ministry, always excepting Roon, and hoped that the conflict over army reform, becoming acute, would do away with the tender beginnings of constitutionalism in Prussia. Military wishes coincided with those of the Junkers, who had fought this development and in particular all attempts to make them contribute to the expenditures for army reform by paying a land tax. They wanted a larger army as "the corn bin" for their younger sons, but would not be taxed for it. A former commander of the guards army corps and member of the Upper House told the King that he had battled long nights in prayer with God and that the voice above had ordered him to vote against the tax bill because it was trespassing on the privileges of the Junkers.[25]

Despite such threats on the Right, the Landtag resolved, in the beginning of 1862, no longer to grant annual appropriations for the enlarged army and insisted on the two-year term of service and on discussing the items of the military budget. This was unbearable to Roon: "The feeling of the Army must not be hurt, for by the ruin of the army-spirit Prussia will become Red and the Crown will roll into the dirt." This spirit would suffer if the Crown yielded merely on the point of money. The proud self-confidence must be preserved "which springs from the dependence upon the King alone and not upon parliament." At the bottom of his heart Roon was convinced that the "liberal crowd, the vulgar Philistines" did not care for high stakes.[26] So the King was persuaded to dismiss semiliberal ministers, to call a conservative ministry, and to dissolve the Landtag, in the hope that an energetic influence of the bureaucracy upon the elections would produce a more compliant parliament. When it became evident even before the elections that the popular vote would go against the Crown and that the King was considering abdication, Field Marshal Wrangel, who was to have commanded the march upon Berlin planned the year before, told the King quite plainly that the army would not allow him to abdicate and would mutiny if he did.[27]

But some of the higher officers in the Prussian army, representing a higher military intelligence than that of the simple-minded Wrangel, drew back. They viewed with much less equanimity the prospect of an open conflict with the newly elected Landtag and its liberal majority and shrank from the necessity of violating the constitution in case the Landtag should withhold money. They knew full well that a two-year term of service was sufficient for mere military drill.

The ministry, including Roon, were willing to accept this compromise, but not the King, who considered a three-year term the
only panacea against the "revolutionary infection of the army."
Feeling unable at his age to carry on the conflict, however, the King
resolved to abdicate in favor of the Crown Prince, the son-in-law of
Queen Victoria. The Prince, on his part, was just enough of a liberal
to shy from such power and possible revolution. He declined to
accept the crown from his father's hands, warned him against
Bismarck, and hastily retired to a happy family life. The weakness
of the wearer of the crown seemed to presage opening the gates to
the rising tide of liberalism even in Prussia. In that event, the
prolonged privileged existence of the Junker nobility would be
threatened.

At this critical juncture, Roon called in the greatest of all Junkers,
Bismarck, who frankly admitted the identity of class and personal
interest when he said during the Revolution of 1848-9: "I am a
Junker and I want to draw advantage from that." [28] He was to save
the rule of the Crown for army and Junkerdom, as Roon reminded
him, recognizing "the old chivalrous duty of salvaging the King even
if, as now happened, he should willfully run into danger." Bismarck,
telling the King he felt like a "Kur-Brandenburg vassal who sees his
feudal lord in danger," at last convinced him of the necessity of
averting parliamentary government, if need be by a period of
dictatorship; rather was he determined to go down with the King
than leave him stranded in the battle over parliamentarism.[29]

The King allowed himself to be saved and reseated by this
demoniac person, though the memory of Charles I, Strafford, and
Louis XVI made him uncomfortable—fearful lest a block be prepared for himself and Bismarck, his Strafford, in the Berlin Opera
Square. Again and again Bismarck had to steel him for the fray:
"Charles will always remain a noble historical figure; after having
drawn his sword for his rights and lost the battle, with head unbowed
he confirmed his royal intention with his blood. Your Majesty is
under the necessity to fight. You cannot capitulate. You must oppose
surrender if need be under bodily danger." [30]

The new Prime Minister, after September 1, 1862, was personally
not at all decided about the necessity of the three-year term of army
service, but he was decided about the necessity of following the
King in his headstrong military opinions, even if the latter should
insist upon a ten-year term. For the King must save nobility and
army—that is, the army as the King wanted it—and defeat the
liberal bourgeoisie.[31] When the overwhelming liberal majority of the
Landtag withheld the "army money," Bismarck proceeded to govern
without its grants. Overleaping, so to speak, Cromwell's civil war
period, he proceeded to a vigorous foreign policy for Prussia in

Germany. He told the budget committee that Prussia alone, with her unfavorable geographic conditions, could no longer provide the armaments which Germany needed for her security, that all Germans must share this burden. This goal would not be approached by speeches, societies, majority resolutions; a serious fight was unavoidable, a fight which could be settled only by iron and blood. He wanted the parliamentarians to place "the largest possible weight of iron and blood in the King's hand so that he could throw it into the right scale of the balance." [32] But this King, generally considered a military pedant, was the last person the Diet was ready to trust with iron and blood, with arms and the men. So they withheld money and confidence from Bismarck and hoped yet to achieve their own aims through the defeat of his daring policy.[33] They offered the government more men than it wanted, but less of their time— power, but not might.

Then the liberals found that the military counselors of the King would not really and seriously "discuss" such propositions with them. In discussion and oratory the military mind is peculiarly weak. Ulysses S. Grant was a feeble and embarrassed speaker. So was Roon; before he became War Minister he worried his friends on this account but, as his son wrote, "he proved that a gifted Prussian soldier of character can do all that is in his duty and that he learns to overcome all difficulties, because it has been ordered so." He used to tell the Diet that he was not making a speech but was merely talking on the business in hand. He overcame the difficulties so well indeed that after a few years he was considered one of the best parliamentary speakers, making the arguments which the army considered necessary, while holding the opinion that "the time of speeches was the time of the downfall of the ancient world." [34]

The tactics of the liberals could not be as revolutionary as their aims. They did not dare to proceed to a tax strike and direct antimilitaristic appeals to the recruits and soldiers. Times were too prosperous for Prussian business to be jeopardized by such notions, which might again stir the laborers to activity as in 1848-9. Incidentally prosperity allowed the government to finance the reformed army from the growing income of the old taxes, avoiding demands on the Diet for new taxes or on the bankers for loans, and escaping the inevitable denial. Only Krupp offered it credits.[35]

After this real victory the only serious concern of the rulers was to keep the army reliable. "They tremble before every noncommissioned officer who reads a democratic paper," a liberal historian and parliamentarian wrote at the time; "before every word in parliament which might seduce the soldiers, but before nothing else. From their own standpoint they are quite right; as long as the army keeps intact the people can apply no material force. Their regime

will last until the army pronounces itself for the constitution or until
it cracks in a foreign war—unless fortune should favor us, as it did
the English in 1688 with the Prince of Orange." [36]

To make the army immune to liberal influence, Manteuffel and
Roon, who was hoping that abrupt measures might provoke revolutionary putsches, obtained a cabinet order of September 1863, forbidding all members of the army to exercise the franchise which
the constitution had granted them. To Roon the withdrawal of the
army "from the dangerous election agitation" seemed more important than a possible loss of progovernment votes.[37]

This palpable pretense of making the army "unpolitical" was one
of the governing tricks of the Prussian conservatives, who possessed
themselves more and more of the bureaucracy, civil as well as
military. They played on the growth of the expert in many fields
and claimed for themselves the sole expertness in military and
diplomatic questions, as against the amateur versatility on which
liberalism based its title. Bismarck, himself always ready to pronounce his opinion on military affairs, including strategic questions,
taunted the liberals by saying that he found their readiness to form
opinions "coupled with the equal amount of ignorance about the
things in question," and that "it was a dangerous, though now widespread, error that in politics whatever is invisible to the reason
of the reasonable men, is revealed to the political dilettante by naïve
intuition." [38]

Diplomatic and military successes of Prussia from 1850 to 1871
made this pretense of exclusive expertness finally acceptable to the
German nation. Even after the catastrophic defeat of the bureaucracy
in the First World War, the nation continued to be patient with it
and, under the law for the restoration of the Civil Service in 1933,
allowed the National Socialists to remove political foes and pack the
bureaucracy with their job-hungry and unexamined followers.

Having won a complete victory over the Prussian Diet and defied
parliamentary control over the army, Bismarck captivated the less
intransigent liberals by his successes, by defeating Denmark and
Austria, and by establishing the North German Confederation—
the union of German hearts for which the bourgeoisie yearned. And
there was nothing like success in wearing down any residual opposition to the further consolidation of the military position. In the
course of time, the Chief of the General Staff shook off his subordinate role. During the war with Austria, in 1866, a royal cabinet
decree empowered him to give orders directly to commanding
officers, thus eliminating the Minister of War entirely in matters of
command, and making Moltke, as Chief of Staff, the supreme army
leader in action.

By His Successes in Handling Mass Armies Moltke Raises the Military in Popular Esteem

With parliamentary control through financing reduced to a nominal check—in Prussia and later in the North German Confederation and the German Empire—and with the Military Cabinet and General Staff well insulated against the civil bureaucracy, Moltke carried forward the work of integrating and perfecting the military machine. Leaving the Danish service and entering the Prussian as one would enter a new industrial concern with more chances for promotion, Moltke worked rather than conspired in the manner of generals without Caesarian ambitions, which included Lee, Grant, and MacMahon, Moltke served the army not so much as a Prussian but as the employee of a big corporation; he was an officer first and a Prussian second. He welcomed the Revolution of 1848 because of its tendency toward German unity, but condemned the democratic desires as the symptoms of "a cholera pervading Europe," and resented criticisms of the Prussian army, his employer. Moltke, like Roon, could apply his thought to earning money by writing books, or a story, by drawing maps, or translating. Given the limitations of the Prussian army, he was a self-made man, though devoid of the customary crudity. For long years his struggle for promotion in this army—to which he had been admitted as "a poor acquisition," or so his superiors thought from his modest exterior—remained unrelieved by war, "without which the military profession will be a sad one in the future," as Moltke wrote in 1848.[39]

For this reactionary army, Moltke thought out the potentialities of the new weapons, less for the purposes of immediate destruction than for the handling and moving of masses by railways and telegraph. There was as little romanticism in technology for Moltke as there was for Grant. With the help of the new aids he made armies manageable up to a hitherto unknown size. Montecuccoli had considered an army of 30,000 men the maximum size; Turenne regarded one of 50,000 as "inconvenient for him who commands it and for those who compose it." Marshal Saxe and General Moreau believed that an army should not outgrow the number of 40,000; to lead an army of 100,000 men, Gouvion Saint-Cyr thought, "calls for such moral and physical strength that one cannot hope to find them combined in one single man." [40] The new armies left the old ones far behind in size; the Franco-Prussian War was opened on the German side with 480,000 men as against the French armies of 300,000. And the new armies were not only very much larger but also much faster. The Crimean War, declared in March 1854, did not really start before September; the American Civil War was almost as slow in starting; but the Prussian wars of 1864, 1866, and 1870-1 were quickly opened and soon over.

The many new highways were one means of acceleration, and railways provided another. Moltke had founded a railway section in the General Staff and, following American experiences with construction corps, he created in May 1866, the new railway troops, the first in Europe and placed under the immediate orders of the General Staff of the army.[41] So great was the speed-up that more conservative generals like Roon were afraid that the soldiers would die of exhaustion unless speed were moderated.[42] Mobilization plans, including the all-important opening movements of a war, were drawn up in the manner of timetables. They were yet sufficiently flexible to allow for changes up to a short time before the outbreak of war.

Besides showing how vast masses of men could be quickly brought into battle action and demonstrating the power of the soldier as administrator, Moltke devised methods for the control of armies by telegraph and message from a post far behind the lines. The new way was to send orders from a distant general headquarters, from a general who could not at any moment appear on the field of battle and interfere with actual execution. In other words, Moltke brought supreme command to a focus and enabled the Chief of Staff to direct from a single center, through fanlike controls, enormous bodies of men and operations covering hundreds of miles. The underlying principle of this generalship was concentration, which allowed dispersal and supreme control, and still permitted initiative to the commanders of single armies.

Although Bismarck, Roon, and Moltke were not democrats, for purposes of warfare they believed that man equals man, as between armies, not within them. This equation underlay their concept of international competition and in particular Moltke's plans. It was his idea that "durable success can only be obtained if one enters the war from the outset with numerical superiority"; whereas the French before 1870 believed that their lesser strength—300,000 as against 480,000 Germans at the opening of the war—would be outweighed by the better quality of their troops. They largely measured quality by the longer service term of their men—seven years up to 1868 and five years afterward—as against three years in North Germany, two in Württemberg, and only a year and a half in Bavaria. After her disaster France, too, embraced the numerical principle, which had given Prussia victory at Königgrätz—221,000 Prussians against 215,000 Austrians—and at Sedan, where fully 250,000 Germans overwhelmed 140,000 Frenchmen. Larger armies, concentration of forces and command, and delegation of authority to subordinate commanders with managerial responsibility were signs of a new stage in warfare.

When Moltke had won immoderate praise from the public, the voters, fascinated by his victories, elected him, with other victorious generals, to parliament in 1867. Now the people became inclined to believe in a superior kind of planning which crisis-beset capitalism did not know how to provide but which seemed to be inherent in successful military institutions and enterprises. This supposition was the psychological basis of popular faith in the capacity of officers for red-tape cutting and in their general versatility. In contemplation of such victories as Moltke's, the public yielded to a doctrine entirely contrary to the earlier bourgeois ideas: namely, that the officer is the only fit person to judge questions of defense, that he is not excluded from other functions on that account, that he is in fact more versatile than members of other professions. He even took charge of theaters, for, as if to taunt the Prussian bourgeoisie, so proud of its artistic tastes, the Prussian kings from 1850 to 1918 entrusted the direction of royal theaters to the Von Hülsen family. One of these Hülsens, a general of infantry, contributed so zealously to the entertainment of his royal master as to cause his own demise; dressed up as a ballerina and performing a *pas de ballet* before the Kaiser, the fifty-six-year-old general was seized by heart failure in the midst of his act.

No group took advantage of this change in convictions more eagerly than the conservatives. To make the greatest possible use of Moltke's prestige, Junker leaders claimed him in 1870 "as the finest wrapper-tobacco" for their interests.[43] This was about the same time that Grant permitted himself to be used as a wrapper to lend appearance to the rather odorous cigar of corrupt party politics in the United States.

The Military Entrenched in the Constitutional System

To obtain the consent of the masses to the rule of the notables, Bismarck took a leaf out of Napoleon III's book of recipes on plebiscites and based the parliament of the North German Confederation, the forerunner of the Second Reich, on manhood suffrage. He did this not for democratic purposes but with Caesarian intentions, sure that he would find the masses everywhere as obedient as the agricultural workers from old Prussia east of the Elbe, both at the polls and in army service. He still conceived of the masses as largely rural. As Lassalle's friend, Countess Hatzfeldt, wrote to Karl Marx, Bismarck did not know the industrial worker; he did not foresee the consequences of this franchise, being under the impression that he could manipulate it in Germany as Napoleon had done in France. That was an error, she thought, for manhood suffrage would sooner or later lead to democracy, a republic, and socialism in Germany, after the industrial workers outnumbered the rural laborers. But when in 1866 Bismarck established manhood suffrage for the Reichstag, the rural workers still numbered 3,430,000 as against 770,000 in industries and 1,000,000 in the handicrafts.[44]

The mere form by which the King exercised his authority in Germany, Bismarck told Roon in 1869, "has never had a particular importance for me; but to see that he does exercise it, I have applied all the strength which God has given me." [45] The King was made Commander-in-Chief in the North German Confederation as unrestrictedly as he had been in Prussia. "For reasons of public safety" he could at any time declare a state of siege and suspend the personal rights of the citizens. Conscription was extended over the territory of the Confederation to procure, for the next ten years, a peacetime army of 1 per cent of the total population of 1867, that is, 300,000 men and 13,000 officers. In order to save himself and the Minister of War from an annual battle about the budget, Bismarck called for a fixed, "iron budget"—a grant of 225 thalers ($169) per head for the next ten years—after which time the army budget as well as its strength was again to be fixed in relation to the growth of population.

Bismarck denied the Reichstag "the right to call in question every year the existence of the Prussian army," and Roon told the parliamentarians that, even if the enemies of army reorganization had come to see the error they had long entertained, still this did not give any guarantee that the army would not be endangered again. Therefore the constitution of the Confederation had to provide for liberating the army from dependence on the vote of Reichstag members. In the arrangement the government did not take all budgetary rights from them, but rather it proposed to appeal to their magnanimity. Bismarck's demands, however, were too much for the "military piety" even of the liberals. As Twesten protested: "On the one hand military power, firmer and more extensive than ever, concentrated in the hands of the warlord, and on the other general, equal, direct suffrage: those are the means by which France has built up Caesarian dictatorship." [46]

Troubled by complications of his foreign policies, which made him anxious to avoid conflicts at home, Bismarck conceded to the Reichstag more budgetary rights than he had contemplated at first: the iron budget for the army was granted only up to 1871. Thereafter a new law was to fix the peacetime strength and the army budget was to be voted by the Reichstag periodically, always, however, on the basis of the army organization as laid down in the constitution: three years of service with the colors, four years in the reserve, and five in the Landwehr. If, after 1871, the Reichstag refused to approve the budget for an army 300,000 strong, the same income from the member states was to be at the disposal of the Confederation. To that extent a repetition of the previous Prussian conflict within the union was prevented in advance.

Nevertheless, this hazy compromise between an executive power which desired to exclude civilians entirely and a parliamentarism which strove for power contained new germs for conflict. With such a struggle in view the compromise had been engineered by the Prussian conservatives, who consciously calculated on a clash in order to do away with parliamentarism. The conservatives trusted that a conflict would sooner or later break out and that the army, triumphant in the field, would sweep away liberal institutions and re-enthrone the King of Prussia in full absolutism.[47]

Actually, the Prussian Crown obtained a vast accretion of power through the constitution of the Confederation. The sphere of parliamentary control over the Minister of War was narrowed, as compared with that in the Prussian constitution. Prussia in turn was affected by the creation of the union and allowed the responsibility of the War Minister to become atrophied from lack of use. The new military powers were now vested in the Prussian Military Cabinet, controlled by the *Bundesfeldherr,* the irresponsible Commander-in-Chief of the Confederation, who in 1871 became the German Emperor. This Cabinet became more than ever the bureaucratic institution for military absolutism in Berlin. It exercised its power most decisively as the exclusive *personnel* bureau, using royal prerogative as a fulcrum if swayed by the humors of a monarch, which might be dangerous, as in the case of William II's moods. It was completely withdrawn from the public eye and popular control and soon even escaped the scrutiny of Bismarck. For such irresponsibilities, Bismarck had opened the doors wide when he excluded the well-considered advice of a parliament.[48]

Bismarck admitted the dangers of such constitutional arrangements to the state he had created and to his own position therein, but his Junkerdom and the desires of the military would not admit of any other settlement. In rejecting parliamentary discussion and repelling parliamentary influence in matters of foreign and military policies, he pretended to be listening to the immediate voice of the German nation, maintaining that it was the duty of the several governments in Germany "to satisfy the national self-confidence of Germany to the extent that it exists. If a people feels hurt in its honor, honor is wounded and corresponding action is necessary: national feeling and national honor are powers which cannot be measured in a logical manner." [49] If they cannot be measured logically, they can be used with calculation. And this is the reason why this greatest of all Junkers, full of contempt for the masses, conceded to the German nation one feudal possession—the feeling of honor. But he did not concede to it, as Hitler did after him, a second feudal distinction—that of having the only good *blood*. Bismarck granted the people *honor*. Hitler even more magnanimously granted them *blood* and *honor*.

After the establishment of the German Empire in 1871 "by the Princes" assembled at Versailles to celebrate the victory over France, the Prussian military system, including the obligation of universal service, was made general throughout the Empire. The principle of fixing the size of the army at a given ratio to the population and allowing a definite sum annually per capita of the army for maintenance was continued until 1874. In that year, when a bill was up for codifying military jurisprudence, the conservatives sought to incorporate in the bill the old rule of an army based on a fixed ratio to the population and sustained by a definite annual allowance per man. This project, if enacted, would have made the army and its finances permanent and put them beyond the reach of the imperial parliament.

Consequently a violent dispute rose among the parties. The deadlock was broken by a compromise which combined a certain degree of permanence for the army and periodical review by the parliament. The term of the authorization for the army and its finances was fixed at seven years—later at five years. Thus, at the expiration of each term a terrific struggle took place between the parties of the Right and the parties of the Left over the new army bill, and down to 1914 these occasions provided tests of military strength in politics. It could not be said that the German military got all they wanted at each successive contest in the parliament. Good bargainers never fix their lowest price at the outset; but given the situation in 1914, as to men and materials, it was fairly evident that the military had all the men and materials they could conveniently manage, considering their deliberate curtailment of the officer list by the exclusion of "undesirables" for class and other reasons of policy.

As an estate the German army increased in size as in independence between 1871 and 1914. The Kaiser, combining civil and military authority, stood outside of parliamentary control in the choice of ministers and officers for the army. The functions of an imperial ministry of war were retained by the Prussian War Office —the old setup as essentially evolved under Manteuffel, Roon, Bismarck, and Moltke; but three south German states kept war ministers of their own to the end of the First World War. The Imperial Chancellor remained to the end a personal appointee of the Kaiser, and all efforts to establish parliamentary government and a responsible ministry were defeated, although after the *Daily Telegraph* affair of 1908 the tendency in this direction gained momentum.

Augmented in size, well supported by public funds, the military estate remained largely in the hands of the officer class that had been in the saddle before and soon after all Prussian army reforms. Nowhere else in Western Europe was the army so completely isolated from political interference, while guaranteeing the political power of the class from which the dominating officer type sprang. Nowhere was the army more solidly organized and the public mind more effectively militarized. Although the perfect "harmony of people and army" was occasionally jarred by criticism, ridicule, and attacks from the Left, especially from the Social Democrats, the German military had the power, the organization, and the popular support which easily turned the war of the mass army into the war of the embattled German nation.

If that mass army failed to overwhelm France and Russia in 1914, the misadventure was due largely to two things. First was the refusal of the military before the war to bring the mass army up to its utmost strength because not enough officers "of class" could be found to take charge of the additional men available, and the military were unwilling to descend to "little-suited elements" and thus expose the officer body to "democratization." [50] Secondly, the power of the mass army was diminished by the rise of the German navy and its demands, which cut in on the military budget, diminished the amount of materials that would otherwise have gone to the army, and, by bringing Great Britain into the competition, made it impossible for the mass army, large and powerful as it was, to crush France and Russia. It is scarcely an exaggeration to say that, in the tangled play of events, the German navy defeated the German army. At all events, had the navy refrained from draining the imperial treasury, the mass army would have been, if not larger, certainly better equipped with heavy guns and all the material means with which no mass weight or mass enthusiasm for death can dispense save by courting, indeed assuring, its own destruction.

The French Professional Army Is Tried Out Against the German Mass Army (1870-1)

While the Prussians were perfecting their mass army, always in fear of its democratic potentialities, the French military under Napoleon III were preparing their professional army, likewise in fear of evoking mass discontent. The Bourbons had abolished conscription after the Restoration in 1814. This abolition the July Monarchy had continued. Although the social uprising in 1848 had been followed by a declaration in favor of universal service, Napoleon had suppressed the popular movement and preserved a professional army on its ruins. After the Prussians had crushed Austria in 1866, Austria and France, both losers in that war, set in motion a new armament cycle. Both empires, compelled to make concessions to popular elements while enrolling them for war, proceeded to make constitutional reforms within, Napoleon moving step after step in the direction of a parliamentary regime, as the price of an army reform bill which put him in somewhat the same position as the Prussian Crown in 1862, but with a different outcome. The process was completed in April 1870, when France had become a constitutional monarchy along English lines.

It was hardly the French army that had wanted this new order. The War of 1866 seemed rather to have demonstrated the military superiority of the aristocratic order prevailing in Prussia. Ardant du Picq, the ideologue of French discipline, whose teachings were to take their greatest effect only after 1870-1, wrote after Königgrätz in favor of the Prussian order from a military point of view:

Has an aristocracy its *raison d'être* if it is not military? No. The Prussian aristocracy is *military,* nothing but that; it may receive plebeian officers into its ranks, but under the condition that they allow themselves to be absorbed. Is not an aristocracy essentially proud? If it were not, it would doubt itself. The Prussian aristocracy is proud, then; it wants distinction through force; and to dominate, always to dominate more, is among its conditions of existence. One dominates by war; it needs war (at its own hour, that is; the chiefs have the tact to choose the moment) and it wants war. . . . Every nation having an aristocracy, a military aristocracy, is organized in a military way. The Prussian officer is the perfect officer as gentleman (*gentilhomme*), as noble; through instruction and examination he is more capable, through education more dignified. . . . Prussia, with all the veils which hide the thing, is a military organization led by a military corporation. Each nation that is organized democratically is not organized militarily; it is, as opposed to the other, in a state of inferiority for war.[51]

At any rate, the French army adhered to a belief in its own features, especially a long-term service as the basis of superior quality. Neither the Prussian victories nor those of the Americans in their Civil War had convinced it that there was a value inherent in sheer numbers. According to Ardant du Picq the Americans had merely "shown us what will become of modern battle with armies immense but without cohesion. Among them the want of discipline, of traditional and solid organization has produced . . . things like entrenched *tirailleurs* fighting over long distances. To fight at a distance is natural to man—lasting one, two, three days, till some false movement, the weariness of the minds, leads one of the two parties to cede ground to the other." [52]

The French military men's horror of mere numbers was shared by the French bourgeois, who did not care to have their sons serve in the army. If one of their sons drew a "bad number" in the lot that fixed the annual class of recruits, he could buy a substitute. Thus without introducing general conscription, the army, according to a bill adopted early in 1868, was to be brought up to an eventual strength of eight hundred thousand in case of war, whereas a mobile guard of four hundred thousand, composed of those whom the lot had spared, was to form a reserve for home defense—a reserve that was not actually organized or trained when the war came in 1870.

The governing elements of the French bourgeoisie gladly accepted the arrangement for a professional army. "The society in which everyone is a soldier is a barbaric society," declared Thiers. "In the countries where everyone is a soldier, everyone is a bad soldier. . . . Without specialization, no army at all"; a statement that provoked this echo on the Left: "Thus to die for the rich would be the specialty of the poor." [53] Professionalism seemed to be well suited to the acquisitive inclinations of the time. Though French society had its sense of noble obligations, general military duty was not yet among them. Aside from such a duty, France seemed to be governed by the *point d'honneur*. To a defender of the order existing under Napoleon III it offered the unique spectacle of a society "in which the point of honor has become the principal guarantee of good order and makes for the fulfillment of most of the duties which religion and patriotism have lost the power to command. If our laws . . . are generally observed, when the young soldier docilely joins the colors and remains faithful to them; . . . if the Frenchman performs properly most of his duty to the state, it is the point of honor that we have to thank for it." [54] The admission of so much honor had usually been the forerunner or the concomitant of greater demands to be put on those who were conceded honor; and this again proved to be the case in and after 1870.

By 1867 French preparations were incomplete and war plans were arranged for defensive purposes. Bismarck thought the time for war not appropriate and Moltke acquiesced, expressing his conviction, however, that avoiding the war now would cost many more German lives ultimately.[55] Unless he could score some signal diplomatic success without it, Napoleon in France wanted the war no less than the Prussians, for, as he wrote to his War Minister in 1869, on an occasion which he thought appropriate to extend his sway over Belgium:

France feels reduced in her power since the successes of Prussia; she might find now an occasion to restore her influence under the best possible conditions, without however stirring the Germans by openly unfolding her standard against the German struggle for unity. The dexterity of the French government ought to be applied, therefore, to finding an occasion when the fight does not direct itself clearly against Germany [that is to say: against Prussia alone].[56]

The candidacy of a Hohenzollern prince for the Spanish throne seemed to offer to both parties the fortunate occasion either to score a resounding diplomatic victory or to start the war which was "in the air," and for which both felt ready in 1870. The German prince in Madrid was approved by the military leaders in Berlin as opening the possibility of forcing France to leave part of her army, however small, at the Pyrenees. Napoleon, on the other hand, fancied that he could score on this occasion, that a mere dynastic question like this would not stir German national feelings so deeply as to unite south and north behind Bismarck. "Here they want the war absolutely," wrote the Austrian military attaché from Paris. The Emperor, the Empress, the Ministry, and the masses were tired of the armed peace. "Bismarck has only the choice now between war and a second Olmütz." Mobilization of the first degree was ordered in Paris, in the belief that that would make war unavoidable.[57]

Bismarck, who had deliberately used the Spanish question from the beginning as "a trap for Napoleon," [58] was not willing to let the French turn into a triumph the renunciation of the Hohenzollern candidacy, which the Prussian King, as the head of the family, granted them. He knew how to turn what seemed a *chamade* into a *fanfare*. He made it appear that the King had granted the French all reasonable demands in order to keep peace and that only far-reaching, humiliating demands had moved him—a venerable, peaceful old man—to show the French ambassador the door. This picture, drawn by Bismarck's skill, with its suggestion of French outrage against the fatherly figure of the former "grapeshot prince," was sufficiently lurid to stir all Germany; Europe, in its peace wishes, was equally moved by the appearance of peacefulness on the part of the Prussian King. Revelations on Bismarck's part about the French intentions against Belgium even won British sympathies for the German cause.

On both sides the armies were ready, if not ardent, for war. Count Waldersee, then military attaché in Paris, had for years "passionately" yearned for war with France.[59] The French officers, as the later Marshal de Castellane relates, were obsessed by hopes for advancement: "I expect continually to be either the victim of a bullet or the possessor of a pair of gold-tasselled epaulettes." [60] On both sides military leaders welcomed the war when it arrived, for each group felt certain that it would win at the given moment. Before Bismarck sent the Ems dispatch, he had asked Moltke the very natural question (which, however, prewar diplomacy maintains it did not put to the military in July 1914), "whether, as things stood, we might hope to be victorious." And when he showed the Chief of Staff the new text, making war inevitable, the shriveled Moltke, Bismarck says, "became quite young and fresh again. He had got his war, his trade." [61] War was to him, as Hindenburg remarked of himself during the First World War, as refreshing as a mineral-water cure.

In spite of the warnings of the French military attaché at Berlin, Colonel Stoffel, extreme confidence reigned at Paris. Marshal Lebœuf declared the army ready "down to the last gaiter button." French mobilization was believed to be quicker than the German which, as it seemed to them, had stalled in 1866. The French Foreign Minister, the Duc de Gramont, took leave of the wife of the German ambassador with the hope that "after a few pistol shots along the frontier everything will be over, and we shall shake hands then." The French were to win a battle or two, for their army was far less prepared for a prolonged conflict than the German, and then were to offer peace to Prussia, allowing her to do in Germany as she pleased, while France took Belgium and a few other concessions which Bismarck had been denying her.

But this polite duelistic-diplomatic settlement was prevented by the unchaining of two nationalisms, not yet reshackled. And German nationalism quickly overbridged the line of the Main River, against which, as the seemingly insecure seam of the new Germany, the French had thought to direct their operations. The German armies proved to be not a coalition, as had been expected, but the war army of a nation.

In spite of all the differences involved in or explained by the national character of the two parties, the "man material" on both sides proved to be about equal at the opening of the war, as it was to be henceforth with the industrial Western European nations in their wars. The German preponderance consisted, first, in artillery, which could stay outside the reach of the French guns and thus force the French infantry to deploy at an early moment, whereas the Germans could hold their columns together much longer. Secondly, it consisted in numbers and organization, particularly in mobilization, and the effective arrangement of the higher units of army corps, divisions, and brigades; on the French side these units were poorly prepared for war. Preparation carried German mobilization through in perfect form and preserved the timetable. On the contrary the French troops arrived in great disorder on the frontier.

In spite of the complicated structure of German politics, things had been so well arranged that German leadership was not hampered by political considerations. The south German states were willing to have their troops assemble in the southern regions of the Rhineland and the Palatinate, north of Strasbourg, whence a French invasion of the south might be feared but could easily be checked by a German thrust in the French flank from the north. On its part, the French command had to pay all manner of respect to the exigencies of a regime none too stable, under which before long two political centers of divergent tendencies evolved—Paris and the Ministry on the one hand, and on the other, the army in the field—whither the Emperor had gone. Much effort was directed toward winning allies in Austria and Italy, but they did not dare to follow up earlier arrangements. In covering French provinces there was also a dispersion of troops in local short "lines," considered "naturally" impregnable by thinkers still caught in the tactics of the eighteenth century. The two main French armies remained separate in Alsace and Lorraine and allowed themselves to be beaten separately.

Even with the comparative shortness of fronts, the latter proved to be inviolable; neither party ever succeeded in a frontal attack.[62] Moltke, from the beginning, pursued great enveloping maneuvers permitted by his numerical strength. Though the willfulness of generals, like Steinmetz on the occasion of Spichern, upset some of his plans, he nevertheless succeeded in bottling up the larger parts of the French armies in Metz and in Sedan. Where frontal attacks were tried, they proved to be very costly—the so-called bayonet attacks of a Prussian brigade at Vionville cost it 62 per cent of its strength in the unheard-of relation of three dead to four wounded. This brigade fired only four cartridges per man on the occasion as against eighty per French infantryman; if shells and mitrailleuse bullets are excluded, only one of every 763 infantry bullets hit its man.[63]

Such are the statistics which supported Hegel's remark that "the soldier fires into the blue," and indicated the ever-expanding use of industrial products in warfare. One or two men per meter were sufficient to hold the front. Their machines were producing accidents and chance was causing death. To evade it, after having incurred heavy losses, the Prussians, in the midst of the war, introduced forward movement by bounds in intervals of running and lying down.

It cannot be said that the generals realized to the full the industrial materialization of warfare to which bourgeois thinkers had long been pointing. Dean Swift had perceived as early as 1712: "nothing else in the modern way of making war, but that the side which can hold out longest, will end it with most advantage. . . . If you will count upon sacrificing so much blood and treasure, the rest is all a regular, established method which cannot fail." [64] This materialist explanation of war was now taken over by the new enemy of the military, socialism, whose greatest thinker on military questions, Friedrich Engels, tried to show

that force is no mere act of will but calls for very real conditions before it starts to work, in particular tools, of which the perfect one overcomes the imperfect one; that furthermore these tools must be produced, which means at the same time that the producer of more perfect tools, *vulgo* arms, beats the producer of more imperfect ones.

In other words, the victory of force rests upon the production of arms and on industrial conditions generally, placing material means at the disposition of force. The development of arms from the invention of powder to the rifled breechloader has caused fundamental changes in the political conditions of dominion and servitude; and the changes in soldier-material have brought new forms of warfare. So impressed was Engels with the development of armament which the Franco-Prussian War had demonstrated that he felt it had now reached its limits. [65]

Most militarists, being conservatives in politics, are antimaterialist. They cannot help accepting in the end, however, the materials of war pressed upon them by industries. Yet they are always ready to use men against material—that is, even more men against more material, thus neglecting to explore the potentialities of the latter. This fact was illustrated in the Franco-Prussian War. Vainly but royally hurling men against one enemy wing, William I's personal interference at Gravelotte caused terrible hecatombs. [66] Observing the scene of war from general headquarters, Bismarck felt that "many of our generals have abused the devotion of the troops in order to secure victory"; that, on occasion, in order to gain victory for themselves alone they would not wait for the arrival of more troops under a rival general or composed of a rival "nation" like the Saxons to co-operate with them. Moreover, he found out that the calculations of the General Staff amounted to this: "Even if the whole 500,000 men whom we have now in France were to be wiped out, that should merely be regarded as the loss of so many pawns, so long as we ultimately won the game." [67]

This was a logical conclusion from military considerations of victory, once the premises of a war commencement were granted, but it naturally frightened Bismarck as the statesman who not only had to win the war but also to get something by it. At Sedan he told the German princes present that "this day secures and confirms the German princes and the conservative principle." Nevertheless he had to consider the relation between cost and achievement, warfare and diplomacy, during the war. With an eye on the diplomatic scene, Bismarck thought that the battles were far too bloody, and that some army leadership was clumsy, misusing "the immortal bravery" of the men: "Only fist and no head, and still we win. But we cannot spare so many as we lose, particularly officers, if we want to go to Paris. It is a waste of the best soldiers of Europe. . . . Every man is so valuable. We do not at all know yet how things are going to go." [68]

The Chancellor, the greatest of all Junkers, could never share the readiness to victimize as many soldiers as might be necessary to insure victory. He was indeed impatient to see enemies killed; he was convinced far too many of the French were made prisoners, but he thought there ought to be a limit to the victims on his own side even in the competition and conflict of armies. In this view he was confirmed by Count Waldersee, who watched the war from the entourage of the King-Emperor. At the beginning of February 1871, he found that his own "passion" for war was still strong, though he admitted "that by now enough blood has been shed. The feeling, however, when the moment arrives in which one sees peace approaching, is certainly something oppressive." [69]

In the end, the Franco-Prussian War seemed to demonstrate two fundamental propositions to military men and civilians. The mass army of "quantity" outflanked, surrounded, and defeated the professional army of "quality." The hostilities of the war marked the death blow to the hopes of old military men, with a nostalgia for the primitive and feudal, that a combination of genius, morale, and good sense in a well-led professional army could, by *élan*, dash, and "glorious charges," defeat masses, superior in number, effectively organized, and competently directed with mechanical precision. The outcome foreshadowed, if military men had possessed foresight or even good memory, the level of the First World War, with its inviolable front as merely the dividing line between the debit and credit sides of bookkeeping, where commensurable items are successively entered, balancing one another for a long time until the items—men plus materials—on the one side finally outbalance those items on the other. If such an upshot was not clearly discerned, at least the French realized that henceforward they must oppose a mass army to the mass army on the other side of the Rhine. That proposition had been well established by 1871.

The second proposition evolved out of the war experience was that an overwhelming defeat in modern warfare, in all likelihood, means a violent overturn in the regime so discredited. After Sedan the Second Empire was replaced by a republic which, in turn, was threatened by the uprising of the Paris Commune. Although that upheaval of the Commune was put down by the army, in ferocious eagerness to restore its reputation at least at home, with an even greater torrent of blood than that in June 1848, this memory remained with the working classes of Europe. It was revived in Petrograd, Moscow, Berlin, Vienna, and Budapest, when society there had likewise been shaken to the bottom by defeat in the First World War.

Defeated by a Mass Army, France Turns to the Mass Army

While the war with Prussia was still raging, French leaders, having overthrown the Napoleonic Empire, were forced to face a change in military organization. After the two French field armies had been annihilated, the new government of the republicans was told by the Germans to surrender Alsace and Lorraine as the price of peace. Unwilling to begin the Third Republic with a damaging peace as a heavy mortgage, they decided to oppose the Germans with an appeal to the masses, as in 1792-3. They resorted to universal conscription, which did away with all previous exemptions, so comfortable to the middle classes. Once more, France became the military power which developed immense popular strength; in the midst of war she started a fresh international competition in mass force and impact.

The Carnot of this war—"the Carnot of the defeat" as his enemies called him—was Gambetta, a parliamentarian and an advocate, a complete military amateur, and almost as much of a foreigner to France as Scharnhorst and Gneisenau to Prussia, or as Napoleon, another of the Italians who had never ruled France for her good, his foes declared, and who, some said, was a Jew.[70] Gambetta was aided by De Freycinet, equally young, a mining engineer with no previous military experience. Both demonstrated the versatility even in army matters which the class they represented was accustomed to claim in parliaments, meetings, and newspapers. Their way of warfare was energetic but amateur and therefore costly to France, Moltke commented, not without a reminder that the professional way of warfare was more economical.[71]

In invoking the revolutionary memories of 1792, Gambetta and Freycinet made the re-established National Guard an embodiment of the nation in arms. Through it France was armed, the warmaking part and the revolution-preparing part being for a time identical. They called up *francs-tireurs,* conceived somewhat in the spirit of the Prussian Landsturm of 1813. They made use of other "republican" war experiences by imitating arrangements of the American Civil War as the most recent "people's war." In their eagerness for numbers, they had, as George Sand said, "far too many men to

have enough soldiers": that is, men well enough exercised and
equipped; there were 250,000 *mobilisés* by the time of the armistice.[72]

In spite of the handicaps inherited from the late Empire, the
republicans were able to put up for months a resistance by which
they kept the Germans largely on the defensive, since the latter
were not nearly so ready to draw on their man power reserves.[73]
In such circumstances, the Germans applied their main strength to
the siege of Paris, even more the center now of government and
organization than in the days of the first Napoleon, and since fortified, rather because of French centralism than for other more
purely military reasons.

Bismarck had not been in favor of marching on Paris and be-
sieging it; he thought he could obtain peace if the army was kept
in the eastern provinces of France. But once Paris was invested
he, put under "a military boycott" by the generals, as well as Roon,
pressed for a prompt beginning of the bombardment in order to
shorten the war and thus preclude the danger of an intervention
by neutral powers. Thinking that Paris would finally be forced by
hunger to surrender, Moltke wanted to postpone the opening of
the bombardment; he demanded instead that greater military forces
be put at his disposal to pursue the war if necessary toward the
foot of the Pyrenees. He insisted that, as compared with France,
the man power resources of the German people had not been sufficiently tapped. Against such demands Roon wanted strategic considerations to be fitted to the forces already available, for reasons
of domestic policy, in which memories of 1848 played their role;
he objected to drawing too heavily on the family heads of the
Landwehr, not to speak of the Landsturm.

Eventually the mass levies of Gambetta failed, Paris capitulated
to the Prussians, Alsace and Lorraine were exacted as the price of
victory, and the French set to work on the problem of reconstructing their military forces along with their political institutions. Although the professionals had been defeated in the war by the Germans, they quickly re-established themselves in the favor of the
French bourgeois by suppressing the Commune. With the leadership of this nucleus readily accepted, despite the imperialist and
royalist elements in it, French politicians began the reform of the
army with the overhauling of 1872.

The reform of 1872 sprang from two needs of *revanche*—against
the foreign enemy and against the domestic foe. For those purposes
the French governing classes put the nation—that is, potentially,
the resources of the nation—at the disposal of the military experts
who had brought defeat indeed but salvation after it, the latter deed
serving to cover up the ignominy of the former. The interior ex-

perience determined the forms and ideologies of discipline, whereas the exterior one determined the organization, tactics, size, and equipment of the French army. It was hoped to amalgamate the quality which the old army was believed to have represented, despite its late defeat, with quantity typified by the German army. Since numbers were the most easily measurable feature of armies, the decision of the French Assembly of 1872 to have an armed force as numerous as Germany's set going the competition in which each increase of peacetime effectives induced every potential enemy to follow suit, arguing in terms of balance of power politics. As Freycinet, the War Minister, said, "what the foreign nations around us have done, does not allow us in turn to avoid the necessity of doing"; or as a French general put it in 1913: "It is necessary to answer the Germans by analogous measures."

Although the military had always been hankering for large peacetime effectives, considering the ex-soldier as more or less lost for all truly military purposes, this desire happened to fit well the democratic principle that man equals man, that one soldier equals another on this side of the frontier and balances another on foreign soil. "Democracy, that is, the power of number: in the interior against the opposition, in the exterior against the enemy. . . . Political supremacy tends more and more to belong to the greatest number; instead of fighting, one counts." Battle thus becomes more than ever the final comparison of numbers in actuality, and the transformation into reality of what has been calculation on paper.[74]

The handicap on France in this race with Germany was her diminishing birth rate, by 8 per cent from 1875 to 1893 (class of 1913), and other numerical inferiorities, so that in 1914 she had only 7,842,000 men of service age, colored races included, as against 15,000,000 in Germany. To equalize the more numerous enemy France turned to seeking allies, to expending more on her army— forty billion francs from 1870 to 1914, as against the equivalent of thirty-two billion on the German side—and to building up the allied Russian army by loans. Finally, in 1913, she resorted to prolongation of the service age from two to three years, thus again trying, as Jaurès pointed out at the time, to carry on competition in a field where it was hopeless for her to succeed in the long run.

The strain put on the French people by this military service was far higher than in Germany, where in 1911 the government called out only 53.12 per cent of those bound to serve, as against 82.96 per cent in France at the same time. Under the German army law of 1913, only 1.2 per cent of the total population served with the colors, in army and navy, as against 2.10 per cent in France. Yet by doubling the strain France was able to achieve a peacetime strength which, on the eve of war, almost equaled that of Germany

—582,500 as against 596,780. In 1910, 10,000 fully serviceable Germans were not called to the colors, while none such were left uncalled in France; 83,000 were considered only conditionally serviceable in Germany, whereas France drafted most of her men in this category. The German General Staff calculated at the beginning of 1913 that in case of a European war Germany could at once send into the field 1,544,652 men as against 1,449,000 in France, 127,000 in Great Britain, 460,000 in Russia, as far as the German frontier was concerned, 90,000 in Belgium—altogether 2,126,000 men.[75]

It was her declining birth rate that had made France so eager to seek the Russian alliance. This alliance was confirmed by a military convention signed by the two chiefs of staffs in 1892, who were allowed a scope of co-operation beyond what Bismarck had or would have conceded to war experts. Their successive arrangements, paralleling those of the Central Powers, speeded mobilization and perfected the preparations for another war. In 1901 Delcassé prepared the way for another agreement of the general staffs, according to which the Russian army in case of a Franco-German war would be ready on the German frontier in eighteen days instead of twenty-eight as before—a period to be shortened by another four days after the construction of new railway lines with the help of a French loan.[76] Further developments on both sides so perfected the mechanism of a future war that, once released, there could no longer be any halt as this would lessen the chances of one's own victory, according to the judgment on both sides.

In an alliance between an autocratic government like Russia and a free country like France, deemed socialistic by many Russians and continually shaken by Cabinet changes, the common conservative character of the officers could serve as a cement. So also could the longer tenure of office in France for chiefs of staff. A French chief of staff thought it only a pleasantry when a grand duke asked him, with reference to a republican war minister: "When are you finally getting rid of that animal of a war minister?" In general the alliance rather strengthened imperialist and reactionary tendencies in France, where Delcassé lost almost as much patience with the parliamentary procedures as did the generals. Certainly it did not weaken the Russian autocracy, always suspicious of "revolutionary" France.[77]

The competition with Germany after the War of 1870-1 led France not only to bid against her as at an auction, but also to imitate her. Renan called for imitation in the days of defeat: "The victory of Germany has been the victory of science and reason . . . Prussia is the best model. . . . We need a military law closely copying, as far as general lines are concerned, the Prussian system." The committee report on the service law of 1913 rejected the ex-

ample of the Swiss militia, recommended by politicians of democratic inclinations: "If we should be in need of light from abroad
in order to improve our military institutions, it is from the side of
Germany that it must come and where we must look." Voices were
not wanting, even military voices, to state that France had "much
more imitated than created" in her military policy, that she spent
her military budgets unwisely, that is, in far too large a measure
for the upkeep of her permanent army in uncomfortable, unhealth-
ful barracks—she held the record in soldier morbidity and mortality
—and not enough on modernization of armaments, particularly
of heavy artillery.[78]

It was also claimed that through overimitation of a foreign military power, France neglected military potentialities which her body
politic possessed. When the Socialist proposal for introducing militia-
like features in the army was turned down by pointing to the example of Germany, Jaurès exclaimed: "Republican and democratic
France will then be forever condemned by its General Staff to model
her military institutions upon the type which the German Empire
and the Prussian monarchy consider superior! She is condemned
then, in order to assure her independence, to reduce first to servitude all her genius!" Competition in effectives, he pointed out, was
hopeless for France; she ought to look instead for her greatest
military strength to a total military organization of the nation.

France might have done that, but Germany could not, on account of her class situation; the elections of 1912 had carried over
one hundred Social Democrats into the Reichstag. Leaving aside
the question of how far the French class situation furthered the
system of the large barrack army, Jaurès's reference to Germany's
social conditions as limiting her military potentialities was strikingly
illustrated by the now famous letter of January 20, 1913, in which
the Prussian War Minister rejected the proposal of the General
Staff for forming three new army corps. That, he explained, would
mean a larger number of officers, many of whom would have to
be drawn from "circles hardly fit"; and this, "aside from other
dangers, would expose the officer corps to democratization." Thus
the "rage for numbers" on the French side was only met to a
limited extent and reluctantly on the German side by similar increases. As early as 1904 the Prussian War Minister thought that
the development of the army with respect to the formation of new
regiments had now come largely to an end.[79] The German army,
in its governing circles, considered itself "saturated."

Apart from introducing such German features as general conscription and the one-year volunteering of the educated and well-
to-do—later swept away as a privilege by the demand for equalizing military burdens—France also adopted what was thought to
have been one of the main causes of the German success in the

Franco-Prussian War: Moltke's emphasis on the offensive, at a time when the French had been inclined too much to the defensive. Actually this was not the case, but the belief was stronger than the factual experience and history warranted.[80] As long as the memory of actual experience helped, the "preponderant superiority of fire" was well recognized by French tactical rules, such as those of 1875. But as memory dimmed, "the heroism of the military writers had to manifest itself on paper by the firm resolution to realize the impossible."

In particular, officers who had not taken part in the war decided that troops, energetically led, could overcome any obstacles and ignored the demoralizing effect produced by the increasing losses which masses must sustain under modern firing conditions. In accordance with this idea tactics were changed in 1894, mass attacks were preferred and initiative on the part of *tirailleurs* was discouraged. Against such doctrines, taught by Foch and others, experiences in the wars between 1871 and 1914 did not prevail. Nor did such "materialistic" protests as that of Colin: "The great transformations of combat and war and their evolution are due to the progress of arms or, more generally, to all the material objects of which use is made in combat." [81] Like bourgeois thought generally, military ideas and speculation had become antimaterialistic, even anti-Comtiste.

Indeed, two distinguished writers, Ardant du Picq and Friedrich Nietzsche, both victims of the Franco-Prussian War—the one killed and the other precariously surviving—forcefully protested against the materialization of warfare. Nietzsche, as a representative of the still rather new phenomenon—the militaristic civilian—preached the "Will to Power," a politization if not a militarization of Schopenhauer's "Will to Live." He was in fact father to some of Foch's principles of war: "The will to conquer: such is victory's first condition." In many ways, Nietzsche gave meaning to the existing and expanding military institutions for a still small sector of the European bourgeoisie. Comte had denied such a meaning when he declared that the most decisive measure of the positivist order was "to suppress definitely the army and replace it by some eight thousand gendarmes, who would suffice to maintain in a dignified way the material order, public as well as private." [82] On his part, Nietzsche praised war, at least the "good war which sanctifies any cause" and "the desirable education through danger." [83]

Speaking of Ardant du Picq's spiritualization of war, his will to conquer, his contention that to be sure of victory *is* victory, Barbey d'Aurevilly, a neoromantic decadent, put the French version of the case:

Never has a man of action, of brutal action, and in the eyes of universal prejudice, more splendidly glorified the spirituality of war. When mechanics, abominable mechanics, take possession of the world and grind it through their stupid and irresistible wheel-works; when the science of war has reached unknown proportions, through the fact of newly discovered and perfected machines, here is a head sufficiently master of its thought in the midst of the agitated modern world not to allow itself to be oppressed by these horrible discoveries which, as it would seem, make the Fredericks and the Napoleons impossible, and which deprave even the soldier. . . . It is forever the soul of man elevated to its highest power by discipline; it is the Roman cement of this discipline which makes indestructible walls out of men; it is the cohesion, the solidarity among soldiers and leaders; it is the moral authority in the impulse which gives certainty of victory.[84]

With the predilection of the military mind for taking its doctrines from the expert or from history rather than from contemporary civilian thought, French military teaching after 1871 turned to Clausewitz. Foch discovered him and taught his doctrines at the French Staff College, which he headed after 1908, without much regard to the date and setting of Clausewitz. As far as the Prussian's war philosophy and war psychology were intended to preserve martial valor in periods of peace, his teachings were doubtless useful to the French. Indeed, they paralleled Ranke's demand that the historian produce compassion within himself for historical individualities by asking the soldier to produce within himself a feeling of the essence of war. But Clausewitz's theories at this late time led the French pupils to neglect more recent experiences and worked as a brake on the systematic search for new power sources outside that of drilled man power, trained for the offensive *à l'outrance*. These teachings also encouraged the neglect of such elements as the moral and economic, and systematic inquiry into the actual strength and merit of the new firearms. Foch and the majority of French officers felt sure that these weapons were bound to heighten the offensive, whereas the American Civil War had already demonstrated the growing effectiveness of defense over attack.[85]

Thus in France a military voluntarism grew up, with an emphasis on will power for offensive action only. The intellect became a mere subordinate means to overcome and rule out considerations of losses, to pour scorn on the comparative strength and effectiveness of men and machines and other material circumstances in the path of the will to the offensive. The intellect, once serving the preservation of life, thus turned the will to life into the negation of life. This was, in effect, the military outcome of Schopenhauer's system of pessimistic voluntarism. Stated in his terms: the world as the military conceived it was largely will and idea, not material. In the case of Foch, however, this outlook was more probably the consequence of a Jesuit Catholic authoritarianism that assumes a dogma, "a work of faith," [86] within the bounds of which reasoning is allowed, but not beyond—a faith that knows how to justify any sacrifices, however great.

Much later, Foch was to admit that "the idea of offensive action first, last, and all the time, might be enough for the private soldier's catechism," but that it did not suffice as a rule for the general or the High Command, which in 1914 met with useless repulses and cruel losses as a result of its exclusive passion for the offensive.[87] From his position as the preceptor of the French army, Foch had been dethroned in 1911 by a still more *"offensiviste"* teaching which declared that henceforth the French army would return "to its traditions"—obviously forgetting Napoleon's dictum of 1805 that all his care "will be to gain victory with the least possible bloodshed" but recalling his boast that he could afford to spend hundreds of thousands of men. The French army, declared the extremists, "no longer knows any other law but the offensive. . . . All attacks are to be pushed to the extreme . . . to charge the enemy with the bayonet in order to destroy him. . . . This result can only be obtained at the price of bloody sacrifice. Any other conception ought to be rejected as contrary to the very nature of war." [88]

Against this teaching as official it was useless to advance protests, such as those of J. Colin and Emile Mayer, the latter hiding behind pseudonyms and in foreign journals. They reminded their colleagues of the steadily growing fire effect of arms, but they were disregarded in the army and outside. Civilian thought in France as elsewhere in Europe concerned itself little with military tactics. As far as civilians felt called upon to shape the army, they imagined that they could act through parliament with its political and budgetary control. The limits imposed on military expenditure before 1914 rather tended to support a military doctrine which mainly called for men, more men, cheap men, and not for strong machinery—not even for a new camouflaging uniform to replace those symbols of the combination of French parliamentary thriftiness and General Staff voluntarism: the red pantaloons of France. Nothing was so splendid as those red pantaloons to help the German gunners find their aim; they made the *poilu* so visible; only the blood he shed was invisible against them. Not until plenty of it had been shed, after war had taught its own requirements, a lesson dearly paid for, did the necessary changes take place, some soon, some late. Only after France had learned economy in the expenditure of men and liberality in the expenditure of material, only after the civilian element had forced this change upon the military, was the way opened for victory.[89]

About 1910 a French captain, in considering the probable wars which France would have to fight, saw in the main two forms: first, the immediate and decisive battle, fought and won by the barracks army; second, the campaign of several months, fought and won by the "armed nation." He decided for the first conception, which naturally favors the peacetime career officer and herewith lauds "a violent and immediate effort which must without delay lead to the definitive solution. . . . It is only the mobilized professional army, assembled by calling in the youngest classes of the reserve, which counts in the capital test. . . . In our preparation it is proper to devote all our care to the army of the barracks." In keeping with this doctrine *La France militaire,* a professional journal, commented that it was about time "that their own affairs are left somewhat more to the military themselves." [90]

What were their *own* affairs? The very openness of the demands of labor for higher wages and better working conditions has caused other groups in society to seek a more discreet veiling of their own demands. Industries which want to raise the proceeds of their capital investment declare their weakness and infant or national character, and call for protection; so does agriculture, insisting that agricultural autarchy is part of national defense and ought therefore to be furthered by peacetime tariffs. The wishes of official bureaucracies are for a safe tenure of office, as a rule, rather than for more salaries or more offices. Thus indirectly an increase in salary is achieved. Promotion is not only an occasion for higher compensation; it is at the same time an honoring of the promoted person. A salary is more nearly an honorarium to a bureaucrat than the day laborer's wages. The worker's remuneration is considered on the settlement of a single deal, and too much feeling of solidarity on the part of wage earners is often resented by the employer. But the *esprit de corps* of a bureaucracy is generally allowed, even if it includes the furtherance of very material professional interests. Bureaucracies are nearly always expansive and those which have to do with foreign affairs usually are imperialistic: for example, diplomatic branches and, even more, armies, navies, and colonial administrations.

The social structure of the French army brings out this situation more clearly than that of other armies. In Germany, Austria-Hungary, Russia, and England, the officers were to a far larger extent than in France mandatories of ruling classes; the payment they received before 1914 was often small in monetary terms, for they were serving in the interests of classes, generally as sons of these classes—classes which obtained and secured profits through the existence of the army and other bureaucratic institutions.

To take the typical Prussian case: the Junker's son served for a lieutenant's small salary. It was not large enough to provide for the life he was expected to live; to make up for the deficiency, his father sent him a monthly allowance from the proceeds of his estate.

These proceeds were safeguarded by political measures such as protective tariffs. William II admitted the connecting links when he approved the augmented German grain tariffs in 1902, saying: "They are bound up with the preservation of the basis for the further existence of the officer corps. He could not forsake the sons of fathers who had bled for the Prussian Crown on the battlefields." [91]

The French army was far more directly professional and therefore the interest of the officers was more immediately effective in army organization and doctrine. The 1870's witnessed lively discussions of the question whether the infantry battalion should consist of four or, as heretofore, six companies. The reduction of the number of companies per battalion, which seemed preferable from the tactical standpoint and was eventually introduced, would have put 1,210 captains *à la suite,* and would have reduced the chances of promotions for the lieutenants to that extent. The War Ministry proposed to have two captains per company and to introduce a new grade of *captain-commandant.* A deputy protested: "What would you have them do? They'll just go to the cafés." A way out was found by adding a fourth battalion to the existing three. That added several millions to the budget, but as the committee report said: "All the officers are placed."

Yet the measure had several fateful consequences. As a general and war minister later admitted, it brought about an abnormal promotion and carried officers into positions which they ought never to have reached. Besides, the Germans considered this rise in the number of *cadres,* by simultaneously reducing the peacetime establishment of the company from ninety to sixty-six men, a warlike measure; indeed it led to the "War in Sight" episode of 1875, famous in diplomatic history.[92]

By 1909 serious ill-humor had grown up between infantry and artillery in the French army, because in the infantry there were only 128 captains and staff officers per 100 lieutenants, while in the artillery, "profiting from its prestige as the learned branch," there were at least 160. The question whether the battery should have four or six guns had been decided in such a way that, as a deputy put it, the artillery received more colonels than cannon. When it was pointed out that Germany had 3,798 field guns as against France's 2,400—that is, 144 per army corps as against 120 in France—a general calmed those who were inclined to trouble their minds and the consciences of officers by declaring that "we have enough artillery; we have rather too much of it." [93]

To a complaint in the 1880's about the "profusion of grades" in the corps of the engineers, which counted 226 staff officers and 532 captains where the Germans had only 87 and 178, respectively, the parliamentary *rapporteur* of the army law answered: "The organization of the engineers must be determined by the service conditions of peacetime, by far the most important ones from the standpoint of the personnel."

To increase the chances of promotion, the French army law of 1873 laid down the rule that no general was to hold the command of an army corps longer than three years—a dubious measure, perhaps, from the standpoint of the service—except by special resolution of the Cabinet. The right of decision was placed in the Cabinet in order to protect the War Minister "against pretensions which are irresistible in tenacity," as one general declared who knew his comrades very well; there were then 280 aspirants for 18 jobs. At the same time, army commands for peacetime were suppressed in order to spare the feelings of generals who, having reached that post at the end of a long service, would have to be removed at the moment war was declared—a removal which they would consider as "an insult to their long and honorable services, an affront made to their white hair."

All along from 1871 to 1914 the parliament was the prisoner of the professional interest, which determined almost exclusively the organization of the army. Outside ideas of reform did not prevail against it. As Gambetta, the leader of the republicans, well-intentioned toward the army, warned France: "There are numerous offices and situations which are not to be impaired and disturbed. If there appears an innovating system which tends to threaten them, to upset their arrangements, to place an obstacle in the way of their future, efforts are immediately made to avert all the attempts at progress and reform, in such a way that the question itself is not judged by its merits, but merely from the standpoint of professional interest." [94] Hence, while France had a mass army in 1914, professional conceptions predetermined the uses to be made of it, at least until bitter experience taught other lessons.

Renovations in Great Britain and the United States

Neither Great Britain nor the United States escaped the impacts of army reorganizations and competition on the Continent. Both clung to the standing army of volunteers, more or less effectively under civilian control. But both were moved to reshape their systems and to look beyond the limits of the regular army. More immediately concerned with Continental affairs, Great Britain led off in her work of reconstruction. Under Gladstone's leadership, Edward Cardwell started his reform of the British army in 1869, when it had increased from 120,000 to 137,000 owing to the panic fear of a Napoleonic invasion which plagued England. Against such a catastrophe the majority, including Palmerston, considered "a large yearly expenditure for army and navy an economical insurance." [95]

The system of selling officers' commissions was abolished. A modicum of education was made a requirement, instead of the power of patronage which had to a large extent paralyzed the operations of education and talent in England. If not higher in England than in Prussia, the educational requirements for officer candidates were more strictly applied and they seemed too high to some later army men, such as Haig or Henry Wilson, a true Junker even if from Ulster.

The British army of this time displayed bravery in the distant corners of the earth, but little leadership. On this point a German observer remarked near the middle of the nineteenth century: "In battle, often nothing is left to the British officer but to take over the functions of the common soldier, i.e., to become a *sabreur*. One sees here the lack of ability replaced by bravery." Accordingly England's contribution to military literature of the didactic kind was unimportant; it was computed by the same observer at only one per cent compared to 50 per cent on the part of Germany and 25 per cent on the part of France at the same time.[96]

With a view to increasing the effectives, a short-term service of twelve years, of which three or six were to be spent with the colors and nine or six in the reserve, was introduced by Cardwell, and thus a rejuvenation of the army started there as elsewhere. The standing army, formerly "a costly receptacle for veterans," was to be henceforward "a manufactory for making soldiers." [97] Like capitalist enterprises, every nation was then busily piling up reserves, and young ones at that, for an emergency, and was trying to make its army standardized and its parts interchangeable. This effort succeeded least in England, where the army, a congeries of regiments, long retained relics of its earlier proprietary system; but some gains were made in the reform of 1870.

Until that year, the British army was under dual control: (1) the Commander-in-Chief, whose function was made permanent in 1793 for the purpose of combating the Revolution and who was provided with the purely military office of the so-called Horse Guards; and (2) the Secretary for War, with the War Office, composed of civilian officials. In 1870 and to 1895 the Commander-in-Chief was the Duke of Cambridge, a near-relative of the Queen and like the latter an obstinate enemy of Cardwell's reforms. Nevertheless the reformed Parliament forced Gladstone's Cabinet to insist that "it is of course necessary for the Commander-in-Chief to be in harmony with the government of the day." Only with great reluctance did the Queen and her entourage, hating to lose so much patronage, surrender the fiction "that the Sovereign's hand bore the sword, and that the wearer of the crown through a Commander-in-Chief had rights of control over the army, not quite dependent on Parliament and Secretary of State." To disabuse Her

Majesty of this opinion was Gladstone's not very pleasant duty, long remembered against him.[98] The old arrangement was replaced by the complete supremacy of the Secretary for War, fully responsible to Parliament, even over the Commander-in-Chief, and thus apparently in favor of parliamentary control.

Actually, this responsible parliamentary officer became in time the prisoner of the military experts who took over the War Office and made its personnel largely military, particularly in the higher positions. Entering his office as a civilian, generally without any previous knowledge or even interest in military affairs—an ignorance which most such ministers in England, with the exception of Haldane and possibly Campbell-Bannerman, seem to have shared —the Secretary for War had to take his information, and therewith often his views, from the permanent and military officers of his department:

If he is not conversant with the business, they can . . . let him see as much or as little of the details as they please; they thus gradually acquire complete power in their several departments, and they are practically irresponsible. . . . The bulk of the superior officers now employed in the War Office is Military; many hold their appointments for limited terms, and will return to their military duties. Their interests are therefore more identified with those of the military, who apply for increased pay or allowances . . . or other benefits than was the case under the old system.[99]

Nevertheless, the reforms of Cardwell worked a consolidation of the ramshackle agencies in Britain's war system. A general staff in the Continental fashion was set up, in spite of Campbell-Bannerman's earlier resistance; it added to England's entanglements as the latter had foretold when he said that these general staffs were "constantly and necessarily concerned in watching the military conditions of their neighbours, in detecting points of weakness and strength, and in planning possible operations in possible wars against them," and that there might be a temptation on the part of a general staff to create the "general military policy" in the ambitious sense of the phrase, for which England had no use.[100]

More of an imperialist than Campbell-Bannerman was Haldane, in the War Office from 1905 to 1912. Before the close of his term, he had established a compact military organization, composed of two branches: the regular army and the territorial force. Despite sharp demands from some military men for universal service, especially in view of the impending conflict in Europe, Haldane did not venture beyond the tradition of voluntary service. ·It took the menace of defeat in 1916 to bring the British government and the British people to accept the bitter medicine of conscription—the mass army with all that the institution implied.

Although far more remote from the competitive advance of mass armies in Europe than Great Britain, military men in the United States were not indifferent to the movement of military thought and events across the Atlantic. Both before and after the Civil War, they had read Jomini and Clausewitz and studied the use of mass armies. After the United States embarked on "the new course of empire" in 1898, especially after the employment of armed forces in suppressing the insurrection in the Philippines and the Boxer Rebellion in China, the idea of a larger and more effective army engaged the minds of the few who concerned themselves with military affairs. This idea took concrete form while Elihu Root was Secretary of War, from 1899 to 1904, under the presidents who had sponsored the new expansion of the United States.

During Root's administration, the old army was shaken out of its long sleep, the standing army was enlarged and reorganized, a General Staff was created to plan and co-ordinate its operations, and the once almost independent state militias were completely subdued to the standards and methods of the federal military system. Even the name of the militia was changed to National Guard.

Conscription, if occasionally mentioned in esoteric circles, was not adopted; no mass army was created, but the number of effectives immediately at the disposal of the federal war command was materially increased. Moreover the future was forecast, for the act of 1903, as amended in 1908, declared that all able-bodied male citizens and all resident aliens who had declared their intention to become citizens, between the ages of eighteen and forty-five, shall be incorporated in "the militia" and that the total male population so covered shall be divided into "the organized militia," recruited from volunteers, and "the reserve militia"—both branches subject to the call of the President to repel invasion, suppress rebellion, and "execute the laws," including, of course, a law declaring war. By 1912 the strength of the regular army of the United States stood at 92,000 and it was estimated that about 90,000 men and officers out of the 120,000 in the National Guard could be put into the field for immediate action—making 182,000 in all.

According to socialist criticism, the infection of militarism had reached the United States by 1898 at the latest. "There, as everywhere," wrote Jaures in the summer of that year, "capitalism, necessarily aggressive and combative, is leading to militarism" expressed in armaments and standing forces.[101] If there was militarism, there was easily as much of the civilian sort—expressed in dicta like Theodore Roosevelt's that universal military service for America as in Germany "was a good thing" (1907)[102]—as of the military kind, though the new General Staff was quickly learning the motivation and techniques of propaganda.[103]

In the First World War the long preparations of the military organizers in
the several nations involved met the
supreme test. If the record of that
conflict be viewed from the military
angle alone, due regard might be paid
to the achievements of leaders and to
the heroism of the following masses.
To consider the purely militaristic aspects of the war means, however, a
concentration upon the errors revealed
in the course of that struggle, the waste
of heroism and misapplication of resources, material and human; the survival of anachronistic notions and institutions to impede efficiency; the
freedoms taken by the military in the
absence of civilian control. Above all,
it entails reiteration of the fact that,
by and large, the experts had been expecting quite another kind of war.

Few of the seers had looked for a
contest so prolonged. Thus in 1910,
General Bonnal had regretted that apprenticeship to war through war,
though the ideal form of instruction,
could hardly be expected henceforth,
since it must embrace "a period of
several years. This condition will not
be found again in the wars of the future, necessarily of very short duration." [1] Not only did the war stretch
out beyond the foreseen limits, but it
proved to have a radically new character, rendering obsolete many of the
preparations so carefully made in advance, calling for materials and efforts
upon which most planners had never
calculated.

In the first weeks of the war, probably the majority of the generals declined to admit the nature of the conflict in which they were engaged. Only
gradually were the blindest discarded,
and rarely were these put aside before
they had cost their respective nations

8
Militarism in the War of Embattled Nations

countless numbers of the best soldiers. The worst wasters were generals close to the retirement age to whom had been entrusted German and French reserve divisions, bodies by their very nature most in need of energetic and resourceful leaders. In France, up to the end of September 1914, two army leaders, seven corps commanders, and some twenty commanders of divisions were *limoged*.[2] Lucky the army whose chiefs could with Foch claim one merit: to have forgotten what they had taught and what they had learned before 1914.[3]

The Upsetting of Military Preconceptions

One of the first blows to established ideas was the discovery that that highly cherished branch of the service, the cavalry, was in fact useless. It was found that three times as many cavalrymen had been raised in peacetime for the French army as could be employed as such in war.[4] Out of these mounted or dismounted soldiers, it was difficult to make infantrymen or artillerists; they were, however, in a measure utilized for police purposes, to impress the war-weary civilian populations, as they could not impose upon the enemy.[5] Some officers were put into airplanes, thus being given greater horsepower, but not always to the advantage of aviation. When the French Ministry of War decided to regulate promotions for aviators according to their flying hours, the squadron commanders sent their favorites to fly their quota behind the front regardless of the waste of oil and gasoline, until "interfering" parliamentarians, industrialists, and socialist civilians informed the Ministry that this waste and sport must cease.[6]

The last old-style cavalry battle took place early in the war, in Galicia, with the two most technically backward nations, Russia and Austria-Hungary, as contestants. When later the Austrian cavalry was ordered to dismount, the last Emperor of Austria promised that when peace came his cavalry would again receive its specific character in a form corresponding with its traditions, its glorious spirit, and its war experiences.[7] After some early actions, whatever remained of the cavalry proper waited for years for its employment, but no sector of an army was ever so utterly crushed that the cavalry had a chance to ride it down. If further evidence of the futility of cavalry for modern warfare is required, it is furnished by the insistence of the Allies in the Treaty of Versailles that the Reichswehr contain a large percentage of horsemen.

As for the pampered guards, they went under before the field-gray and khaki mass of the armies, proving to be not appreciably better or worse than other regiments: where the elite principle of the guards was adhered to and tried out, it demonstrated its worthlessness. When Russia formed a veritable guard army in 1916, with a duke as artillery commander, and attacked the Germans on the Stokhod River, the outcome was a fiasco. For an Allied observer it was "humiliating to think that the splendid Guardsmen, physically the finest human animals in Europe and all of the best military age, were driven back by such weedy specimens as the German prisoners we had seen." [8] In their internal antirevolutionary function the guards were no less a failure; the Russian guard divisions were among the least stable elements in 1917.

While the horse and the guard principle were sorrowfully abandoned, the armies had to take, also reluctantly, to the ignominious spadework for which they were not trained. Only with difficulty and energy could those officers who realized the importance of trenches persuade the troops to dig themselves in.[9] And for some time the need for cannon and ammunition was underestimated, especially by the French and British. When the military committee of the French Chamber asked the director of artillery in the War Ministry whether the available field guns were sufficient to meet all eventualities, he replied that the supply was adequate, in fact excessive, at the front. When the deputies expressed their surprise and their conviction that for the purpose of victory a powerful artillery was imperative, this same director of artillery replied: "Victory we shall gain by the breasts of our infantrymen." Nevertheless, the committee urged increases in machinery and suggested the retirement of the complacent director.[10]

Nor were the generals able to grasp the necessity for reorganizing industries in the interests of victory, at the beginning of the war at least. When the necessity was urged upon them, they were unwilling to surrender the skilled workers serving in the armies.[11] Without the organizing and promotion abilities of civilians, such as Walter Rathenau, Lloyd George, and Albert Thomas, the dire need of the troops for arms, munitions, and other war materials would not have been met.

Not every efficient arm or type of material which the industries had to offer was demanded and welcomed by army leaders. The history of warfare taught in the schools had largely passed over the instructive experiences with hand grenades and mine throwers in the near past, though the latter had been used at the siege of Port Arthur in 1904. Twice the British War Office rejected a quick-firing trench mortar, the so-called Stokes gun, which Munitions Minister Lloyd George had to force upon it after the Germans had led the way.

Other war products were applied without testing out or thinking out their potentialities and limitations. Thus the Germans employed the U-boat and poison gas prematurely and too experimentally. By using them on a small scale they revealed the secret of their power and their peril and gave the enemy time for developing defensive measures as well as imitating. Half a year after the original use of poison gas at Ypres by the Germans, the Allies were partly equipped with this new agency of warfare. Against this outcome Ludendorff had been warned by Haber. The latter proposed to introduce mustard gas only if there was a reasonable hope that the war would end within a year—a period within which Germany could keep a monopoly over its formula and its application. Haber knew that otherwise the Allies would be in a position to turn this weapon against the Germans, who had introduced them to it. It was sheer luck for the Germans that it took the Allies sixteen months instead of twelve to outfit themselves adequately with poison gas; by that time it was too late for successful and overwhelming use of this effective weapon on their part.[12]

With respect to motorized tanks, that idea early occurred to a civilian in South Africa, on the frontier of European civilization, and in France proposals for the construction and utilization of tanks came from the civilian front at the end of 1915. But General Headquarters turned them down as "engines not susceptible of lending themselves to any military use." Pressed by parliamentarians, the War Minister, Millerand, an ex-Socialist, ordered some tanks to be built and finally the military men accepted them. When Winston Churchill in 1915 described his idea of "land cruisers" to a French general and his staff, they laughed heartily, once he had gone: "Your politicians are even funnier than ours." [13] It was difficult to get them adopted even by a few English generals, despite the fact that the promoters of tanks were officers, for such officers were juniors and mere engineers. When at last tanks were used in combat, they were not employed on a scale that promised a smashing break-through. On the contrary, they were tried out experimentally, in 1916, that is, on a small scale. As in the case of poison gas the secret of their power and possible decisive effect was disclosed to the enemy. But on the other side, official blundering and delay occurred. For reasons never fully known, among them Ludendorff's slight interest in tanks, the Germans did not take to this weapon with alacrity and effectiveness.[14]

The resistance of the officers to new war engines was doubtless rooted in the tradition of peacetime, in the conviction that it is necessary to govern everything moved into battle. And many of the generals who had never grasped the mechanics or the tactical potentialities of such machinery were afraid of losing control over it. At the outbreak and for the first two years of the First World War the Germans were decidedly superior in the number and in the use they made of their machine guns in reducing the effect of

Allied attacks. Even so, Haig thought them a "much overrated weapon," and Kitchener conceded merely that four per battalion might be an advantage. At last, however, Lloyd George, a civilian politician like Bismarck, found himself unable to suffer silently the waste of men mowed down by the German machine gunners. It might be "bad form," but he felt compelled to interfere and insist upon more machine guns for the British forces. "Take Kitchener's maximum, square it, multiply the result by two—and when you are in sight of that," he said, "double it again for good luck." [15]

Hesitation on the part of officers to embrace new means of warfare did not spring from any moral restraint in the matter of human destruction—such a restraint as some men in earlier generations had felt and actually exercised. Older military leaders, somewhat dreading "the uncertain continuance of reason," had shared to a certain extent the hesitations of Dr. Johnson on the issue of aviation:

If men were all virtuous . . . I should with great alacrity teach them all to fly. But what would be the security of the good, if the bad could at pleasure invade them from the sky? Against an army sailing through the clouds, neither walls, nor mountains, nor seas, could afford any security. A flight of northern savages might hover in the wind and light at once with irresistible violence upon the capital of a fruitful region that was rolling under them.[16]

By 1914, however, self-restraint in the use of war agencies had been much diminished. Officers agreed with Clausewitz that "to introduce into the philosophy of war itself a principle of moderation would be an absurdity." The use of atrocity, with which propagandists charged the enemy, had been advocated and taught before 1914 by a French lieutenant colonel: "Terrify, in order to terrify and destroy. The immediate object of fighting is to kill and to go on killing, until there is nothing left to kill." [17] To this plea a British major general made his contribution: "War is a relapse into barbarism. There is no disloyalty in war save that which forbears to spare; no morality, save that which ends quickly. Love and sentiment are out of place in the struggle for existence. . . . It is the exercise of the sterner barbaric qualities which governs the day. Atrocities are the last recourse of strategy in its efforts to force an enemy to its knees." [18] And an American lieutenant general added his opinion: "To carry on war, disguise it as we may, is to be cruel; it is to kill and burn, burn and kill, and again kill and burn." [19]

The advocates of such ferocity, of the liberation of pent-up animality, did not shrink from the thought of using revolution in warfare, a means which had seemed too radical to Napoleon. When he sat in the Kremlin, he did imagine fomenting rebellion among the Russian serfs, the Tartars, and Ukrainians, by issuing a proclamation of emancipation; but starting such an upheaval seemed to him dangerous, and he remembered he was not a maker of revolutions, but their liquidator. Even under the desperate circumstances of the Hundred Days he did not dare, as he later admitted, to call up the Revolution in France, which might or might not have saved him, but which was the last means at his disposal.[20] So, too, in 1871 Bismarck did not befriend the revolution of the French Commune, which he suspected of backfiring potentialities. Such hesitations did not hamper the German rulers in 1917, who blithely transported the Bolsheviks, barred from transit through their territory by the Entente nations, through Germany to Russia in a "sealed train." Like mustard gas, which they adopted, only more rapidly, the Russian Revolution was fired back at them.

It was not, then, sentimentality that led military men to waver in adopting new instruments of death and destruction. It was their preoccupation with traditional routine; they were immersed in obsolete theories and also heavily bureaucratized. Having been trained by written orders and commands, the generals in the First World War, after an initial period of "pure command," showed an inveterate tendency to conceive of the conflict as "a paper war," as Ludendorff called the endeavor to manage masses of men and materials by decrees handed down from above in formalistic settlement of claims and complaints. Both the higher and lower commands gave out written and printed orders by means of which they attempted to settle great battles and the smallest trifles alike. In turn, the execution of these orders had to be reported in writing; this inflicted an additional burden on the fighting troops and induced them to report large affairs with no greater care or conscience than small affairs. In vain did Ludendorff demand, in November 1917, "self-limitation on the part of the higher commands and strengthening of the spontaneity and sense of responsibility on the part of the lower." [21]

With paper-commanding went also the rule of promoting by traditional seniority rather than by the one military test of performance in war. The self-governing traditions in the Western countries and the need of selecting officers, even for fairly high posts, from men who had not served in the army, relieved the Anglo-Saxon forces greatly from the rigidity of the seniority rule. But in the German and French armies, where the professional interest was strong, proposals to overcome out-of-date seniority were rejected. A German fighting leader urged vainly in December 1917:

It does not matter how peacetime lists are made out, or what provisions are made for the development of the professional soldiers after the war. But now freely to reach the only valid aim—

victory—all available powers are essential and it is important to refrain from holding the most efficient officers within their narrow sphere of activity merely on account of the date of their commission. It is important to bring them more quickly into places of higher command.

The Military Cabinet in Berlin, however, was not to be moved by such propositions.[22] Younger and, in particular, reserve officers, the "temporary gentlemen" as they were described in the English army and as they were thought of by other professionals, were not put to the highest services which they might have rendered. It was true that the practice of coupling a young general staff officer or adjutant with an old commander—the reproduction of the Hindenburg-Ludendorff arrangement on a lower level—often gave the younger man all the power that the older man was supposed to have. Although this was a gain, the stubbornness and stiffness of old age still interfered with the elasticity and adaptive abilities of the younger officer.

On the German side the inner conflicts and tensions within the customary self-governing arrangements of the army were settled without outside interference and in accord with traditions rather than true military requirements. On the other side the Western parliaments kept the doors open for the exercise of their influence when conflicts among officer groups threatened to become dangerous. Thus, when the French army introduced gas in warfare and a violent clash ensued between the Third and the Fourth Bureau of the War Ministry over the question as to which bureau was to order gas masks, the army committee of the Chamber of Deputies interfered and pointed out the folly of the dispute.[23]

When the militaristic way is followed in war, there are high losses in men and little inclination to think of reducing them by the most effective and persistent application of machines and materials. Two sets of considerations may induce man power economy: (1) the good civilian politician wants to save the men among the people who elect and re-elect him to a place in the government; (2) the good general wants to save soldiers who have learned the business of fighting, if only to use them in a greater emergency.

Where the desire for and capacity to use mechanical aids did not exist and no large industry was available for supplying arms, both the waste of manhood and the dissipation of the scant available materials for war occurred, as in Russia. There a plethora of men and a lack of man power economy both in peace and war had always been a striking feature of military affairs. Charles XII and his few Swedes were at length simply smothered by the Russian masses. Russia's vast conquests, marked by so few victories, were always noteworthy for the larger heaps of soldiers' bones as compared with the imperialist expansions of other countries. At the opening of the First World War the Russian command was convinced that its supply of men was so generous that it did not matter how many soldiers were led to their death in all the divergent operations from eastern Prussia to Galicia—an overestimation which the Allies shared in their constant cry for Russian offensives.

Where the Germans expended metals the Russians expended lives, sighed a Russian general in 1915, mindful of the Russian inferiority in artillery. On the eve of the war the Russian army had 60 heavy batteries and the German army had 381; the Russian infantry division had only half as many guns as a German division. On the northern front from Riga to Dvinsk in October 1917, the Russian army had 7 howitzers and 11 heavy guns for every ten versts of front, as against 14 and 24, respectively, on the German side; the average relation of bayonet strength on the eastern front between Russia and the Central Powers was as 60 to 38.

On the eve of the Russian Revolution, the Russians had 5,457 light and 1,946 heavy guns on the eastern front; the Germans and their allies had 5,070 light and 4,060 heavy guns. This was at a time when the Allies on the western front had 2,176 light and 6,396 heavy guns as against 4,349 and 5,510, respectively, possessed by the Germans. On a certain section along the Riga front the Russians, at the beginning of 1917, had never less than 92 battalions; the Germans at one time had only 22 to 25 and, in the middle of October 1916, held the Riga-Dvinsk front with less than one-fourth the infantry men possessed by the Russians.

Moreover, the immunity from all outside control which the Russian army enjoyed, joined to the popular belief in the inexhaustible wealth of the Russian state, led to a ruthless waste until even materials finally ceased to be available in any reasonable quantity. As before the war, the Russian soldier was considered cheap. Whereas prior to 1914 the expenditure for military equipment per man amounted to 497 gold rubles in Germany, 457 in Austria-Hungary, and 375 in France, in Russia it amounted only to 289 for 1897-8. The lack of economic management in Russia had brought about saving measures in the army with the result that there were inadequate preparations for wartime forces, a shortage of competent noncommissioned officers, and a consequent reckless expenditure of blood when fighting had to be done.[24]

Recruits were sometimes sent to the trenches without the necessary arms and told to wait until enough of their comrades had dropped out of the ranks to furnish them with rifles. Often they had to wait under German fire and then were captured as unarmed men. Such experiences of technological inferiority provoked in the Russian soldier and many of his commanders the natural if unhealthy feeling that "the Germans could do anything." [25] Toward the end of the struggle the revolutionary conviction that he was considered too cheap was heightened for the Russian soldier by the evidence of high industrial profits at home. Nor was a comparable opinion always foreign to the German.

Officers and Civilians in the First World War

Power, position, success even of the most deceptive kind, and the adulation which the masses bestowed upon them, turned many officers of the war into politicians. This was true of no less a person than Haig who, "with a soldier's distaste for politics," struggled for a long time against becoming involved, but finally became enmeshed as Commander of the British army. Needless to say, he was a Conservative in all respects except that of holding a membership card in the party. Haig regarded Bonar Law as "a straightforward, honorable man"; the Liberal, Lloyd George, as "astute and cunning, with much energy and push, but shifty and unreliable"; Ben Tillett, the labor leader, with more favor, since Tillett seemed to be "quite converted from his anarchistic views" and resolved to get "the labour clan to help end the war." [26]

Indeed, very few officers would have turned their sympathies in nonconservative directions, even if other parties were as anxious to win the war, for differences of opinion sprang from divers notions of how to conduct the campaigning. When officers identified themselves with conservatism and conservatism with officers, that did not necessarily constitute the best military way to achieve victory, even though officers liked to maintain that it did. It was, at bottom, an assimilation of military thought to previously cherished social and economic thought. The line of conflicting opinions drawn between the military and civilians in the war was, in truth, a prolongation of party struggles with other means, even if the parties were not always aware of the fact.

The party which, before August 1914, seemed to be the most powerful opposition party in the world, the German Social Democrats, surrendered without a murmur its own conception of the way to win the war. It cast off all that Engels had advised when he said the party ought to insist at the outbreak of war on being led in a revolutionary way, that everyone should be drawn into service, that the armed nation should assume control over domestic and foreign policies. With astonishing alacrity German and other Social Democrats gave their sanction to the war credits demanded. German liberalism remained equally passive.[27]

But the bourgeois in the Entente countries, except Russia, refused to remain passive. They were determined to win the war in the light of their own image. As the warmaking party in America, the Democrats kept a pronounced Republican general, Leonard Wood, not to speak of the ex-Republican President, Theodore Roosevelt, out of war glory—politics and the requirements of service happily coinciding, as Wood was obviously the Secretary of War's "most insubordinate subordinate." [28] In England a politician of the army, Henry Wilson, had prepared for war by bringing about a truce in the party battle and moving the Conservatives to put pressure on the Liberals for the support of France in the July crisis. He liked to be told, from the English as well as from the French side, that he was "more responsible for England's joining the war than any other man." [29]

Only for a time did the politicians of the Western Powers allow the soldiers to run the war entirely as they thought they had planned it. It is true that, when the question of a committee for the co-ordination of Inter-Allied warfare was proposed in November 1915, Sir Edward Grey surprised even Henry Wilson by objecting that the two foreign ministers who were to sit on the committee should dictate to the soldiers—rather should the soldiers dictate to the Foreign Offices.[30] On the other hand, Lloyd George did not hesitate to enter upon the jealously watched precincts of Kitchener's office and take upon himself a task that did not belong to his own department, though it fairly screamed for action: the need for guns and an adequate munitions supply. Convincing himself that the military would not or could not grasp the significance of war machines and materials, he dared, at an hour when Kitchener's prestige still stood high, to face the handicap under which the civilian politician labors in wartime—the handicap of which the military were taking advantage without scruples.

As always, the war did little or nothing to exalt the civilian politician above his due. He was not a popular figure, for the soldiers and their leaders got the glory and the worship. His business was largely to shoulder the blame for their failures. Under war conditions it was deemed disloyal for the citizen to utter a word of criticism against military and naval experts and yet thoroughly patriotic to abuse a civilian minister who might know or do something about winning the war.[31]

As one of the ministerial "poltroons," Lloyd George took his stand against the military demand for men first, and in favor of munitions first. In so doing he encountered the sneers of Henry Wilson, who said that "the loss of men might have been a good reason for not entering the war, but a bad reason for not fighting when in war." It was the most conservative, reactionary generals who called incessantly for more men, ever complaining that their supply was too low, though they did not always know what man power they or their Allies already possessed. Haig excused himself and Gough during their breakdown in the German offensive of March 1918, by charging the government with failure to provide enough men: "Well, Hubert, one can't fight without men." [32]

Despite military sneers, the civilian minister, Lloyd George, called on the generals to accept and make use of the vast number of machine guns and other weapons he could furnish, men to be multiplied by machines—a modern industrial principle to be applied to warfare. Living in the past with respect to fighting, the majority of the generals replied by at first insisting upon a simple addition of rifles and bayonets for wiping out a corresponding number of Germans: "The only thing worth talking about is killing Boches. . . . The only way to end this war is to kill Germans and not Turks. The place where we can kill most Germans is here," on the western front.[33] On other fronts the generals opposed fighting that might have become decisive.

As a result of such bickering, the maintenance of civilian supremacy was always precarious among the Western Powers, except in the United States, where it was never seriously jeopardized, not even in moments of bad temper on the part of the generals who early and late berated American diplomacy as "poor as usual" and national leadership as inadequate. But even for American officers war was a partial liberation from the politician. When General Harbord was told, after his arrival in France, that Pétain "despises politicians and has risen in spite of them," he thought: "We have that same idea." He was confident that "inefficiency is inseparable from democracy," although he seems never to have pondered on the inefficiency of other forms of government.[34] To his colleague General Bullard, the American Expeditionary Force "was the product of many brains but of one will. Its like could be provided only where but one will governed, not ever in a democracy. Democracy means mediocrity. This was superiority." [35] So a cryptic militarism, glorying in personal expansion, gave no consideration to the democratic sources of success, or to the democratic processes which entered into the selection of leaders, including generals, or to the military values available in a democracy. Without rebuke Henry Wilson could tell Lloyd George in November 1915, that "the present government stank in the nostrils of the whole army and that if he was to break away and raise the standard of victory he would have a unanimous army behind him." [36]

Luckily for the civilian politicians, the generals suffered defeats in the field, from time to time—defeats which, despite the help of modern propaganda technique, could not be turned into victories. Disasters gave civil ministers the opportunity to review and give orders to the generals—a contingency which the latter resented above defeat. Before Nivelle's offensive of 1917 Henry Wilson was persuaded that the politicians, whose rotation in office had left Nivelle and his staff absolutely indifferent, if it had not amused them, would unload Nivelle "if our coming offensive does not succeed or is only moderately successful. . . . What a scurvy crowd!" [37] Battles lost or won, the commanding officers did not intend to lose any prestige themselves. In times of victory they preferred to think of themselves as grand politicians; in times of defeat they liked to retire to their positions as military officials with a firm tenure of office—officials to whom defeat is merely an accident in the routine due to "the lack of men."

Among the officers the authority of parliaments sank lower than that of ministers. Parliamentarians to whom the generals had been running for favors reversed the order by racing to the military head-quarters to catch, if in reflection only, some of the adulation that generals received. Thus Bassermann, who preceded Stresemann as leader of the German National Liberals, assured Hindenburg and Ludendorff and their staff that in the coming victorious peace the Foreign Office must be made subordinate to the General Staff. General Harbord came to the conclusion that American politicians, who had resorted to the American Commander in France for in-spiration when about to speak on Liberty Loans, were merely de-serving Democrats on a trip at government expense; that among seven such politicians just "one was a man of more than average intelligence, who eats with his fork, is not angry because the *petits pois* are round instead of square, and who seems to have heard of the places he is visiting before he came." The general, who himself noted in his diary inanities about French history, found it hard to condescend to the level of politicians. Perfectly hopeless and help-less they were in his eyes, although no doubt democratic and deserv-ing.[38]

Only occasionally did parliamentary authority reassert itself. All through the war the military committee of the French Chamber, with an ex-general as chairman, had the greatest difficulty in getting a hearing for its desires before the army leaders—desires not only constitutionally justified but materially warranted as well. When the members, for instance, expressed the wish to visit the front and the war zone, Joffre declared that "he would not let himself be invaded by civilians," even though they swore to abstain from interference with the military operations. When individual members traveled in the forbidden zone, some of them were placed under arrest by a general. The committee had to seek a reconciliation with Joffre and to agree to send only such members into the war zone as were distinguished for their moderation; that is, no Socialists.

In this controversy the Commander defended his right to exclude parliamentary control by writing that "in war the authorities and responsibilities cannot be divided. The general-in-chief is responsible to the government which can relieve him if it disapproves of his actions; there can be no other control during the action." On its part the committee denied claiming such rights "during the action" and stated that it merely wished to find out for itself about the real conditions of the soldiers at the front, from whom it received information widely at variance with the optimistic statement of the War Ministry. It merely wanted to know the bitter truth, to perform its role of responsibility to the nation, and to encourage the soldier by its presence in the danger zone—notably at Verdun in March 1916, where the committee was welcomed by officers and men alike.

Heartened by that experience, the committee, implored by the War Ministry not to insist too strongly on its constitutional rights, sent some of its members as observers to the front, where they were admitted by a few authorities. Foch, for instance, if not by others, such as the Commander-in-Chief, who did not want them to make inquiries into the mutinies of 1917. Only in October 1917, were the constitutional rights of the committee acknowledged by the Commander-in-Chief, and the exercise of their functions permitted by all the generals.[39] Then Clemenceau opened the doors wide to civilian energies, including his own, which he demonstrated by numerous pilgrimages to the front, symbolizing the unity of front and hinterland.

But until the end this civilian war energy was far from welcome to many generals, most of whom were unable to recognize the intimate relation between military power and power resources, as Clemenceau and Lloyd George understood it. Clemenceau complained that there was in the war no Gambetta or Jaurès to serve as a tribune, as orator, playing upon the emotions of the masses and explaining to them at each crisis of the war the nature of the crisis and the new efforts demanded of the people.[40] Though completely militarized, Germany lacked the spellbinder whose leadership might have summoned the soldiers to a final supreme effort; when the German crisis approached, officers were nominated to "instruct" the soldiers by speeches which achieved nothing but a new low level in the history of oratory.

Without the forceful intervention of civilian ministers, certain war engines and other war potentials would not have been recognized or mobilized or utilized to the best advantage. The military committee of the French Chamber was compelled to inform the French generals, who had prepared no industrial mobilization, that to achieve a high output in the war industries skilled workers, reduced, for instance, at Le Creusot from eleven thousand to seven thousand by the mobilization, must be kept at manufacturing; that just any kind of labor would not do; that it was more conducive to high production for the workmen sent from the army into the war industries to be placed on piece wages instead of military pay. By this action they raised output by 16 per cent.

The committee also busied itself with aviation, insisting on more bombing planes in order to bombard Essen, which might be as feebly defended against air attacks as Le Creusot and other plants proved to be. It also concerned itself with the state of things in respect to metals, thus raising a conflict between the commission seeking information and the War Ministry attempting to keep information from it. But the commission kept a certain control over the largess which the military dispensed out of the nation's riches, saving by its handling of copper alone, according to the ministry of armaments, 500,000,000 francs for the French Treasury.[41] If the American Congress had not completely abdicated its actual power over war expenditures, the appalling waste of the taxpayers' money described by General Hagood might have been avoided, despite American readiness to invest a maximum sum of money for the winning of the war.[42]

If the story of civilian and military relations during the war and in the pursuit of war and victory teaches anything with respect to making and winning war, it offers a clear warning against the surrender of excessive authority to the military arm of government. A comparison of the constitutional arrangements in Germany, where the Kaiser dropped out of the seat of power presented him by Bismarck, and in the Western nations does not speak well for the union of political and military direction in the same hands. Total mobilization in the military way inevitably means the immobilization of certain war energies latent among civilians. These may appear irregular, disorderly, political—all that the term "civilian" means to officers as a term of opprobrium. But they are indispensables of power. Democracies which keep their armies open-minded will be better equipped for war than authoritarian governments run for military men who may have more money and men at their disposal to prepare, but may lack the elasticity to recognize the true character of the war when it arrives.

The increase in the technical tasks of generals in modern warfare overburdened them and made them correspondingly incapable as statesmen, a truth revealed by comparison between Wellington and any of the generals of the First World War. But though the development toward technical specialization was proceeding so rapidly, the public did not want to do without its heroes, and the generals were no more inclined to stay out of politics. They entered it, as they insisted, to win the victory, the secret of which, so Schlieffen maintained, the military alone possess. Yet they neither had that secret in fact, nor could they be trusted with the right political use of victory. Can a worse conception of victory be imagined than the one which Ludendorff advanced with respect to the East and embodied in the Treaty of Brest-Litovsk, or the policies he later pursued in his conduct of affairs? In the formulation of Clemenceau's closest military adviser, "the decisions of generals are functions of the decisions taken by the statesmen."[43] Wherever that civilian supremacy was lost, even peace lost its meaning. It was then conceived in military terms—as giving the army the entire credit for the peace first of all and, on the basis of that assumed competence, everything it might desire in the line of annexations, fresh causes for more war, honors and other rewards, and gigantic military budgets, incident to an army-made peace. According to this scheme of things, power, if it escapes the military at all, must pass to the civilian groups most friendly to the military.

Only one general, Tasker Bliss, an American, well understood that an army-made peace would instigate a new war. It was his belief that the United States went into the war to destroy militarism. So he declared: "It may soothe our guilty souls . . . by saying that Prussia did it first. That kind of plea was first made in the Garden of Eden and it no more clears our skirts of sin today than it did then. Looking to the future, the curse of the world today is European militarism." He warned his civilian superior at home, the Secretary of War, late in October 1918, that on the Allied side the trouble lay in the fact that the military elements were on top and that if they were allowed to make their will prevail they would do things which, if done by Germany, would shock the sense of justice of the world. More than that, their power would lead to a perpetuation of armaments and the standing threat of war: "The military party"—he meant the military party everywhere—"is demanding more and more with every day's success. There is nobody to impose any check."[44]

War as the occasion for such military supremacy the generals were loath to see cut short by any real peace. They did not want to have the day arrive too soon when fighting would cease and they would be feeling "thoughful and utterly lost";[45] when that "creature," Lloyd George, already "supposed to be making a wild grab for civilian control of the armies," would be on top as the Inter-Allied generals whispered;[46] when Clemenceau would be forever in a position to say to Foch: "Keep silent! It is I who represent France," as he had done before an Inter-Allied conference in 1918, where the general mixed the purely military exposition expected of him with political expectorations.[47]

A speech of Bethmann-Hollweg announcing Germany's readiness to discuss peace terms at the end of 1916, vague and guarded as it was, frightened Henry Wilson by the specter of peace it might invoke. It looked even more dangerous for the military "that a President, Wilson, has barged in and asked all belligerents for their terms." [48] When the French Socialists planned to participate in the 1917 Socialist Conference at Stockholm, Pétain insisted, with the French Prime Minister, that they must not be allowed to attend it, that he would no longer be able to control the army if the soldiers heard about French and German Socialists engaged in conversations.[49] In such critical moments, the military on both sides felt in danger of the greatest defeat military institutions as such could sustain—namely, a draw.

Peace at "too early" an hour might have brought out the general bankruptcy of all "plans," the fact that since the autumn of 1914 war had been pursued as a gamble in which no one won, in which each gambler staking his utmost in the game hoped to get the utmost out of it by wearing out his opponent first—in which each gambler hoped for sheer good luck in some unforeseen contingency. Even after the failure of their great March peace offensive of 1918, Hindenburg and Ludendorff continued to attack in other places, the former excusing the procedure in his blundering way: "Further we also wanted so to shatter the enemy's structure by closely connected partial blows that it must after all sometimes break down." [50]

On both sides the army leaders shied away from thinking of peace. When Trotsky made his famous declaration at Brest-Litovsk that Russia was terminating the war without concluding peace, the diplomats of the Central Powers, though greatly startled, were ready to admit that a state of peace between the powers was thus restored. But General Hoffmann protested saying that an armistice had been concluded with the Russians in the intention of leading up to peace; since peace had not been attained, the intention of the armistice had not been fulfilled; and since the armistice was ending automatically, "hostilities *must* begin anew." Headquarters fully approved Hoffmann's view and forced the civilian authorities to agree.[51]

In such ways the road to victory, as distinguished from peace—an increasingly empty victory except for the generals and military institutions—was kept open. Victory came closer to the Western Powers, not through great military achievements, but by bits of "luck" first enjoyed by Ludendorff with the breaking of the Russian Revolution, and then enjoyed by the Allies as Wilson led America into the war and Bulgaria began to sue for an armistice. In this hour, Henry Wilson feared that the Germans would follow the Bulgarian example and yield prematurely. He hoped to God that they would not sue for peace "as one never knows what the politicians will do," for they had found his own armistice terms excessively severe.[52] When the Germans finally proposed an armistice, the majority of the commanding generals, Haig excepted, declared in favor of fighting on until peace could be dictated on German soil; that was said to be "so conforming to strategy and the experience of past wars."

Clearly the generals were not waging the war as a war to end wars. Only when hard pressed by the civilian politicians did Foch admit that there was no reason to fight on for harsher armistice conditions. The continuation of the fighting would have cost some fifty thousand to one hundred thousand French lives, he thought, not realizing until later that even harder terms could have been wrung from the Germans because they were already more drastically beaten than he himself knew at the time. He acknowledged that after all Great Britain and France had reached their own aims and that "only the Americans were disappointed. Their generals had not yet earned the laurels they had hoped for." [53]

War Failure of the Aristocracy

As far as the prewar armies were run by the aristocracies, they were discovered to be the least prepared for the war that came. One of the worst features of the French army was Marshal Franchet d'Esperey, but his political and aristocratic connections helped him to fall upstairs, even if his appointment to the command of the Salonika army put a heavy strain on Inter-Allied relations.[54] The only talented general in the Austrian army was Conrad von Hötzendorf, recently knighted, whom General Hoffmann called a man of genius full of ideas himself but unsupported by a good army. In the German army the most obvious failures were members of the old aristocracy: Moltke, Falkenhayn, Von Prittwitz und Gaffron, Waldersee; they stand out in contrast with the single bourgeois failure, Lieutenant Colonel Hoesch of the Marne. Three of the most successful generals with noble names, Von Kluck, Von Mackensen, and Von Lietzmann, had not been nobles long. Hindenburg belonged to the old Prussian nobility, but he represented merely antiquities of diverse kinds combined for purposes of war politics.

Largely new blood flowed through the veins of the chiefs of staff and the war technologists, the major generals and colonels: Ludendorff, who declined elevation to the nobility; Hoffmann; Tappen; Bauer; Groener, the military head of the railways; Kundt, who later reformed the Bolivian army; Grünert; Heye; Hell; Wetzel; Buchmüller, a retired lieutenant colonel and the greatest German artillery specialist; Schabel, specialist for gas shells; and Heuschkel, a first lieutenant specializing in the trench mortar. To this group belong Hitler's best military organizers before 1933: Röhm and Hierl. The bourgeois officers thought none too highly of the noble officers who rose to prominence, such as Von Seeckt and Von Schleicher. Landless princes who wanted to have states for themselves carved out of the vast territories in the East were received by these nonnobles with the cynicism of the king-makers *à la* Napoleon.[55]

Nor did such German bourgeois military men highly esteem the titled nonentities placed over them as recipients of good salaries, public respect, honors, and devotion, especially the three crown princes who commanded armies on the western front. In the end they did not even inform Hindenburg as to where the army corps stood; his quarters Hoffmann pointed out to a visitor with the words: "Here the Field Marshal has slept, before the battle of Tannenberg, after the battle of Tannenberg and, between you and me, during the battle of Tannenberg also." [56] The actual arrangements were made without these nonentities, between the chiefs of staff directly, over the telephone.

These "nonpolitical officers" by no means restricted themselves to purely military affairs. As early as the beginning of August 1914, Moltke came to the conclusion that "he would have to take the political direction into his own hands." [57] And his second successor did so, one of the general headquarters politicians, Colonel Bauer, justifying his action by an exegesis of Clausewitz and his celebrated definition of war as "nothing but a continuation of political intercourse with other means." This thesis, Bauer believed, must not be interpreted "as if the one who is directing war must be subordinated to the one who is directing policies . . . for war might very well be such a deep-cutting and decisive act of policy that it throws into insignificance all other sides of policy, or puts it into its service. This is altogether the case with respect to the war of 1914 to 1918." [58]

Contradictions to such claims were rare and weak, despite Bismarck's well-known conflicts with the overreaching ambitions of what he called "the technical army direction." The confidence which the German people put in Hindenburg, "Germany's fashion attraction," [59] was overwhelming: more than ten times as great as that in the Chancellor, the Pan-Germans maintained.[60] The resistance of persons entrusted by the Reich constitution with the function of controlling the military, namely, the Kaiser and the Chancellor, became increasingly feeble. The supreme war lord practically abdicated. Hindenburg and Ludendorff, playing consciously on their glory and popular favor, took over the Supreme Command and dominated the unwilling monarch, who sighed before his intimates for the day that he would not have to see this "sergeant-major mug" of Ludendorff any more.[61]

From that time "military necessity," as the first war Chancellor, Bethmann-Hollweg, excused himself, "was the word by which every act of the increasing preponderance of the Supreme Command was justified, till finally nonmilitary demands were also based on the argument that otherwise the responsibility for further leadership in the war could not be carried." With the argument of "responsibility" Ludendorff obtained and defended a position of dictatorship for the Supreme Command, which had no place in the Reich constitution as shaped by Bismarck. This responsibility Ludendorff conceived as carrying no obligations to any one person or body of persons, but as a responsibility for what he called "the life of the German Fatherland" and for victory. As such a dictator he dominated everyone else, from the Kaiser down, by the threat of resignation. When he did not obtain victory, he disappeared without giving account except in memoirs.[62]

Before this dictatorship had been completed in Germany, politicians had overrun the headquarters of Hindenburg-Ludendorff, seeking the authority which these two enjoyed for the support of their own policies. Men who advocated a peace of understanding found little favor there. When Hoffmann could not stand such proposals any longer he broke out "that this accursed flabbiness of our government, which, by the by, stinks to heaven, will not do in the long run." [63]

Instead of peace by negotiation, the Supreme Command embraced the "victory peace program" of the industrialists who wanted to extend control over Briey-Longwy and Belgium; of the agrarians who wanted lands for settlement in the thinly-populated East; of the navy, which demanded unlimited submarine warfare and control over the Belgian coast with a view to threatening England; of the army itself, which wished for greater security by the annexation of territories as "barriers" in the East and in the West; of the Pan-Germans, whose victory program included all this and still more. In a word, the Supreme Command gave heed to the propagandists of this program—the Pan-Germans who, with a general now at their head, and a Fatherland party behind them, led by Tirpitz and Kapp of Kapp Putsch fame, began to indoctrinate the German people.

Never were the upper classes more imperialistic, more Pan-German than at this time. They were anxious indeed for a military dictator to be the *Semper Augustus* of the Second Reich, the agent of expansion in East and West, in contempt of what the Pan-Germans called "the insane catchword of the self-determination of peoples." [64] The Kaiser was then thought to be no longer fit to fill such a role; in fact, a meeting of some of the highest officers, held early in 1918, discussed the question of putting him in tutelage. Neither was the Kaiser considered adapted to the post of dictator at home—a post which the Pan-Germans and the politician officers believed no one could fill better than Ludendorff.[65]

Yet Ludendorff had had no political experience. That he was no politician, "we all know," General Hoffmann jotted down in

1917, "for that he is far too impulsive. With him always something must happen at once, whereas the politician must wait and see." [66] Having become a dictator overnight, Ludendorff readily pinned his faith to proposals promising immediate results, which looked thoroughly military, even in nonmilitary spheres. Labor's demand for higher wages signaled by the Ruhr industrialists and manhood suffrage during wartime he considered treasonable. The militarization of the industrial plants, he imagined, would, by contrast, have a favorable effect in restoring among the workers the concept of authority to which they must bow. The shades of Bismarck and Stumm, with their anti-Socialist legislation, were stalking General Headquarters, along with an imperialism against which Bismarck had fought, if not always successfully.

Only by realizing all aims—the suppression of labor, and what was left of liberalism and a dictatorial peace like that at Brest-Litovsk—could the German governing classes now hope to maintain their old power. Ludendorff was eager to help them; in fact, so enthusiastic that the pseudo politician in him blinded the vision of the general. In keeping with his illusions he allowed the declaration of an unlimited U-boat warfare; after the peace of Brest-Litovsk, he kept in the East over a million German soldiers whom he could ill spare from the West where they might have completed the successes of March 1918, before the American masses began to take an active part in the war.[67]

These policies collided with the German soldiers' hopes for peace "without victory" and without defeat. They began to suspect that "the fatheads who sit at home" were responsible for the prolongation of the war: "They want a regular victory. Then the upper crust will have more hopes and become yet richer than they are already. They ought to come here and have the chunks of iron play around their ears." The faith of the front fighters that the war was fought for the whole nation was shaken. In intercepted soldier letters the officers could read as early as the summer of 1917 such notions as this: "Russia might be dearer to one than the fatherland. Messrs. Pan-Germans sit on the high horse. But they may be glad that we don't pull them off their big estates one of these days. Another fifteen billions of war loans and Germany is pawned to her rich. Europe is a huge insane asylum. Starvation makes me whistle: *Hunger über alles in der Welt.*" [68]

Thus the strong victory policies clashed with those of the democratic elements in the Reich who, if not for it in the beginning, learned as in Russia to want peace and a peace of understanding without annexations and indemnities and a parliamentary government at home—aims diametrically opposed to the policies which Ludendorff had in mind and equally opposed to his dictatorship, which filled for a time the place the Kaiser had once held but evacuated, a place that Hitler was to occupy soon. Drawing to the very limit on the strength of public confidence in his military abilities, Ludendorff, up to the very day of Germany's defeat, threw himself athwart democratization, against manhood suffrage in Prussia, against the demand of the majority parties in the Reichstag that the War Minister be made responsible to the Reichstag, against the insistence that the Emperor's role as Commander-in-Chief be restricted. Against all this Ludendorff set his face like flint. He backed the opposition to manhood suffrage which the Prussian die-hards maintained to the bitter end—one member by pointing to the closed ranks of the German people as "demonstrated on the battle-field where no classes are known." Under the delusive impression that German victories had been won in March and April 1918, the favored classes voted down the suffrage reform. Not even a plural vote was granted to soldiers as an equivalent for their blood. Only when German defeat had become obvious in September 1918, did the die-hards and the Supreme Command itself, directing an appeal to the Prussian Upper House, indicate that they were ready to con-cede reform and even to order a complete system of parliamentary government. The "revolution from above" had started; one from below was to start.

Now the despised parliamentarians of the Reichstag majority were either expected to produce victory or a will for victory. "Stir up the people!" Ludendorff told the ministers. "Cannot Ebert do it?" Or the parliamentarians were to insist upon an immediate peace, which the generals knew was necessary to get the army home—a peace which, because of the odium of signing, the military were absolutely unwilling to take upon themselves. On the third of October, Hindenburg told the Chancellor that he could not assume the responsibility if a catastrophe should occur within a week. On the twentieth, however, he protested against utterances ascribed to him to the effect that Germany could not put up resistance any longer; the latter statements must be denied publicly.[69] As soon as the generals finally convinced the bewildered civilian ministers that they, the ministers, had to sue for peace, they produced alibis for themselves, maintaining that a better, more honorable peace would be obtainable next year. These were the days when the chimera of the *Dolchstoss* (stab-in-the-back) was conceived, to conceal the follies of the military and put the blame for defeat on civilians.

Nationalism and Class Feeling in War

One of the main considerations in psychological preparedness for future wars, arising out of the First World War, is nationalism or chauvinism, the identification of every subject with the nation in peace and war. The nationalization of armies had gone far since the

English resolved to keep foreign troops from serving in the British Isles (1756-7) and since the French Revolution had repatriated an adventurer like Augereau, who had served in five and deserted from four armies. But on the eve of the First World War the nationalization of the soldier was still short of completion.

Nor was it intended to be complete, for all the great military powers had either their Irelands or their irredenta. Germany had her numerous Polish, Danish, Alsatian, and Lorraine soldiers from her eastern, northern, and western provinces. Russia had her Poles, and Austria her Czechs and Croats. For purposes of Germanization in peacetime, recruits from the non-German populations, to a considerable extent, were sent to serve in garrisons distant from their homes and recruits from the interior were placed in the frontier garrisons. In the latter part of the war, army corps largely composed of Alsatians were dispatched to fronts where they did not have to fight the French, and individual soldiers from Alsace-Lorraine were ordered eastward after some deserters from among them had betrayed German plans of attack in the West. Though the minorities in the Reich had belonged to the political opposition and had little for which to thank the governing groups and parties, they fought rather well on the whole and certainly better than the suspicious directors of the war supposed.

England also had her nationalizing difficulties. One of the principal reasons advanced by the English military against home rule for Ireland, before and after the war, was the accompanying loss of recruits for England's sixteen Irish battalions. Without home rule, recruitment from Ireland never exceeded 25 per cent of the comparable effort of Great Britain. London deemed it inadvisable to extend conscription to Ireland after it had been introduced, although Henry Wilson was convinced that the supervision of troops from the governing nation over a recalcitrant minority could be effective—an army of 2,500,000 men fighting in five theaters of war supervising from 100,000 to 150,000 conscript recalcitrant Irish. How far the pronounced Irish character of certain British regiments determined their use on the different fronts in the First World War—or in certain parts of the British Empire, such as India, where in 1920 numbers of Irish in the Connaught Rangers mutinied—is hard to ascertain. But no doubt that factor was important. There was also among the governors in London some fear, if slight, bred of Sir Roger Casement's agitation for the Irish Legion. Throughout the war the English kept a force in Ireland for safety.[70]

In Russia, the plethora of men for the armies, more imaginary than real considering the wasteful treatment that Russian man power underwent, as well as the dread of national revolutions, freed certain non-Russian races—10 per cent of the total population of the Empire—from conscription. These included the Finns (after 1910), the inhabitants of Turkestan and of large sections of the Caucasus. On the other hand the Poles, Jews, Letts, Estonians, Armenians, and Georgians had to fight, and they constituted one-third of the Russian army recruits, serving as a rule far from their home regions. Whatever Russian nationalism might have gained by excluding some of the subject races from the army, its intensity was still not very high.[71]

Before the war, Russian military writers urged that more be done for Russian nationalism, that, for instance, in all the army maneuvers "the enemy" always be called German, that the entire Russian people be made to understand that the future war would be directed against Germany, and that everyone be made to feel "that the German Empire must be annihilated, even if we must lose hundreds of thousands thereby." [72] But Czarist officials, such as the Minister of the Interior who signed the ukase for a general mobilization in July 1914, at the insistence of the army, doubted that those attempts at making the Russian people more patriotic had been very effective. Rather was he inclined to believe that the ideas of the Revolution were more easily comprehended by the people than victory over the Germans.[73]

Certainly great numbers of Russian soldiers lacked the national feeling which embraced allegiance to the whole community and extended its loyalty to cover the imperialistic Greater Russia. During the Revolution of 1917 soldiers were heard to say: "We are from Tambov, or Penza. The enemy is far from our province. What is the point of fighting?" Probably this peasant localism as much as an active patriotism moved some 260,000 Russian prisoners of war to attempt flight from German prison camps. Homesickness, no less than nationalism and the inhuman conditions surrounding the captive soldier, held sway in these camps.[74]

Of all the great military powers, France had the most homogeneous population. She had no minority within her boundaries to weaken her political and national potential. Instead she possessed an irredenta beyond the Vosges. Yet France seems to have been the first Western nation to employ exotic races as soldiers in her wars, as she had been the first Christian nation to ally itself with the Turk. In the eighteenth century, a French administrator in India, cut off by the British navy from getting reinforcements at home, enrolled the Sepoys—Mohammedan natives led and drilled in the European way.[75] Napoleon I used foreigners lavishly; his campaigns cost the lives of only one million "pure" Frenchmen as against the lives of from three to four million foreigners fighting his wars.[76] By drawing first on the numerous political refugees which the July

Revolution had attracted, and later on the adventurous of all the Western nations, France acquired new auxiliaries of varied numerical strength, the Foreign Legion counting in 1914 some nine thousand men. They were used as unsparingly as auxiliary troops always are. The Zouaves marked the beginning of France's *armée noire*, growing in importance as the French birth rate sank.

On the eve of the First World War, the colored troops in the French service amounted to about 9 per cent of her effectives. During the war, France drew from her colonies and protectorates 544,890 soldiers and 221,668 laborers—from the Senegal rather than from North Africa. They proved valuable in attacks and during the better seasons, though less useful under constant fire and inclement weather. Their death rate rose very high and in numbers their losses equaled those of Belgium and the United States combined.[77] It was obvious from the availability of those auxiliaries, enlarged by Americans who entered the French army prior to their country's official participation in the war, that, for sheer military reasons, it was advisable for France to keep alive her ancient cosmopolitan attractiveness. She could not afford to destroy the appearance of equality, regardless of race and color, under which the black army was ostensibly serving France.

On the other hand, Germany, with little occasion for employing Negroes during the war and none afterward, began early in the war to denounce the use of colored troops, and could easily combine the military interest and the race ideology of the "black shame." It is more than doubtful, however, whether her race propaganda ever aroused the resentment of many other peoples against the use of non-Caucasian races or recalled their memory of earlier protests against the use of aborigines. Long ago revolutionary Americans had cried out against the British employment of Indians, and a parliamentary opposition had been voiced by Chatham though he himself had turned the Indians against the French just eighteen years before.[78]

But that was well-nigh forgotten history and the German revival of the issue certainly did not restrain military men from efforts to enlist the greatest possible number of colored troops, such as the Bengal lancers whom Lord Curzon wanted to see on Unter den Linden, the Gurkhas who were to camp at Sans Souci, and the conscripted American Negroes. About the value of the Negro as a soldier, however, there were differences of opinion between the American draft commissions, which sent them into the armies, and the military commanders who directed Negro regiments.[79]

Other ingredients of the American melting pot had sometimes given the militarists and politicians, such as Theodore Roosevelt, pause: would they bestow their allegiance upon the Union, or would they retain their loyalties to their native lands? A Democratic politician during the Venezuela crisis of 1895-6, which Cleveland had precipitated, thought that a war with England would offer a good opportunity to test the recent immigration and to ascertain whether "free republican institutions are to be submerged by hordes of modern Goths and Huns among us." [80]

Despite such doubts the regular American army had always enrolled large numbers of emigrants, often soon after their arrival in the United States, and as in the case of auxiliaries slight appreciation for their labor had been shown. In 1917-18 deep distrust of the German-American element in the population was manifest, for naturally this element had least desired the war. Generals like Robert Lee Bullard shared the popular distrust and took care that considerable numbers of enlisted men and officers of German origin were held in the United States. At the front Bullard was surprised to find a young German-American, who had been only five or six years in the United States, fighting loyally, in spite of the fact that he had two brothers in the German army.

No data appear to exist from which to derive conclusions respecting either the fighting values or the deficiencies of the various nationalities which composed American society, from which to decide whether or not they were drawn to the American cause by stories of German atrocities. At all events General Bullard himself fell victim to these tales and employed them as propaganda in the army to offset the risk of having his soldiers think that the French and English had misrepresented the Germans, especially since so many of his men had lived quietly among their German fellow citizens in America and had found them neither cruel nor brutal.[81]

From the standpoint of national cohesion, the weakest army was the Austro-Hungarian, with its recruits drawn from ten linguistic nationalities. As early as 1895 an official of Galicia had declared "war an impossibility for Austria. Should we be attacked, we must accept the situation with God's help, but an aggressive war on account of Constantinople or some other Balkan question is madness. A state of nationalities can make no war without danger to itself. Among a conglomeration of nations victory or defeat causes almost equal difficulty." The aristocratic Badeni realized that only in peace could the aristocracy which governed the double monarchy preserve itself in that juggling of one nationality against another—preserve the 10 per cent against the 90 per cent on whom the former were living before 1914.[82]

But as if to demonstrate that this system could no longer survive, those who had so long thrived by it decided for war. And the German General Staff, none too well informed as to the inner state of the Austro-Hungarian monarchy and army, and acquainted with only a few generals and staff officers, did not take into account the earlier critical judgment of Waldersee, who saw in her army the prospects of a slow but sure process of disintegration.[83] As late as 1913 it was believed in Berlin that the Austro-Hungarian officer corps "forms the main and at this time still quite effective counterbalance against the polyglot character of the army. It is distinguished by loyalty, unpretentiousness, and knowledge of service, and has the confidence of its inferiors. The rank and file are disciplined, willing, patriotic, largely loyal to the Emperor and not yet touched by antimilitaristic agitation." [84]

Nevertheless, large parts of this very army were in fact indoctrinated with Pan-Slavic ideas. Only German, Hungarian, and Bosnian regiments could in fact be employed equally on all the fronts. Instead of being reamalgamated, as hoped, by the war against Serbia, whole regiments, mainly Slavic, deserted to the enemy. It was found advisable to use Croats against the Italians, not against Russia. Regiments with Italian recruits were sent to the Russian front. Disputes and desertions made for the disintegration of the Hapsburg monarchy, which had long ago, as Trotsky put it, hung out "a sign for an undertaker not demanding any high qualifications of him"—meaning that even the Russians could beat the Austrian armies at times.[85]

The most positive repudiation of allegiance to the Emperor came from the Czechs, who outnumbered all other deserters. A Prague regiment of infantry on the Carpathian front in the winter of 1914-15 was reduced within twenty-four hours from 2,000 to 150 men; in the words of Conrad, "without firing a shot it was taken prisoner, or rather called for in its trenches, by something like a Russian battalion." [86] Out of the Czech prisoners and deserters special legions were formed to fight for the Allies, by whom they were "somewhat misused," according to an admission from that side,[87] in combats with the Bolsheviks as well as the Central Powers. But they had the satisfaction of shedding their blood for the cause of national emancipation and a revolution of their own. Violent, even terroristic, nationalism had helped to start the war and it aided in destroying many governments that had fanned its passions.

The hostility of national officers within the coalitions likewise hampered military efficiency. The history of all coalitions is not only "a tale of the reciprocal complaints of allies" [88] but also a tale of common energies wasted. Personal and national jealousy, ill will, and bad faith on the part of the allied commanders have always stood in the way of their united effort and, indeed, developed among them contempt for one another, rising in some instances as high as Marlborough's declaration to his adversary, Marshal Villard, in 1705, that Margrave Ludwig of Baden, leader of the Imperials, had broken his vow and that he could hold only him responsible for the wreck of all his plans.[89]

Down to the French Revolution the supranational solidarity of officers often smoothed out conflicts of state and army interest. But the national character of armies in the First World War threw out that lubricant of inter-army relations if occasionally officers forgot their international antipathies in a common hostility for politicians, such as Kitchener and Joffre, Henry Wilson and Foch all cherished. In this hostility they would support one another; for instance when Lloyd George asked Foch awkward questions about the source of the high losses in the English army under Haig, the French general, instead of elucidating the problem, "played up very well as regards Haig and would not give him away." Or again a mere conversation would unite generals like Foch and Wilson against favoring a politician, such as the Radical-Socialist General Sarrail.[90]

Except as far as mitigated by careful propaganda, nationalism in war, in its exterior aspects, takes the form of a violent assertion of the collective ego against the ally as well as against the enemy. In the First World War nationalism thus became a corrosive force typical of all war coalitions. From the things he had seen and heard, Montluc, as early as the sixteenth century, concluded that "when two princes undertake the conquest of a Kingdom, they never agree; because each one thinks always that his companion wants to cheat him and so they distrust each other. . . . Always there is reproach and two nations do not agree easily." [91]

Apart from political and economic objectives, conflicts within coalitions are concerned either with the relative expenditure of lives and materials in the common enterprise, with the question of common war plans, or with the division or unity of command. "Allied armies," Clausewitz wrote in respect of a possible war of the Eastern Powers against the July Revolution, "are more in need of unity of action than the army of a single master. When they do not act in separate theaters of war, but rather act in common, the unity is the more difficult to preserve the wider are the spaces which they fill." In his time, where common reactionary policies could be relied upon as cohesive principles for the armies, Clausewitz thought that a supreme command was conditioned largely by the matter of space; over a distance of from 150 to 225 kilometers such authority was possible, but not over one of 750 kilometers.[92] Almost in the same degree that the distance was overcome by the progress of communication, the discordant force of nationalism, hidden within it, increased in power during the First World War.

The "Nibelungen faith" promised by the Kaiser to Vienna so lightheartedly before 1914, despite Bismarck's warnings against Austria's far-reaching egotistic policies, was not easily translated into terms of military co-operation. Austrian failures led to the steady extension of German command over Austrian troops, to the insertion of Germans in some twenty places on the southern half of the eastern front, and to innumerable features in the liaison arrangements. Such German domineering was endured by the old Viennese aristocracy, the members of which scarcely shone in this war business with respect to efficiency, but it was irksome to them.

Near the end they got hold of the young Emperor Charles who, to the papal nuncio in Berlin, was a rather poor ruler who "would just about do for government" if only the power of the high aristocracy could be broken. Asked if the German army command did not have a recipe for the aristocratic disease, General Hoffmann replied that he knew none except strychnine.[93] Making use of the Emperor's and their own Catholic connections with the high aristocracy of the Western Powers, the Viennese aristocracy tried to bring about, under cover, a peace with those powers favorable to old Austria, despite the promises of the Allies already given to the revolutionary organizations of the Austrian nationalities. They addressed themselves, through the relatives of the Empress, to the French government, accompanying the gesture by removing the able and loyal Chief of Staff, Conrad, and overthrowing the energetic Tisza in Hungary. More or less gladly they endured the pacifist strikes against German annexationism as exhibited at Brest-Litovsk, and they did their bit for the defeat of the Central Powers.

The peace endeavors of the Austrian high aristocracy were in many respects identical with attempts at an earlier peace on the part of various interest groups within the warring nations. Akin to their gestures were Lord Lansdowne's effort in 1917 and the preceding Russian attempt to meet German negotiators at Stockholm in the autumn of 1916—a project of liberals in the Russian Duma with whose peace policies, though not with their other aims, the Czar and his entourage were in complete agreement.

Such schemes revealed the "save-the-skin" mentality operating in governments with a view to recovering ground through peace; this alarmed the military, who insisted that these peace parties must be stopped. The motives of the Russian peace groups were, no doubt, deeply rooted in the disappointments bound to occur in coalition warfare. Before the year 1914 was over, the British military attaché in Petersburg met Russians who hinted that a French offensive was retarded because the Western governments had "decided with diabolical cunning that Russia must waste her strength so that she may not emerge too strong from the war." Later, after the Russians had several times attacked in vain, just to help the Allies and for no reason of their own, the British officer was told: "We Russians are so noble-minded that we attack at once if any one asks us for help, but no one has ever helped us when we were in difficulties." [94] When, following the downfall of the Czar, the Russian liberals, hitherto so eager for peace, pretended that they placed their faith in the Allies, they really shared the suspicion of the war-weary masses directed against the war aims of the Entente as capitalistic and imperialistic. This marked the death of the sympathies that had provoked warlike Pan-Slavism; soon after their accession to power Russian liberals were willing to betray "heroic Serbia" in order to bribe Bulgaria with Serbian territory and so purchase her desertion from the Central Powers.[95]

Not until the Russians had practically dropped out of the war did the Western Allies set up an organ for the purpose of co-ordinating their war efforts and policies—the Supreme War Council—on November 7, 1917, the day of the Bolshevik Revolution. Unity of command, repeatedly emphasized by Clemenceau, was deemed an impossible achievement on the English side even by such a Francophile as Henry Wilson, who was convinced since the beginning of that year that his own country "was now the most important of the Allies, in money, in fleets, in shipping, in coal and (almost) in armies." Each member of the coalition feared that a supreme war commander from one of the Allies would spare the troops of his country or pursue in other ways its separate interest, would try to save enough men from the war to influence the peace makers. "At the peace it would never do for France to have no army at all left," Joffre blurted out in 1916 while discussing the use of the Allied reserves.[96]

As soon as the Americans came in, the older and more war-wearied partners fervently hoped that the newcomers would make the necessary human sacrifices in the main. In that expectation they were eager to have American troops sent to the front as soon as they arrived in France. But, true to coalition psychology, the American officers resented this "loss of our national identity in the war" and none more stiffly than General Pershing. A number of the American generals—with the notable exception of Bliss, sitting on the Supreme War Council, and to a certain extent Wood—argued against this arrangement quite politically. They wondered whether the President at Washington fully realized "what it will mean to get a division or two annihilated under the British flag, with Ireland in arms against conscription and our people none too warmly inclined to the British Alliance." [97]

Firmly they withstood what they interpreted as attempts of the war-experienced Allies to patronize them and assume superior airs with them, although the Allies were convinced that the best value would be got out of the newcomers if they would fight in the beginning in close connection with war-seasoned troops and under experienced commanders or with French generals as counselors by their side. Indeed, it was alleged that by declining to render this promptest kind of help Pershing endangered Allied success; the point is arguable and the contention has been supported with a good deal of force by Lloyd George. Less debatable is the opinion that the Americans paid a very high price in American lives and probably in Allied lives by their insistence on the preservation of their army's national identity and by refusing to accept the Allied plan. According to General Mordacq, Clemenceau's close military adviser, it cost them in the Argonne in September 1918—where Pershing had got stuck and wanted to free himself from his impasse without help—more than twenty-five thousand dead.

This determination on the part of Pershing "to fight his own battle and win his own victories with his own army" the French general explains very sympathetically as national *amour propre,* as springing from the fear that the war might be over in a few months and glory thus escape the great American nation and Pershing himself: could one reproach him for such a human sentiment even if he carried it a little too far? [98] The professional soldier of the Allied Powers understood what to others may have seemed more professional than human: the actions of the American generals, in want of laurels, as they drove their men into last-hour attacks, enthusiastically executing all the orders of the Inter-Allied High Command which the hour of panic, induced by the German victories, had finally created. Since victory was rapidly acquiring a rarity value, Pershing had his soldiers attack right up to the time of the Armistice, "No matter how many armistice and peace talkers the Germans may send us," and remained bellicose after the Armistice. He favored continuing the war in the best "grandstand" style, the premiers of the exhausted nations remarked. One of Pershing's subordinates had his army attack until the last minute of the war, until eleven o'clock in the morning of November 11. Then, when all was over, he returned to his headquarters "thoughtful and feeling lost," yet ready to claim the credit which he thought the day's bulletin had denied him. [99]

Given such nationalism within the coalition, only terrible losses and dire necessity brought the Allies to such unity as was attained. The great thrust of March 1918, by Ludendorff, as in the case of other coalition battles, was directed against the point of junction between the two Allied armies with no supreme commander, and his thrust, finding the Allies unprepared, achieved a great tactical success. It was this smash that helped the Allies to overcome their resistance to close co-operation and unity of command; five days after the attack Foch was made co-ordinator of the armies on the western front. After another dangerous German thrust he was made Commander-in-Chief of the Allied Forces in France. His rise to the post of generalissimo of all the forces operating against Germany was a promotion soon to embarrass the peacemakers, for they discovered that they had elevated Foch too high. As soon as victory was in sight they themselves discarded the thought of coalition. Then Lloyd George and Henry Wilson agreed that they had "pandered and bowed too much to President Wilson"—their savior.[100]

The inward nationalism of armies in war tends to make soldiers forget party, class, and other differences, to forget that wars may be wars of governing classes, caused by them and undertaken in their interest. "I know no parties any more; I only know Germans," the Kaiser announced to the Reichstag on August 4, 1914. On both sides officers were inclined to rejoice that wars rid them of the party nuisance, the class curse, the conflict of sections.

When at an earlier time Leonard Wood saw, among his Rough Riders, outlaws, "New York swells," New Mexican cowboys, men from south of the Mason-Dixon line, "all working and as chummy as can be," he was delighted; he believed that "all the cost of this war is amply repaid by seeing the old flag as one sees it today in the South. We are indeed today once more a united country." [101] Such rationalizing was true to form, for one of the prerequisites of modern armies and their victory is the appearance of classlessness. In their conflicts there is no longer any place for such bodies as the British yeomanry of Napoleon's age, which "had come into being mainly through the desire of the farming class to escape being placed on the same level with their labourers through the ballot." [102] As far as they remain intact, class institutions have to be less obvious and care has to be taken that military distinctions are not confounded with them.

In every army, of course, certain ranks must of necessity command and others obey. The upper ranks, from the nature of their composition as well as their function, enjoy privileges, even in war; they receive higher pay; they have better quarters, better food; they carry no kits; they get more orders and medals. To a certain extent class privileges and military requirements coincide. In normal and in victorious times and in short wars the appropriateness of this coincidence is generally admitted, particularly if there is some provision for promotion from the lower to the higher ranks.

But this functional easement is never without its risks for the purposes of warfare. The greater freedom of movement, for instance, that the officer enjoys by not having to carry the heavy baggage of the men—sometimes amounting in weight to sixty pounds or more (the Russian soldier carried ninety pounds in 1904-5)—may tempt him to demand too much of his men and outrun them in attacks. It may encourage him to force them up to enemy positions in a condition of complete exhaustion. Again, the aloofness from material hardships enjoyed at headquarters and the comfort brought by the automobile, while giving officers greater ease and mobility, increase the temptation to forget the limitations on the exactions that can be effectively wrung from troops. They may induce officers to disregard the economy of strength which, in former armies, the commanders, undergoing similar bodily exertions with their men, so closely controlled. In this escape of modern officers from privates' burdens, a German general found one of the weightiest reasons for the failure of the march on Paris in 1914: "The main thing after all was to keep one's own troops capable of action. But of that no command thought in the blind competition for the final victory. The age of automobiles and telephones made the commanders and their assistants callous to the condition of the man dependent on his lungs and legs." [103]

The strict military way of warfare requires the good officer to avoid everything that might seem to be giving him undue advantages. Nevertheless the German rank and file in the First World War were kept apart from their officers in the use of restaurants, hospitals, stairways and entrances, church seats, railway compartments, barber shops, baths and beaches, lavatories and bordellos. Consequently in the summer of 1916, after Verdun—which shook the German soldiers' morale—complaints came to the Supreme Command about the unequal feeding and much ill-treatment of soldiers, including indulgence in abusive terms respecting the patriotism of the men. In response, Ludendorff, in March 1917, issued an order advising officers not yet informed that the soldier at the front was feeling dishonored by discriminatory signs in restaurants and barber shops—which feeling, the general admitted, was justified: "It is hard, even vexing to the subordinate, when, as soon as he has left the trenches, he finds a ridiculous separation of the classes taking place again."

Another order, signed by Hindenburg, declared that many officers and staffs continued to give, as in peacetime, elaborate dinners obviously prepared from army rations: "Considering the heavy exterior and interior struggle which the German people undergo, we must above all avoid spreading in the army that dissatisfaction which arises from a gradation of the several classes of society. This is most easily nourished when the agitators at home and in the field can connect their pernicious activity with the stomach question. We must not give them any basis for that." So the officers were instructed to avoid the appearance of privileges, if not commanded strictly to renounce them.

All attempts, however, to assure equal food for men and officers in the German armies remained unheeded despite appeals even from conservative parliamentarians. In 1917 the Bavarian War Minister refused to order all ranks fed from the same kitchens; that, he said, would be tantamount to proof of a wide and deep distrust of the disinterestedness and sense of justice on the part of the officers; their "undiminished eagerness for the service must be preserved"—obviously the way to that went through the stomach. Even so, the officers' "sense of justice" clashed with the soldiers' understanding of ethics and civilian notions of equality in sacrifice. "Do not think that we do not know our duty toward our nation," wrote a burgher to Ludendorff in August 1918. "We know it. But: the tremendous injustice done on the front systematically destroys our old most sacred feelings of duty." [104]

An ample supply of food saved the Western Powers from hunger as a basis of soldier resentment. The officers on their side received better fare than their men, and the English frankly insisted that officers with higher duties be better fed. This fact led a Prussian Minister of War to suppose that the German egalitarians were thinking of something besides merely winning the war,[105] but in truth the Old Prussians of the German army were really invoking an English practice in defense of all their unequal practices. The Supreme Command, possessing more authority in Germany than anyone since Frederick the Great, knew this situation and yet hesitated to send out an order which the officers might elude. They admitted to themselves that "it is an old experience that the overwhelming majority of the soldiers are satisfied when they are well fed" and that all other questions of the day counted for little with them; that "the superior who obtains for himself special privileges, who is particularly conspicuous, contributes above all to discontent when doors are opened for agitation." [106] Still they could pretend surprise that the rank and file, suffering hunger and want, refused to fight and die any longer for Pan-German war aims.

Another feature of inequality in the presence of death was almost as common in the democratic armies as with the Germans—the *embusqués,* as the French called them, that is, officers and men who sought, obtained, and tried to keep posts in places less dangerous to life and limb. This desire for safety caused an inflation of staffs, so luxuriantly provided with personnel, indeed, that early in 1918 there was, on the English staffs, one combatant to every three *rationnaires* and Lloyd George had to order a purge. A preferred ambush for shirkers consisted of posts in the administrative branches of the armies, where the officeholders endeavored to maintain themselves by doing their superiors favors. A knowledge of foreign languages opened the way to highly desirable positions in the unduly large liaison missions. Most of these positions were held by officers, Mordacq asserts, "almost all belonging in the golden book of our nobility or to our high finance." Certainly many of them were adepts in the "art of pulling the barons out of the fire," as described by a contemporary French libel.[107] In recognition of this form of evasion bitter jesting words circulated in the German army: *k.v.*, that is, *kriegsdienstverwendungsfähig* (fit for front service), *keine Verbindung* (no pull); *g.v.*, *garnisondienstverwendungsfähig* (fit for garrison duty), *gute Verbindung* (good pull); *a.v.*, *arbeitsdienstverwendungsfähig* (fit for labor service), *ausgezeichnete Verbindung* (excellent pull).

The American army was not long enough in the field to experience the ugly mass phenomenon of the rank and file turning bitterly against military rank as class privilege. But on that side also signs of this resentment appeared. Some American politicians thought that, even with the draft, "we should send comparatively few men outside the United States and we should select those to be sent largely from the street-corner loafers who are not particularly good anyhow." [108]

Perhaps acquainted with such conceptions as well as with the recrudescence of class emotions in European armies, several civilian politicians anxious for victory, such as Samuel Gompers, feared that class differences would be embodied in the army. Gompers proposed that soldiers taken from the working population be sent to France under the leadership of foremen and trade union heads instead of being placed under college men who would be mostly "moneyed men," inclined to bring out the unfortunate distinction of class against mass. He thought that his scheme would assure the solidarity, the spirit of the corps, and good fellowship; that it would prevent the perpetuation of a "forbidden form of aristocracy"; that it would bridge the gulf between the officer and the private—"the lack of the opportunity for the officer to know the man in his quality of son, father, brother, husband, or neighbor." Needless to say, the War Department rejected this proposal, declaring that war and industry were professions too diverse for the foreman to be an officer, while omitting to mention that the bond salesman's college training was hardly a better basis for the metamorphosis.[109]

The better, more understanding officer makes sparing use of his privileged position; when work is to be done he works beside his men. This is a modern development. In the eighteenth century the soldiers themselves found it "almost painful to see their officers lay their hands to any but officers' work. Such things were not seemly for gentlemen." [110] And not every officer, of course, displayed the co-operative spirit in the First World War. On the contrary, some of them took advantage of their position to overwork tired soldiers for their own personal comfort or that of their colleagues. Seldom did the eye of the inspector note the luxuries thus secured or, if it did, still more rarely did corrective action follow.[111]

For a long time the rank and file in the German armies were willing to concede special privileges to their officers but a protest, rising from an almost silent and secret objection to an angry explosion, was provoked when honors became a mere appendage of rank, particularly when officers and other men outside the sphere of danger received decorations along with the so-called "front pigs," when officers and men got the Iron Cross without having shown any courage to justify it. In the mind of the common soldier the suspicion grew that he was not only working for the comfort of the officer but also dying for his honor. And this suspicion was nourished by such observations as were inevitable when staff officers had themselves transferred to the front in order to win an order or a cross as "crusaders." [112] Playing at bravery merely tended to make the Iron Cross, once "the spur to the most intrepid deeds," a piece of tinsel, a symbol of the common soldiers' bondage.

Even within the officer body dissensions developed between the professionals and the "temporary gentlemen" of the reserve, who were seldom employed on staffs. In the German army a third and particularly disturbing category of officers was created in the war by the institution of the sergeant-major lieutenant. This long-serving, noncommissioned officer had had a rigorous service experience, but he was inexperienced in the arts of drinking and being decorated— arts readily acquired by the young college graduates who came "down the line." As substitutes for war experience the young collegians were wont to display an imperious tone and cutting manner to the men in the ranks.

Resentments arising from officer privileges and seeming class distinctions naturally increased with the passing of time. In the beginning of the First World War, as in every other war, no danger was felt to be too great to face, even by the common soldier. The Rough Riders had liked to chant: "Rough-tough, we're the stuff! We want to fight and we can't get enough." The German soldier chalked on the sides of his box cars: "More declarations of war still accepted." There was a grand moment of romantic challenging with the whole world as foe. Yet in that as in every war, there came a reaction. Courage was worn thin and the spirit of the men became like that described by a German military writer after the Franco-Prussian War: "In August one asked: 'Who may go along today?' Two months later: 'Who does go along today?' And in January: 'Who must go along today?'" The "many enemies, much honor" vogue was bound to weaken, and the change was ominous.

The soldier of the World War I armies brought to his work a

stronger bent toward criticism than his forerunners had displayed. At the start of the war he may have been bored with his peacetime privilege of democratic faultfinding or, seeking new excitements, have taken this right for granted and forgotten that it was a privilege; but the memory revived as he encountered conditions similar in fact or in appearance to those he had considered hateful in peace. In the armies of the democratic countries, certain rights to criticism were preserved—rights based on the rotation of parties in power and the idea that "we are going to change this afterwards" and "we will not be under officers any more, these merely temporary leaders"; once the war is over "we will be civilians again." It matters not whether such opinions were sound, judged by postwar applications; they were influential during the war.[113] And they were a source of strength to the armies of democracy—a strength upon which those who propose to introduce a totalitarian dictatorship in war may well ponder before they undertake to corrode rank-and-file hopefulness by the excess government so tempting to the military mind. In the two world wars the military minds of democratic countries at least had to stand a great deal of parliamentary criticism.

In contrast with the men of the democratic armies, German soldiers of 1914-18 could look forward to no reasonable assurance that the return of peace would reduce the dominance of the military in any essential respect. They felt certain that, even in the event of a German victory, they would be held to the colors for many years. In fact, German policies in the East after November 1917, warranted that belief. No doubt, soldiers in the armies of the Reich were at first content with entrusting their fate to their officers. But as the war went on they began to lose their confidence as they watched the officers directing German politics and fitting themselves into the pattern—the class structure of society—which the soldier hoped would be modified by the common enterprise of war. At home the parties of opposition to the German military class kept the so-called *"Burgfrieden"*—peace within the besieged castle; thus they were tying their hands more tightly than the political parties among the Western Powers and diminishing their influence over the direction of the war and the lot of the rank and file. In the rare and secret meetings of the Reichstag committees, politicians could demand that officers be instructed to regard as treason the premeditated neglect of their men, but they could not go before the public with complaints against the officers without running the risk of being promptly charged with the loss of the war.

When, after initial successes, officers openly took up the defense of the nondemocratic institutions of Germany and adopted the several annexationist and imperialistic war aims, the situation altered on the home front and the battle front. The masses, civilian and military, had believed they were fighting a defensive war and would at least be recompensed by manhood suffrage. Now they were told about Pan-German aspirations and class dominion. Naturally they could not penetrate very far into officer politics, such politics being veiled behind a screen called Hindenburg; but enough became known to shake the confidence of both soldiers and civilians in officer leadership and turn it from the Supreme Command and the government to the parties that opposed the war of annexations and demanded electoral reform with parliamentary institutions.

Nor was the situation essentially different in the Austrian army, where the aristocracy, as far as it refrained from trying to make peace behind the back of its ally, hankered for imperialistic gains in Poland, or in the Russian army where the imperialistic objectives of the Allies, as well as the ambitions of the Czar and the liberals with eyes on Constantinople, finally disgusted the masses. Having no effective opposition parties to voice their war weariness, the Russians reverted in an anarchic way to a mass individualism[114] which was seized upon by the most radical peace party, the Bolsheviks, and made the basis of its rise from a group of doctrinaires to a party of power.

At this stage of war weariness, nationalism encountered the peril of being replaced by internationalism. In August 1918, the Deutsche Werkmeisterverband, a conservative organization of factory foremen, warned the Supreme Command that there existed in the army "great masses of politically corrupted men to whom it is a matter of indifference whether they are Frenchmen or Englishmen." And infantrymen were heard to say in September of that year: "It is all the same whether we are Germans, Frenchmen, or Englishmen." [115] So the policy of replacing or covering up class competition by national competition failed in large parts of the German army; the old national antagonism was no longer dynamic. Behind the struggle of the embattled nations, soldiers detected the struggle of class interests and began to ask the devastating question: What is all this suffering for and who is to benefit from it? They became ready to listen to those who could furnish the answer.

Struggles Within the Officer Class

Against the civilians—"the frocks," the parties of opposition, and especially the socialists—a closely united front was seemingly presented by the officers in the First World War. Yet behind this camouflaged front, a frantic, ruthless, unscrupulous, interminable jealousy operated on all sides to divide the generals battling for their individual recipes for victory and the officers of lower rank seeking advancement and decorations while the war raged. These conflicts, "war within war," demonstrated the bearing of peace-time army life, "the school of cold climbing," on actual military preparation for war. Among the officers of the German General Staff the distrust of one another became so deep and wide that the orders most fraught with risk to themselves were carefully given not in writing but over the telephone—at the receiving end of which two officers recorded the instructions, one as a witness. "Fights on all sides!" exclaimed one of Ludendorff's handymen, Colonel Bauer, "imbecility, jealousy, and quarrels of the depart-ments." [116]

In its sociological aspects war life among officers in the war ran true to tradition. A jurist in the camp of Wellington, himself *hors concours,* observed that

the officers in the lower branches of the staff are sharp-set, hungry, and anxious to get on and make the most of everything and have a view even in their civilities. I have tried not to see much that I could not help seeing and which gave me a moderate opinion of the profession which has not the independence I flatter myself I have seen in all the most respectable at the bar. There is much obsequious time-serving conduct to anyone who is in office, or is thought to have a word to say to Lord Wellington. . . . I am thought a formidable person to whom it is well to be civil and who can often be of service to others.[117]

Everyone at all familiar with staff life will agree that this char-acterization of the competitive relation between the lower ranks of officers and their behavior toward their superiors is accurate. It is one which, according to military convention, should not be written down and yet is true and will probably remain true. Nev-ertheless this competition in the lower ranks of officers is like a struggle of pygmies compared with the leonine strife in the higher ranks, carried on behind nearly every front of every war and amply revealed in the memoirs of superior officers. Warfare turns the chronic state of jealousy among officers and officer cliques into an acute state. The perpetual "war in peace," treated innumerable times in the typical prewar officer novel, thus becomes "war within war."

There was, for instance, the conflict within the Prussian army after 1807 between the reformers, like Scharnhorst, Grolman, and Gneisenau on the one side, and the conservative Prussians, like York and Kalckreuth on the other, the former openly accusing one of the latter group of having caused the Duke of Brunswick to lose the battle of Auerstädt and to be altogether in the French interest for reasons of vanity.[118] This contest was carried over into the wars of 1813-15. When York received an order, signed upside down by Blücher, who was ill in bed, he protested: "One sees, the old man is insane again. Therefore, it is really Gneisenau who commands us; that we must not suffer." In return, York and his staff accused the much younger Gneisenau, Blücher's chief of staff, of artfully concealing the glorious deeds of York in the army reports; whereupon Gneisenau retorted that "one gets along best with York if one lives in open enmity with him." At all times a difficult subordinate, York, by his obstinacy and disobedience, clearly added to the defeats of the Allies at the hands of Napoleon in February 1814.[119]

As for himself, Napoleon took the manifold jealousies among his generals as a matter of military nature, though he constantly avoided recognizing its menace to victory, particularly when he was not on the spot. He himself nourished a number of hatreds for other generals, such as Moreau, Bernadotte, and Kleber—aversions strongly reciprocated. "The renown of Kleber tired him," wrote Bourrienne. "He knew the way in which Kleber expressed himself about him." During the bloody and futile siege of Acre, Kleber said to Bourrienne: "Your little bitch of a Bonaparte who is no higher than my boot is going to enslave France. Look what a d———d expedition he has made us undertake." [120]

Except for the affection which Napoleon had or at least displayed for Desaix, it seems impossible to find indications of any true friendship and comradeship among the leaders of the Napoleonic armies. Each marshal or general appears to have had far more enemies to combat among his peers and his subordinates than foreign enemies. Saint-Cyr was generally considered a "very bad comrade"; he left Vandamme unsupported after Dresden. Generals Reynier and Destaing, who had both served and quarreled in Egypt, had a duel after their return in which the latter was killed.

Ney had to thank his own blunt and honest nature for many of his personal foes, among whom were some of the judges who were to condemn him to death in 1815. His gruff nature got him into trouble with Bernadotte, whose "desertion" from the French army seems to make him the personification of faithlessness among Napoleon's generals, in the eyes of French military writers. Bernadotte, Ney's biographer says, wrote Ney a letter that amounted to "a monument of perfidy." [121] Soult, "who would not at any price call upon the good services of Marshal Ney in order to destroy the English army, contented himself with following the latter when it started retreat on its own account and assisting from afar its embarkment in the port of Coruna." Later when Ney, as a man of good faith, in the spring of 1809 concocted a plan against the

English with Soult, "he did not reckon with the perfidiousness of the latter" who left him in the lurch—"an unimaginable atrocity," as Ney called it, believing that only the inactivity of the enemy had saved him from the disaster which had without doubt been prepared against him by Soult. This view was shared by Ney's generals, one of whom wrote that Soult "saw no hope to save himself except in the misfortune of his neighbors" and that there was no disloyalty of which he was not capable. It was also shared by all the ranks in fact and led to bloody encounters between men and officers of the two marshals' armies.[122]

Conflicts intensified when one of the marshals was subordinated to another if only for a short period, especially when their respective jurisdiction was not clearly outlined. Thus Ney protested against his corps being placed under Murat's command even for a time: "It would be very cruel to me to make me give up, by passing under the command of Prince Murat, a part of that glory which I can promise myself; such a misfortune would destroy all my powers." And the exercise of *amour propre* endangered the success of the operation ordered by Napoleon, for Murat in his own vainglory claimed still more authority over Ney's corps than he had been granted. The outcome was a challenge to a duel which was stopped when the parties realized how singular a duel would be between officers facing an enemy.[123]

The animosities of Davout were no less sharp and if possible more numerous than those of Ney. Davout deemed himself betrayed by Bernadotte at Auerstädt in 1806, where he won the battle against great odds and in spite of treachery on the part of Bernadotte, who withheld two reserve divisions from participating in the battle though they were not under his orders. Among his foes Davout counted Marmont, likewise rated as "a bad comrade" by others; on the other hand, Marmont had been warned of Davout's faithlessness by Junot. The jealousy of Berthier kept Jomini, in many respects his superior, from rising in the French army and was also directed against Davout. Against Berthier's orders Davout had won a battle and saved the army, incurring "hence a terrible hatred." Berthier and Murat the Emperor considered the "authors of the failure of the campaign of 1812." With Soult he quarreled violently even during the desperate Hundred Days.[124] Yet Napoleon was not at all displeased by the lack of harmony among his generals; indeed their accord would have alarmed him.

In cases where Napoleon had to be absent, he did not particularly enjoin co-operation upon his generals. In the Peninsular War differences among them often prepared defeat, as at Talavera, and led them to thwart rather than to help one another. Soult found Suchet reluctant to obey. Soult and Marmont at first resolved to co-operate, but after less than a week parted company "upon terms of mutual suspicion." The sole common front which Napoleon's marshals and generals in Spain could find was against the Emperor's brother, King Joseph, at Madrid, and his chief of staff, Jourdan; their eagerness in this union was only rivaled by their desire to throw the responsibility for defeat upon someone else. If no one else was available, a subordinate might be made a scapegoat and driven to suicide by the unjust reproaches of a marshal or of a colleague who had withheld his help.

Before Wellington had fully asserted his authority, dissensions among the British officers were no less common and virulent. Wellington had started his career by attempts to displace Dalrymple, the first British Supreme Commander in the Peninsula, and to install Moore, for whose supersession by Wellington not long afterward many officers were intriguing. From the politics of these officers and their practice of shouting their opinions about orders of the Commander-in-Chief, from their jealousies and egotisms, Wellington suffered in his turn. But in his determination to create and uphold authority within the British army, so riven with political dispute, he seldom visited mistakes upon recalcitrant and inefficient generals; instead, however unfairly, he laid their blunders upon their subordinates.[125]

An especially fertile source of complaints and recriminations had always been the special relationship between the commander-in-chief and his chiefs of staff. The latter were prone to tire of the ungrateful role in which they served the glory of their general, when things went well, and as the scapegoats when things went wrong. Despite his usually harmonious relations with Blücher, Gneisenau thought he had reason to grumble about the old man's ingratitude. He shared the grievances of Müffling, the second on Blücher's staff: "Who should have thought that the magnanimous Prussian army had so many commanding officers who want to have the reports filled with names and deeds; that is, who regard the great affairs of their country from such a low point of view and who for the sake of the great cause cannot forget their own precious selves." How often was the mere decision overrated and the preparation for it by the General Staff unappreciated! [126]

A century later the relations of the higher officers remained essentially the same. The first great defeat of the Russians in the First World War, at Tannenberg, was in some respects due to a personal feud between Samsonov and Rennenkampf. They had quarreled at Mukden in 1905, when it was said that Samsonov boxed Rennenkampf's ears for having been faithless to their common trust. To get even Rennenkampf refrained from marching to the support of Samsonov, his enemy, in the crucial hour of Tannenberg.[127] Internal conflicts of that kind between commanding officers continued as long as the Czarist army and its heir, the White armies, existed,[128] and contributed powerfully to their failure. On the side of the Reds, the deathly conflict between Stalin and Trotsky started in this very same Civil War.[129] As a rule the public did not learn much of the truth about official camaraderie before the memoirs were written.

Troubles among officers sometimes grew out of differences of opinion over the preferable style of warfare and choice of theaters of war—every general, as Napoleon remarked, tending to believe that the important point of the battle or campaign is where his particular command is situated. At other times troubles sprang out of doubts allowed to percolate to the outside by one party, or both, respecting the competence of the rival and the justice of his claims for successes attributable to others. As early as August 11, 1914, Haig, an army corps commander, confided to his diary that General French was "quite unfit for this great command at a time of crisis in our nation's history"; yet he was resolved to be thoroughly loyal and perform his obligations "as a subordinate should, trying all the time to see Sir John's good qualities and not his weak ones." But his own and other generals' misgivings relative to the competence of French eventually came to the ears of the British government, which removed French and put Haig in his place. It may be improper to inquire whether Haig, whose own enemy was Henry Wilson, always succeeded in pursuing his aim of keeping his loyalty intact; it has been questioned.[130]

In the French army, conflicts among generals were less acute during the First World War, for so many rivals had been removed from the arena before the war had actually begun; but conflicts frequently occurred. Differences between such generals as Foch and Sarrail were political as well as military, if a distinction can be made.

By withholding a command in France from General Wood, the American army avoided a terrible dispute prepared by the composition of the prewar officer corps. The elimination of older generals and other officers through an examination of their fitness, incidentally or intentionally, had much the same effect in curtailing controversies as the French elimination measures. But it cost General Bliss, who presided over the committee which decided war promotions by selection instead of seniority, many friendships and brought him many irate letters including some from the wives of old officer friends thus passed over. To these complaints he could only reply that "no regular officer has any claim, as a matter of right, to any assignment or promotion." [131] This conciliatory disposition caused General Harbord, a Pershing man, early in 1918, "more worry than the anticipated German offensive," though it helped General Bliss to get along with the imperious Pershing. On his part, Pershing, soon after America's entrance into the war, commenced to "can" many officers—that is, dispatch them to Cannes —in much the same spirit as the French sent their 138 general officers to Limoges; and the Americans did not take their "canning" amiably.[132]

As a matter of fact, relations among American generals, as between Pershing and Peyton March, for instance, could on occasion be as strained as between classes or states. General Bullard's division was once relieved by a division whose command was so faultfinding and critical of his shortcomings "and made such bad reports of us to our common military superiors that for long afterward we were kept explaining, fighting our own people behind while we fought the enemy in front." It proved "the most irritating experience" of his life, General Bullard said—"a vicious blow from behind." [133] The stab in the back came in this case from the spot where the good comrade was supposed to stand.

If the Americans were spared a large amount of wrangling among their generals, that good fortune was due to the short duration of their participation in the war, rather than to an innate friendliness within their officer corps. They were in truth no less inclined to divide on the one side of the ocean in this matter than their colleagues on the other side, as the story of interofficer relations during the previous American wars only too clearly evinces.

The case of McClellan is illustrative. As long as he belonged to the Union army, McClellan, haughty, ambitious, unbridled, provided the worst quarrel center. He expressed himself about his colleagues in such angry words as these: "I don't know whether Scott is a dotard or a traitor! He cannot or will not comprehend the condition in which we are placed. . . . I must confess a double motive for desiring the defeat of Wadsworth [in politics]. I have a thorough contempt for the man and regard him as such a treacherous miscreant that I do not wish to see the great State of New York disgraced by having such a thing at its head. . . . Halleck is turning out just like the rest of the herd, is very dull and very incompetent." General Pope ascribed his defeat to "the treachery of McClellan and his tools." In turn, McClellan considered it "something of a triumph that my enemies [Pope and McDowell] have been put down so completely." McDowell, with whom he really had little reason to quarrel, McClellan simply regarded "as a scoundrel, a liar, and a fool who, in seeking to injure me, has killed himself." [134]

Most authors of the military memoirs and biographies on the side of the victorious powers in the First World War have been mindful of the reputation and prestige of their armies and have tended to pass over lightly the wretched disputes with former colleagues dead or alive. But German generals or colonels, not bound by such hesitations, despite warnings from their fathers against the writing of memoirs, threw discretion to the winds and uncovered the gigantic "war within war," on their own front at least. Once the army as a corporate ego had been split up, if temporarily, the urge for personal apology produced more literature per epaulette than had ever before appeared among the German "generality." Those who could not do their own writing were, as in the case of Hindenburg and the Crown Prince, assisted by ghost writers.

For a short cut through this material composed after the events, the historian may well follow the conflicts in the pages of General Hoffmann's notes—records largely contemporaneous with the events he treats. Hoffmann was the high, though not quite the highest, General Staff officer, serving as a critical and even acid expert under noble and princely commanders of no great personal importance, like Hindenburg and a prince of Bavaria. From the beginning of the war, Hoffmann believed that if a good idea of his own led to victory the credit would go to the commanding general and the blame for failure to himself and his kind; he regarded the whole credit system as unjust. He also thought that some generals had either all the luck, like Von Kluck, whose light wound was only a phase of his usual good fortune in that it gave him added glory while invaliding him, or all the honor, like Mackensen, who was given the command over the army in Serbia. Of Mackensen, Hoffmann wrote: "Since all the attainable honors, titles, and orders have already been visited on his head in short succession, the only thing left to do for him is to make him Prince Eugene after the taking of Belgrade." That even accidentally some general, really intelligent on his own account, might be promoted to be field marshal, Hoffmann could not believe possible.

Of Hindenburg, Hoffmann was so critical that his remarks could not be printed while the old man lived. In fact his personal desires, animosities, and antipathies were so sharp that it appears dubious which was primary with him, his opinions or the material difference that set him, as well as Hindenburg-Ludendorff, against Falkenhayn, the Commander-in-Chief, and the Supreme Command— the same conflict between "easterners" and "westerners" that raged within the Western Powers. To Hoffmann, the war on the part of the Germans was a "war of missed opportunities," of the failure of Falkenhayn to seek decision in the East, where Hoffmann served throughout the war, when it could be clinched there with relative ease.

As early as December 1914, after the successful battle of Lodz,

Hoffmann felt confident that, if the Supreme Command would give *Ober Ost,* the Eastern Command, two more army corps, Russia could be eliminated as an enemy. He went to Falkenhayn and begged for them "on his knees," but was dismissed like a bothersome poor relation and after that received the most necessary things only in driblets or not promptly. "The mistake was that General Headquarters had not remained in Berlin where it still belonged— thus, absolutely uncalled for, France became forever the master theater of war and we remained the sideshow."

When Falkenhayn rejected his plans, Hoffmann felt that it was because "the East should not achieve too much success." From that time on, and not merely after Verdun, he always called General von Falkenhayn "that criminal," responsible for the useless sacrifice in the West and the quarrels with Conrad, for belittling in press bulletins the successes of the eastern army based on ideas contrary to those of the Supreme Command.

When that Supreme Command took from the Eastern Command certain districts under the latter's government, it answered protests by saying that such demands represented nothing but the megalomania of Ludendorff,[135] who had quarreled with everyone before 1914, when he served on the General Staff. This action the Eastern Command resented for military reasons: "By way of force we got the Field Marshal to employ the threat of his resignation—he did not want to until Ludendorff threatened to hand in his own." That elicited nothing except slippery telegrams from Falkenhayn, "who is so firmly in the saddle with His Majesty that no other opinion besides his own is worth anything," and who seemed to hope that the Eastern Command would suffer somehow "malheur and a little defeat." So the strife between the two went on and on.

At last the Field Marshal told Falkenhayn the truth for once. "Nothing much will come from that, I presume, and we shall all be the sufferers in the end; but he could not suffer forever from the small and big meannesses." While Hindenburg and Ludendorff tried to establish the record of their victories, on which they were determined to rise before their glory paled, Hoffmann listened to the tales of Tirpitz, the "father of the lie," who was visiting headquarters in the East. Of Tirpitz, Hoffmann writes:

When one hears him the world is yet worse, far more flabby and without direction than one had thought. When one looks down at all the evil conditions, the mutual jealousy, the calumny and the hatred of all the influential people for one another, one must always remember that things are far more maddening among the others, the English, French, and Russians, or else one might be frightened to death. Part of it Tirpitz probably contributes with his own lies in order to make the best possible impression for himself. The struggle for power and personal position seems to spoil the character of all people. I think only the man on his own acres, who does not have to climb and to be a servant to anyone, can remain decent; for good weather cannot be obtained by lip service.

For the eastern campaign of 1916—for the moment in late spring when the pinch of food scarcity would be felt in Germany and when there was need of a victory again—Hoffmann worked out a plan to be submitted to the Supreme Command: "I should like to win victories once more. This victory I could have if we obtained seven to eight divisions." And Falkenhayn's chief of operations muttered: "The Eastern Command always wants to attack where there is nothing." [136] Falkenhayn himself was determined to throw his force to the West, where people, Hoffmann thought, hated him "even more than we do." In fact Falkenhayn was bent on the enterprise against Verdun, "which he will carry on under his own name and that of the Crown Prince in order to put himself into a favorable light with the latter."

After Verdun had proved a ghastly failure, popular unrest forced the Emperor to replace Falkenhayn by Hindenburg and Ludendorff. Then Hoffmann took over Ludendorff's position in the East and inherited his conflicts with the Supreme Command, whose directors, disagreeing violently with Hoffmann in his stand on the Polish question, threatened the Kaiser with their retirement. In the end they made Hoffmann aware of their wrath in a way which showed him that "great men can be very small." Hoffmann dates their antagonism from his last interview, early in 1918, with Ludendorff who had mentioned his doubts whether he should first grope around in the West for soft spots or concentrate everything for a tremendous thrust in one place. "Your Excellency, every ensign who would treat the question in that way," Hoffmann remarked on the occasion, "would certainly fail his examination." [137]

Ludendorff's disfavor struck others, besides Hoffmann, who questioned his victory formulas. Among them was Groener, the foremost German military expert on railroads, who believed early in 1918 that nothing was obtainable but a draw. This was all the more reason for having Groener replace Ludendorff in October 1918. For Ludendorff's removal, men in his closest circle such as Colonel Bauer, once his most confidential emissary, began to work as early as July 1918, when they had become certain that their chief had failed. This conviction Hindenburg at last shared. He did not believe that the loss of the war was Ludendorff's fault, but did nothing to save his impetuous "helper." Unthanked by the Marshal and the Kaiser, Ludendorff broke out into a rage against his chief and passed angrily from the scene.[138]

When, after the war, Hindenburg and his bureaucratic ghost writers set down for the contemplation of the German nation this declaration: "Loyalty is the marrow of honor," it was received with awe: "It's the Emperor who has said that." But the lofty sentiment can hardly be said to characterize the relations among officers during the war. As far as the declaration was intended to do that, it was part of the process of reromanticizing the war, which according to popular conceptions makes devoted comradeship the rule. So strong was this antihistorical, primitive faith that the German popular mind observed with great regret Ludendorff declaiming against Hindenburg, his superior, if not the exclusive, power in this partnership. While the old man lived, that thrust at him created embarrassment.

After Hindenburg's death, however, the Reichswehr, for the sake of preserving the conventions and strengthening valuable popular beliefs in the unity of command, arranged for the appearance of a reconciliation between the dead field marshal and the living general, declaring: "One who wants to understand the generalship of Hindenburg and Ludendorff in the right way must view their work as a unity." [139] The desirable *fable convenue* of unfailing loyalty among officers seemed once more restored; a more realistic description of it might be suggested by the inscription on the grave of a sixteenth-century King of Denmark-Norway in the Cathedral of Roskilde—*Trewe ist wiltprett*, Loyalty is a game.

Shifting Responsibility for the War and Its Outcome

The German command and the army in general, the latter at least after October 1918, knew very well how thoroughly and hopelessly beaten they were. They knew their own true state and the plight of the starved civilian population. This they knew far better than the Allies who to the very last overestimated the strength of the Germans in both respects. The opinion of the situation prevalent among soldiers was expressed in the last letter belonging to a collection written by fallen German students: "I hope that armistice comes soon; we here wait for it hourly. This is no honest war and combat any more. And if the gentlemen at home, who still want to make war, only knew how it looks out here, in what condition our soldiers are, they would not fabricate such phrases." [140]

Even prior to November 1918, the numerical and material superiority of the Allied armies was fully admitted in the German army. It knew that it had lost the war and it even knew that it was conquered. The first truth remained undeniable, but not the second. As far as that was admitted, rarely on paper, it was taken back and a gradual change of mind in this issue was effected. Was the army not still far within the enemy country? Was not the Reich free from foreign soldiers? Was not the retreat orderly? Was welcome not offered by civilians in the rear? Were the soldiers not greeted at the Brandenburg Gate as our "heroes unbeaten in the field"? For a person whose historical training had included controlling memory, his own and that of others, it was wonderful to observe this rapid development in the soldiers' convictions about defeat, the Gorgon face of which was still engraved upon his brain.

In this change of mind were embedded the roots for the belief on the part of the field soldier in what was soon to be called the *Dolchstoss,* the stab-in-the-back, the domestic betrayal that brought the German army to its knees—to some Germans a falsehood and a sheer legend, to others a bitter truth. The slogan, "Unbeaten in the field," became promptly acceptable, highly flattering to proud field soldiers, not to mention others actively hostile to the revolution which had upset their power, defended to the last. Acceptance of the belief widened as many soldiers, who had long cursed the war, acquired a longing to be heroes—each a Siegfried—after the war and not what officers called "November criminals."

Earlier and non-German writers and statesmen, not imbued with that violent modern antimaterialism that admits no materialistic causation, had discovered and declared that hunger may and does defeat armies. In fact it defeated the Scottish Rebellion in 1746 and damaged the Pretender, whose followers were chased from the fertile lowlands into the infertile highlands and were cut off from French supplies by British warships, while the flow of British supplies over the sea route was insured. At Culloden the starved Scots were too weak to keep their rendezvous at the appointed time. A distinguished historian of the British army, which of all armies has been most often supported by the navy, considers it an axiom that "if an army is starving, its dissolution as a disciplined body is only a question of time" and that "when one army is full and another starving, lead and steel are hardly needed to decide the victory." [141]

Napoleon often said that the only revolution which could become really dangerous was one motivated by an empty stomach. Looking at hungry Germany, Austria, and Russia in 1919, Woodrow Wilson declared to the Peace Conference which continued to starve them: "So long as hunger gnaws, foundations of governments crumble." [142] Admitting that "everything wears out in the long run, even heroism," [143] generals have usually insisted on having armies well fed, stating this need less naïvely perhaps than old Montluc, who lived before the age of military hypocrisy, but no less categorically: "If you [the captains] want the soldiers to perform great fatigue-duties and do not furnish anything to sustain them, it will come about that, human bodies not being made out of iron, they will leave you on the road, or if you come to battle they will be so weak that they can serve you only very little. But if you carry refreshments with you and accompany them with remonstrances, you will not only make them march but run if you desire. And thus one must never excuse one's self by pointing to the soldiers: for there is no man in Christendom who has experienced this more than myself. And I have never seen faults happen through them that had not been done by the captains." The old practitioner of war thus advised captains not to throw the responsibility for failures upon the soldiers but to trace them to their own mistakes.[144]

While Montluc warned the captains to keep close watch over their rear formations, where disorder was always apt to start, later generations, approximating total war and thereby drawing into the rear ranks nearly every individual in the warmaking nation, have found it convenient to transfer the blame for defeat, for a break in the morale, for desertion from the war, further and further away from the army itself, to the civilians and the depot battalions in their midst. In a purely military respect it is probably true that "the crisis of confidence always starts among those who do not fight. Marmont says that it was always the men of the last rank of the phalanx who gave the signal for flight. This phenomenon has again appeared in the great war and, generally, military clerks and similar employees have been the first to flee. . . . The crisis grows singularly with the greater distance from the battlefield." [145] But the accusation on the part of the general did not stop there; Bonaparte told the soldiers on the 18th Brumaire: "Liberty, victory, and peace will restore the French Republic to the rank which it once occupied in Europe and which ineptitude and treason alone could make her lose." [146]

A representative of the defeated Russian army placed treason equally far in the rear, saying that in Russia "the farther away from the firing line, the greater the pessimism," at the top as well as at the bottom; "the country was completely demoralized. No longer could it offer any source of encouragement to the army; it could only contaminate it with its spirit of dissolution." Guchkov, later War Minister of the provisional government, a liberal more eager to carry on war than to forward liberal plans, wrote General Alexeiev in August 1916, that "in the war, disintegration is doing its full work, and the government is decaying at its foundation. No matter how good the conditions now may be at the front, the rotting rear is once more threatening . . . to drag down your gallant front and your clear strategy, nay, the whole country, into that impassable swamp from which some time ago we extricated

ourselves after mortal peril." [147] The Bolshevik Revolution saved
Russia from the troublesome public discussion of war guilt and
defeat by the home front—a question dear forever afterward to
White Russian nostalgia. This same service victory performed for
France.

The failure of Nivelle in April 1917, ascribed by some generals
to the defeatist press said to be under the influence of German
propaganda, produced a serious crisis of confidence in the French
army and nation. A commission, composed of generals including
Foch, for inquiry into the conditions under which the attack had
taken place, reported that "the action of the general-in-chief had
been spoiled, counteracted, by parliamentary interventions." But
this acquittal of the general by the generals did not calm the agitation. As another general, turned historian, recorded, "influences
which have remained mysterious proceeded to spread that state
of mind from the rear into the army. . . . Toward the end of
May, an insidious propaganda crept into the families, the stations,
the depots, wherever the service could be reached. . . . The Supreme Command itself was caught by an uneasiness. It felt itself
surrounded by this dull and unseizable ferment, which might set
tumbling with one single blow the results of such efforts." [148]

Pétain succeeded in restoring the morale of the French army—
certainly one of the greatest victories in the war. But it is evident
that the generals in France, eager to defend their prestige, had
also laid out their plans for defeat and the stab-in-the-back accusations. In their plot was included the melodramatic dark foreign
element which, in the German version, thrusts the dagger into the
back of the fighter, the dagger being especially chosen because it
is the most un-German weapon, later to be identified in Germany
with the hidden hand of Marxism, Jewry, Catholicism, Freema-
sonry, and other scapegoats. Austrian generals made use of the
same stage weapon as giving the Imperial and Royal army the
"coup de grace in the back." [149] In the middle of October 1917
Ludendorff wrote that "the bad morale has first come from the
interior and has reached the army from there"; but he added: "I
am perfectly conscious that inversely the morale which the soldiers
on furlough brought home was abominable." Still later, after the
National Socialists made the stab-in-the-back legend more or less
official history in Germany, to this same dagger was ascribed the
fatal butchering of German pigs in 1915; the wicked advice of
Jews and misguided agronomists really designed to save other foodstuffs was said to have caused the death by hunger of 750,000
Germans.[150]

As has been pointed out, one can least expect from generals any
confession of faults, errors, and mistakes. No such admission was

elicited from Kolchak after the Bolsheviks had caught him and tried him by court martial in Siberia. The beaten general strongly denied errors on his part. Likewise Hindenburg wrote to his wife in June 1918: "It will not be my fault if the war does not end favorably for us." Whose then? The Field Marshal will decide that later.

The first scapegoat chosen by the members of the Supreme Command for their mistakes was not a military man, not a Prussian, not a Protestant, not a Jew. It was Erzberger, a Catholic from the south of Germany, a prewar critic of German colonization and militarism, an advocate of peace through understanding as the papacy had envisioned it, the parliamentarian *parlementaire* of 1918. From the moment when the war began to terminate in defeat, the Supreme Command strove to avoid being identified with the ungrateful task of gathering up the wreckage. No member of it was on the Armistice Commission; no general was leader among the group sent to the Allies with the white flag, and those officers who had to go along soon tried to free themselves from all connection with the necessary act of humiliation. For the service to the beaten army which he assumed with the confidence of a hopeful patriot, Erzberger was killed some years afterward by soldier assassins.

Other scapegoats were picked in due time by Hindenburg, the high priest of Prussia's army Moloch. With an amazing dexterity and sureness, this augur handled the sacrificial knife, not even sparing the Kaiser. When that special sacrifice later caused some remorse, it was remembered against Ludendorff's successor, Groener, a non-Prussian, that he was the first who had dared to express the knowledge and conviction of the majority of generals that "the army does not stand any longer behind His Majesty and that the oath to the flag is nothing but a fiction." He was, as the ex-King of Württemberg noted in his journal, quite right, "but he should have said to the Marshal: 'Take a Prussian to speak these things out.'" In their solidarity the Old Prussians knew how to avoid such an admission. Not they, not Hindenburg, had demanded the Kaiser's abdication, but Groener, the Chancellor, a Prince of Baden, and his Cabinet in Berlin—the same men who had entered upon the armistice negotiations, had sent Erzberger to treat with respect to them, and had accepted Foch's armistice conditions. In their common flight from responsibility, which they had proudly claimed as long as victory seemed to smile upon them, they were powerfully assisted by the behavior of the Allies. The latter not only desisted from carrying the war into the Reich, thus demonstrating to the German people that they were the victors; they also refrained from demanding that the German army through its leaders sue for the armistice, come to sign it, and take the blame as other capitulating generals had been forced to take the blame in other wars. By 1945 they thought they knew better and insisted that German generals and admirals sign the surrender document.

A French historian of the Reichswehr concludes:

A well-struck image impresses itself upon memory better than abstract reasoning. The more confusing a situation is, the more necessary it is to give it a symbol. If Marshal Hindenburg had come himself to hand his sword over to Marshal Foch in the same way as Napoleon III was forced to do after Sedan, no doubt Germany would have understood that she was beaten in the military sense. In agreeing to negotiate with Erzberger, we have accorded the General Staff an unexpected immunity and have obliged the young German Republic to assume for itself all the burden of the defeat. We ourselves have given the first impulsion to the stab-in-the-back legend.[151]

To the end of his own negotiations, Foch refrained from demanding any active participation of the German Supreme Command in the armistice arrangements. When the German delegation later brought officers from the Command with them to France, he would not receive them and insisted upon dealing with the original delegation from the Forest of Compiègne. Foch's reasons and reasoning are not revealed. But militarism, shaping action coldly and objectively, could have done no better than it did in December 1918, when it provided itself with a basis for its own continuation by leaving the honor and the legend of the German General Staff intact and inviolate—the honor and legend of its "victory in the field."

Such actions on the part of the Allied Powers enabled Hindenburg to go on with his exculpations and accusations. They permitted him to join without a blush the reactionary parties in the Reich in charging the Left parties with having undertaken "the secret, deliberate decomposition of navy and army as the continuation of similar tendencies existing in peacetime. . . . An English general was right in saying that the German army has been stabbed from behind." Although this English general took the Marshal to task for making such an assertion, the "embodiment of reliability" never corrected himself.[152] In such circumstances the German parties of the Left were powerless to prevent the resurgence of the army, first in prestige and then in other powers. Many of their followers, moreover, had been in the old army and were disinclined to aid in dishonoring it, in whose shadow a new military machine was being reared.

Never did beaten generals escape with so much honor as in

postwar Germany. Many times in the past, after wars, generals had been accused of treason and cowardice and condemned to prison or death; this had been true in Prussia after 1806-7, when the civilians raised the cry about traitors. Among the ancient Greeks, unlucky generals were frequently treated severely by discouraged civilians. The mercantile Carthaginians had beheaded them. They also had rough handling by the French revolutionists, in the Hanse towns and Venice, and by the British on a few occasions. Only the militant Romans in olden times and the militant Japanese in modern times—the latter after the first battle of Shanghai—spared them.

During the wars with Napoleon, British ministers constantly considered the question whether they should accept responsibility for military failures or cast the blame wholly upon the military commanders. Canning, the more bourgeois minister, proposed to place all the blame upon the generals; since the maintenance of government was the first object of government, military officers responsible for defeat were to be recognized as the guilty parties, or if that was not done, the Ministry or the Secretary of War was to play the role of the scapegoat and retire in disgrace. Being the representative of a city electorate, Canning operated on the assumption that generals, paid and equipped for war, who did not achieve its ends, should be discarded. On the other hand the more aristocratic minister, Castlereagh, insisted that the officer aristocracy remain free from such ungentlemanlike censure. Castlereagh felt that the officers—members of the group from which he himself sprang—could not always be held responsible for not delivering victory. A historian of the British army considers that only Castlereagh was a gentleman.[153]

As Napoleon said, after a battle each party has its accounting, and Castlereagh was willing to have the officers do the accounting. He thought they could do this in an honorable way—perhaps by having their general staff write histories of the war in question—but Canning voiced the growing demand of the citizenry, which had hired them, for its own accounting of their service. And less hidebound officers, such as the Prussian reformers after 1807, maintained that those commanders who had surrendered fortresses without resistance or had capitulated in the field should be brought before courts martial. They believed that this course would purge the army of incompetence and cowardice. Others wanted to have at least the causes of defeats examined. "It is not that misfortune would be inadmissible. We are by no means in Carthage," said the Prince de Ligne, too much a *grand seigneur* to be merely an officer with professional interests. "But without pushing the examination that far, it would be good to know why a defeated general was defeated. I do not suspect his good faith; but if his capacity is in doubt, it might even be necessary to make an example of him. Is he not responsible for the death of several thousands of men?" [154]

Despite the democratic demand for settling the responsibility for the loss of war and the loss of men, the demand has usually been frustrated by the officers. Benedek took upon himself the onus for the defeat of 1866, though it was far less his own than that of the Austrian aristocracy, which ran the army. The parliamentary committee of inquiry, set to work after the French defeat in 1870-1, elicited some remarkable admissions by officers with respect to their unpreparedness. Thus the War Minister of 1870, Marshal Lebœuf, confessed that he had not thought war could break out while he was minister and that the Foreign Minister had not asked for his advice on the war.[155] Public pressure led to a judicial prosecution of Marshal Bazaine and his condemnation to death by a court martial, though not for treason as the public voice had demanded; he was condemned for failure to do his duty in the presence of the enemy. His sentence was reduced to twenty years' imprisonment, from which the Marshal made his escape without any difficulty. The disgrace of other officers was overcome with the help of the Red scare started by the Commune. Then a coalition of parties, including the monarchists, elected as President of the Republic MacMahon, a general who had been even less victorious than Hindenburg. So the army's prestige was rapidly rebuilt and soon the Commune seemed to have been its only enemy in war.

Rebuilding the German army's prestige was a similar process. As in the French parliament, so under the new parliamentary system of Germany, providing for civilian supremacy over the war minister, as inquiry into the "causes of the German collapse" was undertaken. But the impressive findings of the parliamentarians in fifteen volumes—an amazing source of facts for military history—weighed little as compared with the military demagogy of the stab-in-the-back legend, to the force of which the arbitrary determination of the war-guilt question by the Allied and Associated Powers at Paris powerfully contributed. The tendency among large masses of the Germans to identify themselves with the army and its old leaders, and to accept the stab-in-the-back thesis, was enormously strengthened by the decision of the Allies to base the peace of Versailles not "on Germany's defeat but on Germany's responsibility for the war."

The so-called war-guilt question wears two aspects: exterior and interior. The exterior aspect is concerned with the issue: by what measures in relation to foreign powers did any one power bring about war if in fact it did? The internal aspect is concerned with the issue: by what kind of errors and faults did the diplomats, the army, and the groups cause the loss of the war? By placing the responsibility for starting the war on Germany, the Allies, thus abetting the tendencies of militarism to ascribe its troubles to sources external to itself, largely suppressed the conscientious pursuit of the question of domestic responsibility in Germany and enabled the defeated German diplomats and officers to regain at home their honor, their reputation, their authority, and popular faith in their efficiency, competence, and innocence.

To establish and fortify their contentions, a work of propaganda was begun in Berlin under the guidance of Alfred von Wegerer, a former officer, aided by government funds. The undertaking was handled effectively both within and outside of Germany. Abroad it was sustained by the historically incorrect Allied thesis, to say nothing of its deliberate misrepresentation with respect to responsibility for bringing on the war.

Within Germany this propaganda suppressed a large part of that heart-searching and technical inquiry into causes of defeat which was necessary for a true liquidation of the war. If conducted in a military way an inquiry should have led to such pertinent questions as these: was Ludendorff a general in the sense of Clausewitz's definition; that is, the field marshal "whose eye comprises, on the one hand, all state relations; whose mind, on the other hand, is precisely conscious of what he can achieve with the means available; whose prescience includes insight into ways of gaining the utmost"? [156] Or if the German generals, who held military and political affairs in an iron grip, were geniuses, how did it come about that they knew nothing about the stab-in-the-back preparations which according to their contention caused the German defeat, that they were ignorant of those preparations while they were going on? Should not a genius have recognized this danger in time and have averted it? [157] All such rational questions were left unanswered. The German people turned for satisfaction instead to the slogan, utterly at variance with the actual character of the German defeat: "Unconquered in the field; beaten at home."

It did not occur to sponsors of this slogan, and they could never be persuaded, to consider how ungenerous it was to the masses. However, one of the more truthful German officers told the Reichstag: "No one would have dared at the beginning of the war to expect from the soldier what he afterward had to endure for years as a constant necessity. There simply seemed to exist no limits, till the moment arrived when a quick breakdown commenced. Not to have foreseen this was a psychological error, an error on the part of the men of the Supreme Command who, in their indomitable will for victory, lost at last all estimate of what was attainable." [158]

Hindenburg and Ludendorff never admitted that error or any other, great or small. They clung to their own myth and appeared

stubbornly conceited as compared with Napoleon, who acknowledged in January 1814 that he had really failed in his plans to make
France dominant over the entire world: "These projects were not
commensurate with the limited force of our population. The entire
population *en masse* should perhaps have been called to arms, but
I admit that the course of social existence . . . does not permit the
transformation of a whole people into soldiers. I have erred and
I must suffer. France has not sinned in anything. She has generously
donated her blood to me. She has not refused me a single
sacrifice." [159]

The war-guilt question is not academic. It is a prerequisite of
modern warfare, the warfare of democracies. As General Harbord
later noted, though not without misgivings: "Propaganda is perhaps
a necessary influence in the waging of modern war." [160] At all
events, leaders in a war relying upon popular support must lay the
guilt of starting it upon an unrighteous enemy. Propaganda did not
arise from the spirit of absolutism. A writer under Spanish
absolutism once argued:

This scrutiny, which of the two factions has a better cause, is
admissible in a democratic or an aristocratic state where sovereignty is divided up among rivals; but in a monarchical state all
that is best and wisest will follow the authority of the prince, in
whom is the sole sovereignty. . . . Seeing that the right to make
war is a prerogative of princes who have no superiors, discussion
of the equity of the cause is inappropriate.[161]

In the armies of absolutism, soldiers were expected to fight without "a just cause," but such a cause had to be supplied to the forces
fighting against it. They had to be persuaded that the wars they were
waging were just, useful, honorable, and advantageous. Otherwise,
why fight at all? In the beginning, the Americans charged the
British with firing the first shot at Lexington. It was part of the
preparation for the American Revolution to print, as did the
Journal of the Times, numerous stories of British cruelty.[162] To
furnish part of the moral equipment for the revolutionary army, the
American Congress issued the Declaration of the Causes and the
Necessity for Taking Up Arms—a statement to the army of July
6, 1775.

So likewise the French revolutionists and Napoleon took great
care to make their wars appear as "just and necessary," started by
the enemies of France, who committed acts of aggression and fired
the first shot. Marshal Ney, according to a biographer of 1911,
"developed this beautiful idea that the French soldier does not fight
well except for a cause thought by him to be interesting and just."
And he issued an order to his generals in 1805 that "the intelligence

and the nature of the French armies demand that they be well informed about the cause that obliges them to fight, and only when the aggression is legitimate can one expect marvels of valor from them." [163]

This same beautiful idea all the later armies endeavored to apply among their reasoning soldiers, wherever and against whatever nation they were sent to fight. When Lord French was appointed Viceroy for Ireland in May 1918, Lloyd George impressed upon him "the wisdom of putting the onus for the first shooting on the rebels." [164] Failing to fire the first shot might be a military disadvantage but it could certainly be turned into a great political advantage. To implant in their own army the conviction that it is not the aggressor, and to arouse in the opposing army doubts about its war being defensive in a political respect, became the prime endeavor of the wartime propagandists. It was the starting point of the Allied propaganda directed against the German soldier who, somewhat to the surprise of the Allies, was quite as positive as their own soldiers about the responsibility of his foes as aggressors.[165] Since propaganda is a function largely of politicians, civilians became its supreme directors.

To most of the officers this was distasteful business, alien to their nature and foreign to their knowledge of war. If, however, they had studied propaganda directed against other armies before 1914, they would have found this contest of ideologies neither new nor an affair of the "dark powers" to whom, in his astounding historical ignorance, Ludendorff attributed so many things which might better have been laid at his own door. Propaganda was a fairly regular feature of the wars of the French Revolution and the Empire. The inventive Lord Cochrane, while sailing along the French coast, towed kites laden with pamphlets to be blown by favorable winds to the French on shore.[166] When the French and the Prusso-Russian forces were lying opposite each other in eastern Prussia, in the Spring of 1807, the Allied troops threw over to the hard-suffering French printed material inciting them to desert. During the investment of Hamburg, in 1813-14, the besiegers undertook what the biographer of Davout calls "this underhand war of false news and lying bulletins"—the more effective since their news about the defeats of France happened to be true.[167]

Although some of the later wars were too short to invite startling propaganda work against the enemy, the art was not lost. Bismarck, in 1870-1, employed special French papers to impress the French population. In order to undermine Russian morale in the war of 1904-5, the Japanese translated Reuter dispatches about the Russian revolution at home and spread them out before the enemy lines where the Russian patrols picked them up—"a very practical method to get around the Russian censorship." "Noble be man, helpful and good!" remarked General Hoffmann, an observer of that war on the Japanese side.[168]

Being one of the few officers with actual propaganda experience in wartime, Hoffmann, after the February Revolution of 1917, had proclamations printed to tell the Russian soldier at the front about the troubles at home: "The poor people would not have learned it otherwise and that would indeed be a pity." [169] Duma members who inspected part of the front in April 1917, reported that "the propaganda carried on by Germany through her ordinary and involuntary agents and spies in the rear, as also her propaganda at the front, under the pretense of armistices and fraternizing, have done their pernicious work. The soldiers are no longer eager to fight nor prove their willingness to sacrifice themselves for the sake of free Russia. . . . Everyone is weary of fighting and the Bolsheviks insist on the immediate ending of active military operations. Their chief aims are to undermine the belief of the army in the govern-ment, the Allies, and the Duma." [170] In turn the Russians employed propaganda against the German troops, but with little effect. It is defeated, not victorious armies, that are most readily infected by enemy appeals.

Propaganda may confirm in the mind of the soldier a conviction of a defeat already existing, or sensed, but it cannot produce that conviction or suspicion unless defeat and heavy losses in battle, coupled with hunger and want, have prepared the way for it. Then and only then does the soldier fit the facts and circumstances with which he is familiar into a world outlook contrary to that of his superior officers. This is shown by the Russian and German ex-periences. The promise of the Revolution in Russia, in particular the Bolshevik upheaval, was new to the disaffected soldier and yet adapted to his state of mind, for he had resolved to escape from a war, apparently lost, into "peace, freedom, and land." Given his disorganized state of mind in 1917, it needed only a spark to set him off.

On the other hand, the German soldier was really not aware of defeat until near the military breakdown of 1918; hence Allied propaganda left him cold. Insofar as he desired a change in the domestic structure of Germany, his conceptions embraced more than the mere political ideology of democracy prepared by the literary professors of Allied propaganda. This was especially true of the Social Democrats in the German army, for they were well acquainted with capitalistic and imperialistic practices among the nations that now made "a war for democracy." For them the war could not be a conflict of black and white; it cut across both sides of the forces deadlocked at the front.

It is not possible, of course, to determine with anything like scientific exactness the effect of propaganda on the conduct and outcome of the fighting. Propaganda did fix some ideas in the heads of officers and soldiers, although there is no way of knowing how many of them were really affected by it. For example, from some source General Pershing acquired the thesis that the Allies were innocent in 1914 and that the Central Powers were black as sin in starting the war; in fact, the thesis was embedded so deeply in his mind that he was never able to modify it, to say nothing of removing it. Moreover, Ludendorff and Hindenburg, having lost the war as commanders, were only too happy to have a scapegoat and to lay the responsibility for their own mismanagement on Allied propaganda. But there is no real evidence to support the Hindenburg-Ludendorff thesis and apology. All along the German High Command regarded President Wilson's ideological essays and grand promises of a liberal peace as so much camouflage. Neither the Supreme Command nor Prince Max, the new Chancellor, believed that Wilson represented the actual spirit and intention of the Allies or that he could "make good" at the peace table. In the hour of defeat they merely grasped at Wilson's promises, as drowning men grasp at straws—for the want of something better.

It seems in keeping with the facts to say that the rank and file of the German soldiers, as far as they were aware of the ideological battle amid the smoke and confusion of real battle, took a similar view of the situation. Near the close they knew "through their skins" that they were going under for lack of fresh troops, munitions, and food supplies. They were more poignantly aware of that lack than they were of the fine hopes held out by the leaflets showered down upon their heads, along with shrapnel and poison gas. To the conservatives among the German soldiers the Allied appeal for a revolution on their part was a call to treason; to the Social Democrats it was a capitalist device designed to hoodwink them. In such circumstances, it is reasonable to conclude Allied propaganda was negligible in producing the disintegration of military morale that accompanied decimation of German ranks by fire, war weariness, and hunger. The German soldier may have been lacking in imagination, but he could not see in the airplanes that dumped political tracts upon him angels of mercy soaring above the bursting shells and well-fed Allied and American troops that drove his weak and weary body remorselessly backward.

However considered, it is now clear that the propaganda was playing with fire. In substance and intent it was an appeal for revolt on the other side and no one could say how far revolt might spread. That was an essentially novel aspect in the conduct of war, and it could work two ways. A sound conservative instinct had led commanders in previous wars to halt on the brink of revolutionary devastation and to look beyond the day of battle to "a settlement among gentlemen" after the decision in the field. Now on the Allied side, the upheaval in Russia was "a horrible lesson" to the military. And on the German side the Russian explosion, combined with revolutionary outbursts at home in the autumn of 1918, gave military men a bitter taste of the fruits of propaganda, from whatever source it originated. Appeals designed to disrupt may consolidate, and appeals designed to consolidate may disrupt. Charges of war guilt from one side may be countered by similar charges from the other.

Yet it is doubtless true that propaganda has become an indispensable part of setting mass armies and nations in motion and keeping them in motion, and that in this propaganda must be appeals to enemy soldiers to overthrow their own military and civil governments. It appears equally true that, when such appeals coincide with the bitterness of defeat in an enemy or allied country, explosions as incalculable and devastating as war itself are likely to occur. The more of militarism there is in war, and the less of the military way, the more certain would seem to be the prospects of social dissolution promoted by propaganda.

By comparison, war propaganda directed against the Germans in 1939-45 was almost more ineffective than on the earlier occasion. On the whole, this seems less due to the cohesive force or fanaticism which National Socialism, as a system of ideology and terror, induced in the fighting forces but rather, to speak in very general terms, to the sense of complete otherness and estrangement which filled every fighting force. The ancient supranational solidarity among fighting men was still more weakened than in the First World War, largely due to the action of civilian warmakers and directors who would not allow it sway. Hitler preferred to end the Hague Conventions on warfare—to which the Russians were not signatories—and Roosevelt insisted on the unconditional surrender of all Axis forces, despite some soldiers'—and propagandists'—plea for a "hope clause" that would induce the enemy to give up resistance more readily.

Peacemaking by the Generals

If, as Clemenceau said, the making of war was too serious an affair to be left to the generals alone, the making of peace was an even more serious business. What was to be the role of the generals in peacemaking? Not the least difficult and delicate part of the work at the Paris Peace Conference consisted in subduing and in other ways demobilizing the generals. As soon as the end of the war was

in sight the century-old conflict between the military and congressional diplomacy was renewed—the reasserting of civilian
authority which Gneisenau had greeted in 1814 with the statement:
"One knows too well how these diplomats are, with what kind of
ravenous hunger this sort of people reaches for negotiations, and
how reluctantly having once entered upon them, they give them
up." [171] Contrary to the convictions of the "frocks" about the end
of their generals' usefulness, in the autumn and winter of 1918 the
latter still perceived numerous occasions for the use of their expertness.

The sun of military glory was inevitably sinking into an eclipse
behind the moon of civilian policy. There was nothing left for the
military except to go into politics themselves, after the example of
Henry Wilson who, in accordance with the justice which is called
"poetic," found his death in that field rather than in battle; or to
curse and grumble if the civilians proceeded against the advice which
they asked of the soldiers. When at the Inter-Allied Conference at
San Remo in 1920 "the frocks" thought they had done good work,
"we soldiers," according to Henry Wilson, thought "they are all
rotters. Nothing is decided. . . ." The soldiers' advice to knock out
Bolshevism, by methods which included arming Russian prisoners of
war in Germany, was turned down, and "we soldiers" regarded this
as tantamount to "a tacit agreement to Bolshevism . . . a most
dangerous thing." [172] This same civilian opposition to an anti-
Bolshevik crusade, shared though it was by an influential *pétrolier*
like Sir Henry Deterding, buried a plan of General Hoffmann,
pursued to his dying day in 1927, to have one great army of Englishmen, Frenchmen, and Germans march against the Bolsheviks. When
the English Cabinet did not accept the advice proffered by the
soldiers, Henry Wilson pronounced them "a miserable crowd. My
contempt for their brains, knowledge, pluck, and character deepens
every day. They will ruin England and the Empire." It was doubtless
with full professional feeling that Pershing whispered to Wilson, in
the shade of the London Cenotaph: "This is my first happy moment. No frocks here." [173]

In France Foch promptly fell out with the radical Clemenceau.
He did his best to prevent the election of Clemenceau, "the father
of the victory," to the French presidency, to which he had himself
aspired without getting much further than Pershing in his similar
aspiration.[174] When the Big Four fixed the demilitarized zones
without asking the military and failed to keep them informed about
the labors of the conference, Foch and Henry Wilson were angrier
than ever with the "frocks," over whom they had scored a triumph
by having their way in establishing the strength of the Inter-Allied
occupation forces on the Rhine. "Foch and I are much too strong

and cunning to be beaten over such a manoeuvre," Wilson exulted. So strong did Foch feel, with the backing of the popular election sentiment, that he threatened to hand in his commission as Commander-in-Chief of the Allied armies if the peacemakers did not heed his demand for the Rhine as France's military frontier and his protest against a number of articles in the Peace Treaty—largely the items which had cost Clemenceau the greatest trouble to obtain for France. Pétain was to be designated as his successor, but the Marshal did not resign the highest position he would ever attain.[175]

The services and posts left open to the military for a time were for purposes mainly honorific, such as the Inter-Allied Supreme Command which Foch retained. As if to show that his high office was still needed, he thought that the Germans might reopen the war and that, therefore, the stay of the homeward-looking American troops in France had better be prolonged. While they waited for the Germans they might be employed to clear up the devastated regions.[176] By sharpening the conditions under which the Armistice was to be continued, Foch tried to provoke the Germans into reopening hostilities, much as the latter had done after Trotsky proposed to avoid making a formal peace and to use the armistice as a *modus vivendi* between Russia and Germany. As a matter of fact, Foch thought that he could make peace with Germany much faster than the civilians and even outdo the Germans at Brest-Litovsk; he maintained it could all be arranged within three days and by three articles providing for German demobilization, a hundred billions in indemnity, and occupation of the Rhineland, with everything else to be settled later.

But the civilians were not much impressed by the peacemaking abilities of Foch. Woodrow Wilson asked him "affectionately" at the end of a discussion on the prolongation of the Armistice "to act more as a diplomat than as a soldier." Henry Wilson, who was present, remarked that "the old boy's face was a study" and heard him say in an audible whisper: *"Ce n'est pas commode, Henri."* On another issue the obstinacies of Foch moved the American President to remark that he might no longer entrust the American army to a general who did not obey his own government. They stirred Lloyd George to declare that, in his Rhineland policies where he had the separatists supported by agencies of the French army, Foch was confounding policy and strategy.[177] If, as Lloyd George admitted, the civilian governments stumbled into the war in the summer of 1914, so it may be said that the military men had stumbled through the war.[178]

THE MILITARY AND POLITICS

So far we have been concerned with the evolution of military interest from the feudal array, through the standing army and the mass army, to embattled nations with militarized mentalities. In the written history of this development the military usually appear as somewhat separated from government and politics—from the civilian statesmen, diplomats, and populace. It is evident of course in the development itself that absolute monarchs have played a dual role as civil rulers and as commanders of armies: Frederick the Great, for example. It is also evident that military men have sometimes risen to civil power and combined at the same time the functions of civil government with those of war, as did Napoleon Bonaparte, the artillery officer. Often, especially in the United States, the military officer has passed completely out of military service to high office in the civil government: George Washington set this example—for Andrew Jackson, William Henry Harrison, Franklin Pierce, and down the list of military men in the presidency down to Colonel Theodore Roosevelt and Dwight D. Eisenhower. Occasionally, as in the case of MacMahon in France and Hindenburg in Germany, the hero of defeat has been elevated to the headship of the state.

These relations between the military and politics are so well known and so apparent as to need nothing more than a passing notice here, important as they have been in the advance of the military toward a position of dominance in modern societies. But there is another aspect generally neglected by students of both civil government and armies. This is the subject of the various connections, often under-

9
Military Officers as Politicians

ground, between military officers and politics. On the one side, these connections bear upon the immediate business of armies—such as organization, supplies, the promotion of officers, public relations, and class affiliations. On the other side, the connections between military men and politics have a bearing on the general public policies to which the military and warfare are popularly supposed to be subordinate—ends of which armies and war are popularly imagined to be the mere means or servants.

The Theory of the Military as Nonpolitical

It is a common assumption in the civilian world, as well as a pretense on the part of the military, that "soldiers are so little politicians generally." [1] If only party and parliamentary politics are in review, or those formal political deliberations from which most states have excluded their active soldiers, a nonpolitical character for the soldier is somewhat credible. Even without an express prohibition it would appear doubtful whether officers as a type have the ability, the suppleness, the temperament, or the time for a continuous application to politics. The absence of such gifts, tastes, and opportunities, of which the military man has himself been aware, has sharpened his criticisms of the civilian politicians and officials, such as the British major general's outburst: "Politicians make us soldiers sick, soldiers being perchance too straight and honest for them." [2] The rather simple-minded Haig, so little a politician that he could hardly have consorted much with that fraternity, wrote home from the Boer War that he wished "to disband the politicians for ten years. We would all be the better without them." When the peace was concluded with the Boers, it seemed to him to be so civilian in character that he condemned the politicians for their clemency, though, in point of fact, Kitchener was largely responsible for this mildness while the civilian, Milner, had opposed it. [3]

Officers' judgments on parties and party politicians have run true to form since the time of Marlborough. Accomplished politician and diplomat though he was, Marlborough had his troubles with the Whigs, who supported his wars, but with whom he did not sympathize politically; and he had difficulties with the Tories, to whom he inclined, but who supported the navy rather than his establishment. As he told his wife, this experience made him no party man. His impartiality, he said, "is not designed to get favour, or to deceive anybody, for I am very little concerned what any party thinks of me; I know them so well that if my quiet depended upon either of them I should be most miserable, as I find happiness is not to be had in this world, which I did flatter myself might have been enjoyed in a retired life. I will endeavour to leave a good name behind me in countries that have hardly any blessing but that of not knowing the detested names of Whig and Tory." [4]

Nevertheless, though debarred from formal association with parties, the army in every country forms to some extent a class or "estate" with positive professional interests and corresponding views on state and society. Group interests and personal interests force every army to be "in politics" in the larger sense. This the War Minister of Japan, and head of the most political army on the eve of the Second World War, confessed: "It is impossible for soldiers, who are part of the nation, to be entirely unconcerned about politics." But he insisted or promised that "their views must be expressed only through the War Minister. My assistants have connections with other departments of the government for purposes of investigation and study, and it is necessary, from the broader viewpoint of national defense, that they express opinions. Junior officers must make inquiries, but only the War Minister translates the results into action." [5] The Minister carefully refrained from mentioning other military politics than the interdepartmental.

As in other professions, a large proportion, perhaps even a majority, of officers may be unpolitical as so-called experts or specialists, fully absorbed by their specific tasks, are inclined to be. But in fact, while waiting for action during intervals in their true business, war, they have more leisure than most experts in which to apply thought and wish to political activity. And since the early days in the history of modern military expansion they have had in fact an elite at work in politics—an informal group representation, that "terrible organization" of professional interests which Carnot learned to fear.[6]

This elite has not been an open organization, since that was forbidden by concepts of duty and expediency; but groups, cliques, camarillas, schools within armies, have taken it upon themselves to voice, represent, and realize military interests, through politics, without having any mandate conferred upon them by the majority of officers, save, perhaps, the assumption that most of the men agreed with them. Such cliques have established and maintained contacts, usually well screened, with the civilian political groups holding or striving for power. Thus the jealous Gates, in the trying times of Valley Forge, gathered a cabal of officers around himself with the intention of removing Washington from command, and the ringleaders found some members of the Congress ready to listen to them. In monarchies, such camarillas have almost always understood how to get hold of the monarch himself, as they did in Russia or Prussia. Where the monarch is not so readily managed, he may be threatened and even treated with violence, as he was in Serbia in 1903.

In such extreme cases officer politics takes the form of conspiracy, either against governments at home or abroad. Serbian officers, including the chief of the information department of the General Staff, who had himself founded the nationalistic secret society, "Unity or Death," helped to prepare the murderers of Sarajevo. It was the same department in France which persecuted Dreyfus. Revolutionary and other unsettled conditions have turned generals into traitors to the country they were serving, as in the cases of Charles Lee, Benedict Arnold, Pichegru, or Lafayette. More regularly, officer politics pursues minor objects, such as improvements of pay and living conditions, the winning of favors, and transfers. As Clemenceau's closest military adviser, General Mordacq, described the opposition of officers to the attempts to rejuvenate the French officer body during and after the war: "Always haunted by that spirit of camaraderie which, in the army, has done us so much harm, certain high functionaries hesitated to apply the red-hot iron where it was needed." [7]

The very barriers in the way of officer politics have provoked a great deal of anonymous activity on the part of officers, such as the writing and publishing of brochures and articles. These may be penned with the consent of the officer's superiors, as were the reactionary pamphlets of Roon's friend, Lieutenant Colonel von Griesheim, the "Berlin Cavaignac," who in 1848 extolled the superior qualities of the Russian army in order to frighten the Frankfurt parliament. Again, in *Only Soldiers Help Against Democrats*, published in 1848, he exalted the old Prussianism.[8] Sometimes, however, anonymity has been used to cover opinions which the governing hierarchy did not want to have discussed.

The natural tendency of armies is not only toward a self-government brooking no outside influences, but also toward the extension of their power beyond their own circles. Bismarck, who knew them so well, observed that many officers considered all things outside the army "as alien enemies." [9] In an age which has highly cherished democratic self-government, the army organization has often sought praise as being democratic itself. The Prussian army, for instance, liked to point to such of its features as the election of officer aspirants by the whole officer corps. Even the Russian officer corps of 1914 was said not to be "really a distinct class. Men of humble origin were to be found even among the generals occupying high positions. . . . The corps was fundamentally very democratic" in spite of some regulations "which had been drawn up under strong German influences." [10] Yet in reality such egalitarian rudiments in officer relationships were due to feudal hangovers rather than to democratic influences.

The Politics of Promotion

Sovereigns and other constitutional commanders-in-chief may be powerful agents for the advancement of specific officers. But they cannot intervene for the great majority of officers, as the latter are far too numerous, and such arbitrary interference might turn out to be harmful for the corporate interests of the officers as a whole. This was illustrated by experiences with the mad Czar Paul. One day he invited a private of his guard into his sleigh saying: "Get in, Sergeant!" "But, Your Majesty, I am only a . . ." "Get in, Lieutenant!" replied the Czar. By the time the astonished soldier had climbed into the sleigh he was a captain, and he stepped from the sleigh in the evening a general. After a few days, however, the general was invited for another ride as a colonel and at the end of the drive found himself fallen to sergeant.[11] As a rule, the officer body has preferred its regular, predictable mode of promotion.

The innate organizing tendency in armies is aristocratic, with an inclination to set up and recognize gerontocratic arrangements, for instance, to have generals take over political as well as other responsibilities. A general may enter with impunity upon political activities which would break and ruin an officer of lower rank. In the higher grades the relation between generals often takes on a political rather than a disciplinary character; generals of a lower rank may contradict generals high up, on occasion, as Henry Wilson "answered back" to Kitchener, having "no intention of being bullied by him, especially when he talks such nonsense as he did today." Wilson welcomed a promotion which would, as a matter of course, give him additional power for politics.[12]

Only in revolutionary times and countries is this rule broken in favor of pushing ahead younger officers or even noncommissioned officers, as in Serbia in 1903, in Cuba in 1936, when Sergeant Batista rose rapidly, or in the case of Ensign Krylenko in Russia. Again, a generalship has been regarded as the sign of an achievement, if not of martial glory, which in more recent times has been won rather sparingly by officers of lower rank; the latter when they have achieved glory have often become a sort of peacetime embarrassment to the authorities. For example, Lawrence of Arabia suffered neglect and disavowal—humiliations that might have been exploited by men with fascist intentions in search of a figurehead.

Whatever may be the system of ‘ overhead political control, seniority as determining the officers' promotion is part of the general gerontocratic arrangements in armies. Its application is intended to equalize competition during peacetime among officers in the lower ranks who are supposed not to show any such remarkable differences in talents as to warrant exceptions. In time of peace the armies have more or less adhered to seniority up to the rank of captain or even major; in higher grades the officer may exhibit peculiarities that bring about his advancement out of line or his retirement on a pension. In the pre-1914 German army there was the so-called "major's corner" at which the officer might be wrecked or, if he turned it successfully, allowed clear sailing ahead. It was an elimination race in which the inefficient or nonbelligerent were cast off along with those who would not conform, who might be talented for war but were a nuisance in peace.

In many armies service in war and the colonies, including "little wars" in China or Morocco, have counted double and thus made the ambitious men the more desirous to participate in overseas enterprises. Leonard Wood wrote from Cuba to the American Secretary of War that if there was to be war in China in 1900 he wanted to be in it instead of fossilizing in his administrative work in Cuba. When complications arose with Mexico in 1914, Pershing would not stay marooned at the Presidio but craved "for a chance to get into whatever might develop," assuring Wood, the Chief of Staff at Washington, who did not sympathize with him, of his loyalty.[13] Such employments, even if they had been humdrum, enabled an officer to forge ahead. Joffre owed the Supreme Command in the French army in 1912 mainly to the circumstance that he, an engineer officer, had exercised his talents for building barracks in the colonies where the service years counted double.[14]

To rise far in the army all those arts are required which enable the officer to stand out favorably under inspection and which "make the army in peacetime the school of cold-blooded climbing," as Bernhardi expressed it.[15] Every army possesses in great numbers the *arriviste* "who never varies in the manifestations of his moral weakness: haughtiness with respect to the small ones, ill will toward his peers, and bowing and scraping, not to say platitudes vis-à-vis the great." [16] In the lingo of the German army he is the bicyclist—treading below and bowing above. Those who detest the demoralization of peacetime careerism hope for war to bring moral "purification," reveal the worth of officers, put a stop to servility and job hunting, and political wire pulling, and restore true comradeship likely to become brittle beneath the brilliant surface of *esprit de corps* shown to the outside world. It is war, wrote General Bonnal in 1910, "provided it lasts long enough, which cleans the hearts, tempers the characters, and, different from peace, gives to true merit the place which it deserves." [17] Yet a large if not the major portion of the actual participants in the world wars might well argue that their very duration destroyed the rebirth of comradeship clearly manifest in the first months of hostilities.

The history of the personnel policy of the armies is crowded with attempts to reconcile the effort to end the "lock step of seniority" by retiring the unfit, with the aim of making the tenure of office secure enough to attract candidates. The gerontocratic arrangements have naturally been opposed to premature retirements, the once small American army providing no exception to this tendency. When Elihu Root planned to have one vacancy in three filled on the basis of merit and fitness, to be determined by some board authorized to exclude favoritism, "the great majority of officers opposed this so vigorously that for eleven years they have defeated it." [18]

Retirement, frequently regarded by its victims, in the absence of objective criteria of fitness and ability, as undeserved and premature, has brought tragedy into many an officer's life and family. Lily Braun described how her father, a Prussian general commanding a division, was unlucky enough to win a maneuver battle over the young Emperor and to express views contradictory to the Emperor's on the use of cavalry masses. One sad March morning her father summoned his family to his side and told them about the misfortune of his retirement, which had arrived instead of the hoped-for higher command. "There the proud strong man was sitting utterly crushed behind his desk," she said, "a convulsive sobbing shook his body; his pale face was overrun with tears. He held out the blue letter to us. He was a broken man. Never again did he become his old self. His life had no meaning any longer. Only for our sakes, I believe, has he endured it at all." [19]

To those who survive the weeding-out processes of peacetime, war brings the severer test. The history of the older wars, though not the Napoleonic wars, is crowded with generals who received and retained command on account of seniority, combined often with good health and high connections. In the revolutionary age, coalition warfare produced the fatal tendency to send into the field old generals who had proved their inefficiency but could claim precedence, even the highest command, over the senior generals of the associated armies.[20] Only in recent times has retirement become more ruthless. In the First World War the democracies retired their generals far more quickly after failures than did the Central Powers, among whom the generals were and remained so much a part of the governing system and such exponents of ruling-class politics that they could not be dismissed by the dozens. Napoleon's maxim, *"Dur aux grands!"* had not yet penetrated Central Europe.

Incapacity of the Military for Political Oratory ("La Grande Muette")

Aside from the praetorian moments, strong as they have been in politics, armies have never been so powerful as they might have been had they openly exercised the force which they represent. The period from 1871 to 1914, full of prejudice against violence, as Sorel says, witnessed very little of the frank application of military force as a pressure in politics. A few military revolutions in the Latin American countries, the expulsion of the first Bulgarian prince in 1886, the murder of a royal couple in Belgrade in a military conspiracy, and the Revolution of the Young Turks in 1908, constituted about the sum of political military violence during those years. Generally armies appeared to be obedient to the existing governments, both parliamentary and otherwise, the spokesmen of the former reminding them on occasions that military governments have always been short-lived. In other words, the military accepted the governments as frameworks within which their interests could be secured, often by identifying them with those of the governing groups.

Where the class situation has been fairly harmonious, as in Anglo-Saxon countries, army officers have accepted the nominal supremacy of parliamentary bodies, though scarcely ever without grumbling. Exasperated by the "masterful inactivity" of Congress before the outbreak of the War of 1898, the Army and Navy departments at Washington took measures which were not only designed to prepare for hostilities but also to bring war closer. Congress countered such tendencies by asserting that after this war the enlarged army would be reduced to its original size.[21]

Habitually the Anglo-Saxon armies have also accepted, without open protest, the civilian secretaries of war. But they have looked upon them as liaison officers to obtain from parliamentarians what they themselves have deemed essential in money and men. On occasion the officers have thought, as Henry Wilson did in 1901, that the inner working of the War Office was "exceedingly unsatisfactory. The whole idea of governing the army by a civilian, whose training has been political expediency and who knows less about the Army than I do about the Navy, is vicious in theory and hopeless in practice." In taking this view, Wilson chose to ignore the basic function of the parliamentary War Minister, Haldane, who in a few weeks learned enough of military affairs to present convincingly the army's budgetary demands to Parliament. Rather, thought Wilson, should the commander-in-chief of the army, once or twice a year, present his own case in the House of Lords, and "the country would then be in possession of the expert's view of the case and could judge as to its proper course of action." [22]

This theory of military capacity for politics presumes, among other things, that the collective intelligence of the country is more enlightened than that of a civilian War Minister, or that it can be captured more easily for military demands by a general than by a civilian cabinet member, or that a general can persuade masses better than the cabinet. At any rate, it points to a certain inferiority of the military class in its relations with the governing groups and forces. It indicates a conflict between the commanding class and the discussing class, when the interests of the two happen to conflict, and an inequality in the soldier's equipment for persuasion without application of violence. "Since it is necessary to tell you, these same discussions which astound you constitute our honor," Clemenceau told Boulanger. "They prove above all our eagerness to defend the ideas which we believe just and fertile. These discussions have their inconveniences, but silence has more. Yes, glory to the countries where one speaks! Shame to the countries where one is silent!" [23] When Boulanger tried to discuss from the same tribune he proved a dismal failure.

On the Continent, the weakness of the generals has been more marked than in England; the Continental nobility remained singularly devoid of great speakers, whereas the English aristocracy produced orators, to some extent, among generals in its midst, Marlborough being a striking instance. Even in France, a country so naturally rhetorical, "men of war are in general deprived" of the "habit of the word," as Marmont explained. Enraged at the importance given to the word by the voluble civilians, Marmont insisted that their silence did not mean that the men of war were "very inferior in point of intelligence," for "the faculties necessary for commanding armies are unquestionably the highest, the most sublime." [24] Napoleon himself, on the 18th Brumaire, was overawed at first by the assembly he intended to dissolve; hesitating, stammering, he was extricated from a very awkward situation by his brother Lucien, an experienced parliamentarian. The only words at the instantaneous service of the officer being those of command, he is not facile in speaking from the platform.

Military eloquence, at earlier times taught in military schools,[25] is more effective when used for writing bulletins or proclamations. Even then the author-general often persuades by declamation, not by reasoning. Bourrienne was convinced that most of the time the soldiers did not understand what Napoleon said; they did not know what it meant, for instance, when they were told they had won back Pondicherry and the Cape of Good Hope on the Elbe and Oder. "But they said to one another: the Emperor has said that. . . . So prodigious was the enthusiasm, or rather the fanaticism, with which Napoleon knew how to inspire his soldiers." [26]

This side of army oratory is a part of military ritual, and is probably understood by as few soldiers as is the Latin of the Catholic Church services by the believers. Wellington, who knew the power and function of the spoken word, was asked whether there had been any difference between the French and English armies in their susceptibility to harangues. He thought not: "The proclamations you read of in the French army were much more seen in the papers than by the soldiers—they were meant for Paris. Besides, we too have our orders of the day. As to speeches—what effect on the whole army can be made by a speech, since you cannot conveniently make it heard by more than a thousand men standing about you?" [27]

Such considerations and the desire not to appear as an imitator of Napoleon led his foe, Scharnhorst, to propose, as part of an early Prussian army reform, the printing of a weekly war newspaper to publish reports of successes apt to incite courage and hope in the army. Since the Prussian officers could not speak effectively to their men, this paper was to be read to the soldiers by the quartermaster-sergeant.[28] As a modern general, Schlieffen believed there was somewhat more room for the spoken word even during battle. While the battle went on and the outcome was awaited, Schlieffen thought the supreme commander ought to address "stirring words" to the lower commands.

Just before the First World War, the officer-orator appeared in greater numbers than ever before. Military men found it necessary to enter the oratorical contest between classes and groups, but though they were ready enough to orate they were impatient of and unprepared for discussion, not to speak of heckling. To this extent, the military oratory of that period was the forerunner of fascistic oratory; fascists from the very first excluded discussion and threw hecklers out of meetings.

In Russia, oratory was the smallest part of the equipment of the governing classes. During the war, they were unable to counter the oratory of Kerensky and the Bolsheviks. Military officers proved peculiarly unable to address their men; most of them, as Brusilov admitted in 1917, had "no political experience, and many more do not know how to talk to their men. All this keeps them from reaching a mutual understanding." [29] In contrast, the Anglo-Saxon countries deliberately furnished military speakers quiet occasions, at the ends of dinners, for presenting their aims and needs with no interruptions; there, as in some other lands, nationalistic organizations and veterans' societies provided such openings, safe from the contradiction which calls for ready wit and a wide range of knowledge such as parliamentarians possess to a disturbing degree.

Yet even in democratic countries the officers found it constitutionally difficult to expound such ideas as they entertained: Foch used to express himself "by vehement discharges, like machine-gun explosions, riddling the interlocutor with a hail of short phrases, violently elliptical and one might say apocalyptical." [30] Akin to him was Kitchener, with his "rambling and cryptic discourses," [31] and Manteuffel, the Chief of the Prussian Military Cabinet, of whom it was said that "his knowledge is extremely small, but the little he knows he knows for certain." [32]

The Second World War heard but little of the military orator, though the totalitarian leaders when exhorting would remind their hearers that they, too, had been or were forever soldiers. The one great soldier-orator emerging in the war was Charles de Gaulle— rather than MacArthur. In him, the old Gallic preferences emerged once more—*rem militarem et argute loqui*—for he proved a particularly effective speaker over the new mass communication medium, the radio, easily the superior in this as in other respects of his one-time rival, General Giraud, a typical *muet*.[33] On occasion, an outstanding general would be forced to speak by his civilian superiors; the Truman Administration was fond of making its chiefs of staff deliver speeches—which must be distinguished from the lecture. They would obey, though with an occasional confession that they would have preferred to remain silent. "It is work and I don't like to make them," General Bradley confessed to senators. "I feel it is my duty to make them once in a while, and that is why I make them. When I retire, I don't expect to ever make any (Laughter)." [34]

The Military and Journalism

Military dislike of contradiction has made journalists, as the producers of written public criticism, particularly obnoxious to officers, in peace as well as in war. As a rule, officers have considered this latest set of "clerks," these hated ink slingers without bureaucratic or other restraints, as thoroughly venal, irresponsible, and ignorant, if not traitorous; their criticism is rarely taken as the expression of serious patriotic misgivings about the state of an army or the way of winning a war. Rather it is regarded as a libel at least.

In the early days of journalism, Marlborough at first resolved not to appear concerned over the ill use he experienced at the hands of pamphleteers, but then he wrote home from the field that the government must prosecute a rogue who had written against him. If that could not be done, he would "find someone that will break his and the printer's bones, which I hope will be approved by all honest Englishmen, since I serve my Queen and country with all my heart." The rogue in question was not very long afterward flogged to death, though not, apparently, by the bravoes of the Duke.[35] In a like manner Stendhal's Lucien Leuwen, dreaming about his military future in the 1820's, is determined to treat the "journalist who raises doubts about the bulletin of the last battle like a traitor, the ally of the enemy."

It became almost the habit of officers in the first half of the nineteenth century to handle disagreeable journalists with the riding whip. It is said that Karl Marx one day received the visit of two outraged noncoms, but escaped the intended beating because he carried a pistol. The constant want of respect for military authority which journalists voiced for the less vocal classes moved one of the calamitous Austrian archdukes, shortly after the Austrian defeat in 1866, to condemn the "endeavors of a subversive press to make ridiculous the discipline and the severe forms of service indispensable to every army." [36] When some German newspapers took the liberty of attacking the Kaiser, the Chief of his peacetime headquarters, General von Plessen, thought that "there ought to be shooting right away," and the monarch responded by saying that he would have such editors "challenged by his aides if they published articles which insulted him." [37] Actually the state attorney, prosecuting on the basis of the *lèse-majesté* paragraph of the criminal law, spared the aides this task.

This low opinion held of journalists, however, never kept the military from stooping to employ them, from giving them news or money, often private money such as Waldersee—who married an American fortune—possessed in abundance, or secret funds[38] which sometimes were used to oppose rival branches of the same government.[39] Of all army offices the French War Ministry apparently employed journalists most extensively, and with such abandon that the Ministry and General Staff became the prisoners of unscrupulous papers whom they had supplied with secret materials.

That these colonels and generals whom discipline bade be silent, even under injustice and outrage, that these great professional taciturn men started public and scurrilous controversies with the help of journalists, that was the sure symptom of the most serious evil which can plague armies; they, then, created for war, wear themselves out in peace.[40]

In reality, the complaint of military men about the dependence of their army on "the wind of public opinion" is usually not well substantiated. Even Roon, who wanted to see the army freed from this dependence, called a friendly Berlin paper "the faithful guardian of soldiery against everybody." [41] No officer with any political inclination has ever objected to favorable trade winds of public opinion, or has refrained from trying to raise them. The Prince of Prussia, later King and Emperor William I, secretly contributed to the *Wehrzeitung* some articles in defense of the Prussian army reform he was planning. After armies became more literate, it was less and less possible to exclude reading matter from the barracks. But newspapers of the day were unwelcome; the more Left the less welcome. Lucien Leuwen is told by his colonel not to allow himself to be seen reading newspapers in public, except a government *Moniteur*.

To feed the moderate "reading hunger" of the soldier and indoctrinate him at the same time, periodicals like the Prussian *Soldatenfreund* (Soldier's Friend) were founded in the 1830's. This one pleased the Czar so much that he sent the editor a diamond every year.[42] Military trade journals, which in former times had received poor support from officers, during the nineteenth century displayed a renewed vitality, particularly those representing the officers' interests most directly, like the *Spectateur militaire* founded in 1826, and later *La France militaire*, the Prussian *Wehrzeitung* and *Militärwochenblatt*, the *Army and Navy Journal*.

Such military journalism, however, did not check the ability and inclination of newspapers to expose or to caricature conditions within the army—an ability and inclination which made them both hated and feared, especially in wartime. Down to the Crimean War, battles, sieges, and other operations had largely taken place without admitting civilian observers and reporters. Napoleon was his own reporter, the inventor of the first bulletins.[43] Officers were convinced that civilian reporting could not be wholesome in any way and were sure it would betray secrets to the enemy. Their animosity was increased during and after the Crimean War when war correspondents appeared and immediately felt it their duty to denounce to the public at home the shocking organization and conduct of the armies. General Wolseley retaliated by calling the correspondents "those newly invented curses to armies . . . that race of drones who are an encumbrance to an army; they eat the rations of the fighting men, and do not work at all. . . . These gentlemen, pandering to the public craze for news, render concealment most difficult." [44] But the soldiers commented on Wolseley's appetite for self-advertisement, praising his opposite, Roberts: " 'E's little but 'e's wise; 'e's a terror for 'is size; and 'e does not advertise." [45]

To control the pressmen, who came in with the telegraph, exciting wrath among military men, censorship was established in wartime. To this dominion journalists finally succumbed, chafing at the suppression of their scoops or at the absence of common sense in the average censor, of whom Henry W. Nevinson gives this description from the time of the Boer War:

Unpunctual, unbusinesslike, never present where they ought to have been found, irritable and discourteous, heartily despising the work on which they were themselves employed, regarding the correspondents as something between traitors, scoundrels and bores, anxious only to thwart them in every possible way, favouring papers with whose politics they agreed, or from whose mention they might hope to get some advantage . . . appointed to the Censorship because they are obviously unfit to be appointed to anything.[46]

Fearing the printed word and hating even a hint of criticism, officers were unprepared for the task when the hour struck to make use of the press or other publication for positive war purposes. The co-operation of officers with pressmen and their contribution to propaganda were of a poor sort, poorest where the social distance between officer and reporters was greatest—in Germany and Russia. The military failures among the officers of the Reich threw a part of the burden of the stab-in-the-back legend upon the newspaper. After their defeat generals lashed out at the Jewish journalist in particular, charged him with being largely responsible for the loss of the war, and made him the scapegoat for Pan-Germany.[47] Taking advantage of this scapegoat thesis, the National Socialists made the thesis of the generals into an article of universal belief.

The Nazis as warmakers did away with the private war reporter altogether by making him a soldier sharing all risks and hardships —by April 1940 no less than 23 such front reporters had been killed in action. They produced an enormous amount of reportage, having sent, it was announced in April 1942, 38,000 despatches and 1,000,000 photos to German papers.[48] Like the Nazis, the Russians kept foreign reporters away from the fronts except on the occasion of a few guided tours along quiet fronts, while the Western Allies considered them good, or at least indispensable, morale builders who must be suffered—if not respected—and, when necessary, censored.

The General as Politician

Finding himself hampered by the tightness of military organization and by the exigencies of politics, the officer is likely to reveal his natural inclination to contradict where he is not in a position to command. The violent swearing in the armed forces is in itself partly the consequence of the hierarchical form of organization of those forces, to the coherence of which little is contributed by simple veneration and obedience. Normally the use of expletives is taken for granted as the functioning of safety valves. Officers up to the rank of colonel are expected to do that as well as their duty. It has been said, with considerable justification, that the officer curses first and most his superiors, next his inferiors, his peers, the home government, and, lastly, the enemy.

But only from the general upward do cursing, contradiction, and the expression of violent opinions, as a rule, take on a political character—hence the phenomenon of the "political general" as exemplified by Waldersee, Leonard Wood, and Henry Wilson. This type of soldier-politician takes the liberty of contradicting and contravening everyone, even the supreme war lord, be he William II or Woodrow Wilson, and seeks to shape the course of politics, at least as far as it affects the army and warfare. When President Wilson stated in a note to Germany, that in his view the aims of Germany and the Allies were the same, General Wood, after campaigning against Wilson from the vantage point of the Plattsburg camp, declared to a dinner assembly: "We have no leadership in Washington," [49] hinting that he could provide it.

The general as the officer transmuted into politician without losing the advantages of his rank often becomes so powerful that the political head of government can hardly tell him to be silent or dismiss him in a disciplinary way. In any case, he has to be treated in a political manner. Bülow's fear that Waldersee might interfere with his candidacy for the chancellorship made him send the latter as *Weltmarschall* to head the international troops in China, where he remained for over a year, until Bülow had safely landed in office. President Wilson never called Wood to order; he simply kept the general out of the theater of war and the limelight.

Indeed, neglect or transfer has always been thought one of the best ways to reduce the ambitions of such political generals. When Marchand, of Fashoda fame, a hothead inflamed by public acclaim and demonstrations, returned to France from Africa with open criticism of the government which had "let him down," and seemed about to become a hero for the nationalists, the government, not unafraid of the commotion, gave him an honorable employ in the expeditionary force sent to China. When the limelight still flickered on Marchand, the Combes Ministry found it necessary to send him to a far-distant colony where it would not reach him. He resigned with *éclat,* protesting against this "moral assassination," and tried to get into parliament. For this purpose he devised a platform calling for a proportional vote for families, as the cells of society, and proclaimed himself an enemy of both "excessive individualism and *étatisme,* which would destroy private initiative." But he was "not gifted for electoral politics" and failed more rapidly than Boulanger.[50]

When Clemenceau resolved to remove Nivelle, the frightful failure of 1917, from Paris and even its neighborhood, he remembered the utility of distance. Nivelle had "political relations and if he was not sent away discussions about him were sure to arise. The command of the North of Africa was a beautiful command, particularly interesting . . . and it was beyond the Mediterranean." [51] The still broader Pacific served to keep General MacArthur out of American politics, though not completely.

Military Men in Parliaments

One of the ways for officers to effect military designs under a parliamentary regime is to enter the legislature, usually after the termination of their active service, for in most armies such open interest in politics has been forbidden and even voting rights suspended. The moderate constitutionalism of the early nineteenth century often gave officers dispensation from the uncongenial burden of electioneering by appointing them to the upper house of the bicameral systems. There they became the peers of representatives of other groups, though they hardly ever lost the professional feeling that their comrades in the army were their only true peers. When they took up such careers, therefore, it was largely because they feared the power of parliament, rather than because of a natural interest in politics. They disliked deliberations which they deemed the "fatal crushing of the elite by numbers, of characters by the average, of vigorous souls by the others." [52] The officer had been taught resolution, not deliberation; to do something, whatever it might be, has been considered better in the army than doing nothing—a doctrine quite contrary to that of parliaments and civilian bureaucracies. While serving as military governor of Cuba, Leonard Wood confirmed from his own experiences that ancient military view that "action, right or wrong, seemed always preferable to inaction; and generally less dangerous." [53] Perhaps where there was so much to do, as in Cuba after 1898, Wood's rule for administration that "to do nothing is always a mistake," was less pernicious than it might be in other places and times.

Whatever the true military conception of politics may be, most modern parliaments have contained a sprinkling of ex-officers. The old British parliaments always had a number of officer members and in the reformed parliaments the practice continued; that of 1868, for instance, counted thirty-four members who were or had been in the army, and eighteen belonging to the militia or reserve forces.[54] Moreover, a certain supraparty solidarity showed itself in "meetings of the military members of the House." The French Chamber between the wars of 1870-1 and 1914-18 regularly included some twenty to thirty ex-officers, not to mention reserve officers. If the number in the Reichstag was somewhat smaller, the discrepancy was made up for by officers from the reserve and the Landwehr, who almost without exception were, or pretended to be, friends of the army and its demands. This was particularly the case in the Conservative and National Liberal parties. The leader of the latter from 1905 to 1917, Ernest Bassermann, predecessor of Stresemann, was a major in the reserve, the highest rank a reserve officer could reach—if not high enough to be ever noticed by the Emperor himself.[55] More ominously, among the 107 Nazis swept into the Reichstag by the elections of September 1930, 15 were retired officers.

A study of the constituencies represented by such members would probably bring out the fact that they were in most cases elected by a rural population, unopposed and unheckled. When the Conservatives ran some of the victorious generals of the War of 1866 in Berlin districts, they were all overwhelmingly beaten by Progressives. Only in times of crisis is civilian criticism silent and the Boulangers may be elected wherever they care to be. Eastern Prussia or Ulster, which sent Henry Wilson to Commons in 1922, are ideal regions for officers; there they may count on election; there they are likely to be viewed as "natural" parts of the government. After inspecting the Memel region, which Moltke the "Taciturn" later represented in the Berlin parliament, Roon wrote in 1865 that the population "is disposed to submit to the authority which has power and the will to apply its power; but that has been wanting till now. Not always have the best organs been sent into this semi-Siberia. . . . That explains the rural agony in which these stout, hard, and obstinate Lithuanians find themselves. . . . It is not art to confound this raw mass; but if it be shown the strong hand, it is and becomes as dutiful and obedient as one may wish. In general, false liberalism has power over the mass only as long as it is allowed to open its mouth impudently and by that augment the illusion that right and strength are supporting it." [56] After this region had been worked over, it provided the ideal constituencies for German officers.

Once within a parliament, the former officer could impose himself on the political parties as a military expert and often most effectively in committees. When parliaments go into the details of military affairs, thinking to establish more control over the forces, the theoretical supremacy of the government may be shattered by the influence of former officers in their midst. Generally they are given occasion to fix the details because they "understand" such questions best, and the details are the substance of military policy.[57] Officers so privileged do not as a rule displease their former comrades.

Besides, armies can always trust to finding some militarists among the civilian politicians. Men like Poincaré pleased General Gallifet, for whom energy and love of the army were the measuring rods for public men: "Poincaré is a little bit too much of a lawyer, but his spirit and his heart are military; he has will power." He was the only man, besides Waldeck-Rousseau, under whom the General would agree to serve as War Minister. Others like Ribot and Méline were "bourgeois who do not understand and do not love the army." [58] In the main, love for the army is considered sufficient qualification for statesmanship, whatever the military men may think of the personality of such a politician.

In the United States the army once had an exotic friend, Congressman Julius Kahn of California, one of the most militaristic members of the House before 1914 and after. Through his marriage Kahn was related to officers and he took it upon himself to defend the demand for an army increase in 1919-20 by reviving the ancient argument that it would protect the United States from the consequences of foreign trade competition: "We are trying to expand our trade, and nothing stirs up trouble so much or so quickly as getting the trade from another country. That frequently brings war, and the only salvation is to be prepared to defend the rights of the country at any time." [59]

Such parliamentarians, the army's friends, are the natural approach for favor-seeking officers; members and chairmen of the parliamentary committees on military affairs are sought after in particular. Usually, flattered in their ambition to be "experts," they can be persuaded to present as their own any policy worked out by officers. For example, the Chairman of the Military Affairs Committee of the Senate, George E. Chamberlain, espoused in 1913 the military concept of competition in foreign politics, which was not the traditional American foreign policy, and demanded more effective measures of mobilization.[60]

In military influence on questions of general policy there has been little difference between the various countries, regardless of the degree of parliamentary control. But there has been a difference in the way outside influence could be made to work in favor of individual officers. In Germany direct parliamentary exertion was largely excluded by the existence of the Military Cabinet, to which the better families had to turn in search of favors. In France, on the other hand, officers worked energetically on deputies and senators or even newspaper editors who might appear more useful instruments for obtaining promotion and transfers of a protégé than many a general.[61] During the First World War the chief of Clemenceau's Military Cabinet was overrun by senators and deputies looking for safer places for their constituents in the army and he had to send them all away, so he says.[62] The ambitious American officer likewise has had "a congressman or senator whom he kept warm for emergencies," or other politicians who worked for his promotion, not to speak of possible friendship with the Commander-in-Chief, the President. Such connections helped Leonard Wood to jump over 509 of his seniors, and Pershing, through his father-in-law, to rise from a captaincy straight to a brigadier generalcy.[63]

Without questioning the merits of such generals, it remains doubtful whether personal qualities alone would have carried them so far. Connections are necessary to give them opportunities to prove their mettle. There is at least a nucleus of bitter and general truth in Wolseley's saying that, for an English officer not highly connected, the only chance to get ahead was to do his best on every occasion to get himself killed,[64] and in Lord Fisher's caustic dictum: "Favoritism is the secret of efficiency."

To lay down the general rules for the selection of officers for the national army, if not also for the ratification of specific appointments by the executive, as in the United States, has been a legitimate task of parliamentarians, and if well done, it would insure the homogeneity of parties and the army. On the whole, this homogeneity has been best attained by the American system of having members of Congress nominate candidates for West Point. In most other countries there has been a wide divergency between the parliament as the representative of the nation and the army as its exponent. Generally speaking, parliaments have been far more "Leftist" than armies, and armies have been more royalist and imperialist than the parliaments. Where this cleavage became too wide a crisis usually ensued.

The Ulster crisis in England was solved by a backing down on the part of Parliament and by a world war.[65] In France the Dreyfus crisis brought out into the open the long-veiled contradictions between army and Republic, an army in which the nobility and the clericals, largely excluded from the civil offices of the state, were at times more influential than the republicans. Over a thousand of the descendants of the *émigrés* of the 1790's were serving in the army in the beginning of the twentieth century, presumably still not above fighting the Republic. And this Republic nursed and privileged its own enemies, especially in the matter of promotions, which was in the hands of commissions of officers, not of parliaments and the changing war ministers. It was part of the "revision" of the Dreyfus case to change the arrangements for the selection and promotion of officers, to push ahead the convinced republican officers who had sometimes suffered for their loyalties, and to retard those known as monarchist or clerical.

In its effort to get at army opinions the personnel cabinet of the French War Ministry used the Masonic lodges as agencies to discover the political reliability of the twenty or thirty thousand officers and to report on their "philosophical and political standpoint." Such reports led to long lists of proscriptions; although this operation produced scandals, the Republic was afterwards able to impose its authority over the officers generally and to convince them that it was the only form of government fit for a French army to exist under and to defend in war. Both Right and Left, Nationalists and Socialists, finally agreed that, as Jaurès pronounced it, devotion to the Republic was the crowning virtue of the officer, that with the constant growth of technical problems, which the modern officer had to meet, the principal republican affirmations were work and science.[66]

Intervention in the affairs of officers on the part of the parliamentarians, as when the U. S. Marine Corps went into the lobbies of Congress, has ordinarily been taken for granted by civilians as part of the community of interests and political trading in the governing groups. American presidents "have always used the Army and the Navy for trading stamps";[67] yet this is removed from public control, as it generally takes place behind the curtain of politics and is only now and then uncovered. However carried on, the meddling of the parliamentarians encounters stubborn difficulties when it goes too closely into the internal affairs of military service. It required the action of members of the permanent opposition in prewar Germany, informed by soldiers, to bring to public attention and mitigate such abuses as the mistreatment of privates and the bad feeding of the men.

Parliamentarians have also run into difficulties in trying to bring out the inefficiency and lack of organization which usually become obvious in colonial warfare: for example, in the French expedition to Madagascar in the 1890's; the American enterprise in the Philippines in 1898-9; and the German suppression of an insurrection in Southwest Africa in 1904-7. In seeking to discover those responsible, parliamentarians have often unearthed scandals. Defeats have also given rise to parliamentary commissions of inquiry and none to a more serious searching of hearts than in France after 1870-1, and in Germany after 1918. As a rule, military men have resented all such inquiries, maintaining that exposures would lay bare things which ought to be kept secret, that they would lower prestige abroad—a pretense that the opposition in France, speaking through Jaurès, met by saying that those who prepare for the future debacles and commit the faults are not likely to be the men to point them out.[68]

The Conservatism of Military Politicians

Almost all the military officers in European parliaments have been associated with the parties and groups of the Right and reaction, like the monarchist groups in France. Only a few have turned out to be strict liberals. In general, if the interests of the army have conflicted with those of the party, they have reverted to the army. During the Dreyfus crisis, a member of the Right, protesting in defense of the army, slapped the face of a republican Minister of War in parliament who happened to be a general. Another member of the Right, a general only recently put on half-pay by the same Minister, declared this action an infamy, "and since this man is a soldier, it is an outrage to the army. . . . The whole army is revolted by the cowardly attack committed in its name." [69] Another picture of the army interest in Parliament was furnished by the British House of Commons on March 11, 1836: Hume moved for a reduction of the army by five thousand men; he was opposed by Captain Bolders, M.P., Colonel Perceval, M.P., and Captain Dunlop, M.P., but supported by Major Beauclerk, a liberal and former infantry officer, who demanded that the reduction should take place in the cavalry.[70]

The structure of politics in the different countries has made for great formal differences in the share of officers in parliamentary governing. In the United States their share has been smallest. Officers rarely have entered politics unless this has previously been their trade. On the contrary, politicians have become officers in order to round out a reputation already established. Theodore Roosevelt rushed into the Cuban War to win the martial glory which carried him through the Governor's mansion at Albany— when his party seemed sadly in need of someone with a war halo —to the White House. At the same time the Republican administration of the war exhibited a preference for reserving the "heroism" of 1898 for Republicans—"accidentally" they claimed, though the Rough Riders, led by Roosevelt, were mainly loyal party men; the outstanding Democrat, Colonel William Jennings Bryan, never got as far as Cuba. It suggested carping when Theodore Roosevelt later complained that the Democrats took revenge on his party colleague, Wood, and made the First World War a "very exclusive war" for themselves by keeping Roosevelt and Wood both at home, "as Republican presidents past and potential." [71]

It is the need for a constant application to politics, which the American party system has evolved, that prevents latecomers from rising rapidly. Successful admirals, such as Dewey, whom the navy would have liked to present to the country as a presidential candidate, and generals, such as Wood and Pershing, whom the army would doubtless have been happy to see in the White House, may be hopeful candidates, even if they do not win nomination. But an ex-officer as such may not be even that. A good war record, real or manufactured, is convincing to the American electorate, but a good peacetime service record is not—a fact probably due to the sound instinct that in military matters only wars count.

The failure of Leonard Wood demonstrated the difficulties of circumnavigating civilian politics in an approach to power in

America. His fairly late and rather unconventional entrance into the army, his ability to lift himself into preferred positions and the limelight of the battlefield, showed no little political acumen. Wood knew how to inspire people better than the cold and retiring Pershing, who did not arouse enthusiasm in the voters, though he gained respect for his war success obtained without great scandal or discontent. But if Wood "was enough of a politician to put the politicians on their guard," as his biographer admits, "he was not enough to beat them at their own game. He took a hand, moreover, only at intervals, and an effective politician is a politician day and night. . . . The strategy of politics, the game of give and take, were dark to him. . . . He lived for a while under the happy delusion that party discipline was like army discipline and that policies approved by the President were all but enacted already. . . . He had devoted friends at both ends of the Capitol and bitter enemies; but he made no effort to win over his enemies except with facts and logic." His opinions were ill received in 1920, especially his idea that war as an institution was not dead, as the pacifists maintained, and that men were merely tired of it for the time being.[72]

The rank and file of the army officers of the great European powers have identified themselves with party interests only in a general way, as a rule without open party membership, active or otherwise; it has been considered by many of them Balkan to mix in party politics. Like Wellington, who declined to have "violent party men" as generals, officers have usually felt that "we must keep the spirit of party out of the army, or we shall be in a bad way indeed," [73] but they have generally been as conservative by instinct as the Duke himself. In France, in particular, up to the Dreyfus case, whoever showed too active an interest in supporting the republican government was noted down as "playing politics." [74] In Germany, up to the death of Emperor Frederick III, in 1888, there had been a number of liberal officers, even generals like Von Stosch, who insisted that his own liberalism, inherited from Gneisenau, could be squared with the duties of a Prussian officer. But this death robbed liberalism of its hope to obtain influence within military spheres.

Under William II, conservatism was the required world view of the officers, no less than membership in the established churches. As the same rule was extended to the reserve and Landwehr, the army became an agency for conservative politics in Germany. A lawyer who defended a journalist in a political *cause célèbre* was stricken from the list of reserve officers and afterward could not obtain the necessary confirmation from the government when a town elected him burgomaster. A burgomaster who had not prevented the tenant of some town property from letting Socialists hold a meeting therein was also stricken from the lists of the reserve.[75]

In France, similar means were used to discipline reserve officers who opposed the army's stand against Dreyfus. They were punished on the basis of a law forbidding officers to address themselves "to their military superior or publish against him libelous writings." They claimed that as free citizens of a free country they were at liberty to discuss acts of the military as well as civil authorities, and that the former had no power over them while they were in the reserve; but their claim was disallowed.[76] Thus in both countries the sphere of influence of the regular army was extended far and wide over all those who had connections with it.

Their peacetime enemies the armies have almost unvariably found on the Left, though there have been a few friends of the armies even there. Clemenceau, one of the great havoc makers in European politics, took care never to attack the army openly, except in the Dreyfus case. Little as he thought of its intelligence, and deeply as he had waded through the mire of the Panama scandals, he spared the army in order to use it when he should attain power. Besides, he was no enemy of the armament industries. The army was a political cleaning fluid to just such politicians as Clemenceau or those of Tammany Hall who have always been friendly to the army. In general, however, armies have seen their enemies on the Left, just as the Left has come to view them as foes.

Conservatism in politics, which means of course affiliation with the upper classes, has all along produced a certain conflict between military men as political conservatives and military reactionaries, and military men concerned above all with the perfection of their profession: that is, with evoking from their respective nations the utmost power for armies. There is thus perpetual conflict between militarism supporting and depending on conservatism with its regularized inequalities, and that military thought which recognizes the power-source for war purposes in individualism, in that equalitarianism which admits the opportunity to rise. "The power state itself, as it exists since the French Revolution," said Burckhardt, "postulated equality even when it left to the nobility the civil and military jobs as spoils." [77] Does it also postulate liberty? That is the question.

True military men have recognized that from the standpoint of mustering the greatest possible war strength, the nation should be made homogeneous, that class differences should be little emphasized or so harmonized as to allow the least dissipation of domestic energies. But this war image contradicts conservatism. Fascism saw this problem and sought to fuse the nation by proclaiming equality, in the common blood or the common history merely, though not in freedom, while at the same time freezing classes in the *status quo,* withholding liberty from them, and creating new privileged groups—in the various gradations of party membership.

In old Russia, Radko Dmitriev thought that the Rumanian army was "not much good owing to the cleavage between the classes." Yet he could not see the class differences in his own Russian army, where there was more than one figure like Prince Dolgoruki, Commander of the Don Cossack Division in the First World War, "a rich man with large estates, but no other apparent claim to responsible command." [78]

Few military men have been fully aware of the problem of military potentials hidden in domestic party conflicts and have tried to face it squarely; most of them have avoided it by putting up a show of neutrality, saying they merely serve the state and are above all party strife. This attitude has been particularly adopted during the trial periods of new regimes, like the French Republic after 1871 and the German Republic after 1918, when the military ostensibly sat on the fence waiting to see where the advantage would lie, while numerous officers intrigued underground to give direction to affairs. In France, when a Bonapartist deputy protested that "the army is above existing institutions," the President of the Chamber replied: "Nothing is above the institutions; nothing above the laws of the country, and nothing is more revolutionary, more factious, than putting the military force above the laws." It took a long battle before the French Republic forced the army to recognize the primacy of her laws, and before she rid herself of her own Hindenburg, Marshal MacMahon, who was protecting and shielding the generals who were ready to make a *coup d'état* in 1877.[79] In Germany after 1918 nearly all the high military officers despised the Republic, while appearing to serve it punctiliously, and did their part in the movement to overthrow it.

Military Crisis Phenomena

When the social history of the great economic crises is written, their effect on the armies, the uses of the armies, the opinions about the armies in such times, should receive special treatment. Bismarck's plans for a *coup d'état* before and in 1890 should figure in that history no less than the use of troops in strikes. Boulangism was one of the crisis phenomena in the military sphere. It brought out mass tendencies toward welcoming dictatorship, offered to the general on horseback. At the same time when in Germany an imperious Chancellor was trying to discredit parliamentarism, in France a parliamentary system had itself discredited and disgusted the nation with its constant change of cabinets, its scandals, including the traffic in honors and decorations which the son-in-law of the President had organized.

In the crisis lasting since 1882, which brought out Boulanger, dissatisfied groups remained without relief for their woes from the Chamber. No help was forthcoming for labor either, which undertook many strikes and lost almost as many, or for the peasantry, which suffered from low prices and foreclosures, or for the small traders, who complained, like Hitler's adherents, about the competition of big department stores. To these and other dissatisfied elements must be added the army, which Boulanger had won through several minor material and psychological improvements, including the return of drums, which a predecessor had abolished. The various groups with grievances turned with anticipation to the unsoiled, elegant figure of this general, a soldier not implicated in any dirty deal, beautiful to see on review, France's "first popular War Minister" (1886-7), the first to declare that the soldiers were to share their meals with the laborers on strike, among whom they were sent, as Boulanger said, in order to protect labor against itself.

French nationalism, incited by Franco-German incidents, made Boulanger, who at bottom did not wish for war, *le Général La Revanche*. Bismarck also considered him in that light, expecting him to become the military dictator that France had had several times before, though the German General Staff did not share this view, expecting, instead of a French attack in the winter of 1887-8, a turn of Boulangism into civil war. Foreseeing that 1888 would pass without a war, Waldersee wrote that he was "mean enough to regret this." [80]

When the parliamentarians, who had originally brought the general to the Ministry, Clemenceau among them, became aware of the growing dangers of his popularity, they tried to get rid of him by declaring that he was indeed *la guerre* and removing him from the Ministry. He was sent to the provinces, but he departed only to return as a parliamentarian himself. He got himself elected where and by whom and as often as he wished, for he was something to all groups: urban and rural, petite bourgeoisie and labor, big landowners, anti-Semites, and at last to the clericals and royalists, and the army itself, who wanted him as their Monck; while the *plébiscitaires* wanted him as their Caesar, the revolutionary saw in him their Cromwell and the patriots their *Général La Revanche*.

But Boulanger put himself in the way of his own final success: he engaged in parliamentary discussion before he proceeded to close the era of discussion. He proved feeble and mediocre in debate. He missed the short nocturnal moment when power was close to his hand, when the Ministry trembled, the army and the police were thought unreliable, and when the time had come to act illegally, to show the civilian courage needed for a *coup d'état* instead of the military courage which exhibits daring only under orders. After that he opened himself to ridicule, to police trickery, which drove him into panic and despair, and finally abroad, into the arms of his *maîtresse,* "where all ambition dies," on whose grave he was to end his life in 1891.

Thus the French Caesar-Cromwell-Monck, and his symbols, lost themselves in the fog, as one of the disappointed royalists wrote: "The black horse, the idea of *revanche,* the grand saber, the talisman promised to all the unhappy and all the conquered, the star, have become Chinese shadows. And General Boulanger, whose express mandate it was to lead, without waiting, drums beating, the elections toward battle and victory, has destroyed all hopes and has not created the expected 'other thing.' " [81] By 1890 Boulanger and even Boulangism were passé, the Republic was saved once more, and the military-political leader was made impossible in France until, long afterward, Lieutenant Colonel La Rocque was to appear in another crisis.

A fresh economic depression set in by 1890, lasting into 1894, the year in which the Dreyfus case broke out. This was a social as well as economic crisis, started by the Panama scandals, in which parliamentary politicians were involved. The memory of Panama worked against Dreyfus, as a member of a race which had shared, though not inordinately, in the loot and mud of the Panama episode; it worked in favor of the officers who fought against a revision of the case. When accused of criminal action toward Dreyfus, they defended themselves by announcing they were free from the prevailing sordidness. One general said: "If the officers were really knaves, they would have been found in all the *cochonneries* which have been committed in France for ten years and more."

For a long time the French bourgeoisie, in the strange forgetfulness which accompanies the cycles of economy, closed its eyes to this second Boulangism in the making, and to its dangers for the Republic. Instead of drawing the parallel, as Esterhazy feared, the French nation was ardently resolved to see at least one palladium of purity and integrity preserved: the army. In a bourgeois world where religious belief, the belief in the Word of God, was steadily diminishing, where so recently the business man had failed in his word and had turned swindler, there was the more readiness, the more resolution to trust to the noble word of the soldier. "We take his word for it" had replaced the older bourgeois distrust of the soldier. For a considerable time the rodomontades of the soldier had disappeared from literature. The soldier no longer appeared a liar, a swashbuckler. In the process of secularization the resolution, "the word they shall let stand," was now turned away from God to the warrior.

With this determination, the people were blind to the greatest collective crime which an army has ever committed, committed in the establishing and defense of a governing officer set, committed through the army's greatest weakness: the administration of military justice. In the late 1870's, when the memory of the recent defeat had dimmed and the more ancient military traditions had reasserted themselves, an officer prototype was in the ascendance in whom various traits were amalgamated, aristocratic, clerical, and *bourgeois gentilhomme*. This French officer type was not so different from that of Germany as the different structure of French politics and society should have made him. The central seat of his power was the General Staff, more the permanent cell of political will on the part of the army than the War Ministry proper. Into this inner sanctum Dreyfus penetrated, carried there automatically by his superior intelligence and good marks rather than by connections. He was the only Jewish officer employed in this office where he was not wanted and where anti-Semitism was outspoken enough, a solitary individual, much envied and little loved, with practically no friends in the army, far less at home there than in his own family.

Alfred Dreyfus was a rich Alsatian-Jewish industrialist's son, who had declined to take up his share in the management of the family plants, and went to France rather than to Germany because a Jew might more easily become an officer there. He was resolved to serve and to endure as if to atone for his money, bringing along as part of his heritage his ability for hard work, but none of those critical talents with which other outsiders have benefited armies. Bourgeois enough to choose the artillery as his branch, he was not bourgeois in his concepts beyond that. All this was amalgamated with a will to conform to the nobleness which he never ceased to see in the military profession. His perfectly uncritical belief in its honor and in the nation made him surprisingly unaggressive in the assertion of his innocence. As Léon Blum said, Dreyfus himself would not have been a *Dreyfusard;* he was himself in many ways a militarist, and all his tragic experiences did not suffice ever to make him critical of army institutions and regulations. But his ideal attitude did not make him any more acceptable to the officers of the General Staff. He remained foreign among them; his very foreignness made him suspicious and made him the traitor, when a traitor was looked for.

For many reasons, and to many groups, Dreyfus was the ideal traitor. The French mind is obsessed with the traitor, insisting on finding him even where inefficiency or negligence might have wreaked havoc. To the anti-Semites—and many believed that the majority of the French nation was at the time anti-Semitic—the Jew had ever since Judas been *the* traitor; to the anti-Semitic nationalist, he was the internationalist who, through the "Jewish international," was trading the secrets of the diverse general staffs, like other goods, from country to country. As if to demonstrate the feudal hangover in this nationalism, it declined to find the true traitor, Esterhazy, guilty. Even though Esterhazy was somewhat of an international adventurer, in an age of nationalism which excluded foreigners from the army, his noble, though illegitimately acquired, name protected him from the suspicion which persecuted the honestly nationalistic Jew from lost Alsace.

If the General Staff could "prove" the treason of such a *roturier,* it could at the same time prove for a long time to come its own worth, the exclusive worthiness of the officer type it preferred. It could then govern France, or the parties which endorsed its doings could do so. To convict, to punish this chosen traitor, to keep his innocence from being established, military authority and military justice were misused to the utmost. The usual forms of procedure were neglected, exonerating circumstances were withheld, documents falsified, witnesses intimidated and ostracized, the military judges prejudiced from above, in order to insure the condemnation of Dreyfus and exclude revision of the case which, as a military court of revision declared, could not be done "for want of proof of innocence." The perpetrators of the crime convinced the army and wide circles outside that to put the chiefs in the wrong would wreck the army. A belief was built up that public procedure would endanger national security and public order, that revision would be detrimental to the "honor of the army" and would mean war, for publicity would bring out the Kaiser's own supposed role in employing Dreyfus and thus make him go to war.

On the whole the French nation, condemning Dreyfus even before his peers had done so, approved of this exercise of military justice for a long time. Where it took Voltaire three years to establish the innocence of Calas, it took the *Dreyfusards* twelve. Assurances on the part of foreign powers, their sovereigns, diplomats, and attachés, that they had never employed Dreyfus as a spy, were not accepted. The violence and distrust of nationalism did not believe in a foreign word of honor, whereas it trusted any such word of its own military authorities. Against this determination, civilian ministers did not have the courage to accept foreign assurances and defend their honesty before the excited country. In cabinet after cabinet there was no trace of civilian courage to be found that would rise up against the War Minister; shirking his responsibility, and doubting the "proof" of Dreyfus' guilt at the same time, Gabriel Hanotaux, the Foreign Minister, became ill and went to bed.

The situation of classes and parties in France, the very detach-
ment of a man like Dreyfus from any groups, postponed revision.
The bourgeois parties were afraid to take up his case in the face
of public frenzy. The Socialists, who could usually be trusted to
rise in such a case were not interested in Dreyfus, saying he "would
have massacred us like all the rest"—as he probably, almost certainly, would have done. To them, it was a quarrel of soldiers;
Dreyfus belonged to the capitalist class, the enemy class, and the
Dreyfus affair they viewed as a rivalry between bourgeois factions;
it was no business of labor. The more generous Jaurès finally persuaded the socialist groups that it was, that to let this affair go by
was endangering the Republic and handing it over to the generals,
as the inactivity of the bourgeois parties threatened to do.

The original force behind revision, the force ready to attack the
militaristic infatuation of French nationalism, came from the "in-
tellectuals," as they were then called in contempt, a name which
has clung to them since, men of literature and science, leaders of
reason against the saber; men like Anatole France, who became
a *Dreyfusard* "because the methodical and scientific work of the
intellect was in his eyes the only certain reality," and was sure that
"we shall be right because we have reason on our side." The ideas
of the equality of all Frenchmen before the law, the natural, un-
alienable and sacred rights of man and citizen, were revived, ener-
gized despite the derision which the auxiliaries of the army poured
upon "the poor ideological vanities of 1789." These rights were
defended against the reactionary "clerks," tired of liberty, and
therefore become civilian militarists, like Barrès and Brunetière, to
whom "scientific method, and respect for truth" only covered up
the pretensions of individualism and intellectualism, the forerunners
of anarchy. In vain did the latter call up the army against parliament; all the political energy of the army had gone into the fight
against Dreyfus, in which the end was thought to justify all means.
The officers insisted that military justice was something different
from other forms of justice. But the intelligence of the army was
not the equal of civilian intelligence, once Dreyfus had been removed from their jurisdiction.[82]

Militarism in France at the time produced a rather vocal antimilitarism, which as a rule is silent. But in the long run the Dreyfus
crisis turned out to be a crisis of purification for France and her
army. In spite of all that was granted to the army in lives and
money, the civilian supremacy over it was strengthened; it was a
Dreyfusard, Clemenceau, who held the army in his reins in 1918
and 1919. And the army itself became finally republican, at last
ready to recognize in the Republic the strongest formation for war
and a generous supplier of men and money. Foch admitted that
in saying: "The republican government is the strongest in war since

it is the one which puts to work the maximum of the national force." [83] Through such harmonization, Republic and army survived together.

Under the low-hanging clouds of yet another socio-economic crisis, a battle between liberalism and army took place in England. The ensuing War makes it impossible to say whether the "Strange Death of Liberal England," taking place in the spring of 1914, was merely a catalepsy of English liberalism, or the demise. The officers from Ireland, Junkers from the western hinterland of London, but not very different from those born east of Berlin, threatened to resign *en masse* if the government insisted upon enforcing home rule in Ireland as granted by Parliament against the Ulstermen. Henry Wilson, one of them, told the Secretary of State for War "that the Government are done, that they have bumped up against 100,000 men who are in deadly earnest and that, as neither the Cabinet nor Englishmen are ever in earnest about anything, Ulster was certain to win." [84] And it did win, through the silent group dictatorship of the officers which, real though it was, Baldwin obviously did not reckon when he boasted that England in the last three hundred years of her history has had only ten years of dictatorship.

The liberal majesty of the law was dethroned by the sword law of the Ulster Junker because the British army was not liberalism's own. Liberalism has sometimes made wars without losing control of armies, but it has not made armies. When it made the greatest of all wars, war undid liberalism, whose earlier defeats at the hands of militarism were suffered even before the First World War—in England no less than in Germany, where, about the same time, the Reichstag censured by a vote of 293 to 54 the treatment of the Zabern case● by the government without in the least affecting all-powerful German militarism. If, as has sometimes been maintained, the Ulster question made the German government hope for British weakness in a war and thus precipitated in Berlin the resolution for war, the Zabern incident must also have strengthened French desires to free maltreated Alsace-Lorraine from the Prussian saber rule and thus for war.

● Overbearing Prussian officers in the Alsatian garrison town of Zabern had clashed rather violently with the civilian population, offending against its civic rights and sentiments.

Important as are the activities of individual officers in promoting military interests and creating military psychology among civilian politicians, they are collateral to the regularized relations of the military establishment to the state. Whether the government is democratic and nominally provides for civilian control over the military, or is more or less autocratic and intimately affiliated with the military class, it contains departments or agencies of a bureaucratic character for maintaining constant connections between the tax-paying and potential arms-bearing population on the one side and the economy and operations of military organization on the other.

Theoretically, at least in democratic countries, the civilian legislature and executive, or parliament and premier, determine the national policies to be defended and promoted by arms, and the military establishment merely conforms to and executes these policies. Practically, the process is not so simple; indeed, it may be reversed. In the case of any specific government, democratic or autocratic, pulling and hauling take place within the civil-military setup and, as a rule, confusion reigns as to the location of the center of real and efficient power within the conflict of interests. It is not often that civilians outside the government, or even members of parliaments who do not serve on military committees, know what is actually happening in the civil-military tug of war over money, supplies, men, and equipment. Nor is it possible to gain much information on this subject, for historians have strangely neglected it and treatises on government and war pass over it lightly. Nevertheless, there are available clues to the deeper and more

10

Protection and Promotion of Military Interests Within the State

fundamental phases of what is called the military policy of a state or a government and its shaping.

The War Ministry and Conflicts Over the Services

The official mediator between armies on the one side and parliaments and the peoples on the other is the war minister, or secretary of war, with the war office or war ministry or ministry of defense as the highest administrative office of the military force. An ideal definition of the qualifications of such a personage, as laid down by another sort of minister, demands that he should be

the representative of the physical power of the nation animated by spiritual strength; therefore he must keep this power always active and further its development by his activity; but neither must he waste it, he must not misuse it and degrade to playthings those powers dedicated to the holiest purpose. The most complete knowledge and grasp of these powers, and of those who give life to them, the most perfected ability to use and to apply them suitably, and the highest respect for the nation which provides these powers, must guide his way of acting; for these requirements are to ensure to the people the safety of their existence. A difference between the army and the people must be an abomination to him, for the state is lost in the very moment when the people imagines this difference. The soldier who insists on more right than any other representative of the supreme power, degrades himself; the highest triumph is achieved when it can be said: the soldier is completely assimilated as a citizen.[1]

Speaking more practically, the war minister in liberal countries is the personification of parliamentary control over the army, be it complete or not. He is a member of the cabinet and either responsible together with it to parliament, as in England and France, or not responsible, as in the United States. In England and France administration and command are united in the person of this minister. He must be a civilian in England where, to insure civilian supremacy, the Commander-in-Chief is excluded from the House of Commons. He is a civilian in the United States, although a former officer, out of service, may be called to the post. In France this is optional, with a growing tendency to entrust the office to generals, though the war ministers of the First World War were civilians. But before French generals accept the portfolio, they sometimes obtain the approval of a number of army chiefs; at least one of them, during the Dreyfus crisis, resigned because he was in agreement with the army rather than the government.[2] A candidate for the old Japanese Ministry of War or other Cabinet post would ask for the opinion of the generals who, from the rank of lieutenant general upward, formed the governing set of the army politicians. If their advice should appear an intrusion into politics or contrary to the will of the Emperor, it could always be declared as given in the personal capacity, as friends of the candidate.[3]

Whatever the formalities, most generals as war ministers have considered themselves to be temporary representatives of the army in the cabinet. "Don't call me *M. le Ministre*, but General," said Gallifet to a French bureaucrat; "Minister, I am that for a few days only; but General I shall remain all my life." He remained in office for some eleven months and then left it with the curse: "*M*————! I have enough of it."[4]

In Russia the war minister had to be a general until 1917, in Prussia until 1918, and he had to be a general in Japan, where this rule had been followed since the establishment of the constitutional monarchy. In the two latter countries, the war minister was regarded as not responsible to parliament but only to the monarch, or head of the state. Whereas in old Prussia-Germany the ministry, including the war minister, was not responsible to the Reichstag, in Japan the Cabinet was responsible to the Diet; only the war and naval ministers were exempted.

Since parliamentary responsibility is a check on military self-government, it has generally been opposed by military men. In the early stages of the Russian Revolution, the Czar demanded that the ministries of defense and foreign affairs be exempted from answering to any parliamentary system that might be established. Theoretically, as experience shows, the war minister may be either a representative of the army in the cabinet or in parliament, or in both, or a representative of the cabinet and parliament in the army.

The general as war minister is the highest of all the office generals. Napoleon abominated this type. But since his day generals as war ministers have multiplied, sharing fully in the growth of bureaucratism. Wherever a civilian politician has become war minister, the highest ranking office general has usually acted as the representative of the army, to treat with the minister and the parliament. This was the role played by officers such as General von Schleicher, and the holders of the office of adjutant general in the United States army, such as General Ainsworth in the 1900's, who engaged in a constant feud with the new office of the General Staff, "was a past master in the seductive art of politics and had an extraordinary hold on Congress."[5]

The civilian minister of war is naturally expected to shape the army according to the ideas which his party and his chief, the prime minister or president, entertain with reference to the most desirable military force. But in no country did a party or cabinet chiefs in the time between 1872, when the basic French army reform was finished, and 1914, show any great understanding, initiative, or will of their own in respect to army affairs. No such directive drive came from even the most energetic chiefs of government, like Gambetta, Jules Ferry, or Waldeck-Rousseau in France, or in England; nor was it displayed in the United States, where a Theodore Roosevelt might be exceedingly friendly to military wishes, but lacked specific ideas of military organization. In this period of liberalism just two civilian war ministers were conspicuous for taking the trouble to devise an army reform which had become unavoidable—Elihu Root and Richard B. Haldane.

Most war ministers were mere representatives of the army in the cabinet, rather than agents of the cabinet in the army. They allowed the military element to shape cabinet policies, to determine its own organization, and to defend its own interests. Very little serious initiative in matters of military organization and reform, hardly any clear notions about the best possible military policy for their country's needs, came from the throng of parliamentarians who crowded the political stage between 1870 and 1914. Liberalism itself allowed the idea of the division of labor to enter even general military policies, and looked with indifference or hostility upon all civilian proposals to reform military institutions—projects such as Jaurès, or Bebel, or Raiberti sponsored. In other words, liberalism tended to ally itself in military affairs, more than in any other field, with conservatism.

The division-of-labor idea parallels the parceling out of money and men through parliaments. Like most other groups within a nation, armies want the maximum for themselves. Probably they have been more insatiable in their demands, more ruthless and inconsiderate than other departments. Such, at least, was the conviction of Bismarck, who begged his trusted colleague, Roon, when the latter left Berlin for a long vacation, to recommend to his deputy "the standpoint of a statesman who does not ask in his wild departmental patriotism: 'What else can I get?' . . . but 'What *must* I have and what can I postpone?' " It proved a vain request. While Roon was absent Bismarck met nothing from the War Ministry but office patriotism, "which considers everything not given to the military as enemy territory." [6] It has always been the painful task of cabinets and parliaments to harmonize departmental demands, taking good care at the same time to guard themselves against reproaches of having neglected the country's defense.

To a certain—though scarcely measurable and not easily comparable—extent, the share of the total budget that goes to the army expresses the strength of that army in home politics. As measured by pre-1914 national budgets, this relative strength appears in the year 1897-8 in the percentages that went to the armies: in Germany 17.3; in Austria-Hungary 17.6; in Russia 24.3; and in France 28.6, or in a relation of 100:102:140:165.[7]

Within the cabinet the usual task of the war minister consists in persuading his colleagues of the justness of the army's demands and in obtaining the largest possible slice of the total annual budget for his department. By the end of the nineteenth century all countries except Russia had passed out of the army's happy times of the mid-century, when the Austrian Emperor Francis Joseph could remove the portfolios of army and police from the Cabinet and take these affairs into his immediate charge. The adjutant general whom he entrusted with the army interests declined even to discuss his budget with the Finance Minister, saying: "What a thing costs we know as well as you; it is your business to get the money." [8] It was a comfortable system for the army, though very ruinous to Austrian finances.

All along after those "happy times" war ministers were regularly irked by the annual budget, or estimates, laying down the strength of the army and the expenditures for it on the basis of general political conditions—the program on which liberalism has insisted, following the English example. But in old Prussia Roon decided that he would not allow such an "un-Prussian" regime to be established: "In my opinion there is nothing worse for Prussia than to get involved in the doctrinaire swindle. From the mud bath of a revolution she may arise with new strength, but in the cloaca of doctrinaire liberalism she will rot past recovery." [9] The Prusso-German solution of the budgetary problem was the septennate, later the quinquennate, arrangements between army and Reichstag, whereby the peacetime strength of the army and the corresponding budget were fixed for a term of seven, later five, years, and thus became undebatable during that period. Advocated as a way of insuring "steadiness" in the affairs of the army, it actually served to spare the military bureaucracy the struggle to defend the army strength annually. Moreover it made reductions practically impossible, even if the international situation had permitted them, for at the end of each of the long periods a fright could be worked up to drive away thoughts and hopes of cuts and reductions.

The most exasperating answer to his demands which a war minister could hear was "There is no money," or "There is no real reason to spend more money this year than the year before." General von Einem, Prussian War Minister from 1903 to 1909, described his ministerial experience in this relation. When he came into office the Chancellor, Bülow, asked him to demand only the most necessary things for the army, for the general political situation was completely quiet and Germany was just emerging from an industrial depression. But the War Minister and Tirpitz merely judged that the Chancellor did not have the courage to demand higher taxation from the country; they felt sure that money was overflowing the land, even if not pouring into the Reich treasury, and that only a false sense of economy prevented the cabinet from supporting many of the demands of the General Staff.[10]

Armies vs. Navies

Particularly painful is the task of obtaining a full share of the national defense budget for the army in the face of the demands of the navy. In England and the United States, the navy traditionally received the lion's share of the annual defense appropriations: traditions, defense geography, and a predilection among liberals for this branch conspired to maintain that proportion. Only in London could a war minister be inclined to ask for more ships, instead of soldiers, at a time when his military assistant, Henry Wilson, wanted more soldiers and thought England had ships enough.[11] In Germany, after 1900, the army was forced constantly to reduce its demands in favor of the navy—the spoiled child of the Kaiser and also of the Reichstag and the German bourgeois generally.[12] The Kaiser and the bourgeois were captivated by Tirpitz's salesmanship and were taught to consider naval expenditure more "productive" by the argument that a larger share of this outlay went to the industries than that of the army budgets; the army money went rather for salaries and for foodstuffs and horse feed, which benefited agriculture instead. Again, the navies could be immediately useful in collecting bad debts abroad, whereas the utility of the army was only realized when war or insurrection broke out.

The subordination of all officers to the common supreme war lord in Germany excluded the possibility of an open conflict between army and navy such as raged publicly in Japan. But this cloaking of the inner conflict between the two branches could not conceal the strategic consequences of the rise of the navy as a war instrument to an importance almost equal to that of the army. As early as 1898 this shift was clearly recognized by Waldersee when he observed that in the navy "the idea is more and more cultivated that future wars will be decided on the seas. What, however, does the navy intend to do if the army should be beaten either in the West or in the East? Thus far the dear gentlemen prefer not to think." Nevertheless, the divergent tendencies of the two branches were "harmonized," like competing interests, but their comparative importance for defense or offense was never settled from the higher standpoint of a determined Reich defense policy. The persons who were in a constitutional position to make this decision, the Kaiser and chancellors, were, by character and mentality, incapable of coming to a decision. Consequently to each branch of the defense forces went "something," largely according to the pushing and intriguing abilities of the officers at its head.

In liberal countries, the tendency was to favor the navies, in part because this branch seemed the more trustworthy; the larger funds handed to the armies appeared to be more readily convertible into a power which could be used against the government in case of political conflicts. It was a liberal principle to restrict the demands of offense forces by constitution and law, to prevent them from obtaining an immoderate share of the country's wealth, and to keep them subordinate to civil power; it seemed less dangerous to favor the navies. This was certainly one of the considerations which led Great Britain and the United States to develop sea power. Admiral Pratt of the United States navy stated the case as he understood it: "Those countries whose fate depended upon sea power have at heart been liberal thinkers and lovers of free democracy [Japan?] whereas the more strictly land-locked nations . . . have been governed more by what may be called military influence, and have been exponents of the more autocratic forms of government." [13]

By comparison, naval officers in the European countries have been of more modest origin than army officers. In the United States the officers of both forces have come from the same strata of American society. Before the purchase system in the British army was abolished, it was thought that the officers of the army must be reliable, well-to-do members of the ruling class, in order to insure their rendering help if called upon in civil disturbances at home. The origin and family of the naval officers, however, did not seem so important, for "no political crisis has yet arisen when the navy has been called upon to aid or to restore Civil Authority. . . . The constitutional history of the two services is essentially dissimilar. The debates on the army are redolent with political strife; and tho' every increase to the army has been resolutely opposed, there has been no annual contest as to the number of seamen to be maintained. . . ." The scrutiny of Parliament fell with far greater jealousy upon the lists of the candidates for command in the army than in the navy.[14]

As if to avoid having this good constitutional agency of war tainted by too much contact with the army, it was equipped with a landing force of its own, the marines, a curiously amphibian force, which owes its origin, if not its continued existence, more to political considerations than to military designs. Its reputation for a certain amount of refractory behavior and lawlessness seems to have arisen from a reluctance on the part of the authorities to discipline the marines as strictly as soldiers, and from their free use in "backward countries" on the more defenseless peoples.[15]

The differences between armies and navies constitute only a few of the many conflicts to which the military *esprit de corps* is likely to lead. No groups have more disdain for other bodies than do armed forces taking positions on such varied fronts—against civilians, foreigners, traders and other capitalists, and industrial workers. Within their own ranks they conduct smaller though hardly less bitter feuds—as between infantry and cavalry, cavalry and artillery, guards and the line, line and Landwehr, and all against the train. In the United States army, for example, there have been sharp struggles between the regulars and the volunteers,[16] between the graduates of West Point and nongraduates such as Dr. Leonard Wood, whose rapid promotion moved a general to congratulate naval cadets publicly for serving in a branch of the service which did not turn doctors into admirals.[17]

In peacetime this cohesive corps spirit eventuates, as a rule, in expansive demands on the part of each branch of the army. In wartime it appears in a tendency to impose its will, its specialist concept of operations, upon all the forces employed. With the plans of the leader for the concerted, that is, highest, effect of the common endeavor, the power tendencies of the separate branches often interfere.[18]

Many, if not most, of the war enterprises have suffered from rivalries and divergences between the army and navy offices and the forces engaged side by side in the field. The Second World War was to witness "the battle of the Smiths" on Saipan in 1943, the widely aired conflict of an army and a marine general of that name. Perhaps it is a heritage of the days when the members of the aristocracy undertook to command both branches of war that has made naval officers in modern times claim knowledge of land warfare and undertake command over land expeditions in ventures where they were supposed only to co-operate with the army. When the military men in Cromwell's expedition to the West Indies in 1655 failed in their attempt on Santo Domingo, Admiral Penn proposed to take the place with sailors. Of this the military would not hear: "All ranks in the fleet now abused the army for rogues, and the worst feeling grew up between the two services. . . . Finally the expedition sailed away in shame to Jamaica." Penn, openly saying that he would not trust the army, seized the weakly defended island, whereupon the two forces quarreled for another six weeks.[19] Again, during the unsuccessful expedition of the allies against Toulon in 1707, undertaken against his own desires, Prince Eugene complained that the admirals, "even though they do not understand land warfare, still stick to their original opinion." [20] Such conflicts at last led to a ruling in favor of the specialist, namely, that in land enterprises the senior military officer was to take command over all naval officers regardless of rank.[21]

Whereas in England the encroachments of one force on the other more often came from the navy, on the Continent the army was in general the more domineering party. When Prussia founded her navy, generals were at first put at the head. In landlocked Russia the superiority of the army was scarcely disputable. When the unexpected issue of the campaign of 1812 called for an explanation, for a hero and a scapegoat at the same time, General Kutuzov was glorified and Admiral Tchitchagov, who had commanded an army, was chosen as the victim. It was the unlucky admiral who was called to account for the dark spots which appeared in the glorious picture of this campaign.[22]

Even the greatest military thinkers and generals have not emancipated themselves from a misunderstanding of the war power of a navy—a misunderstanding which may be traced back to professional jealousy and narrowness. The mishandling of France's naval resources by Napoleon went hand in hand with his dislike for the naval profession generally. Jomini apparently hated "the maritime despotism" exercised by England so much[23] that the action and effect of navies did not figure in his picture of war. Among the greater generals, only Marlborough possessed an over-all concept of war, including the uses of both land and sea forces. Most generals have remained purely military experts, and admirals have likewise been limited.

The co-ordination of the two forces, scarcely attempted before 1914, had to be brought about afterward by the political heads of governments. The degree to which this was achieved was largely due to their energy. For a time during the First World War the civilian heads of the German Reich succeeded in restricting the U-boat warfare which threatened to bring the United States into the conflict; then Ludendorff, replacing Bethmann Hollweg by what was practically a military dictatorship, unleashed the submarines which, as naval officers promised on their "naval officers' *parole d'honneur,*" would keep the American soldiers away from Europe. When they failed to do that, officers in General Headquarters and other high positions—some of them long before convinced that Germany would have been better off if Tirpitz had built more submarines and fast cruisers and fewer battleships for naval parades —were ready to sacrifice the entire German navy as the price of a favorable peace with England. It was hoped that England would take to the cheap bait of "our maritime renunciation." Then, in July 1918, the whole hatred of the army for the navy, and the "visionaries" of sea power, broke out in judgments highly unfair as far as the actual services of that arm in the war were concerned. "Our naval policy before the war was radically wrong and the main reason for England's hostility. . . . During the war the fleet has cost us men and money. I don't see any military benefit in it." This judgment came about twenty years too late.[24]

Taxation for Armies

The tendency toward stricter control of military budgets was especially marked among liberals when the bulk of the expenditure passed to members of classes not their own. For a long time comparatively little went back to groups represented by the liberals—the bourgeois and urban workers. Friends of large budgets indeed pointed out that one-third of all taxes paid for army expenditure were returned to the tax-payer in some form;[25] but liberals and socialists could of course, reply that often enough they were not favored by the forms or returns of taxation, that military expenditure flowed, not to their middle class and urban groups, but to a bureaucracy, to certain industries, and to agriculture. Besides pointing to the money paid out for horses and feed, grain and meat, the German and French armies had a peculiar way of courting the favor of agrarians: they paid for actual or pretended damage done to crops during the maneuvers. France took over this policy of granting subventions to the agrarians from Germany, along with so many other things which she borrowed after 1871.[26]

The fond belief in the possibility of controlling armies from the outside, by way of the purse strings, instead of by entering armies consciously and with a definite policy, gave liberals and socialists some expertness in military budgets, whatever their ignorance or indifference might be in other military matters. This made them redoubtable to the war ministers who, when not responsible to parliament, still needed the consent of parliament to the budgets. It was the most disagreeable of the German minister's duties to defend his demands against the penny-mindedness, the detailed scrutinies, of such budgetary experts as Eugen Richter, or the later Matthias Erzberger, not to speak of the socialist critics. The officers considered such men as their enemies, "dangerous" on account of their oratorical gifts and their wide knowledge in budgetary questions,[27] for they forced the army to abandon its early cavalier attitude toward monetary matters, and prevented it from applying money for other purposes than those for which it had been granted.

After 1918, when the violent search for a scapegoat began in Germany, to bear the responsibility of defeat, parliamentary critics were chosen as convenient and welcome victims by the generals, who denied any shortcomings on their own part and attributed nearly all the faults of the prewar German army to the stinginess of parliament, unwilling to tax the German nation sufficiently. This accusation was made in terms so violent that officers and other militarized German youth, after 1918, murdered such prewar critics and exposers of the army as Erzberger and Liebknecht.

Actually, the accusation was unjustified. The European bourgeoisie, in Germany and everywhere else, all the more as 1914 approached, had been willing to grant almost all the armament expenditures demanded. In autocratic Russia the Duma made no use of its budgetary rights to further its own power, but enthusiastically voted the army bills—the last, of 800,000,000 roubles in March 1914, after a secret conversation between the Prime Minister and the party leaders.[28] So also did France, with its parliamentary government which, after the war, did not altogether escape the reproach of war guilt, however readily it had agreed to the sums asked of it. The amounts granted by the French parliament between 1905 and 1914, totaling 1,683 million francs, were only 40,000,000, or some 2 per cent less than the amounts demanded by the War Ministry.[29] Indeed, the French parliament, through its discretion, made possible the introduction of the 7.5 cm. cannon after 1897; it granted at first 30,000,000 francs, "adroitly obtained" by the War Minister under the pretext of repairs to artillery material, and then more millions to make possible the buying and introduction of this weapon without arousing attention.[30]

The same was true in Germany. There, a member of the German National Liberal Party in the Reichstag asked the General Staff, early in 1913, whether the latter was really satisfied with the army bill as the War Minister had presented it; his own party thought the demands did not go far enough. The Chief of Staff and Ludendorff were ready to welcome all such party support. But the War Minister actually refused to take advantage of this encouragement; he was disinclined to demand the three additional army corps which parliament might have granted.[31]

Certainly, the prewar parliaments could not be justly accused of parsimony in their expenditures for defense. Their faults in defense politics lay in quite other directions. The interparliamentary competition in generous spending appears from the following survey of outlay for defense in pre-1914 Europe (in millions of pounds):[32]

	1858	1883	1908	1913
Great Britain	23	28	59	77
France	19	31	44	82
Germany	5	20	59	100
Italy	2	12	18	29
Austria-Hungary	11	13	21	24
Russia	19	36	60	92
Other States	16	23	38	82
Total	95	163	299	486
Average Price Level (1913 = 100)	110	95	90	100
European Population, in Millions	278	335	436	452

The General Staff as the Military Directorate

Far more removed from any parliamentary control than the minister or secretary of war is the General Staff—an institution fully developed after the rise of the mass army in warfare. Upon this bureaucratic-professional body falls the supreme task of supervising military preparations and the general direction of operations in wartime. It does, or should, carry the burden of advising the heads of the government respecting war potentials and the possibility of winning any specific war upon which the government decides. No other agency of government in the modern state bears heavier responsibilities in peacetime, and especially in the hour of crisis when war decisions are being weighed and settled by the civil heads of government.

Yet concerning the nature and operations of this war-preparing and war-directing body relatively little is known outside military circles. Among the victorious powers in the First World War, there was scant consideration of the role, good or bad, of their own military authorities in assenting to the making of war in July 1914. Victory is a posterior harmonizer of conflicts—a harmonizer that leaves the civilian population uninformed. But it was otherwise in Germany, where defeat brought about a searching inquiry into the causes of defeat.

In their examination into the origins of a war that ended in disaster, some few Germans raised the fundamental issue: should not the office that, in 1914, presumably possessed the best insight into the probable course of the war, the General Staff, have presented an estimate to the government which would have furthered a postponement of conflict? A spokesman of the old General Staff answered this pertinent, patriotic question by saying that he did not see how the government could have evaded it permanently; evasion would merely have strengthened the will to attack on the part of the enemy.

"That, however, is a question of policy," he said. "Before the war the General Staff could merely point again and again to the tremendous military efforts of our enemies and their clearly recognizable war aims. It had to realize and warn that the strain put on our military sinews was not sufficient, that our enemies were far superior. And that it has done with all decisiveness and even with acrimony [in another place it is admitted that the Chief of Staff, the younger Moltke, could have pushed the demands for three more army corps with much more energy] but with insufficient success. Further its competence and power did not reach." [33]

This was a none too courageous retreat into the compartment of bureaucratic competency, from which the General Staff could and did step boldly forth on other "political" occasions. In July 1914, instead of declaring that the war was too risky and should not be made then—and certainly not without the three additional army corps which the War Ministry had refused to demand the year before—the Staff appears to have encouraged the Austrian Chief of Staff, Conrad von Hoetzendorff, to proceed. After forty-three years of laborious preparation for war, the Staff could not admit unpreparedness to the civilian bureaucracy, to say nothing of admitting it to the nation. And was there not the example of Frederick, surrounded by a world of enemies, and yet victorious? It inspired German General Staff officers like Von Kuhl to gamble on a favorite outcome.

From the materials brought forth in many inquiries, it would appear that none of the powers was convinced that July 1914 was for it the very best moment for the war. It cannot be maintained, for instance, that Germany really chose the moment when her crops were harvested; as a matter of fact they were not harvested in large parts of the country. Moreover, it would have been better for her to choose, if she had the choice, the "roadless season," the thawing period of spring, when Russia could not have moved her masses through the mud. But no power thought the moment positively prohibitive; none expected in 1914 that it would be beaten. The heads of the French and English armies were sure, as Grey relates, that together they could win, even without Russia.[34] The diplomats finally resolving upon war must all have assumed before July that their own and their Allies' general staffs and admiralties were not against a war for reasons of general or momentary unpreparedness, that as conditions stood they saw a reasonable chance of victory.

This time, the diplomats apparently did not ask the general staffs specifically, as Bismarck used to do. It does not appear that to any leader was put that straight question which Caillaux presented to Joffre during the Agadir crisis of 1911: "General, it is said that Napoleon only gave battle when he thought that he had at least a sixty per cent chance of victory. Have we a seventy per cent chance of victory if the situation drives us into war?" Joffre replied: "No, I do not think we have it." Caillaux: "That's good. We shall then negotiate." [35]

Fearful of having their respective countries appear as aggressors, they did not—or at least it is not documented if they did—ask their military departments in July 1914: "Shall we or can we make the war now because our country is best prepared for it and may not be again in such a good position?" When the test came, the general staffs, afraid of losing prestige, or completely enslaved to the mechanical preparations for mobilization, would not confess to any qualms. The absence of such objections again indicates that the First World War started at a moment in military competition when all parties were running abreast in the arena and felt tempted to spurt ahead. As a matter of fact, the "stalemate" character of the war was preceded by a stalemate in preparation, when the balance of power was so even that each side could believe itself ready and the other about to attack.

If the assumption of the inevitability of war furnishes one of the main reasons for the existence of military institutions, the wish to undertake it at a moment of supposed superiority is the merely logical consequence drawn from this assumption by military men. Bismarck opposed the idea of a "preventive war" as the equivalent to committing suicide because one was afraid of death. Hardly a statesman or diplomat owned to having such a war intention before 1914, for each was striving not to have his own nation appear before the public as the aggressor. But they did generally admit a feeling of the inevitability of a clash and were encouraged in the feeling by their general staffs and generals. As early as 1902, well in advance of the Anglo-French Entente, Lord Roberts was sure, as he watched the German maneuvers, that war between England and Germany was inevitable.[36] Winston Churchill, Clemenceau, Paleologue, Poincaré, Izvolski, Admiral Fisher, and Henry Wilson had come to a similar conclusion.

In most cases the belief in the inevitability of war coincided with an equal assurance on the part of the general staffs that the other side could be beaten. The English Ambassador in Petersburg, Sir Arthur Nicolson, told the Russian Foreign Minister in 1909, so shortly after the Russo-Japanese War, that Great Britain, France, and Russia were more than equal to every combination.[37] French generals, in 1913, as Henry Wilson reported to Nicolson, were of the opinion that it would be better for France if the war were not postponed too long.[38] On the other side, Schlieffen, the Prussian War Minister, and Holstein in 1905, during the First Moroccan crisis, were inclined toward war with France while Russia was in a bad state, but they could not persuade the Emperor and Chancellor.[39] Conrad von Hoetzendorff begged permission in 1907 to overthrow Italy—"alas in vain" as far as permission from Berlin was concerned—and again on many a subsequent occasion he wanted to tame Serbia.[40]

Conrad and Field Marshal von der Goltz united during the imperial maneuvers of 1913 in "the sharpest condemnation of our peace policies, which had missed the last favorable moment for breaking loose," that is, during the Second Moroccan crisis of 1911. They regretted that Schlieffen's proposals had been disapproved; so did General von Eisenhart-Rothe, who ascribed that rejection to

Bismarck's old advice against a preventive war—advice which he considered out of date.[41] An influential group in Germany, therefore, were of the opinion that the most favorable moment for war had already passed by 1914. But there were circles in the Reich which considered the signs propitious and expected from a war an improvement in internal politics—an opinion not shared by Bethmann-Hollweg, who felt instead that war would add to the power of Social Democracy and might upset many a throne.[42] Certainly after Sarajevo, the General Staff at Berlin was disposed to consider it a happy circumstance for war to break out immediately; the situation and prospects, some members believed, could not be improved. Moltke is reported to have declared himself for war, urging that the conjuncture would not soon again be so favorable to Germany, inasmuch as neither France nor Russia had completed the work of military organization.[43]

Russia too had a group of "war hawks," imbued with clear military and imperialistic aims—to obtain the Straits and to wash off the stain of the ignominious defeat in 1904-5. They now felt ready for war and victory, better equipped than ever, better than in the autumn of 1912. At the latter date, the Russian military attaché in Paris told his Austrian colleague in 1913, Austria ought really to have attacked and had committed a grave fault in not doing so: "At that time sentiment was not yet prepared in Russia. Now all Russia is bitter against Austria, and in the most distant Volga garrisons the recruit is drilled to hate Austria, of whom he had perhaps not heard up to then." [44]

Militarist nations, notably Japan, which attacked a Russian fleet before the declaration of war in 1904, have least shunned the odium of aggression; the Anglo-American nations have feared it the most. But the latter have had their advocates of preventive wars. Many "very reasonable, quiet Englishmen" wanted war at the time of the Fashoda episode, when England was still the most powerful nation on the seas, and complained that neither Salisbury nor any other minister had a right to pass over the propitious moment for war, thus sacrificing the interests of the country.[45] Lord Fisher maintained that the German navy ought to be "Copenhagened" in time, though this was hardly possible without opening war abruptly and unannounced. That the thought was also in other minds is evident from the speech of the Lord of the Admiralty, Lee, who told his constituents in February 1905, that if war should break out, the British navy would strike before the other party had had time to read about it in the newspapers. The very influential Sir Eyre Crowe in the Foreign Office was, on July 27, 1914, frankly an advocate of a preventive war.[46]

The readiness of the General Staffs and numerous diplomats for the "inevitable" naturally weakened the hold of the brakes which could be applied to moves closer toward war. The mechanism of mobilization, partial and total, as developed during the nineteenth century in the best timetable style, had become united with the older feudal principle that the sword must not be made and drawn in vain, and it kept the military always in a quiver lest their own mobilization be set in motion too late. As Roon wrote to a party leader of the Prussian conservatives some months before the actual outbreak of the war with Austria in 1866: "When armaments are once in train, the outward thrust will either be followed by the beginning of a fight or, what is worse, by being ridiculed, if the sharpened sword is returned to the sheath without results." [47]

Honor and prestige of the professionals once engaged, that is, the psychological mobilization started, it was hardly possible to put the mechanism in reverse. "I foresee," the Czar complained to the Kaiser during their last exchange of telegrams at the end of July 1914, "that I shall very soon be overwhelmed by the pressure exerted upon me, and be forced to take extreme measures which will lead to war." [48] On the German side, Moltke answered a suggestion of the Chancellor that preparations against France be stopped, by saying that if that should happen the Kaiser would have "a crowd of men but no army." [49] In France, Messimy, the War Minister, told Viviani, whose readiness for war was somewhat less decided than that of others, that it was too late for any interference with the order of mobilization, for "the mechanism had been started." [50]

Mobilization was in fact admitted as more or less identical with war; so it was conceived in Berlin, where it terminated the vacillating, though growing, resistance of the Foreign Office to the war desires of Moltke, one of whose subordinates declared on July 29: "We are sliding slowly but surely into a mobilization." [51] But it would amount to *post factum* moralizing to decide at which moment the military preparations for war took on the character of culpability. From the standpoint of military competition during July 1914, every step forward toward mobilization on the part of one power was considered by the others a handicap to their own preparations, if not at once followed up and countered by similar measures.

"Every hour of delay makes the situation worse, since Russia gains advantage," Moltke told an emissary of Conrad on July 30, in order to move the Austrians toward a further mobilization of their army.[52] Partial mobilization, undertaken on earlier occasions, seemed in that hour less feasible to the general staffs, among other reasons because all the Great Powers believed that any war within Europe could not be localized. No mobilization for a partial war had even been planned. Russia had no such plan against Austria alone; Germany none for a war with Russia alone. Since the armies could only do that for which they had themselves prepared, Russian military men —the General Staff rather than the War Minister—thought nothing else possible except a total mobilization. Only under the command of the Czar did they bring themselves to ordering temporarily a partial one. Yet by means of this limited mobilization a vast deal of preparation could be achieved, as Messimy, himself a former member of the General Staff, advised the Russian ally.[53]

Soon a new wave of military and diplomatic influences, sweeping over Europe, wrung from the Czar the order for general mobilization. A decisive factor in this decision was the conquest of the Czar's Foreign Minister by the military in St. Petersburg, who convinced him that it was "better not to fear to provoke war by our preparations for war, and by pursuing these carefully, than to give an occasion for war by fear and thus be surprised by war."[54] Although Russian military men thought that Russia was not prepared for war up to the maximum in July 1914—that point they had intended to reach only after two more years of peace—they were sure that Russia was sufficiently ready.

From July 31 diplomacy was primarily concerned with guiding the several peoples and their "slow imagination" to this general resolution for war on the part of the military and diplomatic bureaucracies, and with making the enemy out as an aggressor and one's self as the victim whose efforts for peace had failed. France evacuated a boundary zone of ten kilometers' depth, though not to the full extent of her announcement, without thereby in any way compromising her planned military operations.[55] England waited until Germany had violated Belgian neutrality, a step which the military men among her enemies knew long before that she was going to take[56]—a step for which the British army had been reformed and prepared to counter.

Planning for War

In all countries of the world that have military establishments, the heads of such agencies are constantly planning for the next war. In the nature of things they must do so and, in planning, must have before them "the enemy" or "the enemies" against which the coming war is to be directed. Ideally, at the close of one war, the civil government should secretly designate "the enemy" or "the enemies" in the next war and supply the military with the appropriate men and equipment. Practically, in democratic countries, this is difficult, if not impossible, for the politicians are not always able to foresee events and contingencies; nor are they always certain that they can "swing" their party or the country into line with their predeterminations. In autocratic and totalitarian governments, political directors theoretically enjoy the power to assure their general staffs on the point of "the enemy" or "the enemies," but even they are uncertain as to contingencies in international relations and as to their own power against the possibility of a palace or popular revolt; besides an autocrat or dictator, whether a Czar or a Napoleon, is likely to be constantly disturbed by personal passions and vagaries which communicate confusion to the army managers.

Nevertheless, planning for the next war is a part of the business of every military establishment. Almost as long as bureaucracies and standing armies have existed, they have recommended themselves to their contemporaries and to posterity on the score of their prescience, as being able to plan for the future. One of the statemen's main qualities was said to be looking far ahead for the welfare of those who lacked such a gift. This claim has more often been raised on the Continent, as in Richelieu's *Testament politique,* than in the Anglo-Saxon world—one reason being possibly that in the latter the process of secularizing political thought was slower; Calvinist predestination excluded the self-praise of prescience. As a Scottish nobleman wrote home from Mainz in 1743: "There is a great deal of chance in all military affairs, and a weakness often attending the wisest heads to bring about the ends of providence." [57] Be it religious or be it wordly, both elements appear to mingle curiously in Marlborough, who declared: "Providence makes the wheel go round, and I hope the blessing of God will make us succeed much better than we can propose to ourselves." [58] This disinclination to claim prescience persists in the English, who will not cross the bridge before they get to it and who maintain that they gained their Empire in fits of absent-mindedness, whereas the Continentals managed to convince themselves that the Anglo-Saxon empires were achieved by carrying out logical lines of policies, perhaps in a Machiavellian planner's way. Whatever is most foreign to ourselves seems always most thoroughly planned.

On the Continent, Metternich claimed that he, as the *homme d'état* distinguished from the *homme d'affaires,* had "made politics a science and art according to rational method, which makes possible a computation of the future." Only his downfall, brought about by an unforseen revolution, shook Metternich's own trust in his ability to calculate the future in politics.[59] The last German Kaiser did not envisage his own downfall and the coming of war. On the eve of the war, he still pretended that the "gift of looking into the future occurs often among sovereigns, rarely among statesmen, almost never among diplomats." [60]

What the prescient military, like the civilian statesmen, have promised the peoples is, of course, security. In a way they early took it upon themselves as part of their governing function to furnish that consolation which Christ had promised: In this world you fear, but be confident I have overcome the world! Or as Mohammed more definitely assured the faithful. "God alone is great: I testify there are no gods, but God: and Mohammed is his Prophet. Come to prayer: come to security." Yet the governors of nations must take the precaution not to give their peoples an excessive feeling of safety. "If the peoples were too much at their ease, it would be impossible to hold them within the rules of their duty," wrote Richelieu, summing up his lifetime's experiences with giving and holding back security.[61]

The preferred militaristic way of utilizing the mass feeling of insecurity is through raising a scare, preferably that of a threatened invasion, and maintaining that a danger exists which none but expert generals can gauge. Since history is not written along such lines, it cannot be said how often the raising of such a scare has reason behind it. But it can be said that it is a permanent trick of any permanent military bureaucracy, early or late. Charles I wanted to use it in order to introduce the standing army in England, which Parliament did not intend to grant. To overcome their resistance, he maintained that an invasion of northern England by the Scots was impending and that "it was incumbent upon him to provide for the Defence of the Kingdom by raising sufficient forces to repel the attacks of his enemies. There was little probability that the Scots should think of invading England, if they were left unmolested; but it was necessary to excite the English with the dread of an imaginary danger." [62]

To such claims, general or specific, by absolutism and its bureaucracy, even such thinkers as Spinoza fell victim, when he conceded that whereas "liberty or strength of soul are the virtues of private persons, the virtue of the state is security." [63] With the growth of the secularization and capitalization of life, the craving for security grew and it provided the strongest *raison d'être* of standing armies, police, and other organs of security, in spite of the skepticism with which they were viewed by the freer minds. "You do believe then that the police agents foresee everything, know everything?" Napolon asked an officer of his entourage at Elba. "The police invents more than it discovers." [64]

And army officers have not been above such inventions. Perhaps the most notorious of fictions was manufactured shortly after Napoleon spoke. This was the pretended conspiracy of Lyons in 1817, in which figured one of the oldest generals of the Empire, Canuel, taken over by the Bourbons, distinguished by nothing but his cruelties in the Vendée, where he had marched for the Republic in blood up to his ankles, and afterward declared himself ready to wade in up to the knees for the Bourbons. Canuel conspired with a civilian prefect to uncover a vast "conspiracy," though only the slightest indications of it were available. Grossly overstating the seriousness of the troubles, which their own agents had largely started, they announced themselves the saviors of the kingdom. With ruthless illegality, they had an officer murdered whom they had "framed" as the head of a sham conspiracy because they feared he was going to uncover their own doings. Except by dismissal, none of the provocateurs was punished, and Marshal Marmont, the King's commissioner, demanded Canuel's head in vain.[65]

Meditating upon the fact that the men of his time became less ready for death and eternity while they were preparing for military death, it occurred to Pascal's Christian skepticism that men through their agitations more often fall into the pitfalls they seek to avert than attain the safety they try to prepare for:

When I have sometimes applied myself to consider the divers agitations of people, the perils and the pains to which they expose themselves, at the court, in war, out of which grow so many quarrels, enterprises bold and often bad, etc., I have found out that all the misery of people springs from one thing, which is, not knowing how to remain at ease, in a chamber. A man who has enough goods to live on, if he knows how to remain at home with pleasure, would never leave it in order to go across the seas or to the siege of a place. One would buy so dearly a commission in the army only because one finds it insufferable not to move out of town; and one seeks the conversations and the distractions of gambling only because one cannot remain at home with pleasure. . . . But when I have thought closer, there is one very effective reason which consists in the natural unhappiness of our feeble and mortal condition, so miserable that nothing can console us if we think of it from nearby.[66]

While Pascal's all-embracing understanding led to an all-forgiveness, the politically more activist thinkers of the eighteenth century found in plans for the case of war actual, positive causes of war. To the Abbé Galiani, forethought was the cause of the present wars of Europe: "If one would only take the trouble not to foresee anything, all the world would be tranquil, and I do not believe that one would be more unhappy because one would not make war." The Abbé was the open-eyed contemporary of wars such as those for Silesia, which Frederick concluded to make because he had so magnificent an instrument at hand in the Prussian army. Rereading Galiani some hundred years later, Nietzsche on the contrary was not afraid "to foretell a few things and thus, possibly, conjure up the cause of war." [67]

The history of armies planning for war follows two main lines of military endeavor: to know the enemy and to eliminate accident in war by having thought out and provided against eventualities, so that as little sphere as possible will be left for the vagaries of Fortuna. In order to know the enemy's strength or weakness and intentions, spying is necessary, either through accredited diplomats and attachés, through scanning war news and literature, or through regular spies. While piercing the enemy's secrets, one's own must be kept inviolable. "Above all other things," wrote Frederick, "the one who is to draw up a plan of operation must possess a minute knowledge of the power of his adversary and of the help the latter may expect from his allies. He must compare the forces of the enemy with his own numbers and those of his allies so that he can judge which kind of war he is able to lead or to undertake." [68] He must know the enemy's country or other possible theaters of war by acquiring maps, learning the depth of rivers, the capacity of bridges.

Obtaining information began to be considered of the greatest importance in the Renaissance, when a Frenchman wrote a novel for the military education of young noblemen, in which he recommended that a prince spend one-third of his income for spying.[69] Its development parallels that of general news reporting; in either case news had to be divested of its fabulous character. In wartime the enemy's movements and distribution of strength had to be found out by the most active spying, by reconnoitering, or aerial observation and subterraneous listening in—the latest developments enforced by the increasingly impenetrable character of the fronts. In 1914-18 the belligerents on the eastern front sent spies over the frozen lakes; in 1939-45 the air-drop became a favored method.

Through the advance in spying, the inner secrets of an enemy's plan become more and more readily available. Even the great Schlieffen Plan, laying out the German march through Belgium, was sold to the French General Staff, but was bought on the understanding that it was only a *Kriegsspiel,* a war-game problem. Driven by an obsession with their own offensive plans, the leading French generals planned for something quite different, whereas Schlieffen later had thought out for himself a "Schlieffen Plan" which the French might follow to meet his own. One single French general after him, in 1911, tried to match him in this, but the rest ignored the question. Again, the Russians, about 1905, got hold of a *Kriegsspiel* which was actually to be played against them in the First World War—Tannenberg.

It was not the fault of the spies that both these war games were not recognized as actual war plans, and if Kitchener, "by divination," had concluded that the Germans intended to carry their wide-sweeping campaign through Belgium, north of the Meuse, he either did not or could not persuade the French to take this plan seriously.[70]

Even so this invasion was expected by the Allies. Never is all the information offered, or even collected, by the intelligence departments put into service. That assembled in the British War Office on the Boers and the possible theater of war in South Africa, after the Jameson Raid, was not used when the actual Boer War came around.[71]

To be fully prepared, ready for every military contingency, is in the nature of things impossible. The general staffs have to restrict themselves and their plans and studies to the more probable operations. Even so, omissions of a most striking kind occur. This was illustrated when Foch admitted during the war that every part of France had been studied by the French Staff and himself as a theater of war—except French Flanders. "They never thought a French army would ever have to fight there." It has, on the other hand, become a stylistic feature in military biography to state that the hero in question, while employed in preparing for war, had worked out some plans which "were actually adopted during the war." [72] Such praise would appear much less impressive if the one scheme applied were contrasted with the many unapplied and unconsidered ones about which so little is heard afterward.

A balance of the errors, knowledge, and lucky guesses, on the part of the belligerents in the First World War, would include such items as these: no side thought that the war would last four years and over, and would call for such masses of material as it did, but rather that two to three months and three battles, with three hundred shells per gun, would suffice. The French reckoned with the German march through Belgium, but more in a general way than for their own specific countermeasures; the suppositions, however, on which the German General Staff had based its calculations of initial French movements, proved generally true. The calculations of the French about the initial strength of the German armies were wrong by 50 per cent; the Germans did not underestimate the potential help America could bring to the Allies, but they miscalculated the shipping available for a prompt transportation of American troops.[73]

After the data on the enemy, always fragmentary and incomplete, have been obtained and an idea of his intentions formed, comes the projection of one's own operations. For that, however, a profound knowledge of one's own country, its institutions and interests, is essential. This certainty is not so easily attained by the armies as would at first appear. Where the military profession, the political government, and the civilian bureaucracy have a tendency to grow apart, a reminder of the obvious is due:

The art of warfare and policy join hands in order to determine together the plan of war in general. Whosoever takes the one or the other alone for his guidance, goes astray. . . . How far, for instance, does a victorious attack lead? Is it permissible to follow it up as far as possible against all the enemies? A soldier who is nothing but a soldier, says: yes; the statesman, however, sees further and knows the limits which policy puts to conquests only too often. The success of arms does not blind him; he thinks of the princes whose interest suffers from the success, he offers them security, he lulls them to sleep. He does not make war unnecessarily general, and undertakes in time the steps which guarantee a safe permanent peace.

Hard as it is to believe, this advice was written by a soldier for the use of his colleagues.[74] And Clausewitz, observing tendencies to keep the military side of a great strategic operation separate from the policies, had to repeat with great earnestness: "War is no independent thing; the main lineaments of all great strategic plans are of a political nature, the more so the more they include the totality of war and the state." [75]

Through the mutual understanding of the war and the political departments, the future enemy is chosen, if indeed the former has not already selected one, or is not preparing for war with more nations than the latter has suspected. In Berlin, for instance, the General Staff thought, at least for a time after 1898, that a war with the United States was more probable or feasible than the Foreign Office did; the officers of the Staff were therefore pondering and preparing plans for such a war, including transportation, landing places, and so on; they supposed they would at least be prepared for a war with the "country of unlimited possibilities," [76] and against a shock like that experienced later by the British War Office, when the Doggerbank incident of 1904 revealed the "lack of definite and detailed plans for dealing with probable, and with possible, national emergencies that prevailed at that time." [77]

A peculiarly delicate point to arrange between military and political departments is the understanding between allies for the case of future war. It is a modern problem, largely dating from the Franco-Russian Alliance of 1892, and involves considering how closely the mechanism of mobilization and initial operations should be interlocked. In general, military departments naturally have wished for the closest and longest co-operation before the outbreak of war, thus obviating the traditional miseries of coalition warfare; but the diplomats have been loath to sign away so much freedom of action and to surrender it to an ally who might have an undue desire for war.

This reluctance was strong in both the armed camps into which Europe was divided before 1914. It was strongest under Bismarck, in his relations with Austria, whom he did not want to encourage in warlike ambitions by allowing close co-operation and conversations on the part of the two general staffs. It was weakest within the Franco-Russian Alliance. Yet in each case the party better prepared and armed for war lost a large part of its initiative for war or peace to the other party, which was more ready to undertake war than its military preparations made advisable. On both sides the rasher, weaker party was encouraged and allowed to take a perilous initiative.

The reluctance on the part of the diplomats and cabinets to see their respective countries too deeply involved in advance of war undeniably caused a military weakening of these alliances. There were, for instance, no fixed arrangements between Berlin and Vienna about the specific employment of the Allied forces, with the result that far too many Austro-Hungarian troops were sent against Serbia in August 1914.[78] Among the Entente Powers little thought had been given to the problem of how to maintain connections between East and West during a war; consequently Archangel, the only port that remained open, was not equipped before the war for receiving the shipments which the insufficiency of the Russian war industries made so urgently necessary. But the general political situation allowed France without specific understandings to withdraw all her troops from the Italian and Spanish borders and to calculate on an undisturbed transportation of her African troops.

Even the English with their disinclination to build bridges for future crossing had to decide certain objects for which army and expeditionary force existed—the general object of a mere maintenance of the balance of power in Europe being no longer sufficiently definite. Their generals, insisting on "the absolute necessity for our mobilizing the same day as the French," held conversations about the case of war with the latter and the Belgians; their naval attachés conferred with the Russians. Haldane thought that "by organizing, war may be prevented." But, because it might mean conscription, he was against "an alliance with France for the specific case of German aggression," which Henry Wilson was advocating for reasons of greater military efficiency. Conscription could be introduced in England only in the midst of war, and after such violent experiences as the invasion of Belgium by the Germans. Only in wartime could it be imposed, liberals thought before 1914, and that, Henry Wilson told them, would be too late.[79] Certain kinds of nonpreparedness, for instance, that of the British public for the invasion of Belgium, are equivalent to a vast amount of military equipment.

When the army leader is penetrated by the guiding principles of his country's policies, acquainted with the policies of the prospective enemies, and in possession of sufficient information concerning his own country's and his enemy's strength and designs, he may proceed to the conception and elaboration of a plan of action as the basis of all preparations for commencing a war. It may be tested somewhat through operative studies and peacetime maneuvers. Test mobilizations, however, have been discarded as too apt to have political consequences. The effect of accident and chance has to be put off as far as possible. Up to 1914 the mobilization plan was a schedule which, indeed, functioned undisturbed within the reach of one's own railway system, but which, soon after the initial movements, was somewhat disturbed by the independent will of the enemy. In subsequent wars, this moment could not be postponed so long owing to the growth of aviation; the troop trains could not leave their home stations unmolested; the period of noninterference was incalculably shortened.

For the period prior to 1914, the elder Moltke's thought about the initial movements in war is classical:

In every operation our will is soon met by the independent will of the adversary. The latter we may limit, when we are ready for and resolved to take the initiative, but we cannot break it, except through the medium of tactics, through battle. The material and moral consequences of every large battle are, however, of such far-reaching kind, that through them usually a completely changed situation is created, a basis for new measures. No plan of operations reaches with any certainty beyond the first encounter with the enemy's main force.

Moltke warded off the immoderate expectations which the public in a society with little faith in planning, be it divine or socialistic, continued to put in military plans: "Only the layman believes that he sees in the course of a war the accomplishment of an original idea, conceived beforehand, considered in all details and adhered to until the end." [80] Ever is the militarism of modern nations ready to trust the plans of the general. Hindenburg was popularly believed to have spent his vacations in the lake and swamp regions around Tannenberg, into which he drove the Russian armies, and to have been selected for this special knowledge. In fact, he became commander of the German eastern forces merely because he was next on the waiting list and would suit the imperious temperament of the chief of staff chosen for him, Ludendorff.

Again, after the First World War, the idea spread that Foch, "in his far-seeing, superior strategy," had consented or even invited the Germans in May 1918, to occupy the salient of Château-Thierry. The same American general who attributes this notion to the desire of laymen to admire heroes, himself indulged in the idea that the Germans had chosen far ahead, during peacetime visits of officers, the exact points which they held in the autumn of 1918 in the

Pont-à-Mousson sector not far from the Franco-German boundary.[81] A modern Oxenstierna would have to remark: "You cannot believe with what little planning the world is governed."

What is more: there is inherent risk in war plans—namely, the temptation to see in the prepared program the sole condition of success and thereby become its victim. Against this obsession Napoleon warned when he declared he had never had a plan of operations—which of course he did have, at least to cover initial movements and the broad aim.[82] The still greater risk is to plan for the future war merely in terms of past wars, to expect recurrent features of former campaigns. A caution was given by the Marshal Saxe about peacetime generals: "When they come to the command of armies, they are all new and in default of knowing how to do what is necessary, they do what they know." A similar warning was uttered in 1909 by Lieutenant Colonel E. Mayer, one of the antagonists of Foch:

We ought to teach our future army chiefs that they will enter into a campaign without knowing according to which rules the war will be made. Battles will take charge of teaching them, provided that they are still capable of learning, which is to say, provided that they have intelligence, free and open, that they have judgment and resolution, and that, moreover, their army has discipline. . , . The unforeseen is what has to be foreseen the most.[83]

Actually before 1914 the foreseeable war was overlooked, as if through a concerted determination to avoid looking into its Gorgon face. The war plans were conceived as if to avoid thinking about the probability of a stalemate of nations, along positions and trenches. An imaginary picture took form—a picture of a war in which Germans and French were to interpenetrate one another's territories, flanking and wheeling, charging and feinting. But the true picture of the coming war would have been a head-on collision, after which both parties remained with interlocked bumpers, unable to move for years.

The freezing of the fronts in the First World War reduced the planning of strategic motion to a minimum and introduced another sort: the planning of destruction engineering, the investment of material against men and men against materials, both on the largest scale possible. The way to exclude accidents which might prove fatal was then largely sought in an extra application of materials and men. If the plan failed, nevertheless, there was a strong inclination on the part of generals to ascribe it to perfidious outside influences, generally of a civilian character. This charging of misadventure to others ranged in scope from Haig's accusation that a *Times* report had drawn the German fire upon an English artillery observation point during the fluctuating battle at Festubert in 1915,[84] to Ludendorff's wholesale "stab-in-the-back" accusation. The groundwork for such a sweeping legend was laid in the Allied armies as well as the armies of the Central Powers. When Joffre, himself only a moderately successful general, felt compelled to admit the loss of morale in the French army after the bloody failure of Nivelle's offensive in 1917, he attributed this loss "to the changes in command and to the active interference of the politicians." [85] The military alibi and counteraccusation can be clearly observed.

The Vision of the Short War

Whereas socialist critics of military affairs, long before 1914, in common with a very few military writers, pictured the coming war as a long-drawn-out butchery, the existing armies imagined it as an operation which was in part, at least, planned and would soon be over. Armies of conservative, if not reactionary, professionals were serving a more or less liberal order of society and economy and accordingly thought out war plans which this society and economy would be able to stand. Schlieffen was sure that protracted wars were "impossible at a time when the existence of the nation is based on an uninterrupted functioning of commerce and industry and when by a quick decision the machinery brought to a stop must be started again. A wearing-out strategy cannot be undertaken at a time when the maintenance of millions calls for billions." [86] The French General Staff and Foch in his *Principes de la guerre* did not reckon any more than the Germans on a war of long duration. The governing school of military thought everywhere believed in the brief conflict and prepared for that. Only a small and uninfluential minority thought otherwise of war of the twentieth century; the older Moltke had as early as 1890 expressed the fear that it might become a Seven Years' or even a Thirty Years' War.[87]

The prospect of such wars the civilians would not face. They seemed only willing to take upon their nation and its economy a war which would leave a margin of men, money, and materials to spare. Liberal parliaments authorized large armies in the fond hope that they would quickly decide the war. As Thiers said in 1873: "The war ought to be made by the active army," that is, not by the armed nation. Resting on the belief in a short war, parliaments were the more ready to leave to professionals the organization of the army and the planning of future strategy. Sharing this expectation, the professionals created carefully trained armies of limited numbers, aiming, as the general presiding over the *Comité d'infanterie* said in 1913, if possible "to enter upon the campaign without reservists." By comparison, the French relied more upon the barracks army and esteemed the reservists less than the Germans; the faith in the *troupier* which had misled them before 1870 still persisted.

Having organized such troops, the military planned to make a war in the image of the barracks army. And they gave to the bourgeois the picture of a limited and professionalized war in a manner that persuaded him to accept their plans of a short and violent offensive, whereas he probably would have spurned the idea of a tenacious, prolonged, and exhaustive defensive.

A military writer and deputy, Driant, at the end of 1912, gave the Chamber of Deputies this ferocious and yet hopeful, and thus Darwinian, vision of the best possible army and war:

The victorious army will be the one which, scornful of reserves and fortresses, will first jump at the throat of the enemy and will at once obtain the moral superiority that forces the events. And nothing indicates that for such purpose hundreds of thousands of men are needed. The first great battle will decide the war and the war will be short. It is necessary that the concept of the offensive penetrate the soul of our nation. It is therefore necessary that all the solicitude of the country and of the government be directed toward the active army.[88]

True to form, the bourgeoisie, economical, eager for limited liability in all things, recognized in the promise of a good, hard but short, heroic war, a philosophy that promised something for almost nothing—victory as the result of moral training, which the military took upon themselves, and not at the price of all worldly goods, as the yet only dimly suspected "total war" would soon demand. Said Foch: "Victory equals will power. A battle won is a battle in which one declines to admit being beaten. . . . Victory goes always to those who merit it by the greatest force of will and intelligence." [89] The way to victory was through the attack, and that only; the attack was victory more than half won. Not: attack when and where you are strongest, but: attack always and everywhere. The offensive thus took on a value of its own; it became an article of faith, especially with the devout Catholic Foch. "Those are happy who are born believers, but they are few," he said one day, teaching and trying to suggest to his audience that belief is acquired through will power, like muscles, like instruction.[90]

This belief was in its nature utterly religious in that it considered the material side of warfare, at least before August 1914, to be comparatively unimportant or irrelevant. If will power failed to overcome bullets, the slain soldier was yet saved, religiously. It is not surprising that this Catholic general, whose brother was a Jesuit priest, had a feudal background or allure—through his marriage he acquired a château. Nor is it surprising that he was chosen for the directorship of the Ecole de Guerre, the central institution for indoctrination, by Clemenceau, the iron-willed skeptic, the anti-Vatican politician to whom the swamp odor of Panama was still clinging. Hoping to make use of the militant Christian, Clemenceau told Foch: "You will make good officers for us; the rest does not count." [91] But did it not count?

The offensive à outrance doctrines of Foch, overworked if possible by his successors at the Ecole de Guerre and by the Command, lost France 664,000 dead in the sixteen months from August 1, 1914 to November 30, 1915, as against 683,000 in the thirty-five months from then to the armistice, or 156,000 per month in August and September 1914, as against 27,500 for the monthly average from July to November 1918.[92] After the offensive policy had had its full tryout—"glorious to us but without great profits," as the conventional French historians write about it—soldiers mutinied and civilians and nonprofessionals reclaimed direction of the war in 1917. "An end must be put to ambitions and bold plans, the grand appearance of which only poorly hides emptiness and lack of preparation," declared War Minister Painlevé publicly in July 1917; an end must be made to pretended Napoleonic concepts which in a few days waste and cut to pieces armies made out of nations in arms. Thereafter Pétain, the "military economist," was to prevail with his guiding idea, "to let the enemy take the initiative of attack and then act yourself on the counteroffensive." He was a general with a business sense of realities, material and psychological, and an appreciation of the means which the industries put at the disposal of the generals.[93]

In fine, with a short war in mind, the military men in prewar years selected and adopted some so-called experiences of warfare between 1871 and 1914, and utterly failed to see other and supreme lessons. The Russo-Japanese War seemed to be a war of normal duration, about one year. It seemed to prove that war could not last very much longer, for the Japanese were weak financially and the Russians had a revolution at home. The noncomparables with Western countries were overlooked, namely, that in a European war the richest and most stable nations would be involved. The general staffs thought so little of this aspect that they would say, with General Mordacq, *"L'argent, on en trouve toujours"*—there will always be money.[94] They had read Clausewitz on how to make war without money, or remembered experiences of the American and French revolutions, without realizing that, in the meantime, money had become stabilized on the basis of gold, and that creditor nations in an age of Liberalism could not accept financial anarchy.

It appears that only the civilian bureaucracy was to some extent prepared for eventualities in this field. According to Helfferich, the Ministry of Finance in Germany was expecting financial mobilization. But the military bureaucracy was far from reckoning with economic and financial preparations. The general staffs made a few proposals touching vague industrial or economic plans for war and then rested on this alibi. Apparently obtaining, storing, and distributing foodstuffs, raw materials, training workers, redirecting industry and commerce—all that did not belong under the military categories and was not worthy of the closest military consideration. No plans for manufacturing war machines were included in the mobilization plans: the French powder factories, though state owned, received no minute instructions for mobilization day; they were merely expected to go on producing along the old lines. The circumstance that a vital chemical like phenol was coming from Germany was ignored.[95]

In the selective process which the closed mind of army leaders applied to the study and judgment of recent warfare itself, certain features were excluded. Trench warfare was by no means a novelty; trenches had been used at Plevna in 1877, in the Boer War, in Manchuria, in the Balkan Wars. A French colonel wrote after the War of 1904-5: "The combatants had to have recourse to the movement of vast masses of earth; they have disappeared from the battlefield. . . . The trench is the shield of the moderns."

Even earlier, in 1902, Emile Mayer published in the *Revue militaire suisse* an article on the future war which no French military journal would have published, for in it he smashed the official image of the future war by delineating it as a war of trenches, of inviolable fronts,

putting face to face two human walls, almost in contact, only separated by the depth of danger, and this double wall will remain almost inert, in spite of the will of either party to advance, in spite of the attempts to achieve this. Unable to succeed in front, one of these lines will try to outwing the other. The latter, in its turn, will prolong its front, and it will be a competition about who will be able to reach farthest. . . . The line will stop at a *point d'appui*, at a sea, at mountains, at the frontier of a neutral nation. From this moment on, there will be so to speak no reason for the fight to stop, at least for one side. Exterior circumstances [the entrance of the United States into the European War!] will bring the end of the purely defensive war of the future.

Another truthful picture of the future war was depicted later by the French Colonel Montaigne in 1912: war will assume the features of a siege war, in which perfection of technique, power of material, and abundance of supplies, combined with perseverance and tenacity of the fighters, will play the main role; the battles will be weeks in duration, probably close to a frontier, and will possibly degenerate into a barbarian battle *d'usure,* in which the victory will go to the people best able to feed the combat, to throw the last soldier into the furnace. "The battle will be decided by exhaustion." [96]

In spite of many such warnings, planners for the First World War went on the old way. In many regiments on both sides of the Vosges, the recruits of autumn 1913 had never used a spade for digging in, not to speak of forming regular trenches and positions, before August 1914. To the commands, even the cheap ground around military camps seemed too precious for that. When a pupil of Schlieffen draws from this neglect the consoling conclusion that it had been a common fault of all parties to overestimate the war of movements in relation to the war of position,[97] he leaves unmentioned the fact that this form of warfare had been elaborately pointed out to the several general staffs in time.

Nor did the general staffs more effectively foresee that the use of munitions would be incomparably larger than ever before, or the need of much heavier artillery, or the utility of arms like bomb-throwers and mine-throwers, which had been applied long before in the siege of Port Arthur. So also the use of barbed wire was overlooked, although the war in South Africa had taught combatants the value of this material when they chanced to find it available in large amounts—the frontier of Western civilization thus adding a new element to warfare. Another warning sign—the invisibility of the armies—was neglected. That feature of warfare had grown to an alarming degree in South Africa and Manchuria. Kuropatkin "could not see anything; he maneuvered in the dark." Still knowledge of this invisibility did not stir the armies of prewar Europe to develop new ways of scouting. Aviation remained a kind of sport. If the younger Moltke was in favor of the airplane rather than the airship, this did not signify a strong and systematic support for aviation in the German army.

Invisibility on the battlefield, which the French declined to increase by surrendering their historical red pantaloons, merely supplied new arguments for prolonging the existence of vast masses of cavalry as scouting forces. True, the Russian cavalry had proved a failure in 1904-5, but that was thought a Russian failure merely, not of cavalry as such. Cavalry, the military thought, must not be reduced; it needed only to be reorganized. Reorganization would be difficult enough, however, considering the "rider spirit, opposed to the war on foot. For the ancient school, putting a foot on the ground is downfall. It sees in horsemanship an aim whereas it is only a means. From that follows its obsession with races, horse-shows, carousels, and its disdain for shooting. The public, fascinated by the spectacles which it supplies, pushes it further along this way." But the reorganized cavalry, though with such fantastic hangovers as the hussars or cuirassiers sheared off, would more than ever be called for, it was fancied, because of the long fronts along which the modern and future battles would be fought.[98] For such vagaries there was no excuse. General Max Hoffmann, sent out as a young officer by the German General Staff to observe the war in the Far East in 1904-5, found the actual war very different from the idea he had brought along. He resolved to report home faithfully what he had seen, but was apparently not convinced that "the people in Berlin," his superiors, would learn anything from what the people out there did. Among the people in Berlin was the younger Moltke, who found this kind of warfare "miserable on both sides. . . . There was never such a crazy way of making war as long as the world has stood." [99] In spite of ample warnings, the General Staff, whether in Berlin, Paris, or anywhere else, did not envisage even the possibility of such a war being repeated in the West in the different circumstances provided by rich nations. Uppermost in the military minds was the thought: such a war *cannot happen* here, rather than a conscious determination: such a war *must not happen* here. A widely read German military handbook announced *ex cathedra* in 1911:

That the long-drawn-out frontal battles of the Manchurian War should repeat themselves, that they furnish the example of future warfare, is only to be expected under the improbable supposition of similar fundamental conditions. This disposes of the often heard prophecy that in the future, as in the Russo-Japanese War, the battle around fortified field positions, which even in Manchuria could not obtain decisive importance, will have first rank.[100]

At the end of an inquiry into military planning, the supreme historical question is this: did the unwillingness to look the coming war in the face, though it had been outlined already, and the hope— as yet reasonable in 1905—of avoiding it by some such strategical scheme as Schlieffen's plan, form a conscious part in the psychological and tactical preparation for the First World War? The importance of this question is reinforced by the circumstance that a general realization of the character of the coming war ought to have spread a conviction that this kind of combat would be unendurable and ruinous to victor and vanquished; instead the prospect of war was greeted by the military cheerfully and with a light heart.

Military imagination in those cheerful days apparently ran only as far as victory. It applied little forethought to defeat. It gave little consideration to the disorganization, confusion, and political consequences, revolutionary and otherwise, that might accompany the wreckage. Schlieffen was comparatively farsighted when he conceived that the purpose of his plan was to avoid a second Jena for Prussia. But that a second Jena would mean the revolution for the defeated nation, the military did not tell the people, if indeed they thought of it or any other disastrous upshot. That might have had a deterrent effect on ministerial and popular willingness to undertake a war.

The Military Utility of Ex-Soldiers' Organizations and Special Leagues

In casting about for outside support to the military or militaristic policies deemed desirable, the directors of military establishments, particularly since the middle of the nineteenth century, have relied increasingly upon organizations of veterans and ex-soldiers. They took arms out of the arsenal of their own original enemy, liberalism, by making use of the freedom of press, speech, and association, once these achievements had been won, largely against military wishes.

Although military men are often disgusted with the necessity that compels them to argue their case with anybody, in the press or on the platform, and to make "popular" appeals, they recognize the necessity and accept it, especially when they are on the defensive. Accustomed to run that portion of society which, apart from the prison population, is under the most constant and effective restraint, military men prefer to give orders, but they can, if necessary, negotiate and make appeals to other men not actually in the army.

In so doing, of course, they feel more at home in dealing with ex-soldiers, especially when the latter are well organized and under the management of a limited circle which dominates the rank and file. After all, veterans are united by memories of past wars and other service. They long for honors which the forgetful general public is inclined to withhold. They have interests that seem to be neglected by civilians. They know the value of material equipment from bitter experience and are inclined to support every demand for still more lavish equipment to be given to future comrades-in-arms.

The earliest of such ex-soldiers' organizations—leaving aside the veterans' corporations in the Roman camp towns (*canabae*)—were those of officers, such as the Order of the Cincinnati in the United States. Interest and the memory of a—perhaps only comparatively —glorious past life drew them together more easily than the recollection of unrelieved hardships brings privates into societies. After 1815 one of the generals who had served under Wellington without sharing the Duke's politics, Thomas Graham (Lord Lynedoch), planned a General Military Club for army officers. The government, not at all eager to see an organization grow up containing the germs of a military menace to civilian supremacy, disliked the plan at first, for a body "so extensive, so exclusively military, having at its head the Prince Regent and the Commander-in-Chief, might be objectionable, either in approving or censoring, supporting or opposing" military measures pending in Parliament. A compromise was arranged by the founding of the United Service Club (1817), in which the two branches of the armed forces in a way balanced each other.[101]

It needed that romanticism of mass thought and mass feeling which appeared after the Napoleonic wars, combined with mutual aid tendencies, to lead common soldiers into forming organizations. By 1840, however, the leaders of the pre-March army in Prussia thought such bodies could be quite useful for perpetuating and spreading military spirit. They apparently ascertained that the ex-soldiers, who felt the urge to combine on the basis of their common experiences in the armies, would not be the type to oppose military service and institutions. Once the men had left the service, much as they might have grumbled under it, they seemed glad to romanticize the soldier's life—a life that had taken many a man farther away from his home than he could ever have moved on his own volition. And this romanticism encouraged others to long for the same experience which, after its termination, in retrospect, looked so "wholesome."

The Prussian government recognized this positive feeling as a sign that the nation was becoming satisfied with the military institutions, and a Cabinet order of 1842 told the Kriegervereine (Warriors' Societies) how to organize themselves.[102] The government thus won these societies as auxiliaries for military and other authoritarian purposes, particularly in the villages and small towns where they included a larger percentage of the ex-service men than in the cities, and were led by conservatives rather than liberals. Everywhere the latter were more inclined to join the Schützenvereine (Riflemen's Associations) which, before 1870 in Germany, carried on ancient burgher militia traditions combined with tendencies for German unification. Hence the Riflemen's Associations were not always so much in step with the policy of the Prussian government as the Kriegervereine.[103]

The German ex-service men's organizations served as antiliberal auxiliaries, first, by spreading among the masses the military arguments for each and every army bill and other measures pleasing to the military; secondly, by keeping alive the memory of late battles and the hatred of France. They were "the standing armies of Saint Sedan," as the *Frankfurter Zeitung* called them, when it was proposed to make the anniversary of this battle a national holiday.[104] Still later, with even greater vehemence and under the patronage, that is, supervision and guidance, of ex-officers, they were turned into antisocialist units, excluding everyone known to be a member of the Social Democratic Party.

In the Continental countries, these societies acted as parade troops, originally in civil garb, reviewed by the authorities of the military and civilian bureaucracy. It was the Japanese who first bound closely and systematically with the army all the reservist associations, including the Reserve Officers' Association, which existed in nearly every place and numbered three million members in the 1930's. These associations preserve "the spiritual training" received in the army, the spirit of camaraderie; they impart it to their neighbors, instilling the elementals of military training into the young recruit before he is called to the colors. Their official purpose is "the development of the military spirit and the promotion of military efficiency which in turn will promote social welfare, encourage virtuous customs and habits, and guarantee the stability of national defence." From time to time they are visited by the commander of the military district, who offers guidance through patriotic speeches.[105]

Far more autonomous in their tendencies and aspirations, less obedient to the army, more self-assertive in their desires, have been the veterans and ex-service men's organizations in the United States, such as the Grand Army of the Republic and the Confederate Veterans, or the later Military Order of Foreign Wars of the United States, founded in 1894, the Military Order of the Carabao, and others. The Grand Army included nearly all the veterans of the North; as far as it was an auxiliary of the Republican Party, it received in this quality a consideration—the generous pensions granted to veterans.[106]

More clearly auxiliaries of the armies have been the different types of societies which grew up in the years immediately preceding or following the outbreak of the First World War: the army leagues in the different countries; the Wehrverein in Germany; the Army League and National Service League in Britain, with Lord Roberts at its head and sixty thousand members in 1911; the Ligue pour la service des trois ans in France; the Reserve Officers' Association in Japan; the National Security League and the American Defense Society in the United States.

Most of these societies were apparently founded in imitation of the navy leagues in the various countries, following the English precedent. Being the modern arm and less in the public eye than the armies, the navies had felt it necessary to establish contacts with the public through extraparliamentary groups. In imitation, the new military societies, headed by retired officers and an occasional ex-private, promoted and spread the wishes, hopes, and mentality of the army through civilian political agitation. In practical effect this amounted usually to supporting larger army bills and condemning those actually passed as "completely inconceivable in their short-comings," to use the language of General Keim, founder of the Wehrverein.

Close contact with the armies was established as a rule by admitting ex-officers to the direction of such leagues, men like General Keim, at the head of the Wehrverein, one of the several off-shoots of that imperialistic holding company, the Pan-German League,[107] specifically dedicated to "awakening the whole nation to an understanding of the need for a larger army and of realizing this demand by the pressure of public opinion on the parties of the government." [108] In the United States, the National Security League was organized as late as December 1914. Thus the United States was in this, as in so many military fields, a newcomer, but its leagues made up in speed and zest anything they lacked in the way of historic traditions.

While officers have frequently provided the leadership in these associations, the armament industries, occasionally at least and perhaps often, have helped to provide for their financing. They have done so openly or secretly, depending on the different purposes and tactics of such groups. At least enough is known of the methods and financing of the different army and navy leagues in various countries to warrant the conclusion that the organizations which are directly affiliated with the armies and work openly for their interest are less heavily subsidized by industrial money than societies with vaguer objectives, such as the Air League of the British Empire and the Hands Off Britain Air Defense League, the British Chemical Warfare Defense League, and the United States National Chemical Defense Association. These special associations were little more than screens for the promotion of interested air-mindedness or gas-mindedness.[109]

Sometimes those who started such "ginger groups" and raised the cry "England, Awake!" made use of a double screen, that is, operated under cover through bona fide veterans' organizations, as well as their own organizations. For example, the National Chemical Defense Association once induced the American Legion to serve as the less obvious pressure agency in working on legislators and other persons.[110] And army leagues and national security leagues have not been at all above accepting help from armaments interests.[111] However conceived and operated, not to say manipulated, the innumerable veterans' and other military associations may be, in fact they constitute, powerful agencies for the protecting and promoting of military interests within the state. For their purposes, the military have made ample use of the credit acquired through past martial performances by the veterans, even though the majority of actual ex-service men hardly ever prove organizable. Reliance upon such auxiliaries, however, in turn affects army thought, strengthening conservative tendencies. Content with small, easily led groups of veterans, officers may avoid an appeal to the nation as a whole, the source of real war-power. Moreover, looking and pointing backward to the past war, now almost romantically familiar, the military may more readily forget to turn forward to the unknown, the unpredictable aspects of the next war, thus making it possible for civilian governments and generals alike to blunder once again into a "shape of things" utterly beyond their imagination.

By comparison, the old-style veterans' organizations were far more innocuous, manageable, and peaceful than those other post-1918 mass aggregations in which not a little of veteran sentiment and also interest was stirring—the fascist parties. The military directors, as distinguished from other officers, had not originally wanted them or conceived of them as they arose. A supreme army politician like Von Seeckt, realizing as early as 1916 that veterans' organizations had been poorly used before 1914, thought it "the main thing to preserve the public-spiritedness produced by the army and the war . . . the equality of duty. . . . It is really essential to found a labor party which does not want to attain its aims in a revolutionary fashion, which remains national and co-operates in a decent manner." [112] At most times, Seeckt must have realized, the Nazi Party did not live up to his specifications. A somewhat like-minded general, Pétain, proceeded from the vantage point of Vichy to make the French Legion—the one and only union of the veterans of the two world wars, with a membership of some 1,200,000—the one-party political organization for his interim regime.[113]

The at least potential power of veterans and their organizations in America, daringly challenged by Senator Kennedy's statement that "the leadership of the American Legion has not had a constructive thought since 1918," is indicated by the fact that as of 1956 "about one out of three male citizens between 18 and 50 is a veteran," which places their various organizations together with the National Guard Association "among the most powerful lobbies in the country." [114]

If the writings of statesmen are to be taken at face value, the supreme object of governments previous to the First World War was national security. They were, of course, concerned with matters of domestic welfare and with pushing "national interests" abroad, but all made the attainment of national security their supreme goal. Without security, domestic welfare seemed to be a shadow and the pursuit of foreign commerce or other international objectives fruitless. And how was this security to be won and held? Assuming that actions do speak louder than words, the generally accepted answer was that made by the most powerful and active interest within the state, namely, the organized and consolidated military, with the congeries of supply interests attached to the army and navy. This answer on its face seemed to be less complicated and less difficult than that advanced by the internationalists who look to conferences, treaties, leagues, and tribunals of arbitration and adjudication as offering a way to security for all.

11

The Military as Guarantors of National Security

Armament "Insurance" and War Scares

The very simplicity and apparent feasibility of the military answer made the prewar world almost blind to the fact that the piling up of explosives, armies and navies and their equipment, diplomacies and ideologies, might endanger the safety and tranquillity of the very states and societies which accumulated them. Of all the competition filling this world, that for more security was the hardest to restrict. Where business formed cartels and trusts on an international basis to cut out wasteful and destructive competition, states merely heightened it continuously.

Interests faring well under international arrangements for curtailing competition proposed a similar procedure to the states competing in armaments; the older interests of the nineteenth century that counseled such restriction were those identified with banking capital working on an international basis, like the Rothschilds. Later the internationally combined electric industries also proceeded from the basis of their good results to recommend to governments an imitation of their disarmament. "It is certainly difficult, but by no means hopeless," Rathenau, representing the German electric industry, wrote in 1911, "to find ways to soften the warlike tension by way of apportionment, and seen in this light the thought of disarmament is no utopia." [1] But such interests were not strong enough to impose their concepts in the field of armaments, for they ran counter within the national economy to the armament industries.

The utmost which the industrial armament interests were willing to concede in the line of international agreements was the proposition to raise national armaments before sitting down at the conference table where international curtailment was to be discussed. Stumm, an ironmaster and armor plate manufacturer, for whom there were "no more productive expenditures than those for the army," proposed, before the first Hague Conference, that Germany, in order to be well prepared for a percentage reduction, arm at once and strongly and thus be ready to stand the cut.[2] When disarmament in the air threatened the aircraft industry in England, one of the English spokesmen approached the problem in a similar way: "Disarmament in fact is not negotiated; it is dictated by the strongest Powers. Once we have the strongest Air Force we shall be able to call a halt in competition and then only shall we of the industry be able to turn our activities to the genuine development of aircraft for purposes of peace." [3]

The majority of parliaments seemed satisfied when sufficient money had been granted for "adequate" defense, whatever that might mean, and the funds had been well spent by the armies. To assure them of this was a main function of the war ministers. When a war minister told his parliament that the country was safe, that the army was prepared for all eventualities, that if the enemy should attack and invade he would be met by strong defense legions, the members shouted back at the reassuring minister, as in France: "It does us good to hear you, General!" [4] If such a picture of the future war was somewhat less comforting to parliamentarians and electors, at least the more official view of that war and the preparations for it were more cheerful than the substitute projects which were available but did not receive official approval.

From the generals, at least, parliamentarians received assurances on security. Schlieffen and his school imagined that the future war would be one more pleasing, more in harmony with the general belief in progress than past wars. Whether looking backward or forward, whether conceiving war plans or writing war history, the official forecast was optimistic. General Bonnal, a one-time director of the Ecole de Guerre, wrote in 1910 that modern war owes everything to Bonaparte, that it had regained the character of bloody energy which it had lost under the humanitarianism of the second half of the eighteenth century: "The more violent war is, the shorter its duration and the longer are the periods of peace. War on the Napoleonic model marks, therefore, a progress of humanity." [5]

The military men themselves had gone no further than the parliamentarians in connecting their war plans and policies with security. No military thought in the prewar time, at all events of any systematic character, was concerned with the idea of how a society would look or should be shaped, to be productive of the greatest possible military potency in defense. Altogether the politics of the army, or rather of its officers, in that era was the politics of the specific interests associated with the parties favorable to the military, which granted their demands most readily and criticized them least. If such interests held back, the military could always foment alarms about insecurity in order to obtain larger budgets and overcome the resistance of frightened parliamentarians.

From time to time, it is true, protests were made against war scares. One was openly ventured by Lord Salisbury, whose personal appearance at the Berlin Congress of 1878 displeased Bismarck and made the Iron Chancellor wish that he could have had the noble Lord in the hands of a noncom for half an hour daily in order to give the representative of Great Britain a better carriage.[6] With startling simplicity Salisbury made the annoying remark: "If you believe the doctors, nothing is wholesome; if you believe the theologians, nothing is innocent; if you believe the soldiers, nothing is safe." [7] But beyond the desire to secure the largest possible organization and the largest possible appropriations—beyond shaping their organizing and spending on plans conceived in traditional images—the political vision of army leaders did not go. It was hardly wider than that of racketeers who, for the price of extending "protection," tax those who need it as far as the traffic can bear.

Prepossessed by the politics of their class and surroundings, military men before 1914 had commonly avoided the question whether, with the highest military efficiency in view, a society should be conservative, liberal or socialist; they did not consider how wealth should be distributed, how education should be given, how and where industries should be organized, with reference to the utmost military strength. No such conception existed among the military who talked of "national security." They were actuated only by vague wishes, such as that embodied in Schlieffen's warning of 1909: "For the future battle, be it led with arms in hand or with the help of other means, at least to the outside world a united people of brothers is necessary as well as a great, strong, powerful army, led by a strong hand and filled with absolute confidence." [8]

Instead of thinking about ultimate potentials, armies undertook to "sell" themselves as institutions of security to the civilians of their countries, who did not want to live dangerously, except now and then. The salesmen employed the argument of the insurance agent. As accepted by a civilian and co-bureaucratic political scientist, it ran as follows in 1872: "The value of an army does not consist in what it produces, but rather in the protection and safeguarding of production it provides. . . . If a nation does not care to support its own army, it will be forced to support that of the enemy. . . . The army is the insurance of peace, the army budget the premium which a nation pays for its civilian and economic independence." Put on an actuarial basis, this premium is paid in countries with conscription in the form of one to one and a half years of the male's lifetime. For an average family life of thirty years, beginning from the moment when the male marries, this amounts to an insurance premium of from 3 to 4 per cent of the value of his total economic existence. The premium a nation pays against the danger of war amounts to about half of the premium paid on a capital insured against death; still it protects not only the original capital, but also the acquisition of a second, new capital.[9]

This argument was well received by parliaments, for it served to cover up the fact that armies often created insecurity at the time they were presumed to be providing security. It also strengthened the bourgeois habit of continuing to pay premiums on any insurance policy once entered, lest it lapse. It turned attention away from the fact that armies and affiliated groups were concerned with securing their own existence first and foremost, and with the broader and far from certain national "security" second, if at all.

Although the nations talked of security as need and ideal through the period before the First World War, they never believed they had attained it. The older sense of established safety had vanished and the nineteenth century was swept by spasmodic war panics. The first of these great fears with a military significance arose in the country which was *per se* the safest, namely, England, where in 1847 there opened the series of war scares recurring in the years 1852, 1859-60, 1884, 1889, and 1892-3. In each case the alarmist cry rang out that the country was threatened by French naval increases or plans for such increases designed for the invasion of England. In each case it was subsequently disclosed that no such plans had existed. In some, if not all of these frights, the union of interests was obvious to some of the English people. Thus Cobden detected in the war panic of 1847 the persuasion on the part of "Mr. Pigou, the gunpowder maker, that the French were actually going to attack us." [10] A better expert on military affairs, Joseph Hume, thought it was engineered by half-pay officers in the London clubs.[11] The war alarm of 1892 was a factor in the retirement of Gladstone; having "uniformly opposed militarism" for the sixty years he had been in politics, though he had made limited concessions in the scares of 1860 and 1884, he declined to become as terrified as the majority of his Cabinet by the threats of the opposition. But Parliament doubled the annual expenditure for the navy; as against three million pounds it rose to seven million pounds.[12]

Strange as it may seem, Great Britain originated the modern terror created by the dread of insecurity. This may be charged to the industrial crises which rocked that nation. Sir John Fortescue pictures how the armed forces used such situations: "Civil not less than military administrators wait for what is called a 'war scare' in order to fasten this or that improvement upon a reluctant nation; and actual war serves this purpose still better." [13] Either allied with the bureaucracy or on its own motion, the party in opposition often produced an alarm by accusing the party in power of neglecting the country's defense; in turn, that party might be allied with the armaments interests always so ardent for additional orders that they are not above creating popular fears on their own initiative, in the style of Mr. Mulliner and Herr von Gontard.

Watching such advantage taken of useful insecurity, members of Gladstone's last Cabinet protested. The Chancellor of the Exchequer, Sir William Harcourt, battling with the Admiralty in 1893 over the large program, declared that the true facts of Britain's position were obscured "by the lying statements of *The Times*. . . . The principle of the alarmists is to pile up every conceivable contingency, probable or improbable, on one side and to admit no possible contingency on the other." [14]

The history of war panics in other countries reflects the operations and constellations of interests in armaments. These interests and their ideologues have constantly nursed the feeling of insecurity over the world by taking advantage of every diplomatic incident to make it a reason for more armaments. And as soon as one nation approved the reason and increased its armaments, the others felt constrained to do the same.

The Theory and Practice of Total Mobilization for War

Throughout the pre-1914 period, armies as constituted were emphatic enemies of liberals and socialists, whom they accused of hampering their growth. Being estranged from these parties of individualism and mass unity, the armies failed to attain a competent understanding of the potentialities inherent in the forces they represented. Nor did the parties try to capture the military, whom they scorned as hopelessly conservative.

The concept of a total mobilization for war—as a reserve of universal and ultimate sacrifice—is inherent in the philosophy of liberalism and socialism, but not in that of conservatism. The military were therefore not prepared to demand all of any nation's resources, to envisage utilizing everybody and everything a nation possessed. Total mobilization had been known in earlier ages—to some extent in antiquity and in the seventeenth century during the Thirty Years' War. But officers of the years just prior to the First World War had no such idea. In no country were measures for the industrial and financial side of war comprehensively prepared or planned in minute detail. It did not occur to the military generally, even if it did to a few individuals, that the demand must be vast. Nor indeed did industrialists and financiers propose to mobilize the nation. The separating wall called "division of labor," erected between army and economy, was too high to allow the necessary exchange of ideas. Although the German General Staff did, it is true, suggest in 1905 that a study be made of Germany's food and other raw materials as war supplies, it did not follow up the suggestion.[15] Apparently the General Staff intended merely to provide itself with an alibi before the high court of history.

To such a vital question as the proper geographical distribution of national industries essential to war purposes, the pre-1914 military applied little analysis. Nor was heed given to Napoleon's warning. If not before St. Helena, Napoleon at some stage in his career found it "ridiculous that all the warehouses and manufactories of arms are on the extreme frontier, exposed to being cut off at the very beginning of a campaign by the attacking army."[16] Nevertheless, before 1914 many of the basic war industries were situated close to the borders of the various European nations. By that very circumstance the location of war industries conditioned certain war operations.

The basis of this army miscalculation is not difficult to explore. Officers were aloof from intimate contact with most branches of economy. Many of them were close to agriculture. But few of them, and these few mainly bureaucrats, had contacts with the armament industry and other industries essential to war provisioning. Officers who sprang from manufacturing or trading families habitually made haste to forget their origin; the army's hauteur toward trading money kept the trader's son and the trader's business far apart and prevented the son from recognizing any war-potential in his father's dirty plant. Almost the only war potentials which prewar armies expected to exploit were agricultural products, including the horses, by this time anachronistic, and the output of national armament plants already operating. The officers' common and long identification with agriculture in Europe even excluded the question whether the specific form of national agriculture then prevailing was ideally constituted for providing the army and the nation with suitable and sufficient foodstuffs in the event of war.

Far less did the officers scrutinize industries. During the nineteenth century most of the nations had come to rely on a particular kind of nationalizing for their arms supplies. Increasingly the nationalist spirit, stimulated or not by the interests, had found it unbearable to buy articles abroad. The free-trading British violently resisted the introduction of Colt's clearly superior, but American, firearm, which the inventor tried to sell them in the early 1850's. He learned that the entrenched army purveyors, mostly small producers, were backed by gentlemen "too noble to be publicly engaged in vulgar trade who nevertheless were as greedy for profits as any Cheapside pawnbrokers. And those noble lords were the makers and wagers of wars and the purchasers of the materials for carrying on the wars."

Colt made it worse for himself by declining to let members of the British aristocracy participate in his profits as partners instead of through the commissions and bribes which he offered them.[17] Finally the British bought Colt out, but they were never able to bring themselves to purchase Krupp's steel goods, except in a roundabout way, despite the superiority of the Krupp offerings at that time. Their reluctance was capitalized by Krupp, who sold licenses to the various national producers of arms for the use of his patents. In the late 1880's while the Germans and the French continued to regard American industries as primarily munitions plants for their own needs in case of wars, the Americans began to feel the urge to build warships with home-made armor plate.

Frequently the armies maintained small armament plants of their own, ordinarily in connection with arsenals, the traditional way. The arrangement was for experimental ends rather than a plan for supplying their needs exclusively, nor did it serve as precedent for a nationalization of the armaments industry in their war schemes. France alone produced her gunpowder in public factories. In most other countries the firm opposition of liberals to state industry, as a principle, ran against even a state armaments plant. An English government committee headed by John Morley pronounced itself, in 1887, in favor of private manufacture and of giving more orders to private firms. It was said that this program would not only "stimulate inventors and manufacturers to vie with one another in producing the best possible article, but it tends also to widen the area of production, so that in time of pressure the requirements of the Service would be more readily supplied." Later, the government plants were actually reduced in size and output, and more orders were given to the private plants; proposals to manufacture all the government's arms in the arsenals of Woolwich were refused because it would have "meant practically the wreck of the military arms trade in Birmingham."

In this policy of keeping production private, the liberal hostility to state manufacture synchronized with a forethought for, without planning of, industrial mobilization. Orders given to the private plants in peacetime were to be a measure of mobilization for the national industries, which were deemed "capable of almost indefinite, though not of immediate, expansion. Demand discovers or creates new sources of supply, and the result of an increased demand upon the trade in ordinary times would, therefore, probably be to create an additional reserve of power in emergency." [18]

This consideration eventually gave the arms supply a national character. Armor plate thus had to be home-produced, whatever the shortcomings of that scheme might be from the technical and financial standpoint. In the end, the defense forces were persuaded of the need for armament autarchy, without simultaneously insuring themselves against the high price they would have to pay. When they so "nationalized" their arms supply, they took no steps to provoke on a national basis the stimulating competition that had prevailed on an international basis. Schneider-Creusot in France, Krupp in Germany, and Skoda in Austria-Hungary practically monopolized the supplying of guns for the armies of those countries. Prewar Germany went furthest in this isolationism: for the ten years previous to 1914 she bought practically no armaments at all in foreign markets except through the second-hand trade. Moreover, it appears that the armies actually wanted to buy guns only from monopolistic plants; they positively discouraged competition within the home market, thus in Germany exhibiting an animus against the works of Ehrhardt, Krupp's only serious competitor. The sole dependence upon Krupp was merely another sign of the stagnation which domestic conditions had brought, or were shortly to bring, in the development of the German army.

To a large extent the favoring of Krupp sprang from sheer decadent conservatism. Krupp employed ex-officers who had access to their former colleagues in the War Ministry and other bureaucratic places. The intermediaries "were to procure the necessary information through the medium of comradeship" and to persuade the occupants of swivel chairs that they must convey to Krupp's men information relative to competitors' prices and continue purchasing where they had always been well served. So the military bought, as conservative persons are accustomed to buy, at well-known places. In the circumstances Krupp could fix high prices and make high profits while the traditional, if not genuine, Prussian niggardliness merely grumbled at the cost.[19]

Not all the motives for the preferences shown to native arms makers were free from stain. Lebœuf, Napoleon III's War Minister before 1870—who had pronounced the French army to be perfectly fit for action at the fatal hour—had family relations with Schneider. Taking advantage of the affiliation, he recommended Schneider to the Emperor as the exclusive gun maker for France despite the fact that Schneider had not yet taken on the manufacturing of such steel guns as gave the Prussians their superiority over the French artillery in 1870-1.[20] The German Kaiser's relations with Krupp were close in another way: His Majesty was one of the rare outsiders let in on Krupp's ground floor, if only to the extent of fifty thousand marks.[21] And the elder Moltke, as we now know, in 1874 invested in 41,000 talers worth of 5 per cent Krupp bonds, redeemable at 110.[22]

While other, more circuitous, connections between war lord and arms maker remain obscure, a great deal is now clear with respect to the typical contacts between Krupp and other munitions makers and officers. It is known that bribes were given officers to secure foreign orders and technical secrets from the War Ministry.[23] Poor as a rule, officers were extravagantly feted by Krupp in the Villa Hügel at Essen. This establishment resembled Colt's "Armsmeare" in its splendor and Colt liked to point out to his guests "the industrial dukedom of which he was the overlord." Both Krupp and Colt considered the "entertaining of the officer" highly profitable despite the expense.[24] Relatives of the mighty were also employed by Krupp. The *cadets* had found new offices.[25] This provoked complaint from his competitor Ehrhardt, who declared: "Krupp employs hundreds of officers on leave or inactive, at a high salary, for doing nothing very much. To some families, Krupp's was a great sinecure, providing jobs for the nephews and poor relations of officials who have great influence in the army." [26]

Scandalous as such transactions may appear to moralists, their effect on the efficiency of national defense was apt to be calamitous. When a Prussian commission of inquiry in 1786 proposed that all old contracts be annulled and more favorable ones concluded, if necessary by attracting other industrialists, the King remarked in a marginal note: "The older *concessionnaires,* in particular the large providers, must not be preferred because then the new and small ones cannot arise. . . . After the smallest proved complaint of a regiment the provider must be punished at once and severely. . . . The inspectors must be well paid lest they be bribed." [27] But his descendant, William II, was neither disposed to give such orders nor in a position to enforce them, for instance, to move Krupp to manufacture a pneumatic recoil gun that had been invented.

In extending the network of "security" interests it is an advantage that officers are ordinarily more willing to receive calls from fellow officers than from other salesmen or inventors. In the American army this accessibility led after 1912 to a war of schools. Among the several types of machine guns offered the army, Leonard Wood preferred the Lewis type, the invention of an American officer; though it failed in some American tests, it was sold abroad, where France and England used it as their mainstay during the war. But Crozier, Chief of the Ordnance Department, not so influenced as Wood by "old association in the service with Lewis and his natural inclination toward any underdog appealing for help," backed the competing Benet-Mercier gun, the inventor of which was his friend and the son of a former chief of ordnance. However, it never was developed for practical use.[28]

Numerous army officers have been salesmen of armament firms, if none rose to the eminence of the trader Sir Basil Zaharoff. General McClellan, going abroad after his failure in the field to sell American ironclad steam batteries which the Northern government had rejected, seems to have been the first of his countrymen in this calling. His qualification, in the opinion of his employers, was his "Europoid" character; apparently "his prominence and personal contacts" fitted him particularly well for Prussia and Russia, but obviously not well enough, for he could report no sales in 1867-8.[29] Long afterward, that professional alarmist, now official, now private, Lord Beresford, a director of Henry Andrews, Ltd., sponsored in the House of Commons the proposal to adopt an automatic rifle with the production of which his company was concerned.[30] On the pre-1914 relation between officers and businessmen in England Philip Snowden commented as follows: "There is not a single large firm doing contract work for the Government which has not either upon its Board or in its service a man who has been in the service of the Government and who knows the ropes." [31]

Conditions corresponded in other countries. Schneider employed at Le Creusot on the eve of the war two former admirals, one ex-general, one ex-captain, one honorary director of artillery.[32] In

Germany as well, of course, officers in ever growing numbers became the go-betweens for the industrialist and the bureaucrat, harmonizing relations which in the beginning the elder Krupp had
found none too pleasant. He and the younger Krupp smoothed
the way by marrying a daughter of the latter to a member of the
higher German bureaucracy and by taking more former officials
and their relatives into his directorate or other employs. The affiliation was crowned by the appointment to the head of the Krupp
Works (1909-18) of Hugenberg, who changed several times from
government to private employment, always and everywhere pursuing reactionary and Pan-German policies, by means of which he
finally helped to put Hitler into office.[33]

As the processes of warmaking grew more complicated, these
personal arrangements formed the counterpart to the increasingly
close co-operation between the government technicians and the
private entrepreneurs, induced by the growth of inventions in explosives, metallurgy, and transportation. It was a co-operation in
which the bureaucratic element contributed some designs, but little
invention, and the money for orders, while the industries provided
the ideas and the goods and the salesmanship. If there was some
stimulus to efficiency in such relations there was also danger of
lagging in the international arms competition. When Krupp declined to take an interest in the idea of a pneumatic recoil for
guns, Ehrhardt bought the patents and Krupp for a long time tried
to sell the old guns instead of buying the expensive licenses from
his competitor; those were the years from 1902 to 1905. Unable
or unwilling to wait until the two firms had settled their controversies in lawsuits, the government proceeded to introduce a new
type of gun using the new patent; then German diplomacy helped
Krupp to sell his old-type guns to the Turks at fabulous prices.

In the hands of the arms makers the military and naval bureaucracies were rather helpless. They knew that agreements between
army purveyors often existed [34] and that they had to pay exorbitant
prices in consequence; on occasion they almost abjectly begged
Krupp to lower their quotations—only to be told by the Krupp
directorate that the patrimony of Fräulein Krupp could not be
diminished.[35] That bureaucracies might have controlled prices by
calculation of their own does not seem to have entered their minds
before the First World War. The super-prices they felt forced to
pay were the penalty of their lack of technical inventiveness and
comprehension. None of the revolutionary war inventions have
been the work of officers. The legendary figure of the monk Ber-
thold Schwarz, who is said to have invented gunpowder, heads the
list of nonmilitary inventors of war machines reaching in our time
to Colt, Nobel, the Maxims, and the several contributors who made

the submarine possible. Despite an obvious community of interests, the practical relations between war offices and inventors were discordant, willful, and inimical to the efficiency of the war machine. Except in critical, that is in war, times, officers have been inclined to repulse inventors as cranks and of course they have been overrun by eccentrics. There is the famous case of Lewis, designer of the Lewis machine gun, "impossible to deal with, always, it was said, throwing his invention in the face of somebody and hurting him." [36] There was also Turpin, the inventor of melinite, whose involved story, full of conflict with the French Ministry of War, which he had shocked by his irregular behavior, is among the marvels of military history. His newest invention was refused without examination by Mercier, the War Minister, the highest-placed enemy of Dreyfus, who told the Chamber that his own *"flair d'artilleur,"* his nose for artillery, had rendered an examination unnecessary; the Minister knew without looking at it that the thing was worthless. The Prime Minister had to promise the laughing Chamber that henceforth it would be impossible to reject without examination inventions that might assist national defense. The War Minister thereafter was anxious to live down his chagrin and soon acquired the notion that nothing would serve this purpose better than the prosecution of the Jew Dreyfus.[37]

Despite their obligation to look into the matter of proffered inventions—if security was to be more than a name—the armies remained out of step with the technological process of the times. They were not willing to adopt the most modern machinery or to advocate the purchase of the maximum amount of destructive apparatus.

In part the peacetime imperatives of the armies stood in the way of this advance toward efficiency. Officers were content to govern men—to increase the supply of soldiers with traditional equipment; they did not attempt the severer intellectual task of thinking out the potentialities of war in a mechanized age. Over man power they felt sure of establishing control; they tried men out in maneuvers and tabulated what could be done with them, although they could not put them under real fire. But they shrank from unknown and unexplored, possibly uncontrollable, machinery. They preferred to study men and animals, rather than explosives and armor. Although experiments with material potentials might have been undertaken without the forbidden tryout on man, they were in fact sparing in number and superficial in nature. Hence peace was not a genuine preparation for war.

As a German General Staff officer once remarked: "In peacetime you cannot have enough of light artillery, but in war, as the history of all wars proves, you cannot have too many heavy guns."

The explanation, which he did not provide, lay to a large extent in the circumstance that peacetime maneuvers could demonstrate the "value" of field artillery, largely owing to their equestrian arts, while heavy artillery, being clumsy, could not be easily tested in shooting to pieces the structures and trenches provided. In their eagerness "to show zeal and motion" in such demonstrations, the military answered proposals for heavier artillery by insisting that the greater mobility of the 7.5 would atone for the weaker effect of its projectile.[38]

Undeterred by professionalism of that kind and realizing that French and Belgian fortresses stood in the way of his strategy, Schlieffen refused to accept that decision. He asked himself: Can we be sure that field artillery alone can be effective against fortified positions? Can we expect that heavy artillery will be always promptly available where howitzer fire support is imperative? Since neither answer could be in the affirmative, Schlieffen stood firm for a new procedure—the transformation of the heavy artillery for field use and the introduction of a new howitzer. The experts grumbled or joked about the "mounted foot-artillerist," but despite the thinning out of Schlieffen's plan, something of it was accomplished. The First World War, therefore, found the Central Powers far superior to the Allies in heavy field artillery. For Schlieffen the idea that the old things had "stood the test" was of no avail: "No institution proves true, least of all the old ones. True are only the principles. . . ."[39]

Here again, in the relations between parliamentarians and officers, it was the military, rather than the civilians, who declined proposals for more heavy artillery. In France, such a good field gun had been developed that the War Minister declared in 1909 that the whole heavy artillery was useless; with a sufficient number of shots from the light 7.5 guns all obstacles could be removed. When an army budgetary commission ventured to offer more artillery, a delegate of the General Staff declined the gift: "Thank God, we don't have it. What constitutes the power of France is the swiftness of her artillery."[40]

In their distaste for innovations, the military were not easily brought to befriend the internal combustion engine and adapt it to the purposes of war. For carrying forward the aeronautical experiments which he had personally witnessed in the American Civil War, Count Zeppelin was considered a crank and procured no military support worthy of mention, notwithstanding his rank of ex-officer. If his lighter-than-air principle was eventually outmoded by the heavier-than-air machines, it might have been applied with effect in a war, say of 1910. In that year when French parliamentarians pointed to the military uses of aviation, Foch, Director of the Ecole de Guerre, called "all that sport; for the army the aeroplane is zero." A little later a French general, one of the foremost advocates of the three-year military-training term for France, sneered at the idea of an armored, gun-equipped car, the forerunner of the tank.[41]

The military officer had grown dependent on traditional conveniences, and his fear that he would lose his power to govern in the accustomed mode—over men and horses—and be carried away by materials, handicapped him for introducing the new machinery required for establishing the maximum of superiority. A comparison with the navies and their alertness for new contrivances emphasizes the point. At a time when Britain possessed, with the means already at hand, an overwhelming preponderance at sea against any imaginable enemy, the British navy was far from satisfied; for the sake of modernity and technical perfection it called for dreadnoughts. But among the forces at sea as on land the tradition of convenience and governing extended its sway. This made the British seamen cling to the dreadnought with its ample deck space and cubic footage permitting comfortable cabins for the commanding officer in preference to the dirty hole of a submarine. If Tirpitz had not been such an imperious person, imitative rather than creative, he might have furthered the undersea ship instead of slavishly adopting the British dreadnought; in that case he might conceivably have contributed to the security, instead of to the ruin, of his country.

Besides neglecting or hampering the increase of their own potentials by invention, military officers have strengthened their possible or probable foes by helping the munitions industries to sell their products abroad. In this enterprise they have acted as salesmen, as we have said; they have also acted as instruction officers for other peoples' armies, and as military attachés, previously discussed. By pushing these wares and talents in other lands, it was stated with some justification, they enabled the domestic industry to grow and prepare itself for war mobilization; simultaneously they were often adding to the offensive power of enemies. In Austria-Hungary, by way of illustration, the Skoda Works, unable to keep running at a profit on Austrian army orders alone, got help from the bankers and diplomats for foreign orders. When Serbia refused to give orders to Skoda, that made her an unequivocal enemy of Austria.[42] Thus the care for the war potential itself contributed to the war causes.

The German Emperor approved gladly the mission of General Liman von Sanders to Turkey in 1913 for reasons of prestige and also in the expectation that this officer would be in a position to direct important orders to Germany.[43] Through such military and naval missions, smaller nations, besides becoming appendices of the big military-industrial nations, were set on the militaristic way themselves. The Chilean army stood in that relation to Germany; France instructed and provisioned the Peruvian army; England controlled the instructors and materials in the Turkish and Greek navies; and France instructed the Greek army in 1913.

In Germany, diplomatic support for such ventures was reserved for Krupp but denied to Ehrhardt—a decision based easily as much on imperial favor as upon the estimate of Krupp's value to wartime mobilization. The theory there and elsewhere was that the more armaments products could be sold abroad in peacetime, the more ships were being built on foreign orders at the moment war broke out, the larger would be the national war potential on hand at the crucial hour. In other words, foreign orders presumably prepared the national industrial mobilization. How far military officers were consciously guided by this concept and thought of future war in their endeavors to promote foreign sales, and how far this war potential rose as a by-product of such promotion, cannot be determined in every case. It is certain, however, that the sentimental idea that guns produced by a nation's industries would fire upon that nation's own sons, did not disturb the conventional makers and users of arms. At the request of the Berlin War Minister, Krupp did indeed check the selling of guns to Germany's possible enemies, France, Russia, and Denmark. But this did not exclude occasional deals, with the Kaiser's permission. For instance, Krupp participated in the building up of the Putilov Works in Russia, without which the breakdown of Russia's munitions supply in the First World War would have taken place even sooner than it did.

Sentimental outcries arose against munitions makers, but to a corresponding degree other army provisioners were relieved of the opprobrium once heaped upon them, especially by Napoleon. His own relations to the purveyors were violently contradictory. In a way the Bonaparte dictatorship liquidated the state armament production begun by the Jacobins, but which men like Barras had started well on the road back to private ownership. To insure the completion of this process, the First Consul, faced with an empty public treasury after the 18th Brumaire, was offered and accepted as first aid some eight hundred thousand francs from an army provider.[44] Thereafter he never emancipated himself from the services of the private purveyors, though at times he dispossessed them of large portions of their gains by drastic measures. The provisioning of the army through private entrepreneurs remained, as one of his marshals, Saint-Cyr, wrote, "a source of public scandals and of suffering for the armies." Saint-Cyr himself, War Minister under the Bourbons, returned to the state provisioning of the army against the determined opposition of the private contractors, who tried to discredit the state operation and constantly pointed to the example of England, where all was left to private enterprise.[45]

Generally speaking, the army providers of shoes and leather, cloth and uniforms or foodstuffs retired to an inconspicuous position in the nineteenth century. Ordinarily the armies exercised more control over them than over the arms providers. Only now and then did scandals break out, either on account of the miserable quality of goods delivered—particularly the "embalmed meats" of 1898—corrupt relations of the purveyors with officialdom, or too intimate a connection with parliamentarians. One of the malodorous cases was the Tippelskirch affair in Germany, in which the part-owner of a firm that furnished articles for troops in the German colonies turned out to be the wife of the Prussian Minister of Agriculture, General von Podbielski. The Russian autocracy enjoyed usurious profits, such as huge sums made from armaments sales and contracts by the grand dukes and other members of the Czar's family and the rake-off pocketed by the Czar himself during the Russo-Japanese War. According to Bolshevik computations, nine-tenths of the total war expenditures eventually benefited the Czar.[46] Sometimes abuses of this nature were brought to light by parliamentarians of the opposition, but occasionally by military officials who clandestinely informed the party agitators.

Neglect of Domestic War Potentials

While the military of all countries, nominally engaged in attending to the security of their respective nations, became ever more deeply enmeshed with the supply interests, they were forced by the mass character of the orders they placed—as well as of the aggregations of men they ruled and trained—into increasingly bureaucratic procedures, full of the inertia and formalism of officialdom, except in the always lively pursuit of their immediate and specific interests as a peacetime concern. Besides displaying a lack of the imagination necessary for the utmost use of the material potentials at hand, they failed to exhaust the possibilities of man power. To a large extent this failure was due to two proclivities on their part. In the first place, during the pre-1914 period, like the naval men, they constantly kept their eyes outward and calculated comparable forms and quantities. By so doing they estimated their own degree of preparedness in terms of their own peacetime effectives as against those of the "enemy." In the second place, in spite of the rise of the mass army and the obvious lessons presented by it, the military refused to explore and utilize that potential to the limit. In some countries, the refusal undoubtedly grew out of a fear that such an excursion into potentials would raise democratic, or even worse, perils; elsewhere it seems to have been the outcome of sheer bureaucratic or professional incapacity to envisage the vast resources available and to devise the methods that could swing them into action, either for national defense or for aggression.

Hence the "security" program was marked by the constant desire of all parties to be "equal" to their neighbors in peacetime effectiveness; by this standard the balance of power was measured, and its alterations. As Joseph Reinach said in defending the French three-year term of service of 1913: "It is nothing but the means of bringing forth the effectives which will balance those of Germany." [47] This was the distinctive feature of the years or months immediately preceding the war.

The pace for this special competition was set by the Franco-Russian military alliance. Both countries raised their effective strength. France finally reintroduced the three-year term to have as many available men as the dwindling birth rate allowed, and Russia lengthened the service term by three months in the autumn of 1913, when she had for the first time four classes with the colors. On the other side, the last prewar German army bill did not so immediately raise the peacetime effectiveness; Germany's strength, though growing, would not have overtaken that of France until 1919, when she would have had a preponderance over France of five hundred thousand men. The army laws of both Germany and Austria were not designed to reach their full effect until 1922-3.[48] At the moment, therefore, the Russian danger was growing and the French numerical maximum was attained.

How far these numerical relations, momentary and prospective, heightened or weakened the resolve to make war in 1914 on either side remains an open question. Judging the French army by its own standards, that is, by the number of men immediately available, it was in 1914 in the best condition and had more military reason to make a war than to wait. So at least the diplomats thought in a nation which had reason to dread being involved in war. The Belgian minister in Paris in the spring of 1914 perceived that one of the most dangerous elements in the situation was the return of France to the three-year term of service: "It was put over light-heartedly by the military party, but the country cannot sustain it. Before two years it either has to be given up or there must be war." [49]

Under democratic government, France made general conscription sweeping: in 1911 she called to the colors 82.96 per cent of all men bound to serve, while Germany called only 53.12 per cent. To the democratic masses of France under arms Russia added her masses, which she and many others agreed were her main reliance as an armed nation. In this competition of numbers Germany followed suit without especially strong convictions with respect to the military value of mere numbers of men. Count Leo von Caprivi who, before his Chancellorship, would have commanded an army in case of war, could not believe "that among the army leaders alive there is one who would be able to feed, to move, and to bring together for battle those masses with whom one has become accustomed to reckon now. . . . The number by itself, even if made up of nothing but good soldiers, has its doubtful side." [50]

Whether they were democracies or not, the several Continental nations offered the armies more men than they would or could take and on conditions which were modest, indeed too modest. The officers could draw heavily upon the open reservoirs and resources of the nations and from these materials, in accordance with their own wills, instincts, and traditions, they shaped armies in their own image instead of the nation's image.[51] Thus in each state there existed something of a contradiction: *L'armée contre la nation,* the army against the nation. Yet the contradiction was not completely drawn in that form, for the armies were allied with specific and powerful groups and classes in the nations that supported their lines of action. This is another way of saying that armies are not out of politics. The nations, as represented in parliaments, were either unwilling for class reasons, or too careless, or too ignorant in the absence of a study of military questions, to tell the officers what kind of army they wanted. There were, of course, gradations between St. Petersburg and Washington in the manner of imposing popular will upon the armies; but there remained in all countries, including England, as the Ulster crisis showed, a sphere of remarkably free play for the army.

Nowhere in the great military states were the governing military officers desirous of taking the maximum number of soldiers for war and creating a nation in arms. Other officers, not in power, may have dreamed or demanded such a nation. After the end of his army service, Schlieffen called for such a nation in a magazine article of 1908-9, painting in the darkest hues the military and political situation of the Reich, with the purpose of impressing a newly elected chauvinistic Reichstag. Through Ludendorff as well, the General Staff insisted that Germany must again become a nation in arms as she had been under the direction of great men in times of disaster.[52] But the aim of the high authorities in Germany and in other countries was rather for a maximum control over the soldiers at hand, too lightly identified with a maximum war potential diminished in actuality by their peacetime penchant for ruling and governing as an independent estate.

The product of that desire was the prewar "barracks army" in France, Germany, Russia, and elsewhere. The conviction that man had to undergo two or three years' service in the barracks to acquire the *"esprit militaire,"* to become a soldier, kept vast numbers of men from being prepared for war. In Germany the original short-term exercise of the so-called Substitute Reserve was stopped in 1893 as "militarily unsatisfactory," as furnishing nothing but what Bernhardi called a "military proletariat." [53] The growing threat of war before 1914 led only to an intensification of this barracks regime, particularly in France, where the two-year term was lengthened just before that date in the belief that the war would in the main be fought by the immediately available, trained effectives. These trained men the officers looked upon as their familiar tools, tried out in maneuvers and the barrack yards. When confronted with the possibilities of the far larger, monster armies inherent in modern nations, military commands were filled with horror. For real mass armies they could devise no frame of order and organization, no estimate of their full war potential.

The French General Staff calculated in advance that the classes of 1887 to 1913 contained only 4,829,000 mobilizable men, whereas actually 6,136,000 men of these classes were mobilized in the war. From August 1 to August 15, 1914, only 2,887,000 men were called to the colors and added to the 692,000 men who were serving at the outbreak of the war; but of these 2,887,000, only 1,700,000 were mobilized and only 750,000 actually sent into the field in that fortnight. Thus men for twenty-seven reserve divisions remained unused for the defense of France's frontiers during that crucial time.[54]

The more democratic nation put the heavier burden on its citizenry, including the ruling classes, whose sons had to serve terms as long as all the others: two years and then three. The French army law of 1905 abolished the privilege of a one-year term for high school graduates, which the sons of the well-to-do classes in Germany continued to enjoy. Aware of the growing superiority of the French reserve officers, the German General Staff, shortly before the war, looked forward to abolishing eventually the privileges of the educated and well-to-do. In this way it hoped to even up things against the French. It realized that, even though French officers came from various social strata, in case of war their social, religious, and political antagonisms would be overcome and the whole body tightly unified.[55] The project was not carried out, however, for the Berlin War Ministry would not welcome officers from the lower social strata, even though they might have commanded three additional army corps.

Thus in the competition between France and Germany, the democratic structure of the Republic allowed a better use of man power. Consequently in August 1914, France had two more fighting divisions available for the western front than Germany, not including the Belgian army and the four British divisions. Only the higher industrialization of Germany enabled her to offset this superiority in mass power—by the more effective use of technological potentials, namely, machine guns and heavy artillery. If the Germans had possessed the three army corps that her population could have yielded and thrown them on their extreme right in the August 1914 offensive, "the march to Paris" might have been realized, especially if the original Schlieffen Plan had been followed.

The Schlieffen Plan itself was an outcome of German military policies at home insofar as it sought to replace undeveloped German man power by swift and unexpected movements of the available war army. At the same time it was a function of Germany's foreign policy: it was conceived when Italy's desertion from the Triple Alliance had become obvious and when the French consequently gave up the idea of an offensive along the Alpine front.[56] Schlieffen first mentioned his plan in 1904 and it acquired full shape on account of the experiences in the Russo-Japanese War. Seen in this light, the Schlieffen Plan amounted to making use of rapid mass motion and an avoidance of the prolonged war of positions to which modern technique threatened to lead. National economy, "the machine with its thousand wheels, through which millions find their living, cannot stand still for long," he said at the end of 1905. "One cannot move for one or two years in battles of twelve days' length from position to position, till the belligerents are completely exhausted and worn out, both beg for peace, and both submit to the conditions put up. We must try to throw down quickly and annihilate the enemy." [57] This would not be possible along defensive lines, by standing still in a frontal defense, but only in a war of movements.

Politically speaking, Schlieffen's plan meant a break with the established morality of Europe as the backer of Belgian neutrality. For this the masses in no country—not even Germany—were prepared, whereas the armies and, in part, the diplomats, were, and this unpreparedness for the execution of the Schlieffen Plan proved to be a great anti-German war potential, one not reckoned upon beforehand in Berlin.

By intention the plan was to break the frozen fronts of the balance of powers by outwinging the enemy and thus beating him with a numerically inferior army. As Schlieffen stated it: "In 1870-1 Germany had to fight against a weaker army. In a future war, Germany will have to fight with stronger armies. The enemy can apply our procedure of 1870, *not we*." Contrary to the expectation of the German public, Schlieffen was prepared to let the enemies in West and East invade parts of German territory, a prerequisite in fact to the functioning of his plan, for it forbade any prepared German positions along the Saar-Nied line. His army machine he constructed in the semblance of a gigantic barn door with its weight on the right wing—the right wing and left wing standing somewhat in the relation of 7 to 1 in their strength, a weight that would force the French back to Paris even if they invaded southern Germany, and would at the same time crush an English expeditionary force.

This plan envisaged a short war, in which the German army as constituted would be most effective—one in which Schlieffen was not afraid of the British navy as having any great influence on the decision. Only a prolonged war would permit this instrument to count: "It can destroy German trade almost completely, though not without damaging considerably that of its own country." This was tantamount to saying, in 1904, that in no kind of war would the German navy be of much use, a judgment which did not serve to make Schlieffen a prime favorite with the Emperor. In fact, Schlieffen had to allow the monarch to undertake romantic cavalry attacks in the autumn maneuvers in order to win his fickle heart back from the navy to the army, not because such maneuvers were thought by him to be part of a future war.

Schlieffen's plan of marching through Belgium was the strategy that went with the German Morocco policy, as far as the latter was intended to lead to war—the war which Holstein, Schlieffen, and the War Minister rather sought than cared to avoid, pointing at the time to Russia's defeat in Manchuria and her Revolution at home. But they had to admit to themselves that Bülow "would hardly, and the Kaiser in no way, resolve upon the extreme." "This regrettable pell-mell," as Bülow, the official director of German policies, called the disagreement, led not long afterward to Holstein's dismissal and Schlieffen's retirement. As his successor, the Emperor chose another Moltke, the nephew of the elder leader, who had shown his generalship to the imperial satisfaction in the maneuvers.

Given German methods of avoiding full use of mass potentials, 1905 was the one year of the century in which Germany could still have won the war, most probably, as Schlieffen was convinced, with the army as it was then constituted, that is, without combing the country for all able-bodied men. But later he himself insisted that this was no longer possible: "All men fit for duty must undergo training," as in France. "That does not yet give us superiority over France and Russia, but we have then, in point of raising soldiers, done our duty to the utmost possible. . . . That our army is better than the French and the Russian, that is our hope. But that it is as much superior as the European is to the Indian and the Negro— and this would be necessary considering the relation in strength— would first have to be proved. Up to now we have to thank at least in part our greater number for our successes, 1813-15, '64, '66, '70." [58] Schlieffen's successor also wanted the actual conscript army, but the military judgment on the class situation in the Reich, as expressed by the War Minister, witheld it from him.

Again and again Moltke asked for additional army corps, which were denied him. In their absence he reshaped the Schlieffen Plan, generally speaking in the direction of a more defensive character. He gave up the idea, with which Schlieffen had toyed, of marching not only through Belgium but parts of Holland as well. He was not as ready as Schlieffen to let the enemy invade large sections of the Reich. For that reason he strengthened the left or southern wing, which amounted to about one-third of the German strength in the West, as against one-seventh in Schlieffen's original plan. Thus in every way Moltke's modifications ran counter to the dying Schlieffen's warning: "Make the right wing strong!"

It is not clear how far Moltke had a presentiment of the modern industrial war and, therefore, consciously sought a stronger protection of the German industrial regions in the West and in upper Silesia. But his own plan was in part conditioned, like that of the French, by the exposed situation of the munitions-producing regions. With a backward-looking sagacity one of his collaborators made this observation: "In no case must the enemy be allowed to get to the Rhine; for then our Rhenish-Westphalian industrial region would be extremely endangered, our coal in the Saar and the ore in Lorraine would be lost. . . . Once these regions were lost, warfare would become impossible." [59]

Doubtless Germany was thus better protected and this protection harmonized with the desires of masses uninformed as to the exigencies of combat and of the large economic interest demanding protection. A fatal respect in truth was paid to popular desires in August 1914, when two army corps, badly needed on the Marne, were sent away to eastern Prussia where they were not needed. What is more, without the three army corps which the War Minister refused to create, Moltke continued to adhere to the march through Belgium with his weakened right wing. He lessened the chances of victory, the strength of the military offensive, while he maintained undiminished the painfully offensive political character of this enterprise—possibly too fraught with tragic consequences to justify the one success of this "watered" Schlieffen Plan: that of carrying the war abroad.

The war abroad Moltke undertook to wage without having presented the clear alternatives to the other leaders in Germany. He might have demanded sufficient force and allies to make his plans feasible; he might have resigned in protest over the inefficiency of the means granted him for the eventuality of war. But as late as July 18, 1914, Moltke was still arguing with the Chancellor that Germany need not hesitate to follow France and Russia, that financial considerations need not weigh heavily on a nation which spent billions annually for luxuries and still had tens of thousands of serviceable men free from duty. The demands of the navy for appropriations, he urged, ought to recede "since the great decision of the battle of nations will take place on land, with the army." [60] But this was merely the customary, not particularly optimistic, demand annually made for a larger slice of the budget due in the rhythm of the fiscal year; it was not the outcome of prescience as to the immediately threatening military situation. This situation Moltke did not consider alarming enough to discourage Austria from warlike measures, that is to say, he believed war could still be won with the Germany army as it stood in size, organization, and plan.

An organization for obtaining maximum war strength was excluded not only in Germany but likewise in every other country at that time. In France the reason was the devotion of the officers to the barracks army; in Germany it was the lack of a superior and central direction of foreign and other politics, coupled with the class situation. The last large prewar demands of the German General Staff were turned down owing to domestic politics before they reached the Reichstag, in a conflict between the General Staff on the one side, and the War Ministry, Chancellor, and Reich Secretary for Finance on the other. The bureaucrats were afraid that these demands would not be conceded, even by a Reichstag which had already agreed to the bills of 1911 and 1912 in all essentials. They feared the Left might demand in return an electoral reform in Prussia which the conservatives would not admit. A general in the War Ministry told Ludendorff to his face that if he continued his inordinate demands he would bring about a revolution within a few years.[61]

What were the signs of this revolution, however, aside from the demands of the socialists? Had the electoral reforms been passed and the basis of power widened in Germany, the socialists would in any case still have been excluded from a share in that power. What was so frightening to the military bureaucrats who governed the Reich? It was actually the insistence of the not very numerous bourgeois Left that the military strength of the nation must no longer be identified with the exclusive need of officer families for jobs; that everything should be dropped which served only to meet the flair of the officers for parading and luxury; that the Prussian class electoral law—a deadening weight in the baggage of the mobilized Landwehr man—ought to be abolished; that the service term should be reduced to one year; that officers must be drawn from wider classes of the people; that the ranks must be given a chance to produce officers; and finally that the costs of an extraordinarily large army bill should be furnished by taxing high incomes, great fortunes, and large inheritances.[62]

These were the demands presented by the Leftist bourgeois, but the fact that they were shared by the socialists, and had perhaps originated with them, made them revolutionary in the eyes of the officers of the War Ministry. The latter refused to consider them, as they refused to consider the plans for a larger army presented by the General Staff and elaborated by Ludendorff. That Ludendorff's revolution might take place rather than the socialist revolution was a possibility not imagined in the years stretching between Bismarck and 1914. Meanwhile nothing was done to prepare for mobilizing and officering the great manpower reserves of Germany, ultimately to be drawn upon for war.

Armies and Imperialism

Besides the task of providing the superior power in materials and men required for their security program, the military concerned themselves not a little with the immeasurables and imponderables connected with the commercial and territorial ambitions of the time. Obviously it was one military responsibility to defend given national boundaries and another to prepare for waging wars for territorial expansion in Europe, Africa, and Asia. Bismarck had thoroughly understood the distinction and had resisted excursions of power beyond the borders of Germany. He had foreseen the inevitable clash with Great Britain, shrunk from the possibilities of a two-front war, and recognized the limitations on German military power, great as it was. In the United States, the old army, as it existed before the building of the "new navy" began, regarded its function as that of defending the American continental domain. But as the naval men everywhere commenced to dream of unlimited sea power, the military caught the fever of ambition and, with some noteworthy exceptions, assumed the incalculable obligations of the excursion into the wide world, generally without due consideration of its relation to security at home—presumably their supreme concern. Had not Francis Bacon said long before: "For empire and greatness it importeth most that a nation do profess arms as their principal honor, study, and occupation"? [63]

In rushing into the glamorous, if incalculable "obligations of a world power," the military often rode over the capitalist conservatives who were supposed to be the chief promoters of commercial and territorial expansion. This was the case in the United States as well as in other countries. During the Cuban crisis in 1898, the most conservative of the conservatives, Mark Hanna, opposed war. On the other hand, the officers assembled in Washington "seemed agreed that there was no way out of the crisis except war" and that the so-called Republic which the Cuban insurgents strove to erect should not be recognized but "controlled." [64] When, after that war had been waged, no one really knew why the Philippines should be retained by the United States, the officers tried to furnish the reasons. With no burning desire on their part for annexations, the conservatives were willing to let the army or the navy have a foothold in the Philippines—a foothold which many army and navy officers later admitted created a frightful weakness in American defense. The same complaisance among conservatives toward the imperialism of officers appeared elsewhere, in France, for example, where the noble landowners or the wine growers, not as groups interested in Cochin-China or Algiers, supported military adventures in those regions.

In Germany, with its belated entrance into the imperialistic competition of the nations, this domestic relationship of parties, classes, and groups to imperialism was particularly confused. The conservatives, as agrarians, hated the "dreadful navy," as one of their leaders termed it behind the scenes in the Reichstag; they were not interested in railway enterprises in Asia Minor or Venezuela, which German diplomacy supported, for they feared this would swamp Germany with still more grain. But since the army and navy were interested in such ventures and in imperialism, the conservatives followed their lead, rather than lose the support of such powerful professional groups to the rival National Liberals, not to speak of the ultraimperialistic Pan-Germans. They could not afford, they thought, to estrange the imperialists, from the Kaiser and Tirpitz down. Furthermore, imperialism seemed a welcome distraction from domestic problems. Even against his better judgment Bismarck started his colonial policy, for which dubious commercial enterprises provided nothing but the pretext, in order to rally behind himself the parties which were drifting apart, and also to use the colonial policy as a "lightning rod for the Social Democratic danger." [65] To this extent conservatives also approved it.

The impetus which kept this and other imperialist policies alive in Germany was not provided, however, by the conservatives, but by the bureaucracy and the middle-class Pan-Germanism. To the vision of "a greater Germany" rallied those officers of bourgeois origin who found promotion less easy than noblemen, as well as those who wished a stronger Germany which would incidentally provide reasons for a larger army and opportunities to pacify and govern outlying possessions, thus offering occasions for peacetime distinctions. By the hundreds, officers became members of imperialist societies like the Colonial Society—forcing diplomatic language into a sharper key in colonial conflicts. In somewhat smaller numbers they joined the Pan-German League, which in 1904 had 7 officers among the 276 officials. [66]

Some of the officer members of these societies were dissatisfied even with the ample army bills the Reichstag granted: the former War Minister, Von Einem, and General Keim, for instance. In fact, Pan-Germans were always ready to favor and support still larger army bills and if necessary provide popular scares for the purpose. Their society founded in 1910 Germany's Army League, the Deutscher Wehrverein. When the government showed an inclination to lesson international competition, the leaders of the Army League, generally of a bourgeois or bureaucratic complexion, challenged all such inclinations. They went so far as to anger the governing military bureaucracy which, through the mouth of the Bavarian War Minister, publicly condemned the "machinations of the Pan-German military fanatics." [67] But in effect, they were voicing the wishes of the General Staff, which opposed the bureaucracy, and in particular those of Ludendorff, who came to join them more and more openly during and after the war.

The effect of these chauvinistic, alarmist organizations on the German government and army was by no means negligible. In sharpening the inner competition between the parties, each claiming the most thorough nationalism, they pushed the trends of German policies more and more to greater bellicosity. They added to the war neurosis with their alarmist cry: "Germany, awake!" which is older than Hitler, even older than the Pan-Germans. Leaders of the Pan-Germans, such as Class, satisfied themselves that the whole officer body was resolved to undertake an aggressive war and found it "fortunate that our officers are filled with such a spirit." [68] No group, no man, of the Right in Germany dared appear less "patriotic" than the Pan-Germans; least so the Emperor, who announced to Krupp von Bohlen-Halbach, the head of the Krupp Works, his decision for war with the words: "Now no one could any longer think me not sufficiently resolute." The same rivalry animated those generals whom Henry White heard in Silesia in 1912 exclaiming that the Kaiser had twice made Germany ridiculous in the eyes of Europe: by backing down at Algeciras first, and then at Agadir. The generals announced that they would not allow him to do this a third time, that he would have to fight it out whether he liked or not.[69]

The very belatedness of the German entry into overseas imperialism drove the Pan-Germans into a frenetic effort which other nations with older traditions of such imperialism could escape. But even in those nations, wherever imperialistic or chauvinistic organizations existed, officers belonged to them. Deroulède's Ligue des Patriotes had quite a following in the French army; not a few officers sympathized with his rather ridiculous attempts at a *coup d'état*, though not one was found ready to head them.[70] The steering committee of French colonial expansion, the Comité de l'Afrique Française, a little older than the Alldeutscher Verband, was a more select pressure organization than the latter, having about seventy members. But it strove to popularize Africa in France and to work on neglectful governments, keeping colonial questions alive through any interregnum which might be caused by the change of cabinets. In this group, side by side with parliamentarians, government officials and other "colonials," were navy and army officers, such as General Gallieni.[71] The contacts of this group with the men actually governing, some of whom sprang from it, were far more intimate than those achieved by the Pan-Germans, who, though more numerous, were often considered noisy and maladroit by the rulers of Germany and dismissed as silly nuisances after they had served to stir up public opinion.

Tradition and interest, the tradition of Algiers and the need for opening new reservoirs of soldiery among the colonials, combined to make the French officers enthusiastic about colonial adventures, especially in Africa, from whence native soldier material could be drawn more speedily in an emergency than from distant Indochina. Colonial enterprises were also thought to stimulate the soldier spirit and provide more rapid promotions all along the line. Whoever may have entertained the first design upon Fashoda, it was Colonel Marchand who nourished this "magnificent conception" for some time before he found the official acceptance and the assurance of Hanotaux: "You will fire a pistol-shot toward the Nile; we take upon ourselves all the consequences." [72]

French imperialistic chauvinism was linked with the Russian, years before the official Franco-Russian Alliance was signed. Russia's disapproval of Bismarck, as deep as the French, was voiced by General Skobelev, as early as 1882, in a call for an alliance of all Slavs with France against Germany and Austria-Hungary, designed to open a path to Constantinople through the Brandenburg Gate.[73] Deroulède and Katkov were publicists of the Entente. The Pan-Slavism of Russian officers, displayed in their revolutionary and martial activities in the Balkans, prepared the way for the military convention signed by the French and Russian chiefs of staff in 1892. The change thus brought about in Russia's foreign policies was thought to be balanced at home by a stronger "Russification" of the army, by making the army as far as possible a peasant force, a uniformed mass to which the name "steamroller" was singularly inapplicable. But this program did not save Russia from revolution, against which the Three Emperors' Alliance—Russia, Germany, and Austria-Hungary—would have been the best insurance, and Russian imperialism was compelled to assume the onus of being a primary cause of revolution.

Constantinople, the goal of the Pan-Slavists, was a clear military objective, compared with the vague aims in "the hunt for a national boundary" which led the Russian army, as the driving force of the expansion, into Asia. Russian military demands ran in the direction of more territories, rather than, as among Western countries, of a search for more raw materials. As soon as the "natural" boundary in one place was reached, the safety of Russia, as War Minister Kuropatkin explained to the Czar in 1900, called for the conquest of neighboring territory.[74] This endless driving led Russia to the Pacific, to the boundaries of India, into conflicts with England and Japan, and finally to the War of 1904-5. It resulted also in a positive military weakening of Russia, when she exposed herself to Japanese aggression on the Pacific littoral at Port Arthur and Dalny, "The Distant." By their imperialist chase after The Distant, Russian military men ran away from military security.

Defeated in the East, and drawn by alliances to the West, the imperialistic military turned back to Pan-Slavism as the other way to occupy themselves. Though the military preparations for war were by no means finished in 1912, war passions ran high and Grand Duke Nikolai prepared a great officers' meeting of protest against the moderating policy of the Foreign Ministry and in favor of Pan-Slavism. Only at the last minute was the Prime Minister able to stop it by obtaining the Czar's veto.[75]

It was not alone occidental imperialism, knocking open the closed door of Japan, which brought forth imperialist doctrines in Japan.[76] These doctrines were old, and only needed revival. Side by side with the inward-directed militarism of the Tokugawa period had existed, since the eighteenth century, a school of imperialist thought, the *"Moto-ori,"* which exalted the divine position of the Emperor and considered him destined to extend his power over the other, not divine, rulers of the earth. This school prepared the Restoration in Japan as well as the outward imperialism. It set objectives to be attained as soon as the tools had been acquired through westernization. For some twenty years the leaders of Japan's internal reconstruction, only occasionally providing an outlet for warlike energies among the imperialist elements, maintained the primacy of their task. When they ran into domestic difficulties too great to be mastered in the accustomed way, a war against China was launched in 1894 because, as a Japanese diplomat frankly admitted at Washington, it would improve the situation at home, "by arousing the patriotic sentiment of our people and more strongly attaching them to the government." [77] In its imperialist tendencies the army was closely allied with such groups as the Black Dragon Society, aiming at the Black Dragon River—the Amur—as the line of Japan's Manifest Destiny on the Asiatic mainland.

When the United States opened its latest imperialistic era at the end of the nineteenth century, its army's unpreparedness for war was only exceeded by the army's unpreparedness for imperialism.

Captain Alfred T. Mahan, of the navy, had provided the specific arguments for expansion through the strengthening of sea power, in America or anywhere else; but no one had performed a similar service for the American army. So the winning of the Philippines and other islands found the army utterly unequipped with military arguments for retaining them. Questioned by the American peace delegation in Paris in 1898, General Merritt said he did not know that he had an argument for the acquisition of the Philippines but that he felt the necessity for it: "It might be sentimental. He thought our interests in the Far East would be helped by the cheap labor in the Philippines." Army men in other countries, except England perhaps, would probably have omitted the humanitarian appeal, the missionary ideology of imperialism. Not so the American general. He "did not think our humanity bounded by geographical lines." Yet he was especially conscious of the occasion offered in the East of employing some twenty thousand to twenty-five thousand troops which seemed to be needed to hold part of the archipelago.[78]

In a similar manner, General Chaffee, the leader of the American expeditionary force in China in 1900, thought more of the employment of soldiers and marines than he did of security for the United States, when, contrary to the open door policy of his government, he proposed in Washington that the United States should start, like other Western nations, upon a policy of territorial acquisition in China. If the navy's support of the army man's plan and the military support of the navy's hope for stations in China led to nothing beyond discrediting the open door policy of Hay, the outcome was not due to their lack of zeal.[79]

Official statements and officers' declarations show that the American fighting forces generally interested themselves more in foreign policies than did the rest of the nation. They were doubtless the most willing to concede a primacy of foreign policy over domestic considerations. At least since Mahan's day they took care to emphasize the competitive character of policies, including armament policies, whereas the isolationist traditions of the country generally excluded world competition. And this emphasis was serviceable to the expansive tendencies of the navy and army. In 1912, for instance, the army maintained that its growth had not kept step with the very considerable changes in American policy during the previous twenty years:

Gradually our external problems have been assuming larger and larger proportions. While we were expanding, other nations have been doing the like. . . . Due to this world-wide expansion, the contact between great nations and races tends to become constantly closer. . . . With this close contact comes a competition, commer-

cial, national, and racial, whose ultimate seriousness current events
enable us to gauge. . . . The evidence is clear that the nations and
races capable of maintaining and protecting themselves are the only
ones who can flourish in the world competition.[80]

To maintain the position of the United States as a first-rate power
in this general competition, it was said on behalf of the military, the
army must be reformed so that it can put into the field, immediately
after the outbreak of a war, at least five hundred thousand men. To
its possible specific use the Chairman of the Senate Military Affairs
Committee, Senator George E. Chamberlain, made reference the
following year; in pleading for an enlargement he pointed to the
necessity of making the country safe against a Japanese invasion.[81]
As in Europe, on the eve of the First World War, so in America,
the military concern with "security"—an alleged historic interest
—had been widened into concern with any fight that might possibly
arise out of imperialist competition in the sweeping Darwinian
sense.

In pursuing imperialist aims, military men in all lands sought the
enlargement of their country rather than its greater security. A few
officers did, it is true, tremble for the defense of the metropolis as
they saw energies directed toward colonization. With such fears in
mind, Caprivi and Waldersee wanted Germany to get rid of Samoa
and possibly the whole of East Africa in order to have all strength
available for a two-front war.[82] But officers who entertained such
images of the future were inclined to withhold their views from the
public. Otherwise they might estrange valuable allies of the army
interest and arouse the ire of the navy men, to whom imperialism
gave many opportunities to land marines here and there and thus
display their *raison d'être* in the long intervals between real wars at
sea.

From a cursory survey of the imperialist tendencies of the prewar
armies, it would appear that the German army, particularly its most
influential group, the Old Prussians, was in comparison rather un-
imperialistic for reasons of its own, as far as colonial and kindred
enterprises were concerned. It took its own share of offices in the
colonies, and fought the colonial wars. But it had at the outset no
interest in such adventures as the Baghdad Railway, which might
bring more wheat into the German market and thus endanger the
grain-growing Junkers who provided the army's leaders. The later
alliance with the Turks, which the German army tried to strengthen
through the mission of Liman von Sanders in 1913, was a by-product
of the Baghdad enterprise rather than the outcome of Junker ambitions. There was, indeed, a marked difference in the imperialist
inclinations between the noble officers and the bourgeois officers in
the German army. The bourgeois were as a rule more unreservedly

in favor of overseas enterprises; and the navy, with its far larger number of bourgeois officers, was the most imperialistic element in the Reich forces, as also in the United States. The truth is that the German army scarcely took imperialistic aims seriously until, during the First World War, Ludendorff and others thought that German security demanded control over Belgium, the acquisition of Briey and Longwy, and parts of Russia's western provinces. Owing to the class composition of their officer corps, the armies of the Central Powers were on the whole more conservative even in their imperialist prewar aims than were the armies of France and Russia. Nevertheless, in all countries the imperialist conception was supplanting the domestic security conception in the minds of the military—or at least vitiating its integrity.

Restraints on Armaments

As mass armies arose and were developed, if never to their logical completeness and utmost potential, as the financial burdens of the associated armament rivalries threatened the economies of the participating nations, a countermovement set in—a demand for the limitation or restriction of armaments by international agreements. This movement was by no means confined to pacifists and other opponents of war on humane or Christian principles. It was promoted by "practical men," untainted with pacifism, who saw in the growing rivalry grave dangers to the national security which the military were supposed to be guaranteeing. In time the pressure for arms restriction appeared in governing circles and was then augmented by the pacifists, who discovered in this movement "the first steps to world peace."

Although many military men saw in arms restriction a chance "to dish their neighbors," most of its civilian supporters seemed to regard it as a means of putting a stop to arms competition as one form of dangerous competition. Observing in it a threat to the type of competition in which they were specializing, upon which their expansive interests depended, military men in general viewed the arms limitation advocates as "mollycoddles," "frocks," and "sentimental women." Not content with reliance on the old argument of security in defending their military budgets and preparations, they became philosophers and found in Darwinism a boundless and apparently indisputable *raison d'être* for their existence and interests —for a war of all nations against each and each against all. In so doing they turned Darwinism against their political foes among the bourgeois to whom Darwinism meant a defense of *laisser faire* in economy—a war of all against each at home. Thus the foundation and justification of military institutions and practices were made immediately identical with the very explanation of human existence: the struggle for existence, "natural" selection, and the survival of the fittest—all nature red with blood in tooth and claw. The more hostile life was conceived to be and the more "beneficent" the restless conflict in the jungle, the more armed combat appeared to be necessary, indeed defensible as a good thing in itself and as a way of raising the qualities of the fittest that survived.

Respecting this military universalization of Darwinism, there were some doubts at the time even among men who had employed soldiers to accomplish their designs; they had grown tired, perhaps, of the military and their endless demands upon the state. For example, Napoleon III, in distress, asked his Chambers and Europe generally in 1863, what was the utility of that military system he had himself done so much to set up: "Will the jealous rivalry of the great powers forever obstruct the progress of civilization? Will we always maintain our mutual defiance by exaggerated armaments? Will we forever preserve a state which is neither peace with its security nor war with its chances of fortune?" [83] But Napoleon's greatest antagonist, Bismarck, did not share this despair. He never came to regret this kind of competition. He held Darwin in high esteem, and never emancipated himself from the warlike and military interests of the class from which he sprang.

Generally unwilling to urge war themselves, domestic or foreign, for the mere purpose of giving the fittest a chance to show their fitness, the military have scouted all forms of pacifism and laid the blame for war on others. Moltke ascribed responsibility for modern wars to the activities of parliaments and stock exchanges and other forces which, being modern, seemed repulsive to him. Leonard Wood, who personally wanted the war with Spain in 1898 —a war which the traders and the stock exchanges clearly did not want—declared that "wars do not have their origins in personal likes and dislikes, but are brought about by commercial and race influences; and until competition for trade and land and all questions of race expansion are solved, I do not believe they will pass off the field. Readiness to defend one's interests tends to preserve peace." [84]

At best, military men have deemed the tendencies to harmonization, inherent in some sectors of capitalism, futile and misleading. When William II tried to attract a number of American finance magnates to his court, to improve American-German relations, the younger Moltke thought it all in vain: such meetings would have no influence on the political relations of the two nations, would not smooth out the divergent economic interests of a hundred million people all undergoing the struggle for existence, all wanting to get rich, each at the expense of the other.[85]

Like Leonard Wood, many other officers have maintained that

armies preserve peace, and that they preserve it the better the bigger they are; that the military do not want war, but that war is always in the offing: "No one knows when the game is coming off, but we know it is coming one day, and what is worse, we know we are not getting ready for it." [86] At all events, armies do not, and in the nature of things cannot, want unarmed peace. It is incumbent on their craft, therefore, as a craft to combat as ignoble or dangerous both general and specific proposals for pacification.

For centuries armies have strenuously objected to the extreme form of disarmament known as pacificism. When George Fox converted a number of officers and men in the army of the Puritan Commonwealth to Quaker nonresistance, Monck wrote to Cromwell that they might "prove a very dangerous people should they increase in our army, and be neither fit to command nor obey, but ready to make a distraction in the army and a mutiny upon every slight occasion." Others told Cromwell that on principle the Quakers would not allow their converts to fight, that their egalitarian notions were "the root of disobedience. . . . The whole world is governed by superiority and distance in relations, and when that is taken away, unavoidably anarchy is ushered in." In 1657 the Quaker-infested regiments in Scotland were purged of the converts.[87] Other antimilitary sects such as the Mennonites have fared no better. Although fully informed of their antiwar beliefs, governments have by turns welcomed such sects owing to their thrift and hard work, and driven them out because they furnished "bad examples." Frederick William I, the first of the Prussian soldier kings, "did not want this vermin any more. Their children do not become soldiers." They might be fit as merchants but not for gentlemen.[88] In the main, military men have agreed with Donoso-Cortés, one of the exhumed forerunners of fascism, that "when a nation shows a civilized horror of war, it receives directly the punishment of its mistakes. God changes its sex, despoils it of its common mark of virility, changes it into a feminine nation, and sends conquerors to ravish it of its honor." [89]

While universally accepting the necessity of condemning every form of pacificism, the military have been almost equally united in doubting the efficacy of international law as a world harmonizer. They have found it harmful to their interests in a broad and in a narrow sense. Moltke, whose function was not merely to win battles abroad but to provide justifications for the army at home, said to the liberals of the Reichstag:

Within, the law protects the right and liberty of the individual; without, between states, only power. A tribunal of international law, if it should exist, would still be without executory power and its judgments would finally be submitted to decision upon the battle-field. Small states can rely on neutrality and international guarantees; a large state exists only by itself and by its own strength; it fulfills the purpose of its existence only when it is resolved and armed in order to defend its existence, its freedom, and its right; and to leave a country defenseless, would be the greatest crime of its government.[90]

Enough statements from military men of other nations are available to demonstrate the existence of an international military front against international law as offering security. Their solidarity is, perhaps, best expressed in the language of a British major:

It cannot be too clearly stated that International Law is no protection except to the strong, and that the only laws which great Powers recognise as binding are those of power and expediency. . . . Otherwise, International Law, as a protection to the weak or the unprepared, is, as Clausewitz says, "hardly worth mentioning." . . . The European waste-paper basket is the place to which all treaties eventually find their way. . . . There is no such thing as International Law, for the thing so miscalled is merely international custom.[91]

Nor has that other form of pacific intention called "neutrality," guaranteed or not, always found much respect among military persons. Prince Eugene's march through Venetia in 1701, Napoleon's drive into Italy in 1796, the seizure of the Duke of Enghien in 1804, are examples. The violation of neutrality, an "expedient not the most delicate," as the Prince de Ligne admitted,[92] is too tempting a way of surprise to be shunned forever. During the nineteenth century, however, a strong conviction spread that neutrality ought to be recognized and observed by others. Bismarck played on it successfully when he informed the English of Napoleon III's desire to take over neutral Belgium. The very belief of the masses that neutrality would be respected by belligerents helped to make the idea useful to the designers of military plans, especially when they could think of no other way to break the stalemate of modern war. Waldersee, in 1883, intended in case of war with Russia to occupy Denmark at once.[93] Apparently Bismarck's approval of this intention was as little invited as the later Chancellor's approval of the Schlieffen Plan. On no side has the strictest care for neutral rights always been observed; the attempt of Colonel Luke Lea in 1919 to kidnap the Kaiser and carry him away from Dutch territory was a violation of neutral rights and international law heartily approved by General Bullard, who wished "that the Colonel could have captured the Kaiser. It would have been glorious!" [94]

The only rules of international law which are fairly certain to be observed by armies in time of war are those that appear useful to all parties. Up to 1914 most of the belligerents had adhered to the ruling that hostilities should commence only after a previous warning, a formal declaration of war, although Japan had not observed the rule in making her war on Russia. The plans for mobilization, however accelerated, still allowed the potential belligerents to subscribe to and adhere to the Hague Convention of 1907, with respect to war declarations; but it is now highly unlikely, for technical reasons, that it will be observed in a future war.

From previous ages various unwritten and written codes of warfare, setting limits to permissible violence, have survived. From time to time the rules have been altered to include newer and more deadly weapons, always under loud protest. Pope Innocent II condemned the crossbow as too deadly for Christian warfare in the 1130's; and when the British *Royal Ark,* in 1588, threw "fyreworks" at the Spaniards, the latter protested against so ignoble a method of fighting.[95] For a long time, complaints were raised against the so-called dumdum projectiles, "expressing height of malice rather than martiall prowesse," as a parliamentary report about the siege of Bristol in 1645 phrased it.[96] Similar outcries were made at each change of tactics. After the battle of Ravenna in 1512, the French denounced the Spanish because, instead of giving the customary push at the feudal adversary, to lift him out of the saddle, they directed their onslaughts at the horses. Alas, for chivalric warfare! The Spanish had learned to disregard these niceties of conduct in their struggle with the semibarbarian enemy along the frontier of European civilization.[97] But all these laments were in vain, like the futile cry of Molière's *Bourgeois Gentilhomme,* when his maid servant beat him with a broom: "Thou dost not attack me according to the rules!"

In the nineteenth century, after the papacy and feudalism had lost their power to enforce or modify rules, humanitarianism strove to fill the gap by attempting to bring about general agreements on the banning of certain of the worst elements, such as chain shot in naval war and explosive shells condemned at the Paris Conference of 1856, poison gas and poisoned arms, arms and projectiles apt to cause superfluous injuries and so increase the savagery and bitterness of warfare. But the military representatives of "progressive" powers whose industries were equipped to furnish such war materials or invent new ones, have usually set themselves against the restraints. It was Captain Mahan, representative of the most advanced industrial nation, who, at The Hague in 1899, voted against the exclusion from warfare of the largely untried asphyxiating gases.[98]

In the First World War the Central Powers broke the conventions, and the other side, after making capital by arousing popular moral indignation, followed suit. As a somewhat philosophical American general sums up his lifelong reading of war history: "This is the result of war as long as men have fought or will fight. What they believe 'pays' in securing victory they will use as they will in any other business they choose to engage in." [99] Thus successive ages of invention have regularly swept away most of the supranational amenities and arrangements, largely feudal or religious in origin, which formerly existed and were observed by armies in war, even though never to the extent that later romanticizing generations have chosen to believe.

Among the few survivals among the amenities would seem to be the silent, unwritten understanding between the higher staffs that they will not unduly molest one another, with retaliation available if one party should break the rule. When Prince Eugene in 1702 tried unsuccessfully to kidnap Vendôme in his headquarters, the latter shortly after posted a great number of guns close to Eugene's quarters and forced the Prince, by bombardment for a whole day, to move.[100] During the First World War the soldier was often shocked by the mutual consideration that prevailed between the opposing headquarters: "The staffs in the rear enjoyed additional security. The German and the enemy staffs spared one another since retaliation was at hand." [101] During the war of movements, to be sure, headquarters might still be molested, but this occurred rarely after the war of trenches had fully opened. British Headquarters remained for two and a half years in one place, a spacious and comfortable castle; there the British were left as undisturbed [102] as they left German Headquarters. If a mistake was made, and staff quarters happened to be bombed, the fury of the generals was unbounded. Early in 1915, an old Russian commander, under fire from German planes, was "waxing more and more indignant as each bomb fell. He said that such conduct was a scandalous breach of the customs of war, and if the airman were brought down he would at once hang him up to the highest tree in the village." [103]

Even this happy understanding, this genial survival of an earlier age, was on the verge of termination toward the end of the First World War. Near the closing crisis the officers of a new branch, the tank corps, proposed to Foch, in 1918, to break through the German lines with high-speed tanks, penetrate as far as their headquarters and thus paralyze, from its brain center, the whole German defense of a region. Foch accepted this proposal as the "basic idea of his 1919 plan of campaign." [104] Even though the proposal remained unapplied, none of the old immunity of headquarters survived in later wars.

Still another feudal remnant of the Internationale of the Military went down in the First World War: the readiness to concede to the enemy an honorable character in peace and war. Up to the First World War, though with notable exceptions, defeat in war, as in single combat, was considered quite as honorable as victory, provided the defeated party had fought bravely and according to the rules. The stronger the feudal spirit in an officer corps, the greater the readiness to concede to a brave enemy the "honors of war." In the Walthari saga the heroes of the battle in the Vosges sat down to eat, drink, nurse their wounds, and jest over the limbs they had lost in battle before the sun of the battle day was down. But the bitterness of modern warfare does not permit such amenities; not until December 1928 was a German allowed to visit West Point officially. Pershing remained convinced that the war was undertaken on America's part "in opposition to the continued violation of human and property rights." [105] In a questionnaire sent out by an American magazine, the large majority of the officers addressed reaffirmed their belief in complete German responsibility for the war. The ancient rule of *hosti etiam fides servanda* is ended.

On the German side, officers played a large part in the repudiation of the war guilt laid upon Germany by Article 231 of the Treaty of Versailles. A former officer, Alfred von Wegerer, was entrusted with direction of the counterpropaganda, and only a Jewish grandmother—no propaganda inefficiency on his part—brought about his removal by the Nazis. Other German officers sought to achieve the same end through personal means. Von Papen, a former, or perhaps eternal, cavalry officer, urged a group of French cavalry officers who were visiting in Berlin in 1934 to let bygones be bygones. "Basing his talk on the word *cheval* and its derivatives, chivaleresque and chivalrous, he seemed to attribute international troubles to politicians and officials, and expressed the view that if only politicians and officials were imbued with the same spirit as cavalrymen, there would soon be an end of misunderstanding between nations." [106] But how far was the request of Von Papen part of the German officers' endeavor to re-establish at home their shattered reputations, and how far was it an appeal to genuine traditions? Has the spirit of honorable competition actually prevailed in previous wars? To be more specific, how magnanimously had the Prusso-Germans behaved, after victory?

Since the war-guilt question has been confined by historians chiefly to recent conflicts, it is difficult to generalize on the question. Brest-Litovsk would hardly indicate that the Germans, when in a superior position, were ready to make great concessions to the vanquished. Yet the personal treatment accorded to the Russian delegates on that occasion was certainly far more honorable than that meted out to the German delegates at Versailles. The future of the rights and considerations to be granted to enemies in war is at best obscure. Judging by experience, enemies are to be deemed criminals in advance, guilty of starting the war; the business of locating the aggressor is to begin before or shortly after the outbreak of war; the methods of the enemy in conducting the war are to be branded as criminal, and victory is not to be a triumph of honor and bravery over honor and bravery but the climax of a police hunt for bloodthirsty wretches who have violated law, order, and everything else esteemed good and holy. If civilians are extensively responsible for this new war code, the military have not been negligent in adopting and enforcing it. In any form, however applied, it does not make for the reconciliation of nations or for a firmer belief in the possibility of harmonizing international interests, permanently or temporarily, before or after war.

Such being the attitude of the military on minor phases of pacification, it was not to be expected that they would look with favor on proposals for complete disarmament. Such projects had, indeed, been rejected as utopian long before the modern military had to trouble themselves about them. The religious argument for such disarmament was met by theological reasoning in the sixteenth century. When a count of Nassau, in 1595, proposed to his neighbor peers that they arm their subjects instead of hiring mercenaries, he considered how to overcome objections to armaments in the minds of those to be conscripted. One should impress on them, he decided, "what troublesome and dangerous warfare is going on right now, and that on account of our sinfulness things will remain that way for quite some time to come, and how much therefore depended on a regular military establishment." [107] This belief in the sinfulness in the world, which will not permit total disarmament, provided a principal reasoning of authority down to William II and President Harding. The latter maintained that there "never can come a time when there is not requisite an agency for the maintenance of law and authority and for national defense." [108]

The more materialistic argument that armament expenditure is wasteful and nonproductive has been in the main taken care of by the industrialists themselves rather than by army officers, although the latter constantly point out how "good for business" are military outlays—good, that is, for some business. Stumm could imagine no expenditure more productive than that for armies. Samuel Colt proposed that the crisis of 1837 be overcome by large appropriations for armaments, including his own revolvers. Essentially co-bureaucratic writers like Hans Delbrück were sure that Germany, "bulging with riches," could well afford to arm.[109] And war ministers insisted that nations which spent so much on alcohol and tobacco might well employ their money more nobly for war purposes.

Though total disarmament could be disposed of so lightly, a "most dangerous" proposal was that for proportionate disarmament: for an all around reduction. On the surface, and plausibly argued by men like Thomas Paine, the idea appears eminently fair. Late in the eighteenth century the author of *Common Sense* and *The Rights of Man* proposed a disarmament convention among the sea powers; they were to stop new construction, reduce existing naval establishments by 50 per cent, and take care that no other nations were arming on the sea. Construction of navies and sea war, Paine thought, were incompatible with the life of rational beings; commerce depended, not on navies, but on the trade with other, prospering countries.[110] His plea was very rational, very bourgeois, but not connected up with any specific energetic interest which might start negotiations. At that point the actual resistance of specific interests, those of diplomats and the military, begins.

When military proposals of this sort have been made, they have as a rule emanated from governments anxious to maintain a *status quo* in armaments and power position. In the winter of 1800-1, the summer of 1801, and again in 1802, the triumphant Napoleon was ready for disarmament. The nations of Europe were all one family, and a war between them was civil war. He asked the Prussian and Austrian ministers in Paris whether it would not ease the burdens of their peoples "to reduce proportionally the armies which the Great Powers supported in time of peace." The Austrian answered that his court could wish for nothing better, but that it would be difficult to make the Berlin court assent.[111] A third power was always found to stand in the way of disarmament, even if two pretended to agree.

The war weariness after the close of the Napoleonic hostilities provided the climate for fresh projects of this nature. Czar Alexander I proposed to the Great Powers a concerted reduction of military armaments, but met with a strong though polite resistance. Without daring to pronounce a neat refusal, Metternich told Alexander that standing armies were an indispensable support of governments, admitting, however, that those of inordinate size robbed the state of resources, contained the seeds of revolution, and endangered the peace of Europe. Steps toward actual disarmament, which might vastly have improved Austrian finances, were avoided. Metternich and Castlereagh suspected Russian deception. In truth, Russian military interest might have agreed with the Czar's proposal, for at that time the Russian army was backward in organization—even in 1807 and 1813 it contained Kalmucks, Bashkirs, and other tribesmen armed with bow and arrow—and it was slow in action. The moment was favorable for Russia. Nothing was done.[112]

Other disarmament proposals of nineteenth-century governments had equally specific interests behind them and went little or no further. But there was more apparent momentum behind them, a wide variety and concentration of interests. Parliamentarians, impressed by popular movements, did not wish to leave pacifism forever to the socialists. The papacy, through the encyclical of Leo XIII on June 20, 1894, asked whether the state of armed peace in Europe was really "the natural state of civil coexistence of humanity." To these were added a pressure from financiers, like Bloch, with his *Future of War,* published in 1898, and the notoriously pacifistic Rothschilds.

Finally there was a "movement of military reaction," as the Foreign Minister of Belgium called it.[113] Russia faced the danger of lagging behind in the arms competition and the necessity of spending huge sums to catch up, unless, as it occurred to War Minister Kuropatkin, she could persuade her nearest competitor, Austria, to agree to a moratorium on certain types of guns. From a military point of view this would have been quite safe for Russia, because proportional decrease of armaments would have left her in possession of her numerical superiority—the very advantage that Western Powers sought to match by expediting mechanical progress.

Approaching the Czar with some trepidation, Kuropatkin found him quite sympathetic, confessing that he had long been "against the adoption of new guns in our army." New guns would create a new quasi-industrial proletariat in the army, a more revolutionary element. This antirevolutionary desire and the wish to even up military competition, in which Finance Minister Witte eagerly concurred for financial considerations, speeded along the Russian "peace" proposals without affecting Russian imperial policies. Witte persuaded the heads of the Russian bureaucracy to invite not only Austria but also all the arming nations to join in the standstill. This project, connected with a plan to arbitrate, which was as popular in Western democracies as it had hitherto been foreign to Russian concepts, would, it was thought, take the wind out of the red sails of socialism.

In spite of their innocuous appearance, the Russian proposals were easily penetrated by other military men and stirred up a hornet's nest of angry doubts and protests on the part of all the other powers. Threatening to interfere with the armament business of officers as well as industries, the proposals struck a "socialistic note," the Kaiser said bitterly, and strengthened the internal opposition to all armament bills. The United States, at the close of the Cuban War, found it "impracticable . . . to consider the present reduction of [its] armaments, which even now are doubtless far below the measure which principal European powers would be willing to adopt." Readily yielding, Russia weakened her propositions and assured all the countries that no harm had been meant to their specific interests and that no political questions would be raised, such as the treatment of Alsace-Lorraine or other imperialistic problems. Only "technical" questions, such as the limitation, as distinguished from the reduction, of armaments was contemplated.

Viewing the Russian proposals with wrath or, like Goluchowski, with benevolent hilarity, all the Great Powers were equally determined to kill them before or during the conference. There were degrees of readiness to co-operate among the members of different national delegations, as between Andrew D. White and Captain Mahan, but on the whole all the delegates were apparently resolved to make the conference as unsuccessful as possible without offending Russian susceptibilities. The military and naval members of the delegations were, as a rule, the most hostile to any convention which might be drafted.

The "technical" character given to the conference, at the outset, opened the doors wide to the direct participation of these officers. Taking advantage of the occasion, military and naval officers effectively kept the diplomats from any voice in so-called technical matters, although at the same time they themselves insisted on discussing freely the so-called political questions. While the British and Germans looked after their concerns, Captain Mahan protested against the prohibition of poison gas, against any restriction on the Monroe Doctrine, and indeed against some of the measures his own delegation was especially instructed to press. The activity of the officers went beyond the usual role in which they are visualized at such conferences—that of shoemakers expected to agree on the suppression of shoes. In their zeal they often forgot their national divisions and like members of a professional *internationale* or fraternity united in agreeing to yield as little as possible to the civilians.

Above all things the military and naval experts of each nation endeavored to retain and defend what they considered the specific advantages of their country and the proper methods for its own warfare, while giving no countenance to anything like a reduction in armaments. The British Admiralty and War Office protested even before the opening of the conference against the suppression of certain arms and ammunition which "would favor the interest of savage nations and be against those of the more highly civilized." The American delegation was inclined "to favor to the greatest degree possible every sanction for the liberty of the population of an invaded country to take up arms in its defence, without incurring liability for the action other than that of legitimate belligerence."

Among the officer delegates of the Great Powers, there was an informal but strong understanding—directed if necessary against the civilian heads of the delegations—not to admit any restrictions on what each professional delegation considered its own country's chief strength. Together they quashed some Russian and Dutch proposals for restrictions in arms. But all except the German military delegates took care, as they were instructed, not to make their opposition too public or outspoken. It was left to the German delegate, Colonel Gross von Schwarzhoff, to take over "the spiritual leadership in this opposition," as one of his colleagues said, and voice most energetically and publicly the resistance to any disarmament. Schwarzhoff expressed the opinion that armaments were not impoverishing peoples and that military service was not a burden. On the contrary, the German at least considered it "a sacred and patriotic duty to which he owes his country's existence, its prosperity, and its future." He introduced the questions which have wrecked all attempts at disarmament since the Hague Conference, even when the mandates were more urgent and the intentions somewhat more honest than in 1898-9: What constitutes the military strength of a nation? By what measuring rod can that strength be established and made comparable, as a preliminary to general cutting-down of arms? What goes into all that later has been called the military or war potential, aside from men?

After posing these questions, he pointed to such elements of potential strength as the state of public education, the duration of active service, the number and kinds of drills imposed on the reserves, the railway system and fortification of the countries, the economic resources, the geographic situation, the military duties incumbent upon a country, colonial troops. In such circumstances, the military subcommittee, studying the matter of potentials, found the subject "very difficult," and the rest of the delegations and governments were content to accept that judgment and do nothing. The Americans felt that their armed forces were in every way noncomparable, "so small, relatively to the extent of territory and the number of population, as well as in comparison with those of other nations." [114]

Although the German officer had most effectively achieved the end generally desired by the military and naval experts, the members of his delegation were least successful in escaping the popular odium attached to their rigid stand against disarmament and arbitration. Arbitration, it was thought in Berlin circles, would deprive Germany of the values drawn from the potentials which supported her in diplomatic negotiations and from the speed of mobilization in which she felt superior. However that may be, their attitude made it the easier for other nations, no whit less reluctant to disarm in truth, to throw upon Germany a large part of the responsibility for the failure of the Hague Conference and to make her armaments a measuring rod for all other European and even some American armaments. Germany, the British military delegate asserted,

is the military centre of gravity in Europe, and all ideas effecting any reduction, small or great, in the present burden of armaments on land, must inevitably fail if they do not receive support from Berlin. They do not receive such support; on the contrary, they are met with the plain intimation that Germany will, under no circumstances, be a party to any limitation and still less to any reduction of armaments.[115]

So the delegates parted, confining themselves mainly to pious "vows" for the future reduction of armament burdens, "for the purpose of the growth of the moral and material well-being of humanity." In reality, among the officer delegates, the intimate intercourse with one another at The Hague had stiffened some hostilities and confirmed resolutions to arm. Fisher, for instance, decided on the basis of the Hague experiences that the enmity of the British navy must be shifted from the French to the German navy.[116] For the German delegation "the moral of the Peace Conference" was that "never again must we allow Russia to act as the guardian of Europe and, under the pretense of military burdens, incite the Europeans as well as the socialists against their sovereigns, as has been done in such a shameless way at The Hague." In other words, agitation for disarmament and arbitration was to be outlawed as socialistic, if not treasonable.

The second so-called disarmament conference was convoked and finished with similar twisting and turning on the part of those involved. Theodore Roosevelt was no less an enemy of disarmament and arbitration than William II, the only difference being that he was not so outspoken in his public utterances on this issue; he and other leaders of the Western Powers took more care for the effect which arbitration agreements produced upon "the gallery." The Second Hague Conference hardly touched the subject of military disarmament. In their international solidarity the officers took good care to insure their well-being in case they were captured in a future war. The diplomats of the Western Powers, including the United States, again assured one another that Germany, as Grey told Ambassador Reid, "holds the key" to any step in disarmament. The "great nonsense," as William II called the Conference of 1907, ended with a "vow" declaring the limitation of armaments to be "highly desirable," as against the "greatly desirable" of 1899, the difference between *grandement* and *hautement* corresponding, perhaps, to a rise in armament expenditure of sixty-seven million pounds in the interval between 1899 and 1907.

Even if the German opposition to disarmament and arbitration was again the most outspoken in 1907, the history of the conference, now rewritten in the light of secret papers, does not in any way justify the war-guilt note of the Allied and Associated Powers, on June 16, 1919, which maintained that Germany had been adding to her armaments while other countries had seriously endeavored to achieve international harmony and amity. The statistical and political records of all the powers at that time reveal constant technical progress in armament and advances in their ideological preparation for "a just war," which Theodore Roosevelt proclaimed before the Second Hague Conference, as "in the long run far better for the nation's soul than the most prosperous peace obtained by acquiescence in wrong or injustice." [117]

Bilateral attempts at restriction of armaments have been not much more successful than those which figured on the agenda of international conferences. Two statesmen animated by at least a modicum of intention to avoid the war which the armament competition of their two countries threatened to bring on, Bethmann-Hollweg and Haldane, thought that on both sides the "admirals and generals were pretty difficult." [118]

Later discussions, including the disarmament conferences at Washington in 1921 and at Geneva, were in all essentials prefigured by the Hague meetings. The active opponents of actual restrictions were always soldiers or sailors who wanted armament or rearmament. They were never too fastidious in their argumentation, like the French admiral who in Washington defended the continued use of submarines by saying: "You could not stop the progress of humanity." [119]

THE POST-1918 MILITARIZATION OF SOCIETY

Even while the First World War was in progress, it was evident that the mass armies provided by universal conscription and inflamed by nationalist sentiment, such as the nineteenth century had known, were not sufficient to bring victory or produce the maximum of military endeavor. The combatants were beginning to draw on economic reserves and industrial ingenuity as never before and to study problems of raising psychological resistance among masses. The war was being carried to the civilian behind the lines. By the time peace was concluded, the outlines of a militarism more embracing in its claims and dreams than any of previous times were already drawn.

The 1914-18 war, accordingly, may take its place as the third of the three general blood baths, emancipated or "true wars," as Fichte called them, which have swept the scene clear of age-hardened institutions and ideas, only to make room for mightier organizations and concepts. The first of these waves of destruction, the religious wars, which subsided by about 1648, the date of the Peace of Münster, wiped out the feudal system with its small, impermanent bodies of individualistic warriors; upon the vacated arena were soon built up the standing armies of the new nations, officered by noblemen, with caste honor as the cohesive. Under the second universal deluge, that of the Napoleonic era, concluded in 1815, these limited troops led by exclusive commanders broke down, yielding place to mass armies animated by nationalistic fervor. For a century this development continued, until the War of 1914-18 sucked most of the world into its whirlpool; in its turn, this war proved the inadequacy of existing forms and energies, setting the nations toward a fresh search for new potentials. Scarcely was it closed when a giant concept of military organization came forth: the society-in-arms, regimented down to the very infants, fused by consciousness of some supranational "race," "soil," or "history," economically and mentally mobilized, forever standing in readiness for total war.

At each stage in the development of militarism, a constant exchange or osmosis of thought between nations has gone on. Military organization is the product of highly complex interactions; this is evident from a mere look at the international military vocabulary: the word "infantry" is originally Spanish; "lieutenant" is French; "captain" is Italian and "field marshal" German. It is therefore not easy to assign their several roles to the various peoples. The standing army, for instance, might be called English, for it was first exhibited there in imposing size under the dictatorship of Cromwell; yet a Frenchman, Jacques Cœur, had proposed the idea a century before, and refinements in drill and methods were added by Dutch and Prussians, in turn not unaffected by the Spanish and Swiss. Again, the mass army appeared in startling shape first in France, but Germans had forecast some such plan previously; moreover, as they sought to resist France by her own instruments, the Prussians produced some of the most critical discussions of the subject. Similarly, the new notion of the armed society is the result of a universal conflux of ideas.

Societies have, of course, been placed on a constant war footing in times past; not to speak of Sparta, Sweden rationalized her industries and agriculture under an absolute state in the seventeenth century in order to wage a more efficient war in Germany and elsewhere. The phrases, *guerre absolue* and *guerre totale,* are French; an Italian, Mussolini, uttered the fiercest exhortations to such mobilization of social forces. A most vital contribution was made during the First World War by Americans who revealed to others, in particular the astonished Germans, a unique skill in mass propaganda, won through their special experiences in business advertising and political campaigning. Hitler, after the war in the service of the Intelligence Department of the Reichswehr, acknowledged in *Mein Kampf* the deep impressions made on him by observing the psychological technique of the Anglo-Saxon countries.

In the 1930's all the major nations, in one way or another, were groping toward a more complete utilization of resources and energies than in any previous age. The Germans insisted on war service even of aliens residing in their territory, and so did the French to a scarcely lesser degree. Even the democracies had their plans for bringing industries upon a war footing in case of need, and heatedly debated the question of regulating war profits (which no longer existed for Russia). It was generally seen, also, that airplanes and poison gases carried new threat to the civilians, except perhaps in aloof America; England and France now recognized that the preparedness of the civilian population for sudden attacks was a matter almost as vital as the equipment of armies with guns. Tentative efforts were made in the direction of "thought control," as the Japanese called it, using the new agents, film and radio, education and suggestion, to create and keep up morale.

Yet, from various causes, the scheme of the armed society owed as much to Germany as that of the standing army to England and the mass army to France: the most radical practitioners and thoroughgoing theorists of social embattlement were German. So prodigious and intensive a study of its every phase was made there, and so elaborate a terminology created, that, as a German general declared, no other country possessed even an adequate vocabulary in which to discuss the subject. Among the various fascisms, the German was the most militaristic, for it carried furthest what the Italians call the *"inquadramento"* of the individual, making the private citizen a public unit, whereas in England even the soldier remained a "private." According to its "mythologist," Alfred Rosenberg:

The German nation is just now about to find its style of life for good, a style fundamentally different from what is called British liberalism. . . . It is the style of the marching column, regardless of where and for what purpose this marching column is to be used. . . . It is a mark of the German style of life that no German wants nowadays to feel himself a private person. . . . That is the secret explanation . . . of why present-day Germany is uniformed and marching in columns.[1]

Both Fascism and Communism, depending more than democracies for their daily existence on their armies, attempted a greater penetration of their peoples by military ideas; the masses were organized in a quasimilitary way in uniformed formations under leaders whom the rank and file recognized as permanent, not merely temporary, superiors. Military metaphors abounded in directions and exhortations, such as "victories on the harvest front," the "butter battle," the "March on Rome." But there was some difference in aim between them: the Bolshevik state indeed offered the theoretical promise that the military bondage of the present was only a transition period on the way to a millennium in which all force will be ended; it does not exalt military exertion and expenditure as good in themselves. By contrast, the militarism of the Third Reich expected even theoretically to endure one or two thousand years, for it is the essence of that Empire; there, as Sieburg said "the population sees in the carrier of arms a symbol of itself." [2]

Examples of the armed society came into being in various degrees of perfection; moreover, other nations were spurred by their efforts to prepare for defense along new lines, not merely by heaping up armaments and enlarging armies, but by planning and weighing economic and psychological resources unknown to the relatively innocent pre-1914 era. Yet it was and is by no means certain that the society-in-arms would have to be forced upon the peoples so generally as were the standing army and the mass army in their day. For one thing, the leading rich democracies were not compelled to such extraordinary exertions as the poorer peoples, less favored with natural resources or backward technologically, like Germany and Russia respectively; Great Britain could plan an armaments program as huge as Germany's without reaching very deeply into her pockets or making frenzied appeals to her citizens.

If economic pressure does not bend the democracies in the direction of totalitarianism, neither need they be persuaded by military arguments. On the contrary, there was every reason to suppose, as the French popular front insisted, that democracy was and is preferable from the sheer technical point of view. Democracy preserves many war potentials, such as initiative in business and on the battlefield, and taps many deep sources of energy, intellectual and nervous as well as economic, which may quite conceivably fail authoritarian governments.

Officers and Fascisms

If officers in many countries gave eager support to fascist movements, this did not necessarily argue for the greater war efficiency of such a system over the democratic way. Their predilection was too easily militaristic rather than military: realizing how much fascism did for armies, they often ignored the question whether fascism was also good for war, the ultimate purpose for which armies exist. At times they exhibited a tendency to underestimate the *potentiel de guerre* in democracy, because, though so volcanic when it erupts in war, it may not be so easily ordered in peacetime. This was probably behind the definition of "democracy" written for an R.O.T.C. manual in the American War Department after 1918:

Authority derives through mass meeting or any other form of "direct" expression. Result is mobocracy. Attitude toward property is communistic—negating property rights. Attitude toward law is that the will of the majority shall regulate, whether it be based upon deliberation or governed by passion, prejudice and impulse without restraint or regard for consequences. Results in demagogism, license, agitation, discontent and anarchy.[3]

Fascism fulfilled many an old daydream of officers everywhere; for instance, it abolished the politician, with his awkward queries on budgetary matters, and at the same time it effectively stopped criticism on the conduct of military affairs through press or books and from the platform. That subjection to control and criticism may be excellent for armies, preventing them from premature ossification and decay, is easily forgotten in the enjoyment of the convenience of such arrangements. Again, the fascist form of government brought greater authority, supported by more severe and swift punishments, to those in control; the fascist parties took care of the problems of propaganda and "indoctrination," ever dreaded by the generally word-poor officers. That civilians so ruthlessly punished, so compactly herded, may lose the individualism which seems more and more desirable amid the desolation of the modern battlefield, is also usually ignored, although at least one German major expressed some dissatisfaction with the overexcitement and overdrilling of Nazism which, he thought, might threaten to sap the nervous energies of the Germans.

A further lure was the fact that military men were conceded the highest rank in society under fascism; military institutions furnished the great examples for all other organizations in the state. There was a time in Germany, immediately after the First World War, when as a Reichswehr officer in charge of public relations complained, "the officers, up to then the most respected class, fell lower in the public estimation than any paper on the Exchange." [4] Hitler changed that and restored the officers to that ancient accustomed place, even above the large majority of the dignitaries of his own party.

Besides such apparent conveniences to army men, fascism provided enlarged armies, bringing rapid promotion. It also took care of certain agrarian interests, which officer bodies continued to represent in Europe as they have for centuries. These and other motives led military officers to take an active part in the initial stages of various fascist movements. This was twice the case in Spain, under Generals Rivera and Franco; it was evident in Italy, where General de Bono took part in the March on Rome, and in Germany, where Hitler, a corporal in the First World War, had officers like Röhm and Hierl for his lieutenants, not to speak of military patrons higher up. In France, also, Colonel de la Rocque, scion of an old military family, led or carried the *Croix de Feu* with the blessings of Marshal Lyautey[5] and perhaps of General

Weygand, forming a completely military organization which included a motor and aviation corps; like other "leaders" he claimed for his own group the credit for preserving the national effort during the war, saying that "we," the army men and other combatants, "saved France once, we can save it again." Even in England, that intelligent military writer, General Fuller, joined the unshirted Blackshirts, standing with a vice admiral at the head of Oswald Mosley's list of candidates for Parliament.[6] Officers have been influential likewise in the fascist regimes of Austria, Hungary, Bulgaria, and Yugoslavia.

In Poland, under the dictatorship of her liberator Marshal Pilsudski, the domination of the military was especially clear. The manner in which the dictator made and unmade ministers, and how officers allowed themselves to be treated, is made clear by General Slawoj-Slavkowski in his memoirs, in one of those bursts of revelation for which officers no longer make us wait until the evening of their life. One day, this General obeyed the summons of Pilsudski, who had taken over power in 1926. He entered the room to find the *Kommandant* playing solitaire:

He gave me his hand across the table and pointed to a chair opposite. Without any introduction he then said: "Now then, you become Minister of Interior, the present one will no longer work with this . . . parliament." I sat still, waiting what the *Kommandant* might further say. He remained however silent and only looked searchingly into my eyes. In all modesty I pointed out that I had not come into contact with politics at all and that some one else might be better fitted. The Marshal laughed and said, agreeing with me so to speak: "Politics is not necessary for that, every one makes such a great fuss about you being such an organizer. For that reason you shall become Minister! Present yourself to the Prime Minister. Goodbye!" Then the Marshal, as if tired by this conversation, dropped his head and went on with his solitaire without giving me his hand.

Four years later, the General having in the meantime returned to army service, Pilsudski called him in again and began abruptly: "You leave for the Ministry of Interior. Parliament is to be dissolved, and you have to make the new elections." The General thought he needed more time than the six weeks proposed: "If one receives unexpectedly the command of a regiment, it is hard to lead it to an attack an hour later, particularly if one does not know the terrain and the men." But the elections were made as ordered. Again the General was called in to see the Marshal, who asked him what he wanted now, to retain the ministerial office or return to the army. "Marshal, I shall work as you order." "You are tedious." "I cannot judge, *Kommandant,* for which service I am better fitted. . . . In my service for you I have long forgotten what I should prefer. I am altogether at your disposal and it is certainly good, whatever you, Marshal, decide." "If things are that way with you, you may go where you will, I shall not tell you." The General left disquieted, wondering how the *Kommandant* would decide his fate. "To choose anything, would have been senseless. No such chance with the *Kommandant.*" [7] No thought of personal dignity ever disturbed the General, who submitted to a tyranny greater than that of the old absolutism.

Even where fascisms were not founded by military men, they had the sympathies and the favors, sometimes very material ones, of large groups in the armies, on their way to power, whereas the support given by armies to the liberalism which paid them was practically negligible, except perhaps in Italy, where the few liberal generals were, however, betrayed by the monarch. In Italy, Fascists and officers were brought together by a common aversion to the peace tendencies of liberalism. When Balbo returned from the war, as he wrote, "Just like so many others, I hated politics and the politicians, who in my opinion had betrayed the hopes of soldiers, reducing Italy to a shameful peace and undermining the cult of heroes. To struggle, to fight in order to return to the land of Giolitti, who made a merchandise of every ideal? No, rather deny everything, destroy everything, in order to renew everything from the foundations." [8] The armies, like the Fascists, sought their *revanche—Invictis victi victuri,* as the inscription on the war-dead monument in Berlin University read: "To the unconquered [dead, from] the conquered [living] who will be victorious tomorrow." The Italians demanded *revanche* for ignominies inflicted by foreigners at Caporetto and Versailles, but they meant first a domestic revenge for the peace dictates of their own fellow nationals who had "starved" the armies and certain kindred groups, like large-scale agriculture, by their liberal politics.

Behind fascism in Italy, Spain, and Germany stood, side by side with certain industries, but most influential, the big landowners who consequently were spared expropriations to any considerable extent, in favor of peasant settlement, under that system. Particularly in the latter country have the agrarian interests been intertwined with those of the nobility, and these in turn with the claims of officers in the army and navy. That nexus of interests had been threatened when German parliaments before Hitler began to investigate the *Osthilfe,* the subventions accorded to owners of bankrupt estates in East Prussia. Fearing the publication of reports which would have uncovered scandals and led to the lopping off of state funds for such purposes, all these groups joined behind the Nazis in

January 1933; Hitler was to salvage the ancient connections of the German officer corps.

In Germany, accordingly, the old story of postfeudal nobility in army politics continued. The share of that nobility in the actual direction of the First World War had not measured up to expectations; although it took a highly honorable proportion of war losses as a whole, too many nobles had been cavalry officers to share to the fullest extent in the *impôt du sang*. The small war losses suffered by the cavalry and its officers testify too unmistakably the slight service they did in the war. Of 386 officers in the most distinguished German horse guard regiments, almost completely noble, only 43 died and of these only 9 died with their own regiments.[9]

In the postwar social upheavals, however, the nobles reasserted their claim to direction and commanders at the head of "White" troops showed the people that "the masters' names are still von . . . and von . . ."—Von Lüttwitz, Von Oven, before the scenes, Von Seeckt, Von Schleicher behind.[10] They showed their hand during the Kapp putsch, named after a gentleman whose official occupation had been the securing of credits for the large estates of the Junkers and whose side job was conspiring first for a Pan-German victory, then for a reconstitution of the dominion of old Prussianism. Since this putsch had no mass basis, it failed; seeking to remedy that lack of popular appeal, old Prussianism came to ally itself with the National Socialists. Some of the uprooted *cadets* joined the Nazi Party; these and the scions of nobility in the army took care that the Junker interest was kept intact under fascism, except perhaps in name—for the much-hated title, *Rittergutsbesitzer,* possessor of knightly estate, has been abolished, although not such estates themselves.

Not only did old Prussianism wish to salvage its land holdings, however; it also sought recovery of its former privileges and positions in the army. These had been sorely diminished after 1919 by the reduction of the German army to one hundred thousand under the terms of the Versailles Treaty. That reduction had been a heavy blow to German nobility. Before 1914 the vocation of officer had been the one most frequently chosen by its members, followed by those of landowner, agricultural administrator, jurist (largely in government service), and diplomat. Twenty years later, the line-up had changed to: landowner, jurist, administrator, diplomat, officer. Whereas in 1912, 33 per cent of the nobles of age had become officers, in 1932, when the Treaty of Versailles had reduced the number of commissions to one-tenth of that in 1914, this percentage was only 1.17. But even so, in this same year, 27.15 of the German officers were still noble, vastly more than the percentage of nobles among the Reich population would warrant. Despite such favoring, dissatisfaction grew among the nobles; nearly three times as many of them emigrated after the war as in 1912,[11] but that was a small outlet for their energies. The surplus went to preparing the overthrow of the democracy which hampered the remilitarization of Germany.

Through their close co-operation with the National Socialists, the nobility managed to survive the change to a Third Reich extremely well; in the army, noble officers proved in fact as "long-lived" as before the war, as the army list of July 1936, shows:

1	Field Marshal	noble	1	100	per	cent	
5	Colonel-Generals	"	4	80	"	"	
18	Generals	"	6	33	"	"	
56	Lt. Generals	"	17	30	"	"	
91	Major Generals	"	22	24	"	"	
317	Colonels	"	69	22	"	"	[12]

The reintroduction of the mass army of conscripts naturally reduced the percentage of noble officers; practically all nobles who wanted to become officers were welcomed, but their number was far from sufficient to command the enlarged army, and the percentage of noble officers—23 per cent in the Reichswehr of 1921 [13] and on the increase since then—was bound to diminish in time. But that did not deprive the Prussian aristocracy of the chance to continue to run the army during peace periods. Only during the Second World War, with defeat staring him in the face, did Hitler find this aristocracy, still largely associated with the General Staff, incompetent and treacherous.

It seemed surprising, after the experiences of one world war, and in an era when preparations for warfare were of a more technological character than ever, to see a modern army retain such a large number of noblemen as officers who are not prepared either by tradition or education for the engineering war. A closer examination of their positions shows unmistakably that these nobles were preponderatingly placed in posts of command, of army corps and military districts—in a word, they held the positions important in peacetime, the militaristic jobs, including especially those in the cavalry. Far more often nonnoble officers were placed in technical fields, in the high ranks of the artillery, the air force, the tank troops, at the head of the technical army schools (War Academy, Aerotechnical Academy, Air Warfare Academy), and finally the first chief of the rebuilt General Staff of the army was a nonnoble.

Parliaments and Preparedness

The common enemy of such restless officers was in every case parliamentarism, old or new, and of course the newer the weaker. The shortest shrift of constitutional processes was made on the frontiers of Western civilization, in Iraq, for instance, where in 1936 an army leader "sent a fleet of airplanes over Baghdad, dropped warnings to the Cabinet, demanding that it resign within two hours. When the time elapsed and the Cabinet had not resigned, the planes bombarded the Ministry offices and fully armed troops occupied the city." The Premier was forced to submit his resignation and the King compelled to accept it immediately.[14] One of the outspoken contemners of parliamentarism was Pilsudski, who applied to it the same scatological expressions which William II reserved for the Hague Conference.

In Germany, parliamentary control over military budgets was established in 1919, and thereafter exercised, if not always thoroughly, at least enough to uncover misuses of moneys granted *en bloc* to the army and navy. Reichstag committees, acting largely under socialist pressure, brought out some of the "black" and "blue" special budgets, with their scandals; flagrant among these was the case of the naval captain Lohmann, who had used millions entrusted to him in acquiring a film company to make pictures furthering the militarist spirit. In the years 1928-30, the Reichswehr even had to surrender some eighty million marks of "reserves" it had piled up. Before the Reichstag had finished its work on the so-called *Osthilfe* scandals, threatening to implicate Hindenburg and other Junkers and officers, that body was dissolved, never to deliberate and control again.

Immediately after Hitler's coming into power budgetary publicity was ended in Germany, and all became "secret" about the army. Only by devious calculations could experts compute the use which the German army made of this liberty. Whereas in the budgetary years 1927-8 to 1930-1, the total expenditure amounted on the average to 781,000,000 marks, or about 10 per cent of the Reich's total expenditure, the later armament spending has been estimated at twelve times that much, and its share in the budget (for 1936-7) at 67 per cent.[15] General von Reichenau declared in 1935 that, under fascism, "the size of the armed forces is independent of parliament or majority decisions" [16]—a great relief.

Not only was an end made to embarrassing investigations, which might uncover cases of inefficiency, waste, and mistreatment of soldiers, but the more general criticism of military institutions stopped under fascism. The press was government-controlled and so was all other publishing, including that on military affairs. In Germany, where press and radio showed a decided indifference to military matters after 1918, they were thoroughly militarized. The *encadrement* of the German journalists proved far-reaching; at the head of their national organization (*Reichsverband der deutschen Presse*) and of half of its local branches were ex-officers, once members of the regular army and after that of diverse nationalist-military organizations, including the Nazi Party.[17] Through the Ministry of Propaganda, instructions were given to the press of which the following were typical: "We remind you that all reports about military innovations, as far as Germany is concerned, are undesirable. It is however in the interest of the Reich policy to illuminate the German public constantly about military affairs in the neighboring countries."

It is true that the press, even in democratic countries, was at this time no longer so sharp in military matters as it was earlier, when every time something unpleasant happened in the officer body, the prayer went up: "If only nothing gets into the papers!" [18] But of course under fascism, a breath of complaint would be punished with a severity unknown elsewhere; German criminal law became essentially the establishment of martial law in peacetime, condemning harshly any actions deemed damaging to national health or honor, the "spiritual and psychological bearing of the people" or the "interests of race, soil, army and nation." Not only were anti-military crimes and misdemeanors strictly dealt with, but officers were members of the high *Volksgerichtshof* before which, in a Star Chamber procedure of secrecy, cases of treason, attacks on the Führer, and so on, were adjudicated and punished as Draconically as by a military court in war-time.

Under the other authoritarian form of government, that of Russia, an opposite extreme was reached, that of more civilian control than even democracies pretend to assert. Trotsky had indeed early conceded value to the *spets,* or military expert, praising his services in the Civil War, and for a time such experienced commanders as Marshal Tukhachevsky built up the credit of the Red army until Russia was able to fling a solid weight into the balance of power politics of some of the Western nations. Stalin had always disagreed with Trotsky about the *spets,* preferring a good Bolshevik, though unseasoned in war, to an expert of dubious political views; at length he apparently narrowed his choice to good Stalinists. When the execution of Tukhachevsky and other generals was decreed, the credit of the Red army, upon which the continued existence of the Soviet state depends, was seriously threatened abroad; to many observers at the time it looked like a serious weakening of Russian military power owing to too much civilian control, control induced by a party dictator militarism that could stand no opposition or independent thought.

Quite a different situation was presented in Japan, where the military indeed interfered with the policy-determining function of the government, but did not have one of the most progressive forms of parliamentarism to contend with. In the Meiji era, when power was handed back to the Emperor, and the samurai, who provided the officers for the army, were released from their disciplined bondage of feudalism, a constitution was adopted, shaped most closely after the Bavarian constitution. The Emperor of Japan was made to fill a position in many respects resembling that of his contemporary, William I of Prussia-Germany. The latter was not a little surprised to find that the Japanese Emperor, who followed Prussian institutions closely, yet insisted upon giving his country a constitution, "after this thing had failed in our own country." [19] But the model chosen by the Japanese carefully withheld army and navy affairs from parliamentary control and exalted the supreme war lord role of the Emperor.

In spite of the deification of the Mikado, about whom the soldier was taught that "all other emperors are emperors through usurpation or popular choice whereas ours is a God and of divine essence," the army constantly revolted against what must have been the Emperor's will in the beginning. The army rebelled against the policy givers, at first openly, in 1874, 1876, and 1877; it forced the government into the Chinese War of 1894-5; in 1918 it rushed ten times as many troops into Siberia as the Cabinet had agreed to send, because it did not forecast the outcome of the war as accurately as the civilians. After the war, when a period of civilian ascendancy ensued, the army presently pressed its forward policy in Manchuria, accompanying this with a vigorous propaganda at home and finally confronted the unwilling Cabinet with the *fait accompli* of troops dispatched into Manchuria.

In the later stages of this struggle, a system of terror and assassination was developed which was greeted sympathetically by a German general, who, recalling the similar murders of statesmen by soldiers and militarized youth in post-1918 Germany, acknowledged that "very often in Japanese history long sword and short sword served as regulators of politics, and political murder as corrector of too great ministerial ambition, or as punishment of inefficiency in directing army positions. . . . In military questions where the life of the Empire was at stake, the samurai have not allowed themselves to be trifled with." [20] Generals and admirals represented the army and navy in the Cabinet, though not the Cabinet with the forces; if a soldier in the Cabinet should yield to the weighty considerations of the Cabinet majority, instead of to the pressure of the army and its auxiliaries, his life might be endangered.

The Japanese military, however, were not fascists in the accepted European sense of the term, for they strove to prevent the growth of such private armies as the shirt militias of European fascism. On the other hand, radicals were as readily killed by military assassins as capitalists and statesmen. The Japanese army was in fact opposed to capitalism, communism, *and* fascism; whatever system it supported must be peculiar to its needs, and the struggle between civilian and military assumed shapes outside the classifications of the West.

The forces of civilian democracy were hampered in Japan by the original form of the constitution; parliaments in some other countries were able to maintain their control over military affairs, although there appeared few party leaders in the Western world who had been aroused, even by the First World War, to take an expert and active interest in military questions. No party would appear more deficient in that respect than the British Labour Party. When someone in 1936 intended to inform that party about important events of a military character and begged to be put in contact with its military experts, he was told: "We are a peace party, we have no military experts." This scorn of the politician for the military was returned then in kind: F. S. Oliver, the romantic owner of a great drapery firm, friend of Henry Wilson and other officers, called politicians "mercenary rascals" and announced that "militarism is a fine thing," because it reduces their sphere of operation.[21]

Attempts of the military to transgress boundaries have abounded in England as well as elsewhere. One of the earlier examples was presented by Lord Wolseley, on whom Queen Victoria and Disraeli were agreed that, though he resembled Nelson, he was "an egotist and a braggart." Around 1888, during the naval scare started by Captain Beresford, Wolseley denounced "the system of our government by party—that curse of modern England—which is sapping and undermining the foundations of our country" and preventing the army and navy from attaining proper strength. His courage was not great enough to make this statement publicly, and that slouchy civilian, Lord Salisbury, who was clearly included among those whom Wolseley said the soldier must be taught to despise,[22] protested against the officers' "practice of making statements against the Government under whom they serve and making them in places where they cannot be answered."[23]

A more recent instance of forwardness on the part of the English military was the warning of Henry Wilson in 1921, who told Austin Chamberlain that "it was, to say the least, unwise for the frocks to try the Army too high . . . that we soldiers and sailors . . . strongly objected to the relations with Krassin and Lenin, that we strongly objected to the Cabinet Greek policy, to the Irish, Egyptian and Indian policy." Accusing the Cabinet of working with the King's enemies,[24] he took it upon himself to determine who

those enemies were. But such interference has always run up
against the traditional insistence of all the parties including the
Conservatives on parliamentary prerogatives; the latter party connected the great rearmament program of 1937 with the emphatic
declaration that parliamentary control over money granted would
in no way be curtailed.

In France, the reassertion of military will started the moment
Clemenceau left office; he had already received proof in 1919 that
"to the *militaires,* this war has taught nothing, at least not from
the political point of view. They do not seem to have perceived
the evaluation of the democratic ideas. Militarism is no longer
fashionable. Everybody is aware of that—except the military."
Forty-eight hours after he left office, a plan went into effect which
had been worked out beforehand, taking much of the authority
of the War Minister away and handing it to the Chief of the General Staff.[25] The Republic was fairly lucky in these arrangements
in that they were guided by Marshal Pétain, who seemed a good
republican at the time and kept down agitations in favor of fascism
within the army, to which men like Weygand, "up to his neck in
priests," as Clemenceau said of him, were not unfriendly. Some
civilian reforms, like those of Raiberti, were blocked by the army,
but the latter accepted the defense system of the Maginot Line,
begun in 1929, which was a concept dearer to the civilians than
the military. This provided for an unbroken fortress barrier of steel
and concrete. In addition the civilians impressed upon the military
the necessity of saving the productive means of the nation from
even a temporary evacuation and so hindered the army from in-
dulging again in the dream of a war of a mobile character, an
old-fashioned mobile war, that is. After they had succumbed to
the "Maginot mentality" not even an insider like De Gaulle was
able to win them over to the new-fashioned mobility of *panzer*
warfare. The question: Can France still be invaded? was answered
in the emphatic negative by the army gerontocracy.[26]

The struggle in France continued, even though the general lines
were thus laid down. After the violent outbreak of the Stavisky
scandals, Laval had to warn the staffs of the army to stop political
propaganda—the first time, perhaps, since the liquidation of the
Dreyfus case, that such public warning was found necessary.[27]
Most emphatically, the War Minister of the French popular front,
Daladier, like the English Conservatives, insisted on preserving parliamentary control over budgets, denying that secrecy in such matters was essential to military security. Though a member on the
Right proposed to discuss certain questions in secret committees,
Daladier declared: "The Government is of the opinion that speak-
ing out the truth is the suitable method for strong peoples. . . .

The clear-eyed control of parliament over our military organization is an essential element of French security." [28] Again, the army committee of the French Senate, in its report approving the nationalization of armament industries,[29] expressed its faith in democracy as the foundation of national defense: "We trust that the indivisibility of the material and moral forces in the service of the national defense will be one of the most essential concerns of the government in order that our country will feel always in closed ranks, and ready when the great reveille comes."

A greater confusion seemed to exist in that democracy most remote from immediate threat of war, the United States. No party there formulated so clear a military policy as the Conservatives in England or the popular front in France. For the majority of Congress, it was sufficient to vote ample supplies, and for the minority, to save money; neither forms a military policy worthy the name. This can only come from a willingness to bring together in a clear relationship military policy and foreign policy. What objects of American national interests were to be defended against aggression, beyond the area between Portland, Oregon, Portland, Maine, and Panama? The uncertainty about this larger aim left a large twilight zone in which the military themselves were forced to fumble without the guidance from the civilians which many of them desired.

One retired leader, General Hagood, testified that Congress "has lost its contact with the army and that there are very few members, if any, who really understood and could explain its organization," and although in the Roosevelt era money was easy to obtain for the fighting forces, its purposes remained unclarified. In this situation, according to the General, the army could only hope to acquire as much as possible; its "one consistent policy" was "to frighten Congress into appropriating more money," [30] lest, some day, it be caught unprepared by a vast conflict unleashed by the civilians.

The congressional arguments about budgets tended therefore to center around supplying the army and navy with more of what they had already—men, money, and machines—without discussing other war potentials. Thus it was maintained that the rich United States could well afford a larger standing army than that of Portugal, without mentioning other elements in America's potential which put her far ahead of Portugal. Sometimes the army's wishes might coincide with those of a pork-barrel politician eager for an allocation to his district, even if it be situated along the peaceful Canadian border. But again, the desire of the army to transfer a school to a more suitable location might meet the resistance of a Congressman from the old neighborhood, who denounces the transfer as intended merely to provide officers with better "social surroundings, country clubs and tennis." [31] In the absence of clear-cut objectives, Major C. G. Mettler, treating the broad subject of "The Common Defense," frankly admitted that: "I expect to use all the platitudes, old sayings, historical recollections, and trite experiences I can remember." [32]

It was natural that divisions of opinion should arise within the army on the question of means and arguments to employ in explaining its wants to a civilian population so generally indifferent and inexpert. One wing favored appealing to the public over the heads of the politicians, through Leonard Wood's training camps, for instance, where he did not expect to accomplish much in the way of detailed military instruction but a great deal "in implanting a sound military policy." [33] This method was repudiated by General Hagood, who found unnecessary the sort of teaching at R.O.T.C.'s which sought to demonstrate deficiencies of the army from early American history: "Whatever advantages might accrue from such studies to an institution like the Army General Staff, it is quite evident that, except for the purpose of propaganda, no such instruction is needed by young men who are being given only rudimentary military training to qualify them as non-commissioned officers." [34] Even more a matter for inner conflict was the resort to the plea of army usefulness in case of civil disturbances, a plea which some felt to be dangerous from the army standpoint.

As a Polish general, exiled by Pilsudski, said, in discussing the subject of modern war and democracies, the task of watching over the maintenance of public order may interfere with the army's essential task of preparing for national defense, for, if a party government uses it for its particular ends and confounds the army with the police, the army may incur unjust blame and thus help to further antimilitaristic tendencies. [35] In America the division of military labor has given military police duty to the National Guard, thus relieving the army proper from it, but on some occasions the argument that the army should be strengthened for "domestic trouble" was put forth. The proponents of a measure to authorize the President to increase the enlisted strength of the army during the fiscal year 1935-6, from 118,750 to 165,000, justified their proposal by urging the necessity of allowing the Executive to deal with inner difficulties that might or might not arise. "There are disturbing activities in many sections of the country aimed against the existence of our government," as Representative Buchanan warned the House. [36] A more definite use of this plea was made by Harry Woodring, as Assistant Secretary of War, when he advocated that "economic storm troops be fashioned from the CCC and veterans' organizations under army command." [37] Such arguments were offered to civilians interested primarily in domestic issues and unwilling to concern themselves with ultimate issues of foreign and military policy.

While this general indifference is not surprising in a population so removed from immediate threat of invasion, still the veterans of the First World War might have been expected to show something of the keen interest manifested by ex-servicemen in France. The diverse leading members of American veterans' organizations, who held high federal posts, left no record of initiative of their own in military policy but immersed themselves in domestic politics.

The End of Disarmament

Theoretically, the democracies had so overwhelming a superiority in war potentials that they could have imposed disarmament upon those countries in which militarist officers predominated. This relationship was formulated by President Roosevelt when he said the world was divided into the 90 per cent who are satisfied with the *status quo* and the 10 per cent who seek change. The 90 per cent include within their own boundaries precisely those raw materials without which the 10 per cent could not undertake a modern scientific war.

The realization of such a peace grouping was, however, made impossible by difficulties inherent in the home policies of the three leading democracies, which, though able to maintain civilian control over military matters, could not make up civilian minds to a general co-operation. In England the Tory policies led to isolation and balancing of powers, which prevented such an alignment; at the same time, large Labour and Liberal groups carried isolationist convictions to an extreme which British military policy thought it impossible to uphold. Naturally, Englishmen of all parties were in favor of a peace policy with the aid of the United States. This in turn was frustrated by American traditions of isolation and the deep-rooted belief that in such a *societas leonina* the British would pursue other aims than mere peace. The two Anglo-Saxon countries could not co-operate together under the Kellogg Pact, for instance, which Britain refused to uphold against Japan, or come to an agreement as to the proper weight to be accorded to Soviet Russia in balance of power politics, although President Roosevelt's recognition of the latter was obviously a lead in a direction which Britain would not follow for some time. Nor was it possible for either country to harmonize its interests with those of France.

France was the super-gravedigger of disarmament. Having her strength on land, rather than the sea, she was anxious to see no sequel to the Washington Conference on the Limitation of Armaments at which a treaty was concluded that, as Secretary Hughes confidently pronounced, "absolutely ends the race in competition in naval armaments. At the same time, it leaves the relative security of the great naval Powers unimpaired." [38] The French sent Foch on a trip through the United States to sabotage disarmament[39] and to make people forget that France figured highest in the list of army effectives with 818,000 men. Disarmament, in her view, should be imposed only on the Germans; she was the driving force in those Inter-Allied commissions which inspected the progress of German disarmament, whereas representatives of other powers, so Röhm wrote,[40] "as chivalrous officers betrayed understanding for our situation." She humiliated the German republicans, although maintaining these in power was the only real chance for her own peace and security; she weakened the Republic and was denying it a militarized police which might have counterbalanced the Reichswehr. In so doing, she estranged the Anglo-Saxon nations by her militarism, thus raising the hopes of the German army to play a role in Britain's balancing policies. When Hoover, in 1932, put the cause of economic distress at the door of militarism, which took away tremendous sums from productive investment that could only be redirected by disarmament, France, through Tardieu, sabotaged the American initiative, waving again the dossiers on German rearmament and repeating the demand for American guarantees against an aggressor. Thus a psychological front was formed against France which counterbalanced the technical structure of the Maginot Line—her foreign policy undid her military policy.

French intransigence gave the Reichswehr occasion to develop its chief argument for its own comeback: while Germany had disarmed, her ex-enemies, contrary to their contractual engagement, had not.[41] For a moment only, at Locarno in 1925, was the situation improved. But Luther, the Chancellor, was sent along by Hindenburg to keep an eye on Stresemann and his peace enthusiasm, and the Marshal wrote afterward to a leader of the Junkers that this Locarno broth had been cooked before he entered the presidency, and had to be eaten now, but "As far as I am concerned, I am little edified by Locarno and am trying to guard against the evil within constitutional limits." [42] This was moderate language, compared with Hitler's, when he said that Stresemann ought to be shot for this like a mad dog; the two were agreed that Locarno held too many peace potentialities.

Although recommencing to arm in secret, the Reichswehr was at length able to continue propagandizing publicly, after 1930, always pointing to France's superiority. Reichswehr Minister Groener declared that "peace is endangered as long as disarmament is restricted to one country," while Germany was left "without defense. . . . The unbearable misrelation of armaments within Europe must come to an end." Complaining that German Leftist parties were supporting France's policies, every time they attacked the Reichswehr, he entangled pacifism with the suspicion of treason. Opposition to remilitarization in Germany, or even questioning past performances of the army commanders in the First World War, was avoided as unpatriotic by the most liberal. Whatever the readiness of Brüning to agree to a ten-year moratorium on Germany's agitation for rearmament and revision of boundaries, in return for a big French loan, this compromise was vetoed by the Reichswehr.

Gradually the Reichswehr gathered strength to propose the thesis of "equal security for all nations" in 1931. The French would not hear of that: "One cannot admit that all nations ought to be put on the footing of equal rights," War Minister Maginot of France, warming up the war-guilt question, told the deputies in 1932: "If war-danger is to disappear, it is only just, and even necessary, that those who have been the aggressors should be put under the most severe restrictions, and that the nations who have not attacked and who declined to attack, cannot allow the military clauses of the Versailles Treaty to be called in question." [43]

Since the German thesis that other nations should not be allowed to have anything forbidden to Germany, or vice versa, was not accepted at Geneva, the urgings of the Reichswehr to quit the League of Nations were finally heeded. Germany then left what Hindenburg had already called "the most joked about institution of Europe," and on the Allied side had never been endorsed by generals like Pershing, who "was very open in ridiculing the League of Peace" before his English friends.[44] Since then, the quest of the military for arguments against disarmament on all sides was no longer so difficult. Each party had only to point a finger at some other power. Thus one of the secret orders of the German Propaganda Ministry to the press in 1935 urged: "Again and again desirable are extensive descriptions of the army strengths of Germany's neighbors, as compared with our own numerical inferiority; material obtainable from the War Ministry." [45] British aviation commanders could show convincingly the disparity between their own allotments and those of the Germans, and even in distant America, General Nolan, on the eve of his retirement from the service, greeted the Italian move on Addis Ababa: "As a result of the Italian demonstration we will have less trouble getting appropriations for this important advancement." [46]

The troubles before a renewal of disarmament were vastly increased with every step in the new progress, for the old yardsticks, alas never fixed like a normal meter, became steadily more inadequate as measurements of national potentials. Even as early as 1925 a general like Tasker Bliss, who admitted that militarism, and not merely Prussian militarism, was a cause of war, had to confess himself unable to provide measuring rods for the new situation.

"A mathematical formula to determine the military strength of each nation" was not obtainable, and reduction, if it was to come, could be achieved only through effective arrangements for the peaceful settlement of conflicts.[47] It would, in other words, demand an overarching concept of military policy and a recognition that preparedness was no longer, if it ever was, a matter of technical details—it involves the sum total of society's powers.

The Organization of Economy for War in Germany

All sides were agreed that the next war, even more than the last, would be a war of materials. The question of material preparedness was much complicated by the expectation of an abrupt opening of hostilities—only remote America, it could be said, might still preface war by a declaration of war. How far, then should the mobilization of industries and man power be developed during peace? How much material should be stored? Could a nation pile up sufficient materials and speed up production enough to win a superiority that might enable her to open by a swift but well-prepared move, gaining victory in one and only one battle? Is national autarchy the best preparation, or may it weaken resources? How far is the location of war industries and administrative offices to be made dependent on war probabilities? To what extent should national finances be drawn upon to support the very expensive and wasteful maintenance of industrial preparedness in peacetime?

In industrial planning for war, the fascist and communist states went furthest, with Germany at their head. Germany tended to revert to the so-called Hindenburg program of 1916, which was to balance "the richer means at the disposal of our enemies by applying everything that our land contains in the line of resources, and what industry and the farm can produce, exclusively to the demands of war." Under her Four-Year Plan of 1936, combining military features with promises of a better future in store—which Russian plans similarly emphasized—Germany announced that "powerful factories will be built according to their urgency. We shall begin with those for armament purposes; that is most urgent. Then come factories which are in other ways needed to make the Four-Year Plan a reality. Finally the building of labor settlements. In a world governed by reason this would not be necessary, but the world is insane." [48]

This self-sufficiency program aided agriculture first of all and thus pleased the army directly and indirectly. Not only could the German army absorb all the Junker sons who cared to come, but, to assist further the bluer blood and poorer soil of the Prussian East, labor service was lent to estates there, hundreds of thousands being commandeered to work on the land at nominal wages. The equipment of the army with horses made horse raising very profitable again: whereas Germany exported some ten thousand horses each year in 1930 and 1931, she imported some twenty thousand each year in 1933-5. With the political factor strong in German price formation, this promised well for the agrarian interests.

The effect of remilitarization on industry proved harmful to small businesses, which had put so much faith in Hitler before 1933. No doubt the armies and enlarged bureaucracy gave employment to many sons of the middle classes; but the small and middle-sized industrial producer was not able to satisfy army demands for uniformity in leather goods, garments, and other articles; the manufacturer in turn complained about the exactions of the army and the long-term credits demanded. In an economy which so largely relied on orders for rearmament, the tendency to capital concentration, long marked in Germany, was strengthened by the character of such mass orders placed with industry. The number of German shareholding companies was reduced from 1932 to 1936 by 25 per cent; their capital, however, merely by 14 per cent. The number of small companies with a capital of less than fifty thousand marks was reduced by 31 per cent, that of middle-sized companies by 18, and that of large-sized ones with more than fifty million marks by merely 0.9 per cent. At the end of 1936 the latter category provided for 0.8 per cent of all German shareholding companies; their capital, however, represented 36 per cent of all shareholding capital.[49]

Upon the great industries, which thus appear to benefit more than the lesser, the German plan put many burdens by giving them a "direction." For example, it forced the lignite industry to invest heavily in plants for the production of gasoline from coal, and other industries to remove their plants from the much endangered, but convenient, western frontier regions to the interior. It compelled industries generally to give absolute preference to armament orders. In some branches, these claims even before 1939 reached a degree already far beyond the conditions in the previous war.

As part of the price for putting these heavy burdens upon industry, the subjection of labor was included. A comparison of the movement of nominal production value of German industry and total wages would rather indicate that German labor paid highly for rearmament:

Year	Industrial Production (in billions of marks)	Wage Income
1932	38.5	26.0
1933	41.3	26.3
1934	50.1	29.8
1935	58.2	31.8 [50]

According to this, production increased by 20.3 per cent, whereas total wages gained 5.8. Such disproportion between the cost of material and of the practically forced labor is typical for fascist countries and included that in the army itself. The share of expenditure that goes to officers and men was certainly far less than the 46 per cent of the American army budget of 1937; doubtless this relation of "pay of military components" [51] to expenditure for equipment (31 per cent) was reversed in a fascist state.

The mobilization of labor for industrial and other work went far in Germany. The laborer was enrolled for service only a little less strictly than in the army. He had his "labor book," a pass without which no work was to be given, just as those liable to military duty have their military pass. Hitler's Four-Year Plan of 1936 practically deprived certain categories of labor, including civil engineers, and in particular those in iron industries and building trades, of their former liberty to change employment without asking. It was declared that the individual's ambitions and interests must be subservient to the state interest, which required reduction of labor turnover to a minimum. So far as possible, factory and barracks were run on the same lines, according to Major Dr. K. Hesse, entrusted with the direction of the Department of Military Economy (*Wehrwirtschaft*) in the War Ministry. As he described the German factory system:

Life is no less hard and men are no more softly treated than in military life. Perhaps general conscription and its prolongation to two years has its particular economic importance for the particular reason that it helps to educate these men for fitting in, for conscientiousness, for punctuality, in short for simply doing their duty, and thus is in a position to render industry a decisive service.[52]

Not all industrialists in the Third Reich were satisfied with such dream fulfillment. How far were they and other leaders of the Reich aware that they were about to realize prophecies of industrialists and others in, and contemporaries of, the Second Reich? As early as 1872, Jacob Burckhardt foresaw shop militarism as the logical outcome of the combined German military victories and economic advance. As learned activity seemed to become more fitful, more dilettante, when contrasted with the highly developed efficiency of military institutions, he concluded, "the latter must now become the model of all existence," for government and education as well as for factories:

Most strangely will labor fare; I have a notion which for the time being sounds like foolishness and yet will not leave me: the military state must become a large-scale manufacturer. Those masses of people in the large factories cannot forever be left to their distress and to their raging desires; a certain and regulated amount of misery with promotion and in uniform, daily started and finished with drums rolling, that is what ought to follow logically. . . .[53]

The more educated among the Nazis might rather have read and sought to apply the words of Nietzsche, university colleague of Burckhardt, on the future of the German laborer:

Workingmen should learn to feel like soldiers. An honorarium, a salary, but no pay. No relation between pay and performance. Rather to place the individual, according to his peculiarity, in such a position that he can produce the highest that lies within his gifts. [But the laborer should live as did the bourgeois], and, above them, excelling by their asceticism the higher caste: poorer, then, and simpler, but in possession of the power.[54]

The elder Krupp and Stumm, the greatest ironmaster of the Saar, wanted their laborers in a military, not a patriarchal order. Said the latter:

It has often been maintained, that there is no analogy between factories and the army. I insist on the contrary. . . . In both cases, discipline is a wholly unavoidable first condition if successes shall be achieved. . . . If a manufacturing enterprise is to flourish, it must be organized in a military, not a parliamentary way. . . . As the soldier estate includes all the members of the army from field marshal down to the youngest recruit, and all together march against the enemy, when their King calls them, thus the members of this plant stand together like one man when the time has arrived to fight competition as well as the sinister powers of the revolution. Are we victorious, that is to the advantage of all; do we lose out, we all suffer, and you far more than I myself. Victory, however, calls among ourselves as well as in the army for the severe upkeep of discipline, which here as well as there is not only compatible with loyal comradeship but forms the real basis thereof.[55]

Echoing such sentiments, leaders of German industry in the Third Reich demanded an ever more complete militarization of labor. What was done was not enough for Karl Arnhold, head of the Dinta, the German institution for Taylor methods, and for years the most outspoken representative of a master-in-the-house standpoint of the employer. He recommended going beyond the present quasi-chivalric arrangement, under which the laborer formed part of the "retinue" of the factory chief. Arnhold would militarize the factory completely, advocating among other things that the factory chief or "retinue leader" should open the day, not with trumpet flourishes as some did presently, but with a morning appeal to his men like that of a captain to his soldiers, to tell whatever makes their hearts heavy.[56] The fate of any grumbler, with concentration camps and black lists at the disposal of the employer, would hardly be happier outside than inside the army.

From the army standpoint, this control was supposed to make impossible a return to the conditions in the First World War, when, as War Minister Blomberg said, "while soldiers were winning victories, so-called labor leaders were engaged in high treason." [57] This he told government arsenal workers on an occasion when they were also informed that there was no hope of higher wages for them. In this attitude, of course, the German military were not entirely alone. Many of the military leaders of other powers have expressed their belief that labor, particularly union labor, was the worst, if not the only, profiteer in the First World War. According to retired General Bullard, president of the National Security League, labor began, right from the moment of America's entry into the war, "laying aside all patriotic considerations of the hour," to "bully and dictate to other labor and to the Government. They did the work but literally enriched themselves at the very start. In safety at home . . . in wealth and luxury from the high pay which no soldier had, they were to keep up their bullying and dictation during the war and make in their country's hour of need a record of strikes and labor troubles that were a dishonor to the name of America." [58] As if American generals were resolved that this should not occur again, some of them lent approval to bills in Congress mobilizing or in other ways militarizing labor in case of another war, or putting it under the practically unlimited dictatorship of the President.[59]

Militarization of labor was not regarded by German military officers as alone sufficient to settle that aspect of economic preparedness. The question of war wages conjured up some very ugly reminiscences in the minds of Reich army officers. Captain Schmidt, in a book on *War Profits and Economy,* admitted that "the fact of the untamed profit-intoxication of the privileged decisively contributed to our breakdown in 1918." To minimize the "psychological damage" done by the sight of war profits and profiteers, the Reich must be prepared to grant moderate wage rises in case of war, to keep labor from strikes, which would indeed be disastrous. This, however, raises the problem of controlling industry as well.[60]

Like other fascist officers, those of the Reich were essentially conservative in their concept of property. Despite some revolutionary-sounding threats, such as the ill-fated Schleicher's boast that "the Reichswehr does not exist for the purpose of protecting out-of-date forms of property," the army, and the National Socialists themselves, were essentially nonrevolutionary. Fascism merely expropriated political enemies who were, like the Jews, singled out not for their menace to the state but their weakness. The National Socialist state on the whole refrained from more radical steps; somewhat contrary to the party program, which promised nationalization of industrial plants to some extent, it sold back to private capital the controlling interest which the Reich formerly held over the largest steel company, the Stahlverein. The contention was that a "strong state," which has established the primacy of its policy over all other considerations, did not have to nationalize war industries.[61]

Yet Reich army men did not shrink from the thought of extending powers over economy in case of war, at least to prevent contractors from making excessive profits. In his book Captain Schmidt showed how essential the profit issue is for war; his reasoning led to the conclusion that, to provide for war expenditure by war loans, the national economy must be left great chances for profit, out of which war loans were to be bought. The danger of this process was inflation, an experience unforgettable in Germany. If all war profits were suppressed, this was tantamount to "conscription of property" and would take away the necessary incitement and initiative from the capitalist system. Warfare is impossible without offering a chance, however deceptive, of gain. But the profits must be controlled from the very beginning—less to check their rise than to take care that they are used rightly, for extension of plants, and to be pumped back through war loans, and also for wage raises.

A danger to be guarded against was that radical labor groups might be tempted in war, even more than in peace, to view with favor the Russian Communist system, which knows no profit except for the hero and expert. Military men were not oblivious to the notion that this system might offer advantages to them also. In a Reich military journal, "military communism" for the duration of war was urged as a way of conducting combat without money. In this scheme of "field-gray socialism"

> With the first day of mobilization every German, whether man or woman, old or child, enters the service of the Fatherland. There is no difference any more between the field of operations and home. In war everybody is a soldier whether he stands in the first or last rank. Everybody fights against the enemy with all his power. The State takes over the feeding, clothing and housing of all racial comrades.
>
> All property—land, buildings, machines, means of transportation, horses, cattle, raw materials and so forth—go over to the State for the duration of the war and the State may freely dispose of it for

war purposes. Domestic and foreign moneys and securities must be
delivered to a postoffice or bank within so many days after mobilization.

All commercial deals concluded during war are null and void. The
entire civil administration and judiciary are subordinated to the local
military commanders.[62]

Economic planning by the soldiers, which at first had the eager
support of the financial "wizard" Schacht, who retired or was retired when his measures became too unorthodox, was never brought
into complete harmony (*Gleichschaltung*) with Hitler's war policies.
The blueprinted full industrial mobilization was not started at the
outset of the war, which the Führer hoped to win by way of aggression and the threat of still more aggression, but only later
when it was too late, too late to make up for the basically weak
German and still weaker Italian economic war potential. And then
the Führer's interference with war research and weapon choices,
fortunate as it sometimes proved, was in the final balance more
obstructive than it was helpful.

Militarization and Economy in Other Countries

Like the first mass army of France, which terrified other countries
into imitation, this new German economic planning, far more than
the earlier Russian, forced surrounding Western Powers to consider the same problems. About the totalitarian claims to be put
on nations everywhere in the next war, there could hardly be any
doubt. Dubious was merely the degree to which totalitarianism was
to be approached by other countries in peacetime and how far
autarchy and governmental control was deemed advisable from the
military standpoint.

It was debatable whether the autarchy attempted by Germany
strengthened her for war, or was sapping potentials. The condition
of the German balance of payments forced the Reich into a state
much like that in wartime; the Reich had to exploit, prematurely,
poor deposits of ore, which would be needed in case of a blockade,
though some resources, like the scanty oil wells, seem to have been
sealed. But there could be no protest that the demands of the
"military standpoint to which costs do not matter" [63] might bring
the national economy to the breaking point.

There were many special problems raised by the crowded condition of European countries by aviation. While autarchy in food
production was preached, it was endangered in Germany by with-
drawing hundreds of thousands of acres from cultivation for military camps or fortifications and aviation fields. A somewhat similar

contradiction existed in Britain, for, desiring to grow more food at home, she had none the less to surrender forty thousand acres in 1936 to the British Air Ministry.

Since the most militaristic powers were the poorest, the strain of such mobilization upon the national economy was intense; a far greater proportion of the nation's wealth and labor was absorbed and enjoyed by an all-powerful military force than in other countries. England, richer than Italy or Germany, spent 3.5 per cent of her income for such purposes in 1913, and only 3 per cent in the Locarno year of 1925; even the colossal program of 1937 absorbed only 6.25 per cent. This contrasted with Germany's secret army expenditures, which have been estimated at as high as 21 per cent of the national annual income.

Still, rearmament in Britain meant postponement of a large part of the welfare measures which might possibly have been wrung from the Tories, but it made Britain, as Sir Robert Horne thought, able to argue and "negotiate with a dictator who talks of peace as a result of a forest of bayonets . . . who not merely preaches force as a necessity but as a philosophy and talks of war as a beneficent factor in human progress" or another dictator "who since he has come into power has initiated a system of education in which all schoolbooks inculcate the theory of war and the necessity for preparedness." [64]

Since the three great industrial nations of the West, the United States, Great Britain, and France, could bring forth mighty results without the intense strain of the fascist countries, it was natural for them to avoid anything like that premature extension of governmental control over industries. Since manufacturing for war involved at that time the production of some thirty-five thousand different articles needed for the equipment of a modern army, this was a broad realm over which officers did not greatly desire to reign. Perhaps they did not trust their own technological inventiveness to keep the nation well in the van of progress; if they had nationalized armament industries this would have meant taking over the whole bureaucratized system of industrial research with inventor employees which private industry created. Private enterprise has its drawbacks, including the reluctance of manufacturers at times to develop a new invention which might render existing plants obsolete—as Krupp resisted pneumatic recoil—but despite all this, the armies on the whole would prefer the old system.

Both Americans and British were openly convinced that "the full manufacture in governmental establishment . . . would fail in war and therefore does not appear logical in peace . . . ; that an organization or industry that has produced munitions in peace will be better qualified to produce munitions in war." [65] An Ameri-

can Secretary of War even declared that private manufacturing of
arms and munitions was "a nonmilitaristic way of providing for
the national defense." [66] This may be so, as far as the views of
governing parties and the armies concur; and it does not prevent
the preparation for a war with a totalitarian character, for the
officers already were making blueprint mobilization plans bringing
industries into a scheme of co-operation with the war ministries,
and, in case of emergency, they would not hesitate to replace industrial management in part, where it proved inefficient or non-co-
operative.

In both Anglo-Saxon countries the armies as well as governments declined the much-proposed nationalization of the armament
industry, holding that the suppression of private firms "would deprive the country of an essential part of its war potential." They
also felt that the constant maintenance of government plants in
idleness during peacetime would be even more expensive than paying high prices in peace and war for arms and even subsidizing
private factories.[67] As before 1914, both nations included the private
trade and exportation of arms "as an element in our national security," lending the services of officials and officers at times to
industry for promotional purposes, though at others refusing them
lest military secrets be divulged.

This system requires a certain liaison of officers and industrialists
which is often confusing; it is, for instance, hard to classify General
Sir Herbert Lawrence, formerly Haig's Chief of Staff, in the 1930's
chairman of Vickers, Ltd., and to decide in which capacity, as a
capitalist or a military man, he held forth against pacifism and
nationalization proposals, declaring the prejudice against arms
makers to be "an expression of an honorable, but perhaps mistaken
ideal respecting the sanctity of life and the iniquity of war." [68]
Under fascism, this relationship undoubtedly was as close, but even
more obscure.

Despite all such connections, the armies were forced to face decision in the problem of the highly unpopular profits of the armament industries. Under democracy and even under fascism, this
was the most vital point where military need pressed upon national
economy. In France the army approved of, if it did not induce,
the partial or gradual nationalization of the armament industry,
taking over first those plants obviously "ripe" for it; the experiences or forces behind this resolution are not known in detail, but
the sparing of the De Wendel plants in Briey during the First
World War, insisted upon by the Comité des Forges, had something to do with it, as well as the general resentment of the whole
popular front against the "gun merchant."

Such questions, at least, were spared the Russian state, and for military men there were other things to envy there, such as the richness in raw materials and space, and the strategically-chosen situation of industries, besides the plethora of men and the far-reaching motorization of the Red army (2.6 H.P. per Red Guardist in 1929, 7.74 in 1935). The ample size of military budgets left little to be desired—420 million rubles in 1924, 744 in 1928, 1,450 in 1933, 1,665 in 1934 (as originally proposed, but actually 5,000), and 6,500 in 1935. This strength was offset by the weaknesses of the Russian transportation system, the ravages caused by collectivization in agriculture, when the number of horses sank from 34,000,000 to 15,000,000 from 1929 to 1934. Also liabilities were the peasant character of the recruits, the numerical slightness of the Russian intelligentsia and shortage of experts, and the iron discipline which suppressed discussion but not waves of Stalinist hysteria.

On the whole, the most awkward relationship between army and economy was that in Japan, where the former had only a hazy counterimage of its own desires to put up against capitalism and bureaucracy. Among younger officers, social criticism and even nationalism were dissolved into a fantastic heroic ideology, which was more or less a return to the spirit of Oriental feudalism. Feudalism in the Orient took more care of the community members' rights and honors than the more hierarchical form of feudalism in Europe, but the two are similar in their lack of understanding for and appreciation of business methods and arguments. Moreover, the large peasant element among the officers sympathized readily with the peasantry, hard hit by the world economic crisis, instead of with industry and banking capital. Certain groups of the army, therefore, lent an ear to anticapitalist sounding agitation, though it was not socialistic or communistic so much as an echo of bygone agrarian feudalism. This produced many difficult moments; thus Baron Dan, representative of the Mitsui firm, who argued with the military in 1932 that Japan could not, for financial reasons, undertake new military operations in the Shanghai region, was soon afterward killed by military assassins, as was Finance Minister Takahashi, who had protested against budget increases for the armed forces.[69]

In the East, accordingly, as in the West, the problems of both armies and business were enormously increased by the new tightening of general mobilization plans. Not only business and labor were affected by the all-embracing character of modern preparedness—the civilian, in any walk of life, was also caught in its enveloping web.

Psychological Aspects of Militarization

Without the soldier, the heaping up of materials will be of no avail. But what kind of soldier was needed for the war to come? If it is a short one, he must have great technical skill and mobility; if it is prolonged, he must have immense powers of endurance. In former days any robust country lad answered; since 1914, at the latest, the problem is to find the soldier with the strength of the peasant and the nervous system of the townsman, accustomed to machines and excitement. Moreover, increasing individual responsibility and intelligence will be required. This was the view of German generals like Von Seeckt, who called for "education of a soldierly, autonomous personality, which alone is equal to bear the impressions of a modern war of materials." [70] An Italian colonel agreed:

A time when the subordinate followed the leader, marching at the head, could evolve the concept of implicit obedience. Today, when the leader is invisible and often miles away from his troops, guiding their movements, obedience must exist in interpreting with open eyes the ideas of the commander. Discipline must be shaped by modern tactics, which demand from everyone personal thinking, personal initiative. [71]

Could fascism, with its general militaristic tendency to overgovern men and materials, produce this individualistic soldier? Was it possible to regiment the individual in almost every sphere and leave him the feeling of freedom needed for war purposes? Mussolini proposed just that: "The latter is deprived of all useless and possibly harmful freedom but retains what is essential." [72]

The problem of soldier psychology, upon which fascist military writers concentrated was, however, but one of the angles of the new psychological mobilization. For, as war is now constituted, the civilians must also be prepared for "sticking it out," for endurance of terrible tests, blockade and aerial bombardment, as well as enemy propaganda. An army in action must have behind it an entire society united in will to war. This unanimity is produced in most countries by the widespread horror at the prospects of destruction which will spare no one, not even the sick in hospitals. The question of awakening societal lust for war is thus vastly enlarged; indeed, it has never been quite so easy as many suppose who picture "man" as a beast of prey, ever hungering for blood. In fact, the old standing armies had great difficulty filling their limited ranks with recruits, even by the most brutal methods of agents, and by an organized soldier trade differing little from slave dealing. In the nineteenth century, when nationalist fervor was at its fiercest, the civilians cheered loudly for war, indeed, but for wars in which they did not expect to engage. Now for the first time, when all those who cheer must also suffer, there came a great stillness over mass spirit in most countries.

To add to the problem, the nations have apparently two policies, one at home, preparing for war, and the other abroad, publicly condemning war as a "barbarous means of settling disputes," as the greatest disaster, which "nothing justifies." Fascist nations could solve the contradiction by frankly separating their domestic from their foreign utterances. But in democratic countries, the officer who is preparing for the emergency of a war that may be forced on the nation is inevitably aware of the unresolved conflict in the popular mind and feels it only logical to suppress teachings and policies that turn the public with loathing from any warfare for any cause. To accept indoctrination of peace means surrendering the great war potential without which the officer's material preparations are in vain. The lawgivers of the liberal nations do not concern themselves with this dilemma; they have the tendency to leave the military officials alone to their technical affairs. If preparedness were indeed a matter of technique only, this might be permissible, but political or psychological factors are evidently quite as important.

Proposals of one American military psychologist, declaring that men taught from childhood that war can never be justified "will never make an army," would demand that the schools teach that war is at least acceptable under some circumstances.[73] The fascist powers, however, went far beyond such wishes; the Reich military maintained that war is sublime, "the high summit of military endeavors. War is the natural and ultimate phase of an evolution in the history of mankind. War is the father of all things." [74] According to Mussolini:

Fascism contemplates above all the future and the development of mankind merely from the vantage point of political reality and believes neither in the possibility nor the usefulness of eternal peace. It rejects therefore pacifism, which under a pretense of magnanimity hides the renunciation of combat and cowardice. Only war brings human energies to their highest tension and ennobles those peoples which dare to undertake it. All other tests are only substitutes, which never put men before the highest decision, that of the choice between life and death. Therefore every doctrine which starts out from a premeditated revolution for peace is foreign to Fascism.

The program for re-establishing military value in society in Ger-

many was formulated by the press department of the Reichswehr
Ministry as early as 1931 in these terms: The army's

future depends on the fact that this warlike spirit is kept awake;
that in the midst of a world bristling with arms only he is respected
who is resolved to defend himself against an attack in any case;
that nothing invites foreign attacks more than a spirit of fear and
submission. This is the part which the army can play in the spreading of its own spirit. To step further into the quarrels of the day,
is contrary to its nature. The army stands not in a political front,
only its politically responsible head does so. To assert military
thought in the education of youth and in other measures of the
state, to lead actively the fight against antimilitarism and cultural
bolshevism which undermine the cultural and moral bases of our
national life, to enforce the interests of the army and of defense
in all fields even under the most unfavorable political constellations,
those are the permanent tasks which occupy the Reichswehr Minister and the Reichswehr Ministry.[75]

Militarization of Education

With relief, the seldom very glib-tongued officers turned the problem of such preparedness very largely to the schools, which were
officially handed "the great task of laying the world-outlook foundation to military thought. School and the armed forces are interrelated: the general faculties of a good soldier, the physical, mental
and moral ones, grow up under the severe discipline of the school.
The intellectual type who haughtily smiles over his comrades' exertions in gymnastics and sports has no place any more in the
school of the future."

It was hardly necessary for the Reichswehr to place an order for
a desirable soldier-product with the teachers, who knew what was
expected without being told by General Horst von Metzsch that
"it must be the teacher's ambition that his 'good' pupils become
efficient soldiers. It is contrary to the military idea when the ex-
emplary head of the class later becomes the lowest object of fun
in his military company. . . . The joy in obedience can be im-
planted ex cathedra." Pedagogical journals had already begun to
treat the issue of implanting the war idea in the pupil so deeply
as to survive those trying hours when victory seems far away.[76]

The militaristic education of youth in fascist and communist
countries commenced almost as soon as the child could walk and
united the larger part of youth in semimilitary organizations like
the Young Communist League, with five and a half million members, the Hitler Youth, probably the most military of all, with four
and a half millions, besides the Young Wolves, the Balilla, and
other Italian groups whose "military training forms generations

which obey, not because they are ordered, but that fight because it is their desire," as Mussolini declared.

To make room for this activity, German high-school education, once the solid basis of German learning, was reduced by one year out of nine and by handing over one of six weekdays to the militarist exercises. Besides actual loss of time, further diminution in study was caused by the weariness which children would bring to the classroom. Such studies as were left were to a large degree militarized. Many new university courses were introduced, such as military history, military geography, military policy, and experimental and theoretical ballistics. The teacher of the three last sciences in Berlin University, Professor E. Schumann, was at the same time head of the two Berlin University Institutes for Experimental and Theoretical Physics, head of the Research Department in the Reich Ministry of Education, ministerial counselor in the Reichswehr Ministry, and also director of the Central Office for Army Physics and Army Chemistry. Professor Schumann qualified for this domineering and many-sided position in the German university and military bureaucracy, not by any contribution to the relativity theory, but by a very important ballistic discovery. Another expert in ballistics, General Becker, during the First World War a commander of a 42 cm. battery, then director of the office of the Development of Army Technology and university professor, was the first general in active service to be made a member of the Prussian Academy of Sciences.

Thus ended for the time being the history of the fluctuating relations of armies and educational institutions: They began with an attitude of disparaging hostility of officers toward learning, but now, since officers and their inferiors had become educated and there were five Ph.D.'s among the major generals and colonels of the Reich army (all significantly bearing nonoble names), the process culminated in the complete subjection of learning and education to the armies, at least in some countries. As if it were the function of the exotic armies to bring out with the clearness of caricature the vices of the armies of the Great Powers, the Cuban army in 1936 had impeached a President, who declined the demand of the army for control over the rural school system, which it wanted to take away from the Department of Education. It reminded one of eighteenth-century[77] Prussia, when invalided war veterans were entrusted with the same task, bringing their Frederician barrack discipline into the schoolrooms.

The general trend of this indoctrination was toward an uncritical worship of discipline, leadership, and heroism, not of course to an all-around discussion of military aims and efficiency. The retouching of past military history was necessary in order to prevent uncomfortable questions from arising; this necessity was realized almost as soon as the ink on the Versailles Treaty was dry. Then, in a Reich Cabinet meeting in September, 1919, the question was raised of collecting and editing military documents in the Reich archives. The Reichswehr Minister, Noske, a tool of the generals, declared to his socialist colleagues that "the German people today is nationally so dissolute that everything must be done to rebuild its nationalism. By nothing can this be achieved more effectually than by reviving the proud soldier memories of the World War." This led to a long tussle between the pacific-minded members of the Cabinet and the officers who ran the Reichsarchiv and wanted to write their version of the First World War. When expert civilian historians were sent into the archives to co-operate, the officers complained about the hindrance to their "purely scientific work," through which the "inner values of the old army were to be salvaged for a better future." [78] As they conceived this aspect of the restoration of Germany's military power, outsiders, even historians, were to be excluded. On this the old army, the Reichswehr, and the modern Reichsheer alike have insisted, while the *vox populi* echoes:

When a thousand slew one man,
That is not glory, that is not honor.
Therefore 'twill be said in later ages:
Victorious was in spite of all the German army.

In this field lies the army's own particular part in the work of remilitarizing the German minds. Following in its wake came such philosophers as Count Keyserling, head of a School of Wisdom, according to whom "the idealization of war by peoples become primitive again is no sign of moral decadence, but on the contrary the sign of a new hero-worship and sacrificial spirit. . . . Blind belief is a sign of rejuvenation and increased vitality." [79]

Satisfactory to the army as was all such endeavor, which served to militarize and mobilize the people, it may be questioned how far this really promoted the more specifically military needs of the Reichsheer. A few weeks after the Nazi Ministry of Education had cut down the regular high-school course by a year and was considering a shortening of university studies, the War Ministry published an article in the daily press, signed by a colonel, complaining that "many young men compete for the officer career . . . part of whom demonstrate a completely inconceivable deficiency of the simple elements of knowledge." He indicated plainly to the educators that for the service as officer more was needed than gymnastics; that it was not permissible, as part of the candidates were doing quite ostentatiously, to deny or evade everything spiritual or cultural; that whoever wished to qualify for a professional leader must have the ambition to gain popular respect by general education, the cultivation of broader interests, and good manners.[80]

It would seem a somewhat embarrassing task on the part of the army, when it was served so eagerly, to protest against excess of prostration, but this must have become at length unavoidable. Some army men had to see that Germany might become, as Nietzsche called that of after 1870, "a strength without reason." Apparently, then, it was not enough for true military purposes if German youth learned to solve problems in arithmetic like this: "Day-bombers cover up to 280 km. an hour, night-bombers up to 240 km. Find out the flying time for the distances Breslau-Prague, Munich-Strasbourg, Cologne-Metz." [81] Neither did schooling in obedience appear sufficient to make German youth offer itself in sufficiently great numbers for the aviation service, where the accident rate was, according to British information, five times as high as in the Royal Air Force. Italy was the first state to give up the principle of volunteering for the recruiting of aviators and to apply conscription to this as well as other branches.[82]

Such early experiences with strenuous militarization could be multiplied; a tremendous increase in foot deformities, for instance, attended the endurance testing of youth in heavy hobnail boots.[82] Not only did German authorities hesitate in some matters, but the Russians significantly gave up the "brigade method" of study in groups for a method requiring more independence.[84] Where both Germans and Russians paused, the democracies might well stop to ponder long their own measures in educating youth, when their military complained that their youth did not receive the right preparation for service; that educational policy must be more closely linked to military preparedness; that "it is a challenge to common sense to consecrate billions to national defense, to keep thousands of men under arms, and at the same time to allow that sacred ideal to be outraged, in the name of which these sacrifices are demanded." So wrote the French General Weygand, and Marshal Pétain made similar demands.[85] In England, the industrialist and former officer Viscount Mersey praised the German example as one from which England could learn much.[86]

Paying little heed to such cries, the English Board of Education restricted its new measures to improving general health, for which there seemed much need. In spite of the reduced requirements for admission, 50 per cent of those liable to service during the First World War had to be rejected on grounds of poor health, and conditions seemed hardly to have improved since then, for in the years before 1936, 57 per cent of those volunteering were rejected

—a discovery about the national health, the Labour Party maintained, which the government had only made because it needed more "cannon fodder." Labour thought "the greatest stride towards an improved physique would be to keep the children out of the mines and factories till they have developed their strength." [87] Health policy is indeed good democratic military policy.

Aside from the improvement of the children's health, the Secretary of War, Duff Cooper, called upon the teachers of England not to dwell too much upon pacifist hopes in the course of instruction. The children ought to know that the ideal of permanent peace, not *per se* impossible, could not be reached in the immediate future; they ought to be informed about the different governmental systems and the advantages of the democratic constitution of their own country as worthy of being defended and saved from destruction. The duty of defense as a voluntary act should be placed side by side with other duties taught in schools—Duff Cooper thought one volunteer worth four or five pressed men. The immediate attraction of possibly fighting to "keep the flag of freedom flying in this corner of Europe" [88] appeared, however, severely diminished among young Englishmen by the strong belief that there was too little democratic opportunity within the ranks, "that young aristocrats just out of Sandhurst have a monopoly of the commissions and that there is no place for an eager, intelligent young recruit except in the ranks," where he may be tied down by six or seven years in a blind alley, without a hope of quitting if he does not like it. In consequence there was in 1937 a shortage of fresh recruits, as it was estimated, fourteen thousand less than the thirty-five thousand needed for the regular army.[89]

Race, Honor, and War

With every extension of the military bodies themselves, a corresponding widening of the concept of honor has necessarily taken place. Under the system of the standing army, only the caste of noblemen, from whom the officers chiefly came, were entitled to the highly exclusive honor of the eighteenth century; it was generally withheld from their soldiers, or reluctantly accorded on special occasions. When the mass army appeared, the scope of honor was broadened to the nation. Then even that was not sufficiently embracing: honor must take in all Slavs, all Germans in whatever country, the Italians abroad, or, as with Russia, the proletariat of the world.

The race idea set the frame for the fascist concepts in particular: outside the race there is no honor, within it there may be many grades. A *mésalliance* shuts one out from the exclusive race as it once did from the noble caste. In order to distribute to millions the feeling of honor, which involves that of superiority, it was necessary to single out small groups who were denied this honor and were the objects of scorn from the multitudes of the "elect." This was the function of anti-Semitism in race ideology—it provided the underlings the basis for a mass honor which permitted remilitarization. In Russia it was the bourgeois who was used for the purposes of the Red army.

Never before was honor so generously opened in peacetime. Now all Germans were comrades, *Volksgenossen;* and the call was even issued to all Germanic or Aryan peoples to co-operate. Few heeded it so well as *The Aeroplane,* a trade paper of the British airplane industry, anxious to see the Nazi air fleet built up as a stimulus to British rivalry, which exclaimed: "France is again selling herself to Russia. Never in the present generation will we send or land men or money to save France. But if France aids Russia in an invasion of Europe, we shall help the Nordic peoples of Germany and Austria. Then we shall need a real Air Force!" [90]

Through fascism, a cheap patent of nobility was given to the people, such as kings and princes once claimed, insisting they had "sprung from the grandest race in the world; it goes back to immemorial time." [91] Now the nobility of birth included all members of a race supposed to have come down intact from primeval times in the march through the ages and lands of Europe. "Pure of race, every Ass wants to be now," wrote Cervantes long ago, mocking his own Spain, which in the seventeenth century likewise had its race romanticism in the conflict with Moors and Jews, but more really with money economy.

Though a contradiction in terms, this concept of birth aristocracy for the masses was found so effective that it was adopted even by fascism in England, land of many mixtures, where Defoe ridiculed such pretensions in the eighteenth century, in *The True-Born Englishman.* Mosley added anti-Semitism to his program, and so, to some extent, did Mussolini. Though anti-Semitism had its military uses, it involved the armies themselves in some inner troubles, for these contained Jews in some measure; in the pre-1914 French army, there were five hundred Jewish officers, among whom one, Dreyfus, provoked a storm of antagonism; the proportion was far less in Germany up to the First World War. There only very few Jews became regular officers and only unusual riches won entree to army society. The widespread mobilization of the First World War brought out the war uses of some Jewish energies (Rathenau, Haber, Baruch) in various countries, and even talents of a purely military character, as in the case of General Monash. After the war, the German Reichswehr included some one hundred and twenty officers who had a Jewish parent or wife (Ludendorff's first wife was Jewish), but obviously passing the severe selective test of admission.

When Hitler demanded dismissal of all non-Aryan officers, the army allowed no Quixotic voice of the old-fashioned caste honor of the officer body to interfere with its progress. Only a few German generals realized what war energies might be latent in the Jews— Goering, for instance, who, as Aviation Minister, actually made a Jewish aviation expert, Herr Milch, General and Secretary of State in the Air Force. Mussolini permitted three hundred Jews to hold commissions in his army, from General and Viceroy Graziani and ten members of the General Staff downward.[92] The Red army at one time included numerous Jews—among the political commissars with the army, 10.3 were Jews; among the highest commanders, 3.44; among the medical personnel, 18.6, as against 1.8 per cent among the common soldiers.[93]

With the concept of well-nigh universal honor, to be conferred upon all those with no Jewish relatives or Marxist politics, came a devotion to the uniform, which, to outsiders, appeared frequently like a return to Wilhelminic days. Then the man in uniform was in Germany the wearer of the "honor garment" (*Ehrenkleid*) whereas in the other Western nations officers and noncoms wore civilian garments increasingly; the insignia of honor had tended to shrink to a mere rosette or ribbon. In any case, the Wilhelminic era did not know the uniform for the masses. The assumption of uniforms by fascists made use of the widespread longing for distinction; to the homeless and jobless, and those who saw the future as dark and inglorious, the resumption of khaki and medals seemed like admission to a band of heroes and a splendid past. How dependent fascism was upon shirts and badges was illustrated during the debate in the British Parliament in 1936 on the order bill to prohibit the wearing of uniforms by political organizations; a member reminded the Commons that after the failure of the Pretender in 1745, "one of the ways of punishing the Highlanders and suppressing their political opinions and their movement in favor of the Stuarts was by forbidding the wearing of the kilt" for a hundred years, until the kilt had become harmless.[94] The comparison was aptly drawn between the poor man's feudal or pseudofeudal dependence on the highland chieftain and on the modern *duce*.

With the uniform, Hitler proclaimed that he "returned honor to the German laborer," ominously echoing Rupert Brooke's chant of 1914 that "Honor has come back to earth again." To increase and supervise that sentiment, Social Courts of Honor for craftsmen and for laborers were created to pass on certain conflicts and misdemeanors of employees and employers who as "plant leaders" might have hurt the honor of members of what is officially called their "retinue." These courts often condemned laborers bold enough to insist on rights and opinions to dismissal. And the Social Honor Court of Silesia fined a big landowner sixty marks "because he had boxed the ears of a hired hand and had even whipped him." [95] Before the "restitution" of honor to the German laborer, such an employer would have gone to jail, but punishments were reduced for the employer along with real wages for the worker.

In compensation for wage reductions or hard living conditions there appeared a tendency in all the poorer countries to give medals and distinctions. This was done in Japan, and was in fact recommended by the great General Hideyoshi in the seventeenth century. It was also found necessary in Soviet Russia, where honorific titles were finally restored to officers and honor was added to raised pay to lure the Stakhanovite workers to greater speed. How consciously the Soviets have taken a leaf from Robert Owen's and Fourier's unscientific socialism is not known, but both these early socialists had wished to make use of honor in arousing competition in their projected utopias, in order to obtain the maximum of socially useful labor.[96]

With the wide distribution of medals and honor, there was some danger of lowering their estimation. They were handed out on every occasion and for every kind of merit. An Italian *prix* for the best journalistic performance of the year was given in 1937, under the auspices of the Foreign Minister, to three journalists who had whistled at Haile Selassie when he pleaded before the League. "In this case," the award said, "our courageous journalists have defended not only the honor of the journalist profession but also the honor of Italy and the whole of Western civilization." [97]

Although honor was thus generally bestowed, this did not preclude the possibility of an elite, which the Italian and German fascists considered a necessity in their system. A new German nobility was to be educated in old castles, Order Castles, fitted out for the purpose, where the cream of the Storm Troopers underwent an ascetic and disciplinary education, modeled on that of old Prussia's "Spartan youth" in the cadet schools, and not without the application of Jesuit educational experiences and also the invocation of Cromwell's Ironsides. "In romanticism everything, even the most heterogeneous, may meet," as a philosopher in exile wrote:

New nobility is so to speak being produced on the conveyor belt. What does not grow naturally in the land, is artificially engendered, oil as well as knights, with the sole difference, that artificial oil has merely to take the place of that obtained from the ground, whereas blood and honor have to deceive more, have to make men overlook the want of bread, and the new knighthood does not at all feed the hungry. Instead of bread it holds the fist under their noses. . . . Artificial knights protect natural bourgeois.[98]

As the leader of the Labor Front described the aim of the new Order Castles: "I do not at all want to raise a new priesthood," but "my ideal is rather the political soldier who unites unequivocally within himself the concept of preacher and soldier. That is a mixture as yet never achieved. . . . The only institution from whose realm we could borrow many a good thing for our castles, was the army." [99]

The supreme privilege of such an elite, dueling, once more made legal and was indeed enjoined on the people in Germany. Theoretically, at least, the duel was possible between industrialists and barbers, officers and longshoremen, though it was unlikely that such diverse members of the folk honor community would clash. Nevertheless, the official announcement said that dueling was "no longer a privilege of academicians but a manly settlement of an offense to honor open to all national comrades skilled in arms." [100] The cases of duels actually fought should rather have been indicative of some of the dissensions existing within the groups of fascist rulers. No system of government could stop the conflicts between officers in the armies, least of all fascism, which carried the unscrupulously ambitious to the top. This became evident in the first two wars undertaken by fascism, the Abyssinian and the Spanish. The violent quarrels of De Bono, the original Commander of the Abyssinian venture, and those who provided the reasons for his removal,[101] which verged at one time on a duel, indicate that the stormy chapter of "officers among themselves" would not be closed by fascism.

The race idea was one of the means of government of fascism at home. Its propagation often squared with military interests, as it did when Germans accused France of "race shame," "treason to the race, crime against the European space" [102] in employing the colored auxiliaries which were not available for Germany. But there were hitches in the program; when the understanding with Japan called for a rearrangement of the terminology, a Berlin paper close to the War Ministry wrote, "the race question takes a new turn." And the whole talk of race violation went by the board in the very first war in which the Third Reich took part—in Spain in 1936. There Nazis, as the "blond Moors," inconsistently fought side by side with the Moroccans.

International Honor and War

The inevitable dilemma, that "race" is good preparation for war, but war is not good for the race, was not so squarely faced by the Nazis as by the Russians, who with a heavy heart realized that war would weed out the best in a people.[103] A way out of the problem was pointed out to Germany by a major in the Reich Air Ministry. Discussing the losses of civilian populations through air attacks on modern cities, he concluded that from the eugenic standpoint such attacks were healthy. Since the residential segregation of men was not the outcome of class conditions but of racial inheritance—the poor eugenically are the poor materially—there lived in the desirable quarters a desirable population and vice versa. As the "undesirable parts of the people" lived more densely, they would be hit more frequently by aerial bombardments. Such attacks therefore make for the survival of the fittest. Incidentally, by the nervous strain they caused, they would weed out lives which might be nursed through in quiet times; if those suffering from nervous diseases or the insane could not handle gasmasks or follow other protective measures, their share in the losses would be abnormally high—for the people's future health only advantages could be expected from it.[104]

This is one illustration of the changing concepts of honor since the days when it was limited to a small class, and that class disdained to fight with those beneath it. Another is the violence with which all those opposed to fascism were denounced as criminals instead of honorable foes. Nowadays national war and class war alike know no honor which is common to both sides—the essence, long surviving, of feudal chivalry. The breaking-up of the old supranational concepts began with the end of the First World War. When the Germans concluded armistice and peace with Russia in 1917-18, only the old Czarist officers were considered honorable foes, and they were pitied because the commissars held them in a humiliating position; this respect was not tendered to their superiors, the Bolsheviks. The civil wars between Whites and Reds in Russia were led without any consideration of honor on either side—or, as Denikin, on the part of the Whites, maintained, it was not admitted on the side of the Reds. When the latter left thousands of wounded behind, they wrote on the hospital doors: "Entrusted to the honor of the Volunteer Army." According to Denikin, "they had every reason to trust. *We*—never." [105]

The newness of an adversary makes it infinitely more difficult for the "older" party to concede honor to him, particularly when the new government, like the Bolsheviks, disavows the contractual liabilities of its predecessors. Consequently, Millerand, an ex-Socialist and French corporation lawyer, at the Inter-Allied Conference at Lympne in 1920 declined to deal with them: "Their word and their signature were worth nothing and they had neither honor nor laws." A more military man like Henry Wilson quite approved of this estimate of the "vile brood," [106] all of which did not absolve the politicians from the necessity of dealing with them, or the military of the ex-Entente from conceding them honor and respect when the time came around to co-operate with the Red army.

As honor became more and more confined to the members of the elected race, it was more and more denied to those across the border; the old knightly concept of all foes as equals dissolved, and with it the validity of Christian commands, based on the equality of mankind. Fascist and communist armies alike appealed to honor in secular language. Since 1934 the oath of the German army called "service in the fighting forces honor-service to the German people," and the Soviet Constitution of 1936 declared "military service in the Red Workers' and Peasants' Army" to be "honor-duty of the citizens of the U.S.S.R. and defense of the fatherland the most sacred duty of every citizen." Objecting strongly to this new absolutism of state and race, which ignored the Christian values, the Roman Church protested to Germany in the encyclical of March 14, 1937:

Whosoever takes the race or the people or the state or the form of state, the incumbents of state power and other basic values of the form of human community—which occupy an essential and honor-commanding place within the secular order—out of this their secular scale of values, makes it the highest norm of all, including the religious values, and deifies them through idolatry, reverses and falsifies the God-created and God-commanded order of things. . . . God's commands are valid independent of time and space, of land and race. In the same way as God's sun shines over everything that wears a human face, His law knows no privilege and exception. Governors and governed, crowned and uncrowned, high and low, rich and poor are equally under His word. . . . Only superficial minds can become victim to the heresy of speaking of a national God, a national religion, can proceed to the mad attempt of trying to incarcerate God, the creator of all world, the King and lawgiver of all peoples, before whose greatness the nations are as small as the drops in a water-pail, within the limits of a single people, the narrowness, as defined by blood, of a single race. . . . The highest point of revelation as reached by the gospel of Jesus Christ . . . knows no supplements and no replacing by the arbitrary "revelations" which certain spokesmen of the present time want to deduct from the so-called mythos of blood and soil. . . . With this measure the principle: "Right is what is useful to the people," must be measured.

The old Christian international idea of honor, strangely enough, would appear to survive better in newer countries with less of a feudal heritage, as in the United States, where it was illustrated by an invocation of Secretary of War John Weeks to a graduating class of West Point: "An officer and a gentleman is a familiar term to everyone in and out of service. Be sure that you are both. You cannot be an officer and a gentleman unless you are just, humane, thoroughly trained, unless you have character, a high sense of honor and an unselfish devotion to duty. Be an example of such to every one." [107] Thus the War Minister of a liberal power included among the officer qualities that cardinal virtue of medieval chivalry, *misericordia,* humanity.[108]

This concept is in contrast to that of the variable and restricted honor, as defined by Hitler's own newspaper. "Even loyalty to a treaty cannot always and in every case be considered binding," according to that new formulation:

Loyalty must be an absolute virtue when it refers to absolute values like God, people, race, honor, and to men who personify these values invariably. Loyalty toward variable and second-class values is by physical necessity conditional and can become dangerous and unmoral under certain circumstances. . . . The primitive rigid and formal adherence to treaties in the sense that duties undertaken are to be fulfilled literally under any circumstances, even if by that the highest and ultimate values are suffering and perish, cedes more and more to the demands which equity and healthy feeling of right are entitled to raise.[109]

Fascist powers officially taught disrespect for international treaties as well as the peaceful settlement of disputes. This attitude indeed permitted them success in matters which did not seem worth a war to others; but it had another aspect as well: it wore out a moral war potential, for loyalty to treaties, grown out of the respect for business contracts, has been one of the basic sentiments of democracies, and indignation over broken treaties is part of the emotional force upon which they rely in arousing war fervor among their masses. Honor is the supreme potential and the ultimate protection of societies. Without it, the combat of societies-in-arms would become too frightful to contemplate.

Honor, as old Vico saw it, was the intermediary stage through which mankind must pass, "between the brutal regime of force and the purest laws of abstract justice and duty." [110] To a later French moralist it was indeed the final goal; after it had ceased to be mere "duty to the tyrannical state" and become the reorganizer of moral life, it would become "the supreme vertu, the supreme good." [111] More actually, honor had now become the mark of a return to the same brutal regime of force which Vico thought humanity was leaving behind; honor which formerly regulated and ameliorated combat now prepared and sharpened the conflict of peoples.

In this situation, surrounded by economic, mental, and moral uncertainties, it would have been impossible for any military to say truthfully to the civilian leaders of a nation that they were "ready to the last gaiter button" for war. The gaiter buttons no longer counted in a struggle which threatened to involve mankind's deepest forces. Neither could the civilians say to the military that they were preventing the occurrence of such a war, unless their policy was as far-reaching as the former's preparedness and envisaged peace morale as much as the others considered war morale.

Obviously the Western cycle was reaching a position which was recognized by a Buddhist monk-historian of Japan in 1220, during the feudal period of that country, when confusion was spreading and no one could foresee the outcome. Far in the future, centuries ahead, lay the solution offered by Hideyoshi, who imposed upon that island two and a half centuries of domestic and foreign peace— the longest experience of peace to be conferred upon any great nation of the world—a condition elaborately maintained by codes of honor, to bind energies, and systems of aesthetics, to divert them. In the thirteenth century, all was still chaos; and the monk observed how many men, hard pressed by crises, had rushed to obtain governmental positions which brought them land, titles, and the right to bear swords:

> It came finally to the bad world of a degenerate age, to the military epoch, . . . the period preceding the end of the world. . . . To the noble warriors who had lost their commanders-in-chief and who had nothing to fear, all available land was allotted in their quality of landowning district lords. . . . As the noble warriors have a martial spirit and look menacingly and self-assertively at those who do not please them, there is no one who dares to oppose them. It seems nowadays that the noble warriors are firmly determined on having everything their own way. When these unreasonable abuses go on accumulating till a great disturbance occurs, this world, including ourselves and others, will finally perish.

One of the earliest civilian protests against the sword-bearing class, this account of the old Buddhist father closed, not in occidental fatalism, in gloomy Spenglerian expectation of world downfall, but in the hope for moral regeneration to come: "Most of the noble warriors must think of the path of virtue." [112]

Most of the "noble warriors," however, were apt to insist, and did insist in Hitler's Germany, as before, that

Der Soldate, der Soldate,
Ist der erste Mann im ganzen Staate.

(The soldier, the soldier,
He is the first man in the whole state.)

In Japan, they echoed the words of Iyeyasu, the founder of the old Shogunate: "It is the custom of the country to regard the actions of the military class as the standard of conduct for the nation." [113]

Traditional militarism, as far as the Great Powers were concerned, was everywhere on the wane as the Second World War approached. With the sole exception of Japan, where old-style officer methods and ambitions had only intensified, the armies and navies of the world had learned to shun politics and shrink from "incidents." None of them were eager for the *casus belli* itself.

There was little of that to-the-last-button readiness that had marked the brink of other wars. The American General Staff thought it would not be prepared before 1943 and the German army, hoping to rely on Hitler's assurance of "not risking a major war before 1944 at the earliest," actually never was quite ready for Hitler's kind of war. In the Western world, an English general, familiar with various general staffs, found in 1938 that not one of them would glorify war or wish for it. "They knew too much about it." [1] And also not enough: the uncertainties were too many for generals to predict victory with any assurance. Besides, the war alliances, including the Hitler-Stalin Pact, had not jelled.

The top echelons, commanders and staffs, even among the Axis countries, were far from eager for hostilities to commence. A German military attaché, coming to Berlin in February 1939, found the traditional order of things reversed: "The gallant blades sit clearly in the Foreign Office and the diplomats in the Reich War Ministry; it was here that they fought for keeping the peace—because the means of making the war were absent." [2]

It was now civilians who appeared more reckless and sanguinary by comparison, an eve-of-war phenomenon that had not often before been wit-

13
The Militarism of the Civilians

nessed. Most wars up to 1939 had been welcomed by impatient warriors; they had been wanted chiefly by the armed forces, by commanders and staffs down to ambitious subalterns, rather than by civilians, either rulers or the governed masses. Now the growing enthusiasm for action by party leaders and parties—less among the masses—in the totalitarian countries reversed all this. By a strange shift, the armies of many lands found themselves at the mercy of bellicose civilians, of militarists in mufti.

Could there be, in fact, a civilian militarist? Was it not a contradiction in terms? Most observers felt completely baffled by the spectacle presented in Germany and Italy, by the strong youth movement for war, a juvenile readiness for death—not to say in Freudian language, death-wish—and a determination to find war beautiful and enemies necessary. Hitler provided enemies for the young, more than their elders wanted; "the children," in Reichsheer parlance, formed the Führer's true *comitatus*, ready not only to kill but to die for Germany. As a member of the older generation, remotely involved in the bungling attempts to remove Hitler, wrote about this frustrating zeal of the young: "They only lived in a sort of trance, no longer with a clear consciousness. I myself had thought that in the decisive hour Hitler's Satanic plans would fail because youth would not want to die. The contrary happened. The Devil had an easy game of it, they were ready, everyone, not only to immolate, but to be immolated." [3]

This true youth movement for rearmament and war was seen not only in Europe but in Asia, where young Japanese showed the utmost longing for self-sacrifice. Among women as well, and broad groups of citizenry in the totalitarian countries, this macabre enthusiasm prevailed; it was so curious and unprecedented that foreigners could not believe their eyes, or accept it for what it was. General Smuts, speaking in November 1934, thought the whole uproar in Germany "was probably nothing else but the consequences of an inferiority complex. It is not real militarism, but these are military stimulants for the masses. This wild behavior creates a blessed feeling of satisfaction and relief to those who consider themselves inferior or humiliated by their neighbors across the Rhine." [4]

Difficult as it was to realize, however, the world was witnessing an outburst of that civilian militarism which had long been present, in a limited degree, but had never been taken very seriously even by professionals. There had been many such enthusiasts out of uniform, serving the soldier in fields where the latter was deficient, in the creating of ideology and mood, in combating "false economy" of parliamentary budgets, in attacking pacifism and socialism as far as it identified itself with pacifism. Soldiers often welcomed such support, to be sure: Carlyle received a high Prussian order for his *Frederick;* Moltke would console Treitschke when he had spoken before a listless Reichstag, telling him that he was not alone in his patriotic concern about Germany's safety;[5] and Seeckt, writing in retirement, elevated Nietzsche to a pantheon dedicated to genius, together with Alexander the Great, two Fredericks, Napoleon, Goethe, Bismarck, and Moltke, a genius being by his strange definition "infertile, his emanations designed for or bringing on death." [6] Still, the soldier has not historically been the *demiurgos* of the lay militarists, nor has he admitted them to the management of military affairs, not to mention the actual conduct of war, until the rise of totalitarian government, and then unwillingly.

A Gallery of Civilian Militarists

Civilian militarism might be defined as the unquestioning embrace of military values, ethos, principles, attitudes; as ranking military institutions and considerations above all others in the state; as finding the heroic predominantly in military service and action, including war—to the preparation of which the nation's main interest and resources must be dedicated, with the inevitability and goodness of war always presumed. Such high regard leads to the advocacy of applying military values, organization—notably hierarchical features—to the totality of a nation's life. With the soldier militarist, the civilian shares the contempt for civilian politics, parliamentarism, parties, the hatred of civilian supremacy, of trade, of labor, and of diplomacy. Theodore Roosevelt, when Assistant Secretary of the Navy, thought diplomacy "utterly useless when there is no force behind it; the diplomat is the servant, not the master of the soldier," [7] and the Führer was said to be "so much against most of the German ambassadors that he hardly ever saw them at all"; he would call them "a club of defeatists." [8]

All the military powers of the nineteenth and twentieth centuries produced such lay militarists. They were, indeed, a concomitant of the standing army, though not quite its coevals. While it would be difficult to say where he was born, "the first to make a malady of peace" (Byron, *The Age of Bronze,* 1823), Prussia might claim priority, with Thomas Abbt (*Vom Tod fürs Vaterland,* 1761), and a variety of other university professors, that "spiritual bodyguard of the Hohenzollern," including the biologist Haeckel and Treitschke, the historian. Historians were among the foremost purveyors of militarism, Thiers with his *épopée* of the Consulate and Empire (1845-62), Carlyle whose hero-worship, after the death of Goethe, turned from individual great beings to corporate great beings: the Prussian army and the British navy and army, proofs to him that something had "survived Parliamentary eloquence," in days when "man can do almost all things, only not obey" (*Sartor Resartus*). In the contemporary armed forces, in their hierarchy as "hero-archy," Carlyle saw the chief hope left for the century[9] and the solution of its problems, including labor, which he wanted to see militarized until "there be no unregimented worker" left, with the captains of industry acting over them like officers of the Horse Guards; "wise obedience and wise command" would confer on industrial labor the chivalry of work[10]—a solution of the labor problem dear to many a later "heroic vitalist," such as Nietzsche, Oswald Spengler, down to Ernst Jünger (*Der Arbeiter; Herrschaft und Gestalt,* 1932).

Like Carlyle, Nietzsche belonged to that shock troop of thinkers who came to attack burgherdom, liberalism and also socialism and Christianity, from military positions, so to speak, from which some of the military themselves might have retired, as obsolete. When he proclaimed who were and needs must be the rulers in Europe— the sons of Prussian officers in Germany—what was to provide the cure for European decadence—"militarism, for example, dating from Napoleon, who detected in civilization his natural foe" (*Wille zur Macht,* No. 41)—he foresaw a future with leaders "receiving a strictly polytechnical education, military service: so that on the whole every member of the higher estates is an officer," (ibid., No. 793), with workers learning "to feel like soldiers, receiving an honorarium," rather than wages (ibid., No. 763). However, Nietzsche never meant to support actually existing classes and regimes; what he did was to provide an ideology "free-floating" enough to be annexed by dissident groups, esoteric at first like that of Stefan George and his "circle," and then, debased through demagogy, by fascism and Nazism, to whose demoniac counterfeiting a follower of George tried to put an end: Colonel von Stauffenberg, who came nearest to killing Hitler in 1944, "the doer" who meant to take the curse off Germany and a man in whom many saw the predestined chief of staff.[11]

Individual perhaps more than group dissatisfaction provided the Anglo-Saxon countries with their civilian militarists, such as that romantic draper F. S. Oliver, to whom "militarism was a fine thing," or Rudyard Kipling, whose generally militarophile writing described a militarist dream society in "An Army of a Dream," training for which began among boys of six, providing the highest exaltation when one was "borne along on billows of surging music among magnificent men, in sunlight, through a crowded town whose people, I could feel, regarded us with comradeship, affection —and more." [12]

In *fin-de-siècle* America, Theodore Roosevelt, according to his admirers and detractors, "had an ardent admiration for the military virtues and a keen interest in the Army and in military strategy," together with Leonard Wood chafing "increasingly under the sense that nothing was happening and nothing was likely to happen; and if ever they were to do things worth while it was about time they began." [13] Luckily for them, the Cuban War gave them the sought-for and politically useful military glory and a chance to stand for all that the Populists would abhor most—"imperialism, extravagance, class legislation, militarism, Hamiltonism, of the rankest sort." [14]

Much the weirdest figure among the American, and probably all, civilian militarists was Homer Lea (1876-1912), a frail hunchback with early Napoleonic ambitions, partly dedicated to militarizing the Chinese revolution stirring since 1899, partly to alarmist writing about the "yellow peril" of Japan and the "swarming of the Slav" threatening the world of the Anglo-Saxons (*The Day of the Saxon*, 1912), who were losing their military virtues and values under the influence of commercialism, a form of strife "without honor or heroism." While this "closest American approximation to Bernhardi" (Hofstadter, *Social Darwinism*) found not much acceptance at home, European militarist agitation and thinking had use for him —Lord Roberts; the German Emperor; Lenin, who read him in his Zurich exile; and possibly Adolf Hitler, in whose *Mein Kampf* the amateur historians of ideas have detected Lea's influence. The social historian is more likely to find the links between these two warriors who wanted to fight mankind's battles and their own in their sickly personalities.[15] *Mens insana in corpore insana.*

French civilian militarism ran rather more to organization than into ideology, with Déroulède's Ligue des Patriots (from 1882), the Action Française, the Croix de Feu. Not that they lacked poetry, oratory, and journalism altogether, for as early as 1934 the anti-militarist turned militarist Gustave Hervé asked "How to get rid of this regime of impotency and putrefaction? Who is the chief to emerge in France as he has arisen in Italy and Germany?" By 1936 he had the answer: it was Pétain whom France needed (*"C'est Pétain qu'il nous faut"*).[16] More esoteric and aesthetic—a more detailed analysis of civilian militarism could not omit the admiration for beauty, and the *eros,* in military bodies—were the *"Maximes sur la guerre"* (1930) of René Quinton (1860-1925). To this biologist, a much decorated reserve officer of the First World War, war was "a chapter of love, the natural state of the male . . . to them what the sleeping waters are to the swans: the place of their beauty." His hero transcends the purely military virtues, which "do not yet constitute the hero. What sets him apart is the voluptuousness which he experiences in difficult situations. . . . Heroes hear voices other than those of their chiefs. Even when obedient, they dictate their own missions." They are less part of the professional forces than of the *"levée en masse,"* which brought "a decided progress into the world. . . . While professional armies think only of saving their face, national armies think of saving the world."

Its aestheticism would group the *Maximes* with a whole series of militaristic utterances by literati like Marinetti, who in the Futuristic Manifesto of 1909 proclaimed: "We want to glorify war—the world's only hygiene—militarism, deed, destructor of anarchisms, the beautiful ideas that are death-bringing, and the contempt of woman." [17] There, too, belong D'Annunzio and Enrico Corradini with his *"culto della morale guerresca,"* forerunners of Fascism, and Oswald Spengler, Ernst Jünger, and Arthur Moeller van den Bruck. The last-named, "from the libertinage of literary Bohemianism by his own free will had found the way to Prussian discipline," but this "chief of staff without a commander-in-chief and without an army passed away tragically early and in psychic disarrangement," [18] that is to say, by suicide in 1925, the year of Locarno. Among the Anglo-Saxons another Bohemian writer, D. H. Lawrence, voiced such civilian militarism. This miner's son, shunning actual military service, fleeing from all discipline to the Bohemian regions of the world, nevertheless called for "leaders—this is what mankind is waiting for," a new heroic age with "active training in primitive modes of fighting and gymnastics compulsory for all boys over ten years of age." But "the great mass of humanity should never learn to read and write—never." [19] Heroic analphabetism is, of course, the least desirable qualification for soldiers of modern armies, so far apart were actual armies and dream armies.

Socialist militarists, and there are a few, could naturally look forward only to dream armies, conceived from socialist thought, until that National Socialist Hitler took over an existing army. Socialist language was replete with warlike or military language, but the metaphors could barely hide the antimilitarism and pacifism of leaders and masses, with the exception of a few theoreticians such as Peter Tkachev (d. 1886), "among the first to advance the program of a direct assault" upon the government as it existed in Russia, by means of a centralized fighting organization of professional revolutionaries whose action was to prevent the bourgeoisie from taking over in Russia as it had in Western Europe.[20] It is obvious why he has been called a "forerunner of Lenin," together with George Sorel (1847-1922), who, disgusted with socialism, which "remained a doctrine entirely exposed in words," had turned to militant syndicalism as the fittest vehicle for the overthrow of the present bourgeois society including its armies, "the clearest, most tangible manifestation of the state, most directly connected with its origin." Proletarian violence was to culminate in the general strike of the unions as "the grand Napoleonic battle" in which the class enemy was to be crushed.[21]

Whatever the claims for Lenin as "the great strategist of the class war," [22] the success of the 1917 Revolution was due far more to the weakness of its opponents and the pacifism of soldiers and sailors than to any body of military thought of the Bolsheviks, whose own unpreparedness was not overcome at once, their military or para-military cadres having been only slowly formed. In September 1918, Zinoviev, then head of the Petrograd Commune, would still demand that "to overthrow our enemies, we must have our own socialist militarism. We must win over to our side 90 millions of the 100 of the inhabitants of Russia under the Soviets. As for the rest, we have nothing to say to them. They must be annihilated." [23] When civilians use the terms of violence they are usually more literal in their intention than when soldiers like Clausewitz speak of annihilation, etc., in combat. The Communists and later the Nazis were literalists.[24]

Much more in Communist action and ideology than can be detailed here, must be termed militaristic, not the least its antipacifism. Even its anticapitalism has a tinge of the historical soldier's disdain for the trader: the "phony war" of 1939-40 was to Moscow the upshot of the "Remarque spirit." After 1945 the Moscow governing circles, Stalin participating, would speak in Napoleonic style of that "gentleman shopkeeper," Harry Truman, and look forward to new military inventions "to make it easier to talk to the shopkeeper gentleman." [25]

The highly derivative, not to say dishwater, quality of the ideology of Hitler, the content of his damaged psyche, put him at the end of the gallery of militarists whose bellicosity sprang from deeply unsatisfied lives. Since early childhood, he had "raved more and more about everything connected with war and militarism," and the war of 1914 had come to him like "a redemption from the exacerbating sentiments of my youth." Unlike most other civilian militarists he entered an army and a war which gave the lonely *Lumpen* proletarian the craved opportunity "to join and belong," finding soon enough that he still was an "outsider." A defeated army, no longer choosy in the picking of auxiliaries, gave him his first job, as informer and propagandist. He was soon singing its praises: "What the German people owe to the army may be simply summed up in one single word: Everything," with a special compliment for the General Staff thrown in—"the most tremendous thing the earth has seen up to now." [26]

From praise of the army to promises: he was to free it from the fetters of the Weimar Republic, which was slowly but inevitably turning the Reichswehr away from "the people"—that eternal "part of the nation that does not know what it wants" (Hegel)—and into a "militarist" body. One of the several dubious slogans Hitler rode in on was—antimilitarism, as defined by himself, and acceptable to the Reichswehr, which had long resented the application of the pejorative "militarism" to its own being and doing. In the end this led to a confusion worse confounded about what was and was not militarism.

It would be difficult to decide whether it is more often a psychosomatic strength or weakness in the social thinker that is transmuted into something prescriptive for his or all society. At the bottom of Carlyle's "heroic vitalism" not all was healthy or self-reliant, as when he cried out: "My isolation, my feeling of loneliness, unlimitedness (much meant by this), what tongue shall say? Alone, alone." [27] The "socialization" of the private psyche, of a faulty psychosoma, from which society cannot easily be protected, will be discovered in nearly all the specimens of our gallery, many of them unmarried, still more childless—the childlessness of the great general should be noted in passing—and most of them sick and sickly. No wonder that armed forces seem to them the healthiest of all groups of males when they themselves are struck by ill health, their own and their nations'. Like that lame schoolmaster of antiquity, Tyrtaeus, who sang of Doric virtues, they want to join armed bodies in vicarious ways, or have others join them, thus to win back health. The lonely unconventional thinker craves for, exalts, prescribes for others, the male lonely-hearts society, the most orthodox, most tight-knitted company, after contemporary society has been found hateful, mercenary, commercial, demagogical, democratic, decadent, lacking in a sense of honor and order or respect for "birth." Most in our gallery liked to claim "birth" for themselves, from Carlyle and Nietzsche ("my ancestors were Polish noblemen"), down to Ribbentrop, who had himself adopted by a titled old aunt. Hitler exalted the race superiority of Nordic man, a mass aristocracy, with an overlying "better" aristocracy, that of the SS. All military nations provided for the temporary gentlemanship of the reserve officer corps, a "joinerdom" for pint-size imperialists like Count Ciano, who from time to time left his ministry to engage in the air war. To compensate for what? Hitler seems to have suspected the answer: during the speech-making accompanying the signing of the German-Italian-Japanese Treaty of 1940 the Führer's eyes "strayed two or three times to Ciano's crooked little legs." [28]

Armies at the Doors to Power

The road to power for the totalitarian movements was blazed by para-military formations, to which governments conceded their near-monopoly of uniform-bearing willingly enough. Fighting street and beer-hall battles, murdering opponents, applying violence and threatening more, they lamed much of the opposition. But they would never have reached their goal except for the services, active and passive, of military men, acting either as experts of violence— 15 of the 107 Nazi Reichstag members of 1930 were retired officers —or as gatekeepers at the threshold to power.

Italian officers of the troops occupying Fiume encouraged D'Annunzio in his coup against the disputed city, the first open action of Fascism. A strong group of officers, "including several accused of co-responsibility for the shameful defeat at Caporetto, who wanted to have their careers protected against such accusations," joined Fascism on stage and behind, a movement which promised to do away with politics and pacifism, to which officers liked to ascribe the defeat of 1917.[29] Officers who had joined the movement openly like De Vecchi, a "war ace," and De Bono, leader of the *"Squadristi,"* the storm troopers, persuaded the powers that be that Fascism was "a good thing." These older powers, including the army, watched the March on Rome, arms at rest, either out of benevolence for Fascism, or out of ignorance of its true meaning.[30]

It was a passive attitude Hitler never tired of recommending to the Reichswehr,[31] which was not otherwise very respectful of the Italians whom, as Hindenburg used to growl, "even the Austrians could beat." Its leaders, from the Marshal down, clearly felt the hesitations which officers are likely to entertain when forced to deal with either psychopaths or insubordinate members of the lower ranks, not to mention the ominous combination of the two inside the Nazi Party. But the party's professed utter devotion to everything military, in contrast to the anti- or non-militarism of the other parties in the Weimar Republic, in the end procured them admission to power, the admissive power resting largely with the arms-bearers. "If Germany was to be powerful once more," General von Fritsch wrote later, three battles had to be won—against the working class, the Catholic Church, and the Jews.[32] Not that the military were the only gatekeepers at the portal to power; there were others, industrialists and bankers, bureaucrats and Junkers, one of the latter saying that the Prussian nobility "would not deny itself to a 'German Mussolini' coming from the labor estate," [33] but none were as powerful as they, and Hitler knew them well in their inferior-minded hauteur. When at a later meeting of Nazi bigwigs, Goebbels suggested that General Keitel be consulted, Hitler waved that aside: a man like Keitel, with the brains of a cinema doorman, would not be of much use.[34]

Among the groups who welcomed, rather than admitted, Fascism and Nazism to power, youth—next to women—was the one that knew least what it was doing. In its readiness for *"servitude volontaire"* (De la Boétie), it had become unfastidious in its preferences, for either song—singing as an act of surrender—or such low demoniac company as that of the Nazis. Inside the Reichswehr, among the troops, older officers saw the surge in the Nazi direction growing so strongly that by 1930 they feared "it can't be stopped, it is the *Jugendbewegung*," [35] a movement of youth that, as a semi-Nazi writer put it, was "grateful for every sacrifice expected of it" (Ernst Jünger), and, in its military sector, a movement of the cadets, whose mentality, so often prevailing over better professional insight, according to one general, more perceptive, more outspoken than most military memoir writers, has "cost Germany much blood. If they have been able to impose themselves, until today, this is due to the fact that it is always easier to die honorably than live honorably." [36]

This young submissiveness, even thirst for death, was still more outspoken and also politically influential in the Japanese officer corps, making itself felt despite all traditionally hierarchical-gerontocratic arrangements in Japanese society; as idealists these young officers remained quite impervious to the fact that their stirrings might be motivated by armed forces interests or by those of the classes from which they sprang. The wars they provoked, beginning on the Asian continent, were in a way wars of youth movements, such as the world had not seen since the American War of 1812— as also was the Second World War, which Hitler wanted to start as long as he was still young. Among the Japanese, it was a more archaic warriordom than in the West, confident that its material shortcomings, so obvious in Germany and even more in Japan, would be overcome by "spiritual mobilization," part of which was the instilling of death defiance in the young, which was to culminate in the Kamikaze pilot. "Inadequacy of strength is not our worry," explained General Araki, long-time president of the Army Staff College. "Why should we worry about that which is material?" [37] For a war overwhelming in its "materialism," this was hardly adequate preparation.

Totalitarian Control Over Armed Forces

The illusions as to the totalitarians entertained by the armed forces allowed the latter a certain "closed season" during which they could arm and rearm much as they pleased, along orthodox military lines, and obtain promotions, while keeping down an occasional resentment or disgust over the parties' doings, notably when these threatened their arms-bearing monopoly. Army conservatives in the general staffs hoped that the dictators would not bring on wars prematurely or along two fronts or within Western Europe, which as the German Chief of Staff told his French colleague in 1937, could only profit Bolshevism.[38]

Army and dictator remained more nearly equal partners in Italy than elsewhere. Badoglio, temporarily removed from Rome to a South American embassy for his lukewarm attitude toward Fascism, in the struggle between the old and new forces in Italy became once more Chief of Staff, as such on good terms with his French counterpart, keeping up a common front against Hitler with whom, as Mussolini told Badoglio after the first meeting of the two dictators, there was "no way of understanding. He talked to me of nothing but the Anschluss and of war, in which he wants to employ all the most brutal means of modern technique. He is a barbarian." [39] Mussolini's own barbarism came to the surface with the Ethiopian War for which the forces in Italy joined, the old ones in order to wipe off "the shame of Adua," the new ones for empire and in order to impress Hitler.[40] The anti-Hitler Stresa front of the statesmen and general staffs broke.

The German army directorate's illusions about Hitler lasted until 1938, only a little longer than those of the old warhorse Winston Churchill, who was ready to see the Führer enter history "as the man who restored honour and peace of mind to the great German nation and brought it back, serene, helpful and strong, to the forefront of the European family circle." [41] A tendency in favor of militarism constitutes a weakness on the part of most conservatives —many "better-class people" in Germany regarded the Nazi movement "as a timely revival of nationalism which it will not be difficult for the right people to control and exploit." [42] In much the same way a constant suspicion of militarism in the soldier characterizes liberalism, leading Franklin D. Roosevelt, for instance, to consider MacArthur in 1932 as dangerous a man as Huey Long.[43]

The respective positions of strength in the Reich made Hitler's steps toward control over the Wehrmacht the most devious of all dictatorial ways to power. At the outset he took great care to appear absolutely legal in his actions, obtaining power constitutionally, thus keeping the Wehrmacht from forming a dangerous breeding ground for a *coup d'état,* until the time when he could swamp it with Nazis and the Nazi spirit and thus overcome old and new opposition among the officers.[44] In the ensuing battle for control Hitler knew his opponents and their weaknesses far better than they knew his; their intelligence work proved poor, while his surprises surprised them as much as their foreign counterparts because he applied means and things not in their code, bearing down hard on their vaunted fastidiousness and *corps d'esprit* and honor. Their protest against his opening moves such as the Rhineland occupation made them "for the first time lose credit with him, and very considerably at that," since the expected countermove of the French did not come about.[45] In early 1938 he assumed "immediate command over the whole armed forces" with the OKW (Armed Forces High Command) functioning as his military staff. Now, he could safely break his promise that the Wehrmacht would remain sole arms bearer, forming the SS, his typical dictator's guard, into an independent force, employing generals as an opera manager employs singers eager for performances and high pay. The comparison is by no means farfetched: when invited to join the conspiracy against Hitler in 1942, a brilliant general like Mannstein was willing once he had delivered another aria, so to speak, had captured Sevastopol, which might bring him yet another decoration;[46] in the opposite camp the histrionic Patton would admit that "all very successful commanders are prima donnas, and must be so treated. Some officers require urging, others require suggestions, very few have to be restrained." [47] There was a moral imperviousness in what the majority of these German officers were willing "to take" from Hitler—gifts of money, promotions, decorations no less than the repeated stunning blows against their sense of honor or their professional convictions about the Führer's wild schemes, which ominously called to mind that berserk warrior Charles XII of Sweden. Never could enough officers unite against Hitler in a "general strike of the generals"—they could not bear unemployment. As time went on, they earned the Nazis' increasing contempt as an army that had become "really self-complacent, an end in itself," without belief in large-scale rearmament, which would not take more than one cannon or an additional division at a time.[48]

The dictator's bottomless distrust, his primeval fear of generals, which needed little or no proof of their guilt, drove Stalin to the purge of the Red army's generals and staffs. For his energy and ruthlessness he was duly admired by Hitler—"he knows his models, Genghis Khan and the others, very well" [49]—who only much later, in 1944, could proceed to place commissar-like political officers (*Führungsoffiziere*) in the Wehrmacht. The disagreements between the armies and dictatorships in both Germany and Russia, little as we know about the Russian events (if there was conspiracy, it was even clumsier than the one against Hitler) seem in many respects similar. In both there was the conflict over the army's desire to evolve in its own way as a professional organization, undisturbed by the party, and the wish for a voice perhaps in the choice of enemies: Tukhachevsky once complained publicly that the politicians were "disturbing German-Soviet relations." When Stalin ordered the purge of the generals, he was saying, in effect: It is I who determines who are Russia's enemies. According to observation from American embassy windows at the time: he "must have decided once for all to demonstrate to the army its full dependence upon himself." [50] Belated rehabilitation, following Stalin's death, would still leave it at that and the army in dependence upon a new dictator.

Civilians in Command

While civilian intervention in the Second World War was everywhere in keeping with constitutional institutions, even if doubts persisted whether fraud was used in obtaining the Wehrmacht's unconditional oath to Hitler,[51] it was certainly far more marked and persistent than in previous conflicts. The difference between the civilian leaders' share in the planning and conduct of campaigns between the two world wars is striking. And even if De Gaulle would call Churchill "the Clemenceau of World War II," the contrast was vast between Woodrow Wilson's passivity as Commander-in-Chief and F.D.R.'s unrelenting activity.

Some of this broadening out of civilian power, so unprecedented, may be considered militaristic. Wartime civilian militarism as considered here may be defined as the interference and intervention of civilian leaders in fields left to the professionals by habit and tradition. How far it contributed to ultimate victory or, on the Axis side, to utter defeat, is open to dispute on many points. But there seems no doubt, at least, that in general it led to an intensification of the horrors of warfare. Civilians not only had anticipated war more eagerly than the professionals, but played a principal part in making combat, when it came, more absolute, more terrible than was the current military wont or habit.

Such blame, indeed, may be laid at civilian doors in earlier eras: it was the civilian Louvois, Louis XIV's war minister, who invented the dragonnades inflicted on the Huguenots, and who gave orders to devastate the Palatinate, making the scorched land unable to support war; Saint-Just who, as delegate to the armies of the French Revolution, told them "to march willingly, the feet in blood and tears" and toward "the secret mission of exterminating tyranny in every country"; and Bismarck who uttered bloodthirsty proposals in 1870 to shoot some 13,000 captured *francs-tireurs*. Responsibility for much, if not most, of the intensification of modern warfare also, actual or proposed, must go to civilian warmakers.

The inhumanities ordered by Hitler and Himmler, in which they tried, with less than complete success, to make the army join them, do not derive from a military tradition of warfare, but rather from a vulgar reading of Nietzsche or a continuation of the war idea underlying beer-hall battling against political opponents. "The soldier of the Red army must be regarded as an ideological enemy of National Socialism," the Führer told the generals, "and must not be treated like soldiers of other nations. As such, he was not

to receive any quarter." Generals must therefore eschew any idea
that the war against Russia could be "conducted in a knightly
fashion." [52] The SS would show the army the way, suffering from
"no Christian inhibitions." [53]

"Violence" contrary to established rules of warfare, proved "successful like a new disease" (Auden), spreading in all directions:
the British War Cabinet in the summer of 1940 ordered German
air ambulances marked with the Red Cross to be shot down above
the Channel in order to keep the rescued personnel from returning
to the fight.[54] Russians, notably the partisans, took Stalin's exhortation that "the fascist invaders must be annihilated" quite literally;[55] and it was a Russian civilian, Ilya Ehrenburg, speaking on
the occasion of the Soviet armies' entrance into Germany, who
uttered an exhortation more elaborately ferocious than any attributed to the ruthless military conquerors of old: "Kill! There is
nothing that is innocent in the German. Neither in the living nor
in the unborn. Follow the directive of Comrade Stalin and trample
into the ground forever the Fascist beast in his cave. Break by
force the racial haughtiness of German women! Take them as your
lawful prey! Kill, you brave advancing Red soldiers!" [56]

There are American contributions to this budget of sins, not all
venial: the proposal of a member of the New York bar to have
Germans sterilized *en masse,* the Morgenthau Plan of converting
Germany into a country primarily "pastoral," Bernard Baruch's
proposal to keep Germany and Japan forever "from re-establishing
themselves in the exports of the world," [57] the agreement at Yalta
to have people by the million driven from their homes, when earlier
Americans might have remembered the divine ordinance against
"cutting people off their place" (Job 36: 20). Treatment of prisoners of war was nowhere in full compliance with the Hague
Convention and the obligations of the captor under it. Ancient and
honorable concepts of asylum fared no better. While even the
French in 1940 had resisted Nazi demands for the extradition of
foreigners who had served in their armies, as "contrary to honor
or account of the practice of the right of asylum," a record which
Vichy did not uphold for long,[58] American authorities agreed without compunction to the involuntary mass repatriation of Poles,
Russians, and other peoples. It was a sign of reawakened conscience when during the Korean armistice negotiations they insisted
and obtained that the prisoner of war was free to go where he
wanted:[59] "We will not buy an armistice by turning over human
beings for slaughter or slavery." [60]

Civilians started and gloried in a kind of warfare which to the
regulars seemed "a degenerate form of war" [61]—partisan war,
started by Russians and followed by French, Italian, and other

groups; Anglo-American generals were much relieved not to be forced to fight German partisans. Toward the end, after the atomic bomb had been manufactured, Harry S. Truman "never had any doubt that it should be used," [62] when one doubt, to say the least, might have obtained him some credit in the annals of humanitarianism, and for his Secretary of War "there could be no significant limits to the horrors of modern war." [63]

The most fatal civilian contribution to the making of war since 1939 was the demand for "unconditional surrender." Hitler had wanted it (and the other war lords followed) long before he started his foreign wars openly. "The great masses," he had written in *Mein Kampf,* in the war to come would want "the victory of the stronger and the annihilation or the unconditional surrender of the weaker." [64] He "determined that Poland would and must surrender unconditionally," [65] and the yet unconquered were to fare no better: England was "to be turned into a green island," "pastoralized," to use the later Churchillian expression.[66] Before the soon-expected fall of Leningrad and Moscow Hitler "decided once again" that no capitulation of the two capitals, even if offered, was to be accepted by the army, which was not even to occupy them, but to leave them to rot.[67] Local Japanese commanders were equally harsh in their insistence upon unconditional surrender, in Singapore and the Philippines, whereas the larger aims of the Japanese were far less uncompromising and looked toward a negotiated peace with an America that would not, they naïvely expected, fight the war to a bitter end.[68]

Well before America's entry into the war Roosevelt had convinced himself that no peace with the Axis was possible except on terms of complete surrender, of one side or the other.[69] Remembering 1918 and after, he was determined that the Germans, who liked to think that they had not surrendered in the last war, "this time are going to know it." [70] The Grant-Lee negotiations about unconditional surrender were also much in his mind and admittedly contributed to the formulation of yet another such demand in American history.[71] A wartime Washington civilian-military Subcommittee on Security Problems, considering postwar questions, had concluded that Germany must not again be permitted to get off with conditions and that "unconditional surrender rather than an armistice should be sought from the principal enemy states except perhaps Italy." [72] When the President announced this as a war aim to the Joint Chiefs of Staff, they raised no objections, never made any "study of the meaning of this formula for the conduct of the war, either before or after the President's announcement" at Casablanca, where he had hurriedly obtained approval from Churchill and the British War Cabinet.[73] The demand, meeting almost no opposition at home, though a little more presently in Britain, found its first protests from among field commanders and the makers of "political warfare," ascribing stiffening German resistance to the effects of the Casablanca formula. They wanted a "hope clause" inserted, in order to persuade the Germans to surrender more willingly, piecemeal or *in toto*.[74] But only following Roosevelt's death and German surrender was it possible to modify the demand in a way that "still left the Japanese in their own mind some face and honor." [75] They were then granted a sort of conditioned unconditional surrender, a contradiction in terms but otherwise sound enough, allowing Truman to proclaim unconditional surrender on V-J Day and international jurists to conclude that "Japan's surrender was a negotiated surrender." [76]

On the various post-mortems of the unconditional surrender demand the verdict of the soldiers and the military writers speaking for them had been almost unanimously damning: one of "the great mistakes of the war" (Hanson Baldwin); "these two words—a putrefying albatross around the necks of America and Britain" (General J. F. C. Fuller); a further step along "the decline of civilized behavior" in the conduct of war, "this combination of an *unlimited aim* with an *unlimited method* . . . produced a deepening danger to the relatively shallow foundations of civilized life" (B. H. Liddell Hart).[77] Looking back from the vantage point of the Korean War, during which the United States "deliberately chose to fight a major war in a lesser degree than that of which we were capable," Commander Ralph E. Williams, United States Navy, thought it preferable to the Second World War as one in which "moral hysteria betrayed us into a witless, paranoiac insistence that 80 million Germans and 70 million Japanese were our mortal enemies and must be destroyed wherever they may be found and at whatever cost." [78] Among civilians as well, the later war brought on "a struggle for new concepts of terminating war other than by unconditional surrender" (Senator Fulbright), an ending that would leave a reasonable balance of power in the world, "without knocking out, emasculating, ruining, killing off all your enemies" (General Vandenberg, Air Force Chief of Staff).[79] Ominously, in the now opposing camp, other ideas of terminating war seemed to prevail: in a thesis which the nonmilitary Marshal Bulganin submitted to the Soviet War Academy in 1945 in partial fulfillment of the qualifications for his baton, no doubt was left that in a new war the same conditions would be imposed as those on Germany, only still more relentlessly.[80] Again, civilian demand for war and war ending was more radical than the suggestions of the professionals.

Commanders-in-Chief and Chiefs of Staff

The best function that can be claimed for the civilian war leader between 1939 and 1945 is that of energizer, a role visibly and audibly displayed to the masses through the media of modern communications, through orations and gestures rallying forces behind the fronts. He could also be the backer of efficient generals and admirals and air chiefs, the driver and dismisser of sluggish ones, the winner of new allies in war, the maintenance man to see to the continuance and better functioning of alliances and coalitions, and the supreme director of war economies, on the whole more efficiently producing under civilian than under military management. Seen as a competition of systems, there can be no doubt that the anti-Axis group of heads of states and their aides performed these tasks enormously better than their enemy counterparts.

But were they fully up to their tasks? Societies are never quite their own contemporaries, but full of cultural lags which may be *per se* fortunate or not,[81] and the military part of them in the past has usually been far from up to date, being inclined to fight past wars over again, with the old weapons, the old tactics, in the conflict at hand. While the military in 1939 and after were definitely more open-minded, better able to look ahead to what the war was bound to bring, than in practically all previous prewar times, the case was different with their civilian overlords. This time it was the civilians who brought to war more memories, more preconceptions, mostly dating back to the First World War, including Churchill's rankling and bitter memory of the Dardanelles enterprise, which the army had liquidated. More old-fashioned also were their notions about the desirable relations that must exist between soldiers and civilians in wartime.

The civilians in power were far more resolved to fight the war of 1914-18 over again, including its disastrous determination to gain "complete victory," than the soldiers, who left this ancient militaristic vice to the civilians. There was also a widespread conviction among the warmaking civilians that, as Saint-Just had put it, "you have first to conquer the army if you want it to conquer in turn," [82] and they were all set to conquer it, whether this would prove necessary or not. It proved more essential in the case of the losers than of their opponents. Still another issue of lag entered civilian-military relations at the top: the conception, building, and application of new and unconventional weapons. While there were great variations among the belligerents, there was nearly none of that superciliousness on the military side that had been noticeable before, as expressed in the French general's remark of 1915 after

Churchill had developed his idea of tanks, or "land cruisers": "Your politicians are even funnier than ours." [83]

Whether it was a sign of the "thorough-militarization" of modern society or not, all the heads of states in the Second World War, except in Japan, could look back to earlier military experiences of some sort, with Mussolini, "Marshal of the Imperium," showing the poorest record and Churchill the longest and most variegated. The two ex-Austrians, Hitler and Tito, had fought among the lowest rankers. That other unprofessional Marshal, Stalin, in the Civil War had learned to despise the *spez* as "psychologically unfit to fight a decisive war against the counterrevolution" [84] and later, how to remove and replace generals by the hundred. Franklin D. Roosevelt's experience as Assistant Secretary of the Navy had convinced him that he could do even more easily without a Secretary of the Navy than a War Secretary, and Harry S. Truman had been an artillery reserve officer in the First World War and after. While they might have shared the very common desire of veterans of earlier wars to fight the old campaigns again, their previous experience would seem to have induced in all of them a determination, continued or occasional, to stand up to their professional advisers and either let themselves be persuaded or dissuaded, or stick to their own notions—plans would be too concise a term.

In their relations with the experts, they were often driven by those intuitions which in high places are apt to be heavily fraught with consequence. These impulses were usually rooted in an image of history and as such likely to interfere with the needs of technologically developing war. While Churchill might think back to Marlborough and Clive, while Hitler envisaged war as a prehistoric tooth-and-claw struggle for existence, Roosevelt "had a hunch that Stalin doesn't want anything but security for his country, and I think that if I give him everything I possibly can and ask nothing from him in return, *noblesse oblige,* he won't try to annex anything and will work with me for a world of democracy and peace." [85] The byname of "Junker of Hyde Park" could not have been earned better and more fatally than for this trusting to a knightly quality in a Communist.

The central position of the civilian war lords was still more firmly established by the masses' expectation of the genius in war, the victory-as-miracle created by genius. "The art of the geniuslike captain consists in making possible through the suddenness of his resolutions what at first sight appears impossible" (Mommsen, *The History of Rome,* Book IV), and everywhere the people trusted such captains would appear. The Caesarian-Napoleonic claim that "the general is the soul of the army; he strengthens it by more than one half," [86] was being raised by and for the twentieth-century

dictators, from Hitler to Stalin and on to Peron: Germany and
Italy together could put two hundred divisions in the field, Ribbentrop told visitors in April 1939. "This number must be multiplied
by two considering the leadership of A. Hitler and Mussolini." [87]
A Stalin biography of 1948 was so emended by its subject that it
appeared that "Comrade Stalin's genius enabled him to see through
the enemy's plans and defeat them," exactly what he did not see
in 1941.[88] And it is not likely to be the last echo along the cor-
ridors of history when we hear Peron claim in 1948 that he had
500,000 workers behind him and, "as Napoleon said, with me at
their head that amounts to a million." [89]

Actually, the development of warfare, apart from the demand
for an ultimate pyramidal point of decision and political authority,
held no role for the solitary military genius; he had been replaced
by managerial staffs of experts, a change not all generals liked to
admit. As a German historian operating under the handicaps prevailing in the Third Reich put it, in a warning against Mommsen
and Hitler: "The acquisition of strategical mastership outside a
strict military education is no longer possible today." [90]

The Führer as Feldherr

The officers who rebuilt the German army after 1918 did not build
in a superman, such as Ludendorff thought necessary for the future total war. Ludendorff was not accepted by the army, but rather,
out of hate-love, by Hitler. The best of the officers proceeded from
the essential weakness of Germany's war potential, to overcome the
shortcomings in part by organization, though hardly in case of a
prolonged war. These men were the doubting Thomases in the
army directorate, including among them General Georg Thomas,
head of the War Economy Office, and General Beck, the Chief
of Staff until 1938, who warned against "intuitions" in the conduct
of war, even if they might "appear ever so clever and geniuslike." [91]
Others fell under the spell of Hitler's luck, despite their General
Staff upbringing and the Moltkean warning: "Luck in the long run
is given only to the efficient."

The war as Hitler wanted it was fundamentally a refighting of
1914-18, and he, the veteran of those campaigns, would refight it
as no other veteran had done before him. It was Hitler's own
1914-15 experience in Flanders which made him halt the tanks
before Dunkirk because he considered the terrain unfit for tank
warfare.

What justifies us in speaking of civilian militarism during the
Second World War is above all the exhibition of many of the
worst militarist traits by nonprofessionals like Hitler. He sought

war for war's sake and was determined to fight it during his own best years, when he was most fit, whether or not Germany was; he was eager to undertake war as preventive war, before the others were ready. Added to this was his contempt for the so-called war guilt, for peace-minded diplomacy, afraid only, on his way to war, "that, at the last moment, some *Schweinehund* will make a proposal for mediation," and above all his scorn for "any humanitarian reasoning. We must make our hearts closed and hard" (Speeches to the generals in May and August 1939).

It might appear that Hitler was the creator of that social evil of modern times, total war, but in fact there was once a Hitler before Hitler. He was Francisco Solano Lopez (1827-70), also a civilian, the third in a line of Paraguayan dictators, the first of which had received Carlyle's praise. Solano ruled over a proto-totalitarian society—Indians long conditioned for servitude by the Jesuits—which he as "Supremo" plunged into a five-years war, waged so pitilessly that in the end a population of 1,337,000 was reduced to 221,000, and of these survivors less than 29,000 were adult males. Many features of the Hitler regime may be detected in that of the *Supremo:* injection of the race issue—the pure Guarani Indian fighting against the "monkey" Brazilians with their Negro blood; scorched earth measures; women and children in battle lines, and special units of the maimed—like Hitler's "stomach ulcer" battalions—and units of the deaf, who had to be led by signs. The Supremo had given himself an autodidactic military education, always interested himself in the latest "hardware" for war, preferred "to do everything himself," except leading and fighting in the front lines—"like all Neronic characters he wanted personal courage"—for, like Hitler and Mussolini, he stayed away from actual danger. Like them, too, he clashed with the remnants of the old ruling elements against whom he then directed the hatred of the Guarani who, as a visiting Prussian nobleman observed, "in the cutting down of the upper classes enjoyed a secret Indian pleasure." The demand of his opponents for unconditional surrender helped to prolong the fight, and Paraguay was saved only by the jealousy of the victors and the concern of one or the other for maintenance of the balance of power along the La Plata.[92]

The story of Solano Lopez spares us much of the retelling of Hitler's "intuitive" strategy, his abuse of German strength, and the archetypical distrust of the tyrant even in modern war—Hitler would not trust even weather reports, believing that they were so fashioned by generals that they could be used as further excuse for their stalling in the autumn and winter of 1939-40.[93] He was as regardless of human lives as that primeval forest Nero and as keen as the latter on securing the most up-to-date hardware, while neglecting the first conditions of that continuing research that must go into the planning and construction of modern war engines, this neglect being in keeping with the general Nazi anti-intellectualism. By comparison, scientists like Einstein and Lindemann had far easier access to the authorities, while in Russia the eagerness to enlist scientists for war purposes may have developed somewhat later, making good for original neglect by assiduous later courting.

Sound strategic ideas must be derived from firmly established and considered ratios of strength, the selection of objectives for attack through which the enemy's main strength can be struck or opposed and destroyed—such strikes to be delivered in the most surprising and decisive way, with an economy of means and on the basis of careful planning. Territorial conquests are of secondary importance, even in ages when war economy might make them highly desirable. A preference for early conquests was the failing of much of Axis strategy, together with an overestimation of friendly and contempt for the opponents' strength, Hitler always thinking more highly of the Italian forces, whom "Fascism had enabled to perform extraordinary deeds," [94] than the Wehrmacht. The desire for early conquests—later ones are more to be wished —drove the Japanese southward instead of into bleak Siberia, and moved Mussolini, "in an act of strategic madness," as his old admirer Fuller puts it,[95] to go after territory which he expected Italy to win in the coming peace, Corfu and the Epirus,[96] where he encountered Greek resistance which he could not break unaided.

So largely was Hitler's strategy political-minded and imperialistic —part of the "Cyclopean task which building of an empire means for a single man" and which he had shouldered [97]—that it often missed the basic aim of operations, destroying the enemy's main force, while conversely it proved least wrongheaded when least politically tinged, as in the approval of the successful plan for the opening of the French campaign in 1940. He aimed the first attack on Russia in 1941 at Leningrad and Stalingrad as the "two breeding grounds of Bolshevism" which must be destroyed,[98] instead of Moscow, as the military would have preferred. Contrary to their advice he would not release the hold on Stalingrad, as this would be sacrificing "the whole meaning of the campaign." [99] For "political reasons which my generals cannot understand" he would not allow them to evacuate the Crimea, become untenable, in time. It would have saved thousands of lives, they argued. "Some thousand more or less do not count," not to him.[100]

If at the outset of his warmaking Hitler achieved considerable surprise, among friends and foes, it was more often sociological in nature than military. He discarded the often more unconsciously than consciously preserved heritage of warmaking habits which had excluded certain extreme actions, despite often violent military language. Hitler, the revolutionary from below, wanted the war to be just as violent as the language. "Generals think war should be waged like the tourneys of the Middle Ages," he confided to Hermann Rauschning. "I have no use for knights. I need revolutionaries." [101] Apart from himself, there were few revolutionaries with military talent in the purely military field, and German war conduct kept always a somewhat schizophrenic quality, which Hitler thought to overcome when he took over direct command of the army at the end of 1941, at which time he told the army Chief of Staff: "Anyone can do that little bit of directing operations. The task of the army Supreme Commander is to educate the army in the National Socialist spirit. I know of no army general who could perform this task as I have it in mind. Hence I have resolved to assume the supreme command myself." [102]

The July 20, 1944, conspiracy, as an attempt, in its final meaning, of ending the war that Hitler could not bring to a close, showed him that the split continued and was even deeper than he had thought. As he told a participant in that attempt who had escaped death, though not suspicion, two months later: "I have often bitterly regretted not to have purged my officer corps as Stalin has done. I must make up for that now, it is high time and there is not a minute to lose. One must at last learn how to obey, blindly and without batting an eye. What I demand of the party and the whole people, the army must also do." [103]

It was much too late to attempt purges now and expose the officers to all sorts of indignities, putting above them commanders like Himmler and his fellows. Their obedience was only outwardly.

The Duce as War Lord

The Second World War was of all wars the most materialistic. Matériel and numbers decided its style, its outcome, and not, as the Axis members expected, "the myth of the Heroic Man." [104] Beyond a certain point, heroism, even of the Kamikaze type, was no *Ersatz* for matériel shortcomings. Mussolini was somewhat aware that Italy's war potential was the weakest of all the great powers, hence his promise to Hitler to enter the war was with the understanding that "a long war he could not undertake." But that was nearly the extent of what he had learned in his office as minister of all three services.

He was unaware "of the facts, the hollow kernel within the glittering display," the army's poor discipline and morale, the deep chasm that separated officers and rank and file, the officer privileges (such as separate kitchens) forming part of the price Fascism had paid for the officers' toleration; in short, he was ignorant of the "deficiencies that ought to have kept Italy out of the war," according to German professional judgment.[105] While the Duce's grasp of things military was insufficient, he could always muster for his actions "intuitive reasons of a general character," as he called it, maxims such as that "in politics as in war, those who are absent are always wrong," and of course the excuse in the end, when the Fascist Grand Council was about to depose him, that "the nation's effort had been sabotaged by the General Staff, whose behavior has always been equivocal and secretive," [106] much the same excuse that figures in Hitler's political testament.

Prime Minister and Army

In addition to his premiership Churchill had "arrogated to himself military responsibilities" unprecedented in British history: he was Minister of Defense as well, and besides chairman of the Chiefs of Staff Committee and practically controlled the Joint Planning Committee, an interservice body set up to examine, embrace, or discard strategic possibilities.[107] More recent British war history has become highly critical of the application of these powers in some areas, notably as regards his share and intervention in and interference with plans and operations, an intrusion into military fields which may have hampered rather than improved upon military planning and action. While not denying his indefatigable energies, drive, and resistance force, which saw Britain through the war, generals and admirals complained during the conflict and even more afterward about what army Chief of Staff General Brooke called his "method of suddenly arriving at some decision as it were by intuition, without any kind of logical examination of the problem." [108]

British and American war historians, official or not, in the wake of his proud war memoirs have enumerated a number of his impractical schemes, mostly "peripheral-minded" in their nature,[109] a common feature of politicians' strategy as opposed to soldiers'. Churchill proposed strikes through the Sound and into the Baltic in 1939-40 or against Norway after 1941, which the planners considered unfeasible, given the German *dominium coeli* over these regions; Hitler, however, feared that the British might attack here, which in turn his experts thought unlikely—so very much coincidental was politicians' strategy. Because it derived from history? Seeking for the reasoning behind Churchill's Norway notions, the soldiers were told that "Hitler had unrolled the map of Europe starting with Norway and he, Churchill, would start rolling it up with Norway." [110] Again like Hitler, he had a mania for islands as objectives—they would seem glorious trophies, acquired in the best British tradition, whatever their actual importance in modern warfare. With the words, "This is the time to think of Clive and Peterborough and of Rooke's men taking Gibraltar," he sent off the hapless attackers to the Dodecanese in the autumn of 1943.[111]

Nearly always, Churchill's war thoughts were to a degree historicized: not only had he "never the slightest doubt that he had inherited all the military genius of his great ancestor Marlborough," [112] more unfortunately he also sought mobility in warfare in ways and places where modern logistical considerations proved stifling to genius. Mars in the mid-twentieth century had acquired leaden soles in his sandals, and Wavell used to emphasize in his War Academy lectures that Socrates had called supplies the first care of the general.[113] "I don't want any of your long-term projects, they cripple initiative," Churchill would tell the planners when they pointed out logistic and other obstacles in the way of his ideas and sudden changes, "I sometimes think some of my generals don't want to fight the Germans." [114] They did not always want to fight in the places the Prime Minister preferred, or for the reasons which he preferred, the political ones, as when he sent the ill-fated *Prince of Wales* and the *Repulse* into Japanese-controlled seas.[115] In other ideas for the conduct of the war, this statesman proved far more perspicacious than the greatest of the logisticians, the Americans, who preferred not to think beyond the hour of the achievement of victory.

F.D.R. as Commander-in-Chief

> "Please try to address me as Commander-in-Chief, not as President."
>
> F.D.R. to Cordell Hull [116]

Their constitutional position in total war kept the heads of state in those nations joined against the Axis in continuous occupation with the problems of war. Their function as energizers and unifiers of war endeavor, and as formulators and pronouncers of war policies, is more germane to total war than any other. "He who asserts, as is often done, that politics ought not to interfere with the conduct of war, has no grasp of the direction of great war" (Clausewitz). They gave to the professionals their general ideas about the war and approved or rejected the latter's plans.

Their role became more dubious when their own strategic notions, stemming from political reasoning or chosen "for psychological reasons," came to overrule or interfere with those of their professional advisers. In order to boost morale at home, Roosevelt suggested the Halsey-Doolittle raid on Tokyo, the evaluation of which military historians find difficult enough. His most far-reaching intervention was that in favor of Chennault and his proposals for establishing an air force in China and from there to bomb Japan and Japanese shipping. When General Marshall warned that this would infuriate the Japanese to such a degree that they might undertake land operations deeper into China and even drive Chiang Kai-shek out of his last stronghold, Roosevelt, surrounded by his civilian aides and in possession of "private advice out of China," turned him down: "In a political fight it's not good tactics to refrain from doing something because of something your opponent may do in return." He reminded the Chief of Staff—without exemplification—that he had overruled the military before and now thought he had been right in doing so. What he wanted was in effect to direct United States air forces "to implement a strategy for which the logistical foundation had not been laid." [117]

Aside from this episode and despite an occasional burst of bravado—"You can't leave things to the military; otherwise nothing will be done" [118]—Roosevelt usually accepted the views of the military, directly from them rather than through the civilian secretaries, a way that, while it might have speeded victory, left aside political points of which the civilians might have been more mindful than was he himself in his single-minded pursuit of victory.[119] According to British observation, he "had no great military knowledge and was aware of this fact and consequently relied on Marshall, who never seemed to have any difficulties in countering any wildish plans which the President might put forward." [120]

It was fortunate for the planning and the conduct of the Anglo-American war of coalition that this was the case, for originally, as at the Arcadia Conference (end of 1941), there seemed almost too much agreement between the political leaders. But in the long run the coincidence of views among the chiefs of staff—"particularly those of the same service" [121]—prevailed. They would have F.D.R. on their side and he would meet some of Churchill's proposals to take this or that island by retorting: "All right; but where do we go from there?" [122] It contributed vastly to Allied victory that on their side the professional view prevailed, and on Hitler's side basically political ones.

Marshal Stalin

The historiography of the war is nowhere in a more precarious situation than under totalitarianism; hence little is reliably known about Stalin's actual military role. Was it he who first suggested the war against Finland, which he did approve of, a war with at first sight so clearly a military objective—better security for Leningrad, the second capital, and a stronger share in the *dominium maris Baltici?* The reality of Stalin's leadership is only partly revealed by the downgrading or de-mystification he was made to suffer in 1956. He was certainly a morale builder of size, as captured Soviet generals told the Germans, who in turn recognized in his orders a fundamental trait of dictatorial strategy—to hold out to the last man, no strategic withdrawal *à la* 1812, as the defeat of summer 1941 had been masked.[123]

Not the least of his wartime endeavors was directed at maintaining the party's and his own supreme position, hence the downgrading of all victorious marshals as soon as feasible. He wanted "no new Dumouriez to win the honor of having hurled the enemy back across the country's frontiers"; unity of command was arranged in such a manner that "no Bonapartes or other friends of a *coup d'état* would see their way cleared. Among us we shall never have a Russki," that leader of the northwest front who had forced Nicholas II to abdicate in 1917.[124] As party man, his role could not be considered complete unless he made as well his ideological contribution to the discussion of the war in its latest manifestation; according to Stalin war had gone far beyond the interpretation of Clausewitz who, he wrote, was merely "the representative of the hand-manufacturing phase of warfare," and was now superseded by Stalin, the war-thinker, himself.[125]

Myth-building around the warrior has seldom taken place without the subject's help. No one was more strongly participating in the process than Stalin. Byzantium was still in the East. The glorifiers, usually provided with a military title, wrote glowingly of Stalin's leadership, farsightedness, breadth of vision in planning the war—"how far into the future peered the eagle gaze of the Great Leader"—his ability to deal the enemy blows "of mounting force," his elaboration of "a new type of strategy which supplanted the old and obsolete linear strategy," etc., etc. There were not only the recipes for past victories but also for others to come, those over the Anglo-Saxon warmakers, whose strategy was as faulty as that of the German-Fascist invaders. "The time has long passed when the leaders of the bourgeois armies could contribute anything new and progressive in the sphere of strategy. They cannot, because their aims in war run counter to the development of human society." [126]

Army resentment over this downgrading of the military became a powerful factor in Stalin's own debunking, Khrushchev paying for army support in his rise to power by "revealing" Stalin's—very real—shortcomings in the conduct of war and for Russia's preparedness in 1941. There could have been more, if silent, agreement about one achievement of his: he knew what he wanted to gain in the war for Russia and communism and he obtained most of this.

Soldier Militarism and Nonmilitarism—
The Second World War

As 1939 drew near, military men stood at or hard behind the heads of state in many Latin American countries, in Poland, Hungary, Rumania, Greece, Spain, and Yugoslavia, while officer politics remained endemic in a number of the smaller nations. More often than not, however, this was an inward-directed militarism, not a threat to the general peace. The one remaining stronghold of old-style great power militarism was Japan, her officers staging those "incidents" which other armies and navies had learned to shun while the various fascisms sought them ever since the Italo-Greek Corfu incident of 1923. Behind the scenes military men were dictating to Japan the choice of friends and foes and alliances. "As the real driving force behind Japanese state policy, the officers accepted full responsibility for the alliance [with the Axis] idea, gradually permeating it through all sections of the population," the German ambassador, a major general, reported from Tokyo.[127]

While the warlike adventures of Fascism and National Socialism in Abyssinia and Spain came to a close, and remained without a sequel of further war, the wars which the Japanese army had set off in Manchuria went on from "incident" to "incident," low-burning much of the time, but endless. This was "causally" dangerous because it attracted first accomplices, the Axis partners, and then new open enemies, through the attack on Pearl Harbor, bringing America into the war as no other provocation could have done, since Hitler assiduously shunned incidents, for which F.D.R. was waiting. This was soldier militarism in a belated recoil effect from the exotic world.

Meantime, in the leading nations of the Western world, such traditional militarism as is indicated by the activities of political-minded officers, by their hankering for and provocation of war, was distinctly lessening. Sheer professionalism was the predominant attitude, on the eve of the Second World War, in England, the United States, and Germany as well. German generals on the whole behaved like the most obedient and at times almost passionate professionals, save for a small group of military men who, in partnership with other groups of those in fear of Hitler's death-dealing policies, ineffectually conspired against the regime. The majority neither fostered Nazism nor sought to stem its excesses; doubt most strongly assailed the top echelons, some of the commanders and some of the staffs, those who like sorcerers' apprentices afraid of what they had brought about were, according to Hitler, sabotaging his wars. The rest stood aside from politics, waiting for the "necessary" war and enemies to prove themselves, like the young Reichswehr officer in the Weimar days who, utterly bewildered after a lecture on international understanding, broke out: "But, gentlemen, things can't work that way, an enemy one must have." [128]

At the outset of war, at least, "there is nothing more beautiful than to win," a German general confessed, as so few do, "and we did win, for a time—and did all of us enjoy it, no doubt about it. . . . Many of the present-day heroes of the resistance went along enraptured. Winning pleased, but not the later defeats." [129] On the medium level of the hierarchies the desire to prove, at long last, one's leadership abilities remained exceedingly strong, "the psychological factor that any ardent soldier finds it hard to resist a professional opportunity," a factor on which Hitler "played constantly in order to split the solidarity of professional opinion" arrayed against him. [130]

On the opposing side, this type of commander also existed—"we are not free to moderate at our pleasure our own desire to command," as Thucydides said of Alcibiades—and was represented most succinctly outside Germany by the nearly archaic personality of Patton, "invaluable in time of war, but a disturbing element in time of peace," as a between-the-wars fitness report would say of him. He would regret the invention of the atomic bomb, for it would give "pacifists, politicians and fools a chance to say: 'All we need is a bomb, no Army,' " [131] and would have lamented together with that Japanese military attaché who on V-J Day regretted that war, "this sporting match mingled with heroism," had been revolutionized by the bomb, "no longer leaving room for chivalry." [132]

Under the influence of civilians, there was not much space left for such an outlook on war—Eisenhower would not even speak to the German general surrendering forces under his command in North Africa. Generals had learned not to insist on such traditional points or on various others that seemed still more to fall into the political sphere. The politically minded, politically active general of the Henry Wilson type had practically disappeared from the scene, and even from the wings in Britain and America and, one might say, in Russia. The top rankers had risen largely unknown to the politicians and without their help. At the British Staff College they had been taught to "cut out the politics." [133] With this aloofness went "a marked hostility of the Army towards Members of Parliament" such as General Spears, an M.P. himself, encountered when he sought employment in the army as a "retread," finally becoming liaison officer with the French command, a position not originally planned by the War Office. [134] Montgomery, remembering "how generals had been roughhandled by the politicians in the First World War, was determined to play the politicians at their own game and keep his end up with the public," saw to his own speech-making and other publicity, which he disliked *per se.*[135]

In the United States, the gulf between the Executive and Congress and the military was only slightly less wide and deep than the cleavage in Britain. While the President knew naval officers from his Navy Department years (one of whom, Admiral Leahy, he made his closest uniformed adviser on the war), General Marshall had been brought to his attention only in 1939, by Hopkins, who subsequently received from Roosevelt and Marshall his education "in the military facts of life." [136] In his relations with Congress, Marshall during the war years "virtually dictated the budgets," [137] so anxious was Congress to let the military have all that they considered necessary for victory. No civilian control touched the wartime "immediacy" relations between the President and the Joint Chiefs of Staff, conferring on the latter an abundance of power which they only occasionally tried to extend into new fields, such as that of "political warfare." [138] If the State Department was so largely excluded from Washington war councils, this was not due to a militarism on Marshall's part but to Roosevelt's wishes.[139]

Fundamentally, the Joint Chiefs remained wholly unlike Ludendorff in their abstinence from politics; on the lower echelons only was there an occasional expression of the traditional contempt—less traditional in America than elsewhere—of the soldier for the politician. Even if to the irrepressible Patton "politics was a low form of life, when his position demanded that he receive visiting Congressional committees, he was gracious and charming." [140] The other problem general, to the Washington command, was Douglas MacArthur, a man much harder to keep in his place and in harmony with a "Hitler first" strategy, to the abandonment of which he would apply "every stratagem of political manoeuvre." [141] As the British saw this wartime conflict: "Even with the authorities in Washington, his relations were peculiar. For MacArthur occupied a unique position in the American military hierarchy. . . . This background and his own self-confidence did not incline him to act in the manner of senior commanders. A pronounced consciousness of his position and of political importance which it fostered, gave his relations to Washington something of the flavor of an independent power." [142]

The sometimes nearly desperate resolve of most American generals to remain "military generals" and not become "political generals," exemplified with tragic starkness by Stilwell in China and confirmed in Eisenhower after the Darlan episode, resulted in a single-mindedness directed to the achievement of military victory, to V-E and V-J days, and not a minute beyond. How much did this contribute to America's "winning the war and losing the peace"?

The political involvement of generals and admirals went far deeper in France, where they looked upon their political chief "as an ignoramus to be kept in his place, good enough to make meaningless speeches, but always woefully inadequate in the only role in which he might be useful, that of extracting funds from Parliament for the navy" or the army.[143] The true spokesmen of the army were Pétain and Weygand, the great survivors of the First World War, who felt particularly outraged by the politics and diplomacy of the popular front, including the military alliance with Russia, not because it did not seem to them sufficiently strength-conferring but because, as Pétain declared "by holding out a hand to Moscow, we have held it out to Communism . . . have admitted Communism into the register of avowable doctrines. It is quite likely we shall have an opportunity of regretting it." [144] As conservatives, they backed the *status quo* in French armaments, sans armored corps and dive bomber squadrons, hiding behind the Maginot Line, which was to make all future offensives, German *and* French, futile and an invasion of France impossible. The question *"Une invasion est-elle encore possible?"* was answered in the negative by General Chauvineau, author of a book of this title (1938), and by Pétain, while Weygand, speaking on the archaic occasion of a horse show in July 1939, was equally assuring.[145] Only a few like De Gaulle, who knew "that the military organism, because of the inherent traditionalism in its very nature, will not reform itself of its own accord," but had to receive outside impetus, ineffectually attempted change.[146]

The clear fact that this self-satisfaction lost France the war in 1940, still could not keep her politicians, the clear majority of them, from making Pétain the trustee in bankruptcy of the Third Republic, a trustee recommended by Weygand's and others' fear of a sovietization of France. Vichy fascism, the shortest-lived of the species, was nothing so much as the outcome of retired generals' wish dreams about their country's better, firmer, more authoritarian order, eliminating parliament and parliamentarians who had made the army lose the war; the veterans' organizations would become the backbone of the new order; the head of state would receive from the remaining armed forces an oath as unconditional as Hitler had obtained. Weygand, Foch's one-time chief of staff, outlined the plan that, following the end of France's foreign war, was to terminate the interior one, that of parties, classes and other interests, including the Freemasons.[147] Once more a nation having suffered military defeat wanted to accept a marshal as head of state—MacMahon after 1871, Hindenburg after 1918, and now

Pétain. (Could one add: Lee after Appomattox? The North, as if afraid of something similar, kept Lee forever ineligible.)

One of the besetting sins of wartime militarism has long been a soldiers' nationalism, occurring on all levels, obstructing the successful conduct of coalition warfare, detracting from the sum total of the strength invested in such war. Despite a much presumed community of political doctrine, it proved far more virulent among the Axis powers in the anti-Axis camp. The Italians, for example, would gladly have done without German help, not to mention Germans in command of their forces, in their offensive toward the Suez Canal, and Badoglio and Graziani "wanted to keep the glory of conquering Egypt for themselves. Mussolini backed up their objections" against German assistance and commanders.[148] This may well have cost the Axis control of the Canal.

The Anglo-American coalition of 1941 and after was the most efficient, hence the most successful one in the history of warfare. Only occasionally would a resentment tinged by nationalism erupt, as between Bradley and Montgomery in 1944. At times, the field commanders seemed almost too eager to smooth down such ruffled feathers to suit their superiors at home, as when Churchill in March 1944 sent General Wilson a "fulmination," accusing him "of being too neutral as an Allied Commander and not playing adequately to support his hand in resolving differences with the U. S. on strategical matters," [149] or when General Marshall expressed fear that Eisenhower, in order "to make things go smoothly [with the British] might be going too far in agreeing to disruption of American command and organization." [150] Nationalism will cling to reservations in coalition warfare. To a considerable extent, the NATO organization is intended to overcome this, ahead of war.

A common liberalism proved a better lubricant of coalition war than Axis totalitarianism or the much-proclaimed "democracy" that supposedly united the Western Powers with Russia. Western naïveté had begun by looking forward to a comradeship-in-arms on all levels. Eisenhower, who invoked the very misleading parallel of the crusade, ignoring the military futility and proto-nationalism of the latter, wanted to discover in the ordinary Russian "a marked similarity to what we call an 'average American,' " to believe that past Russo-American relations gave "no cause to regard the future with pessimism. . . . Both were free from the stigma of colonial empire building by force." [151] (A reading of "Easterns" instead of "Westerns" might have corrected this error.) The twofold barrier of Russian war nationalism and Communism made unrealistic hopes, such as those of the American air force, "to put military relations with Russia on the same basis as those with Britain." [152] Stalin wanted no "touching of the cloth," no comradeship-in-arms to develop between capitalist and anticapitalist warriors. It might have made Red army officers more profession-minded, less class-conscious. He had suspected such a danger before.

To no small extent had their previous war experience with the Germans led Churchill and Roosevelt toward seeking and finding the same enemy once more. Again, as in 1914 and 1917, the enemy's preparations for and readiness to go to war seemed centered in the Berlin General Staff. While it would be correct, to a large extent, to see German war strength organized by this staff, it was far less true to call it the seat of the will to war or the instigator of that militarism which Roosevelt had denounced well ahead of war: "You cannot organize civilization around the core of militarism and at the same time expect reason to control human destiny" (Speech of Oct. 25, 1938). Neither he nor Churchill were aware that there was a new militarism in the world, when they proclaimed the eradication of militarism as one of the two supreme aims in the war against Germany, together with the destruction of Nazism, quite as if the one were not the other, too. Hence the declaration of Yalta and Potsdam of "the inflexible purpose to destroy German militarism and Nazism, to break up for all time the German General Staff that has repeatedly [!!] contrived the resurgence of German militarism," hence the indictment at Nürnberg of the General Staff and the High Command of the German armed forces.

In the light of history, the Nürnberg judgment, while arriving at an acquittal—the Russian member dissenting—but declaring the group "responsible in large measure for the miseries and suffering that have fallen on millions of men, women and children," having been "a disgrace to the honorable profession of arms," and having, as German militarism, "flourished briefly with its recent ally, National Socialism," [153] was still strongly under the impact of war propaganda. The court was called a "Military Tribunal," with no military members except a Russian judge advocate. In the court of their truer peers they soon fared far better, with British writers like Captains Russell Grenfell and B. H. Liddell Hart, the latter calling it "one of the surprising features of the Second World War that the German Army in the field on the whole observed the rules of war better than it did in 1914-18—at any rate in fighting its Western opponents." [154]

In an "interior forum," in the context of German history, the German generals must be judged far differently, far more harshly even: for having misjudged Nazism, its nature and its leaders, for not having removed them when it was in their power, for having accepted offices, promotions, checks for 100,000 marks at a time from Hitler, the "fount of honor," though he had members of their estate murdered and defamed, whose guilt the worst of careerists like Blomberg and Keitel readily took for granted. Theirs was a spinelessness, a suffering of the dishonor prevailing once more under Hobbesian conditions of competition—when "honorable is whatsoever possession, action, or quality is an argument and sign of power" (*Leviathan*, X)—which made a former Reichswehr commander say: "These fellows make of me, an old soldier, an antimilitarist." [155] Against all this only a small group of dissidents, the participants of the 20th of July conspiracy, protested. All honor was lost, except theirs.

Beyond the call of honor, this group felt the call for peace, for the ending of a lost war. Hitler the desperado would not give peace back to the Germans and the rest of the world; he was unable to bring a halt to the forces he had set in motion. Terminating war is indeed a difficult problem, one older than the professionalism of arms. In one of the Norse sagas, the speaker of the folk *thing* complains:

This king suffers no one to speak to him and does not like to hear anything but what pleases him. . . . But we, peasants, want that thou, King Olaf, should make peace. If thou dost not want to satisfy our desire, we shall kill thee and no longer suffer unpeace and unlawfulness. For this is what our ancestors have done: They threw five kings into a well near Mulathing, because they were swollen with pride and acted contrary to the law." [156]

There being no institution, no individuality, no "economic man"—he least of all—left in Germany capable of ending the war, they, who came so largely from the General Staff, and hence knew the hopelessness of the struggle better than anyone else, took it on themselves to end the war by ending Hitler. It was a noble office.

V-E and V-J days seemed to bring victory consummated over not only the militarism of the conquered but also all militarism. If there was any left in Germany and Japan, military occupants proceeded to root it out, Eisenhower proclaiming in the first issue of the newspaper that was to serve the re-education of the Germans that together with National Socialism, militarism "must be eradicated from the German world of thought. For all the civilized peoples of the earth war is per se something immoral, the Germans have to be educated to this truism."

While the proud victors believed themselves free of such sinfulness, the conquered had often reason to feel that the soldiery ruling over them exhibited only another sort of militarism —that which appears following unconditional surrender of a place—the Berliners and Viennese joking bitterly that the true inscription on the Russian victory monuments put up in their midst was "To the Unknown Looter." Like a hardy perennial, militarism, still so called by some people, showed a regrowth, more often almost in new and unexpected places than in old ones.

As dissension inside the anti-Axis coalition grew apace, it promptly became a pejorative fitting the other side: to Americans and others in the West, the Communist regimented order of things came to represent the worst kind of militarism,[1] assuming its most radical incarnation in the latest of the Communist states, in Red China and its "people's communes" through which, largely during 1958, labor was "organized along military lines, and things are done the way battle duties are carried out, and the

14
Militarism after 1945

people live collectively." [2] And to the Communists capitalism, and monopoly capitalism in particular, as Lenin had already discerned and Stalin re-emphasized, had militarism for its basic ingredient. It was said to be

not just a temporary side-effect of modern capitalism, but resulted with iron necessity from its essence, represents an inescapable part of its basic economic law. Putrefying capitalism—in its last stages represented by the war-hankering financial oligarchy of the U.S.A. —is ready to rush into warlike adventure. . . . To the socialist state, however, militarism and wars of conquest are essentially foreign.[3]

During the inevitable postwar *malaises,* militarism was discerned in various new military developments. True, there was no longer a basis for many old complaints; critics could no longer quote the old adage that war was too serious a thing to be left to the generals, now that generals heartily agreed with them, urging civilians, including scientists, to assist them; for example, that rather unconventional admiral, H. G. Rickover, amazing Congress by suggesting that it might use defense funds if necessary to increase teachers' salaries.[4] However, old-fashioned pacifists, socialists,[5] and liberals, as if unable to dispense with old enemies, saw danger in the extended role given defense considerations and military men in American policy. "Should we fear the military?" Justice William O. Douglas asked, and was inclined to answer his query in the affirmative: "Today, as a result of our military-mindedness, there is less room for debate —less room for argument—less room for persuasion—than in almost any period of our history." [6] American educators were particularly anxious to denounce the "army mind, that part of the brains within the military orbit that determines policies and directs power," in two directions, "to uniformity, absolute uniformity in all physical things, and to maintaining the status quo, unless making conquests." [7] Another educator of the older generation, Eduard C. Lindeman, speaking during the "cold war," thought that "the discipline expected of us," made militarism "one of the conditioning factors in the lives of children and youth." [8] During that period of actual but undeclared war the American strategy of providing a counterforce to Communist expansion, seemed to some neutrals and even allies as throwing "the onus of militarism and imperialism" on the United States when actually it was Communism that entertained the largest armies and was expanding.[9]

With somewhat more justice, critics might discern old-style militarism in the occasional public proposals of officers to launch a preventive war against Russia as long as the American monopoly of the atomic bomb lasted,[10] or the spying and incident-provoking activity of service attachés, one of whom even so far forgot discretion as to allow his diary to be stolen by a Soviet agent in 1952, a failing for which he was duly court martialed. The much too familiar political penchant of the service attaché—shades of Papen and Peron!—would again be observed after 1945, but largely in the new countries of the Near East, where Egyptian attachés were accused of having tried to hire murderers in Jordan and Libya to assassinate "official personalities." [11] A former military attaché, Lieutenant Colonel Abdel Hamid Serraj, became chief of Syria's military intelligence, from which vantage point he, the "Nasser of his country," as a man of the military left steered his country into union with Egypt.

Paradoxically, the tested military heroes of the liberal powers fared less well as regards their postwar reputation and prestige than the unproven generals and colonels of the new military small powers. De Gaulle went into a prolonged political limbo, "a Caesar sitting on the Rubicon in order to fish in it," as his period of inactivity has been described.[12] Eisenhower's star paled under the critical glare of an economic recession and a second term in the White House, while MacArthur and other ex-generals held no offices but in giant industrial corporations, to demonstrate so to speak that Herbert Spencer's dichotomy of the soldier and the industrialist is no longer valid. A *Heldendämmerung* set in in the West, cutting away the ground from under most militarism, military and civilian, which as hitherto known was always so strongly historicized. Faced by atomic bombs and intercontinental missiles history, in its more obvious aspects, had nothing to teach about future war, in which no central hero figure will be directing campaigns of the old style, and in the expectation of which the superman had become simply infantilistic. The generals themselves did not attempt to revive such old traditions; even MacArthur, in whom something of long ago survived, would never have proposed to militarize the country's society and economy to meet the future war. Indeed, not a little in American preparations for and against war was aimed at preventing it from being militarized. Asked what would have to be done if the Communists should take over all Europe and Asia, General Bradley, when Chief of Staff, thought " 'we'd have to militarize the country completely for 100 or 150 years, and that would be as bad as defeat.' Because he hates the prospect of a militaristic state, he is determined that we shall not be thrown back on the Western hemisphere." [13]

The realistic imagination of such war is deeply upsetting to modern services. Ought they to fight it as hitherto constituted, separately though under Joint Chiefs, or completely unified? And can any *esprit de corps* survive in unified services? (Scottish colonels resigned in 1957 rather than see the regimental trews go). These issues underlie the prolonged intraservice fights in America, probably the worst in the history of military-naval relations. They were never cut short by a *mot d'ordre* from the civilian authority, which was not formulated with any finality so as to end "undesirable branch consciousness or competition." [14]

Civilian indecision prolonged this strife as it prolonged the struggles over MacArthur's Far Eastern consulship. The old awe inspired in Washington by the General blocked the prompt reassertion of civilian control over the Korean War, allowing his concepts to prevail that when you go to war, "the balance of control, the balance of concept, the main interest involved, the minute you reach the killing stage, is the control of the military." [15] Realizing none too soon that this was risking a general war, the President, who could not want such an extension of the conflict, recalled him at last,[16] making up for the delay by the brusqueness of his comment: "You hire them and you fire them." The General's reaction took the form of a protest against "a new and heretofore unknown and dangerous concept that the members of our armed forces owe primary allegiance or loyalty to those who temporarily exercise the authority of the Executive Branch of the Government rather than to the country and its Constitution which they are sworn to defend. No proposition could be more dangerous." [17]

For all its perilous interpretation of the Constitution, and the echoing, in the phrase about the "temporary" civilians, of historical attitudes—of times when other officers held up other "temporary gentlemen" to scorn—the General was speaking out when no longer on active duty and, to all appearances, only for himself. His stand was not fraught with such consequences as that of Seeckt in the Kapp putsch or the British officers during the mutiny on the Curragh in 1914. Probably this pronouncement marks the furthest point reached by militarist thinking in post-1945 America. The obvious intrusion of defense considerations into the affairs of the country, so utterly contrary to earlier peacetime concepts, still was not accompanied by an intrusion of military men into the country's governance. Those who worked in traditionally civilian posts for a time, came by more or less urgent invitation, not because they pushed themselves forward. Nor did the large-scale rearmament programs lead to the "barrack state" or other much apprehended militaristic measures.

It was in France that civilian-military conflict under constitutional government as part of old-style militarism proved most perennial. In the Fourth Republic, under the efforts to salvage an old but damaged prestige and a colonial empire, rioting servicemen could sack and destroy the offices of a Saigon newspaper owing to its pro-

Annamese attitude and its criticism of the conduct of French
personnel on the spot.[18] Following the defeat at Dienbienphu,
General Navarre published a brochure in which he, like Vichy
generals, ascribed the loss of Indochina to the civilians in the government.[19] False military pride combined with an outdated nationalism
—outdated militarily speaking—and with Communists and pacifists
to defeat the European Defense Community idea under slogans like
"EDC revives the German army and destroys the French army."
Weygand, De Gaulle (who called it a "politicians' joke"), Marshal
Juin (who wrote at the time that "the treaty violently offends
national feelings")—"to a man all saw the possibility of glory only
in service to a France which actually existed only in their corporate
imagination, a France of shako and sabres." [20] The bombing of a
Tunisian village in January 1958, due to local initiative oblivious of
all far-reaching consequences, was merely the last outbreak of
military frustration in the fight against yet another Resistance which
with its *mystique* had already robbed the French army of so much
prestige.

Joining Rightist civilian elements, army officers, with the para-
troopers in the lead and navy elements not far behind, in May 1958
set up "committees of public safety" in Algiers and later Corsica,
openly defying the Paris central government, which did not dare, lest
all end in chaos, to call upon the conscript army to deny obedience
to these disobedient officer-politicians. Rather were the majority of
the parties in metropolitan France ready to admit General de Gaulle
once more to power, relying on his promise to maintain essential
liberties. "The army, which has long suffered trial from bloody tasks,
is scandalized by the absence of true authority," De Gaulle told the
moribund French National Assembly.[21] Still, the army did not carry
things to another much expected 18th Brumaire. Following a
plebiscite endorsing him, De Gaulle in October 1958 told the soldiers
bluntly the moment had come to quit political organizations at once
and to stop interfering with the press and other freedoms. They
recognized in him "true authority." Should the new Fifth Republic
succeed, the army's role in its start may yet prove that of a fortunate
catalyst in an unfortunate political process.

Like old styles and fashions exported to distant regions, some
forms of fascist militarism reappeared overseas after 1945. In India
the Rashtrya Swayamsevak Sangh, a Hindu extremist right-wing
militant organization, anti-communist, anti-Moslem, in opposition to
Nehru's Congress Party, gave its members para-military training.[22]
In Argentina, Peronism grew out of an alliance of military junta and
the labor movement, reminiscent of the Nazi Party except that
instead of black or brown shirts they were called "no shirts" or
descamisados; most of the glory went to an army that had seen no

war since 1870 but whose *"coronels"* nevertheless considered themselves "deserving of absolute deification," at the same time bestowing
the honorary rank of general on the "Virgin of Mercedes," the army's
patron saint.[23] Peronism evolved into a Ducedom, until it was
swept away by another military-naval junta. Fundamentally, political
conditions in Latin America in their dependence on the military,
actual or potential, remained much the same as in Hegel's day, when
"the republics were based on military force alone; their whole
history is continuous subversion, all changes being brought about
by military revolutions." [24] Whereas at present there are fewer
strong men in power in Latin America than at most other times of
its turbulent history, many of them having been ousted in the 1950's
by military-naval juntas, the juntas as vehicles of force still remain,
likely and usually inclined to bring on new caudillos.

While within the military scheme of the Western powers guard
troops, where they remained at all, played no great role, several of
the new states introduced them, more in the image of the old body-
guards than the guards reintroduced in Russia as elite troops. Moreover, nearly all the newly independent nations are beset by officer
politics. Much of the customary militarism would seem to have
immigrated there—attaché politics, innumerable frontier incidents
and so on. Whether the underlying cause is called political im-
maturity or the numerical and ideological weakness of the middle
classes in these countries, most of them are susceptible to the political aspirations of or political direction by officer cliques, acting not
unlike Latin American juntas during the past 150 years.

In many respects Marshal Pibul of Thailand was another caudillo,
far away but under the same latitude, balancing himself between
rival military, police, and naval factions whose uniforms did not
keep their members out of lucrative businesses, until ousted from his
patriarchal, amiable dictatorship by the temporarily united groups
in September 1957, directed from behind the scenes by Field
Marshal Sarit Thanarat. A new "National Socialist" party was
formed, the more important Cabinet posts filled with more generals,
with firm adherence sworn to the Western camp and the SEATO
organization. A year later, the Marshal, at the head of a still newer
Revolutionary Party, "comprised of army, navy, air force, police,
and civilian officials, 'in the name of the people' " took over control
more openly, explaining his coup as necessary because of the threat
of Communism and "tension building up within and without the
country," and planned to dissolve the National Assembly.[25]

If centrifugal tendencies are the opposite of modern nationalism,
there would be less nationalism among the officer-politicians of
Indonesia, to whose island-mentality President Sukarno tried to
oppose his own brand of aggressive nationalism by claiming Dutch

New Guinea and dispossessing the remaining Dutch enterprises in the archipelago, thus to make liberation complete. Against this Java-based centralism and the philo-Communist "guided democracy" of Sukarno, some of the other islands and their colonels, strongly anti-Communist, rose in arms early in 1958.

Where Eastern militarism has a common denominator, or causation, or detonator, it is the failure or patent weakness of democratic-parliamentary governance in most of the countries between Turkey and China. Still more weakened by the 1957-8 crisis in capitalist economy, democratic forms of government were replaced by heavily militarized regimes in a whole monsoon of such coups during the autumn of 1958: in addition to Thailand, Burma was taken over by a general, Ne Win, acting, it was reported, at the invitation of Premier U Nu himself, who felt no longer able to master domestic anarchy; both were apparently acting under pressure from a very typical pressure group, "the colonels." [26] Only a little later, President Iskander Mirza of Pakistan, a Sandhurst-trained former officer, came to an understanding with the army's commander-in-chief, Ayub Khan, also Sandhurst-trained, that the army was to take over from the civilian politicians, who were mostly "crooks and scalawags," according to Mirza. As Ayub Khan explained: "We both came to the conclusion that the country was going to the dogs. . . . I said to the President: 'Are you going to act? If you do not, which Heaven forbid, we—the armed forces—shall force a change.' " [27]

Officer politics in the Near Eastern countries had its traumatic experience in military defeat and humiliation for which *revanche* was to be wrung from someone. Kemal Ataturk and Riza Shah Pahlavi, the restorers of Turkey and Iran, became the paragons of the military politicos after 1945, and still more definitely following the defeat in the war with Israel, for which the officers blamed the politicians and the politicians the military, and in the Suez expedition of 1956. Officers formed the vanguard of a youth movement within a civilization where gerontocratic stagnation had prevailed for centuries, until first stirred by the Young Turks.[28] Diverse religious and ideological movements flocked to the support of the officer groups who in Egypt under Colonel Nasser's leadership ousted the effete King Farouk in 1952—Nasser becoming at once the beau idéal of the young officers everywhere—and in Jordan caused the dismissal of the British command of the Arab Legion, the most advanced group, the artillery, providing the shock troop for the *coup d'état*.[29] In Syria, with the behind-scenes direction of the army chiefs of staff and of intelligence, they forced the government to accept arms, and to a certain extent ideas, from Russia and then pushed for an alliance and finally union with Egypt, the civilians at last agreeing in order to put a somewhat less pro-Communist

Nasser above the more pro-Communist officers in Damascus. In the old lands of the Assassins political murder, plotted abroad by military attachés, experienced a revival, with Arab nationalism as its heady hashish, and military youth as the most uncritical swallowers of the opiate, at a time when youth in Germany and Japan could hardly be moved in sufficient numbers to embrace military careers.

An Iraqi officers' conspiracy deposed and murdered their King, young Feisal, and Premier Nuri, supposedly a civilian "strong man," in the summer of 1958, moved into action by the belief that the Iraqi army was to be marched to support the largely civilian Chamoun government, in Lebanon, which was threatened by the Arab element in that country whose politicking with bullets instead of ballots the Lebanese army itself declined to terminate. Peace in Lebanon was restored, following American intervention with troops, when Chamoun was replaced in the presidency by the Moslem head of the army, General Chehab, while in Iraq General Kassem headed a government which almost from the outset was troubled by "the colonels." All over the East, with India the lone exception, parliamentary politicians seemed completely eliminated, an ancient enmity confirmed on new fields of conflict.

The Soviet habit, introduced during the war, of giving civilians military rank, similar to the bestowal by the Nazis of SA and SS rank on civilians, is in its way a reversal of the older systems of military powers to extend military interest and governance into society by way of the reserve officers. It was also intended to limit military power and to lay claim to a share in the recent victory for Generalissimo Stalin, Marshals Beria, Bulganin, Voznesensky, and Voroshilov, and Lieutenant General Nikita Khrushchev, who had served in the armed forces political administration and whose military renown was built up later, when he was "given" a prominent share in the defense of Stalingrad. While this might have furnished the most visible show of control over the military, other supervision, control, and indoctrination was probably more effective, together with the downgrading of popular military heroes like Marshal Zhukov. (In the Soviet film *The Fall of Berlin* the soldier was depicted as having panicked whereas Stalin, all serene, overrules the expert and thus wins the war.) [30]

Army resentment over such Stalinist downgrading and tightened political control came to prove a great help to Khrushchev in his rise over the Stalinists and the reputation of Stalin. The army assisted him through Zhukov and was rewarded lavishly, no one more visibly than Zhukov, who soon became Minister of Defense and a member of the Soviet Presidium. Obviously of great concern to the army, a rewriting of history was brought under way, beginning with the rehabilitation of nearly all the military victims of Stalinist purges. It obtained a decrease in the role of the political officers and almost "full command prerogatives for the professionals." [31] Zhukov himself claimed that the current reversion of the "cult of the individual" must not lead to the denial of the role of leaders generally and military leaders in particular, because such denial would be "doing poor service to the cause of increasing the military ability of the armed forces." [32]

When such views—which to outside observers seemed to indicate that the Russian military "retain continuing capabilities of independent action" [33]—might have foreshadowed a new Bonapartism, of which Khrushchev began to speak in warning tones,[34] the party reasserted itself overnight and in his absence abroad ousted Zhukov from all his offices (October 1957), accusing him of having tried to undermine party control over the armed forces. This was to be strengthened again, "for the further improvement of party and political work within the Soviet Army and Navy, work which is to enhance the might of our armed forces," which is to say that such work was not for control purposes but designed to raise military efficiency. Stalin, Zhukov's old detractor, was partially rehabilitated and his mantle, as far as still wearable, assumed by Khrushchev. The army showed no opposition, no solidarity with the deposed man; officers with hatchet men in their midst like Marshal Konev, were as eager to replace him as were the generals who took the places of those dismissed by Hitler. By February 1958 an army general would broadcast that the army liked the political work, considering "party leadership of the armed forces the source of their strength." [35]

Composition, thought, and behavior of the divers groups of army officers, at most times and in most places, have been greatly under the influence of postfeudal nobility as a complex of ideas, sentiments, and "belonging," membership being acquired by conforming to the code of chivalry, diluted and altered but basically still knightly. A complex whole lived on, extending far beyond the nobility of birth or that "created" in the various monarchical governments. *Esprit de corps* and cohesion of armed bodies, whose members were more exposed to danger and death than practically all other groups in society—hence their "closeness"—were built up and nourished on honor, a sense of inclusiveness and exclusiveness, usually the stricter the higher the rank, which dated back in essentials to knighthood, to the "Middle Ages which are nowhere ended except in the history handbooks," as Anatole France observed in *Le Lys Rouge*.

The concept of "officer and a gentleman" influenced greatly the preparation and the making of war. It slowed up the rationalization of army governance and the introduction and application of more modern equipment, excluded or impeded technological progress or insight or the timely preparation of a war economy, omissions that at the present point of arms evolution might seem more pardonable than at others. Leaving certain, relatively short historical periods apart—those of revolutions and severe, lasting military defeats—the "well-born" officers together with the ones received into their value-setting company, have shown less than full military appreciation of the mass of people or of the government, so often "disorderly," attempted in its image: democracy. Basically, the military estimate of democracy remained that of a feudal age which would concede honor and war-value to the sword-bearing mounted knight alone. Only occasionally could a medieval minstrel singing to town audiences remind his hearers that besides the knights there was the populace as warmaker—including giants who were never knights or mounted, but primeval "warfarers," who marched on foot and did great deeds even if armed only with poles and spears, as in the German epic of King Rother, of about 1150.[36]

Whether or not it was simply estate egotism—supranationally prevailing postfeudal chivalrousness—rather than humanitarianism, working its course in unsuspected ways as a code largely unwritten, that kept war as competition within bounds, certain things were simply "not done" in war. Increasingly, however, the list of taboos became shorter, the authors of such breaches of the rules of war proving most often bourgeois and proletarian civilians, trying to achieve break-throughs to more total, more absolute war. While such attempts had been advocated and made as during the American and French revolutions, officers as professional warmakers have usually succeeded in channeling war back into the dikes of custom.

These dikes were broken once more by the rise of the Soviets in 1917. However great the number of Czarist officers absorbed into the Red army, a new pattern of warmaking was imposed by the belligerents, who thought of war as one existing continually between classes—only temporarily was it switched back to the character of the "great patriotic war" in order to touch energies not otherwise mobilizable—a war that could not end until classes came to an end, with "peaceful coexistence" describing the less acute phases of the struggle. Attenuation of this perpetual strife was not to be considered, hence the Russian nonmembership in the Geneva Prisoners of War Convention of 1929, "an attempt to diminish the rigors of war and to mitigate the fate of the prisoners," as an official American publication defines its purpose.[37] There were moments when Red army officers would still have preferred to be considered members of the supranational fraternity of arms rather than the protagonists of Bolshevism, which the Russian military attaché in London, General Putna, in the 1930's would say "was not of Russian origin at all, but the invention of a German Jew, and had merely found the most fertile soil for itself in Russia." When he fell victim of the 1937-8 purges, it was held against him that while posted in London, he had been "very closely connected" with a German officer serving there, the reporter of this enlightening anecdote.[38]

There were other moments of understanding, equally fleeting, when Western generals like Eisenhower, in the hour of victory, expected that the Russians, "the more contact we have with them, will the more understand us and the greater will be the cooperation." [39] Stalin would suffer no such *camaraderie*. One of the Soviet marshals, Tukhashevsky, trying to make the most professionally out of this pan-hostility, once confided to foreign professionals that, professionally speaking, much might be said in favor of a totalitarian regime—never any trouble about army budgets, etc. Despite this appreciation, he was soon after "liquidated."

The various fascisms, extolling knightly and martial values, offering their armies the largest budgets and fastest promotions, throwing out "the element of moderation" which Clausewitz had seen prevailing in war, seemed at first "to be made for armies": to General Patton they seemed on a par with the Republican and Democratic parties. But becoming warmakers in their own right and frightfulness, these pseudo-military gave the generals who survived them occasion, if not too much reason, to speak of the "tragedy of true soldiery. . . . Always the soldiers were the whipping boys of the dictators." That was General Halder, one-time Reich army Chief of Staff, speaking to his Boswell in 1950.[40] Might not such as he and Marshal Zhukov and others have come to think by now, at this point of evolution of military-civilian relations, that, from the sheer professional point of view, democracies, of the un-Russian sort, are after all the best purveyors of soldiers and the best employers of officers? If they did, this would end much of the dichotomy of militarism and what is truly and necessarily military.

NOTES

INTRODUCTION

[1] E. Fischer and G. v. Below in *Deutsche Rundschau*, CLXII, CLXXL;
E. Guillon, *Nos écrivains militaires* (1899), II, 355.

[2] Mordacq, *Le Ministère Clemenceau*, I, 205.

[3] "One might speak of an exaggerated militarism with respect to the
exaggerated endeavors which countries like France undertake and
which are out of all relation to the number of the population."—
Major Schmitthenner, *Krieg und Kriegführung* (1930), p. 204.

[4] Sir John Fortescue, *History of the British Army*, X, 113.

[5] Wirth, *Le Maréchal Lefèbvre*, pp. 96 f.

[6] *The Seven Pillars of Wisdom* (Amer. ed.), p. 163.

[7] *N. Y. World-Telegram*, Feb. 10, 1937.

[8] H. Fick, *Der deutsche Militarismus der Vorkriegszeit* (1932).

[9] Karl Mannheim, *Archiv für Sozialwissenschaft*, LVII, 119.

[10] Otfried Müller (1797-1840), a Prussian philologist, cit. Max Jähns,
Heeresverfassungen und Völkerleben (1885), p. 48.

[11] H. von Srbik, *Metternich der Staatsmann und der Mensch* (1925), I,
385.

[12] *Reflexionen* (1908), p. 237.

[13] *Servitude et grandeurs militaires* (1835).

[14] Guillon, II.

[15] Béranger, *Les souvenirs du peuple*.

[16] Pierre da la Gorce, *Au temps du second Empire* (1935), pp. 29 f.

[17] *Lehre vom Heerwesen* (1872).

[18] *Cahiers* (1905).

[19] Terraillon, *L'honneur*, p. 153.

[20] For details see J. Reinach, *Histoire de l'affaire Dreyfus*, III, 570 ff.

[21] Maj. D. H. Cole and Maj. E. C. Priestley, *An Outline of British
Military History* (1936), p. 49.

[22] Reinach, III, 557.

[23] Jean de Pierrefeu, *Plutarque a menti* (1923).

[24] H. Hagedorn, *Leonard Wood* (1931), I, 175.

[25] Max Hoffmann, *Aufzeichnungen* (1929), I, 81, 176.

[26] Ibid., I, 53; II, 309; Hoffmann, *Tannenberg, wie es wirklich war*
(1926).

[27] Jähns, *Geschichte der Kriegswissenschaften*, pp. 1889 ff., 1857 f.

[28] Gouvion Saint-Cyr, *Mémoires*, IV, 39.

[29] Von Unger, *Blücher* (1906-8), II, 80.

[30] *Personal Memoirs of Ulysses S. Grant*, II, 276.

[31] Jähns, *Kriegswissenschaften*, p. 1973.

[32] K. Demeter, *Das deutsche Heer und seine Offiziere*, p. 160.

[33] K. Bleibtreu, *Das Heer*, pp. 107 f.

[34] This attitude is dear to many military writers. "Before I could put
my resolution into effect, I received an order from General Pershing
to do just what I had decided to do," writes Gen. Robert Lee Bullard
in *Personalities and Reminiscences of the War*, pp. 296, 317.

[35] Delbrück-Daniels, *Geschichte der Kriegskunst*, VI¹, 244, 248.

[36] Hohenlohe-Ingelfingen, *Aus meinem Leben* (1897), I, 326, 288.
[37] Delbrück-Daniels, V¹, 202.
[38] Bleibtreu, pp. 100 ff.
[39] Delbrück, *Geschichte der Kriegskunst*, IV, 309.
[40] Bourrienne, *Mémoires*, II, 241, 267.
[41] Spenser Wilkinson, *The Rise of General Bonaparte*, pp. 85 f.
[42] Gourgaud, *Journal inédit*, I, 168.
[43] Bourrienne, III, 288, 300 f., 215.
[44] *Mémoires du Duc de Raguse* (Marmont), I, 236 ff.
[45] G. Tarde, *Les lois sociales* (4th ed.), pp. 54 ff., 68, 86.
[46] Monteilhet, *Institutions militaires de la France*, pp. 321 f., 328, 339 f.
[47] William C. Church, *Ulysses S. Grant*, pp. 188 f.
[48] Ardant du Picq, *Études sur le combat* (7th ed.), pp. xi, xx, 2 f.
[49] *The Ghost of Napoleon* (1933), pp. 11, 16 f.
[50] H. Rothfels, *Carl v. Clausewitz* (1920), pp. 62 f.; Jähns, *Kriegswissenschaften*, pp. 2869 f.
[51] *Aus den Papieren Schön's*, I, vii.
[52] 1768, cit. F. Meinecke, *Entstehung des Historismus* (1936), p. 354.
[53] Engels, *Herrn Eugen Dührings Umwälzung der Wissenschaft* (11th ed.), p. 173.
[54] *Zur Kritik der Politischen Ökonomie* (Stuttgart, 1919), p. xlvi.
[55] Marx-Engels, *Gesamtausgabe*, Series 3, II, 228 f.
[56] 1885. *Heeresverfassungen*, pp. 1, 5, 7.

CHAPTER 1

[1] Hans Delbrück, *Geschichte der Kriegskunst*, III, 106.
[2] Boutaric, *Institutions militaires de la France* (1863), p. 212.
[3] 1523. Comines, *Mémoires*, ed. Mandrot, I, 31.
[4] Max Jähns, *Geschichte der Kriegswissenschaften* (1889), p. 335.
[5] *Ibid.*, pp. 1219 f.
[6] E. Cosneau, *Le Connétable de Richemont* (1886); G. Roloff, "Das franz. Heer unter Karl VII," *Historische Zeitschrift*, CIXIII; Jähns, *Heeresverfassungen*, pp. 228 f.
[7] R. Ehrenberg, *Das Zeitalter der Fugger* (1922), I, 112.
[8] 1582. Balthazar Ayala, *De iure et officiis bellicis* (Washington, 1912), II, 96.
[9] G. Schmoller in *Deutsche Rundschau*, XII, 258.
[10] *Manuscripts of the Earl of Egmont* (1920), I, 315.
[11] Adam Smith, *Wealth of Nations*, Book V, Chap. I.
[12] Albert Babeau, *La vie militaire sous l'ancien régime* (1890), I, 29 f.
[13] T. Tomoeda, "Die Grundelemente der japanischen Moral," *Zeitschrift für Politik*, XXV.
[14] Jähns, *Kriegswissenschaften*, pp. 481 f.
[15] Montluc, *Commentaires*, III, 231.
[16] W. Sombart, *Der Bourgeois* (1913), p. 95.
[17] (1611), Act V, scene 1, 2.
[18] *Commentaires*, II, 338; III, 457, 145.
[19] Boutaric, p. 393.
[20] *Commentaires*, III, 435, 477 f.
[21] Babeau, II, 7.
[22] Boutaric, p. 393.
[23] Jähns, *Kriegswissenschaften*, pp. 251 f.; F. Priebatsch, *Geschichte des preussischen Offizierkorps* (1919), p. 8.
[24] E. von Frauenholz, *Deutsche Kriegs- und Heeresgeschichte*, p. 108.

[25] H. Sée, *Modern Capitalism* (1928), p. 82.
[26] Boutaric, pp. 434 f.
[27] Babeau, II, 45 ff.
[28] Ibid., II, 39 ff.
[29] Delbrück, IV, 298; Schmoller, *Historische Zeitschrift*, XXX; K. Demeter, *Das deutsche Heer und seine Offiziere*, pp. 76 f.
[30] C. von der Goltz, *Rossbach und Jena*, p. 136.
[31] O. Hintze, *Historische und politische Aufsätze*, I, 5.
[32] Goltz, p. 134.
[33] H. Speier in *Social Research*, II, 93.
[34] Jähns, *Kriegswissenschaften*, p. 2470.
[35] Ibid., pp. 2466, 2471, 2479.
[36] Hintze, I, 133.
[37] Babeau, II, 80.
[38] Liddell Hart, *Great Captains Unveiled*, p. 219.
[39] Krauske, *Die Briefe König Friedrich Wilhelms I. an den Fürsten Leopold zu Anhalt-Dessau*, p. 313.
[40] Priebatsch, p. 18.
[41] Babeau, II, 202 f., 234 ff., 250.
[42] Boutaric, p. 427.
[43] Jähns, *Heeresverfassungen*, p. 267; Albert Mathiez, *The French Revolution*, p. 5; Babeau, II, 90.
[44] Sée, *L'évolution de la pensée politique en France* (1925), p. 96.
[45] Babeau, II, 83 ff.
[46] Ibid., II, 81, 87.
[47] 1667. Ranke, *Preussische Geschichte*, I, 287 f.
[48] Hintze in *Historische Zeitschrift*, CXII, 513 ff.; Max Lehmann, *Scharnhorst* (1886-7), 58 ff., 120 ff.
[49] C. Jany, *Geschichte der königlich preussischen Armee*, I, 373.
[50] The conclusion of Lehmann.
[51] Preuss, *Lebensgeschichte Friedrich*, III, 349.
[52] Von Unger, *Blücher*, I, 72.
[53] Jähns, *Kriegswissenschaften*, pp. 2444 f.
[54] Lehmann, II, 644 ff.
[55] Demeter, pp. 6 ff.; Delbrück, IV, 296; Goltz, pp. 82 f., 18.
[56] Lehmann, II, 145 ff.
[57] Johs. Scherr, *Blücher* (1863), p. 222.
[58] Ranke, I, 285 f.
[59] L. B. Namier, *The Structure of Politics at the Accession of George III* (1929), I, 5, 31 ff.; *Manuscripts of the Earl of Egmont*, I, 323.
[60] *Correspondence of King George III* (1927), I, 409.
[61] Babeau, II, 5.
[62] *Esprit des lois*, Livre III, Chap. 5.
[63] L. Perla, *What Is National Honor?* (1918), pp. 37 f.
[64] Sombart, *Der Bourgeois*, p. 181.
[65] Winston Churchill, *Marlborough*, I.
[66] Maj. Gen. George B. Davis, *A Treatise on the Military Laws of the U. S.* (3rd ed.), p. 394.
[67] *Essay on Projects* (1697).
[68] *Farrow's Military Encyclopedia*, I, 516.
[69] Babeau, II, 15 f., 25.
[70] Ibid., pp. 138, 223 ff.
[71] Demeter, pp. 120 ff.
[72] Fortescue, II, 296 f.
[73] Jähns, *Kriegswissenschaften*, p. 2315.

[74] Boutaric, pp. 336, 392, 426; Babeau, I, 113 ff., 183, 194 f.
[75] *Rêveries*, written 1732, published 1757.
[76] Terraillon, *L'honneur*, pp. 58 f.
[77] Maxime Leroy, *Histoire des idées sociales en France*, I, 109.

CHAPTER 2

[1] Johann Gottlieb Fichte, *Beiträge zur Berichtigung der Urteile über die französische Revolution* (1794).
[2] *Zum ewigen Frieden* (1795).
[3] *Essai général de tactique;* Max Jähns, *Geschichte der Kriegswissenschaften*, p. 2066.
[4] As to the appreciation of sports for military purposes, see Jähns, pp. 2056, 2077, 2434.
[5] Max Lehmann, *Scharnhorst* (1886), I, 17 f.
[6] C. von der Goltz, *Rossbach und Jena*, pp. 115 ff.
[7] Ibid., pp. 131 ff.
[8] Ibid., pp. 147 ff.
[9] Ibid., pp. 168 ff.
[10] On Bülow see *Historische Zeitschrift*, VI, 59 ff.; W. Rüstow, *Feldherrnkunst des 19. Jahrhunderts* (1878), pp. 178 ff.
[11] *Geist des neueren Kriegssystems* (1799); *Der Feldzug 1805* (1806).
[12] Von Unger, *Blücher*, I, 261.
[13] Bülow, *Feldzug 1805*, I, xxiv.
[14] *Betrachtungen über die Kriegskunst, über ihre Fortschritte, ihre Widersprüche und ihre Zuverlässigkeit. Auch für Layen verständlich, wenn sie nur Geschichte wissen.*
[15] F. von Meerheimb, in *Historische Zeitschrift*, VI, 46 ff.
[16] *Scharnhorst's Briefe*, I, 26; Lehmann, I, 107; ibid., pp. 67 ff.; Jähns, pp. 2167 ff.
[17] On the attempts of the Yankee Count Rumford in Bavaria to make the army more useful in peacetime, see Jähns, p. 2647.
[18] Woldemar Wenck, *Deutschland vor hundert Jahren* (1887), I, 61.

CHAPTER 3

[1] Jared Sparks, ed., *Diplomatic Correspondence of the American Revolution*, VI, 260 f.
[2] *Writings of Washington*, ed. Sparks, IV, 116.
[3] Sir John Fortescue, *History of the British Army*, III, 239 ff.
[4] *Writings of Washington*, VII, 162 ff.
[5] Greene, *Life of General Greene*, I, 223.
[6] Max Jähns, *Geschichte der Kriegswissenschaften*, pp. 1235 f., 1318, 2110, 2159 f., 2166, 2522.
[7] Maj. William A. Ganoe, *The History of the U. S. Army* (1932), p. 33.
[8] Fortescue, III, 157, 233, 361, 380.
[9] *Simcoe's Military Journal* (New York, 1844).
[10] Stephen Pargellis, "Braddock's Defeat," *American Historical Review*, January, 1936.
[11] Fortescue, III, pp. 528 ff., 537.
[12] Max Lehmann, *Scharnhorst*, I, 79 f.
[13] *Der Feldzug von 1805*, I, xl.
[14] *Writings of Washington*, IV, 406, 557; Fortescue, III, 225, 228, 330 f.
[15] Ganoe, p. 54.
[16] Allen French, *First Year of the American Revolution*, pp. 473 f.

[17] Ganoe, loc. cit.
[18] Greene, I, 222 f.
[19] *Writings of Washington*, IV, 112, 131 ff.
[20] Ganoe, p. 12.
[21] Ibid., pp. 58 f., 53, 61.
[22] Ibid., p. 82.
[23] J. Fiske, *The Critical Period of American History, 1783-1789*, pp. 114 ff.
[24] *Life and Correspondence of Rufus King*, I, 65.
[25] Thomas Jefferson Randolph, *Memoir of Thomas Jefferson* (1829), III, 409.
[26] Tim Klein, *Der deutsche Soldat* (1916), pp. 123 f.
[27] *Journal of William Maclay* (New York, 1927), p. 269.
[28] Louise B. Dunbar, *A Study of Monarchical Tendencies in the U. S. from 1776 to 1801* (1922), pp. 43 ff.
[29] Alice Brown, *Mercy Warren* (1898), pp. 296 f.
[30] Noah Webster, *A Letter to General Hamilton* (1800), p. 5. For the Cincinnati and kindred organizations, see Wallace Evan Davies, *Patriotism on Parade: The Story of Veterans' and Hereditary Organizations in America, 1783-1900* (1955).

CHAPTER 4

[1] *Correspondence of King George III*, I, 94 ff.; II, 15 ff.
[2] Liddell Hart, *Great Captains Unveiled*, p. 237.
[3] Sir John Fortescue, *History of the British Army*, IV, 879, 903 ff.
[4] Albert Mathiez, *The French Revolution* (1928), pp. 46 f.
[5] Wirth, *Le Maréchal Lefèbvre*, pp. 41 ff.
[6] Mathiez, p. 48.
[7] Albert Babeau, *La vie militaire sous l'ancien régime* (1890), II, 284 ff.
[8] Ibid., I, 100.
[9] Max Lehmann, *Scharnhorst*, II, 557.
[10] H. Sée, *L'évolution de la pensée politique en France au 18ᵉ siècle*, pp. 190, 192.
[11] Boutaric, *Institutions militaires de la France* (1863), p. 48.
[12] Mathiez, pp. 58, 75 f., 86.
[13] For details see Mathiez, pp. 306 f.; Boutaric, pp. 472 ff.
[14] Max Jähns, *Geschichte der Kriegswissenschaften* (1889), p. 2384.
[15] Susanne, *Histoire de l'artillerie française* (1874).
[16] Phipps, *Armies of the First French Republic*, I, 276 f.
[17] Mathiez, pp. 217, 223.
[18] Massenbach, *Memoiren zur Geschichte des preussischen Staates*, I, 119, 331 ff.; II, p. 356.
[19] Ibid., I, p. 267.
[20] Fortescue, IV, 168 f.
[21] G. Hanotaux, *Histoire de la nation française*, VIII, 60.
[22] Jähns, pp. 2117 ff.
[23] For this discussion see Spenser Wilkinson, *The French Army Before Napoleon* (1915); Colin, *L'éducation militaire de Napoléon;* Hans Delbrück, *Geschichte der Kriegskunst*, IV, 461 ff.
[24] C. von der Goltz, *Rossbach und Jena*, p. 240.
[25] Jähns, pp. 2551 ff.; Goltz, p. 260.
[26] Massenbach, I, 337.
[27] Mathiez, p. 485.
[28] Ibid., p. 482.

[29] Fortescue, IV, 294; Mathiez, p. 503.
[30] Mathiez, p. 377; Phipps, I, 244 f.
[31] Phipps, III, 198 f.
[32] Jähns, pp. 2489 f.
[33] Gourgaud, *Journal inédit,* II, 43 f.
[34] For details see Fortescue, X, 94 ff.
[35] Phipps, I, 42 ff., 56, 61.
[36] Wirth, pp. 43 ff.
[37] Phipps, II, 205, 118, 309, 348.
[38] Bonnal, *Vie de Ney,* I, 96.
[39] Fortescue, III, 204.
[40] Hanotaux, VII, 96.
[41] For details see G. Ferrero, *Aventure, Bonaparte en Italie* (1936).
[42] Bonnal, I, 215.
[43] *Mémoires du Duc de Raguse,* II, 92.
[44] Wirth, pp. 125 ff.
[45] Gouvion Saint-Cyr, *Mémoires,* II, 101 f.
[46] Bonnal, I, 262.
[47] Monteilhet, *Institutions militaires de la France,* p. 74.
[48] *Cahiers du Capitaine Coignet.*
[49] Gourgaud, I, 328.
[50] *Commentaires,* III, 504 f.
[51] Bourrienne, *Mémoires,* IV, 81 ff., 216 ff.
[52] Bonnal, I, 262; *Mémoires du Duc de Raguse,* II, 226.
[53] Bourrienne, VI, 19; Gourgaud, I, 496.
[54] Rudolf Pannwitz, *Die Krisis der europäischen Kultur* (1917), p. 11.
[55] *Mémoires du Duc de Raguse,* VII, 224.
[56] Eckmühl-Blocqueville, *Davout,* I, 7.
[57] Bourrienne, IV, 279.
[58] Ibid., III, 289.
[59] Gourgaud, I, 339.
[60] For the following see Adolf Caspary, *Wirtschafts-Strategie und Kriegsführung* (1932), pp. 89 ff.
[61] Saint-Cyr, III, 259 ff.
[62] Goltz, p. 256.
[63] Hallgarten in *Europäische Gespräche,* III, 564; Pertz, *Stein,* II, 259; Lehmann, II, 325 f.
[64] W. Rüstow, *Geschichte der Infanterie,* II, 296.
[65] Delbrück, IV, 479.
[66] Spenser Wilkinson, *Rise of General Bonaparte,* p. 132.
[67] Caspary, p. 105.
[68] Goltz, pp. 184, 238, 254. For the most convenient statistics of losses see G. Roloff, *Preussische Jahrbücher,* LXXII.
[69] Bourrienne, IV, 112.
[70] Caspary, p. 108; *Mémoires du Duc de Raguse,* V, 223 ff.
[71] Saint-Cyr, III, 62 ff., 231.
[72] Gourgaud, II,33.
[73] Pertz, *Gneisenau,* II, 295.
[74] Phipps, I, 341.
[75] *Mémoires du Général Baron de Marbot* (1891), I, 247 ff.
[76] *Mémoires du Duc de Raguse,* III, 227.
[77] Lt. Col. Balagny in *Revue d'Histoire* (1908-9).

CHAPTER 5

[1] Pertz, *Gneisenau,* II, 409.

[2] Max Lehmann, *Scharnhorst,* II, 407.
[3] Ibid., II, 554.
[4] Tim Klein, *Der deutsche Soldat,* p. 140.
[5] Pertz, I, 307.
[6] Max Lenz, *Napoleon* (1913), p. 157; Pertz, II, 524.
[7] Schwartz, *Leben des Generals Carl v. Clausewitz* (1878), I, 219.
[8] Lehmann, II, 166, 193.
[9] Pertz, I, 399 f.
[10] Ibid., I, 288, 313, 367 ff., 345.
[11] K. Demeter, *Das deutsche Heer und seine Offiziere,* pp. 129 f.; Meinecke, *Boyen,* I, 512 f.
[12] Pertz, I, 319 ff., 489, 614.
[13] Max Jähns, *Geschichte der Kriegswissenschaften,* pp. 2158 f.
[14] Lehmann, I, 322; II, 110, 197.
[15] Pertz, I, 327.
[16] Conrady, *Grolman,* I, 148.
[17] Meinecke, I, 292.
[18] Lehmann, II, 319, 394 ff.
[19] Ibid., I, 51 f.; F. Priebatsch, *Geschichte des preussischen Offizierkorps,* p. 31.
[20] Lehmann, II, 150 ff.; Conrady, I, 168 f.; Meinecke, I, 186.
[21] Lehmann, II, 98 f., 199 ff., 238; Meinecke, I, 393; ibid., II, 194 f.
[22] Lehmann, II, 295 f., 316, 333 ff.
[23] *Aus den Papieren Schön's,* IV, 568, 570, 604.
[24] Ibid., VI, 149.
[25] Priebatsch, p. 66.
[26] K. Bleibtreu, *Das Heer,* p. 57.
[27] Pertz-Delbrück, *Gneisenau,* III, 49, 53 f.; Klein, p. 186.
[28] Th. von Bernhardi, *Aus dem Leben Toll's,* III, 145; Pertz-Delbrück, III, 98.
[29] Meinecke, I, 288 ff., 298 f.
[30] *Aus den Papieren Schön's,* IV, 259; VI, 292.
[31] Clode, *Military Forces of the Crown,* I, 421 f.
[32] Lehmann, II, 597; *Aus den Papieren Schön's,* IV, 259.
[33] K. Birnbaum, *Psycho-pathologische Dokumente* (1920), pp. 130 ff.; Pertz-Delbrück, III, 530; Stanhope, *Conversations with Wellington,* pp. 119 f.
[34] Pertz-Delbrück, III, 543.
[35] Ibid., III, 645.
[36] Lehmann, II, 524 f., 538; *Aus den Papieren Schön's,* I, 167.
[37] Clode, I, 160 f.
[38] J. Hatscheck, *Englisches Staatsrecht* (1905), II, 234.
[39] L. Brentano, *Geschichte der wirtschaftlichen Entwicklung Englands,* III[1], 55.
[40] Sir John Fortescue, *History of the British Army,* X, 233.
[41] Oman, *Wellington's Army 1809-1814,* pp. 73 ff.
[42] Fortescue, IX, 388; Oman, pp. 47 f., 113.
[43] Oman, p. 48; Fortescue, X, 204 ff.; ibid., XI, 30.
[44] Fortescue, XI, 16 f.
[45] Ibid., X, 225.
[46] Clode, II, 197.
[47] Oct., 1813. Gentz, *Tagebücher,* p. 277.
[48] Bernhardi, IV[2], 139 f.
[49] Ibid., IV[1], 192, 220, 271.
[50] Ibid., IV[1], 126 f., 231 f.

[51] Pertz-Delbrück, IV, 398 ff.
[52] Ibid., III, 82.
[53] Ibid., IV, 594.
[54] Bernhardi, III, 196.
[55] Von Unger, *Blücher*, II, 315.
[56] Klein, p. 134.
[57] *Deutsche Vierteljahrschrift* (1859), No. 2, p. 46.
[58] Meinecke, II, 68; Wellington, *Supplementary Despatches*, XI, 62.
[59] Pertz-Delbrück, IV, 598.
[60] *Cambridge History of Foreign Policy*, I, 511; C. K. Webster, *Foreign Policy of Castlereagh* (1925), p. 161.
[61] Pertz-Delbrück, IV, 317, 323 f.
[62] Conrady, II, 261.
[63] Thus Prime Minister Lord Liverpool at the end of 1814. See C. K. Webster, *British Diplomacy: 1813-1815* (1921), p. 247.

CHAPTER 6

[1] F. Meinecke in *Historische Zeitschrift*, LXXVII, 222.
[2] Alfred de Vigny.
[3] Sir John Fortescue, *History of the British Army*.
[4] For a discussion of the comparative value of urban and rural recruits see L. Brentano and R. Kuczynski, *Die Grundlage der deutschen Wehrkraft* (1900); Kuczynski, *Ist die Landwirtschaft die wichtigste Grundlage der deutschen Wehrkraft?* (1905).
[5] *The Republic of the U. S. of America* (1849), II, 250 ff.
[6] Typical of Continental liberalism is Rotteck, *Über stehende Heere und Nationalmiliz* (1816).
[7] Aretin, *Staatsrecht der konstitutionellen Monarchie*, II¹, 157; J. B. Say, *Cours complet d'économie politique*, II, 280 ff.; Bastiat, *Paix et liberté* (1849).
[8] W. Guttmann, *England im Zeitalter der bürgerlichen Reform* (1923), p. 265.
[9] Fortescue, XI, 84 f.
[10] March 3, 1826. *Hansard*, XIV, 1099.
[11] Lord Hardinge, Secretary at War in Wellington's Cabinet; Clode, *Military Forces of the Crown*, I, 339.
[12] Fortescue, XIII, 10.
[13] June 12, 1849. Cobden, *Speeches* (1870), II, 169.
[14] Clode, II, 346; L. von Stein, *Lehre vom Heerwesen*, p. 167.
[15] Varnhagen, *Tagebücher*, V, 298.
[16] Fortescue, XIII, 20 f.
[17] Schwartz, *Leben des Generals Carl v. Clausewitz* (1878), II, 288 ff.; H. Rothfels, *C. v. Clausewitz, Politische Schriften und Briefe*, p. 243.
[18] Meinecke, *Boyen*, II, 300 ff.
[19] Ibid., II, 213, 310 ff., 391.
[20] E. Guillon, *Nos écrivains militaires*, II, 260.
[21] Monteilhet, *Institutions militaires de la France*, pp. 3 ff.; Max Jähns, *Heeresverfassungen*, pp. 378 ff.
[22] 1888. *Gesammelte Schriften*, III, 1 f.
[23] Kingsley Martin, *The Triumph of Lord Palmerston* (1924), p. 75.
[24] Ibid., p. 238.
[25] Fortescue, XI, 513.
[26] Cobden, I, 516 f.; II, 195.
[27] Martin, p. 231.

[26] W. Rüstow, *Feldherrnkunst des 19. Jahrhunderts* (1878), p. 754.
[29] Pertz-Delbrück, *Gneisenau*, V, 38.
[30] Ibid., V, 84 ff.
[31] H. von Srbik, *Metternich* (1925), I, 587.
[32] Varnhagen, I, 28.
[33] F. Priebatsch, *Geschichte des preussischen Offizierkorps*, pp. 37 ff.
[34] Meinecke, II, 359.
[35] Ibid., II, 209.
[36] For the following see R. Schmidt-Bückeburg, *Das Militärkabinett der preussischen Könige und deutschen Kaiser* (1933).
[37] *Hansard*, 1st series, XIV, 679 ff., 1092 f., 1122.
[38] Ibid., 3rd series, XXXII, 981.
[39] Fortescue, XIII, 21.
[40] Clode, I, 104, 145; II, 202, 326 ff.
[41] Meinecke, II, 113 ff.; K. Demeter, *Das deutsche Heer und sein Offizierkorps*, pp. 16, 80 ff.
[42] Fuller, *War and Western Civilization*, p. 67.
[43] Gouvion Saint-Cyr, *Mémoires*, I, lxx f.; VII, 211 f.
[44] Th. von Bernhardi, *Aus dem Leben Toll's*, VII, 230 ff., 251, 256, 266, 518; IV², 26, 357.
[45] *Abhandlungen zur mittleren und neueren Geschichte*, No. 19, pp. 48 f.
[46] Clode, II, 734.
[47] Meinecke, II, 35.
[48] House of Commons Debates for March 3, 1826 and March 11, 1836.
[49] Stanhope, *Conversations with the Duke of Wellington* (1831), p. 17.
[50] *Commission on Military Punishment. Sessional Papers* (1836), XXII, 190.
[51] *Greville Diary*, ed. P. W. Wilson, I, 193.
[52] Maj. Gen. George B. Davis, *A Treatise on the Military Laws of the U. S.* (3rd ed.), pp. 394 ff.; Demeter, p. 318.
[53] Clode, II, 101 f.
[54] Marshal Franchet d'Esperey in G. Hanotaux, *Histoire de la nation française*, VIII, 273; Demeter, pp. 316 f.
[55] Demeter, p. 228.
[56] Ibid., pp. 130 ff.; Meinecke, II, 513 ff.; Stein, pp. 162 f.
[57] Massenbach, *Memoiren zur Geschichte des preussischen Staates*, III, 393.
[58] C. von der Goltz, *Rossbach und Jena*, pp. 238, 241, 244.
[59] Conrady, *Grolman*, II, 29 f.
[60] Schmidt-Bückeburg, pp. 54 f; Gust. Graf v. Lambsdorff, *Die Militarbevollmächtigten Kaiser Wilhelms II. am Zarenhofe 1904-1914* (1937).
[61] Rüstow, *op. cit.*
[62] Clausewitz was entrusted, not with the direction of studies, but with the discipline of the officers attending the Berlin War School. Since he led a very retired life and his face and nose had acquired a very red complexion owing to winter campaigns, it was commonly said that he was tippling from an early hour on behind the closed doors where he wrote *Vom Kriege* and the other works published after his death in 1831.
[63] *Tagebücher*, I, 259 f.
[64] Marx-Engels, *Gesamtausgabe*, Series 3, II, 270 f.
[65] Rothfels, *Clausewitz, Politik und Krieg*, p. 191.

CHAPTER 7

[1] Veit Valentin, *Geschichte der deutschen Revolution 1848-1849* (1930), I, 546 ff.
[2] Ibid., I, 600.
[3] *Denkwürdigkeiten Roon's*, I, 229 f.
[4] *Taft and Roosevelt. The Intimate Letters of Archie Butt* (1930), p. 236.
[5] F. Meinecke, *Weltbürgertum und Nationalstaat* (1928 ed.), pp. 456 ff.
[6] *Historische Zeitschrift*, LXXVII, 225.
[7] R. Schmidt-Bückeburg, *Das Militärkabinett der preussischen Könige und deutschen Kaiser* (1933), pp. 30 ff.
[8] *Denkwürdigkeiten Roon's*, II, 152.
[9] Hohenlohe-Ingelfingen, *Aus meinem Leben*, III, 72.
[10] *Neue Zeit*, Jan. 15, 1909.
[11] K. Demeter, *Das deutsche Heer und seine Offiziere*, p. 20.
[12] Johs. Ziekursch, *Politische Geschichte des neuen deutschen Kaiserreichs* (1932), I, 30 f.
[13] Demeter, p. 21.
[14] Franz Carl Endres, "Soziologische Struktur und ihre entsprechenden Ideologien des deutschen Offizierkorps vor dem Weltkrieg," *Archiv für Sozialwissenschaft*, LVIII.
[15] Schmidt-Bückeburg, pp. 70 ff.
[16] Ziekursch, I, 34 ff.
[17] Max Lenz, *Geschichte Bismarcks* (1902), pp. 116 ff.
[18] Demeter, pp. 24 ff.
[19] Ibid., pp. 87 ff., 260 ff., 96.
[20] *Neue Briefe* (1949), p. 496.
[21] *Prussian Wehrgesetz*, Nov. 9, 1867, Art. 4.
[22] Vernhagen, *Tagebücher*, I, 13; IV, 335.
[23] Heyderhoff-Wentzke, *Deutscher Liberalismus im Zeitalter Bismarcks*, I, 71.
[24] *Denkwürdigkeiten Roon's*, II, 38 ff., 61.
[25] L. Dehio in *Deutsche Rundschau*, November, 1927.
[26] *Denkwürdigkeiten Roon's*, II, 77.
[27] Dehio, *supra*.
[28] Ziekursch, I, 80.
[29] *Gedanken und Erinnerungen*, I, 290, 296.
[30] Ibid., I, 313 f.
[31] Dehio, *Historische Zeitschrift*, CXLIV, 31 ff.
[32] *Gedanken und Erinnerungen*, I, 312.
[33] Dehio, *Historische Zeitschrift*, CXL, 279 ff.
[34] *Denkwürdigkeiten Roon's*, I, 344 f.; II, 10 f.
[35] Wilhelm Berdrow, *Krupp* (New York, 1930), p. 208; Menne, *Krupp*, 93.
[36] *Heyderhoff-Wentzke*, I, 153.
[37] *Denkwürdigkeiten Roon's*, II, 142 f.
[38] Ziekursch, I, 107.
[39] *Gesammelte Schriften*, IV, 121.
[40] Max Jähns, *Geschichte der Kriegswissenschaften* (1889), pp. 2865 f.
[41] Pratt, *Rail-Power*, pp. 122 ff.
[42] Ziekursch, I, 177.
[43] *Denkwürdigkeiten Roon's*, II, 418 f.

[44] Fürst Bülow, *Denkwürdigkeiten*, IV, 122; H. Oncken, *Lassalle* (4th ed.), pp. 303, 393 f.

[45] Bismarck, *Gesammelte Werke*, VI[b], 134.

[46] Ziekursch, I, 235.

[47] Ibid., I, 221 ff.; *Denkwürdigkeiten Roon's*, II, 333 f.; Schmidt-Bückeburg, pp. 96 ff.

[48] Schmidt-Bückeburg, pp. 108 ff.

[49] Ziekursch, I, 244 f., 270 f.

[50] Demeter, p. 30; Hans Herzfeld, *Die deutsche Rüstungspolitik vor dem Weltkrieg* (1923), p. 62 f.

[51] Ardant du Picq (1852-1870), *Études sur le combat* (7th ed.; 1902).

[52] Ibid., p. 104.

[53] Monteilhet, p. 30.

[54] Prévost-Paradol, *La France nouvelle* (3rd ed.; 1868), pp. 357 f.

[55] Ziekursch, I, 269 ff.

[56] *Origines diplomatiques de la guerre de 1870-71*, XXIV, 280.

[57] Oncken, *Rheinpolitik*, III, 405, 427 ff.

[58] M. Busch, *Bismarck: Some Secret Pages of His History* (1898), III, 187.

[59] Waldersee, *Denkwürdigkeiten*, I, 50.

[60] Monteilhet, *Institutions militaires de la France*, p. 120.

[61] Busch, I, 226, 405.

[62] Colin, *Les transformations de la guerre* (1912), pp. 37 f.

[63] Delbrück-Daniels, *Geschichte der Kriegskunst*, VI[1], 191.

[64] *The Conduct of the Allies* (1712); *Works* (Dublin, 1741), V, 69 f.

[65] Gustav Mayer, *Friedrich Engels* (The Hague, 1934), II, 435 f.

[66] Ziekursch, I, 323.

[67] Busch, I, 194 f., 423.

[68] Ziekursch, I, 323; letters to his wife, Aug. 15 and 16, 1870.

[69] Waldersee, I, 124.

[70] J. P. T. Bury, *Gambetta and the National Defense* (1936), pp. 13, 288 f., 265.

[71] Moltke, *Gesammelte Schriften*, III, 113 f.

[72] Bury, pp. 137, 144 f., 303 f.

[73] E. Daniels, *Roon und Moltke vor Paris. Preussische Jahrbücher*, CXXI.

[74] Monteilhet, pp. 116 f., 235 f., 279, 285, 303.

[75] Herzfeld, pp. 9, 47 f., 140.

[76] Abel Combarieu, *Sept ans à l'Élysée* (1932), p. 129.

[77] Ibid., pp. 93, 103, 229, 287, 184.

[78] Monteilhet, pp. 129, 194, 298, 317.

[79] Herzfeld, pp. 6, 63.

[80] Colin, pp. 30 f.

[81] Ibid., pp. 5, 38 f., 42.

[82] Monteilhet, p. xvii.

[83] *Unzeitgemässe Betrachtungen* (1873).

[84] *Cit.* Introduction, *Études sur le combat*, pp. xviii f.

[85] Liddell Hart, *The Ghost of Napoleon* (1933) and *Foch: The Man of Orleans* (1931).

[86] As he called his *Principes de la guerre* (1903); Lt. Col. Émile Mayer, *La psychologie du commandement* (1924), p. 7.

[87] *The Memoirs of Marshal Foch* (1931), pp. lvii f.

[88] Liddell Hart citing Col. de Grandmaison, *Deux conferences* (1912).

[89] Monteilhet, p. 349.

[90] Ibid., p. 270.
[91] Alfred Vagts, *Deutschland und die Vereinigten Staaten* (1934), p. 189.
[92] Monteilhet, pp. 189 ff.
[93] Ibid., pp. 261 f.
[94] Ibid., pp. 191, 262, 184, 188 f.
[95] Philip Guedalla, *Gladstone and Palmerston* (1928), p. 208.
[96] *Deutsche Vierteljahrschrift*, 1859, No. 2, p. 69.
[97] Sir John Fortescue, *History of the British Army*, VIII, 214.
[98] Morley, *Gladstone*, II, 360 ff.
[99] Clode, *Military Forces of the Crown*, II, 512 ff.
[100] J. A. Spender, *The Life of Campbell-Bannerman* (1923), I, 43, 117 ff.
[101] *Œuvres*, I, 191.
[102] *The Letters of Theodore Roosevelt*, ed. Morison, V, 721.
[103] Mary T. Reynolds, "The General Staff as a Propaganda Agency, 1908-1914," *Public Opinion Quarterly*, III, 391 ff.

CHAPTER 8

[1] Bonnal, *Vie de Ney*, I, 194.
[2] G. Hanotaux, *Histoire de la nation française*, VIII, 504.
[3] Monteilhet, *Institutions militaires de la France*, pp. 320 f.
[4] Ibid., p. 315.
[5] Mordacq, *Le Ministère Clemenceau*, I, 235; II, 35.
[6] General Pédoya, *La Commission de l'armée pendant la guerre*, p. 169.
[7] Generaloberst Arz, *Zur Geschichte des grossen Krieges* (1924), p. 143.
[8] Knox, *With the Russian Army*, p. 472.
[9] Max Hoffmann, *Aufzeichnungen*, II, 89.
[10] Pédoya, pp. 63 f.
[11] Ibid., p. 112.
[12] Hoffmann, II, 152, 173.
[13] Spears, *Assignment to Catastrophe*, I, 10.
[14] Pédoya, pp. 136 ff.; Sir Ernest D. Swinton, *Eyewitness* (1932); Arthur Rosenberg, *Entstehung der deutschen Republik* (1928), p. 219.
[15] Liddell Hart, *The War in Outline* (1936).
[16] *Rasselas* (1759), Chap. 6.
[17] C. E. Playne, *The Neuroses of Nations*, p. 297.
[18] Charles Ross, *Representative Government and War*, pp. 4, 6, 8, etc.
[19] Lt. Col. S. B. M. Young in 1902, cit. Kirby Page, *National Defense*, p. 49.
[20] Eugene Tarlé, *Napoleon* (1936), pp. 289 ff., 381; Édouard Driault, *La chute de l'Empire* (1927).
[21] *Ursachen des deutschen Zusammenbruchs*, 2nd series, XI¹, 36 f., 52 f., 75.
[22] Ibid., XI², 38 f.
[23] Pédoya, p. 124.
[24] Knox, p. 80; Golovine, *The Russian Army in the World War*, pp. 30 ff., 141, 209 ff., 227.
[25] Knox, pp. 319, 349.
[26] Duff Cooper, *Haig*, I, 227, 290, 248.
[27] Rosenberg, pp. 75 f.
[28] Palmer, *Newton D. Baker*, II, 240.

[29] Callwell, *Wilson,* I, 153 f., 189, 294.
[30] Ibid., I, 262.
[31] Lord Beaverbrook, *Politicians and the War,* pp. lx, 89 f.
[32] Ibid., pp. 84 f.; Gough, *The Fifth Army,* p. 253; Callwell, II, 4.
[33] Callwell, I, 215.
[34] General Harbord, *Leaves from a War Diary,* pp. 52, 92, 136, 154.
[35] Gen. Robert Lee Bullard, *Personalities and Reminiscences of the War,* p. 77.
[36] Callwell, I, 299.
[37] Ibid., I, 330, 336.
[38] *Leaves from a War Diary,* pp. 129, 236 f., 240.
[39] Pédoya, pp. 14 ff., 26 ff., 109.
[40] Mordacq, III, 165.
[41] Pédoya, pp. 106, 152 ff., 168 f., 191, 287.
[42] *We Can Defend America,* Chap. 14.
[43] Mordacq, II, 98.
[44] F. Palmer, *Bliss, Peacemaker* (1925), pp. 341, 344 f.
[45] Bullard, pp. 302 f.
[46] Harbord, p. 198.
[47] Benoist-Méchin, *Histoire de l'armée allemande* (1936), p. 19.
[48] Callwell, I, 305 f.
[49] *Journal d'Alexandre Ribot, 1914-1922* (1936).
[50] *Erinnerungen,* cit. Rudolf Olden, *Hindenburg* (1935), p. 142.
[51] Hoffmann, II, 214 f.
[52] Callwell, II, 128, 134.
[53] Mordacq, II, 293 ff.; Bullard, pp. 314 f.; Benoist-Méchin, p. 60.
[54] Palmer, *Bliss,* p. 273; Mordacq, II, 99.
[55] Hoffmann, op. cit., in numerous places.
[56] Olden, pp. 128, 132 f.
[57] *Werk des Untersuchungsausschusses,* 2nd series, XI^1, 201.
[58] Olden, pp. 136 f.
[59] Hoffmann, I, 146.
[60] Werner, *Der alldeutsche Verband,* p. 261.
[61] Olden, p. 134.
[62] Rosenberg, pp. 116 f.
[63] Hoffmann, I, 127 f.
[64] Werner, p. 215.
[65] *Werk des Untersuchungsausschusses,* 2nd series, XI^1, 41; Werner, p. 253; Von Eisenhart-Rothe, *Im Banne der Persönlichkeit,* p. 162.
[66] Hoffmann, I, 159.
[67] Rosenberg, pp. 122 ff., 202 ff.
[68] *Werk des Untersuchungsausschusses,* 2nd series, XI^1, 31, 53.
[69] Rosenberg, pp. 147 ff., 207 ff., 226 ff.; Olden, pp. 147 f.
[70] Maj. D. H. Cole and Maj. E. C. Priestley, *An Outline of British Military History* (1936), p. 336; Callwell, II, 80, 301.
[71] Knox, p. 19.
[72] Von Kuhl, *Der deutsche Generalstab* (2nd ed.), p. 72.
[73] Gen. Serge Dobrorolski, *Die Mobilmachung der russischen Armee 1914* (1922), p. 25.
[74] Golovine, pp. 2 f., 8, 204 f.
[75] Sir John Fortescue, *History of the British Army,* I, 178.
[76] Tarlé, p. 354.
[77] *London Times,* Sept. 6, 1919; Kuhl, pp. 11, 17 ff.
[78] Fortescue, III, 244.
[79] Bullard, pp. 291 ff.

[80] A. Vagts, *Deutschland und die Vereinigten Staaten*, p. 511.
[81] Bullard, pp. 32 f., 118.
[82] Rosenberg, pp. 151 f.
[83] Waldersee, *Denkwürdigkeiten*, I, 294, 302; II, 205, 276.
[84] Kuhl, pp. 96 ff.
[85] *History of the Russian Revolution*, I, 19.
[86] Von Cramon, *Unser österreichisch-ungarische Bundesgenosse*, pp. 9 f.
[87] Mordacq, II, 143.
[88] Winston Churchill, *Marlborough*, III, 246.
[89] Ibid., II, 543.
[90] Callwell, I, 292, 249.
[91] Montluc, *Commentaires*, I, 291.
[92] Schwartz, *Clausewitz*, II, 245.
[93] Hoffman, I, 89, 98.
[94] Knox, pp. 193, 409; Golovine, pp. 238 ff.
[95] Trotsky, *History of the Russian Revolution*, I, 272 f.
[96] Callwell, I, 307; II, 22 f., 30; Cooper, I, 303.
[97] Harbord, pp. 215 f., 271.
[98] Mordacq, II, 8, 89, 258, 309.
[99] Bullard, pp. 302 ff., 315.
[100] Callwell, II, 134, 136.
[101] H. Hagedorn, *Leonard Wood* (1931), I, 149, 155.
[102] Fortescue, XI, 100 f.
[103] Artur Baumgarten-Crusius, *Deutsche Heerführung im Marnefeldzug* (1921), p. 55.
[104] *Ursachen des deutschen Zusammenbruchs*, 2nd series, XI^1, 17, 25, 29 f., 40, 69, 78, 118; XI^2, 91.
[105] Von Stein, *Erlebnisse und Betrachtungen*, p. 157.
[106] *Ursachen des . . .* , 2nd series, XI^1, pp. 50, 382.
[107] Mordacq, I, 77, 180; *Ursachen des . . .* , 2nd series, XI^1, p. 173.
[108] Norman Thomas, *War: No Glory* (1935), p. 36.
[109] Palmer, *Newton D. Baker*, I, 225; Palmer, *Bliss*, pp. 141 f.
[110] Fortescue, II, 578.
[111] *Ursachen des . . .* , 2nd series, XI^1, 114; XI^2, 77.
[112] H. Kantorowicz, *Der Offiziershass im deutschen Heere* (1919).
[113] Lt. Col. Mayer, *Psychologie du commandement*, pp. 56 ff.
[114] Trotsky, I, 268.
[115] *Ursachen des . . .* , 2nd series, XI^1, 75, 405.
[116] Olden, p. 136.
[117] *The Private Journal of F. S. Larpent* (1853), I, 110 f.
[118] Conrady, *Grolman*, I, 144 ff., 193.
[119] Ibid., II, 229; Pertz-Delbrück, *Gneisenau*, IV, 187 ff., 70, 111.
[120] Bourrienne, *Mémoires*, I, 161, 177; V, 7, 13 f.
[121] Bonnal, II, 360, 385.
[122] Ibid., III, 131; II, 193, 206, 211 ff.
[123] Ibid., II, 107, 110, 134, 137, 153.
[124] Eckmühl-Bloqueville, *Davout*, II, 223, 235, 432, etc.; *Mémoires du Duc de Raguse*, IV, 46 f., 177.
[125] Fortescue, VI, 240 f., 319 f., 360, 407; VII, 485, 532; VIII, 620, etc.
[126] Pertz-Delbrück, IV, 338 ff.
[127] Hoffman, I, xiv.
[128] Denikin, *The White Army* (1930), pp. 278, 331.
[129] G. Welter, *La guerre civile en Russie* (1936), p. 176.

[130] For this controversy see Cooper, I, 132, 136, 143, etc.; Major French, *French Replies to Haig.*

[131] Palmer, *Bliss,* pp. 173 ff.

[132] Harbord, pp. 200 ff., 218 ff., 277.

[133] Bullard, pp. 174 f.

[134] William S. Myers, *McClellan* (1934), pp. 214, 222, 267, 330, 347.

[135] Eisenhart-Rothe, pp. 106 f.

[136] Olden, p. 133.

[137] The above is based on Hoffmann, op. cit.

[138] Ernst Kabisch, *Groener,* p. 53; Eisenhart-Rothe, p. 111.

[139] Maj. Gen. von Haeften, *Hindenburg und Ludendorff als Feldherrn* (1937).

[140] Oct. 27, 1918. *Kriegsbriefe gefallener deutscher Studenten,* Ph. Witkop, ed. (4th ed.), p. 354.

[141] Fortescue, II, 143 f.; VIII, 623.

[142] Noble, *Policies and Opinions at Paris,* p. 168.

[143] Bonnal, III, 177.

[144] *Commentaires,* I, 180; II, 235.

[145] General Serrigny, *Réflexions sur l'art de la guerre* (3rd ed.), pp. 44 f.

[146] Bourrienne, III, 75.

[147] Golovine, pp. 227 ff., 245, 249.

[148] Marshal Franchet d'Esperey in Hanotaux, VIII, 567.

[149] Arz, p. 373.

[150] R. Walter Darré, *Der Schweinemord* (1937).

[151] Benoist-Méchin, pp. 60 f., 74 f.

[152] Olden, p. 175.

[153] Fortescue, VII, 44 f., 450.

[154] *Préjugés militaires* (ed. Paris, 1914), xxxv.

[155] Monteilhet, p. 53.

[156] Olden, pp. 150, 173.

[157] Hugo Frh. v. Reischach, *Unter drei Kaisern* (1925), p. 276.

[158] *Ursachen des* . . . 2nd series, XI², 70 f.

[159] Tarlé, p. 337.

[160] *Leaves From a War Diary,* p. 236.

[161] 1582. Balthazar Ayala, *De iure et officiis bellicis* (Washington, 1912), II, 15, 22.

[162] Oliver Morton Dickerson, *Boston Under Military Rule* (1937).

[163] Bonnal, II, 49, 80 f.

[164] Callwell, II, 98.

[165] Brig. Gen. John Charteris, *At G.H.Q.,* p. 44.

[166] C. F. Snowdon Gamble, *The Air Weapon,* I, 33.

[167] Bonnal, II, 445, 450; Eckmühl-Bloqueville, III, 456.

[168] Hoffmann, I, 35.

[169] Ibid., I, 161, 166.

[170] Golovine, pp. 256 f.

[171] Th. von Bernhardi, *Aus dem Leben Toll's,* IV¹, 215.

[172] Callwell, II, 163.

[173] Ibid., II, 235, 258, 275, 310.

[174] Mordacq, III, 65, 95, 321; IV, 284 ff.

[175] Ibid., II, 258 ff.; Callwell, II, 183, 186, 191.

[176] Palmer, *Bliss,* p. 367.

[177] Mordacq, II, 225 ff., 233, 321; Callwell, II, 177.

[178] For a more elaborate, over-all treatment of the problem of generals and peacemaking, see Alfred Vagts, *Defense and Diplomacy,* 1956, Ch. 13.

CHAPTER 9

[1] *Sessional Papers* (1836), XXII, 55.
[2] *American Historical Review*, XL, 513.
[3] Duff Cooper, *Haig*, I, 76, 89, 94.
[4] Winston Churchill, *Marlborough*, II, 497 f., 513, 575.
[5] *N. Y. Times*, March 15, 1937.
[6] Monteilhet, *Institutions militaires de la France*, p. 398.
[7] *Le Ministère Clemenceau*, I, 201.
[8] Veit Valentin, *Geschichte der deutschen Revolution*, I, 547 f.; II, 235.
[9] *Denkwürdigkeiten Roon's*, II, 352.
[10] Golovine, *The Russian Army in the World War*, pp. 287 f.
[11] Phipps, *The Armies of the First French Republic*, I, 27 f.
[12] Callwell, *Wilson*, I, 160.
[13] H. Hagedorn, *Leonard Wood* (1931), I, 302; II, 140, 143 f., 147.
[14] Monteilhet, p. 184.
[15] K. Bleibtreu, *Das Heer*, p. 113.
[16] Bonnal, *Vie de Ney*, II, 87.
[17] Ibid., I, 183.
[18] Greene, *The Revolutionary War and the Military Policy of the U. S.* (1911), p. 331.
[19] Lily Braun, *Kriegsbriefe aus den Jahren 1870-71* (3rd ed.; 1904), p. 50
[20] Sir John Fortescue, *History of the British Army*, IV, 295 f., 315, 665; V, 364; XII, 7, 459.
[21] Maj. William A. Ganoe, *History of the U. S. Army* (1932), pp. 372 f.
[22] Callwell, I, 47.
[23] Alexandre Zévaès, *Au temps du Boulangisme* (1930), pp. 110 f.
[24] *Mémoires du Duc de Raguse*, II, 152.
[25] C. von der Goltz, *Rossbach und Jena*, p. 173.
[26] *Mémoires*, III, 254.
[27] Stanhope, *Conversations with Wellington*, p. 13.
[28] Goltz, pp. 171, 173.
[29] Golovine, p. 271.
[30] Jean de Pierrefeu, *Plutarque a menti*, p. 300.
[31] Lord Beaverbrook, *Politicians and the War*, p. 74.
[32] Von Schweinitz, *Denkwürdigkeiten*, I, 242.
[33] G. Ward Price, *Giraud and the African Scene* (1944), pp. 7, 69 f.
[34] 1951. U. S. Senate Hearings, *Military Situation in the Far East*, 811.
[35] Churchill, III, 209.
[36] Freytag-Loringhoven, *Folgerungen aus dem Weltkriege*, p. 82.
[37] J. Haller, *Aus dem Leban des Fürsten Philipp zu Eulenburg* (1926), p. 260.
[38] J. Reinach, *Histoire de l'affaire Dreyfus*, III, 496.
[39] Haller, pp. 204 ff.; O. Hammann, *Der neue Kurs*, pp. 81 ff.
[40] J. Reinach, V, 140; II, 367.
[41] *Denkwürdigkeiten*, II, 410.
[42] *Historische Zeitschrift*, CLV, 298.
[43] E. Guillon, *Nos écrivains militaires* (1899), II, 10.
[44] Wolseley, *Soldier's Pocket Book* (1871).
[45] Maj. D. H. Cole and Maj. E. C. Priestley, *An Outline of British Military History* (1936), p. 229.
[46] *Changes and Chances* (1924), p. 280.
[47] Goltz, *Meine Sendung in Finland* (1920), p. 17.

⁴⁸ *N. Y. Times,* Feb. 10 and Apr. 27, 1940, Apr. 13, 1942.
⁴⁹ Hagedorn, II, 200, 165, 181, 196.
⁵⁰ Abel Combarieu, *Sept ans à l'Élysée* (1932), p. 16; Jacques Dele-becque, *Vie du Général Marchand* (1936).
⁵¹ Mordacq, *Le Ministère Clemenceau,* I, 71 f.
⁵² General Du Barrail, War Minister under MacMahon; Guillon, II, 363.
⁵³ Hagedorn, I, 306.
⁵⁴ Clode, *Military Forces of the Crown,* I, 194.
⁵⁵ Th. Eschenburg, *Das Kaiserreich am Scheidewege* (1929), pp. x f., 31.
⁵⁶ *Denkwürdigkeiten Roon's,* II, 254 f.
⁵⁷ For French examples see Monteilhet, pp. 179 ff.
⁵⁸ Combarieu, pp. 55 f.
⁵⁹ John Dickinson, *Building of an Army,* p. 370.
⁶⁰ Ibid., p. 7.
⁶¹ For a detailed case see Reinach, II, 64 ff., 284 ff., 484.
⁶² Mordacq, I, 52.
⁶³ Hagedorn, I, 133; II, 24; Gen. Robert Lee Bullard, *Personalities and Reminiscences of the War,* p. 46.
⁶⁴ *Preussische Jahrbücher,* LXXII, 546.
⁶⁵ Dangerfield, *The Strange Death of Liberal England* (1934).
⁶⁶ Reinach, VI, 391 ff., 415 f.
⁶⁷ *Taft and Roosevelt. Letters of Archie Butt,* pp. 156 f., 588.
⁶⁸ Reinach, III, 308.
⁶⁹ Terraillon, *L'honneur,* p. 206.
⁷⁰ *Hansard,* 3rd series, XXXII, 210 ff.
⁷¹ Hagedorn, II, 274 f.
⁷² Ibid., II, 105, 331, 344 f.; Bullard, pp. 46 f., 324, 333.
⁷³ Fortescue, VII, 417 f.
⁷⁴ Reinach, VI, 66.
⁷⁵ Walter Schücking, *Die Reaktion in der inneren Verwaltung* (1902).
⁷⁶ Reinach, II, 634 ff.
⁷⁷ *Weltgeschichtliche Betrachtungen,* ed. Kröner (1868), p. 192.
⁷⁸ Knox, *With the Russian Army,* pp. 399, 457.
⁷⁹ Monteilhet, p. 167.
⁸⁰ Waldersee, *Briefwechsel,* I, 173.
⁸¹ The above is largely based on Francis Laur, *L'époque Boulangiste* (1912); Zévaès, op. cit.; B. Weil, *Glück und Elend des Generals Boulanger* (1931).
⁸² The above is largely based on Reinach, op. cit. and Léon Blum, *Souvenirs sur l'affaire* (1935); Weil, *Der Prozess des Hauptmanns Dreyfus* (1930).
⁸³ Monteilhet, p. xiii.
⁸⁴ Callwell, I, 137 f.

CHAPTER 10

¹ 1817. *Aus den Papieren Schön's,* IV, 409 f.
² J. Reinach, *Histoire de l'affaire Dreyfus,* IV, 335.
³ *N. Y. Times,* March 16, 1937.
⁴ Abel Combarieu, *Sept ans à l'Élysée,* pp. 54, 65.
⁵ H. Hagedorn, *Leonard Wood,* II, 95 f.
⁶ *Denkwürdigkeiten Roon's,* II, 352, 384.
⁷ Golovine, *The Russian Army in the World War,* pp. 30 f.
⁸ Robert Binkley, *Realism and Nationalism,* p. 154.

⁹ *Denkwürdigkeiten Roon's*, II, 23.
¹⁰ Generaloberst von Einem, *Erinnerungen eines Soldaten* (1933), pp. 64 f.
¹¹ Callwell, *Wilson*, I, 113.
¹² For this question see Eckart Kehr, *Schlachtflottenbau und Parteipolitik 1894-1901* (1930).
¹³ *U. S. Naval Institute Proceedings* (1929), XV, 757.
¹⁴ Clode, *Military Forces of the Crown* (1869), II, 63, 179 f., 419.
¹⁵ Sir John Fortescue, *History of the British Army*, I, 389 f.; Delavoye, *Life of Thomas Graham*, p. 695.
¹⁶ For examples see *War Diary of George B. McClellan* (1917), pp. 18 f., 35, 43.
¹⁷ Hagedorn, II, 22; I, 147, 233, 238, 260, 416.
¹⁸ Fortescue, XII, 279.
¹⁹ Ibid., I, 264.
²⁰ Arneth, *Prinz Eugen*, I, 431 f., Winston Churchill, *Marlborough*, III, Chap. 14.
²¹ In England in 1853. Fortescue, XII, 492.
²² Th. von Bernhardi, *Aus dem Leben Toll's*, II, 391.
²³ Sainte-Beuve, *Jomini*, p. 198.
²⁴ Max Hoffmann, *Aufzeichnungen*, I, 113, 149; Arthur Rosenberg, *Entstehung der deutschen Republik*, pp. 220, 281.
²⁵ Stein, *Lehre vom Heerwesen* (1872), pp. 19 f.
²⁶ Monteilhet, *Institutions militaires de la France*, p. 196.
²⁷ Von Einem, pp. 69 f.
²⁸ Hans Herzfeld, *Die deutsche Rüstungspolitik vor dem Weltkrieg* (1923), p. 128.
²⁹ Monteilhet, p. 319.
³⁰ G. Hanotaux, *Histoire de la nation française*, VII, 486.
³¹ Von Eisenhart-Rothe, *Im Banne der Persönlichkeit*, pp. 48 ff.
³² *The Economist*, Oct. 19, 1929.
³³ Von Kuhl, *Der deutsche Generalstab*, pp. 123 f.
³⁴ Lord Grey, *Twenty-five Years* (1925), II, 65 f.
³⁵ *Mémoires de Joffre*, II, 15 f.
³⁶ Hagedorn, I, 399.
³⁷ *British Documents on the Origins of the War*, V, No. 761.
³⁸ Harold Nicolson, *Portrait of a Diplomatist*, pp. 288 f.
³⁹ Von der Lancken, *Meine dreissig Dienstjahre*, pp. 55 ff.; v. Einem, pp. 110 ff.
⁴⁰ Conrad, *Aus meiner Dienstzeit*, IV, 188.
⁴¹ *Im Banne der Persönlichkeit*, pp. 40 ff.
⁴² *Bayerische Dokumente zum Kriegsausbruch* (3rd ed.), No. 1.
⁴³ H. Lutz, in *Werk des Untersuchungsausschusses*, 1st series, XI, 194.
⁴⁴ Ibid., pp. 15, 70.
⁴⁵ *Grosse Politik*, XIV, 3940.
⁴⁶ *British Documents* . . . . , XI, No. 170.
⁴⁷ *Denkwürdigkeiten Roon's*, II, 260; similar opinions in Conrad, IV, 150 ff.
⁴⁸ *Deutsche Dokumente zum Kriegsausbruch*, pp. 332, 335.
⁴⁹ Lutz, p. 327; H. von Moltke, *Erinnerungen*, pp. x, 19 ff.
⁵⁰ Sidney B. Fay, *Origins of the World War*, I, 450 ff.; Lutz, p. 337.
⁵¹ Lutz, p. 198.
⁵² Ibid., pp. 228 f., 236 f.
⁵³ Ibid., pp. 254 ff., 267 ff.
⁵⁴ Ibid., p. 279.

[55] Fay, II, 482 ff.
[56] Lutz, p. 395.
[57] *Lives of the Lindsays*, II, 223.
[58] Winston Churchill, *Marlborough*, II, 286.
[59] H. von Srbik, *Metternich, der Staatsmann und der Mensch*, I, 344, 401; II, 347 f.
[60] *Grosse Politik*, XXXIX, 550 ff.
[61] *Testament politique* (Amsterdam, 1691), I, 198.
[62] Rapin, cit. Clode, I, 21.
[63] *Opera Posthuma* (1667), pp. 269 f.
[64] Bourrienne, *Mémoires*, III, 301.
[65] Colonel Fabvier, *Lyon en 1817; Mémoires du Duc de Raguse*, VII, 234 ff., 324 ff.
[66] *Pensées*, ed. Brunschwig, p. 139.
[67] *Der Wille zur Macht*, ed. Kröner, p. 96.
[68] 1748; cit. Massenbach, *Memoiren*, I, 282.
[69] Delbrück, *Geschichte der Kriegskunst*, III, 666.
[70] Bode and Bircher, *Schlieffen* (1937), pp. 190, 199; Callwell, I, 101, 104, 163, 165; *Berliner Monatshefte*, May, 1931, pp. 462 ff.
[71] Callwell, I, 19.
[72] Duff Cooper, *Haig*, I, 119.
[73] Kuhl, pp. 7, 16, 57 f., 211 f.
[74] Friedrich Wilhelm von Zanthier, *Versuch über die Märsche der Armeen etc.* (1778), cit. Max Jähns, *Geschichte der Kriegswissenschaften*, p. 2095 ff.
[75] 1827. Jähns, p. 2856.
[76] Kehr, pp. 354 f.
[77] Callwell, I, 59.
[78] W. Kloster, *Der deutsche Generalstab und der Präventivkriegsgedanke* (1932).
[79] Callwell, I, 103, 112.
[80] *Über Strategie. Kriegsgeschichtliche Einzelschriften*, 3rd series. No. 13.
[81] Gen. Robert Lee Bullard, *Personalities and Reminiscences of the War*, pp. 222 f., 132.
[82] Kuhl, pp. 145 f.
[83] Monteilhet, pp. 320, 333.
[84] Cooper, I, 245.
[85] Callwell, I, 360.
[86] [Schlieffen] *"Der Krieg in der Gegenwart," Deutsche Revue*, 1909.
[87] Kuhl, pp. 130 f.
[88] Monteilhet, pp. 213 ff., 268 f., 291.
[89] A. Grasset, *Préceptes et jugements du Maréchal Foch*, p. xi. The word about "the battle won" may be traced back to the Restoration thinker De Maistre.
[90] Grasset, p. xiii.
[91] Ibid., p. xiv.
[92] Monteilhet, pp. 350 f.
[93] Liddell Hart, *Reputations Ten Years After*, pp. 211 ff.; Monteilhet, pp. 355 f.
[94] *La guerre au 20ᵉ siècle* (1914).
[95] Kuhl, pp. 132 f.; Cooper, I, 109; Pédoya, *Commission de l'armée*.
[96] Monteilhet, pp. 334 ff.
[97] Kuhl, p. 142.
[98] General de Négrier, *Revue des deux Mondes*, 1905, 1st series, pp. 306, 328.

[90] Hoffmann, I, 14 f., 31, 41; Moltke, p. 303.
[100] *Alten's Handbuch für Heer und Flotte*, IX.
[101] Delavoye, pp. 749 ff., 765.
[102] F. Meinecke, *Boyen*, II, 539.
[103] M. Busch, *Bismarck*, III, 249.
[104] *Geschichte der Frankfurter Zeitung*, pp. 237 f., 821.
[105] Kennedy, *The Military Side of Japanese Life*, p. 169; Causton, *Militarism and Foreign Policy in Japan*, p. 92.
[106] Charles and Mary Beard, *American Civilization*, II, 291.
[107] E. Kehr, *Die Gesellschaft*, 1928, 2nd series, p. 225.
[108] Werner, *Alldeutscher Verband*, p. 155; General Keim, *Erlebtes und Erstrebtes* (1925).
[109] For details see Baker, *Private Manufacture of Armaments*, I, 306 f., et passim.
[110] *The Nation* (New York), Jan. 12, 1927.
[111] Baker, I, 306, 342, 444 f.
[112] Rabenau, *Von Seeckt*, I, 359.
[113] *N. Y. Times*, Sept. 1, 1941.
[114] Timothy W. Stanley, *American Defense and National Security* (1956), p. 65.

CHAPTER 11

[1] *Europäische Gespräche*, 1927, p. 273.
[2] A. Vagts, *Deutschland und die Vereinigten Staaten*, p. 1958.
[3] Philip Noel Baker, *Private Manufacture of Armaments*, I, 334.
[4] J. Reinach, *Histoire de l'affaire Dreyfus*, I, 3 f.
[5] Bonnal, *Vie de Ney*, I, 286.
[6] Johs. Ziekursch, *Politische Geschichte des neuen deutschen Kaiserreichs* (1932), II, 85.
[7] Lady Gwendolyn Cecil, *Life of Salisbury*, II, 153.
[8] "*Der Krieg in der Gegenwart*," *Deutsche Revue*, 1909.
[9] Stein, *Lehre vom Heerwesen*, pp. 21 f.
[10] *Parliamentary Debates*, Feb. 26, 1849.
[11] F. W. Hirst, *The Six Panics* (1913), pp. 15 f.
[12] John Morley, *Gladstone*, III, 507 f.
[13] Sir John Fortescue, *History of the British Army*, XIII, 172.
[14] Nov. 20, 1893. A. G. Gardiner, *Life of Sir William Harcourt*.
[15] Hans Herzfeld, *Die deutsche Rüstungspolitik vor dem Weltkrieg*, p. 159; Th. von Bernhardi, *Deutschland und der nächste Krieg*, p. 210.
[16] Gourgaud, *Journal inédit*, I, 286.
[17] Jack Rohan, *Yankee Arms Maker*, pp. 199 ff.
[18] Baker, I, 58 f., 119.
[19] For details see W. Hallgarten, *Vorkriegsimperialismus* (1935), pp. 183 ff.
[20] Baker, I, 37.
[21] Bernhard Menne, *Krupp* (1937), pp. 206 f.
[22] Willi Boelcke, *Krupp und die Hohenzollern* (1956), p. 48.
[23] Baker, I, 143 ff.
[24] Rohan, pp. 88 f., 99, 187.
[25] Menne, p. 208.
[26] F. Delaisi, *Le patriotisme des plaques blindées*, p. 10.
[27] C. von der Goltz, *Rossbach und Jena*, p. 107 f.
[28] H. Hagedorn, *Leonard Wood*, II, 176 f.
[29] William S. Myers, *McClellan* (1934), pp. 480 ff.

[30] Hans Wehberg, *Die internationale Beschränkung der Rüstungen* (1919), p. 343.
[31] *Parliamentary Debates*, March 17, 1914.
[32] Delaisi, pp. 22 f.
[33] For full details see Hallgarten in *Revue Historique*, CLXXVII, 520 f.
[34] For a case of 1808-9 see Pertz, *Gneisenau*, I, 458 f.
[35] Hallgarten, *Vorkriegsimperialismus*, pp. 182 ff.
[36] Hagedorn, II, 177.
[37] Reinach, I, 7 ff.
[38] Mordacq, *Le Ministère Clemenceau*, IV, 70; v. Kuhl, *Der deutsche Generalstab*, pp. 26 f.
[39] Bircher and Bode, *Schlieffen*, pp. 85 f., 102.
[40] Monteilhet, *Institutions militaires de la France*, p. 318.
[41] Monteilhet, p. 319; Liddell Hart, *Reputations Ten Years After*, p. 157.
[42] C. Dumba, *Dreibund- und Entente-Politik* (1931), pp. 218 ff.
[43] *Grosse Politik*, XXXVIII, 15436.
[44] Gourgaud, II, 188; *Mémoires du Duc de Raguse*, II, 106.
[45] Gouvion Saint-Cyr, *Mémoires*, I, xxxvi f.
[46] M. N. Pokrowsky, *Brief History of Russia* (1931), II, 101.
[47] Monteilhet, p. 285.
[48] Herzfeld, pp. 122, 128, 143.
[49] Kuhl, p. 14.
[50] Herzfeld, p. 9; Ziekursch, III, 64 f.
[51] Monteilhet, pp. xi ff.
[52] 1912. Herzfeld, p. 51.
[53] Ibid., pp. 5, 159.
[54] Monteilhet, pp. 344 f.
[55] Kuhl, pp. 27 f.
[56] G. Hanotaux, *Histoire de la nation française*, VIII, 507 f.
[57] General Groener, *Der Feldherr wider Willen* (1930), p. xiii.
[58] For Sch. see his *Gesammelte Schriften* (1906-8), the writings of Von Kuhl and other pupils.
[59] Kuhl, p. 174.
[60] Herzfeld, p. 160.
[61] Ibid., p. 77.
[62] Ibid., pp. 86 f.
[63] *Essay xxix.*
[64] Nathaniel W. Stephenson, *Nelson W. Aldrich* (1930), p. 155.
[65] Fritz Hellwig, *Carl Freiherr v. Stumm-Halberg* (1936), p. 336.
[66] Werner, *Der alldeutsche Verband*, p. 64.
[67] Werner, pp. 153 ff.; General Keim, *Erlebtes und Erstrebtes* (1925).
[68] Daniel Frymann, i.e., Heinrich Class, *Wenn ich der Kaiser wär* (1912).
[69] F. Priebatsch, *Geschichte des preussischen Offizierkorps* (1919), p. 64; Allan Nevins, *Henry White*, p. 324.
[70] Reinach, IV, 301; V, 261.
[71] Eugene N. Anderson, *The First Moroccan Crisis* (1930), pp. 5 ff.
[72] Jacques Delebecque, *Marchand*, pp. 69, 76.
[73] *Historische Zeitschrift*, CXLII, 279 ff.
[74] A. von Hedenström, *Geschichte Russlands* (1922), p. 118.
[75] Eggeling, *Die russische Mobilmachung und der Krieg* (1919), pp. 15 f.
[76] Causton, *Militarism and Foreign Policy in Japan* (1936).
[77] *Europäische Gespräche*, 1931, p. 298.

[78] Walter Millis, *The Martial Spirit* (1931), pp. 377 f.
[79] Vagts, pp. 1095 ff.
[80] U. S. War Department, *Annual Report* (1912), I, 126.
[81] *N. Y. Times*, Sept. 16, 1913.
[82] Waldersee, *Denkwürdigkeiten*, II, 38, 48; Waldersee, *Briefwechsel*, I, 224, 251.
[83] Robert Binkley, *Realism and Nationalism*, p. 260.
[84] Sept. 26, 1914. Hagedorn, II, 149.
[85] H. von Moltke, *Erinnerungen*, p. 296; similar, Max Hoffmann, *Aufzeichnungen*, I, 77.
[86] Hagedorn, II, 152.
[87] Charles H. Firth, *Cromwell's Army* (1902), pp. 344 f.
[88] Otto Krauske, *Briefe des Königs Friedrich Wilhelm I*, p. 205.
[89] 1851; cit. with approval by General Fuller, *War and Western Civilization*, p. 268.
[90] In the Reichstag, Feb. 16, 1874.
[91] Maj. Stewart L. Murray, *The Future Peace of the Anglo-Saxons* (1905), pp. 26, 40.
[92] Charles Joseph de Ligne, *Vie du Prince Eugène de Savoie* (1809).
[93] Waldersee, *Denkwürdigkeiten*, I, 230.
[94] Gen. Robert Lee Bullard, *Personalities and Reminiscences of the War*, pp. 312 f.
[95] Fortescue, I, 29; Major Schmitthenner, *Krieg und Kriegführung*, p. 106.
[96] Firth, p. 261.
[97] *Zeitschrift für die gesamten Staatwissenschaften*, XCV, 563.
[98] F. W. Holls, *The Peace Conference at the Hague*, pp. 118 f.
[99] 1925. F. Palmer, *Bliss, Peacemaker*, pp. 447 f.
[100] Arneth, *Prinz Eugen*, I, 177.
[101] Lt. Otto Dietz, *Der Todesgang der deutschen Armee* (1919), p. 19.
[102] Duff Cooper, *Haig*, I, 208.
[103] Knox, *With the Russian Army*, p. 230.
[104] Fuller, p. 240.
[105] *N. Y. Times*, April 6, 1937.
[106] Ibid., March 27, 1934.
[107] Max Jähns, *Heeresverfassungen und Völkerleben*, p. 354.
[108] Colby, *Profession of Arms* (1924), p. 4.
[109] Vagts, p. 1950.
[110] 1791-2. *Works*, ed. Conway, II, 511.
[111] Goltz, pp. 246, 252 f.
[112] C. K. Webster, *Foreign Policy of Castlereagh*, pp. 70 ff.; H. v. Srbik, *Metternich*, I, 572.
[113] *Belgische Dokumente*, II, 30 f.; for a treatment of the genesis of the First Hague Conference see Thomas K. Ford's article in *Political Science Quarterly*, LI, 354 ff.; Vagts, pp. 1948 ff.
[114] Holls, pp. 78 ff.
[115] *British Documents on the Origin of the War*, II, 229 f.
[116] R. H. Bacon, *Life of Lord Fisher* (1929), I, 276 f.
[117] Message of Dec. 3, 1906.
[118] Richard Burton Haldane, *An Autobiography* (1929), pp. 257 f.
[119] Dugdale, *Balfour*, II, 240.

CHAPTER 12

[1] *Gestaltung der Idee* (1937), 303 ff.
[2] *Neues Tagebuch*, May 4, 1935.

[8] *Training Manual,* No. 2000-2025 for the R.O.T.C.
[4] *Harper's Magazine,* Sept. 1935, p. 398.
[5] *N. Y. Times,* Jan. 9, 1936; *ibid.,* Apr. 30, 1946, for an obituary.
[6] *Frankfurter Zeitung,* Nov. 22, 1936.
[7] Ibid., Jan. 3, 1937.
[8] H. Finer, *Mussolini's Italy* (1935).
[9] C. W. Gässler, *Offiziere und Offizierkorps der alten Armee in Deutschland* (1930), p. 73.
[10] For details see Caro and Oehme, *Schleichers Aufstieg* (1933), p. 112.
[11] Helene Prinzessin von Isenburg in *Archiv für Sippenforschung,* 1934.
[13] Compiled from B. Jacob, *Das neue deutsche Heer und seine Führer* (1936), pp. 162 ff.; for more data on the titled Reichswehr officer, see Braucher, *Auflösung der Weimarer Republik* (1955), p. 258.
[13] Benoist-Méchin, *Histoire de l'armée allemande* (1936), p. 199.
[14] *N. Y. Times,* Oct. 30, 1936.
[15] *The Banker* (London), February, 1937.
[16] *N. Y. Times,* May 23, 1935.
[17] For details see *Neue Weltbühne,* Feb. 4, 1937.
[18] C. von der Goltz, *Denkwürdigkeiten* (1929), p. 37.
[19] Johs. Ziekursch, *Politische Geschichte des neuen deutschen Kaiserreichs,* I, 13 f.
[20] Haushofer in *Cochenhausen,* editor, *Gestalter der Wehrkraft,* p. 139.
[21] Stephen Gwynn, *The Anvil of War* (1936), pp. 64 f.
[22] Wolseley, *Soldier's Pocket Book.*
[23] Sir F. Maurice and Sir G. Arthur, *The Life of Lord Wolseley* (1924), pp. 56, 239.
[24] Callwell, *Wilson,* II, 291 ff., 238.
[25] Mordacq, *Le Ministère Clemenceau,* III, 53 ff.; IV, 48 f., 302.
[26] General Chauvineau, *Une invasion est-elle encore possible?* Preface by Marshal Pétain (1939).
[27] Chambre des Deputés, June 29, 1935.
[28] Debates in the Chamber on the military budgets, Jan. 28, 1937, and ff. days.
[29] *Frankfurter Zeitung,* Sept. 6, 1936.
[30] Maj. Gen. Johnson Hagood, *We Can Defend America* (1937), pp. 83 f.
[31] *N. Y. Times,* May 23, 1936.
[32] *Army Ordnance,* May–June, 1927, p. 426.
[33] Walter Millis, *The Road to War,* p. 95.
[34] *We Can Defend America,* pp. 234 f.
[35] W. Sikorski, *La guerre moderne* (1935), pp. 101 f.
[36] *N. Y. Times,* Feb. 22, 1935.
[37] *The Nation* (New York), June 26, 1935.
[38] Fifth Plenary Session.
[39] Callwell, II, 310; General Fuller, *War and Western Civilization,* p. 247.
[40] *Geschichte eines Hochverräters,* p. 130.
[41] Since 1923 the Reichswehr Ministry had issued a confidential monthly, *Wehrgedanke des Auslands,* to reliable editors in order to show by excerpts from the foreign military journals how much military thought was alive abroad.
[42] Von Oldenburg-Januschau, *Erinnerungen* (1936).
[43] Caro-Oehme, pp. 207 f., 253.
[44] Callwell, II, 209.
[45] *Neuer Vorwärts,* Feb. 17, 1935; *N. Y. Times,* Sept. 6, 1936.

[46] *N. Y. Times,* April 21, 1936.
[47] F. Palmer, *Bliss, Peacemaker* (1925), p. 444.
[48] General Goering, cit. *Neues Tagebuch,* Nov. 7, 1936.
[49] *Wirtschaft und Statistik,* 1937, No. 4.
[50] *Neue Weltbühne,* Sept. 3, 1936.
[51] *N. Y. Times,* May 4, 1937.
[52] *Deutscher Volkswirt,* Oct. 2, 1936.
[53] *Briefe,* ed. Kröner (1935), pp. 348 f.
[54] *Der Wille zur Macht* (1887), ed. Kröner, p. 506.
[55] Fritz Hellwig, *Carl Freiherr v. Stumm-Halberg* (1936), pp. 295 f.
[56] *Neuer Vorwärts,* Nov. 18, 1934.
[57] *N. Y. Times,* Feb. 13 and 24, 1937.
[58] *Personalities and Reminiscences of the War,* p. 18.
[59] Stephen Raushenbush, *The Nation* (New York), Jan. 27, 1937.
[60] Heinz Schmidt, *Kriegsgewinne und Wirtschaft* (1935).
[61] *Frankfurter Zeitung,* April 19, 1936.
[62] *N. Y. Times,* July 18, 1936.
[63] Prussian War Minister von Einem to the Chancellor, June 1906. Reichsarchiv, *Der Weltkrieg 1914-18. Kriegsrüstung und Kriegswirtschaft* (1930). Anlagenband I, 101 f.
[64] *N. Y. Times,* Feb. 26, 1937.
[65] *Nye Committee Hearings on Munitions Industry,* Part 17, pp. 4335 f.; *Army Ordnance,* Aug. 25, 1936.
[66] Dwight F. Davis, March 15, 1928, 70th Congress, 1st session, H. J. Res. 183.
[67] Royal Commission on the Private Manufacture of and Trading in Arms, *Report,* Cmd. 5292; Philip Noel Baker, *Private Manufacture of Armaments,* I, 58 f., 63 ff.
[68] *N. Y. Times,* Feb. 18, 1937.
[69] E. Lederer, "Fascist Tendencies in Japan," *Pacific Affairs,* VII.
[70] *Die Reichswehr* (1933).
[71] Sebastiano Conte Visconti-Prasca, *La guerra decisiva* (1934).
[72] *International Conciliation,* January, 1935.
[73] Capt. John H. Burns, "The Psychologist Looks at the Army," *Infantry Journal,* December 1928.
[74] *Militärwissenschaftliche Revue,* March, 1936.
[75] Major Marcks in *Wissen und Wehr,* January, 1931.
[76] *Deutsche Schule. Zeitschrift der Reichsfachschaft 4 (Volkschule) des Nationalsozialen Lehrerbundes,* special issue beginning of 1936.
[77] *N. Y. Herald Tribune,* Oct. 18, 1936; *N. Y. Times,* Dec. 21, 1936 and ff. days.
[78] Maj. Gen. Dr. H. Haeften, June 20, 1935, *Sitzungsberichte der preussischen Akademie der Wissenschaften,* XIX, 607 ff.
[79] *La révolution mondiale et la responsabilité de l'esprit* (Paris, 1934).
[80] *Frankfurter Zeitung,* Jan. 16 and 17, 1937.
[81] *Handels-Rechenaufgabe aus dem Gebiet des nationalsozialistishen Aufbaues, für das 7. und 8. Schuljahr* (1935); Maj. Ulrich Schmidt, *Wehrgeist in der Schule* (1936).
[82] *Frankfurter Zeitung,* April 26, 1936.
[83] Ibid., May 27, 1937.
[84] *N. Y. Herald Tribune,* June 28, 1936.
[85] Weygand in preface to Liautey, *Le rôle social de l'officier* (1935); for Pétain see *N. Y. Times,* Dec. 9, 1934.
[86] *Frankfurter Zeitung,* Nov. 29, 1936.
[87] House of Commons Debates, Feb. 8, 1937.

[88] *Frankfurter Zeitung,* Dec. 6, 1936; *Manchester Guardian,* Feb. 9, 1937.
[89] *N. Y. Times,* Sept. 20, 1936, Jan. 24, 1937.
[90] Sept. 27, 1933, cit. Baker, I, 243.
[91] Montluc, *Commentaires,* III, 488, writing in the 1570's.
[92] *N. Y. Times,* July 12, 1936.
[93] *Cochenhausen,* p. 193 f.
[94] House of Commons Debates, Nov. 16, 1936.
[95] *Frankfurter Zeitung,* Sept. 18, 1936.
[96] Terraillon, *L'honneur,* p. 215.
[97] *Neue Weltbühne,* April 15, 1937.
[98] Ernst Bloch, *Neue Weltbühne,* Jan. 21, 1937.
[99] Dr. Ley, *Frankfurter Zeitung,* July 19, 1936.
[100] *N. Y. Times,* April 11, 1937.
[101] Ibid., March 2, 1937.
[102] Von Metzsch, *Die Weltangst vor dem Kriege* (1935), p. 7.
[103] D. Fedotoff White, "Soviet Philosophy of War," *Political Science Quarterly,* LXI, 328.
[104] Maj. E. Suchsland, *Archiv für Rassen- und Gesellschaftsbiologie,* XXX.
[105] *The White Army,* p. 199.
[106] Callwell, II, 257, 262.
[107] Colby, *The Profession of Arms* (1924), p. 55.
[108] Speier in *Social Research,* II, 84.
[109] *Völkischer Beobachter,* March 22, 1937.
[110] Terraillon, p. 126.
[111] E. Faguet, *La démission de la morale* (1910), pp. 359 f.
[112] "The Gukwansho" or "Miscellany of Personal Views of an Ignorant Fool," trans. by J. Rahder, *Acta Orientalia,* XL, 196 ff.
[113] J. H. Gubbins, "The 'Hundred Articles' and the Tokugawa Government." *Transactions and Proceedings of the Japan Society,* XVII, 128 ff.

CHAPTER 13

[1] Maj. Gen. A. C. Templerley, *The Whispering Gallery of Europe* (1938), p. 38.
[2] Moriz Faber du Faur, *Macht und Ohnmacht* (1955), pp. 245 f.
[3] Faber du Faur, p. 181.
[4] *Major War Criminals Trial,* XIX, 229.
[5] Rudolf Stadelmann, *Moltke und der Staat* (1950), p. 367.
[6] Rabenau, *Seeckt* (1940), II, 580.
[7] Pringle, *Theodore Roosevelt,* p. 172.
[8] *Major War Criminals Trial,* XXV, 145; XII, 920.
[9] Eric Bentley, *A Century of Hero-Worship,* 2nd. ed., p. 54.
[10] Lippincott, *Victorian Critics of Democracy,* for details.
[11] Walter Görlitz, *Der deutsche Generalstab,* p. 612.
[12] The piece is to be found in *Traffics and Discoveries* (1904).
[13] Hagedorn, *Leonard Wood,* I, 139, 153.
[14] Woodward, *Tom Watson,* pp. 247, 355, 480 ff.
[15] For Lea see article "H.L." in DAB, Claire Boothe's reissue of *The Valor of Ignorance* (1942), and John P. Mallan, "The Warrior Critique of Business Civilization," *American Quarterly,* VIII, 216 ff.
[16] *Les événements survenus en France de 1933 à 1945. Rapport de la Commission d'Enquête palementaire* (1947), I, 14.
[17] Jacques Chastenet, *La France de M. Fallières* (1949), p. 261.

[18] Walter Görlitz, *Die Junker,* p. 47.
[19] Bentley, p. 214.
[20] M. Karpovich, "A Forerunner of Lenin," *Review of Politics,* July 1944.
[21] *Réflexions sur la violence* (1908). For Sorel see most recently Richard Humphrey, *George Sorel: Prophet without Honor* (1951).
[22] Title of a brochure by A. Lozovsky. English edition 1924.
[23] David Shub, *Lenin: A Biography* (1948), p. 324.
[24] For what Voroshilov and Budënny meant by annihilation see William Bullitt's story in 84th Congress, 2nd. sess. House Report, no. 2189, pp. 18 f.
[25] Col. G. A. Tokaev, *Stalin Means War,* pp. 72 f., 115, 118, etc.
[26] *Mein Kampf,* pp. 8, 210, 384.
[27] B. H. Lehman, *Carlyle's Theory of the Hero* (1928), p. 99.
[28] Wiskemann, *Rome-Berlin Axis,* p. 228.
[29] Cadorna to Foch in 1917. General Weygand, *Mémoires,* I, 424.
[30] Hallgarten, *Dämonen oder Retter* (1957), 222.
[31] Wheeler-Bennett, *Nemesis of Power,* p. 211.
[32] *Major War Criminals Trial,* II, 112 f.
[33] Görlitz, *Die Junker,* p. 369.
[34] Hassell, *Vom andern Deutschland,* p. 285.
[35] British military attaché report from Berlin. *Doc.'s on British Foreign Policy,* 2nd ser., I, 512.
[36] Faber du Faur, *Macht und Ohnmacht,* pp. 165, 168.
[37] Ruth Benedict, *The Chrysanthemum and the Sword,* pp. 22 f.
[38] Gamelin, *Servir,* II, 283.
[39] Ibid., II, 162 ff.
[40] Wiskemann, *Rome-Berlin Axis,* p. 49.
[41] *Great Contemporaries* (1935), p. 261.
[42] *Doc.'s on British Foreign Policy,* 2nd ser., IV, 3.
[43] Arthur M. Schlesinger, Jr., *The Crisis of the Old Order* (1957), pp. 417 f.
[44] *Hitler's Secret Conversations,* pp. 402 f.
[45] Bor, *Gespräche mit Halder,* p. 111.
[46] Wheeler-Bennett, *Nemesis,* p. 530.
[47] George S. Patton, Jr., *War as I Knew It* (1947), p. 354.
[48] Himmler speech to SS officials, Aug. 3, 1944. *Vierteljahrshefte für Zeitgeschichte,* I, 365.
[49] *Secret Conversations,* p. 476.
[50] *Foreign Relations of the U. S.: The Soviet Union 1933-1939* (1952), pp. 384 f.
[51] For a discussion of the Wehrmacht oath see *Die Vollmacht des Gewissens* (1955).
[52] *Nazi Conspiracy and Aggression,* VIII, 592, 646.
[53] *Hassell Diaries,* p. 276.
[54] Kesselring, *A Soldier's Record,* p. 74.
[55] Westphal, *Heer in Fesseln,* p. 95.
[56] Adelbert Weinstein, *Ja . . . aber* (1952), p. 31.
[57] Details in *Politics,* Aug. 1945, p. 29.
[58] Paul Baudouin, *Neuf mois au gouvernement,* p. 199.
[59] Mark W. Clark, *From the Danube to the Yalu,* pp. 12 f., 36.
[60] Truman, *Memoirs,* II, 460.
[61] Kesselring, *Record,* pp. 273, 276.
[62] Truman, *Memoirs,* I, 419.
[63] Stimson-Bundy, *On Active Duty,* p. 632. Louis Morton, "The De-

cision to Use the Atomic Bomb," *Foreign Affairs*, XXXV, 334 ff.
[64] English ed. (1939), p. 469.
[65] *Nazi Conspiracy and Aggression*, VIII, 590.
[66] Rintelen, *Mussolini als Bundesgenosse*, p. 80.
[67] *Major War Criminals Trial*, XXXIV, 426.
[68] For this Louis Morton, "The Japanese Decision for War," *U. S. Naval Institute Proceedings*, LXXX, 1327 ff.
[69] Compton Mackenzie, *Mr. Roosevelt*, p. 23, fireside chat of Dec. 29, 1940.
[70] Daniels, *End of Innocence*, p. 271.
[71] Sherwood, *Roosevelt and Hopkins* (Bantam ed.), II, 301.
[72] Feis, *Churchill-Roosevelt-Stalin*, pp. 108 ff.
[73] Cline, *Washington Command Post*, pp. 216 f., 313; Matloff & Snell, *Strategic Planning for Coalition Warfare*, p. 380.
[74] See for this Bruce Lockhart, *Comes the Reckoning* (1947); James P. Warburg, *Germany—Bridge or Battleground* (1947); and Wallace Carroll, *Persuade or Perish* (1948).
[75] *Forrestal Diaries*, p. 55.
[76] Joseph C. Grew in *N. Y. Times*, Sept. 10, 1950.
[77] *The Revolution in Warfare* (1946), p. 60.
[78] *U. S. Naval Institute Proceedings*, LXXX (1954), 250, a prize essay.
[79] *Military Situation in the Far East*. 82nd Congress, 1st. Sess. Senate Committee on Armed Forces & Foreign Relations Hearings (1951), pp. 644 ff., 960, 1416.
[80] Text in *Die Zeit*, Hamburg, July 19, 1951.
[81] R. Aron, *Introduction à la philosophie de l'histoire*, p. 75.
[82] Albert Olivier, *Saint-Just et la force des choses* (1954), p. 186.
[83] Spears, *Assignment to Catastrophe*, I, 10.
[84] Souvarine, *Staline* (1935), p. 211.
[85] William Bullitt, "How We Won the War and Lost the Peace," *Life*, Aug. 30, 1948.
[86] So Napoleon himself. Ranke, *Denkwürdigkeiten Hardenbergs* IV, 293.
[87] *Major War Criminals Trial*, XXXV, 432.
[88] Hallgarten, *Dämonen oder Retter*, p. 290.
[89] *N. Y. Times*, Aug. 15, 1946.
[90] 1937. Gerhard Ritter, *Lebendige Vergangenheit* (1944), p. 96.
[91] W. Foerster, *Generalstabschef Ludwig Beck: Sein Kampf gegen den Krieg* (1953), pp. 43 ff.
[92] The most relevant piece of literature on Lopez is Major Max von Versen's *Reisen in Amerika und der südamerikanische Krieg* (1872).
[93] Helmuth Greiner, *Die oberste Wehrmachtführung* (1951), pp. 51, 69.
[94] Westphal, *Heer in Fesseln*, pp. 154 f., 158.
[95] *Military History of the Western World*, III, 414.
[96] Greiner, pp. 182 ff., 193 ff.
[97] *Secret Conversations*, p. 37.
[98] Bor, *Gespräche mit Halder*, p. 204.
[99] Gilbert, *Hitler Directs his War*, p. 9.
[100] K. Zeitzler in *Europäische Sicherheit*, I (1951), No. 6-9.
[101] *The Voice of Destruction* (1940), p. 11.
[102] Bor, *Gespräche mit Halder*, p. 214.
[103] Adolf Heusinger, *Befehl im Widerstreit* (1950), p. 367.
[104] Fuller, *Military History of the Western World*, III, 364.
[105] Kesselring, *A Soldier's Record*, pp. 120 f., 210.

[106] Alfieri, *Dictators Face to Face,* pp. 1, 43, 282.

[107] Peter Fleming, *Operation Sea Lion* (1957), pp. 138, 163.

[108] Arthur Bryant, *The Turn of the Tide* (1957), p. 12.

[109] Samuel E. Morison in *N. Y. Times,* May 18, 1957; Trumbull Higgins, *Winston Churchill and the Second Front* (1957).

[110] Bryant, p. 274.

[111] John Ehrmann, *Grand Strategy,* p. 101.

[112] Bryant, p. 583.

[113] Field Marshal Wavell, *The Good Soldier* (1948), p. 4.

[114] Bryant, pp. 205 ff.

[115] General S. Woodburn Kirby, *The War Against Japan* (1957), I for details.

[116] Hull, *Memoirs,* p. 1111.

[117] For the details see Charles F. Romanus and Riley Sunderland, *Stilwell's Mission to China* (1953).

[118] Daniels, *End of Innocence,* p. 172.

[119] For this see John J. McCloy, *The Challenge to American Foreign Policy* (1953), pp. 37 f.

[120] Bryant, 325, similarly Walter Millis, *Arms and Men* (1956), p. 277.

[121] Matloff and Snell, *Strategic Planning,* pp. 98, 125.

[122] Samuel E. Morison, *N. Y. Times,* May 18, 1957.

[123] Guenther Blumentritt, "Strategic Withdrawals," *Military Review,* Sept. 1953.

[124] Kyrill D. Kalinow, *Sowjetmarschälle haben das Wort* (1950), pp. 20 ff.

[125] Maj. Gen. F. Isayev, "Stalin's Military Genius," *New Times,* Dec. 21, 1949. Cit. Byron Dexter in *Foreign Affairs,* XXIX, 44 ff.

[126] Robert C. Tucker, "The Metamorphosis of the Stalin Myth," *World Affairs,* VI, 51 ff.

[127] May 20, 1939, *Doc.'s on German Foreign Policy,* ser. D, VI, 541 f.

[128] *Zeitschrift für Politik,* I (1954), p. 343.

[129] Faber du Faur, p. 178.

[130] Liddell Hart, *German Generals Talk,* pp. 19, 174.

[131] Harry S. Semmes, *Patton* (1955), p. 75.

[132] U.P. despatch from Stockholm, Aug. 11, 1945.

[133] Collins, *Lord Wavell,* p. 120.

[134] Major-General Sir Edward Spears, *Assignment to Catastrophe,* I, 27 f.

[135] Lockhart, *Comes the Reckoning,* p. 283.

[136] Sherwood, *Roosevelt and Hopkins* (Bantam ed.), I, 14.

[137] Elias Huzar, *The Purse and the Sword* (1950), 58; Huntington, *The Soldier and the State* (1957), p. 317.

[138] Lockhart, pp. 236, 253 f., 262 for such attempts.

[139] Cline, *Washington Command Post,* 42, 314.

[140] Semmes, 15.

[141] Chester Wilmot, *The Struggle for Europe,* 100.

[142] Ehrman, *Grand Strategy,* pp. 431 ff.

[143] Spear, *Assignment,* I, 61.

[144] Paul Reynaud, *In the Thick of the Fight,* p. 50 ff.

[145] Reynaud, pp. 175 f., 381.

[146] Ibid., p. 286.

[147] Paul Baudouin, *Neuf mois au gouvernement* (1948), p. 224.

[148] General Thoma to B. H. Liddell Hart, in the latter's *The German Generals Talk,* p. 155.

[149] Wilson, *Eight Years Overseas,* p. 198.

[150] Cline, *Washington Command Post*, pp. 293 f.
[151] Eisenhower, *Crusade*, p. 474.
[152] Matloff and Snell, p. 143.
[153] *Major War Criminals Trial* XXII, 522 f., 589.
[154] *The German Generals Talk*, p. 22.
[155] Wheeler Bennett, *Nemesis*, p. 459.
[156] *Vollmacht des Gewissens*, p. 126.

CHAPTER 14

[1] See for this Lt. Col. William R. Kintner, *The Front Is Everywhere: Militant Communism in Action* (1950), and R. Wagra, "Soviet Militarism," *Eastern Quarterly* II, 27 ff., 50 ff.
[2] *Jenmin Jihpao (People's Daily)*, cit. *N. Y. Times*, Oct. 12, 1958.
[3] S. M. Vishnev, *Der moderne Militarismus und die Monopole* (East Berlin, 1955).
[4] *N. Y. Times*, Feb. 11, 1958.
[5] Ray Jackson, "Aspects of American Militarism," *Contemporary Issues* I (1948), 20 ff.
[6] *Look*, March 11, 1952.
[7] Frank Dobie, "Samples of the Army Mind," *Harper's*, Dec. 1946.
[8] *N. Y. Times*, April 18, 1952.
[9] Osgood, *Limited War*, 188, pp. 240 f.
[10] Vagts, *Defense and Diplomacy*, p. 333 f.
[11] *N. Y. Times*, May 4 and June 11, 1957, for examples.
[12] André Maurois, cit. *Die Zeit*, May 1, 1958.
[13] A. J. Liebling in *The New Yorker*, March 3 and 10, 1951.
[14] Vagts, *Diplomacy and Defense*, p. 522.
[15] *Military Situation in the Far East*, p. 45.
[16] Truman, *Memoirs*, II, 416.
[17] Telford Taylor, *Sword and Swastika* (1952), p. 368.
[18] *N. Y. Times*, Feb. 28, 1946; ibid., Feb. 22, 1945, for a similar action of Italian sailors against a Rome socialist newspaper.
[19] François Bondy in *The New Leader*, March 10, 1958.
[20] Edward L. Katzenbach, "The French Army," *Yale Review*, Summer 1956. Daniel Lerner and Raymond Aron, *France Defeats EDC* (1957) for details.
[21] U.P., June 1, 1958.
[22] J. A. Curran, *Militant Hinduism in Indian Politics: a Study of the RSS* (1951) for details.
[23] Felix Weil, *Argentine Riddle* (1944), p. 54.
[24] *Vorlesungen über die Philosophie der Geschichte*, IX, 104.
[25] *N. Y. Times*, Oct. 21, 1958.
[26] *N. Y. Times*, Sept. 27 and Oct. 1, 1958.
[27] *Time*, Oct. 20, 1958.
[28] Majjid Khadduri, "The Role of the Military in Middle East Politics," *Am. Pol. Sci. Rev.*, XLVII (1953), 510 ff.
[29] J.D.L., "The Jordan Coup d'état," *History Today*, Jan. 1957.
[30] *N. Y. Times*, Oct. 6, 1957.
[31] For details see Raymond L. Garthoff, "The Role of the Military in Recent Soviet Politics," *Russian Review*, April 1957.
[32] *N. Y. Times*, July 29, 1956.
[33] The conclusion of a Harvard survey, *How the Soviet System Works*, ed. by Clyde Kluckhohn et al., Cambridge, 1956, as well as of Mr. Allen Dulles of the CIA, in a speech of summer 1957. *N. Y. Times*, March 16, 1958.

[34] Louis Fischer in *The New Leader*, Feb. 10, 1958.
[35] Resolution of C.P. Central Committee, Nov. 2, 1957. Text in *N. Y. Times*, Nov. 3, 1957.
[36] G. Ehrismann, *Geschichte der deutschen Literatur bis zum Ausgang des Mittelalters* (1922), II¹, 310, 279.
[37] Lt. Col. George G. Lewis and Capt. John Mewha, *History of the Prisoner of War Utilization by the U. S. Army* (1955), p. 66.
[38] Geyr von Schweppenburg, *The Critical Years*, p. 14.
[39] Butcher, *My Three Years with Eisenhower*, p. 855.
[40] Bor, *Gespräche mit Halder*, p. 232.

BIBLIOGRAPHY

It is in the nature of this work that it bases itself to a larger extent on military memoirs, biographies, and histories, than on other authors' writings dealing specifically with militarism, various militarisms, as well as antimilitarism. Needless to say, this literature as far as it is accessible has been examined, and the following bibliography collects the latter kind of writing while omitting a bibliography of the former sort of material, which would be too numerous to be listed here. Besides, a large part—that actually used by the author as relevant to his own purpose—may be gathered from the Notes.

BOOKS AND PAMPHLETS

Altrichter, Fr., *Das Wesen der soldatischen Erziehung*. Oldenburg, 1935.

Andrzejewski, Stanislaw, *Military Organization and Society*. London, 1954.

Anonymous (Ludwig Quidde), *Der Militarismus im deutschen Reiche*. Stuttgart, 1893.

Assmus, E., *Die publizistische Diskussion um den Militarismus unter besonderer Berücksichtigung der Geschichte des Begriffes in Deutschland zwischen 1850 und 1950*. Erlangen, 1951. (Dissertation Typescript.)

Baldwin, Hanson, *Great Mistakes of the War*. New York, 1950.

Bebel, August, and Liebknecht, W., *Gegen den Militarismus*. Berlin, 1895.

Benedict, Ruth, *The Chrysanthemum and the Sword: Patterns of Japanese Culture*. Boston, 1946.

Benoist-Méchin, Jacques, *Histoire de l'armée allemande depuis l'Armistice*. 2 vols. Paris, 1936-8.

Bentley, Eric, *A Century of Hero-Worship*. 2nd. ed. Boston, 1957.

Bernhardi, General Friedrich von, *Germany and the Next War* (1912). Toronto, ed. 1914.

Bethcke, Generalmajor Ernst, *Politische Generäle! Kreise und Krisen um Bismarck*. Berlin, 1930.

Bram, Joseph, *Analysis of Inca Militarism*. New York, 1941.

Brauweiler, H., *Generäle in der deutschen Republik*. Berlin, 1932.

Buchheim, Karl, *Leidensgeschichte des zivilen Geistes—oder die Demokratie in Deutschland*. Munich, 1951.

Castellan, Georges, *Le réarmement clandestin du Reich*. Paris, 1954.

Causton, E. E. N., *Militarism and Foreign Policy in Japan*. London, 1936.

Challener, Richard D., *The French Theory of the Nation in Arms*. New York, 1955.

Civil-Military Relations: An Annotated Bibliography, 1940-1952. Prepared under the Direction of the Committee on Civil-Military Research of the Social Science Research Council. New York, 1954.

Colegrove, Kenneth W., *Militarism in Japan*. Boston, 1936.
Craig, Gordon, *The Politics of the Prussian Army: 1640-1945*. Oxford, 1955.
Davies, Wallace Evan, *Patriotism on Parade: The Story of the Veterans' and Hereditary Organizations in America, 1783-1900*. Cambridge, Mass., 1955.
Demeter, Karl, *Das deutsche Heer und seine Offiziere*. Berlin, 1930.
Duffield, Marcus, *King Legion*. New York, 1931.
Ebeling, H., *The Political Role of the German General Staff between 1918 and 1938*. London, 1945.
Ekirch, Arthur A., *The Civilian and the Military*. New York, 1956.
Erfurth, Waldemar, *Die Geschichte des deutschen Generalstabes: 1918-1945*. Göttingen, 1957.
Ergang, Robert, *The Potsdam Führer: Frederick William I, Father of Prussian Militarism*. New York, 1941.
Faber du Faur, Moriz, *Macht und Ohnmacht: Erinnerungen eines alten Offiziers*. Stuttgart, 1953.
Ferrero, G., *Il militarismo*. Milan, 1898.
Fick, H., *Der deutsche Militarismus der Vorkriegszeit*. Potsdam, 1932.
Fried, Hans, *The Guilt of the German Army*. New York, 1942.
Fuller, J. F. C., *Armament and History*. New York, 1943.
Gässler, Christian W., *Offizier und Offizierkorps der alten Armee*. Wertheim a.M., 1930.
Garwy, Peter, *Der rote Militarismus*. Berlin, 1928.
Gatzke, Hans W., *Stresemann and the Rearmament of Germany*. Baltimore, 1954.
Gilbert, Felix, ed., *Hitler Directs His War*. New York, 1951.
Girardet, Raoul, *La société militaire dans la France contemporaine*. Paris, 1953.
Goebel, Dorothy Burne, and Goebel, Julius, Jr., *Generals in the White House*. New York, 1945.
Görlitz, Walther, *Der deutsche Generalstab*. Frankfurt a.M., 1950.
Gohier, Urbain, *L'Armée contre la nation*. Ed. augmentée. Paris, 1900.
Gordon, Harold J., Jr., *The Reichswehr and the German Republic, 1919-1926*. Princeton, 1957.
Grenfell, Captain Russell, R.N., *Unconditional Hatred: German War Guilt and the Future of Europe*. New York, 1953.
Halder, Franz, *Hitler als Feldherr*. Munich, 1949.
Hallgarten, George W. F., *Hitler, Reichswehr und Industrie*. Frankfurt a.M., 1955.
Harmon, A., *Psychologie du militaire professionel*. 2nd. ed. Paris, 1895.
Hass, Eric, *Militarism, Labor's Foe*. New York, 1955.
Herzfeld, Hans, *Die deutsche Rüstungspolitik vor dem Weltkrieg*. Bonn, 1923.
Herzfeld, Hans, *Das Problem des deutschen Heeres*. Laupheim, n.d.
Heusinger, Adolf, *Befehl im Widerstreit: Schicksalsstunden der deutschen Armee, 1923-1945*. Tübingen, 1950.
Höhn, Reinhard, *Verfassungskampf und Heereseid: Der Kampf des Bürgertums um das Heer (1815-1850)*. Leipzig, 1938.
Huber, Ernst R., *Heer und Staat in der deutschen Geschichte*. 2d. ed. Hamburg, 1943.
Hübner, R., *Albrecht von Roon: Preussens Heer im Kampf um das Reich*. Hamburg, 1933.
Huntington, Samuel P., *The Soldier and the State: The Theory and Politics of Civil-Military Relations*. Cambridge, Mass., 1957.

Jünger, Ernst, *Krieg und Krieger*. Berlin, 1930.

Jünger, Ernst, *Die totale Mobilmachung*. 2nd. ed. Berlin, 1934.

Juganazu, P., *L'apologie de la guerre dans la philosophie contemporaine*. Paris, 1933.

Kautsky, Karl, *Sozialisten und Krieg*. Prague, 1937.

Kennedy, M. D., *The Military Side of Japanese Life*. London, 1924.

Kerwin, Jerome, ed., *Civil-Military Relationships in American Life*. Chicago, 1948.

King, Jere Clemens, *Generals and Politicians: Conflict between France's High Command, Parliament, and Government*. Berkeley, 1951.

Kloster, W., *Der deutsche Generalstab und der Präventivkriegsgedanke*. Stuttgart, 1932.

Lagorgette, Jean, *Le rôle de la guerre: Etude de sociologie générale*. Paris, 1906.

Lea, Homer, *The Valor of Ignorance*. New York, 1909.

Lehman, B. H., *Carlyle's Theory of the Hero*. Durham, N. C., 1928.

Lenney, John Joseph, *Caste System in the American Army*. New York, 1949.

Léonard, Emile G., *L'Armée et ses problèmes au XIIII* siècle*. Paris, 1958.

Liebknecht, Karl, *Militarismus und Antimilitarismus*. Berlin 1907, transl. *Militarism*. New York, 1917.

Löwenthal, Eduard, *Der Militarismus als Ursache der Massenverarmung in Europa und die europäische Union als Mittel zur Überflüssigmachung der stehenden Heere*. n.p., 1870.

Lory, Hillis, *Japan's Military Masters*. New York, 1943.

Ludendorff, General Erich, *Der totale Krieg*. Munich, 1935.

Maki, John M., *Japanese Militarism; Its Cause and Cure*. New York, 1945.

Miksche, Lt. Col. F. O., *Unconditional Surrender*. London, 1952.

Mills, C. Wright, *The Power Elite*. New York, 1956.

Monteilhet, J., *Les institutions militaires de la France (1814-1924)*. Paris, 1926.

Morgan, Brigadier John H., *Assize of Arms. I* (no more published), London, 1945.

Morizet, André, *De l'incapacité des militaires à faire la guerre*. Paris, 1921.

Nef, John U., *War and Human Progress*. Cambridge, Mass., 1950.

Obermann, E., *Vom preussischen zum deutschen Militarismus: Ein historisch-soziologischer Beitrag zur deutschen Staats- und Gesellschaftsentwicklung*. Heidelberg, 1950. (Diss. Typescript.)

Osmond, J. S., *Parliament and the Army, 1642-1904*. Cambridge, 1933.

Osseg, Annuarius, i.e., Georg Michael Pachtler, *Der europäische Militarismus*. n.p., 1876.

Patton, General George S., Jr., *War as I Knew It*. Boston, 1947.

Quinton, René, *Soldier's Testament*. London, 1930. Transl. of *Maximes sur la guerre*.

Renn, Ludwig, i.e., Arnold F. Vieth von Golssenau, *Warfare: The Relation of War to Society*. New York, 1939.

Ritter, Gerhard, *Der Schlieffen-Plan: Kritik eines Mythos*. Munich, 1956.

Ritter, Gerhard, *Staatskunst und Kriegshandwerk. I: Die altpreussische Tradition (1740-1890)*. Munich, 1954.

Rovere, Richard H., and Schlesinger, Arthur M., Jr., *The General and the President*. New York, 1951. The MacArthur-Truman controversy.

Rüstow, W., *Der deutsche Militärstaat vor und während der Revolution*. 2nd. ed. Zurich, 1851.

Sapir, Burton M., and Snyder, Richard C., *The Role of the Military in American Foreign Policy*. Garden City, N. Y., 1954.

Schmidt-Bückeburg, R., *Das Militärkabinett der preussischen Könige und deutschen Kaiser*. Berlin, 1933.

Schüddekopf, Otto Ernst, *Heer und Republik*. Hannover and Frankfurt a.M., 1955.

Schulze-Bodmer, Wilhelm, *Die Rettung der Gesellschaft aus den Gefahren der Militärherrschaft*. Leipzig, 1859.

Seeckt, Hans von, *Gedanken eines Soldaten*. Enlarged ed. Leipzig, 1935.

Shanahan, William O., *Prussian Military Reforms, 1786-1813*. New York, 1945.

Smith, Louis, *American Democracy and Military Power*. Chicago, 1951.

Soloviev, Mikhail, *My Nine Lives in the Red Army*. London, 1956.

Sossidi, Elefterion, *Die staatsrechtliche Stellung des Offiziers im absoluten Staat und ihre Abwandlungen im 19. Jahrhundert*. Berlin, 1939.

Speier, Hans, *Social Order and the Risks of War*. New York, 1952. Part III: "War and Militarism."

Stadelmann, Rudolf, *Moltke und der Staat*. Krefeld, 1951.

Tanin, O., and Yohan, E., *Militarism and Fascism in Japan*. London, 1934.

Takeuchi, Tatsuji, *War and Diplomacy in the Japanese Empire*. Chicago, 1935.

Taylor, Telford, *Sword and Swastika*. New York, 1952.

Thomas, Richard H., *Militarism; or Military Fever: Its Causes, Dangers and Cure*. Philadelphia, 1899.

Toynbee, A. J., *War and Civilization*. Selected from *A Study of History*. New York, 1950.

Tuch, Gustav, *Der erweiterte deutsche Militärstaat in seiner sozialen Bedeutung*. Leipzig, 1886.

Vagts, Alfred, *Defense and Diplomacy: The Soldier and the Conduct of Foreign Relations*. New York, 1956.

Vagts, Alfred, *Hitler's Second Army*. Washington, D. C., 1943.

Vigon, Jorge, *Teoria del Militarismo*. Madrid, 1955.

Vishnev, Sergei, *Der moderne Militarismus und die Monopole*. (East) Berlin, 1955.

Waite, Robert C. L., *Vanguard of Nazism: The Free Corps Movement in Postwar Germany, 1918-1923*. Cambridge, Mass., 1952.

Weber, J., *Was ist Militarismus? Eine kritische Darstellung*. Mainz, 1954.

Westphal, Siegfried, *Heer in Fesseln: Aus den Papieren des Stabschefs von Rommel, Kesselring und Rundstedt*. Bonn, 1950.

Wheeler-Bennett, John W., *The Nemesis of Power: The German Army in Politics, 1918-1945*. London, 1953.

Wiede, F., *Der Militarismus: Sozial-philosophische Untersuchungen*. Zurich, 1878.

Wiese, Leopold von, *Die Entwicklung der Kriegswaffe und ihr Zusammenhang mit der Sozialordnung*. Cologne, 1953.

Wollenberg, E., *The Red Army: A Study of the Growth of Soviet Imperialism*. London, 1940.

ARTICLES

Bahrdt, Hans Paul, *"Militarismus. Definition, Analyse, Kritik,"* Deutsche *Universitäts-Zeitung* IX (1954), No. 9.

Baldwin, Hanson, "The Military Move In," *Harper's,* CXCV (1947), 481 ff.

Battine, Maj. Cecil, "What Is Militarism?" *Fortnightly Review,* CXI (1919).

Below, Georg von, *"Klagen über den Militarismus,"* Deutsche Rund-*schau,* CLXXI (1917).

Boller, P. F., Jr., "Professional Soldiers in the White House," *Southwest Rev.* XXXVII (1952), 269 ff.

Brotz, H., and Wilson, E. K., "Characteristics of Military Society," *Am. Journal of Sociology* LI (1946), 371 ff.

Confer, Carl V., "The Social Influence of the Officer in the Third French Republic," *Military Affairs* III (1939), 157 ff.

Dehio, Ludwig, *"Um den deutschen Militarismus,"* Hist. Zeitschr. CLXXX (1955), 43 ff.

Dennery, Etienne, "Democracy and the French Army," *Military Affairs* V (1941), 233 ff.

Dobie, J. F., "Samples of the Army Mind," *Harper's,* CXCII (1946), with rebuttal by J. J. McCloy, "In Defense of the Army Mind," Ibid., CXCIV (1947).

Douglas, Justice William O., "Should We Fear the Military?" *Look,* March 11, 1952.

Engelberg, Ernst, *"Über das Problem des deutschen Militarismus,"* Zeitschr. für Geschichtswissenschaft IV (1956), 1113 ff.

Fox, William T. R., "Civil-Military Relations Research," *World Politics* VI (1954), 278 ff.

Hale, Oron James, "Adolf Hitler as Feldherr," *Virginia Qua.,* Spring 1948.

Hensel, Walther, *"Was ist Militarismus?"* Politische Studien VI (1955-6), No. 68.

Herzfeld, Hans, *"Der Militarismus als Problem der neuen Geschichte,"* Schola I (1946), 41 ff.

Hoopes, Townsend, "Civilian-Military Balance," *Yale Rev.,* XLIII (1954), 221 ff.

Jackson, Ray, "Aspects of American Militarism," *Contemporary Issues,* Summer 1948.

Kehr, Eckart, *"Zur Genesis des Kgl. Preussischen Reserveoffiziers,"* Die Gesellschaft II (1928), 492 ff.

Kennedy, William V., "Antimilitary Literature," *Ordnance,* Sept.-Oct. 1956.

Krebs, Wilhelm, *"Militarismus,"* Zeitschrift für die gesamte Staatswissen-*schaft,* CVII (1951), 698 ff.

Lamy, Etienne, *"L'Armée et la démocratie,"* Revue des deux mondes, June 15 and July 15, 1885.

Lanham, Brig. Gen. C. I., "Our Armed Forces; Threat or Guarantee?" In: John W. Chase, ed., *Years of the Modern: An American Appraisal.* New York, 1949.

Larrabee, Eric, "The Peacetime Army—Warriors Need Not Apply," *Harper's,* March 1947.

Lasswell, Harold, "The Garrison State vs. the Civilian State," *China Qua.* II (1937), 643 ff.

Lasswell, Harold, "The Garrison State and Specialists on Violence," *Am. Journal of Sociology* XLVI (1941), 455 ff.

Lauterbach, Albert, "Roots and Implications of the German Idea of Military Society," *Military Affairs* V (1941), 3 ff.

Mallan, John P., "Roosevelt, Brooks Adams and Lea; The Warrior Critique of Business Civilization," *American Qua.*, Fall 1956.

Meinecke, Friedrich, *"Militarismus und Hitlerismus,"* *Die Sammlung*, March 1946.

"Militarism," *Encyclopaedia of the Social Sciences* X, 446 ff.

Picht, Werner, *"Der Begriff Militarismus,"* *Geschichtswissenschaft im Unterricht* V (1954), 455 ff.

Rehm, Walter, *"Offizier und Politik,"* *Wehrwissenschaftliche Rundschau* VI (1956), 380 ff.

Reinhard, M., *"L'historiographie militaire sous Napoléon Ier,"* *Revue historique* CXVIC (1946), 165 ff.

Reynolds, Mary T., "The [U. S.] General Staff as a Propaganda Agency, 1903-1914," *Public Opinion Qua.*, July 1939.

Ritter, Gerhard, *"Das Problem des Militarismus in Deutschland,"* *Hist. Zeitschrift* CLXXVII (1954), 21 ff.

Rogers, Lindsay, "Civilian Control of Military Policy," *Foreign Affairs* XVIII (1940), 280 ff.

Rogers, Lindsay, "Our Brass-Bound Foreign Policy," *The Reporter*, Oct. 28, 1952.

Rose, Arnold, "The Social Structure of the Army," *Am. Journal of Sociology* LI (1946), 361 ff.

Salomon, Albert, "The Spirit of the Soldier and Nazi Militarism," *Social Research* IX (1942), 95 ff.

Schlesinger, Arthur M., Jr., "Generals in Politics," *The Reporter*, Apr. 1, 1952.

Schlesinger, Arthur M., Jr., "Military Force: How Much and Where?" Ibid., Aug. 4, 1953.

Schüddekopf, Otto Ernst, *"Wehrmacht und Politik in Deutschland,"* *Politische Literatur* III (1954), 232 ff.

Schulte, Aloys, *"Die Herrschaft der militärischen Pläne in der Politik,"* *Süddeutsche Monatshefte*, Sept. 1924.

Somit, Albert, "The Military Hero as President," *Public Opinion Qua.* XII (1948) 192 ff.

Speidel, Helm, *"Reichswehr und Rote Armee,"* *Vierteljahrshefte für Zeitgeschichte*, I (1953), 9 ff.

Spindler, C. D., "The Military—A Systematic Analysis," *Social Forces* XXV (1946), 88 ff.

Sprout, Harold, "Trends in the Traditional Relations between Military and Civilian," *American Philosophical Society, Proceedings,* XIIC (1948), 264 ff.

Storry, Richard, "Fascism in Japan: The Army Mutiny of February 1936," *History Today*, Nov. 1956.

Strunsky, Simeon, "Armaments and Caste," *Annals of the American Academy* LXVI (1916), 237 ff.

Stryker, J. W., "Are the Military Moving In?" *U. S. Naval Institute Proceedings* LXXV (1949), 295 ff., and LXXVI (1950), 1102 ff.

"The U. S. Military Mind," *Fortune* XLV (Feb. 1952).

Vagts, Alfred, "Land and Sea Power in the Second German Reich," *Military Affairs* III (1939), 210 ff.

Vagts, Alfred, "The German Army of the Second Reich as a Cultural Institution," in: Caroline F. Ware, ed., *The Cultural Approach to History*. New York, 1940, pp. 182 ff.

Vagts, Detlev F., "Free Speech in the Armed Forces," *Columbia Law Review* LVII (1957), 187 ff.

Weitenkampf, Frank, "Generals in Politics," *American Scholar* XIII (1944), 375 ff.

Wraga, Ryzard, "Soviet Militarism," *The Eastern Qua.* II (1949).

Yanaga, Chitoshi, "The Military and the Government in Japan," *Am. Pol. Sci. Rev.* XXXV (1941), 529 ff.

INDEX

Abbt, Thomas, 134-5, 453
absolute monarchies: as basis of militarism, 76-7; opposed by French Revolution, 110
Académie des Nobles, 52 ff.
Adams, John, 93
Addis Ababa: Italian attack on, 425
Ainsworth, Fred Crayton, 325
Alexander I, Czar of Russia, 398
Alexander the Great, 32
Alexeiev, Mikhail Vasilievich, *quoted,* 277-8
Alvensleben, Constantin von, *quoted,* 25
American Revolution, 77, 92-100, 110, 284
antimilitarism: of the Enlightenment, 75-6; economic basis of, 77-8
Araki, Sadao, 460
Argenson, Comte d', 53, 60
Argentina: post World War II militarism in, 488-9
Argonne, battle of the, 258
Arnold, Benedict, 296
artillery, 58, 109, 141, 372
Assumptionists, Order of the, 21
Assyria: militarism in, 15
Auerstädt, battle of, 266 ff.
Augereau, Pierre François Charles, 117, 122, 250
Austria, 72; militarism in, 25-6, 60, 64-5; military education, 53; War of 1792, 110-11; strategy in Napoleonic wars, 147-50; problem of divergent national groups in army, 253-4

Bacon, Francis, *quoted,* 383
Badoglio, Pietro, 461, 481
balance of power, 109, 148
Balbo, Italo, 413
balloon: military, 110
Barras, Paul François Jean Nicolas, Vicomte de, 374
Barrès, Auguste Maurice, 20
Baruch, Bernard Mannes, 464
Bassermann, Ernst, 240, 308
Batista y Zaldivar, Fulgencio, 297
Bazaine, Achille, 282
Beaumont, Francis, *quoted,* 51
Behrenhorst, Georg Heinrich von, 88 ff.
Bemis Heights, battle of, 95
Benedek, Ludwig August von, 282
Bentham, Jeremy, 65
Béranger, Pierre Jean de, *quoted,* 19
Bernadotte, Jean Baptiste Jules, 267-8

Bernhardi, Friedrich von, 26, 298, 378
Berthier, Louis Alexandre, 268
Berwick, Duke of, *quoted,* 58
Bethmann-Hollweg, Theobald von, 243, 247-8, 331, 337, 403
Bismarck, Prince Otto Eduard Leopold von, 156, 185, 198 ff., 242, 246-7, 255, 285, 296, 311, 326, 335 ff., 345, 362, 383, 391, 393, 463
Bliss, Tasker Howard, 257, 270-1, 425; *quoted,* 243
Bloch, Johann von, 27, 399
Blomberg, Werner von, 164, 430, 483
Blücher, Gerhard Leberecht von, 117, 133, 142-3, 149 ff., 269; *quoted,* 24, 130, 267
Blum, Léon, French political leader, 319
Boer War, 294, 305, 344, 352
Bonaparte, Joseph, King of Spain, 269
Bonaparte, Napoleon, *see* Napoleon I
Boulanger, Georges Ernest Jean, 301, 309, 317 ff.
Bourcet, Pierre-Joseph de, 78
Bourrienne, Louis Antoine Fauvelet de, 267, 301
Boyen, Hermann von, 135, 162; introduced compulsory military service, 139
Boxer Rebellion, 228
Braddock, Edward, 96
Bradley, Omar, 303, 481, 486
Brandenburg-Prussia, 42-3, 65
Brest-Litovsk, Treaty of, 243-4, 248, 290, 396
Bristol, siege of, 394
Brooke, Sir Alan Francis, 37, 473
Brooke, Rupert, *quoted,* 444
Brunswick, Karl Wilhelm Ferdinand, Duke of, 85, 111, 117, 366-7
Bulganin, Nikolai Aleksandrovich, 491
Bullard, Robert Lee, 239, 271, 384, 430; distrusted German immigrants in American army, 253
Bülow, Dietrich Heinrich von, 307, 327, 380; *quoted,* 87-8, 96
Bunker Hill, battle of, 93, 95, 126
Burckhardt, Jacob, *quoted,* 428-9
Burgoyne, John, 66, 94; *quoted,* 172
Burke, Edmund, 17
Byron, George Gordon, Lord, 32, 453